COMPARATIVE POLITICS TODAY
AP* EDITION

CONTRIBUTORS

OLADIMEJI ABORISADE
Obafemi Awolowa University, Nigeria

HOUCHANG E. CHEHABI
Boston University

WAYNE A. CORNELIUS
University of California, San Diego

RUSSELL J. DALTON
University of California, Irvine

ARANG KESHAVARZIAN
New York University

THAD KOUSSER
University of California, San Diego

A. CARL LEVAN
American University

MELANIE MANION
University of Wisconsin

ROBERT J. MUNDT
Late, University of North Carolina at Charlotte

G. BINGHAM POWELL, JR.
University of Rochester

AUSTIN RANNEY
Late, University of California, Berkeley

THOMAS F. REMINGTON
Emory University

RICHARD ROSE
University of Aberdeen, Scotland

KAARE STRØM
University of California, San Diego

JEFFREY A. WELDON
Instituto Tecnologico Autónomo de Mexíco

TENTH EDITION

COMPARATIVE POLITICS TODAY

A WORLD VIEW

AP* EDITION

G. Bingham Powell, Jr.
University of Rochester

Russell J. Dalton
University of California, Irvine

Kaare Strøm
University of California, San Diego

Longman

Boston   Columbus   Indianapolis   New York   San Francisco   Upper Saddle River   Amsterdam
Cape Town   Dubai   London   Madrid   Milan   Munich   Paris   Montreal   Toronto   Delhi
Mexico City   São Paulo   Sydney   Hong Kong   Seoul   Singapore   Taipei   Tokyo

Senior Acquisitions Editor: Vikram Mukhija
Assistant Editor: Corey Kahn
Editorial Assistant: Beverly Fong
Senior Marketing Manager: Lindsey Prudhomme
Production Manager: S. Kulig
Project Coordination, Text Design, and Electronic Page Makeup: PreMediaGlobal
Senior Cover Design Manager/Cover Designer: Nancy Danahy
Cover Image: © George Diebold/Photographer's Choice/Getty Images, Inc.
Photo Researcher: Poyee Oster
Senior Manufacturing Buyer: Dennis Para
Printer and Binder: R.R. Donnelley
Cover Printer: Lehigh-Phoenix Color

For permission to use copyrighted material, grateful acknowledgment is made to the copyright holders, which are hereby made part of this copyright page.

Library of Congress Cataloging-in-Publication Data

Control number is on record at the Library of Congress.

2 3 4 5 6 7 8 9 10—DJM—14 13 12 11

Longman
is an imprint of

www.PearsonSchool.com/Advanced

Student Edition
High School Binding
ISBN 13: 978-0-13-261248-7
ISBN 10:   0-13-261248-8

The editors and co-authors of the Tenth Edition of
Comparative Politics Today dedicate this book to
the memory of Gabriel A. Almond, a giant in the field of
comparative politics, the originator of the framework upon
which this text is based, and a friend, colleague, and
leader, who passed away in 2002, at the age of 91.

DETAILED CONTENTS

Contributors   ii

A Guide to Comparing Nations   x

A Brief Guide to Analyzing Visuals   xii

AP Correlation Guide   xviii

Preface   xxi

AP* Edition Program Components   xxiii

PART ONE
Introduction

CHAPTER 1

Issues in Comparative Politics   1

What Is Politics?   1
Governments and the State of Nature   2
Why Governments?   3
When Does Government Become the Problem?   6
Political Systems and States   8
The Diversity of States   10
Challenges: Building Community   13
Fostering Economic Development   17
Fostering Democracy, Human Rights, and
   Civil Liberties   23
Looking Forward   25
Review Questions   26
Key Terms   26
Suggested Readings   27
Endnotes   27

CHAPTER 2

Comparing Political Systems   29

Why We Compare   29
How We Compare   29

How We Explain and Predict   30
Political Systems: Environment and
   Interdependence   33
Political Systems: Structures and Functions   35
An Illustrative Comparison: Regime Change in
   Russia   38
The Policy Level: Performance, Outcome, and
   Evaluation   41
Review Questions   42
Key Terms   42
Suggested Readings   43
Endnotes   43

PART TWO
System, Process, and Policy

CHAPTER 3

**Political Culture and Political
Socialization**   44

Mapping the Three Levels of Political Culture   44
Why Culture Matters   50
Political Socialization   52
Agents of Political Socialization   53
Trends Shaping Contemporary Political Cultures   57
Review Questions   58
Key Terms   59
Suggested Readings   59
Endnotes   59

CHAPTER 4

Interest Articulation   61

Citizen Action   61
How Citizens Participate   63
Interest Groups   65

Civil Society   68
Interest-Group Systems   69
Access to the Influential   71
Interest-Group Development   75
Review Questions   76
Key Terms   76
Suggested Readings   76
Endnotes   77

CHAPTER 5

Interest Aggregation and Political Parties   79

Personal Interest Aggregation   79
Institutional Interest Aggregation   80
Competitive Party Systems and Interest
   Aggregation   81
Authoritarian Party Systems   92
The Military and Interest Aggregation   93
Trends in Interest Aggregation   95
Significance of Interest Aggregation   96
Review Questions   97
Key Terms   97
Suggested Readings   97
Endnotes   98

CHAPTER 6

Government and Policymaking   100

Constitutions and Decision Rules   100
Democracy and Authoritarianism   102
Separation of Government Powers   102
Geographic Distribution of Government Power   106
Limitations on Government Power   106
Checking the Top Policymakers   108
Assemblies   108
Political Executives   111
The Bureaucracy   118
Review Questions   122
Key Terms   122
Suggested Readings   122
Endnotes   123

CHAPTER 7

Public Policy   124

Government and What It Does   124
Public Policy Outputs   127

Domestic Policy Outcomes   136
International Outcomes   144
The Complexity of Policy Choice   147
Review Questions   147
Key Terms   147
Suggested Readings   148
Endnotes   148

PART THREE
Country Studies

CHAPTER 8

Politics in Britain   150
Richard Rose

Policy Challenges Facing the British
   Government   152
The Environment of Politics: One Crown
   but Five Nations   156
The Legacy of History   160
The Structure of Government   162
Political Culture and Legitimacy   173
Political Socialization   174
Political Participation   176
Political Recruitment   177
Organizing Group Interests   179
Party System and Electoral Choice   181
Centralized Authority and Decentralized
   Delivery of Policies   185
Why Public Policy Matters   190
Policy Outcomes in Society   191
Review Questions   193
Key Terms   193
Internet Resources   193
Suggested Readings   193
Endnotes   194

CHAPTER 9

Politics in Russia   197
Thomas F. Remington

Ensuring Continuity of Power   197
Current Policy Challenges   199
Historical Legacies   200
The Contemporary Constitutional Order   204
Russian Political Culture in the
   Post-Soviet Period   213

Political Participation   217
Interest Articulation: Between Statism and
   Pluralism   220
Parties and the Aggregation of Interests   224
The Politics of Economic Reform   229
Toward the Rule of Law?   234
Russia and the International Community   236
Review Questions   238
Key Terms   238
Suggested Readings   239
Internet Resources   239
Endnotes   239

CHAPTER 10

Politics in China   243
Melanie Manion

Current Policy Challenges   244
Historical Setting   245
Social Conditions   249
Structure of the Party-State   250
Political Socialization   260
Political Culture   262
Political Participation   264
Interest Articulation and Aggregation   269
Policymaking and Implementation   271
Policy Performance   276
Hong Kong   281
China and the World   282
China's Political Future   283
Review Questions   283
Key Terms   284
Suggested Readings   284
Internet Resources   284
Endnotes   284

CHAPTER 11

Politics in Mexico   289
Wayne A. Cornelius and Jeffrey A. Weldon

Current Policy Challenges   290
Historical Perspectives   291
Political Culture   297
Mass Political Socialization   299
Political Participation   301
Political Structure and Institutions   302
Recruiting the Political Elite   310
Interest Representation and Political Control   311

Political Parties   313
Government Performance   320
Mexico's Political Future   328
Review Questions   329
Key Terms   329
Suggested Readings   330
Internet Resources   330
Endnotes   330

CHAPTER 12

Politics in Iran   333
H. E. Chehabi and Arang Keshavarzian

Current Policy Challenges   334
Historical Legacy   336
Institutions of the Islamic Republic   342
Elections and Parties   346
Political Culture   352
Political Socialization   355
Recruiting the Political Elite   360
Interest Articulation and Aggregation   361
Policy Formulation   364
Policy Outcomes   368
Conclusion   375
Review Questions   376
Key Terms   376
Suggested Readings   376
Internet Resources   377
Endnotes   377

CHAPTER 13

Politics in Nigeria   381
*A. Carl LeVan, Oladimeji Aborisade,
   and Robert J. Mundt*

Current Policy Challenges   381
The Effects of History   383
Environmental Potential and
   Limitations   385
Political Culture and Subcultures   390
Political Socialization   396
Political Recruitment   399
Political Structure   401
Interest Articulation   406
Political Participation   408
Parties and Elections   409
Policy Formation and
   Implementation   415

Nigeria in Africa and in the World   421
Prospects for Development   423
Review Questions   424
Key Terms   424
Suggested Readings   425
Internet Resources   425
Endnotes   425

CHAPTER 14

Politics in the United States   429
Thad Kousser and Austin Ranney

Current Policy Challenges   429
History   432
Social Conditions   435
The Constitutional System   437

Political Culture and Socialization   441
Political Participation and Recruitment   444
Recruitment of Leaders   447
Interest Articulation: PACs and Pressure Groups   448
The Special Characteristics of American
    Political Parties   453
The Policymaking Process in America   461
Policy Performance   465
American Exceptionalism: Myth or Reality?   468
Conclusion   471
Review Questions   472
Key Terms   472
Suggested Readings   472
Internet Resources   473
Endnotes   473

Index   476

A GUIDE TO COMPARING NATIONS

This analytic index provides a guide to where specific themes are addressed in each chapter.

Topics	Chapters 1–7	Britain	Russia	China
History		160–162	200–204	245–249
Social Conditions	3–6	158–159	233–234	249–250
Executive	111–118	164–168	204–206	253–254
Parliament	108–111	169–171	206–208	253
Judiciary	106–107	171	208–210	254
Provincial Government	106	156–158, 186–188	210–212	
Political Culture	44–52	173–174	213–215	262–264
Political Socialization	52–57	174–176	215–218	261–262
Participation/Recruitment	61–64	176–179	218–222	257–258 264–269
Interest Groups	65–76	179–181	222–227	269–271
Parties and Elections	81–97	181–185	204–208	254–258
Policy Process	100–121	185–190	231–234	271–276
Outputs and Outcomes	127–147	191–192	231–234	276–281
International Relations	9–10, 144–147		236–238	282–283

Mexico	Iran	Nigeria	United States
291–297	336–338	383–385	432–435
321–323	368–372	385–387	435–437
307–310	342–345	405	439–440
304–307	344–345	405–406	439–440
323		406	441
303–304		403–405	438–439
297–299	352–355	390–396	441–443
299–300	355–360	396–399	443–444
301–302, 310–311	360–361	399–401, 408–409	444–448
311–313	361–364	406–408	448–453
313–320	346–352	409–415	453–461
302–308	364–368		461–465
320–326	368–375	415–421	465–468
326–328	372–375	421–423	

We are used to thinking about reading written texts critically—for example, reading a textbook carefully for information, sometimes highlighting or underlining as we go along—but we do not always think about "reading" visuals in this way. We should, for images and informational graphics can tell us a lot if we read and consider them carefully. Especially in the so-called information age, in which we are exposed to a constant stream of images on television and the Internet, it is important for you to be able to analyze and understand their meanings. This brief guide provides information about the types of visuals you will encounter in *Comparative Politics Today: A World View AP* Edition* and offers some questions to help you analyze everything from tables to charts and graphs to news photographs.

TABLES

Tables are the least "visual" of the visuals we explore. They consist of textual information and/or numerical data arranged in columns and rows. Tables are frequently used when exact information is required and when orderly arrangement is necessary to locate and, in many cases, to compare the information. For example, Table 1.4 makes data on the income distribution of many nations organized and easy to compare. Here are a few questions to guide your analysis:

- What is the purpose of this table? What information does it show? There is usually a title that offers a sense of the table's purpose.
- What information is provided in the column headings (the table's top row)? How are the rows labeled? Are there any clarifying notes at the bottom of the table?
- Is a time period indicated, such as July to December 2009? Or, are the data as of a specific date, such as January 1, 2010? Are the data shown at multiple intervals over a fixed period or at one particular point in time?
- If the table shows numerical data, what do these data represent? In what units? Dollars spent on

TABLE 1.4

Income Distribution

Middle-income countries have the greatest inequalities; wealthy ones tend to be more equal.

Country	Year	Wealthiest 10%	Poorest 40%	Wealthy/Poor Gap
Germany	2000	22.1	22.2	−0.1
Russia	2002	23.8	20.9	2.9
Japan	1993	21.7	24.8	3.1
France	1995	25.1	19.8	5.3
Britain	1999	28.5	17.5	11.0
India	2004–05	31.1	19.4	11.7
United States	2000	29.9	16.2	13.7
Iran	1998	33.7	19.5	14.2
Nigeria	2003	33.2	14.6	18.6
China	2004	34.9	12.8	22.1
Mexico	2004	39.4	12.6	26.8
Brazil	2004	44.8	9.2	35.6

Source: World Bank, *World Development Indicators 2007*, Table 2-7 (www.worldbank.org); distribution of income or consumption.

social service programs? Percentage of voters who support the British Labour Party? Projected population increases?

- What is the source of the information presented in the table? Is it government information? Private polling information? A newspaper? A corporation? The United Nations? An individual? Is the source trustworthy? Current? Does the source have a vested interest in the data expressed in the table?

CHARTS AND GRAPHS

Charts and graphs depict numerical data in visual forms. The most common kinds of graphs plot data in two dimensions along horizontal and vertical axes. Examples that you will encounter throughout this book are line graphs, pie charts, bar graphs, and timelines. These kinds of visuals emphasize data

relationships: at a particular point in time, at regular intervals over a fixed period of time, or, sometimes, as parts of a whole. Line graphs show a progression, usually over time (as in Figure 12.7, Comparative Growth Rates). Pie charts (such as Figure 9.7, 2010 Russian Federal Budget) demonstrate how a whole (total government spending) is divided into its parts (different types of government programs). Bar graphs compare values across categories, showing how proportions are related to each other (as in Figure 10.5, showing the male and female populations in China by age bracket). Bar graphs can present data either horizontally or vertically. Timelines show events and changes over a defined period of time (such as the list of prime ministers of Britain in Figure 8.2). You will also encounter charts that map out processes and hierarchies throughout this book (as in the structure of the government of Nigeria shown in Figure 13.4.)

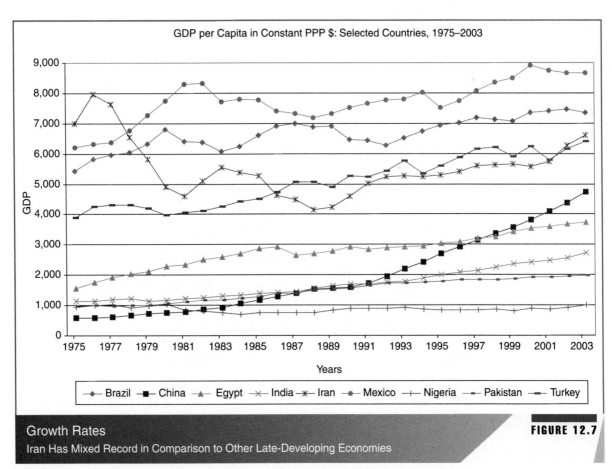

Growth Rates

Iran Has Mixed Record in Comparison to Other Late-Developing Economies

FIGURE 12.7

Source: Based on data from Massoud Karshenas and Hassan Hakimian, "Oil, Economic Diversification, and the Democratic Process in Iran," *Iranian Studies* 38, no. 1 (March 2005): 67–90.

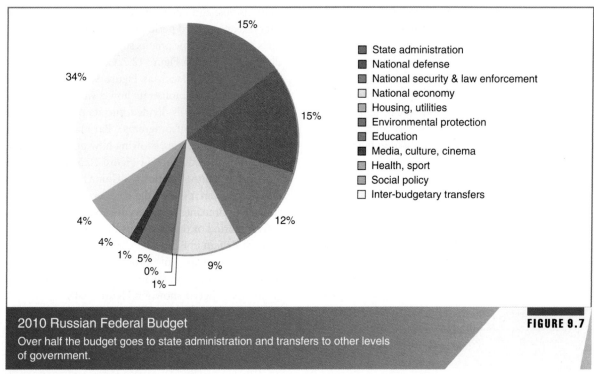

Legend:
- State administration
- National defense
- National security & law enforcement
- National economy
- Housing, utilities
- Environmental protection
- Education
- Media, culture, cinema
- Health, sport
- Social policy
- Inter-budgetary transfers

2010 Russian Federal Budget

Over half the budget goes to state administration and transfers to other levels of government.

FIGURE 9.7

Source: Russian Ministry of Finance, www.minfin.ru.

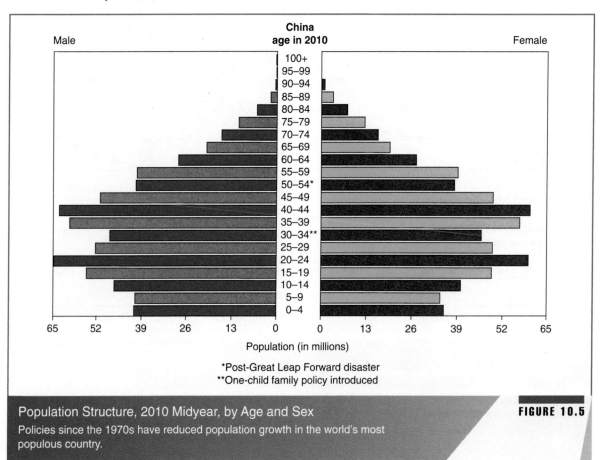

China age in 2010

Male | Female

Population (in millions)

*Post-Great Leap Forward disaster
**One-child family policy introduced

Population Structure, 2010 Midyear, by Age and Sex

Policies since the 1970s have reduced population growth in the world's most populous country.

FIGURE 10.5

Source: U.S. Census Bureau, International Data Base, www.census.gov/ipc/www/idb/country.php.

Many of the same questions you ask about tables are important when analyzing graphs and charts also (see page xiii). Here are more questions to help you:

- In the case of line and bar graphs, how are the axes labeled? Are symbols or colors used to represent different groups or units?
- Are the data shown at multiple intervals over a fixed period or at one particular point in time?
- If there are two or more sets of figures, what are the relationships among them?
- Is there distortion in the visual representation of the information? Are the intervals equal? Does the area shown distort the actual amount or the proportion? Distortion can lead you to draw an inaccurate conclusion on first sight, so it's important to look for it.

MAPS

Maps of countries, regions, and the world are very often used in political analysis to illustrate demographic, social, economic, and political issues and trends. See, for example, Figure 11.4, Drug-Related Killings in Mexico. Though tables and graphs might sometimes give more precise information, maps help us to understand in a geographic context data that are more difficult to express in words or numbers alone. Here are a few more questions to add to those in the above sections:

- What does the map key/legend show? What are the factors that the map is analyzing? Are symbols or colors used to differentiate sections of the map? Maps can express information on political boundaries, natural resources, ethnic groups, and many other topics, so it is important to know what exactly is being shown.
- What is the region being shown? How detailed is the map?
- Maps usually depict a specific point in time. What point in time is being shown on the map?

NEWS PHOTOGRAPHS

Photos can have a dramatic—and often immediate—impact on politics and government. Think about some photos that have political significance. For example, do you remember the photos from the September 11, 2001, terrorist attacks? Visual images usually

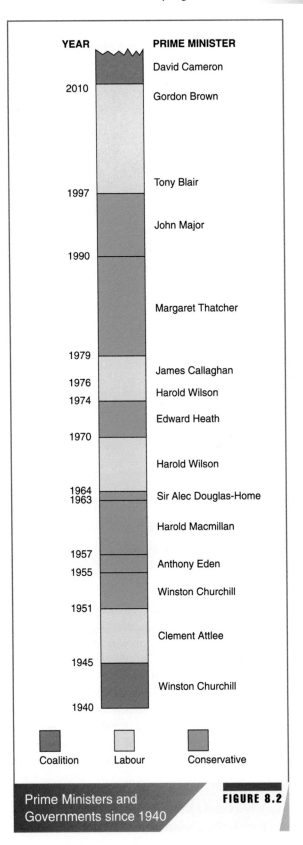

Prime Ministers and Governments since 1940

FIGURE 8.2

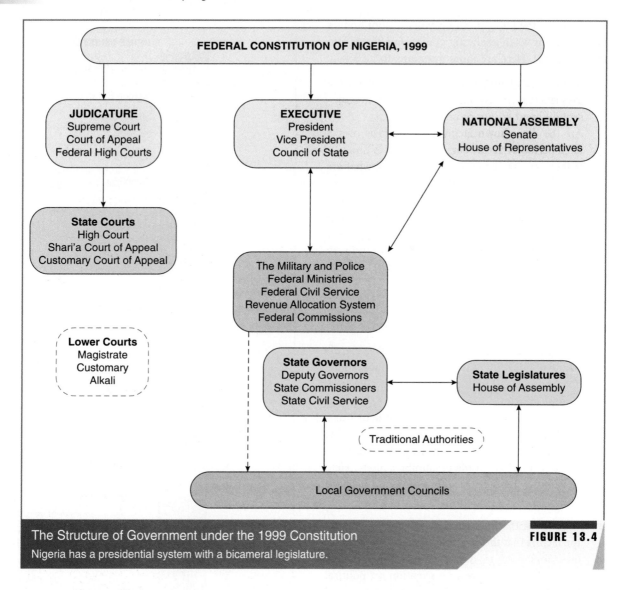

The Structure of Government under the 1999 Constitution
Nigeria has a presidential system with a bicameral legislature.

FIGURE 13.4

evoke a stronger emotional response than do written descriptions. For this reason, individuals and organizations have learned to use photographs to document events, to make arguments, to offer evidence, and even in some cases to manipulate the viewer into having a particular response. The photo of a student protester confronting tanks in Tiananmen Square (page xix) captured the attention of the world and drew attention to the violent response of the Chinese government to the protesters. Here are a few questions to guide your analysis:

- When was the photograph taken? (If there is no date given for the photograph in its credit line or caption,

you may be able to approximate the date according to the people or events depicted in the photo.)
- What is the subject of the photograph?
- Why was the photo taken?
- Is it spontaneous or posed? Did the subject know he or she was being photographed?
- Who was responsible for the photo (an individual, an agency, or an organization)? Can you discern the photographer's attitude toward the subject?
- Is there a caption? If so, what information does it provide? Does it identify the subject of the photo? Does it provide an interpretation of the subject?

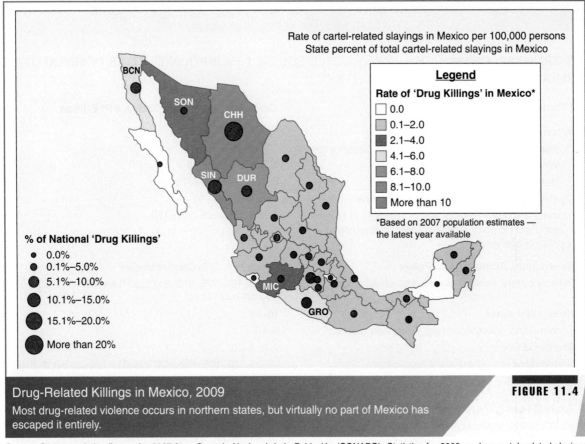

Rate of cartel-related slayings in Mexico per 100,000 persons
State percent of total cartel-related slayings in Mexico

Legend

Rate of 'Drug Killings' in Mexico*

- ☐ 0.0
- 0.1–2.0
- 2.1–4.0
- 4.1–6.0
- 6.1–8.0
- 8.1–10.0
- More than 10

*Based on 2007 population estimates — the latest year available

% of National 'Drug Killings'

- • 0.0%
- • 0.1%–5.0%
- 5.1%–10.0%
- 10.1%–15.0%
- 15.1%–20.0%
- More than 20%

Drug-Related Killings in Mexico, 2009

Most drug-related violence occurs in northern states, but virtually no part of Mexico has escaped it entirely.

FIGURE 11.4

Source: State population figures for 2007 from Consejo Nacional de la Población (CONAPO). Statistics for 2009 on drug cartel–related slayings come from *Reforma* newspaper, Mexico City, compiled by the Trans-Border Institute, University of San Diego, San Diego, CA.

Facing Down the Tanks in June 1989

In 1989, ordinary Chinese participated in the largest spontaneous protest movement the communists had ever faced. A lone protester shows defiance of regime violence in his intransigent confrontation with a Chinese tank.

Jeff Widener/AP Images

GOVERNMENT AND POLITICS: COMPARATIVE COURSE DESCRIPTION OUTLINE CORRELATED TO *COMPARATIVE POLITICS TODAY*, AP* EDITION

AP Topics	*Comparative Politics Today*, AP* Edition
I. Introduction to Comparative Politics	Chapters 1 & 2
Purpose and methods of comparison and classification	10–13, 29–42
Why/ways to organize government	3–8, 23–25, 33–42
Normative and empirical questions	8–10, 29–33, 147–150
Concepts (state, nation, regime, government)	1–2, 8–10, 10–14
Process and policy (what is politics, purpose of government; what is political science/comparative common policy challenges)	1–2, 3–8, 13–26, 127–150
II. Sovereignty, Authority, and Power	Chapters 1, 3, 6, Country studies
Political culture, communication, and socialization	44–58, 173–176, 213–217, 260–264, 297–300, 352–360, 390–399, 441–444
Nations and states	10–14
Supranational governance (e.g., European Union)	9–10
Sources of Power	2–3, 8–10
Constitutions (forms, purposes, application)	23–25, 102–108, 162–164, 204–213, 250–260, 302–310, 338, 342–346, 401–406, 437–441, 461–463
Regime types	46–48, 102–103, 212–213, 333
Types of economic systems	130, 136–138
State building, legitimacy, and stability	8–14, 45–46, 173
Belief systems as sources of legitimacy	16–17, 45–46, 50–52, 216, 250–251, 334–336, 340–341
Religion	16–17, 53–54, 216–217, 291, 333, 357–358, 392–394
Ideology (liberalism, communism, socialism, conservatism, fascism)	2–6, 45–46, 216, 243–244, 250–251, 347–349
Governance and accountability	89–90, 108
III. Political Institutions	Chapters 4–6, Country studies
Levels of government	Chapter 6, Country studies
Supranational/national/regional/local	210–212
Unitary/federal	106, 156–158, 210–212, 298, 302–304, 402–405, 438–439
Centralization/decentralization	302–304
Executives (head of state, head of government, cabinets)	111–118, 164–169, 204–206, 251–256, 307–310, 342–344, 364–366, 402, 405–406, 439–440, 464–465
Single or dual	112–114, 342–344
President	102–106, 197–198, 204–206, 212, 256, 307–308, 342–344, 405–406, 439–440, 460–461, 464–465
Prime minister	102–106, 164–167, 197–198
Legislatures	108–111, 169–171, 206–208, 253, 304–307, 344–346, 405–406, 458–460
Unicameral/bicameral (symmetric/asymmetric)	109, 206–208, 304–307
Organization	109–110, 207, 253, 344–346
Membership (representation)	110–111, 434

AP Topics	***Comparative Politics Today**, AP* Edition*
Parliamentary and presidential systems	102–106, 405–406
Institutional relations	103–104, 116–117, 204–205, 308–310, 440
Elections	83–84, 92–93, 175, 181–184, 213, 225–229, 265–267, 289, 294–297, 313–320, 346–352, 409–415, 444–451, 455, 460–461
Presidential	227–228, 289, 294–297, 313–320, 349, 455, 460–461
Parliamentary	181–184, 213, 225–229, 305, 349–351
Referendums	470
Noncompetitive	92–93, 228–229, 265–267, 346–352, 412–413
Electoral systems	84–85, 304–306, 349–350, 470
Proportional representation	85, 153, 206–207, 304–306
Single member district (plurality, majority turnoff)	84–85, 181–184, 470
Political parties (organization, membership, institutionalization, ideological position)	79–90, 184–185, 224–229, 250–258, 313–320, 346–349, 409–415, 453–461
Party systems	85–93, 224–229, 250–258
Leadership and elite recruitment	110–111, 114–116, 177–179, 218–220, 257–258, 310–311, 340–341, 345, 360–361, 399–401, 447–448
Interest groups and interest group systems	65–71, 75–76, 179–181, 220–224, 269–271, 311–313, 361–364, 406–408, 448–453
Bureaucracies	118–121, 168–169, 172, 189, 256–258, 271–274, 366–367
Military and other coercive institutions	93–95, 202, 235–236, 243–244, 269, 366, 400–402
Judiciaries	
Degrees of autonomy	107, 208–209, 234–236, 254, 382, 406
Judicial review (including European Union in relations to states and citizens)	106–108, 171, 209–210, 323, 441
Types of law	258–260, 323–326, 333, 341, 371–372, 470
IV. Citizens, Society, and the State	Chapters 1 & 3, Country studies
Cleavages and politics (ethnic, racial, class, gender, religious, regional)	13–17, 158–160, 210–211, 230, 249–250, 319–320, 337–338, 391–394, 420–421, 435–436
Civil society and social capital	68–69, 218, 302
Media roles	56, 71–72, 176, 217, 261, 300, 359, 398, 443–444
Political participation (forms/modes/trends) including political violence	61–75, 176–177, 217–218, 264–268, 301–302, 350–352, 363–364, 408–409, 444–447
Social movements	65–66, 335–336
Citizenship and representation	110–111
V. Political and Economic Change	All chapters
Revolution, coups, and war	93–95, 143–147, 203–204, 245–249, 291–292, 340–341, 394, 399–400, 430–431
Trends and types of political change (including democratization)	17–25, 34, 38–41, 57–58, 75–76, 93–95, 95–96, 152–156, 160–162, 200–204, 212–213, 243–245, 258–260, 283, 291–297, 338–342, 399–400, 430–437
Components	57–58, 158–159
Promoting or inhibiting factors	23–25, 57–58, 95
Consequences	23–25, 57–58, 283
Trends and types of economic change (including privatization)	5, 17–23, 58, 160–161, 188–189, 229–232, 244–245, 276–279, 293–294, 367–368, 402–407, 436–437
Components	17–23, 244–245
Promoting or inhibiting factors	17–23
Consequences	17–23, 57, 232–234, 244–245, 282–283

AP Topics	*Comparative Politics Today*, AP* Edition
Relationship between political and economic change	5, 17–23, 34, 58, 229–232
Globalization and fragmentation interlinked economics, global culture, reactions against globalization, regionalism	17, 34, 144–145, 153–155, 199, 391, 431
Approaches to development	17–23, 243–244, 276–278, 320–323, 416–419, 423–424
VI. Public Policy	Chapters 1 and 7, Country studies
Common policy issues	13–26, 41–42, 48–50, 124–127, 152–156, 199–200, 234–236, 244–245, 274–281, 290, 320–328, 334–336, 367–375, 381–382, 415–421, 429–432, 465–468
Economic performance	17–23, 155–156, 199–200, 232–234, 276–278, 320–323, 367–368, 381–382, 415–416, 431–432
Social welfare (e.g., education, health, poverty)	136–141, 191–192, 233–234, 244–245, 321–322, 368–369, 416–418, 466–467
Civil liberties, rights, and freedoms	23–26, 141–142, 171–172, 234–236, 346, 370–372, 420, 437–438
Environment	22–23, 278–279, 467–468
Population and migration	14–15, 158–159, 279–281, 326–328, 334, 435–436
Economic development	17–23, 320–323, 368, 416–419
Factors influencing public policymaking and implementation	120–121, 127–136, 152–156,185–191, 234–236, 271–276, 323–328, 364–367, 395–396, 415–424, 461–465
Domestic	120–121, 136–144, 185–191, 234–236, 271–276, 323–326, 395–396, 415–421, 423–424, 461–465
International	144–147, 153–156, 236–238, 282–283, 326–328, 372–375, 419–420, 421–423, 464

Upon publication, this text was correlated to the College Board's Government and Politics: Comparative Course Description dated Fall 2010. We continually monitor the College Board's Course Description for updates to exam topics. For the most current AP Exam topic correlation for this textbook, visit PearsonSchool.com/AdvancedCorrelations.

PREFACE

We are pleased to be able to offer this AP* Edition of *Comparative Politics Today: A World View* for use in high school Advanced Placement courses. The first seven chapters of this edition offer the general introduction to the field of comparative politics. The country chapters, written by distinguished specialists on the politics of each country, include the countries that are covered on the AP Exam: Great Britain, Russia, China, Mexico, Iran, and Nigeria. We have also included our chapter on the United States, which will help students understand some new concepts by presenting them in a familiar context.

Comparative Politics Today: A World View, AP Edition* has long been used in AP courses. We introduce the fundamental concepts of political system, political culture, political functions and structures, and policymaking that allow us to compare very different kinds of political systems. The "Brief Guide to Analyzing Visuals" helps students understand and utilize the tables, graphs, maps and photographs. We discuss how governments try to achieve such goals as building community, providing security, promoting economic development, protecting rights, and enhancing social justice. We explain how sometimes government becomes part of the problem, rather than the solution. We describe the social, economic, and international conditions that make government more difficult. We also discuss the roles of different kinds of political organizations—interest groups, political parties—and political institutions—legislatures, executives, courts—in the policymaking process. All these concepts are applied and illustrated in the chapters on specific countries.

NEW TO THE AP* EDITION

There are many new features of this edition:

- A substantially revised set of theory chapters (1–7) that introduce the key concepts and theories that are applied in the country studies. Data tables and references been updated, with more of our countries systematically covered.
- Chapters 1, 3 and 7 provide more thorough discussion of globalization and its various elements and consequences.
- Chapter 7 introduces its concept of "political goods" with reference to the United Nations Millennium Goals and more systematically treats policies and consequences, including welfare, fairness, liberty, and security outcomes.
- The number of example boxes has been expanded and the comparisons of patterns across country chapters has been increased.
- All chapters now include study questions as well as a guide to key themes of the chapter.
- The overall length of the book has been shortened to offer a more reader-friendly layout.
- All of the country studies have undergone major revision and updating. A brief summary of the major changes includes:
  - Britain—The 2010 election produced Britain's first coalition government in more than a generation. The chapter describes the new coalition government of Conservatives and Liberal Democrats under the Prime Ministership of David Cameron, and its new policy directions for Britain.
  - Russia—The chapter covers the 2008 presidential election of President Dmitry Medvedev, Vladimir Putin's transition to premier, and the new working relationship between them, as well as the further slide to autocracy.
  - China—Continuing economic growth, international economic influence, and the coming transition to a "fifth generation" of leaders raise further questions for Communist Party control and policies.
  - Mexico—President Felipe Calderón's government struggles to deal with a growing conflict with Mexico's drug trade and the challenges of improving Mexico's economy in the midst of economic hard times.
  - Iran—Ahmadinejad's 2009 re-election as Iranian president increased turmoil in the nation, as economic problems worsen, schisms within Iranian politics deepen, and international pressure mounts against Iran's nuclear program.
  - Nigeria—The new chapter provides expanded coverage of Nigeria's longest period yet under elected civilian rule. It chronicles the 2010 transition to Nigeria's new president Goodluck Jonathan, which took place

in a context of ethnic and religious conflict and policy failures.

■ United States—The new edition gives a more extensive history of the evolution of civil rights in the United States, as well as the historic election of President Barack Obama in November 2008. The election was followed by the new administration's efforts to deal with financial and economic crises while passing ambitious policy innovations such as health care.

FEATURES AND ORGANIZATION

It may be helpful to indicate more specifically where the topics that are designated in the College Board's Government and Politics: Comparative Course Description can be found in the Introductory and System, Process, and Policy chapters in this text. These topics are also covered, as appropriate, in the country chapters. The correlation between the AP Course Description and the presentation in our chapters is provided on page xviii. We recommend that users follow the logic of the book itself, using the introductory chapters in order and taking special note of AP content area topics when these arise. However, it is also possible to address the content in the order of the AP curriculum.

Each of the country chapters is organized following a common framework, making them easy to compare with each other, with the themes in the introductory and theoretical chapters, and with the AP curriculum. See "A Guide to Comparing Nations" on pages x–xi. That common framework begins with current policy challenges and then discusses the unique historical origins of politics in that political system, as well as relevant features of the social and economic environment. The constitutional arrangements and main political institutions are introduced, usually followed by a discussion of the political culture and citizen participation. Interest groups and interest articulation are usually described next, followed by electoral system, parties, and party system. The policymaking process and the roles played by various institutions, with emphasis on the most important ones in the specific country, are the next section. The chapter generally concludes with an overview of public policy and policy performance, domestic and international.

We live in a dynamic and increasingly connected world, with important changes occurring across the globe. This makes it an interesting time to be a student of comparative politics. Events in remote capitals affect our own lives in many ways. At the same time, seeing the many different ways of running political systems and the impacts of different cultural and economic environments helps us understand the nature of our own political system. We hope that this special AP* Edition will be helpful to AP teachers of comparative politics, who have our greatest respect as they challenge their outstanding students to step outside the familiar bounds of American politics.

ACKNOWLEDGMENTS

We are pleased to acknowledge the contributions of some of the many people who helped us prepare *Comparative Politics Today: A World View*, 10e, *AP* Edition*.

We would like to thank the following individuals for their careful review and analysis of this book: Jennifer Horan, University of North Carolina-Wilmington; David Myers, Penn State University; Sanghamitra Padhy, Davidson College; and Ani Sarkissian, Michigan State University. We are also grateful to Frances A. Rubio for research assistance and to Willy Jou for assistance in developing the index for this edition.

Our coauthors wish to acknowledge their gratitude to a number of individuals who have contributed to their respective chapters.

Our thanks also go to the team at Longman and PreMediaGlobal.

The tenth edition of *Comparative Politics Today: A World View, AP* Edition* continues to teach students to understand politics through the conceptual system, process and policy framework that Gabriel Almond introduced. The early editions of this book pioneered the teaching of systematic comparison of the political cultures, structures, processes, and policy performances of the world's political systems. Later editions have described how enormous changes—such as democratization, the break-up of the Soviet empire, globalization, and intensified threats from ethnic and religious conflict—have shaped politics in many nations. Throughout, these editions reflect Almond's creativity and the applicability of his framework to the changing concerns of students of political science. Now that, as he himself planned, his name no longer appears on the title page, the privilege of preparing the new edition passes to us, his colleagues. We believe that this edition reflects and honors its heritage and our continuing debt to Gabriel.

G. BINGHAM POWELL, JR.
RUSSELL J. DALTON
KAARE STRØM

Pearson is pleased to offer students and teachers program components that will make teaching and learning from this text even more effective and enjoyable.

FOR THE TEACHER

Most of the teacher supplements and resources for this text are available electronically to qualified adopters on the Instructor Resource Center (IRC). Upon adoption or to preview, please go to **www.PearsonSchool.com/Access_Request** and select Instructor Resource Center. You will be required to complete a brief one-time registration subject to verification of educator status. Upon verification, access information and instructions will be sent to you via email. Once logged into the IRC enter your text ISBN in the Search our Catalog box to locate your resources.

AP* INSTRUCTOR'S RESOURCE DVD

Includes AP* Instructor's Manual & Test Bank, AP* TestGen, AP* PowerPoints, and AP* Digital Transparency Masters. See descriptions below.

AP* Instructor's Manual & Test Bank

Provides chapter overviews, chapter outlines, learning objectives, teaching suggestions, key terms, discussion and essay questions, and AP-style multiple-choice questions for each chapter. Available on the AP* Instructor's Resource DVD or online for download.

AP* TestGen

This easy-to-customize test generation software package contains all of the AP-style multiple-choice questions from the AP* Instructor's Manual & Test Bank. This fully networkable, user-friendly program enables instructors to view and edit questions and print tests in a variety of formats. Available on the AP* Instructor's Resource DVD or online for download.

AP* PowerPoint® Presentation

Organized around a lecture outline, this electronic presentation contains maps, tables, and figures from each chapter. Available on the AP* Instructor's Resource DVD or online for download.

AP* Digital Transparency Masters

This set of transparency masters contains all of the maps, tables, and figures from the text. Available on the AP* Instructor's Resource DVD or online for download.

FOR THE STUDENT

AP* Test Prep Workbook

Specifically created to accompany *Comparative Politics Today: A World View, AP* Edition*, this student guide contains an overview of the AP program and the College Board's Government and Politics: Comparative exam. It also provides test-taking strategies, correlations between key AP test topics and the AP* Edition textbook, practice study questions, guidelines for mastering multiple-choice and free response questions, practice tests, commentary on taking AP Comparative Politics and preparing for the AP Government and Politics: Comparative exam. Available for purchase.

MEDIA RESOURCE FOR STUDENTS AND TEACHERS

AP* MyPoliSciKit for *Comparative Politics Today, AP* Edition*

AP* MyPoliSciKit is a premium online learning companion that features multimedia and interactive activities that connect concepts and current events. The book-specific assessment, mapping exercises, comparative exercises, *Financial Times* newsfeeds, and MySearchLab encourage comprehension and critical thinking. With Grade Tracker, teachers can easily follow students' work on the site and their progress on each activity. To learn more, please visit **www.mypoliscikit.com.**

Student and teacher access to AP* MyPoliSciKit is provided upon texbook purchase.

High school teachers can obtain preview or adoption access in the following way:

Preview Access

- Teachers can request preview access online by visiting **PearsonSchool.com/Access_Request**, using Option 2/3. Preview Access information will be sent to the teacher via email.

Adoption Access

- With the purchase of this program, a Pearson Adoption Access Card (ISBN: 0-13-034391-9) with codes and complete instructions will be delivered with your textbook purchase.
- Visit **PearsonSchool.com/Access_Request**. Using Option 2/3. Adoption access information will be sent to the teacher via email.

Students, ask your teacher for access.

ISSUES IN COMPARATIVE POLITICS

WHAT IS POLITICS?

Some people love politics. They relish the excitement of political events, such as a presidential election, as they would an exciting athletic contest (the World Series of baseball or the World Cup of soccer, perhaps). Others are fascinated with politics because they care about the issues and their consequences for people in their own communities and around the world. Still others hate politics, either because it sets groups and individuals against each other, or because it involves abuse of power, deceit, manipulation, and violence. Finally, some people are indifferent to politics because it has little to do with the things that matter most to them, such as family, friends, faith, hobbies, or favorite activities. All of these reactions involve kernels of truth about politics. Indeed, most of us react to politics with a mixture of these sentiments. Politics has many faces and can be a force for good as well as evil. The core of politics, however, is about human beings making important decisions for their communities and for others.

This book is about the comparative study of politics. In order to make political comparisons, we need to understand what politics is and what it means to study politics comparatively. Comparative politics thus is both a subject of study—comparing the nature of politics and the political process across different political systems, and a method of study—involving how and why we make such comparisons. We address the first point in this chapter; Chapter 2 discusses the second.

Politics deals with human decisions, and political science is the study of such decisions. Yet not all decisions are political, and many of the social sciences study decisions that are of little interest to political scientists. For example, consider when you go with a friend to an event, such as a concert or a soccer match. You can spend your money on the tickets (to get the best seats possible) or on food and drink, or you can save your money for the future. Economists study the spending decisions people make and perhaps how they reach them. Psychologists, on the other hand, might study why you went to the event with this friend and not another, or who suggested going in the first place.

Political scientists seldom examine such private and personal decisions, unless they have political consequences. Instead, political decisions are those that are *public* and *authoritative*. Political decisions take place within some society or community that we call a *political system*, which we describe below. Yet not all social decisions are public. Most of what happens within families, among friends, or in social groups belongs to the *private sphere*. Actions within this sphere do not bind anyone outside that group and are not controlled by the government. In most societies, your choices of concert partners and food are private decisions.

The *public sphere* of politics deals with collective decisions that extend beyond the individual and private life, typically involving government action. Yet political decisions constantly touch our lives. Our jobs are structured by government regulations, our homes are built to conform to government housing codes, public schools are funded and managed by the government, and we travel on roads maintained by the government and monitored by the police. Politics thus affects us in many important ways. Therefore, it is important to study how political decisions are made and what their consequences are.

In totalitarian societies, like Hitler's Third Reich and some communist states, the public sphere is very large and the private sphere is very limited. The state tries to dominate the life of its people, even intruding into family life. On the other hand, in some less developed nations, the private domain may almost crowd out the public one. Many people in various African nations, for instance, may be unaware of what happens in the capital city and untouched by the decisions made there. Western democracies have a more balanced mix of private and public spheres. However, the boundaries between the two spheres are redrawn all the time. A few decades ago, the sex lives of U.S. presidents or members of the British royal family were considered private matters, not to be discussed in public. These norms have changed in Britain and the United States, but the traditional standards remain in other countries. Similarly, in Britain, certain religious beliefs were considered treasonous in the 1500s and 1600s. Today, religious beliefs are considered private matters in most modern democracies, though not in many other parts of the world. Even though politics may be influenced by what happens in the private domain, it deals directly with only those decisions that are public.

Politics is also *authoritative*. Authority means that formal power rests in individuals or groups whose decisions are expected to be carried out and respected. Thus, political decisions are binding for members of that political system. Governments and other authorities may use persuasion, inducements, or brute force to ensure compliance. For instance, a religious authority, such as the Pope, has few coercive powers. He can persuade, but rarely compel, the Catholic Church's followers. In contrast, tax authorities, such as the U.S. Internal Revenue Service, can both exhort and compel people to follow their rules.

Thus, *politics* refers to activities associated with the control of public decisions among a given people and in a given territory, where this control may be backed up by authoritative means. Politics involves the crafting of these authoritative decisions—who gets to make them and for what purposes.

We live in one of the most exciting times to study politics. The end of the Cold War created a new international order, although its shape is still uncertain. Democratic transitions in Latin America, Eastern Europe, East Asia, and parts of Africa have transformed the world, although it is unclear how many of these new democracies will endure and what forms they might take.

Throughout the world, globalization has brought the citizens of different countries closer together and made them more dependent on one another, for better or worse. Some of the issues people in many societies confront—such as confronting climate change and achieving international peace—are transnational and indeed global. Part of their solutions, we hope, lies in the political choices that people in different communities make about their collective future. Our goal in this book is to give you a sense of how governments and politics can either address or exacerbate these challenges.

GOVERNMENTS AND THE STATE OF NATURE

Governments are organizations of individuals who have the power to make binding decisions on behalf of a particular community. Governments thus have authoritative and coercive powers and do many things. They can wage war or encourage peace; encourage or restrict international trade; open or close their borders to the exchange of ideas; tax their populations heavily or lightly and through different means; and allocate resources for education, health, and welfare or leave such matters to others. People who are affected by such decisions may welcome them or disapprove, and there is often heated disagreement about the proper role of government.

Debates over the nature and appropriate role of government are far from new. They reflect a classic polemic in political philosophy. For centuries, philosophers have debated whether governments are a force for good or evil. In the seventeenth and eighteenth centuries—the time of the English, French, and American revolutions—much of this debate was couched in arguments concerning the **state of nature**.

Political philosophers thought about the state of nature as the condition of humankind if no government existed. In some cases, they thought that such a situation had existed before the first governments were formed. These philosophers used their ideas about the state of nature to identify an ideal social contract (agreement) on which to build a political system. Even today, many philosophers and political thinkers find it useful to make such a mental experiment to consider the consequences of having governments.

These debates have shaped our images of government, even to the present. The contrast between

Thomas Hobbes's and Jean-Jacques Rousseau's ideas about the state of nature is most striking. Hobbes was the ultimate pessimist. He thought of the state of nature as mercilessly inhospitable, a situation of eternal conflict of all against all, and a source of barbarism and continuous fear. He pessimistically argued that "[i]n such condition, there is no place for Industry; because the fruit thereof is uncertain: and consequently no Culture of the Earth; no Navigation, nor use of the commodities that may be imported by Sea; no commodious Building, . . . no Arts; no Letters; no Society; and which is worst of all, continuall feare, and danger of violent death; And the life of man, solitary, poor, nasty, brutish, and short."[1]

Rousseau, in contrast, was more optimistic about the state of nature. For him, it represented humanity before its fall from grace, without all the corruptions that governments have introduced. "Man is born free," Rousseau observed in *The Social Contract*, "and yet everywhere he is in chains." Rousseau saw governments as the source of power and inequality, and these conditions in turn as the causes of human alienation and corruption. "The extreme inequality in our way of life," he argued, "excess of idleness in some, excess of labor in others; . . . late nights, excesses of all kinds, immoderate ecstasies of all the passions; fatigues and exhaustion of mind, numberless sorrows and afflictions . . . that most of our ills are our own work; that we would have avoided almost all of them by preserving the simple, uniform, and solitary way of life prescribed to us by nature."[2]

John Locke's ideas have been particularly important for the development of Western democracies. He took a position between those of Hobbes and Rousseau. Compared with Hobbes, Locke thought of human beings as more businesslike and less war-prone. Yet like Hobbes he proposed a social contract to replace the state of nature with a system of government. While Hobbes thought the main task for government is to quell disorder and protect against violence and war, Locke saw the state's main role as protecting property and commerce and promoting economic growth. He believed government would do this by establishing and enforcing property rights and rules of economic exchange. Whereas Hobbes thought government needed to be a Leviathan—a benevolent dictator to whom the citizens would yield all their power—Locke favored a limited government.

Although these debates began centuries ago, they still underlie current discussions on the appropriate role of government. To some, government is the solution to many human needs and problems—a theme that former U.S. president Bill Clinton often advocated. To others, the government is often part of the problem—a theme that former U.S. president Ronald Reagan articulately argued. To some, government exists to create the social order that protects its citizens; to others, government limits our freedoms. This tension is part of the political discourse in many contemporary nations, including the United States. We explore these contrasting views and different examples of government structures in this book.

WHY GOVERNMENTS?

A recent libertarian science-fiction book begins with the scenario of a group of travelers landing at an airport after a long overseas flight. As they disembark from the plane, they notice that there are no police checking passports, no customs officers scanning baggage, and no officials applying immigration rules.[3] They had landed in a society without government, and the puzzle was what having no government would mean for the citizenry. The answer is a great deal (see Box 1.1). As philosophers have pointed out, there are many reasons why people create governments and prefer to live under such a social order. We shall discuss some of these, beginning with activities that help generate a stable community in the first place and then those that help this community prosper.

Community- and Nation-Building

One of the first purposes of governments is to create and maintain a community in which people can feel safe and comfortable. While humans may be social beings, it is not always easy to build a community in which large numbers of people can communicate, feel at home, and interact constructively. Governments can help generate such communities in many different ways—for example, by teaching a common language, instilling common norms and values, creating common myths and symbols, and supporting a national identity. However, sometimes such actions create controversy because there is disagreement about these norms and values.

BOX 1.1

U.S. Government's Top Ten List

Paul Light surveyed 450 historians and political scientists to assess the U.S. government's greatest achievements in the past half century. Their top ten list is as follows:

- Help rebuild Europe after World War II
- Expand the right to vote for minorities
- Promote equal access to public accommodations
- Reduce disease
- Reduce workplace discrimination
- Ensure safe food and drinking water
- Strengthen the nation's highway system

- Increase older Americans' access to health care
- Reduce the federal deficit
- Promote financial security in retirement

Several of these policy areas will be discussed in Chapter 7, but note that the first of these accomplishments had to do with the country's external environment: rebuilding Europe after World War II. Other achievements include important public goods (safe water, highways), as well as promoting fairness and building a social safety net.

Source: Paul Light, *Government's Greatest Achievements of the Past Half-Century* (Washington, D.C.: Brookings Institution, 2000) (www.brookings.edu/comm/reformwatch/rw02.pdf).

Nation-building activities help instill common world views, values, and expectations. Using a concept discussed more in Chapter 3, governments can help create a national **political culture**. The political culture defines the public's expectations toward the political process and its role within the process. The more the political culture is shared, the easier it is to live in peaceful coexistence and engage in activities for mutual gain, such as commerce.

Security and Order

Hobbes believed that only strong governments can make society safe for their inhabitants, and providing security and law and order is among the most essential tasks that governments perform. Externally, security means protecting against attacks from other political systems. Armies, navies, and air forces typically perform this function. Internally, security means protecting against theft, aggression, and violence from members of one's own society. In most societies, providing this is the function of the police.

Providing security and order is a critical role of modern governments. While governments worldwide have privatized many of the services they once performed—for example, those involving post offices, railroads, and telecommunications—few if any governments have privatized their police or defense forces. This shows that security is one of the most essential roles of government. The international

terrorist attacks in New York City and Washington, D.C., on September 11, 2001, and subsequent attacks and attempted violence in London, Madrid, and elsewhere underscore the importance of security.

Protecting Rights

John Locke considered property rights to be particularly critical to the development of prosperous communities. Without effective protection of property rights, people will not invest their goods or energies in productive processes. Also, unless property rights exist and contracts can be negotiated and enforced, people will not trust their neighbors enough to trade and invest. Anything beyond a subsistence economy requires effective property rights and contracts. Therefore, Locke believed that the primary role of government is to establish and protect such rights. Similarly, contemporary authors argue that social order is a prerequisite for development and democratization.[4]

Effective property rights establish ownership and provide security against trespass and violations. Such rights must also make the buying and selling of property relatively inexpensive and painless. Finally, people must have faith that their property rights can be defended. Thus, many analysts argue that one of the most restrictive limitations on development in the Third World is the government's inability (or unwillingness) to guarantee such rights. Peasant families in many societies have lived for generations on a plot of land but cannot claim ownership, which erodes their incentive and opportunity to invest in the future.

Although Locke was most concerned with economic property rights, governments also protect many other social and political rights. Among them are freedoms of speech and association, and protection against various forms of discrimination and harassment. Indeed, the protection of these rights and liberties is one of the prime goals of government—with other factors such as nation-building, security, and property rights providing a means toward this goal. Governments also play a key role in protecting the rights of religious, racial, and other social groups. Human development stresses the expansion of these rights and liberties, and governments play a key role in this process.

Promoting Economic Efficiency and Growth

Economists have long debated the government's potential role in promoting economic development. Neoclassical economics shows that markets are efficient when property rights are defined and protected, when competition is rigorous, and when information is freely available. When these conditions do not hold, however, markets may fail and the economy may suffer.[5] At least in some circumstances, governments can ameliorate the results of market failure.

Governments may be especially important in providing **public goods**, such as clean air, a national defense, or disease prevention. Public goods have two things in common. One is that if one person enjoys them, they cannot be withheld from anyone else in that community. The second is that one person's enjoyment or consumption of the goods does not detract from anyone else's. Consider clean air. For most practical purposes, it is impossible to provide one person with clean air without also giving it to his or her neighbors. Moreover, my enjoyment of clean air does not mean that my neighbors have any less of it. Economists argue that people in a market economy therefore will not pay enough for public goods because they can "free-ride" on the goods that others provide. At the very least, people will not pay for public goods until they know that others will also contribute. Analysts therefore often claim that only government can provide the right quantity of such public goods.

Governments can also benefit society by controlling the **externalities** that occur when an activity incurs costs that are not borne by the producer or the user. For instance, many forms of environmental degradation occur when those who produce or consume goods do not pay all of the environmental costs. Polluting factories, waste dumps, prisons, and major highways can impose large costs on those who live near them. NIMBY ("not in my backyard") groups arise when citizens complain about these costs. Governments can help protect people from unfair externalities or ensure that burdens are fairly shared.

Governments can also promote fair competition in economic markets. For example, governments can ensure that all businesses follow minimum standards of worker protection and product liability. In other cases, the government may control potentially monopolistic enterprises to ensure that they do not abuse their market power. This happened in the nineteenth century with railroad monopolies, and more currently with technology monopolies, such as Microsoft, or telecommunications companies. In these cases, the government acts as the policeman to prevent the economically powerful from exploiting their power. Sometimes, the government itself may become the monopolist. In some markets, very large start-up or coordination costs mean that there should be only one producer. If that producer may also easily abuse its power, the government may set itself up as that monopolist, or impose tight controls. Telecommunications have commonly been a government monopoly in many societies, as have mail services and strategic defense industries.

Social Justice

Governments can also play a role in dividing the fruits of economic growth in equitable ways. Many people argue that governments are needed to promote social justice by redistributing wealth and other resources among citizens. In many countries, the distribution of income and property is highly uneven, and this is particularly troubling when there is little upward mobility or when inequalities tend to grow over time. Brazil, for example, has one of the most severe income inequalities in the world, an inequality that grew in every decade from the 1930s to the 1990s but has recently receded a little.

Under such circumstances, social justice may require a "new deal," especially if inequalities deprive many individuals of education, adequate health care, or other basic needs. Government can intervene to redistribute resources from the better-off to the poor. Many private individuals, religious and charitable organizations, and foundations also do much to help the poor, but they generally do not have the capacity to tax the wealthy. Governments do, at least under some circumstances. Many tax and welfare policies redistribute income, although the degree of redistribution is often hotly disputed (see Chapter 7).

Some theorists argue that such transfers should attempt to equalize the conditions of all citizens. Others prefer governments to redistribute enough to equalize opportunities, and then let individuals be responsible for their own fortunes. Yet most individuals agree that governments should provide a social safety net and give their citizens opportunities to reach certain minimum standards of living.

Protecting the Weak

We commonly rely on the government to protect individuals and groups that are not able to speak for themselves. Groups such as the disabled, the very young, or future generations cannot effectively protect their own interests. Governments, however, can protect the interests of the unborn and prevent them from being saddled with economic debts or environmental degradation. In recent decades, governments have become much more involved in protecting groups that are politically weak or disenfranchised, such as children, the old, and the infirm or disabled, as well as nonhumans—from whales and birds to trees and other parts of our natural environment. Thus, governments in many countries have increasingly intervened to protect children from abuse or exploitation in their families, in schools, or in the workplace.

WHEN DOES GOVERNMENT BECOME THE PROBLEM?

Governments can thus serve many political functions, yet their intervention is not always welcomed or beneficial. When and how government intervention is necessary and desirable are among the most disputed issues in modern politics. During the twentieth century, the role of governments expanded enormously in most nations. At the same time, criticisms of many government policies have persisted and sometimes intensified. Such skepticism is directed at virtually all government activities, especially the economic role of government. **Anarchism** and **libertarianism** are two political and philosophical traditions that are critical of the role of modern governments. But they differ in their main concerns. Libertarians see the greatest problem of government as its encroachment on individual freedoms, whereas anarchists are concerned primarily with the threats that governments pose to social communities.

Destruction of Community

Whereas some see governments as a way to build community, others argue that governments destroy natural communities. Government, they hold, implies power and inequality among human beings. While those who have power are corrupted, those without it are degraded and alienated. According to Rousseau, only human beings unfettered by government can form bonds that allow them to develop their full human potential. By imposing an order based on coercion, hierarchy, and the threat of force, governments destroy natural communities. The stronger government becomes, the greater the inequalities of power. Such arguments stimulated criticism of communism as limiting the potential and freedom of its citizens. Others argue that strong governments create a "client society," in which people learn to be subservient to authorities and to rely on governments to meet their needs. In such societies, governments patronize and pacify their citizens, as seen in many developing nations today.

Violations of Basic Rights

Just as governments can help establish many essential rights, they can also use their powers to violate these rights in the most serious manner. The twentieth century witnessed enormous progress in the extension of political, economic, and social rights in societies worldwide. At the same time, however, some governments violated basic **human rights** on an unprecedented scale. The millions of lives lost to political persecution is the most serious example of this. Such horrors happened not only in Nazi extermination camps and during Stalin's Great Terror in the Soviet Union, but also on a huge scale in China, Cambodia, and Rwanda, and on a somewhat smaller scale in Saddam Hussein's Iraq, as well as in the Sudan and in Afghanistan under the Taliban.

These extreme abuses of government power illustrate a dilemma that troubled James Madison and other Founders of the American Revolution: the challenge of creating a government strong enough to govern effectively but not so strong that it could destroy the rights of its citizens. They understood the irony that to protect individuals from each other, societies can create a government that has even more power to coerce the individual. Libertarians are especially concerned about the abuses and violations of basic freedoms that large governments may thus entail.

Economic Inefficiency

Governments can help economies flourish, but they also can distort and restrict a state's economic potential. President Robert Mugabe, for instance, has destroyed the economy of Zimbabwe, which was once Africa's most prosperous state, and similar examples exist in many struggling economies. Economic problems might arise even if government officials do not actively abuse their power. Government regulation of the economy may distort the terms of trade and lower people's incentives to produce. Further inefficiencies may arise when governments actually own or manage important economic enterprises. This is particularly likely if the government holds a monopoly on an important good, since monopolies generally cause goods to be undersupplied and overpriced. Moreover, government industries may be especially prone to inefficiency and complacency because management and workers often have better job protection than those in the private sector. Therefore, they may worry less about the economic performance of the firm. Such experiences have caused citizens in both developing and advanced industrial economies to worry about the performance of government monopolies and stimulated calls to restrict the economic role of governments.

Government for Private Gain

Society also may suffer if government officials make decisions to benefit themselves personally, or select policies to get themselves reelected regardless of whether those policies would be the best for the society. A politician or political group may use the government to reap benefits unfairly at the public's expense—what is called **rent-seeking**. *Rents* are benefits created through government intervention in the economy—for example, tax revenue or profits created because the government has restricted competition. Rent-seeking refers to efforts by individuals, politicians, groups, firms, or organizations to reap such benefits. The idea is really quite simple. For instance, a local mayor plans an economic development project that will benefit his friends or supporters who own suitable land or who will supply contracts for the project. Rent-seeking can impose large costs on society because policies are chosen for the private benefits they produce rather than for their social efficiency and because groups may expend great resources to control these spoils of government. Rent-seeking may turn into outright corruption when influence is traded for money or other advantage (see Box 1.2).

BOX 1.2

Rent-Seeking and the Case of Mobutu Sese Seko

What happens if politicians use their power in their own self-interest or to benefit individuals or groups that support them? President Mobutu Sese Seko (1930–1997) of Zaire offers a tragic example of the costs that rent-seeking politicians can impose on their societies. After seizing power in a 1965 coup, Mobutu ruled the large African state of Congo (which he renamed Zaire) for more than thirty years. During his long rule, President Mobutu used government funds, including aid from Western states such as the United States, to amass a huge personal fortune, which he invested abroad. In addition to large sums of money, he is reported to have owned about thirty luxury residences abroad, including a number of palatial estates on the French Riviera. Meanwhile, living standards in Zaire, a poor country despite significant natural resources, plummeted, and the country was racked with epidemic disease and civil war. Mobutu was finally overthrown and died of natural causes shortly after his ouster.

This kind of political exploitation is a particularly serious problem in poor societies. Holding political office is often an effective way to enrich oneself when political watchdogs such as courts and mass media are too weak to constrain government officials. Besides, many developing societies do not have strong social norms against using government for private gain. On the contrary, people often expect those in government to use their power to benefit themselves, their families, and their neighbors. Even in many advanced democratic societies, public officeholders are expected to appoint their supporters to ambassadorships and other public posts, although civil-service rules designed to reward merit may in part constrain such appointments. The temptations of officeholding are great. Despite legal rules, press scrutiny, and citizen concerns, few governments anywhere finish their terms of office untainted by some corruption scandal. In Lord Acton's famous words, "Power corrupts, and absolute power corrupts absolutely."

Vested Interests and Inertia

Government-created private gains are difficult to change or abolish once they have been established because some people enjoy government jobs, contracts, or other favors that they otherwise might not have had. The larger the government and the more attractive the benefits it provides, the more likely it is that such **vested interests** will resist change (unless change means even larger benefits). Therefore, any government will foster officeholders and beneficiaries with a vested interest in maintaining or enlarging the government itself. Such groups may become a powerful force in favor of the status quo.

Vested interests make it difficult to change government policies or make them more efficient. Once established, agencies and policies often live on far beyond their usefulness. For example, when the Spanish Armada threatened to invade England in 1588, the government established a military observation post at Land's End in southwest England. This observation post remained in place for four centuries! In the United States, the Rural Electrification Administration was created in 1935 to bring electricity to rural America. Although the country had long been electrified by then, the agency persisted for almost sixty years until it was finally merged into the Rural Utilities Service in 1994.

Vested interests are particularly likely in political systems that contain many safeguards against rapid political change. While the checks and balances in political systems such as in the United States are designed to safeguard individual rights, they may also protect the privileges of vested interests. Yet even political systems that contain far fewer such checks may exhibit an excess of political inertia. Britain is an excellent example. Until recently, the House of Lords represented the social groups that dominated British society before the Industrial Revolution more than two hundred years ago (noblemen, bishops, and judges). Only in the last few years has Britain begun reforming the House of Lords to eliminate features that reflect Britain's feudal and preindustrial past.

POLITICAL SYSTEMS AND STATES

We began by discussing governments, but governments are only one part of a larger political system. Since the term **political system** is a main organizing concept of this book, it deserves a full explanation. A system by definition has two properties: (1) a set of interdependent parts, and (2) boundaries toward its environment.

A political system is a particular type of social system that is involved in the making of authoritative public decisions. Central elements of a political system are the institutions of government—such as legislatures, bureaucracies, and courts—that formulate and implement the collective goals of a society or of groups within it.

Political systems also include important parts of the society in which governments operate. For example, political organizations, such as political parties or interest groups, are part of the political system. Such organizations do not have coercive authority, except insofar as they control the government. Likewise, the mass media only indirectly affect elections, legislation, and law enforcement. A whole host of institutions—beginning with the family and including communities, churches, schools, corporations, foundations, and think tanks—influence political attitudes and public policy. The term *political system* refers to the whole collection of related, interacting institutions and agencies.

The political systems that we compare in this book are all independent states (we also more casually refer to them as *countries*). They represent some of the most politically important countries in the contemporary world. At the same time, they reflect the diversity of political systems that exist today. A **state** is a particular type of political system. It has **sovereignty**—independent legal authority over a population in a particular territory, based on the recognized right to self-determination. Sovereignty rests with those who have the ultimate right to make political decisions.

External sovereignty is the right to make binding agreements (treaties) with other states. For instance, France's external sovereignty means that it can enter into treaties with other states. The city of Bordeaux, however, does not have this right (nor do other subnational units of government in France). Internal sovereignty is the right to make political decisions having to do with one's own citizens. For example, the French government has internal sovereignty so that it can impose taxes on French citizens.

Yet states mold and are molded by a domestic environment and an international environment. The system receives inputs from these environments and shapes them through its outputs. The boundaries of political systems are defined in terms of persons, territory, and property. Most people have citizenship rights in only one country, and such citizenship implies a bundle of rights and obligations related to that state. Similarly, territory is divided between states. A given piece of land is supposed to belong to only one country. Of course, disputes over citizenship, territory, and property are by no means uncommon and are among the most frequent causes of international conflict.

Every state faces some constraints on its external and internal sovereignty. For example, with the increasing integration of France into the **European Union (EU)**, the French government has given up parts of its sovereignty to the EU, for example by adopting the common currency of the euro, and this loss of sovereignty is a major topic of political debate. In the United States, we confuse things a bit by calling the fifty constituent units "states," even though they share their power and authority with the federal government in Washington, D.C., and enjoy much less sovereignty than France.

We often think of the world as a patchwork of states with sizable and contiguous territories, and a common identity shared by their citizens. A nation is a group of people, often living in a common territory, who have such a common identity. In **nation-states**, national identifications and sovereign political authority largely coincide—the state consists of individuals who share a common national identity. We have come to think of nation-states as the natural way to organize political systems, and often as an ideal. The national right to self-determination—the idea that every nation has a right to form its own state if it wants to do so—was enshrined in the Treaty of Versailles at the end of World War I.

Nation-states are often a desirable way to organize a political system. The national right to self-determination, however, is a relatively modern invention born in late medieval Europe. Until the end of the Middle Ages, Europe consisted of many very small political systems and a few very large ones, whose territorial possessions were not always very stable or contiguous. Nor did states always consist of people with the same national identity. But gradually, a set of European nation-states evolved, and the 1648 Treaty of Westphalia established that principle for the political organization of Europe. The nation-state thus emerged as the dominant political system during the eighteenth and nineteenth centuries in Europe.

Europe did not transform itself into distinct nation-states accidentally—indeed, the governments of the emerging nation-states had a great deal to do with it. They sought to instill a common national identity among the peoples they controlled. They did so, often heavy-handedly, by promoting a common language, a common educational system, and often a common religion. While this process of nation-building was often harsh, it produced a Europe in which the inhabitants of most states have a strong sense of community.

Many societies in the developing world today face similar challenges. Especially in Africa, the newly independent states that emerged in the 1950s and 1960s had very weak national identities. In many parts of Africa, large-scale national communities simply had not existed before these areas were colonized by Europeans and others. Even where such national identities did exist, they were rarely reflected in the boundaries that the colonial powers (such as Britain, France, and Portugal) drew between their possessions. After independence, many new states therefore faced huge nation-building tasks.

There are additional challenges to contemporary nation-states. After World War II, the states of the world have experienced an increasingly rapid process of **globalization**, in which they have become more open to and dependent on one another. Globalization has many faces (see Chapter 7). One is increasing trade in goods and services, which means that many of the products we buy are made in China and many of the telephone calls we make are answered in India. Outsourcing and loss of local jobs have been among the negative consequences of this aspect of globalization. Globalization also means migration across state boundaries, which has increased greatly in recent decades and caused controversy and conflict in many societies. Finally, globalization means that citizens of all (or most) countries increasingly have to share in cultures that have developed elsewhere (see Chapter 3). Globalization has lowered the prices of many products and increased the richness of life, but it has also created serious challenges for many states. Some, such as North Korea and Myanmar, have sought to isolate themselves from its effects. Others have responded in a more accepting manner. Most of the industrialized countries of Europe have thus gradually created a common market economy and a set of supranational political institutions, such as a common parliament and a common court of justice. The EU originally consisted of six countries—France, Germany, Italy, Belgium, the Netherlands, and Luxembourg—but has expanded to twenty-seven members, with several additional states currently applying for membership.

The **United Nations (UN)**, formed at the end of World War II in 1945, has also acquired new responsibilities with globalization and especially since the collapse of the Soviet Union in 1991. As of early 2010, UN forces were peacekeepers in sixteen countries. These operations—involving more than 120,000 peacekeepers—seek to separate combatants in domestic and international conflicts, settle disputes, and form effective governing institutions. The UN has increased authority over world security, constraining, supporting, and sometimes replacing the unilateral actions of individual states. Yet while the sovereignty of states may be diminishing, they are still the most important political systems. That, of course, is the main reason that they are the subject of our study.

THE DIVERSITY OF STATES

Today, just about the entire surface of the world is covered by independent states. There were 192 UN "member-states" in 2010.[6] A few countries are not members of the UN (for example, Taiwan and the Vatican), and ongoing independence movements could create even more states. When the United States declared its independence in 1776, most independent states were European (see Figure 1.1). Much of the rest of the world existed as colonies to one of the European empires. In the nineteenth and early twentieth centuries, the number of states increased, principally in Latin America, where the Spanish and Portuguese empires broke up into twenty independent states. In Europe, newly independent countries emerged in the Balkans, Scandinavia, and the Low Countries.

United Nations Building

The United Nations is the most inclusive organization of states. As of 2010, the United Nations had 192 member states, represented by the flags flying outside its headquarters in New York City.

Joseph Sohm/Visions of America/Corbis

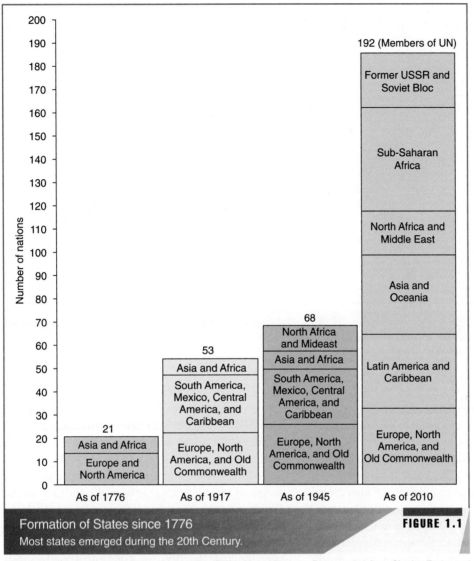

Source: For Contemporary Members, Information Office, United Nations. Data to 1945 from Charles Taylor and Michael Hudson, *World Handbook of Political and Social Indicators* (New Haven, CT: Yale University Press, 1972), 26ff.

Formation of States since 1776
Most states emerged during the 20th Century.

FIGURE 1.1

because of its strict neutrality policy—but there have been few newly independent countries over the past decade.

All these countries—new as well as old—share certain characteristics. They have legal authority over their territories and people; most have armies, air forces, and in some cases navies; they collect taxes and spend money; and they regulate their economies and maintain public order. Countries send and receive ambassadors; most belong to international organizations. But they also vary, often profoundly, in physical size, histories, institutions, cultures, religions, economies, and social structures—factors that shape their politics.

States come in all sizes. The smallest legally independent political entity in territory as well as population is Vatican City, the headquarters of the Catholic Church, with less than half a square kilometer of turf and fewer than a thousand residents. The contrasts between geographic size and population size can be graphically seen in the following two maps. In Map 1.1, the countries of the world are displayed, as we often see them, according to their size. Russia, with its landmass extending over eleven contiguous time zones, is the world's largest state, with more than 17 million square kilometers. The United States, Canada, and China are among the next set of countries, with around 9 million square kilometers each.

Between the two world wars, new states came into being in North Africa and the Middle East, and Europe continued to fragment as the Russian and Austro-Hungarian empires broke up. After World War II, the development of new states took off, especially with the independence of India and Pakistan in 1947. By 2010, 126 new countries had joined the 68 states that existed in 1945. The largest group of new states is in Sub-Saharan Africa. More than twenty new countries formed in the 1990s—mostly the successor states of the Soviet Union, Yugoslavia, and Czechoslovakia. Four states have joined the UN since 2000—most notably Switzerland, which until 2002 had stayed out

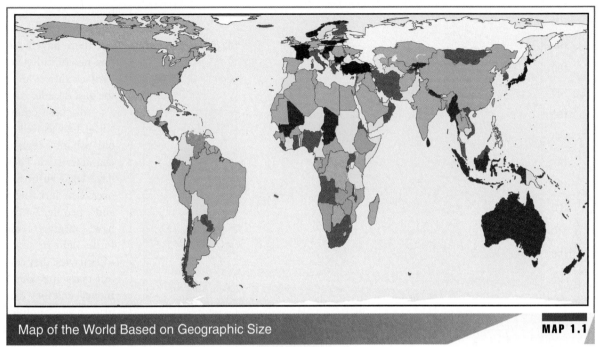

Map of the World Based on Geographic Size

MAP 1.1

Source: Copyright © *The Real World Atlas*, Thames & Hudson, Ltd., London, 2008.

Many of the established democracies in Europe are relatively small (Britain has 242,000 square kilometers and Germany 349,000).

Map 1.2 instead displays the world's states by their population size. Instantly, China and India balloon in size because of their large populations. China alone accounts for about a fifth of the world's population (with 1.3 billion people), and India is not far behind (with 1.2 billion). Important European democracies such as Britain, France, and Germany look much smaller because their populations only number between 60 and 80 million. Even more dramatically, Australia shrinks from a continent in the first map to a small dot in the second because of its small population (21 million). And although the United States has roughly the same territory as China and is larger than India, it is much smaller than these Asian giants in population (310 million and a distant third in the world). And while Russia has almost twice as much land as any other country, its population (142 million) is less than half that of the United States and shrinking.

The political implications of these striking contrasts in population size and geographic area are not always obvious. Size matters in politics, and big states are often more powerful than small ones. Yet big countries do not always prevail over small ones: the United States broke away from Britain when the latter was the most powerful country in the world; both Britain and the Soviet Union tried to conquer Afghanistan and failed; Cuba has challenged the United States for almost fifty years; Israel stands off the much larger Arab world; and tiny Vatican City has great power and influence in spiritual and moral affairs. Nor do area and population size determine a country's political system. Both little Luxembourg and large India are democracies. Autocratic (nondemocratic) regimes are similarly found in small, medium, and large countries. These enormous contrasts in size show only that the states now making up the world differ greatly in their physical and human resources.

A state's geographic location can also have important strategic implications. In the sixteenth through nineteenth centuries, European states typically required a large land army to protect themselves from the threats of their neighbors. These countries had difficulties developing free political institutions, since they needed a strong government to extract resources on a large scale and keep the population under control. Britain was protected by the English Channel and could defend itself through its navy, a smaller army, lower taxation, and less centralization of power—

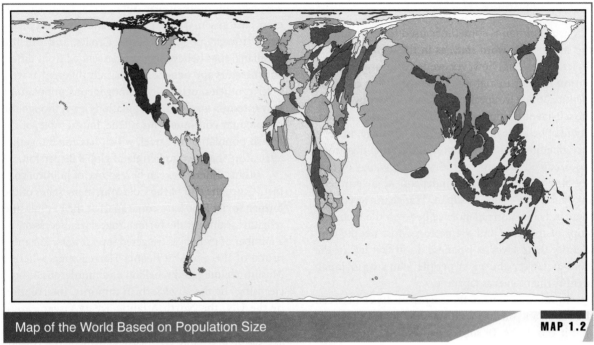

Map of the World Based on Population Size

MAP 1.2

Source: Copyright © *The Real World Atlas*, Thames & Hudson, Ltd., London, 2008.

which aided political liberalization. Most peoples of Asia, Africa, and Latin America were colonized by the more powerful Western nations. Those that had the richest natural resources, the most convenient locations, and the most benign climates tended to attract the largest numbers of settlers. Areas that were landlocked or more geographically inhospitable were less likely to be colonized but have also often remained poor and isolated from world markets.

CHALLENGES: BUILDING COMMUNITY

Whether they are old or new, large or small, most of the world's states face a number of common challenges. The first is building community. Most states do not have a homogeneous population, and instilling a sense of shared identity can be a serious challenge. Second, even the wealthiest states face the challenge of fostering continued economic and social development. Finally, most states face significant challenges in advancing democracy and civil liberties. These challenges should be familiar from our discussion of the purposes and dangers of governments. In the remainder of this chapter, we discuss these challenges successively.

One of the most important challenges facing political systems worldwide is to build a common

identity and a sense of community among their citizens. The absence of a common identity can have severe political consequences. Conflicts over national, ethnic, or religious identities are among the most explosive causes of political turmoil, as we have witnessed in Northern Ireland, the former Yugoslavia, Rwanda, and elsewhere. But while building community is a pervasive challenge, some countries are in a much better situation than others. Japan, for example, has an ethnically homogeneous population, a common language, and a long national political history. A large majority of the Japanese share in the religions of Buddhism and Shintoism, and the country is separated by miles of ocean from its most important neighbors. Nigeria, in contrast, is an accidental and artificial creation of British colonial rule and has no common precolonial history. The population is sharply divided between Muslims and Christians; the Christians are divided equally into Catholics and Protestants. There are some 250 different ethnic groups, speaking a variety of local languages, in addition to English. Obviously, the challenges of building community are much greater in Nigeria than they are in Japan. Although few countries face problems as complicated as those of the Nigerians, the community-building challenge is one of the most serious issues facing many states today.

States and Nations

The word *nation* is sometimes used to mean almost the same as the word *state*, as in the *United Nations*. Strictly speaking, however, we wish to use the term **nation** to refer to a group of people with a common identity. When we speak of a "nation," we thus refer to the self-identification of a people. That common identity may be built upon a common language, history, race, or culture, or simply upon the fact that this group has occupied the same territory. Nations may or may not have their own state or independent government. In some cases—such as Japan, France, or Sweden—there is a close correspondence between the memberships of the state and the nation. Most people who identify themselves as Japanese do in fact live in the state of Japan, and most people who live in Japan identify themselves as Japanese.

In many instances, the correspondence between the nation and the state is not so neat. Nor is it obvious that it should be. In some cases, states are *multinational*—consisting of a multitude of different nations. The Soviet Union, Yugoslavia, and Czechoslovakia were multinational states that broke apart. In other cases, some nations are much larger than the corresponding states, such as Germany for most of its history or China. Some nations have split into two or more states for political reasons, such as Korea today and Germany between 1949 and 1990. Some groups with claims to be nations have no state at all, such as the Kurds, the Basques, and the Tamils. When states and nations do not coincide, it can cause explosive political conflict, as discussed later. At the same time, the presence of several nations within the same state can also be a source of diversity and cultural enrichment.

Nationality and Ethnicity

There is a fine line between nations and *ethnic groups*, which may have common physical traits, languages, cultures, or history. Like nationality, **ethnicity** need not have any objective basis in genetics, culture, or history. German sociologist Max Weber defined ethnic groups as "those human groups that entertain a subjective belief in their common descent because of similarities of physical type or of customs or both, or because of memories of colonization and migration. . . . [I]t does not matter whether or not an objective blood relationship exists."[7] Similarly, groups that are physically quite similar, but differ by language, religion, customs, marriage patterns, and historical memories (for example, the Serbs, Croats, and Muslim Bosnians) may believe they are descended from different ancestors and hence are physically different as well. Over centuries, originally homogeneous populations may intermix with other populations, even though the culture may continue. This is true, for example, of the Jewish population of Israel, which has come together after more than two millennia of global dispersion.

Ethnic differences can be a source of political conflict.[8] Since the end of the Cold War, many states of the former Soviet Bloc have come apart at their ethnic and religious seams. In the former Yugoslavia, secession by a number of provinces triggered several wars. The most brutal of these was in Bosnia-Herzegovina, where a Muslim regime faced rebellion and murderous "ethnic cleansing" by the large Serbian minority. Intervention by the UN, the North Atlantic Treaty Organization (NATO), and the United States contained Serbian aggression and led to an uneasy settlement, but considerable tension remains. Similar tensions and violent aggression occurred in Kosovo as well.

In many developing countries, boundaries established by former colonial powers cut across ethnic lines. In 1947, the British withdrew from India and divided the subcontinent into a northern Muslim area—Pakistan—and a southern Hindu area—India. The most immediate consequence was a terrible civil conflict and "ethno-religious" cleansing. There still are almost 100 million Muslims in India and serious religious tension. Similarly, forty years ago, the Ibo ethnic group in Nigeria fought an unsuccessful separatist war against the rest of the country, resulting in the deaths of roughly a million people. The Tutsi and Hutu peoples of the small African state of Rwanda engaged in a civil war of extermination in the 1990s, with hundreds of thousands of people slaughtered, and millions fleeing the country in fear of their lives.

The migration of labor, forced or voluntary, across state boundaries is another source of ethnic differentiation. The American descendants of Africans forcefully enslaved between the seventeenth and the nineteenth centuries are witnesses of the largest coercive labor migration in world history. In contrast, voluntary migration takes the form of Indians, Bangladeshi, Egyptians, and Palestinians seeking better lives in the oil sheikhdoms around the Persian Gulf; Mexican and Caribbean migrant workers moving to the United States;

and Turkish and North African migrants relocating to Europe. Some migration is politically motivated, triggered by civil war and repression. Two scholars refer to the contemporary world as living through an "Age of Migration,"[9] comparable in scale to that of the late nineteenth and early twentieth centuries.

Table 1.1 provides examples of politically significant "ethnicity," broadly defined, in our selected twelve countries. Five sets of traits are included, beginning with physical differences, then language, norms against intermarriage, religion, and negative historical memories. The table illustrates the importance of each distinction to ethnic identity. The most important bases of distinction lie in intermarriage, religion, and historical memories. Language differences are of great importance in four cases and of some importance in six; and finally, and perhaps surprisingly, physical differences are of great importance in only two cases. Recent migration has made such previously homogeneous states as France, Japan, and Germany more multiethnic. Other countries, such as the United States and Canada, have long been multiethnic and have become even more so. Indeed, globalization and migration seem destined to increase the diversity of many societies worldwide.

Language

Language can be a source of social division that may overlap with ethnicity. There are approximately five thousand different languages in use in the world today, and a much smaller number of language families. Most of these languages are spoken by relatively small tribal groups in North and South America, Asia, Africa, or Oceania. Only 200 languages have a million or more speakers, and only 8 may be classified as world languages.

English is the most truly international language. Close to one-third of the world's population lives in countries in which English is one of the official languages. Other international languages include Spanish, Arabic, Russian, Portuguese, French, and German. The language with the largest number of speakers, though in several varieties, is Chinese (with well over a billion speakers). The major languages with the greatest international spread are those of the former colonial powers—Great Britain, France, Spain, and Portugal.[10]

TABLE 1.1

The Many Faces of Ethnicity
Identity is sometimes based on physical differences, sometimes on language, sometimes on neither.*

	Physical Differences	Language	Norms Against Intermarriage	Religion	Negative Historical Memories
Brazil: Blacks	XX	O	XX	X	X
Britain: South Asians	X	O	X	XX	X
China: Tibetans	X	XX	XX	XX	XX
France: Algerians	X	X	XX	XX	XX
Germany: Turks	X	XX	XX	XX	O
India: Muslims	O	X	XX	XX	XX
Iran: Kurds	X	XX	XX	XX	XX
Japan: Buraku-min	O	O	XX	O	XX
Mexico: Mayan	X	X	XX	X	XX
Nigeria: Ibo	O	X	XX	XX	XX
Russia: Chechens	X	XX	XX	XX	XX
United States: African-Americans	XX	X	XX	O	XX
United States: Hispanics	X	X	X	O	X

*Salience is estimated at the following levels of importance in affecting differences: O = none or almost none; X = some; XX = much.

Linguistic divisions can create particularly thorny political problems. Political systems can choose to ignore racial, ethnic, or religious differences among their citizens, but they cannot avoid committing themselves to one or several languages. Linguistic conflicts typically show up in controversies over educational policies, or over language use in the government. Occasionally, language regulation is more intrusive, as in Quebec, where English-only street signs are prohibited and large corporations are required to conduct their business in French.

Religious Differences and Fundamentalism

States also vary in their religious characteristics. In some—such as Israel, the Irish Republic, and Pakistan—religion is a basis of national identity for a majority of the population. Iran is a theocratic regime, in which religious authorities govern and religious law is part of the country's legal code. In other societies, such as Poland under communism, religion can be a rallying point for political movements. In many Latin American countries, the clergy have embraced a liberation theology that fosters advocacy of the poor and criticism of government brutality.

Table 1.2 indicates that Christianity is the largest and most widely spread religion. Roughly one-third of the world's population belongs to the Christian church, which is divided into three major groups—Roman Catholics, Protestants (of many denominations), and Orthodox (e.g., Greek and Russian). The Catholics are dominant in Europe and Latin America; there is a more equal distribution of Catholics and Protestants elsewhere. While the traditional Protestant denominations have declined in North America in the last decades, three forms of Protestantism—Fundamentalist, Pentecostal, and Evangelical—have increased there and especially in Latin America and Asia.

The Muslims are the second largest religious group and the most rapidly growing religion. Between one-fourth and one-fifth of the world's population is Muslim, and it is primarily concentrated in Asia and Africa, with growing numbers in Europe also. Islam has become revitalized in Central Asia, and Muslims have been particularly successful in missionary activities in Sub-Saharan Africa.

Religion can be a source of intense disagreement, since beliefs may take the form of deep personal convictions that are difficult to compromise. Religious groups often battle over such issues as the rules of marriage and divorce, childrearing, sexual morality, abortion, euthanasia, the roles of women, and the regulation of religious observances. Religious communities often take a special interest in educational policies in order to transmit their ideas and ethics. On such issues, religious groups may clash with one another as well as with more secular groups. Although religious groups can coexist peacefully, and are often the source of exemplary acts of compassion and reconciliation, some may also commit acts of violence, cruelty, and terrorism.

TABLE 1.2

Faiths of the World
Adherents of All Religions by Six Continents (mid-2009, in millions)

Religion	Africa	Asia	Europe	Latin America	North America	Oceania	Total	Percentage
Christians	483.4	345.2	585.4	542.3	280.7	27.6	2,264.4	33.2
Muslims	408.0	1,066.3	40.8	1.8	5.6	0.6	1,523.2	22.3
Nonreligious and Atheists	6.7	608.7	97.0	19.8	41.7	4.9	778.7	11.4
Hindus	2.8	928.5	1.0	0.8	1.8	0.5	935.5	13.7
Buddhists	0.3	456.7	1.8	0.8	3.6	0.6	463.8	6.8
Jews	0.1	5.9	1.8	0.9	5.7	0.1	14.5	0.2
Other	108.1	709.6	3.3	20.2	6.2	0.8	848.2	12.4
Total	1,009.4	4,120.9	731.3	586.6	345.3	35.1	6,826.6	100%

Source: Adherents as defined in *Encyclopedia Britannica 2009.*

BOX 1.3

The Origins of "Fundamentalism"

Fundamentalism is today often associated with militancy and even violence in the clash between religious groups, but its original meaning was less dramatic. Fundamentalism got its name in the decades before World War I when some Protestant clergymen in the United States banded together to defend the "fundamentals" of religious belief against the secularizing influences of a modernizing society. This was a reaction to new biblical scholarship at the time that questioned the divine inspiration and authorship of the Bible, and to the expansion of science and Darwinist theories of evolution. These church leaders were also distressed by the apparent erosion of morality and tradition in the United States. In 1920, a journalist and Baptist layman named Curtis Lee Laws appropriated the term "fundamentalist" as a designation for those who were ready "to do battle royal for the Fundamentals." The fundamentalists affirmed the inerrancy (the absolute truth) of the Bible and formed enclaves to protect themselves from error and sin. Religious fundamentalism has recently emerged in some form in all major faiths in reaction to social modernization.

Even societies in which most people supposedly belong to the same community of faith may be split by conflicts between "fundamentalists" and those who are more moderate in their beliefs. **Religious fundamentalism** has emerged in some form in all major faiths in reaction to social modernization (see Box 1.3). Judaism, Christianity, and Islam are all "religions of the book," although not exactly the same book. The Jews believe only in the Old Testament; the Christians add on the New Testament; and the Muslims add the Koran to these two. While each religion disagrees over the interpretation of these texts, Jewish, Christian, and Muslim fundamentalists all believe in the truth of their respective sacred books. Some want political life to be organized according to these sacred texts and doctrines. There are also Hindu and Buddhist fundamentalists. The rise of fundamentalism has affected the entire world. Israel, for example, struggles with militancy among Jews as well as among the Muslim and Palestinian population. India has frequent confrontations between Hindus and Muslims, and Nigeria between Muslims and Christians.

Religious symbols can often become a rallying point for groups with other grievances, such as poverty or ethnic discrimination. Religious and other extremists employ violence in many forms, from threats and property destruction to assassination and destructive suicide. These acts of terrorism are intended to stagger the imagination, frighten, and weaken the will. From this point of view, the September 11, 2001, attacks on the World Trade Center and the Pentagon involved not only suicide pilot-hijackers but also aircraft filled with volatile fuel and innocent passengers converted into immense projectiles. These attacks were followed by terrorist assaults in Bali, Madrid, London, Riyadh, and other cities. Dealing with international terrorism by religious and other extremists is now a challenge that faces many nations worldwide.

FOSTERING ECONOMIC DEVELOPMENT

Two major forces are transforming political systems and nations, and the lives of their citizens; they provide major sources of comparison across the nations in this book. The first is the process of economic development, and the second is political democratization.

A political system cannot generally satisfy its citizens unless it can foster social and economic development. Thus, as significant as nation-building may be, economic and social development are exceptionally important. Economic development implies that citizens can enjoy new resources and opportunities, and that parents can expect their children to do at least as well as themselves. Many people expect government to improve their living conditions through economic growth, providing jobs, and raising income standards. However, development can also create social strains and damage nature. Yet the success of governments—both democratic and autocratic—is often measured in economic terms.

In affluent, advanced industrial societies, contemporary living standards provide for basic social needs (and much more) for most of the public. Indeed, the current political challenges in these nations often focus on problems resulting from the economic successes of

Fostering Economic Growth

With the Chinese government encouraging economic growth and foreign investment, the Shanghai skyline is now a mix of high-rises and construction cranes.

Wolf Kern/VISUM/The Image Works

the past, such as protecting environmental quality or managing the consequences of growth. New challenges to social-welfare policies are emerging from the medical and social-security costs of aging populations. For most of the world, however, substantial basic economic needs still exist, and governments focus on improving the socioeconomic conditions of the nation.

Over the past two to three decades, globalization, democratization, and marketization have transformed living conditions in many nations more than in any similar period in the past. The United Nations Development Program (UNDP) combines measures of economic well-being, life expectancy, and educational achievement into its Human Development Index (HDI).[11] The HDI shows dramatic improvements in life conditions in many regions of the world over the past three decades (see Figure 1.2 and Table 1.3). East Asia and South Asia have made substantial improvements since 1975. For instance, in 1975, South Korea and Taiwan had a standard of living close to many poor African nations, and they are now affluent societies. Even more striking is the change in the two largest nations in the world. China improved from an HDI of 0.52 in 1975 (the same as Botswana or Swaziland) to 0.77 in 2007 (close to Russia or Brazil); India improved from an HDI of 0.41 to 0.61. These statistics represent improved living conditions for billions of people. At the same time, however, living conditions have changed less in Sub-Saharan Africa over this period. Though

Nigeria's score rose from 0.32 to 0.51, much of it due to improving oil revenues, it remains among the poorest countries in the world. And the HDI for Russia stagnated in the 1990s, though it has since improved.

The process of economic development typically follows a similar course. One element is a transformation of the structure of the labor force. The five advanced industrial countries in our comparisons all have agricultural employment of less than 10 percent of the labor force. Poor countries, in contrast, often have more than two-thirds of their labor forces employed in agriculture. In addition, economic development is typically linked to urbanization as peasants leave their farms and move to the cities. In nations undergoing rapid economic development, such as China, urban migration creates new opportunities for the workers but also new economic and social policy challenges for the governments.

The UNDP's Human Development Index provides a means to compare the differences in current life conditions across the twelve comparison nations in this chapter (Table 1.3). Perhaps the most striking feature of this table is the wide gap in living standards that still exists across nations worldwide. For instance, the **gross domestic product (GDP)** per capita, which is a measure of national economic development, is about twenty times higher in the Western advanced industrial democracies than in Nigeria.[12] Similarly, there are notable gaps in life expectancy and educational opportunities

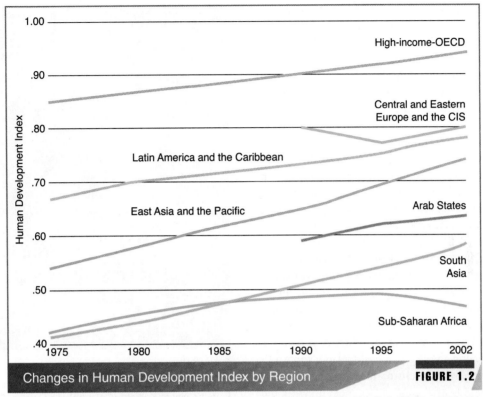

Changes in Human Development Index by Region

FIGURE 1.2

Source: United Nations Development Program, *Human Development Report 2004* (New York: United Nations, 2004), 134.

TABLE 1.3

The Race for Social Progress
Human Development Indicators show improvements in many countries.

Nation	Life Expectancy	Percent Enrolled in School	GDP/capita (USD, ppp)	1975 HDI	2007 HDI	2007 World Rank
United States	79.1	92.4	45,592	0.867	0.956	13
Japan	82.7	86.6	33,632	0.857	0.960	10
United Kingdom	79.3	89.2	35,130	0.845	0.947	21
France	81.0	95.4	33,674	0.853	0.961	8
Germany	79.8	88.1	34,401	—	0.947	22
Mexico	76.0	80.2	14,104	0.689	0.854	53
Russia	66.2	81.9	14,690	—	0.817	71
Brazil	72.2	87.2	9,567	0.645	0.813	75
China	72.9	68.7	5,383	0.525	0.772	92
Iran	71.2	73.2	10,955	0.566	0.782	88
India	63.4	61.0	2,753	0.412	0.612	134
Nigeria	47.7	53.0	1,969	0.318	0.511	158

Source: United Nations Development Program, *World Development Report 2009* (New York: United Nations, 2009) (www.undp.org).

between the affluent Northern societies and the developing nations in Africa and Asia. In highly industrialized countries, education is virtually universal and practically everyone over age fifteen can read and write. In India and Nigeria, less than two-thirds of the adult population has this minimal level of education. Moreover, the countries with the fewest literate citizens also have the fewest radios and television sets—even though these devices do not require literacy. Economic development is also associated with better nutrition and medical care. In the economically advanced countries, fewer children die in infancy, and the average citizen has a life expectancy at birth of around eighty years (almost eighty-three in Japan). Improvements in living conditions have substantially increased life expectancy in many low-income nations, such as Mexico and China. However, the average life expectancy for an Indian is sixty-three years, and for a Nigerian less than fifty years. Material productivity, education, exposure to communications media, and longer and healthier lives are closely interconnected.

In order to become more productive, a country needs to develop a skilled and healthy labor force and to build the infrastructure that material welfare requires. Preindustrial nations face most urgently the issues of economic development: how to improve the immediate welfare of their citizens yet also invest for the future. Typically, these are newer nations that also face the challenges of building community and effective political institutions. Political leaders and celebrities such as Bono and Angelina Jolie have mobilized public awareness that these differences in living conditions are a global concern—for those living in the developing world, for the affluent nations and their citizens, and for international organizations such as the United Nations and the World Bank.

Problems of Economic Development

Wealth, income, and opportunity are rarely evenly distributed within nations, and the unequal distribution of resources and opportunities is among the most serious causes of political conflict. A large GDP may conceal significant poverty and lack of opportunities. A high rate of national growth may benefit only particular regions or social groups, leaving large parts of the population even less well-off than before. Parts of the "inner cities" of the United States, the older parts of such Indian cities as Delhi and Calcutta, remote and landlocked parts of many African states, many rural

Poverty

Indian babies lie on the sidewalk beside a busy street in the city of Kolkata (Calcutta), 14 October 2004. India has become one of the ten fastest-growing developing countries, yet its per capita income remains low and one quarter of the population lives below the income poverty line.

Sucheta Das/Reuters/Landov

areas in China, and the arid northeast of Brazil all suffer from poverty and hopelessness, while other parts of these countries experience growth and improved welfare. Moreover, there is some evidence that rapid economic development tends to increase such inequalities.

A country's politics may be sharply affected by internal divisions of income, wealth, and other resources. Table 1.4 displays income distributions for our twelve comparison countries. Generally speaking, economic development improves the **equality of income**, at least past a certain stage of economic growth. Wealthy nations like Japan, Germany, and France have relatively more egalitarian income distributions than middle- or low-income countries. Still, the wealthiest 10 percent in Japan receive about the same total income as the poorest 40 percent receive. This is a large gap in life conditions between rich and poor, but the gap is even wider in less affluent nations. In Mexico, a middle-income country, the ratio is closer to

Income Distribution				TABLE 1.4

Income Distribution
Middle-income countries have the greatest inequalities; wealthy ones tend to be more equal.

Country	Year	Wealthiest 10%	Poorest 40%	Wealthy/Poor Gap
Germany	2000	22.1	22.2	−0.1
Russia	2002	23.8	20.9	2.9
Japan	1993	21.7	24.8	3.1
France	1995	25.1	19.8	5.3
Britain	1999	28.5	17.5	11.0
India	2004–05	31.1	19.4	11.7
United States	2000	29.9	16.2	13.7
Iran	1998	33.7	19.5	14.2
Nigeria	2003	33.2	14.6	18.6
China	2004	34.9	12.8	22.1
Mexico	2004	39.4	12.6	26.8
Brazil	2004	44.8	9.2	35.6

Source: World Bank, *World Development Indicators 2007*, Table 2-7 (www.worldbank.org); distribution of income or consumption.

three to one; in Brazil it is more than five to one. The United States is at a middling level of inequality, higher than Japan and the countries of Western Europe but lower than most of the rest. The table also suggests that a nation's political characteristics make a difference. India has consciously worked to narrow inequality, which places it higher in the table, while inequality in China has steadily increased.

Although industrialization and high productivity may eventually encourage a more equal distribution of income, the first stages of industrialization may actually increase income inequality. As economies modernize, they create a dual economy—a rural sector and an urban industrial and commercial sector, both with inequalities of their own. These inequalities increase as education and communication spread more rapidly in the modern sector, which may contribute to the political instability of developing countries. Moreover, there is no guarantee that inequality will diminish in later stages of development. In Brazil, for instance, income inequality increased for decades, even as the economy developed. In the United States and Britain, income inequality has increased substantially since the 1970s. In Russia and other postcommunist societies, the development of new capitalist markets was accompanied by new income inequalities. Inequality is an issue that many nations face.

Various policy solutions can mitigate the hardships economic inequality causes in developing societies. If there is equality of opportunity and high social mobility, inequality may decline over time and may not seem so oppressive to younger generations. Investments in education can therefore lessen these problems. Also, Taiwan and South Korea show how early land reforms equalized opportunity early in the developmental process. Investment in primary and secondary education, in agricultural inputs and rural infrastructure (principally roads and water), and in labor-intensive industries produced remarkable results for several decades. A comparative advantage in cheap and skilled labor enabled Taiwan and South Korea to compete effectively in international markets. Thus, some growth policies mitigate inequalities, but it can be very difficult to put them into practice, especially where substantial inequalities already exist.

Another correlate of development is population growth. As health care improves, living standards increase, life expectancies lengthen, and populations grow. This is a positive development because it represents improved living conditions for these people, but rapid population growth also can pose policy challenges for many developing nations.

Table 1.5 puts this issue in sharp relief. The table divides the world population into three strata: low-income

	In 1990		Projected to 2015	
Economic Development Level	**Number**	**Percentage**	**Number**	**Percentage**
Low-income economies	1,777	33.9	2,794	39.4
Middle-income economies	2,588	49.3	3,299	46.5
High-income economies	887	16.8	1,007	14.1
Total	5,252	100.0	7,100	100.0

TABLE 1.5

Population by Economic Development Level in 1990 and Projected to 2015 (in millions)
The ranks of the poor are growing.

Source: World Bank, *World Development Report Indicators 2005*, Table 2-1 (www.worldbank.org), population dynamics.

economies, middle-income economies, and high-income economies. In 1990, the low-income countries had a population total of almost 2 billion, or about a third of the total world population. In contrast, the high-income nations had about a sixth of the world's population.

Some projections estimate that world population will increase by 2015 to 7 billion and that the poorer countries will see a more rapid rate of growth. In 2005, Hania Zlotnik of the UN population division estimated that "out of every 100 persons added to the [world's] population in the coming decade, 97 will live in developing countries."[13] Rapid economic growth in the developing world can create significant burdens for these nations.

These prospects have produced a development literature that mixes both light and heat. Economist Amartya Sen warns of a "danger that in the confrontation between apocalyptic pessimism on one hand, and a dismissive smugness, on the other, a genuine understanding of the nature of the population problem may be lost."[14] He points out that the first impact of "modernization" on population is to increase it rapidly as new sanitation measures and modern pharmaceuticals reduce the death rate. As an economy develops, however, changing conditions tend to reduce fertility. With improved education (particularly of women), health, and welfare, the advantages of lower fertility become clear, and population growth declines.

Fertility decreased in Europe and North America as they underwent industrialization. Today, the native populations are decreasing in many European nations because fertility rates are below levels necessary to sustain a constant population size. This pattern also appears to be occurring in parts of the developing world. Thus, annual population growth in the world has declined over the last two decades. The rate of population growth in India, for example, rose to 2.2 percent in the 1970s and has since declined. Latin America peaked at a higher rate and then came down sharply. The major problem area is Sub-Saharan Africa, which continues to experience very high birth rates.[15] Yet, even the fertility rate in Africa has recently dropped dramatically because of the tragically rising death rate from the AIDS epidemic.

While population growth rates appear to be slowing, governments are addressing this issue in different ways. China adopted a coercive policy of limiting families to a single child, which in urban areas produced dramatic results at great costs. India followed a collaborative approach involving governmental intervention and education to affect family choices.[16] Kerala in southern India shows what can be accomplished by the collaborative approach, where expanding education (particularly among women) and otherwise improving living conditions has reduced fertility more than in China.

Economic growth can have other social costs. For instance, advanced industrial societies are dealing with the environmental costs of their industrial development. Despoiled forests, depleted soils and fisheries, polluted air and water, nuclear waste, endangered species, and a threatened ozone layer now burden their legislative dockets. With increasing industrialization and urbanization in the developing world, many of these environmental problems could worsen. Thus, economic development can impose serious environmental costs as well as benefits. At the same time, some environmental problems are even more acute in less developed countries, where rapid increases in population and urbanization create shortages of clean air, clean water, and adequate sanitation.[17] Thus, economic development generally improves the living conditions of the public, but in the process it produces new policy problems that governments must address.

FOSTERING DEMOCRACY, HUMAN RIGHTS, AND CIVIL LIBERTIES

The second major force transforming contemporary political systems is the process of democratization, which includes the enhancement of human rights and the expansion of freedom. Democracy is the form of government to which most contemporary countries, more or less sincerely and successfully, aspire. A **democracy**, briefly defined, is a political system in which citizens enjoy a number of basic civil and political rights, and in which their most important political leaders are elected in free and fair elections and are accountable under a rule of law. Democracy literally means "government by the people."

In small political systems, such as local communities, it may be possible for "the people" to share directly in debating, deciding, and implementing public policy. In large political systems, such as contemporary states, democracy must be achieved largely through indirect participation in policymaking. Elections, competitive political parties, free mass media, and representative assemblies make some degree of democracy—some degree of "government by the people"—possible. This indirect, or representative, democracy is not complete or ideal. But the more citizens are involved and the more influential their choices, the more democratic the system.

The most important general distinction in classifying political systems is between democratic systems and **authoritarian** (also known as **autocratic**) systems. Autocracies lack one or several defining features of democracy. In democracies, competitive elections give citizens the chance to shape the policymaking process through their selection of key policymakers. In

Environmental Challenges
A farmer drives his tractor in front of the Dukovany nuclear power plant in the Czech Republic, 31 March 2004.
Peter Endig/dpa/Landov

authoritarian systems, the policymakers are chosen by military councils, hereditary families, dominant political parties, and the like. Citizens are either ignored or pressed into symbolic assent to the government's choices.

Authoritarian states can take several forms (see Chapter 6). In **oligarchies**, literally "rule by the few," important political rights are withheld from the majority of the population. South Africa until the abolition of apartheid in the early 1990s is a good example. Other authoritarian states, such as Egypt, are **party**, **military**, or **personal dictatorships. Totalitarian systems**—such as Nazi Germany, or the Soviet Union under Stalin, or North Korea today—are systems in which the government constricts the rights and privacy of its citizens in a particularly severe and intrusive manner.

As societies become more complex, richer, and more technologically advanced, the probability of citizen involvement and democratization increases. In the first half of the twentieth century, most Western states were transformed from autocracies or oligarchies to democracies. After World War II, a second democratic wave—which lasted from 1943 until the early 1960s—saw both newly independent states (such as India and Nigeria) and defeated authoritarian powers (such as Germany and Japan) set up the formal institutions of democracy.[18]

Another round of democratic transitions began in 1974, involving Southern Europe, East Asia, Latin America, and a number of African states. Samuel P. Huntington speaks of this latest move toward democracy as a "Third Wave" of worldwide **democratization**.[19] The most dramatic changes came in Central and Eastern Europe, where in a few short years the Soviet empire collapsed, the nations of Eastern Europe rapidly converted to democracy, and many of these nations have now joined the European Union. A few years earlier, much of Latin America had shifted from dictatorships (often military) to democracy. The People Power Revolution in the Philippines and the end of the apartheid regime in South Africa were equally dramatic.

As a result of these three democratization waves, democracy has become a common goal of the global community (see Figure 1.3). As late as 1978, only a third of the world's independent countries had competitive party and electoral systems. Communist governments, other single-party governments, and other authoritarian regimes dominated the landscape. By 2004, almost two-thirds of states had a system of electoral democracy, and human rights and liberties were similarly spreading to more of the world's population.[20] However, this democratization trend has come to a halt over the past few years, so we should not be overconfident about further progress in democratization around the world.

This democratization process results from a combination of factors. Economic development transforms societies in ways that typically encourage democratization by creating autonomous political groups that demand political influence, by expanding the political skills of the citizenry, and by creating economic complexity that encourages systems of self-governance. Social modernization transforms the political values and political culture of the public, which increases demands for a more participatory system (see Chapter 3). New democracies are also much more likely to endure when founded in economically developed societies.[21]

Democracy is not an all-or-nothing proposition, however. No democracy is perfect, and we can speak of shades or gradations of democracy. Democracy typically does not come about overnight. It often takes time to establish democratic institutions and to have citizens recognize them and comply with the rules of the democratic process.

It can be especially difficult to consolidate democracy in less economically developed societies. Not all of the newly democratizing countries are succeeding beyond the first few years. In some, democratic processes fail to produce stable institutions and effective public policies and give way to some form of authoritarianism. In Nigeria, military coups overthrew democratically elected (but badly flawed) governments in 1966 and again in 1983, and redemocratization did not happen until 1999. Nigeria is by no means unique. Transition can move in either direction, toward or away from democracy. The recent wave of democratization is supported by the more favorable environments of more modernized societies and because there are now more democracies in the world to support new democracies. However, democracy is difficult to sustain when severe economic or political problems face a nation, or where the public remains uncertain about democracy.

Even when states democratize, there is no guarantee that they will grant human rights and civil liberties to all their people. In some countries, majority rule turns into a "tyranny of the majority" against ethnic or religious minorities. Therefore, democracies have to

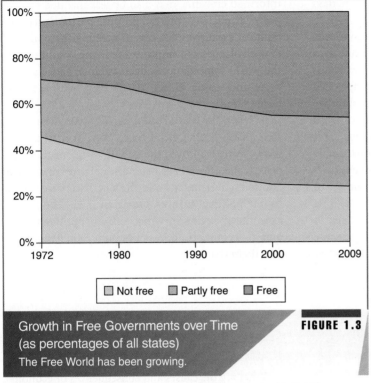

Growth in Free Governments over Time (as percentages of all states)
The Free World has been growing.

FIGURE 1.3

Source: Freedom House, *Freedom in the World 2010* (www.freedomhouse.org).

Western industrial societies favor gender policies that guarantee equal access for women in society, the workplace, and politics. The UN and other international organizations have become advocates of women's rights. But gender norms often vary across cultural zones. The UN's statistics indicate that many developing nations hesitate to grant equal rights to women, restricting their education and involvement in the economy and politics.[22] Restrictions on women's rights are even starker in many Arab states, where they often clash with social norms and religious beliefs. Ironically, improving the status of women is one of the most productive ways to develop a nation politically and economically (see Box 1.4), for example by improving educational and health standards and stabilizing birth rates. In short, expanding human rights is an ongoing process in the world today, and there is much room for further progress.

balance between respecting the will of the majority and protecting the rights of the minority. Even when political rulers sincerely try to promote human rights and civil liberties (which is by no means always the case), they do not always agree on the nature of those rights.

A good example of the spread of rights and liberties—and cultural differences in the definition of rights—involves gender issues. Governments in

LOOKING FORWARD

The last several decades have been a period of tremendous social, economic, and political change in the world. Economic development, improved living standards, the spread of human rights, and democratization improved the life chances and life conditions of billions of individuals. In most of the world, the average child born today

Women and Political Development

BOX 1.4

If a poor nation could do one thing to stimulate its development, what should it do? Opening the fiftieth session of the United Nations Commission on the Status of Women in 2006, UN Deputy-Secretary General Louise Fréchette said the international community finally comprehends that empowering women and girls around the globe is the most effective tool for a country's development. She stated that studies have repeatedly shown that by giving women equal education and work opportunities, and

access to a society's decision-making processes, a country can boost its economic productivity, reduce infant and maternal mortality rates, and improve the general population's nutrition and health. These results are achieved because women's education and participation in the labor force increase family output, increase the likelihood that children will be better educated and benefit from health care, improve nutrition in the family, and better the quality of life for women and their families.

Source: UN News Center, February 27, 2006.

can look forward to a longer, better, and freer life than his or her parents—especially if she is a girl.

At the same time, continuing social, economic, and political problems remain. Progress in one area can create new opportunities, but also new problems in another. Economic development, for example, can sometimes stimulate ethnic strife and destabilize political institutions. Economic development can also disrupt social life. And the process of development has been uneven across and within nations. Many basic human needs still remain in too short supply.[23]

Even in the affluent democracies, as one set of policy issues is addressed, new issues come to the fore. Western democracies struggle to address issues of environmental quality, changing lifestyles, and the challenges of globalization. A more affluent and better informed citizenry may also be less inclined to trust political parties, interest groups, parliaments, and political executives. Success in meeting these old and new challenges can improve the living conditions for the world's populations, decrease international conflict, and come closer to meeting the ideals of humankind.

Governments and politics have played a large role in human societies of the past. Some of their policies have greatly improved the quality of life of their citizens, while others have been disasters. Yet one way or another, governments and their activities are central to our political futures. Our goal in this book is to examine the ways in which citizens, policymakers, and governments address the policy challenges that face them today.

REVIEW QUESTIONS

- What is politics?
- What are the contrasting images of the "state of nature" of humankind?
- What are the potential positive and negative outcomes of government activity?
- What are the main challenges that countries face in building a political community?
- What are the causes and consequences of economic development?
- What are the causes and consequences of democratization?

KEY TERMS

anarchism
authoritarian
autocratic
democracy
democratization
equality of income
ethnicity
European Union (EU)
externalities
globalization
governments
gross domestic product (GDP)
human rights
libertarianism
military dictatorships
nation
nation-states
oligarchy
party dictatorships
personal dictatorships
political culture
political system
public goods
religious fundamentalism
rent-seeking
sovereignty
state
state of nature
totalitarian systems
United Nations (UN)
vested interests

SUGGESTED READINGS

Cornelius, Wayne, et al., eds. *Controlling Immigration: A Global Perspective.* Stanford, CA: Stanford University Press, 1995.

Dalton, Russell, and Doh Chull Shin, eds. *Citizens, Democracy, and Markets Around the Pacific Rim.* Oxford: Oxford University Press, 2006.

Diamond, Larry, ed. *Developing Democracy: Towards Consolidation.* Baltimore: Johns Hopkins University Press, 1999.

Horowitz, Donald. *Ethnic Groups in Conflict.* Berkeley: University of California Press, 1985.

Huntington, Samuel. *The Third Wave: Democratization in the Late Twentieth Century.* Norman: University of Oklahoma Press, 1991.

———. *The Clash of Civilizations and the Remaking of World Order.* New York: Simon & Schuster, 1996.

Lijphart, Arend. *Patterns of Democracy.* New Haven, CT: Yale University Press, 1999.

Linz, Juan, and Alfred Stepan, eds. *Problems of Democratic Transitions and Consolidation.* Baltimore: Johns Hopkins University Press, 1996.

Przeworski, Adam, et al. *Democracy and Development: Political Institutions and Well-Being in the World, 1950–1990.* New York: Cambridge University Press, 2000.

Putnam, Robert. *Making Democracy Work: Civic Traditions in Modern Italy.* Princeton, NJ: Princeton University Press, 1993.

Sachs, Jeffrey. *The End of Poverty: Economic Possibilities for Our Time.* New York: Penguin, 2005.

United Nations. *World Development Report.* New York: Oxford University Press, annual editions.

Weiner, Myron. *The Global Migration Crisis: Challenge to States and to Human Rights.* New York: HarperCollins, 1995.

Zakaria, Fareed. *The Future of Freedom: Illiberal Democracy at Home and Abroad.* New York: Norton, 2003.

ENDNOTES

1. Thomas Hobbes, *Leviathan,* ed. C. B. Macpherson (New York: Penguin, 1968), 186.

2. J. J. Rousseau, *Second Discourse on Inequality, The First and Second Discourses* (New York: St. Martin's Press, 1964), 109–10.

3. Martin Greenberg and Mark Tier, *Visions of Liberty* (New York: Baen Publishers, 2004).

4. See, for example, Fareed Zakaria, *The Future of Freedom: Illiberal Democracy at Home and Abroad* (New York: Norton, 2003).

5. See, for example, Douglas North, *Institutions, Institutional Change, and Economic Performance* (Cambridge: Cambridge University Press, 1990); Mancur Olson, "The New Institutional Economics: The Collective Choice Approach to Economic Development," in *Institutions and Economic Development,* ed. C. Clague (Baltimore: Johns Hopkins University Press, 1997); S. Knack and P. Keefer, "Institutions and Economic Performance," *Economics and Politics* 7 (1995): 207–29.

6. The Vatican is not a member of the UN but maintains a permanent observer mission at the UN headquarters. Taiwan was expelled from the UN in 1971 to accommodate mainland China (the People's Republic).

7. Max Weber, *Economy and Society,* ed. Guenther Roth and Claus Wittich (Berkeley: University of California Press, 1978), 389.

8. Even before the end of the Cold War, ethnic autonomy movements in parts of old countries—such as the United Kingdom (the Scots and Welsh) and Canada (the Quebecois)—sought to break free or achieve greater autonomy.

9. Stephen Castles and Mark J. Miller, *The Age of Migration: International Population Movements in the Modern World* (New York: Guilford, 1994).

10. Erik V. Gunnemark, *Countries, Peoples, and Their Languages: The Geolinguistic Handbook* (Gothenburg: Lanstryckeriet, 1991).

11. United Nations Development Program, *Human Development Report 2005* (New York: United Nations, 2005). See also www.undp.org for additional data and interactive presentations.

12. The per capita *gross national product (GDP)* is the total economic output per person, corrected for exports and imports. Rather than the traditional measures computed according to the exchange rates of the national currencies, the *purchasing power parity (ppp)* index takes into account differences in price levels from one country to another. Most analyses assume that the GDP/ppp statistics are more comparable measures of living conditions. The income gap increases, however, if one uses the traditional exchange-rate measure of GDP.

13. Hania Zlotnik, "Statement to the Thirty-Eighth Session of the Commission on Population and Development," April 4, 2005 (www.un.org/esa/population/cpd/Statement_HZ_open.pdf).

14. Amartya Sen, "Population: Delusion and Reality," *New York Review of Books,* 22 September 1994, 62ff.

15. World Bank, *World Development Report, 1998–1999* (New York: Oxford University Press, 1999).

16. Sen, "Population: Delusion and Reality."

17. Regina Axelrod, David Downie, and Norman Vig, eds., *The Global Environment: Institutions, Law, and Policy* (Washington, D.C.: CQ Press, 2004); Yale Center for Environmental Law and Policy and Center for International Earth Science Information Network, *2005 Environmental Sustainability Index: Benchmarking National Environmental Stewardship* (New Haven, CT: Yale University, 2005) (www.yale.edu/esi/).

18. While many countries became formally democratic in these years, most of them quickly lapsed into authoritarianism. Many of these would-be democracies failed in their first decade; another "reverse wave" in the 1960s and early 1970s swept away some older democracies (Chile, Greece, and Uruguay, for example) as well.

19. Samuel Huntington, *The Third Wave: Democratization in the Late Twentieth Century* (Norman: University of Oklahoma Press, 1991).

20. Freedom House, *Freedom in the World 2004* (Washington, D.C.: Freedom House, 2005) (www.freedomhouse.org).

21. Seymour Martin Lipset, "Some Social Requisites of Democracy," *American Political Science Review 53* (September 1959): 69–105; Larry Diamond, "Economic Development and Democracy Reconsidered," in *Reexamining Democracy*, ed. G. Marks and L. Diamond (Newbury Park, CA: Sage, 1992); Tatu Vanhanen, *Prospects of Democracy* (New York: Routledge, 1997); Adam Przeworski et al., *Democracy and Development: Political Institutions and Well-Being in the World, 1950–1990* (New York: Cambridge University Press, 2000).

22. See United Nations Development Program, *Human Development Report 2005* (New York: United Nations, 2005) (http://hdr.undp.org/reports/global/2005/), Tables 25–30, and associated discussion.

23. Many of these issues are addressed by the United Nations' Millennium Development Goals. Visit the UN Web site (www.un.org/millenniumgoals/) or see United Nations, *Millennium Development Goals Report 2005* (New York: United Nations, 2005) (http://unstats.un.org/unsd/mi/pdf/MDGBook.pdf).

COMPARING POLITICAL SYSTEMS

WHY WE COMPARE

The great French interpreter of American democracy, Alexis de Tocqueville, while traveling in America in the 1830s, wrote to a friend explaining how his own ideas about French institutions and culture entered into his writing of *Democracy in America*. Tocqueville wrote: "Although I very rarely spoke of France in my book, I did not write one page of it without having her, so to speak, before my eyes."[1] Tocqueville taught us that the only way we can fully understand our own political system is by comparing it to others. Comparing our experience with that of other countries deepens our understanding of our own politics and permits us to see a wider range of alternatives. It illuminates the virtues and shortcomings of our own political life. By taking us beyond our familiar arrangements and assumptions, comparative analysis helps expand our awareness of the potentials, for better or worse, of politics.

On the comparative method, Tocqueville offered this comment: "Without comparisons to make, the mind does not know how to proceed."[2] Tocqueville was telling us that comparison is fundamental to all human thought. It is the methodological core of the humanistic and scientific methods, including the scientific study of politics. Comparative analysis helps us develop and test explanations and theories of how political processes work or when political change occurs. The goals of the comparative methods used by political scientists are similar to those used in more exact sciences such as physics. But political scientists often cannot design experiments, a major path to knowledge in many natural sciences. We cannot always control and manipulate political arrangements and observe the consequences. We are especially limited when dealing with large-scale events that drastically affect many people. For example, researchers cannot and would not want to start a war or a social revolution to study its effects.

We can, however, use the comparative method to describe the political events and institutions found in different societies and to identify their causes and consequences. More than two thousand years ago, Aristotle in his *Politics* contrasted the economies and social structures of Greek city-states in an effort to determine how social and economic environments affected political institutions and policies (see Box 2.1). More contemporary political scientists also try to explain differences between the processes and performance of political systems. They compare two-party democracies with multiparty democracies, parliamentary with presidential regimes, poor countries with rich countries, and elections in new party systems with those in established democracies. These and many other comparisons have greatly enriched our understanding of politics.

HOW WE COMPARE

We study politics in several different ways: we describe it, we seek to explain it, and sometimes we try to predict it. These are all parts of the scientific process, though as we move from description to explanation and prediction, our task gets progressively harder. Each of these tasks may use the comparative method. The first stage in the study of politics is description. If we cannot describe a political process or event, we cannot really hope to understand or explain it, much less predict what might happen next or in similar situations.

BOX 2.1

Aristotle's Library

There is historical evidence that Aristotle had accumulated a library of more than 150 studies of the political systems of the Mediterranean world of 400 to 300 BC. Many of these had probably been researched and written by his disciples.

While only the Athenian constitution survives of this library of Aristotelian polities, it is evident from the references to such studies that do survive that Aristotle was concerned with sampling the variety of political systems then in existence, including the "barbarian" (Third World?) countries, such as Libya,

Etruria, and Rome: "[T]he references in ancient authorities give us the names of some 70 or more of the states described in the compilation of 'polities.' They range from Sinope, on the Black Sea, to Cyrene in North Africa; they extend from Marseilles in the Western Mediterranean to Crete, Rhodes, and Cyprus in the East. Aristotle thus included colonial constitutions as well as those of metropolitan states. His descriptions embraced states on the Aegean, Ionian, and Tyrrhenian Seas, and the three continents of Europe, Asia, and Africa."

Source: Ernest Barker, ed., *The Politics of Aristotle* (London: Oxford University Press, 1977), 386.

Description may sound easy and straightforward enough, but often it is not. In order to describe a political event or institution well, we need to use words and phrases that our audience can understand clearly and in the same way, and which they can apply broadly. In order to describe politics, we thus need a set of concepts, a **conceptual framework**, which is clearly defined and well-understood. In other words, we want our concepts to be **intersubjective** (understood and used in the same way by different subjects) and **general**. The easier our set of concepts is to understand, and the more broadly it can be applied, the more helpful it is to the study of politics. Conceptual frameworks are not generally right or wrong, but they may be more or less useful to the task at hand.

HOW WE EXPLAIN AND PREDICT

Once we are able to describe politics with the help of the conceptual framework that we choose, the next task is to explain it. Explanation typically means answering "why?" questions. More precisely, explaining political phenomena means identifying causal relationships among them, pointing out one phenomenon as the cause or consequence of another.[3] It is often important to be able to go beyond description to explanation. For example, we might be interested in the relationship between democracy and international peace (see Box 2.2). Description can tell us that in the contemporary world, peace and democracy tend to go

together. Democratic states are mostly (though not always) peaceful, and many peaceful states are democracies. But we do not fully understand why this is so. Are democratic states more peaceful because they are democratic, are they democratic because they are peaceful, or are they perhaps both peaceful and democratic because they are more prosperous than other states, or because they have market economies, or because their citizens have values (a political culture) that support both democracy and peace? A good explanation helps us find the right answer to such questions. Ideally, we want to put many political relationships in causal terms, so we can say that one political feature is the cause of another, and the latter is an effect of the former.

Theories are precisely formulated and well-supported statements about causal relationships among general classes of political events—for example, about the causes of democracy, war, election victories, or welfare policies. Theories need to be testable, and a good theory is one that holds up after continued tests, preferably after a series of concerted efforts to prove it wrong. **Hypotheses** are causal explanations that have not yet been proven. In other words, they are candidate theories that have not yet been adequately tested or confirmed. Yet scientific theories are always tentative; they are subject to modification or falsification at any time as our knowledge improves. Theories are often modified and made more precise as we test them again and again with better and better data. A well-tested theory allows us to explain confidently what

BOX 2.2

Statistical Methods

A popular contemporary research program known as *democratic peace research* illustrates the pros and cons of statistical and case-study research. It has been of primary interest to international relations scholars, who took the diplomatic history of the Cold War period and asked whether democratic countries are more peaceful in their foreign policy than authoritarian and nondemocratic ones. Many scholars in the democratic peace research group took the statistical route. They counted each year of interaction between two states as one case. With roughly half a century of diplomatic history involving a state system of 100 countries or more, they had a very large number of cases, even after eliminating the many irrelevant cases of countries that never, or rarely, had any relations with one another. Political scientists Andrew Bennett and Alexander George drew these conclusions after surveying the statistical research:

> Statistical methods achieved important advances on the issue of whether a nonspurious interdemocratic

peace exists. A fairly strong though not unanimous consensus emerged that: (1) democracies are not less war-prone in general; (2) they have very rarely if ever fought one another; (3) this pattern of an interdemocratic peace applies to both war and conflicts short of war; (4) states in transition to democracy are more war-prone than established democracies; and (5) these correlations were not spuriously brought about by the most obvious alternative explanations.

Although much was learned from the statistical studies, they were not as successful at answering "why" questions. Case studies make clinical depth possible, revealing causal interconnections in individual cases. Careful repetition of these causal tracings from case to case strengthens confidence in these relationships. Thus, Bennett and George concluded that the best research strategy uses statistical and case study methods together, with each method having its own strengths.

Source: Andrew Bennett and Alexander George, "An Alliance of Statistical and Case Study Methods: Research on the Interdemocratic Peace," APSA-CP: *Newsletter of the APSA Organized Section in Comparative Politics* 9 no. 1 (1998): 6.

happens in specific cases or sets of cases—for example, that two countries have a peaceful relationship because they are democracies, or perhaps the other way around (see again Box 2.2).

Political scientists often develop theories as they seek to understand a puzzling case or an interesting difference between two or three political systems. For example, Tocqueville was intrigued by the fact that democracy was so widely supported in the United States, while it was fiercely contested in his native France. Researchers also often generate hypotheses about the causes and consequences of political change by comparing countries at different historical periods. In his other famous study, Tocqueville contributed to a general theory of revolution by comparing prerevolutionary and postrevolutionary France.[4] Theda Skocpol, on the other hand, based her explanation of the causes of revolution on a comparison of the "old regimes" of France, Russia, and China with their revolutionary and postrevolutionary regimes.[5]

But for an explanatory hypothesis to become a useful theory, we generally want it to explain not only

the case(s) on which it was based, but also other cases (revolutions, wars, elections, etc.) that fall into the same set. Hypotheses are therefore tested against many different kinds of political **data**. Researchers in political science distinguish between studies based on large numbers (large *n*) and small numbers (small *n*) of cases or observations. In large-*n* studies, particularly when the number of cases is beyond twenty or thirty, it is often possible and helpful to use statistical analysis. Such studies are usually referred to as *statistical studies*; small-*n* studies are usually called *case studies*. Many small-*n* studies examine only a single case, whereas others compare two or three or four (or occasionally more).

Statistical analysis enables us to consider possible alternative causes at the same time, accepting some and rejecting others. Large-*n* studies often have a sufficient number and variety of cases to enable the researcher to examine the relation among the variables associated with each case. **Variables** are the features on which our cases differ—for example, "religious heritage: Christian, Muslim, or Buddhist" or "rank in the

UN Quality of Life index," or "income per capita." Large-*n* statistical studies thus allow us to be more certain and precise in our explanations. On the other hand, we need the depth that case studies provide. Small-*n* studies permit investigators to go deeply into a case, identify the particularities of it, get the clinical details, and examine each link in the causal process. They encourage us to formulate insightful hypotheses for statistical testing in the first place. They allow us to trace the nature of the cause-and-effect relations (sometimes called "causal mechanisms") better than large-*n* studies. In this manner, political scientists may come to know not only whether democracies are more peaceful than dictatorships, but more precisely why democratic leaders behave in the way that they do. Most researchers recognize that these methods are complementary (see again Box 2.2).

The final and most challenging task in the scientific process is prediction. Prediction is testing hypotheses against data that were not known by the researchers who developed these explanations, often because the events had not yet happened. It is generally far more difficult to formulate predictions about events that have not yet happened than to explain events whose outcome we already know. This is both because we never know whether we have captured all the relevant factors that might affect the future and because the world itself may change as we try to understand it. Often political actors learn from the mistakes of the past, so that the same patterns do not necessarily repeat themselves. Yet political scientists have made improvements in the act of prediction as well as in description and explanation. Many researchers have, for example, observed the close relationship between economic conditions and the results of U.S. presidential elections. When economic conditions are good (low inflation and unemployment, high growth), the candidate of the incumbent party tends to win; when times are bad, the opposition party tends to prevail. This theory is sufficiently strong that it allows researchers to make fairly precise and reliable predictions about the electoral result after observing economic conditions a few months before the election. Yet sometimes the predictions get it wrong, as they did in the 2000 presidential election, when most researchers predicted that Democratic candidate Al Gore would win handily. Such failed predictions imply the need to revise the theory to take additional factors into account. Successful predictions greatly increase our confidence in a theory,

as well as being interesting for their own sake or to guide policy.

An example may suggest how you might go about theorizing in comparative politics, going beyond "just mastering the facts." It is well known that rich countries are more likely to be democracies than are poor countries; democracy and economic development are strongly associated. But there are many possible reasons for this association. Some persons have suggested that this relationship comes about because democracy encourages education and economic development. Others have argued that as countries develop economically, their new middle classes or their emerging working class are more likely to demand democratization. Yet others have seen that both democracy and economic development are commonly found in some regions of the world, such as Western Europe, while both tend to be scarce in the Middle East and Africa. This fact suggests that certain cultures may encourage or discourage both of them.

Yet the causal nature of this association is important, for reasons of both science and policy. Fostering economic development and securing democracy are two of the significant political challenges that we discussed in Chapter 1. Let us therefore consider how Adam Przeworski and his associates examined the full experience of democracies, nondemocracies, and transitions between them in the world between 1950 and 1990.[6] Their statistical analysis led them to conclude that the explanation for the association between democracy and prosperity did not lie in regional effects or in superior economic growth under democracy. Moreover, countries at any level of development seemed able to introduce democracy, although economically developed countries were somewhat more likely to do so. Instead, Przeworski and his associates argue that the key to the relationship lies in the greater fragility of democracies in economically poor societies. Democracy can easily be introduced in poor societies with less educated populations, but it is often replaced by some kind of dictatorship. In rich countries, on the other hand, democracy tends to survive once it has been introduced. These democratic failures in poor countries produce a strong association between development and democracy. We still need to understand exactly why democracy is more precarious in less developed societies, but we are making progress in understanding the causal relationship between development and democracy, as well as the failures of democratization in poor countries.

Comparative analysis is a powerful and versatile tool. It enhances our ability to describe and understand political processes and political change in any country. The comparative approach also stimulates us to form general theories of political relationships. It encourages and enables us to test our political theories by confronting them with the experience of many institutions and settings.

POLITICAL SYSTEMS: ENVIRONMENT AND INTERDEPENDENCE

In this text we compare political processes with a systems framework. Specifically, we do that with the help of a structural-functional framework. To do so, we need to discuss three general concepts that we use throughout this book: (1) system, (2) structure, and (3) function. A **system**, as we defined it in Chapter 1, is an object with interdependent parts, acting within a setting or an **environment**. The **political system** is a set of institutions and agencies concerned with formulating and implementing the collective goals of a society or of groups within it. **Governments** are the policymaking parts of political systems. The decisions of governments are normally backed up by legitimate coercion, and governments can thus typically compel their citizens to comply with their decisions. (We discuss legitimacy at greater length in Chapter 3.)

Figure 2.1 tells us that a political system exists in both an international environment and a domestic

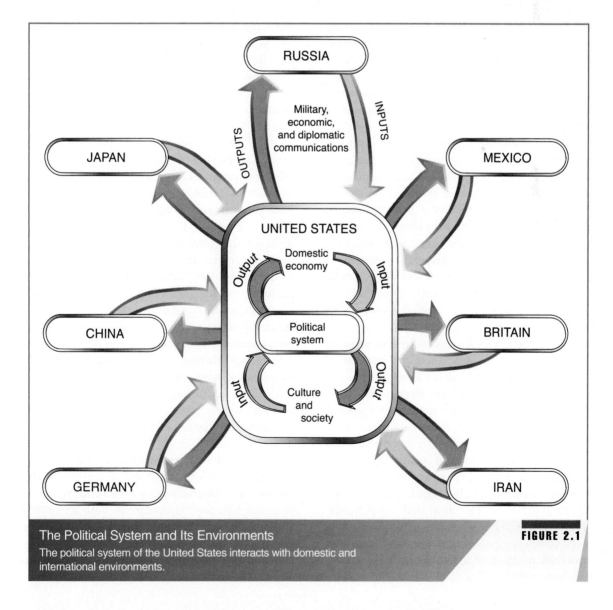

The Political System and Its Environments
The political system of the United States interacts with domestic and international environments.

FIGURE 2.1

environment. It is molded by these environments and it tries to mold them. The system receives **inputs** from these environments. Its policymakers attempt to shape them through its **outputs**. In the figure, which is quite schematic and simple, we use the United States as the central actor. We include other countries as our environmental examples—Russia, China, Britain, Germany, Japan, Mexico, and Iran.

Exchanges among countries may vary in many ways. For example, they may be "dense" or "sparse." U.S.–Canadian relations exemplify the dense end of the continuum in that they affect many of the citizens of these countries in significant ways, while U.S.–Nepalese relations are far sparser.

Relationships among political systems may be of many different kinds. The United States has substantial trade relations with some countries and relatively little trade with others. Some countries have an excess of imports over exports, whereas others have an excess of exports over imports. Military exchanges and support with such countries as the NATO nations, Japan, South Korea, Israel, and Saudi Arabia have been of significant importance to the United States.

The interdependence of countries—the volume and value of imports and exports, transfers of capital, international communication, and the extent of foreign travel and immigration—has increased enormously in the last decades. This increase is often called **globalization**. We might represent this process as a thickening of the input and output arrows between the United States and other countries in Figure 2.1. Fluctuations in this flow of international transactions and traffic attributable to depression, inflation, protective tariffs, international terrorism, war, and the like may wreak havoc with the economies of the countries affected.

The interaction of a political system with its domestic environment—the economic and social systems and the political culture of its citizens—is also depicted in Figure 2.1. We can illustrate this interaction in the U.S. case by the rise of the "high-tech information-based economy." The composition of the U.S. labor force, and consequently its citizenry, has changed dramatically in the last century. Agriculture has declined to under 2 percent of the gainfully employed. Employment in heavy extractive and manufacturing industries has decreased substantially. Newer, high-technology occupations, the professions, and the service occupations have increased sharply as proportions of the labor force. The last half century

has also witnessed significant improvements in the educational level of the U.S. population. Many more young people complete high school and go on to college. Moreover, people move more easily from one region to another. These and other changes in the U.S. social structure have altered the challenges facing the U.S. system and the resources available to meet these challenges.

These changes in the economy and the citizenry are associated with changes in American **political culture**. (Political culture—the attitudes, beliefs, and values of the people in a country—is discussed at more length in Chapter 3.) People want different things from politics. For example, an educated and culturally sophisticated society is more concerned with quality of life, the beauty and healthfulness of the environment, and similar issues.

At the same time, the globalization of the economy leads to demands from firms and workers in some industries for protection of their jobs. Natural disasters, such as the hurricane that devastated New Orleans in 2005, spur calls for the national government to lead reconstruction. Man-made disasters, such as the huge oil spill that contaminated the beaches of the Gulf of Mexico in 2010, also stimulate calls for government action to limit the environmental and economic damages and prevent future disasters. Local issues are seen as the responsibility of the entire country. People live longer. An aging population demands that governments do more to help with medical benefits. In input/output terms, socioeconomic changes transform the political demands of the electorate and the kinds of policies that it supports.

Thus, a new pattern of society results in different policy outputs, different kinds and levels of taxation, changes in regulatory patterns, and changes in welfare expenditures. The advantage of the system-environment approach is that it directs our attention to the **interdependence** of what happens between and within countries. It provides us with a vocabulary to describe, compare, and explain these interacting events.

If we are to make sound judgments in politics, we need to be able to place political systems in their domestic and international environments. We need to recognize how these environments both set limits on and provide opportunities for political choices. This approach keeps us from reaching quick and biased political judgments. If a country is poor in natural resources and lacks the capabilities necessary to exploit what it has, we cannot fault it for having a low industrial output or poor educational and social services. Each country chapter in the second half of this book begins by discussing the current policy challenges facing the country and its social and economic environment.

POLITICAL SYSTEMS: STRUCTURES AND FUNCTIONS

Governments do many things, from establishing and operating school systems, to maintaining public order, to fighting wars. In order to carry on these disparate activities, governments have specialized **structures** (which we may also refer to as *institutions* or *agencies*), such as parliaments, bureaucracies, administrative agencies, and courts. These structures perform

functions, which in turn enable the government to formulate, implement, and enforce its policies. The policies reflect the goals; the agencies provide the means to achieve them.

Figure 2.2 locates six types of political structures—political parties, interest groups, legislatures, executives, bureaucracies, and courts—within the political system. These are formal organizations engaged in political activities. They exist in most contemporary political systems. This list is not exhaustive. Some structures, such as ruling military councils or governing royal families, are found in only a few countries. Some, such as Iran's Council of Guardians, are unique to one country's political system.

We might think that if we understand how such structures work in one political system, we can apply this insight to any other system. Unfortunately, that is not always the case. The sixfold classification in Figure 2.2 will not carry us very far in comparing political systems

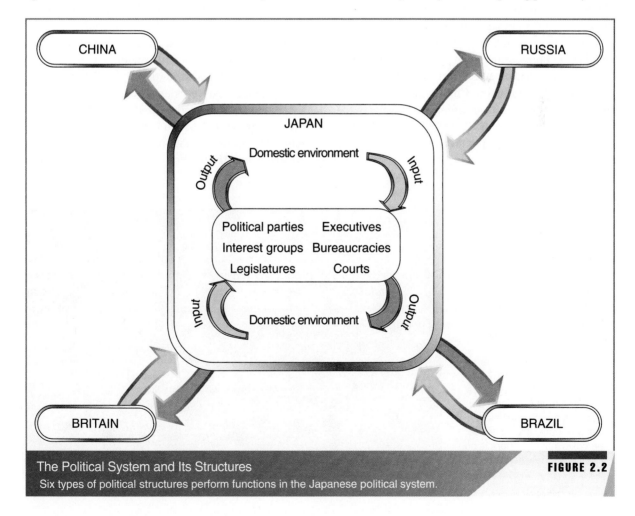

The Political System and Its Structures

FIGURE 2.2

Six types of political structures perform functions in the Japanese political system.

with each other. The problem is that similar structures may have very different functions across political systems. For example, Britain and China have all six types of political structures. However, these institutions are organized differently in the two countries. More important, they function in dramatically different ways.

The political executive in Britain consists of the prime minister and the Cabinet, which includes the heads of major departments and agencies. These officials are usually selected from among the members of Parliament. There is a similar structure in China, called the State Council, headed by a premier and consisting of the various ministers and ministerial commissions. But while the British prime minister and Cabinet have substantial policymaking power, the State Council in China is closely supervised by the general secretary of the Communist Party, the Politburo, and the Central Committee of the party, and has far less influence over public policy.

Both Britain and China have legislative bodies—the House of Commons in Britain and the National People's Congress in China. Their members debate and vote on prospective public policies. But while the House of Commons is a key institution in the British policymaking process, the Chinese Congress meets for only brief periods, ratifying decisions made mainly by the Communist Party authorities. Usually, the Chinese delegates do not even consider alternative policies.

There are even larger differences between political parties in the two countries. Britain has a competitive party system. The majority members in the House of Commons and the Cabinet are constantly confronted by an opposition party or parties, competing for public support. They look forward to the next election when they may unseat the incumbent majority, as happened in 1997, when the Labour Party replaced the Conservatives in government, and in 2010 when the Labour Party was in turn replaced by a coalition of Conservatives and Liberal Democrats. In China, the Communist Party controls the whole political process. There are no other political parties. The principal decisions are made within the Communist Party. The governmental agencies simply implement these policies.

Thus, an institution-by-institution comparison of British and Chinese politics that did not spell out the functions that the various agencies perform would not bring us far toward understanding the important differences in the politics of these two countries. Each country study in this book therefore includes a figure that shows how some of the major structures select and control each other. Another figure illustrates how they fit into the policymaking process.

Figure 2.3 shows the functions of the political process that we can use to compare all political systems. The center of Figure 2.3 under the heading "**process functions**" lists the distinctive activities

Chinese National People's Congress

Delegates applaud below a screen that displays the very lopsided results of voting on the final day of the National People's Congress in Beijing's Great Hall of the People, March 16, 2007. This photo shows the importance of a structural-functional perspective as votes in this "legislature" have little influence on policymaking. There is no real choice between alternatives.

Elizabeth Dalziel/AP Images

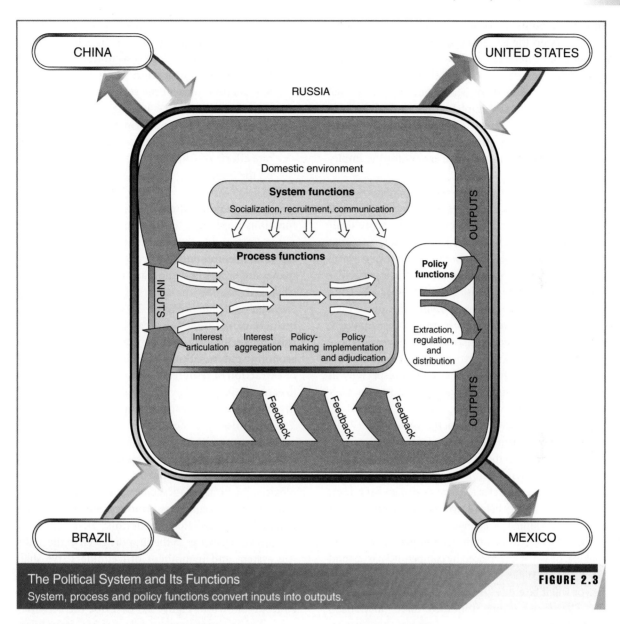

The Political System and Its Functions

System, process and policy functions convert inputs into outputs.

FIGURE 2.3

necessary for policy to be made and implemented in any kind of political system. (We discuss each concept in greater detail in Chapters 4, 5, and 6.) We call these *process functions* because they play a direct and necessary role in the process of making policy.

- **Interest articulation** involves individuals and groups expressing their needs and demands.
- **Interest aggregation** combines different demands into policy proposals backed by significant political resources.
- **Policymaking** is deciding which policy proposals become authoritative rules.

- **Policy implementation** is carrying out and enforcing public policies; **policy adjudication** is settling disputes about their application.

Before policy can be decided, some individuals and groups in the government or the society must decide what they want and hope to get from politics. The political process begins as these interests are expressed or articulated. The many arrows on the left of the figure show these initial expressions. To be effective, however, these demands must be combined (aggregated) into policy alternatives—such as lower taxes or more social security benefits—for which substantial political support can be mobilized. Thus, the arrows on the left are consolidated as the process moves from interest articulation to interest aggregation. Governments then consider alternative policies and choose between them. Their policy decisions must then be enforced and implemented, and if they are challenged, there must be some process of adjudication. Any policy may affect several different aspects of society, as reflected in the three arrows for the implementation phase.

These process functions are performed by such political structures as parties, legislatures, political executives, bureaucracies, and courts. The **structural-functional approach** stresses two points. One is that *in different countries, the same structure may perform different functions.* A second is that while a particular institution, such as a legislature, may specialize in a particular function, such as policymaking, *institutions often do not have a monopoly on any one function.* Presidents and governors may share in the policymaking function (and in the extreme case, each may be a veto power), as may the higher courts (especially in states that feature judicial review of statutes for their constitutionality).

The three functions listed at the top of Figure 2.3—socialization, recruitment, and communication—do not directly concern the making and implementation of public policy but are of fundamental importance to the political system. We refer to them as **system functions**. In the long run, they help determine whether the system will be maintained or changed. For example, will the military be able to maintain its dominance of policymaking, or will it be replaced by competitive parties and a legislature? Will a sense of national community persist, or will it be eroded by new experiences?

The arrows leading from these three functions to all parts of the political process suggest their crucial role in underpinning and permeating the political process.

- **Political socialization** involves families, schools, communications media, churches, and all the various political structures that develop, reinforce, and transform the political culture, the attitudes of political significance in the society (see Chapter 3).
- **Political recruitment** refers to the selection of people for political activity and government offices. In a democracy, competitive elections play a major role in political recruitment. In authoritarian systems, recruitment may be dominated by a single party, as in China, or by unelected religious leaders, as in Iran.
- **Political communication** refers to the flow of information through the society and the various structures that make up the political system. Gaining control over information is a key goal of most authoritarian rulers, as shown in the elaborate efforts of Chinese leaders to control content on the Internet.

Understanding the performance of the system functions is essential to understanding how political systems respond to the great contemporary challenges of building community, fostering economic development, and securing democracy that we discussed in Chapter 1.

The right side of Figure 2.3 illustrates the consequences of the policy process. The outputs are the ways in which policy decisions affect the society, the economy, and the culture. They include various forms of **extraction** of resources in the form of taxes and the like, **regulation** of behavior, and **distribution** of benefits and services to various groups in the population. The **outcomes** of all these political activities reflect the way the policies interact with the domestic and international environments. Sometimes, these outcomes are the desired results of public policies. But the complexities of policy and society sometimes result in unintended consequences. Among these may be new demands for legislation or administrative action, or increases or decreases in the support given to the political system and incumbent officeholders. We shall return to the policy level after providing an example of a structural-functional comparison. The functional concepts shown in Figure 2.3 describe the activities carried on in any society regardless of how its political system is organized or what kinds of policies it produces. Using these functional categories, we can determine how institutions in different countries combine in making and implementing public policy.

AN ILLUSTRATIVE COMPARISON: REGIME CHANGE IN RUSSIA

Figures 2.4 and 2.5[7] offer a simplified graphic comparison of structures and functions in Russia before and after the breakdown of communist rule in the Soviet

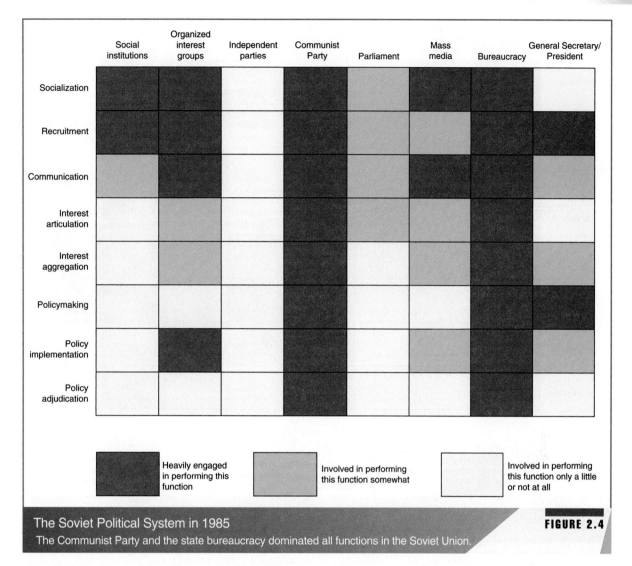

The Soviet Political System in 1985

The Communist Party and the state bureaucracy dominated all functions in the Soviet Union.

FIGURE 2.4

Union. They use our comparative method to illustrate the way a political regime changed significantly in a short period of time. The point here is to illustrate how we can use the tools of political analysis, rather than provide the details of the Russian case (which is discussed in depth in Chapter 12).

The figures depict the changes in the functioning of the major structures of the political system brought about by the collapse of communism. These include two revolutionary changes. One is the end of the single-party political system dominated by the Communist Party of the Soviet Union, which held together the vast, multinational Soviet state. The other is the dissolution of the Soviet Union itself into its fifteen member republics. As a result of these two remarkable events, Russia, the republic that was the core republic of the old union, became an independent noncommunist state.

Figure 2.4 therefore shows how the basic functions of the political system were performed in 1985, when the Soviet Union was a communist state. The Communist Party was the dominant political institution, overseeing schools and media, the arts and public organizations, the economy, and the courts through a massive state bureaucracy. For this reason, all the cells of the chart in the column marked "Communist Party" are shaded dark, as are the cells under the column marked "Bureaucracy." Although social institutions—such as the family, workplace, arts, and hobby groups—exercised some influence over such system-level functions as socialization, recruitment, and communication, it was the Communist Party and

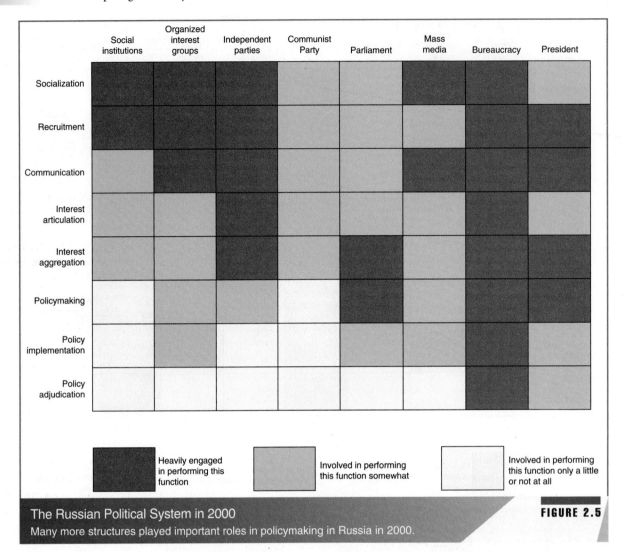

	Social institutions	Organized interest groups	Independent parties	Communist Party	Parliament	Mass media	Bureaucracy	President
Socialization	■	■	■	▨	▨	■	■	▨
Recruitment	■	■	■	▨	▨	▨	■	■
Communication	▨	■	■	▨	▨	■	■	▨
Interest articulation	▨	▨	■	▨	▨	▨	■	▨
Interest aggregation	▨	▨	■	▨	■	▨	■	▨
Policymaking	□	▨	▨	▨	■	▨	■	■
Policy implementation	□	▨	□	□	▨	▨	■	■
Policy adjudication	□	□	□	□	▨	▨	■	▨

■ Heavily engaged in performing this function

▨ Involved in performing this function somewhat

□ Involved in performing this function only a little or not at all

The Russian Political System in 2000

FIGURE 2.5

Many more structures played important roles in policymaking in Russia in 2000.

the state bureaucracy that dominated process-level functions. Under their tutelage, the mass media in 1985 were a key agent of communist political socialization and communication. Parliament was a compliant instrument for ratifying decisions made by the party and bureaucracy. No other parties were allowed by law in addition to the Communist Party. The only organized interest groups were those authorized by the party. The party's general secretary was the most powerful official in the country.

By 2000, the political system had undergone fundamental changes, as shown in Figure 2.5. Many more structures played a role in the political process, as is immediately evident by the larger number of cells that are heavily shaded. In particular, Parliament, independent political parties, and regional governments had all acquired important new policymaking powers. The freedom enjoyed by ordinary citizens to articulate their interests and to organize to advance them had expanded enormously. The Communist Party, no longer an official or monopolistic party, had declined substantially in power and was reduced to the role of an opposition party in the parliamentary game. The lighter shading for the Communist Party in Figure 2.5 shows its diminished influence. The state bureaucracy remained an important element in the political system, although adapting itself to the new trend of movement toward a market economy by adopting quasi-commercial forms.

The presidency has been a dominant policymaking institution in the new Russia, as shown in Figure 2.5. The Parliament, although fairly representative of the diversity of opinion in the country, was frustrated in its policymaking and oversight roles by the inertia of the vast state bureaucracy, by its inability to compel compliance with its laws, by its weak links with the voters, and by the president's political power. Nevertheless, Parliament played a much greater role than before in aggregating interests and policymaking, as demonstrated by a comparison of Figures 2.4 and 2.5.

An updating of Figure 2.5 would show the eclipse of parties, Parliament, and the mass media by the president and the bureaucracy after 2000. This movement in a more authoritarian direction, although not back to communism, would be shown by fewer dark-shaded columns in the middle of the figure. These further developments are discussed in detail in Chapter 12.

The brief comparisons presented here illustrate the use of the structural-functional approach. This approach enables us to examine how the same functions are performed in different countries, or in the same country at two different points in time. Similarly, we may examine changes in the functions performed by the same structures over time or across different political systems. In a country undergoing as rapid and dramatic a transition as Russia in the 1990s, this framework demonstrates substantial changes in the distribution of power.

Neither the analysis of structures nor that of functions is complete without the other. A structural analysis tells us the number of political parties, or the organization of the legislature. It describes how the executive branch, the courts, the bureaucracy, the mass media, interest groups, and other structures of a political system are set up and by what rules or standards they operate. A functional analysis tells us how these institutions and organizations interact to produce and implement policies. This kind of analysis is especially essential when we are comparing very different kinds of political systems.

The country chapters of this book do not present formal structural-functional sketches like Figures 2.4 and 2.5. But at the core of each chapter is a set of discussions of these functions and the structures that perform them. We can see these in the section headings of the country studies and in the analytic guide at the beginning of this book. These tools make it possible to compare the workings of the very different political systems in this book.

THE POLICY LEVEL: PERFORMANCE, OUTCOME, AND EVALUATION

Now, what differences do these variations in political structures and functions make for the citizens of the different states that we analyze? This question directs our attention to the **policy level** of the political system. We call the outputs of a political system—its extractions, distributions, regulations, and symbolic acts—its *policy performance*. We have to distinguish among these efforts, the things a government does, and the actual outcome of these efforts. Governments may spend equal amounts on education and health, or defense, but with different consequences. Government efficiency or corruption plays a role in the effectiveness of politics. But so do the underlying cultural, economic, and technological conditions.

Climbing the Wall

The wall dividing California and Mexico illustrates the input-output model of comparative politics. The two men are trying to escape from the poverty of the Mexican economy. The wall is part of the output of the American political system, intended to frustrate illegal immigrants. The two figures show that outputs do not necessarily produce the intended outcomes.

Les Stone/Sygma/Corbis

Americans spend more per capita on education than any other people in the world. But their children perform worse in some subjects, such as mathematics, than do children in some other countries that spend substantially less. The United States spent enormous sums and many lives on the war in Vietnam in the 1960s and 1970s, as did the Soviet Union on its war in Afghanistan in the 1980s. Yet both countries were held at bay by far less well-equipped armed forces or guerrilla groups resolved to resist at all costs. Because of these costly failures, the United States and the Soviet Union were weakened internally. In the latter case, the costs of the war in Afghanistan contributed directly to the downfall of the communist regime. The outcome of public policy is thus never wholly in the hands of the people and their leaders. Legislatures may vote to wage a military conflict, but neither their votes nor the promises of political leaders can guarantee success. Conditions in the internal environment, conditions and events in the larger external world, and simple chance may frustrate the most thoughtfully crafted programs and plans. Each country study in this book concludes with a discussion of the country's performance, describing both policies and their outcomes.

Finally, we must step even further back to evaluate the politics of different systems. Evaluation is complex because people value different things and put different emphases on what they value. We will refer to the different conditions, outputs, and outcomes that people may value as political "goods." In Chapter 7, we outline a typology of various kinds of political goals and political goods. These include goods associated with the system level, such as the stability or adaptability of political institutions, and goods associated with the process level, such as citizen participation in politics. Finally, we consider and describe goods associated with the policy level, such as welfare, security, fairness, and liberty. To evaluate what a political system is doing, we assess performance and outcomes in each of these areas. We must also be aware of how these broad outcomes affect specific individuals and groups in the society, which may often be overlooked if we simply consider national averages.

A particularly important problem of evaluation concerns building for the future as well as living today. The people of poor countries wish to survive and alleviate the suffering of today but also to improve their children's lot for tomorrow. The people of all countries, but especially rich ones, must deal with the costs to their children of polluted and depleted natural resources as the result of the thoughtless environmental policies of the past.

REVIEW QUESTIONS

- How do the main elements in the environment of a political system affect the way it performs?

- Why are we unable to compare political systems simply by describing the different structures we find in them?

- What are the functions performed in all political systems as policies are made?

- What is the difference between outputs and outcomes of policy?

- How do we use theories to explain political events?

KEY TERMS

conceptual framework	hypotheses	policy implementation	regulation
data	inputs	policy level	structural-functional approach
distribution	interdependence	policymaking	structures
environment	interest aggregation	political communication	system
extraction	interest articulation	political culture	system functions
functions	intersubjective	political recruitment	theories
general	outcomes	political socialization	variables
globalization	outputs	political system	
governments	policy adjudication	process functions	

SUGGESTED READINGS

Brady, Henry E., and David Collier. *Rethinking Social Inquiry: Diverse Tools, Shared Standards.* Lanham, MD: Rowman and Littlefield, 2004.

Collier, David. "The Comparative Method," in *Political Science: The State of the Discipline II*, ed. Ada W. Finifter. Washington, D.C.: American Political Science Association, 1993.

Dogan, Mattei, and Dominique Pelassy. *How to Compare Nations: Strategies in Comparative Politics.* Chatham, NJ: Chatham House, 1990.

Goodin, Robert E., and Hans-Dieter Klingemann. *A New Handbook of Political Science.* New York: Oxford University Press, 1996 (Chapters 2 and 3, and Part 4).

King, Gary, Robert O. Keohane, and Sidney Verba. *Scientific Inference in Qualitative Research.* New York: Cambridge University Press, 1993.

Lichbach, Mark, and Alan Zuckerman. *Comparing Nations: Rationality, Culture, and Structure.* New York: Cambridge University Press, 1997.

Little, Daniel. *Varieties of Social Explanation: An Introduction to the Philosophy of Social Science.* Boulder, CO: Westview, 1991.

Przeworski, Adam, and Henry Teune. *The Logic of Comparative Social Inquiry.* New York: Wiley, 1970.

ENDNOTES

1. Alexis de Tocqueville to Louis de Kergolay, 18 October 1847, in *Alexis de Tocqueville: Selected Letters on Politics and Society*, ed. Roger Boesche (Berkeley: University of California Press, 1985), 191.

2. Alexis de Tocqueville to Ernest de Chabrol, 7 October 1831, in *Selected Letters*, 59.

3. For some related and alternative concepts of explanation, see Daniel Little, *Varieties of Social Explanation* (Boulder, CO: Westview, 1991).

4. Alexis de Tocqueville, *The Old Regime and the French Revolution,* trans. Stuart Gilbert (New York: Doubleday, 1955).

5. Theda Skocpol, *States and Social Revolutions* (New York: Cambridge University Press, 1979).

6. Adam Przeworski et al., *Democracy and Development: Political Institutions and Well-Being in the World, 1950–1990* (New York: Cambridge University Press, 2000).

7. Figures 2.4 and 2.5 and the text of this section were contributed by Thomas Remington.

POLITICAL CULTURE AND POLITICAL SOCIALIZATION

If you have ever traveled to a foreign country, you were probably surprised by how many of the normal things in your life were different there. The food was different, people wore different clothes, houses were constructed and furnished differently, and the pattern of social relations differed (for instance, whether people talked to strangers or stood in queues). You were observing how social norms shape what people eat, how they dress, how they live, and maybe even on which side of the road they drive.

Similarly, each nation has its own political norms that influence how people think about and react to politics. To understand the political tendencies in a nation, we must begin with public attitudes toward politics and their role within the political system—what we call a nation's *political culture*. Americans' strong feelings of patriotism, the Japanese deference to political elites, and the French proclivity for protest all illustrate how cultural norms shape politics. The way political institutions function at least partially reflects the public's attitudes, norms, and expectations. Thus, the English use their constitutional arrangements to sustain their liberty, while the same institutions were once used as a means of repression in South Africa and Northern Ireland.

When a new regime forms, a supportive public can help develop the new system, while the absence of public support may weaken the new system. The content of the political culture has been a very important aspect of the transitions to democracy in the past two decades, as new democracies needed to develop democratic orientations and behaviors among their citizens. It is hard to sustain democracy without a nation of democrats.

Chapter 1 stated that one main goal of any government, and a special challenge for a new government, is to create and maintain a political community. In part, this involves developing common structures and systems (such as a single economy), common political institutions, and common political processes. For the public, this involves developing common worldviews, values, and expectations among the public that together comprise the nation's political culture. Thus, studying political culture partially explains how a political community is created and sustained.

In this chapter, we map the important parts of political culture. We then discuss political socialization: how individuals form their political attitudes and thus, collectively, how citizens form their political culture. We conclude by describing the major trends in political culture in world politics today.

MAPPING THE THREE LEVELS OF POLITICAL CULTURE

A nation's **political culture** includes its citizens' orientations at three levels: the political system, the political and policymaking process, and policy outputs and outcomes (Table 3.1). The *system* level involves how people view the values and organizations that comprise the political system. Do citizens identify with the nation and accept the general system of government? The *process* level includes expectations of the political rules and decision-making methods, and individuals' relationship to the government. The *policy* level deals with the public's policy expectations for the

Political Culture There are three levels of political culture, which tap different orientations toward politics.	**TABLE 3.1**

Aspects of Political Culture	Examples
System	Pride in nation National identity Legitimacy of government
Process	Role of citizens Perceptions of political rights
Policy	Role of government Government policy priorities

government. What should the policy goals of government be, and how are they to be achieved?

The System Level

Orientations toward the political system are important because they tap basic commitments to the polity and the nation. It is difficult for any political system to endure if it lacks the support of its citizens.

Feelings of national pride are considered an affective, emotional tie to a political system. National pride seems strongest in nations with long histories that have emphasized feelings of patriotism—the United States is a prime example (see Figure 3.1). Such a common sense of identity and national history often binds a people together in times of political strain. The figure indicates that high levels of pride exist in nations with very different political and economic systems, such as Vietnam, Canada, Poland, and Turkey. Large majorities in most countries are proud of their nations. In contrast, national pride is low in Japan and Germany, two nations that have avoided nationalist sentiments in reaction to World War II regimes and their excesses. And Russia's resurgence in the past decade has substantially improved levels of national pride from earlier surveys in the late 1990s and early 2000s, while Moldova's continuing struggles since independence are signaled by the weak sense of national pride among its citizens.

Feelings of popular **legitimacy** are another basis for a stable political system. Citizens may grant legitimacy to a government for different reasons.[1] In a traditional society, legitimacy may depend on the ruler's inheriting the throne or on the ruler's commitment to religious customs. In a modern democracy, the legitimacy of the authorities depends on their selection by voters in competitive elections and on the government's following constitutional procedures. Theocratic regimes, such as Iran, base their legitimacy on adherence to religious principles. In other political cultures, the leaders may base their claim to legitimacy on their special wisdom or ideology, which is typical for communist regimes or countries that emerged from recent national independence movements. Thus, legitimacy presumes an agreement on the broad form of government that defines the political system and thus the standards of legitimacy: monarchical rule, a tribal system, a communist order, or a democratic system. Based on these different principles, people in widely differing political systems can still express support for their political systems because they are using different standards of legitimacy.[2]

Whether legitimacy is based on tradition, religion, elections, or ideology, feelings of legitimacy reflect a basic understanding between citizens and political authorities. People obey the laws; in return, the government meets the obligations set by the terms of its legitimacy. As long as the government meets its obligations, the public is supposed to be supportive and act appropriately. If legitimacy is violated—the line of succession is broken, the constitution is subverted, or the ruling ideology is ignored—the government may expect resistance and perhaps rebellion. A political system and a government with high legitimacy are typically more effective in carrying out policies and are more likely to overcome hardships and reversals.

In systems with low legitimacy, people often resort to violence or extragovernmental actions to solve political disagreements. Legitimacy is lacking where the public disputes the boundaries of the political system

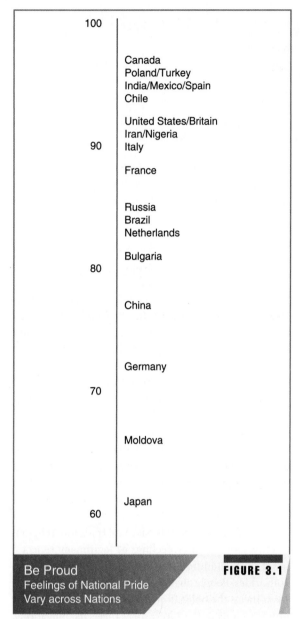

Be Proud
Feelings of National Pride
Vary across Nations

FIGURE 3.1

Source: Selected nations from the 2005–2008 *World Values Survey* and the 2000–2002 *World Values Survey* for Nigeria. Figure entries are the percent "proud" and "very proud"; missing data are excluded from the calculation of percentages.

(as in Northern Ireland or Kashmir), rejects the current arrangements for recruiting leaders and making policies (as when Ukrainians took to the streets in 2004 to 2005, demanding new democratic elections), or loses confidence that the leaders are fulfilling their part of the political bargain (as when the Thai opposition battled the government in 2010).

The Soviet Union disintegrated in the early 1990s because all three legitimacy problems appeared. After the communist ideology failed as a legitimizing force, there was little basis for a national political community without a common language or ethnicity. Similarly, the loss of confidence in the Communist Party as a political organization led many people to call for institutional reform. Finally, shortages of food and consumer goods caused people to lose faith in the government's short-term economic and political policies. Soviet President Mikhail Gorbachev failed in his efforts to deal with all three problems at the same time.

The Process Level

The second level of the political culture involves what the public expects of the political process. Whether you are English or Nigerian, what do you think about the institutions of your political system and what is expected of you as a citizen?

One of the great advances in comparative politics research is the relatively recent expansion of our knowledge of the political culture in developing societies, and this has transformed our understanding of political culture on a global scale. Until then, researchers worried that the cultural bases of democracy were essentially limited to those nations that were already democratic, and thus the prospects for further democratization were limited.[3] Researchers reached this conclusion by assuming that economic development and affluence were prerequisites for democracy, and that autocratic states persisted because the public tolerated or even supported autocratic government.

However, as public opinion surveys have become more common in developing nations, our images have changed. Cross-national studies of political culture document broad support for democratic principles and norms even in many autocratic nations.[4] Democratic norms emphasize the importance of a participatory process, majority rule and minority rights, and the values of political tolerance. Moreover, as more nations democratize (refer back to Figure 1.3) and alternative regime forms lose their legitimacy, democratic norms have diffused to even more societies. Many of the nondemocratic forms of governance are no longer widely accepted. Communism still has strongholds in China and Cuba, but it has lost its image as a progressive force for global change.

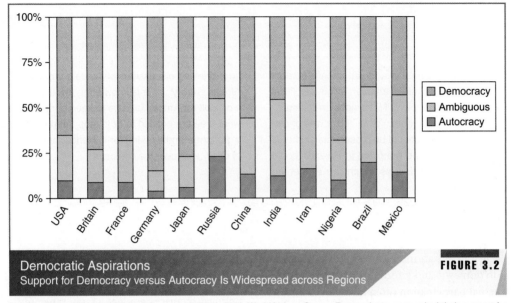

Democratic Aspirations
Support for Democracy versus Autocracy Is Widespread across Regions

FIGURE 3.2

Source: 2000–2002 *World Values Survey* and 2005–2008 *World Values Survey*. Respondents were asked their support for either democracy or autocracy (either a nondemocratic leader or military regime); the ambiguous category is those who express equal approval for both.

Consequently, current research finds that support for democratic norms is widespread in many developing nations in Africa, East Asia, and Latin America.[5] The World Values Survey asked respondents in more than 60 nations to state their approval of democracy and two nondemocratic regimes (military rule or rule by a strong leader). Figure 3.2 displays respondents (from the nations covered in this book) who prefer democracy, prefer either nondemocratic regime, or have mixed opinions.[6] In the established democracies, citizens express overwhelming support for democracy, but even here there are some citizens who are ambivalent about the regime form and about a tenth who actually prefer some autocratic form of government. In the developing nations in this book, the picture is more mixed. Only small percentages favor an autocracy over democracy, with the most autocrats in Russia (23 percent). However, a fair number in these developing nations give equal ratings to democracy and autocracy. Among the seven developing nations, only in Nigeria and China do a majority clearly prefer democracy. It is not a positive sign for democracy in Brazil and Mexico, for example, if less than half of the public prefers democracy over autocracy. Democracy often receives plurality support in these developing nations, but there is clearly a need to increase public support for democracy.

Furthermore, we should be cautious about taking support for democracy at full face value in less democratic nations. Even if most of the people in the world today seem to favor a democratic political process, they differ in their understanding of how the democratic process actually functions. Expressions of support for liberty and tolerance are easier than actually supporting these values when applied to your political opponents. Cultures also differ in how those principles should be applied. In some nations, the public expresses support for equal rights for women, but then imposes Shari'a restrictions on women. Still, the breadth of democratic aspirations is strikingly different than our images of developing nations in the past. These patterns seem to reaffirm Amartya Sen's claim that democracy is a basic human striving—something many scholars doubted a few short years ago.[7]

Another aspect of political culture is the role of the individual in the political system. At one time, social scientists considered the population in developing nations as largely disinterested or even unaware of politics because they were concerned with sustenance and lacked access to political information.[8] Again, this image has softened in recent years as research has documented considerable political interest even in unexpected places (see Box 3.1). The spreading norms of democratization and the development of a global

BOX 3.1

A Small World

With a radio deep in a rural village, a person is abreast with a bomb blast in Bombay, and can follow a political crisis in Moscow. . . . People will take sides on issues far beyond their national borders. Whether the wife of dictator Ferdinand Marcos should be prosecuted or should be pardoned; whether the genocide in Rwanda could have been averted are issues which are enlivening beer-drinking discussions on a scale unprecedented in African history. . . . This knowledge revolution is making it difficult for African leaders to keep people ignorant of what they are entitled to or to stop them from demanding change and working for it. Hence there are shivers of change all over the continent.

Source: A Ugandan government official cited in Bruce Gilley, *The Right to Rule: How States Win and Lose Legitimacy* (New York: Columbia University Press, 2009), 78.

marketplace connect an increasingly larger share of the world to domestic and international politics.

Still, actual participation often involves resources, skills, and norms of active citizenship that are in short supply in many developing nations. Consequently, research shows that industrialization, urbanization, and improved living standards develop the cultural bases of active citizenship.[9] Exposure to modernity through work, education, and the media shapes an individual's personal experiences and sends messages about norms in other societies. It encourages citizen participation, a sense of individual equality, the desire for improved living standards and increased life expectancy, and government legitimacy based on policy performance. It also frequently disrupts familiar ways of life, traditional bases of legitimacy, and political arrangements that limit political engagement. In addition, the secularizing influences of science can alter economic and social systems, which then reshape the political culture. This **modernization** trend has powerful effects as it penetrates societies (or parts of societies).

This modernization process is spread unevenly across the globe. The recent economic growth in East Asia is transforming the political culture and political behavior in these nations. In contrast, modernization has proceeded more slowly and uncertainly in Africa and Arab nations. Some political leaders in these nations even reject the principles of modernization as incongruent with their national values. However, there is persuasive evidence that where social and economic modernization occurs, it transforms the political culture to emphasize self-expression, participatory values, and autonomy.

The Policy Level

What is the appropriate role of government? If you ask political theorists, you get a wide range of answers—from the minimal state to the all-encompassing polity (see Chapter 1). And if you travel to other nations, you quickly realize that there is wide variation in how people answer this question.

Public images of what constitutes the good of society and the government's role in achieving these goals influence the policy activities of a country. Should government manage the economy, or should private property rights and market forces guide economic activity? Should the state intervene in addressing social and moral issues, or should it follow a minimalist strategy? The ongoing debates over "big government" versus "small government" in democratic states, and between socialist and market-based economies, reflect these different images of the scope of government.

We can illustrate differences in policy expectations with an opinion survey question that asks whether the government is responsible for providing for everyone versus individuals being responsible for providing for themselves (see Figure 3.3). The range in opinions is considerable; more than three-quarters of Russians believe government is responsible, compared with only two-fifths among Americans, Canadians, Britons, or the French. In general, people in developing nations and in the formerly communist nations of Eastern Europe are more supportive of a large government role—reflecting both their social condition and their past political ideologies. In some Western nations, traditions include a large role for the government. In general, however, support for

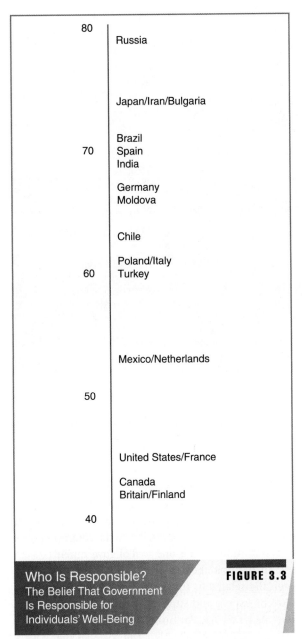

80
Russia

Japan/Iran/Bulgaria

Brazil
70 Spain
India

Germany
Moldova

Chile

Poland/Italy
60 Turkey

Mexico/Netherlands

50

United States/France

Canada
Britain/Finland

40

Who Is Responsible?
The Belief That Government
Is Responsible for
Individuals' Well-Being

FIGURE 3.3

Source: Selected nations from the 2005–2008 *World Values Survey*; missing data are excluded from the calculation of percentages.

Some policy goals, such as economic well-being, are valued by nearly everyone. Concern about other policy goals may vary widely across nations because of the nation's circumstances and because of cultural traditions. People in developing countries are more likely to focus on the government's provision of basic services to ensure public welfare. In advanced industrial societies, people are often more concerned with quality-of-life goals, such as preservation of nature and even government support for the arts.[12] One basic measure of a government's performance is its ability to meet the policy expectations of its citizens.

Another set of expectations involves the functioning of government. Some societies put more weight on the policy outputs of government, such as providing welfare and security. Other societies also emphasize how the process functions, which involves values such as the rule of law and procedural justice. Among Germans, for example, the rule of law is given great importance; in many developing nations, political relations are personally based, and there is less willingness to rely on legalistic frameworks.

Consensual or Conflictual Political Cultures

Although political culture is a common characteristic of a nation, values and beliefs can vary within it. Political cultures may be consensual or conflictual on issues of public policy and, more fundamentally, on views of legitimate governmental and political arrangements. In some societies, citizens generally agree on the norms of political decision-making and their policy expectations. In other societies—because of differences in histories, conditions, or identities—the citizens are sharply divided, often on both the legitimacy of the regime and solutions to major problems.[13]

When a country is deeply divided in its political values and these differences persist over time, distinctive **political subcultures** may develop. The citizens in these subcultures may have sharply different points of view on some critical political matters, such as the boundaries of the nation, the nature of the regime, or the correct ideology. They may affiliate with different political parties and interest groups, read different newspapers, and even have separate social clubs and sporting groups.

In some instances, historical or social factors generate different cultural trajectories. For instance, *ethnic, religious,* or *linguistic* identities in many parts of the

government action generally decreases as national affluence increases.[10]

Policy expectations also involve specific issue demands.[11] Indeed, each country study in this book begins with a discussion of the policy challenges facing the nation and the public's issue concerns. This sets the agenda of politics that responsive governments should address.

Cuba Si!

Cubans wave flags at a pro-government rally organized by the Castro government.

Jose Goitia/AP Images

world shape citizen values.[14] Moreover, as such groups increase their political skills and self-confidence, they may express their identities and demand equal treatment. In fact, the processes of globalization might actually heighten these cultural contrasts.[15] Where political subcultures coincide with ethnic, linguistic, or religious differences—as in Northern Ireland, Bosnia, and Lebanon—the divisions can be enduring and threatening. The breakup of Yugoslavia and the impulses toward autonomy and secession among ethnically distinct regions (such as in Scotland or separatist movements in Africa) all reflect the lasting power of language, culture, and historical memory to create and sustain the sense of ethnic and national identity. The exposure to values from other cultures also may intensify one's own self-image, which may increase cultural tensions. Although such exposure may eventually lead to greater tolerance, that outcome is not guaranteed.

WHY CULTURE MATTERS

Political culture does not explain everything about politics. Even people with similar values and skills might behave differently from each other when they face different situations. Nor is political culture unchangeable. However, cultural norms typically change slowly and reflect stable values. Thus, political culture is important first because it encapsulates the history, traditions, and values of a society. To understand how most people in a nation think and act politically, we can begin by understanding their political culture. Political culture can create the common political community that is one goal of government.

In addition, the distribution of cultural patterns is typically related to the type of political process that citizens expect and support. This is the principle of *congruence theory*. For instance, support for a democratic system is typically higher in societies that have a more participatory political culture. Authoritarian states are more likely to endure where people lack the skills or motivations to participate and the state discourages their participation. These cultural norms represent the "rules of the game" for the political system, and the system works better when citizens accept these rules. Where political structures and political cultures are mutually reinforcing, a stable political system is likely to emerge.

We can illustrate the logic of congruence theory in terms of the relationship between political culture and

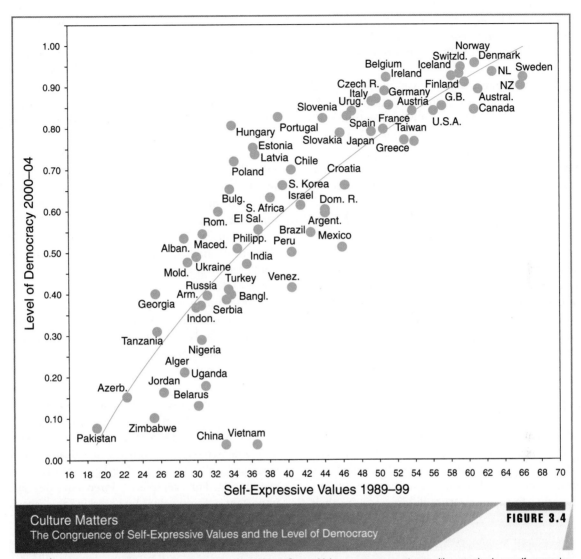

Culture Matters
The Congruence of Self-Expressive Values and the Level of Democracy

FIGURE 3.4

Source: The self-expressive values measure is from the *World Values Survey*; higher scores represent more citizen emphasis on self-expression. The level of democracy measure is a composite of the ranking of democracy by the Freedom House and other national rankings. Higher scores indicate a higher level of democratic development. For additional discussion of these measures, see Ronald Inglehart and Christian Welzel, *Modernization, Cultural Change, and Democracy* (New York: Cambridge University Press, 2005).

the democratic development of a nation (Figure 3.4). The horizontal axis of the figure displays the public's adherence to self-expressive values, reflecting the participatory norms we discussed earlier. The vertical axis represents the democratic development of the nation based on a variety of expert evaluations. You can see that participatory norms and democratic development are interrelated. The nations in this book that are in these analyses differ between the established Western democracies, democratizing nations (such as Mexico and Eastern European nations), and nondemocracies

(such as China and several Middle East nations). Structure and culture do overlap in these nations.[16]

Do democracies create a participatory democratic public or does such a political culture lead to a democratic political system? It works both ways. For example, immediately after World War II, Germans were less supportive of democracy, but political institutions and political experiences transformed their culture over the next generation.[17] At the same time, democracy endured in Britain during the strains of the Great Depression and World War II, at least in part because the British public supported the democratic process. The important conclusion is that there is normally a relationship between political culture and political structures.

Beyond shaping the structure of the political system, a nation's political culture also influences the style of politics and the content of policymaking. We have stressed how the policy elements of a political culture can influence the content of policy. In addition, research suggests that cultural factors, such as social trust and engagement, influence the efficiency and effectiveness of government.[18]

Finally, culture can also divide nations and regions of the world. Samuel Huntington divided the world into different civilizations defined by their religious and cultural traditions.[19] He then predicted that these cultural differences will be a major source of international conflict in this century. While culture may have the power to divide, it also has the potential to build a common political community as people interact and learn which values they share.

POLITICAL SOCIALIZATION

Political cultures are sustained or changed as people acquire their attitudes and values. **Political socialization** refers to the way in which political values are formed and political culture is transmitted from one generation to the next. Most children acquire their basic political values and behavior patterns by adolescence.[20] Some of these attitudes will evolve and change throughout their lives, while other attitudes will remain part of their political selves throughout life.

At any specific time, a person's political beliefs are a combination of various feelings and attitudes. At the deepest level, there are general identifications, such as nationalism, ethnic or class self-images, religious and ideological commitments, and a fundamental sense of rights and duties in the society. At the middle level, people develop attitudes toward politics and governmental institutions. Finally, there are more immediate views of current events, policies, issues, and personalities. All these attitudes can change, but those in the first level usually were acquired earliest, have been most frequently reinforced, and tend to be the most durable.

Three points about political socialization deserve mention. First, the socialization process can occur in different ways. **Direct socialization** involves an actor explicitly communicating information, values, or feelings toward politics. Examples of direct socialization include civics courses in the schools, public education programs of the government, and the political information campaigns of interest groups. Communist political systems also heavily use direct indoctrination programs (see Box 3.2). **Indirect socialization** occurs when political views are inadvertently molded by our experiences. For example, children normally learn important political values by observing the behavior

---

Socializing Values   **BOX 3.2**

Communist East Germany had a special ceremony for eighth-graders to mark their passage to adulthood. The heart of the ceremony was the endorsement of the following four pledges:

- As young citizens of our German Democratic Republic, are you prepared to work and fight loyally for the great and honorable goals of socialism, and to honor the revolutionary inheritance of the people?
- As sons and daughters of the worker-and-peasant state, are you prepared to pursue higher education, to cultivate your mind, to become a master of your trade, to learn permanently, and to use your knowledge to pursue our great humanist ideals?
- As honorable members of the socialist community, are you ready to cooperate as comrades, to respect and support each other, and to always merge the pursuit of your personal happiness with the happiness of all the people?
- As true patriots, are you ready to deepen the friendship with the Soviet Union, to strengthen our brotherhood with socialist countries, to struggle in the spirit of proletarian internationalism, to protect peace and to defend socialism against every imperialist aggression?

of their parents, teachers, and friends. Or, people may learn by observing the political and social context that surrounds them, watching what governments do and how other citizens react.

Second, socialization is a lifelong process. Early family influences can create an individual's initial values, but subsequent life experiences—becoming involved in new social groups, moving from one part of the country to another, shifting up or down the social ladder, becoming a parent, finding or losing a job—may change one's political perspectives. More dramatic experiences—such as relocating to a new country or suffering through an economic depression or a war—can alter even basic political attitudes. Such events seem to have their greatest impact on young people, but people at any age are affected to some degree.

Third, patterns of socialization can unify or divide. Governments design public education systems, for instance, to create a single national political culture. Some events, such as international conflict or the death of a popular public figure, can affect nearly the entire nation similarly. In contrast, subcultures in a society can have their own distinctive patterns of socialization. Social groups that provide their members with their own newspapers, their own neighborhood groups, and perhaps their own schools can create distinctive subcultural attitudes. Divisive patterns of socialization can lead to a political gap among members of a nation.

AGENTS OF POLITICAL SOCIALIZATION

How do we learn our political attitudes? Individuals in all societies are affected by **agents of political socialization**: individuals, organizations, and institutions that influence political attitudes. Some, like civics courses in schools, are direct and deliberate sources of political learning. Others, like playgroups and work groups, affect political socialization indirectly.

The Family

Most of us first learn about politics through our families. The family has distinctive influences on attitudes toward authority. Participation in family decision-making can increase a child's sense of political competence, providing skills for political interaction and encouraging active participation in the political system as an adult.

Similarly, unquestioning obedience to parental decisions may lead a child toward a more passive political role. The family also shapes future political attitudes by defining a social position for the child: establishing ethnic, linguistic, class, and religious ties; affirming cultural values; and influencing job aspirations.

The nature of the family is changing in many societies. Family sizes are generally decreasing, which changes the pattern of family life. In addition, there has been a marked rise of single-parent families, especially in the advanced industrial democracies. The political impact of these structural changes on family socialization patterns is still unclear.

Social Groups and Identities

Our social characteristics also shape political orientations because these reflect different social needs, experiences, and social networks. For instance, social divisions based on class or occupation affect our life changes and political orientations. For instance, industrialization in Britain created a working class that lived in particular neighborhoods, worked at the same factories, and visited the same pubs. This working class developed its own forms of speech, dress, recreation, and entertainment, as well as its own social organizations (such as social clubs, trade unions, and political parties). In addition, labor unions provide an organizational base for informing their members on the politics of the day. Similarly, the life experience of the rural peasantry in many less developed nations is radically different from that of urban dwellers. Often, these social divisions are politically relevant; identifying yourself as a member of the working class or the peasantry leads to ties to groups representing these interests and distinct political views about what issues are important and which political parties best represent your interests.

The religions of the world are also carriers of cultural and moral values, which often have political implications. The great religious leaders have seen themselves as teachers, and their followers have usually attempted to shape the socialization of children through schooling, preaching, and religious services. In most nations, there are formal ties between the dominant religion and the government. In these instances, religious values and public policy often overlap. Catholic nations, for instance, are less likely to have liberal abortion policies, just as Islamic governments enforce strict moral codes.

Religious institutions of many kinds offer valuable moral and ethical guidance that individuals often need to make choices in complex societies. Religious affiliations are often important sources of partisan preferences and can guide people in making other political choices. Where churches teach values that may be at odds with the controlling political system, the struggle over socialization can be intense. These tensions can take a wide variety of forms: the clash between secular and religious roles in the French educational system, the efforts of American fundamentalists to bridge the separation of church and state, or the conflict between Islamic fundamentalists and secular governments in Algeria and Egypt. In such cases, religious groups may oppose the policies of the state, or even the state itself.[21]

In addition, gender shapes social experiences and life chances, and in many nations provides cues about issue interests and political roles. Gender differences in politics have narrowed in many industrial nations, although they persist in many less developed nations.[22] The modern women's movement encourages women to become politically active and change social cues about how women should relate to politics. The lessening of gender differences in self-images, in parental roles, and in relation to the economy and the political system is affecting patterns of political recruitment, political participation, and public policy. Especially in the developing world, the changing role of women may have profound influences in modernizing the society and changing political values.[23]

Social identities are also often linked to membership in a racial or ethnic group. Whether it is an African-American in the United States, an ethnic Pakistani living in London, or an Asian businessperson in South Africa, their distinctiveness partially defines their social and political identity. Ethnic and racially oriented groups provide social cues and information for members of these communities. In many instances, their identity creates a social network of interactions and life experiences that shape their values, while specific groups represent their interests in the political process and provide a network for political socialization and education.

Schools

Schools are often an important agent of political socialization. They educate children about politics and their role in the process, and provide them with information on political institutions and relationships. Schools can shape attitudes about the political system, the rules of the political game, the appropriate role of the citizen, and expectations about the government. Schools typically reinforce attachments to the political system and reinforce common symbols, such as the flag and Pledge of Allegiance, that encourage emotional attachments to the system.

When a new nation comes into being, or a revolutionary regime comes to power in an old nation, it usually turns to the schools as a means to supplant "outdated" values and symbols with ones more congruent with the new ideology.

In some nations, educational systems do not provide unifying political socialization but send starkly different messages to different groups. For instance, some Muslim nations segregate girls and boys within the school system. Even if educational experiences are intended to be equal, segregation creates different experiences and expectations. Moreover, the content of education often differs between boys and girls. Perhaps the worst example occurred under the Taliban in Afghanistan, where for several years young girls were prohibited from attending school. Such treatment of young girls severely limits their life chances, and ensures that they will have restricted roles in society and the economy—which was the intent of the Taliban system. The current Afghanistan government reversed this policy and included girls in the education system, but this is still resisted in parts of the nation.

Education also affects people's political skills and resources. Educated people are more aware of the impact of government on their lives and pay more attention to politics.[24] The better educated have mental skills that improve their ability to manage the world of politics. They also have more information about political processes and participate in a wider range of political activities.

Peer Groups

Peer groups include childhood playgroups, friendship cliques, school and college fraternities, small work groups, and other groups in which members share close personal ties. They can be as varied as a group of Russian mothers who meet regularly at the park, to a street gang in Brazil, to a group of Wall Street executives who are members of a health club.

A peer group socializes its members by encouraging them to share the attitudes or behavior common to the group. Individuals often adopt their peers' views because they like or respect them or because they want to be like them. Similarly, a person may become engaged in politics because close friends do so. One example of peer networks is the international youth culture symbolized by rock music, T-shirts, and blue jeans (and often more liberal political values). Some observers claim that it played a major role in the failure of communist officials to mold Soviet and Eastern European youth to the "socialist personality" that was the Marxist–Leninist ideal. Likewise, the "skinhead" groups that have sprouted up among lower-class youth in many Western countries have adopted political views that are based on peer interactions.

Interest Groups

Interest groups, economic groups, and similar organizations also shape political attitudes. In most industrial countries, the rise of trade unions transformed the political culture and politics, created new political parties, and ushered in new social benefit programs. Today, unions are active participants in the political process and try to persuade their members on political matters. Other professional associations—such as groups of peasants and farmers, manufacturers, wholesalers and retailers, medical societies, and lawyers—also regularly influence political attitudes in modern and modernizing societies. These groups ensure the loyalty of their members by defending their economic and professional interests. They can also provide valuable political cues to nonmembers, who might identify with a group's interests or political ideology. For instance, when a group that you like (or dislike) publicly supports a policy, it gives you information on the likely content of the policy.

The groups that define a civil society are also potential agents of socialization. These groups might include ethnic organizations, fraternal associations, civic associations (such as parent–teacher associations), and policy groups (such as taxpayers' associations, women's groups, and environmental groups). Such groups provide valuable political cues to their members and try to reinforce distinct social and political orientations. They also provide settings to learn about how making political choices in small groups can be extended to politics. For instance, Vietnam has an active network of social groups that socialize individuals into the norms of the communist regime, while civil society groups in the United States are treated as democracy-building organizations. In addition, these groups—using the media and other sources—send out large quantities of information on political, social, and economic issues to the public and elites.

Meet the Press

European leaders meet with the press at the EU Summit held by EU President Herman van Rompuy on the financial crisis.

Andia/Alamy

Political Parties

Political parties normally play an important role in political socialization (also see Chapter 5). In democratic systems, political parties try to mold issue preferences, arouse the apathetic, and find new issues to mobilize support. Party representatives provide the public with a steady flow of information on the issues of the day. Party organizations regularly contact voters to advocate their positions. In addition, every few years, an election enables parties to present their accomplishments and discuss the nation's political future. Elections can serve as national civics lessons, and the political parties are the teachers.

Partisan socialization can be also a divisive force. In their efforts to gain support, party leaders may appeal to class, language, religious, and ethnic divisions and make citizens more aware of these differences. The Labour and Conservative parties in Britain, for example, use class cues to attract supporters. Similarly, the Congress Party in India tries to develop a national program and appeal, but other parties emphasize the ethnic and religious divisions. Leaders of preindustrial nations often oppose competitive parties because they fear such divisiveness. Although this is sometimes a sincere concern, it is also self-serving to government leaders, and is increasingly difficult to justify against contemporary demands for multiparty systems.

Authoritarian governments often use a single party to inculcate common attitudes of national unity, support for the government, and ideological agreement. The combination of a single party and controlled mass media is potent: The media present a single point of view, and the party activities reinforce that perspective by directly involving the citizen. In a closed environment, single-party governments can be potent agents of socialization.

Mass Media

The mass media—newspapers, radio, television, and magazines—are important in socializing attitudes and values in nations around the globe. The mass media are typically the prime source of information on the politics of the day. There is virtually no place so remote that people lack the means to be informed about events elsewhere—in affluent nations, the public is wired to the Internet; satellite dishes sprout from houses in Iran; and inexpensive transistor radios are omnipresent even in Third World villages far removed from urban centers.

There is one thing that most people in the world share in common: we sit before our televisions to learn about the world. Television can have a powerful cognitive and emotional impact on large public audiences by enlisting the senses of both sight and sound. Watching events on television—such as the broadcasts of government affairs or the war in Iraq—gives a reality to the news. Seeing the world directly can shape political attitudes.

Today, the Internet provides another powerful source of news for those with access to it.[25] The Web provides unprecedented access to information on a global scale, especially in developing nations with limited traditions of a free press. One can hardly travel to any city in the world and not see Internet cafés or WiFi access. At the same time, the Internet empowers individuals to connect to others and to develop social and political networks. This may be why autocratic governments struggle to restrict unfettered access to the Internet (see Box 3.3).

Access to information thus becomes an important political commodity in the contemporary world. Western democracies put a premium on freedom of the media, even if they frequently complain about what the media reports. In many European nations, the government still manages television and radio stations because it views the media as a public service. Autocratic governments typically seek to control the media and what they can report, as well as the public's access to information. Similarly, the communist regimes of Eastern Europe tried to limit access to news reports from the West because they feared it would undermine their regimes, and the democracy movements were strengthened by the image of another way of life in the West. In the contemporary world of Internet and satellite broadcasting, it is becoming increasingly difficult for governments to control the spread of information.

Direct Contact with the Government

In modern societies, the wide scope of governmental activities brings citizens into frequent contact with various bureaucratic agencies. Surveys of Americans find that about a third have contacted a government official in the preceding year, and online interactions with government are increasing dramatically.[26] Citizens contact a wide range of government offices, from federal officials to state and local governments to

BOX 3.3

The Great Firewall of China

The People's Republic of China has the largest number of Internet users of any nation in the world, and this fact has government officials worried. Chinese "netizens" find themselves surfing in the shadow of the world's most sophisticated censorship machine. A large Internet police force monitors Web sites and e-mails. On a technical level, the gateways that connect China to the global Internet filter traffic coming into and going out of the country. Even the Internet cafés are now highly regulated and state-licensed, and all are equipped with standard surveillance systems. Google was one of the Western companies that initially provided keyword-blocking technology to prevent access to offending sites. Pornography was banned, but also searches for the word "democracy" or "Tiananmen Square." After struggling with censorship requirements, Google removed its search computers from China in early 2010 and relocated them to Hong Kong. But China continues to restrict Internet access through Chinese-based search engines.

school boards and the police. In addition, the government touches our lives in a myriad of other ways, from running the public schools to providing retirement checks to providing social services. The degree of government intervention in daily life, and hence the necessity for contact with government, varies greatly across nations as a function of the political system and the role of government in the society.

These personal experiences are powerful agents of socialization, strengthening or undercutting the images presented by other agents. Does the government send retirement checks on time? Do city officials respond to citizen complaints? Are the schools teaching children effectively? Do unemployment offices help people find jobs? Are the highways well-maintained? These are very direct sources of information on how well the government functions. No matter how positive the view of the political system that people have learned as children, citizens who face a different reality in everyday life are likely to change their early-learned views. Indeed, the contradictions between ideology and reality proved to be one of the weaknesses of the communist systems in Eastern Europe.

In summary, the country-specific chapters in this book all examine the patterns of political socialization for several reasons. The sources of political socialization often determine the content of what is learned about politics. If people learn about new events from their friends at church, they may hear different information than people who rely on the workplace or the television for information. The role of these different socialization agents and the content of their political messages also vary systematically across nations. In addition, the ability of a nation to recreate its political culture in successive generations is an important factor in perpetuating the political system. Finally, cultures change when new elements are added to the process of political learning. Thus, socialization provides the feedback mechanism that enables a political culture to endure or change.

TRENDS SHAPING CONTEMPORARY POLITICAL CULTURES

A political culture exists uniquely in its own time and place. Citizens' attitudes and beliefs are shaped by personal experiences and by the agents of political socialization. Yet in any historical period, there may be trends that change the culture in many nations. The major social trends of our time reflect both general societal developments and specific historic events.

For the past two decades, a major new development is the trend toward democracy in Eastern Europe, East Asia, and other parts of the developing world. This **democratization** trend reflects long-term responses to modernity as well as immediate reactions to current events. Modernization gradually eroded the legitimacy of nondemocratic ideologies, while the development of citizens' skills and political resources made their claim to equal participation in policymaking (at least indirectly) more plausible. Thus, many studies of political culture in Eastern Europe and the former Soviet Union uncovered surprising popular support for democratic norms and processes as the new democratic system formed.[27]

Ironically, as democracy has begun taking root in Eastern Europe, citizens in many Western democracies are increasingly skeptical about politicians and political institutions. In 1964, three-quarters of Americans said they trusted the government; in 2010, less than a fifth of the public say as much—and the malaise is spreading to Western Europe and Japan.[28] At the same time, public support for democratic norms and values has strengthened over time in most Western democracies. Thus, these publics are critical of politicians and political parties when they fall short of these democratic ideals. Although this cynicism is a strain on democratic politicians, it presses democracy to continue to improve and adapt, which is ultimately democracy's greatest strength.

Another recent major trend affecting political cultures is a shift toward **marketization**—that is, an increased public acceptance of free markets and private profit incentives, rather than a government-managed economy. One example of this movement appeared in many Western European nations and the United States beginning in the 1980s, where economies had experienced serious problems of inefficiency and economic stagnation. Margaret Thatcher in Britain and Ronald Reagan in the United States rode to power on waves of public support for reducing the scale of government. Public opinion surveys show that many people in these nations feel that government should not be responsible for individual well-being (see again Figure 3.3).

Just as Western Europeans began to question the government's role in the economy, the political changes in Eastern Europe and the Soviet Union reinforced this trend toward marketization. The command economies of Eastern Europe were almost exclusively controlled by state corporations and government agencies. The government set both wages and prices and directed the economy. The collapse of these systems raised new questions about public support for marketization. Surveys generally find that Eastern Europeans support a capitalist market system and the public policies that would support such an economic system.[29]

Globalization is another trend affecting political cultures of many nations. Increasing international trade and international interactions tend to diffuse the values of the overall international system. Thus, as developing nations become more engaged in the global economy and global international system, the development of certain norms—such as human rights, gender equality, and democratic values—increases.[30] People in developing nations also learn about the broader opportunities existing in other nations, which can spur cultural change as well as economic change. Thus, although globalization has been a deeply divisive political issue for the past decade in many nations, the Pew Global Values Survey found broad support for globalization among citizens worldwide—especially in developing nations where it is seen as improving living standards and life chances.[31]

Clearly, political culture is not a static phenomenon, so our understanding of political culture must be dynamic. It must encompass how the agents of political socialization communicate and interpret historic events and traditional values. It must juxtapose these factors with the exposure of citizens and leaders to new experiences and new ideas. But it is important to understand the political culture of a nation, because these cultural factors influence how citizens act, how the political process functions, and what policy goals the government pursues.

REVIEW QUESTIONS

- What are the three key elements of a political culture?

- Why does political culture matter?

- Why is the process of political socialization important?

- What are the main agents of political socialization? List the possible agents of socialization, and then compare their relative importance across two different nations included in this book.

- What are the major trends in cultural change in the contemporary world?

KEY TERMS

agents of political
   socialization
democratization
direct socialization

fundamentalism
globalization
indirect socialization
legitimacy

marketization
modernization
political culture

political socialization
political subcultures

SUGGESTED READINGS

Almond, Gabriel A., and Sidney Verba. *The Civic Culture*. Princeton, NJ: Princeton University Press, 1963.

———, eds. *The Civic Culture Revisited*. Boston: Little Brown, 1980.

Booth, John, and Mitchell A. Seligson, *The Legitimacy Puzzle in Latin America: Political Support and Democracy in Eight Nations*. New York: Cambridge University Press, 2009.

Bratton, Michael, Robert Mattes, and E. Gyimah-Boadi. *Public Opinion, Democracy, and Market Reform in Africa*. Cambridge: Cambridge University Press, 2004.

Dalton, Russell. *Democratic Challenges, Democratic Choices: The Erosion of Political Support in Advanced Industrial Democracies*. Oxford: Oxford University Press, 2004.

Gilley, Bruce. *The Right to Rule: How States Win and Lose Legitimacy*. New York: Columbia University Press, 2009.

Horowitz, Donald. *Ethnic Groups in Conflict*. Berkeley: University of California Press, 2000.

Huntington, Samuel. *The Clash of Civilizations and the Remaking of World Order*. New York: Simon & Schuster, 1996.

Inglehart, Ronald, and Pippa Norris. *Sacred and Secular: Religion and Politics Worldwide*. Cambridge: Cambridge University Press, 2004.

Inglehart, Ronald, and Christian Welzel. *Modernization, Cultural Change, and Democracy: The Human Development Sequence*. New York: Cambridge University Press, 2005.

Inkeles, Alex, and David H. Smith. *Becoming Modern*. Cambridge, MA: Harvard University Press, 1974.

Jennings, M. Kent. "Political Socialization," in *Oxford Handbook of Political Behavior*, ed. Russell Dalton and Hans-Dieter Klingemann. Oxford: Oxford University Press, 2007.

Jennings, M. Kent, and Richard Niemi. *Generations and Politics: A Panel Study of Young Adults and Their Parents*. Princeton, NJ: Princeton University Press, 1981.

Klingemann, Hans Dieter, Dieter Fuchs, and Jan Zielonka, eds. *Democracy and Political Culture in Eastern Europe*. London: Routledge, 2006.

Norris, Pippa, ed. *Critical Citizens: Global Support for Democratic Government*. Oxford: Oxford University Press, 1999.

Norris, Pippa, and Ronald Inglehart. *Rising Tide: Gender Equality and Cultural Change around the World*. New York: Cambridge University Press, 2003.

———. *Cosmopolitan Communications: Cultural Diversity in a Globalized World*. New York: Cambridge University Press, 2009.

Pharr, Susan, and Robert Putnam. *Disaffected Democracies: What's Troubling the Trilateral Democracies?* Princeton, NJ: Princeton University Press, 2000.

Putnam, Robert. *The Beliefs of Politicians*. New Haven, CT: Yale University Press, 1973.

———. *Making Democracy Work: Civic Traditions in Modern Italy*. Princeton, NJ: Princeton University Press, 1993.

Rose, Richard, Christian Haerpfer, and William Mishler. *Testing the Churchill Hypothesis: Democracy and Its Alternatives in Post-Communist Societies*. Cambridge, UK: Polity/Baltimore: Johns Hopkins University Press, 2000.

ENDNOTES

1. This concept of legitimacy and its bases in different societies draws on the work of Max Weber. See, for example, Max Weber, *Basic Concepts in Sociology*, trans. H. P. Secher (New York: Citadel Press, 1964), Chapters 5–7.

2. Bruce Gilley, *The Right to Rule: How States Win and Lose Legitimacy* (New York: Columbia University Press, 2009).

3. Lucian Pye and Sidney Verba, eds., *Political Culture and Political Development* (Princeton, NJ: Princeton University Press, 1965); Samuel Huntington, "Will More Countries Become Democratic?" *Political Science Quarterly* 99 (Summer 1984): 193–218.

4. Ronald Inglehart and Christian Welzel, *Modernization, Cultural Change, and Democracy: The Human Development Sequence* (New York: Cambridge University Press, 2005); Pippa Norris, ed., *Critical Citizens: Global Support for Democratic Government* (Oxford: Oxford University Press, 1999).

5. Inglehart and Welzel, *Modernization, Cultural Change, and Democracy*; Russell Dalton and Doh Chull Shin, eds., *Citizens, Democracy, and Markets around the Pacific Rim* (Oxford: Oxford University Press, 2006); Yun-han Chu, Larry Diamond, Andrew J. Nathan, and Doh Chull Shin, eds., *How East Asians View Democracy* (New York: Columbia University

Press, 2008); Michael Bratton, Robert Mattes, and E. Gyimah-Boadi. *Public Opinion, Democracy, and Market Reform in Africa* (Cambridge: Cambridge University Press, 2004).

6. For the list of nations in the World Values Survey, see the project Web site: www.worldvaluessurvey.org.

7. Amartya Sen, *Development as Freedom* (New York: Knopf, 1999).

8. In prior editions, we discussed the differences among parochial, subject, and participatory roles, and the concentration of parochials in less developed nations. Current research leads us to consider this categorization as too stark, as technological and communications changes have spread political information and interest on a broad global scale.

9. Inglehart and Welzel, *Modernization, Cultural Change, and Democracy*.

10. Ronald Inglehart, *Modernization and Postmodernization* (Princeton, NJ: Princeton University Press, 1997), Chapters 6–7.

11. Ole Borre and Elinor Scarbrough, eds., *The Scope of Government* (Oxford: Oxford University Press, 1995).

12. Ronald Inglehart, *Culture Shift in Advanced Industrial Societies* (Princeton, NJ: Princeton University Press, 1990).

13. Even within established Western democracies, there are internal differences in the appropriate role of government, the role of the citizen, and the perceived goals of government. See Max Kaase and Ken Newton, *Beliefs in Government* (Oxford: Oxford University Press, 1995).

14. W. Kymlicka and N. Wayne, eds., *Citizenship in Divided Societies* (Oxford: Oxford University Press, 2000); Donald Horowitz, *Ethnic Groups in Conflict* (Berkeley: University of California Press, 2000).

15. Amy Chua, *World on Fire: How Exporting Free Market Democracy Breeds Ethnic Hatred and Global Instability* (New York: Doubleday, 2003).

16. See also Inglehart and Welzel, *Modernization, Cultural Change, and Democracy*.

17. Kendall Baker, Russell Dalton, and Kai Hildebrandt, *Germany Transformed* (Cambridge, MA: Harvard University Press, 1981).

18. Robert Putnam, *Making Democracy Work: Civic Traditions in Modern Italy* (Princeton, NJ: Princeton University Press, 1993); Robert Putnam, *Bowling Alone: The Collapse and Revival of American Community* (New York: Simon & Schuster, 2000).

19. Samuel P. Huntington, *The Clash of Civilizations and the Remaking of World Order* (New York: Simon & Schuster, 1996); see also Fareed Zakaria, *The Future of Freedom: Illiberal Democracy at Home and Abroad* (New York: Norton, 2003).

20. See Gabriel A. Almond and Sidney Verba, *The Civic Culture* (Princeton, NJ: Princeton University Press, 1963), Chapter 12; M. Kent Jennings, Klaus R. Allerbeck, and Leopold Rosenmayr, "Generations and Families," in Samuel H. Barnes et al., *Political Action* (Beverly Hills, CA: Sage, 1979), Chapters 15–16.

21. Such fundamentalism is often a defensive reaction against the spread of scientific views of nature and human behavior, and the libertarian values and attitudes that accompany these views. The influence of fundamentalism has been most visible in Muslim countries, but also in Christian countries. Broadly speaking, fundamentalism seeks to raise conservative social, moral, and religious issues to the top of the contemporary policy agenda.

22. Pippa Norris and Ronald Inglehart, *Rising Tide: Gender Equality and Cultural Change around the World* (New York: Cambridge University Press, 2003).

23. Martha Nussbaum and Jonathan Glover, eds., *Women, Culture, and Development* (New York: Oxford University Press, 1995).

24. For example, see Sidney Verba, Norman H. Nie, and Jae-on Kim, *Participation and Political Equality* (New York: Cambridge University Press, 1978); Pippa Norris, *Democratic Phoenix: Reinventing Political Activism* (New York: Cambridge University Press, 2003).

25. Pippa Norris and Ronald Inglehart, *Cosmopolitan Communications: Cultural Diversity in a Globalized World* (New York: Cambridge University Press, 2009).

26. Aaron Smith et al., "The Internet and Civic Engagement," Pew Internet and American Life Project (September 2009) (www.pewinternet.org).

27. Richard Rose, Christian Haerpfer, and William Mishler, *Testing the Churchill Hypothesis: Democracy and Its Alternatives in Post-Communist Societies* (Cambridge, UK: Polity/Baltimore: Johns Hopkins University Press, 2000).

28. Norris, *Critical Citizens*; Russell Dalton, *Democratic Challenges, Democratic Choices: The Erosion of Political Support in Advanced Industrial Democracies* (Oxford: Oxford University Press, 2004).

29. See William Zimmerman, *The Russian People and Foreign Policy: Russian Elite and Mass Perspectives* (Princeton, NJ: Princeton University Press, 2002), Chapter 2; Raymond Duch, "Tolerating Economic Reform," *American Political Science Review* 87 (1993): 590–608. Russian support for marketization noticeably lags behind that of most Eastern Europeans.

30. Wayne Sandholtz and Mark Gray, "International Integration and National Corruption," *International Organization* 57 (Autumn 2003): 761–800; Mark Gray, Miki Kittilson, and Wayne Sandholtz, "Women and Globalization: A Study of 180 Countries, 1975–2000," *International Organization* 60 (Spring 2006): 293–333.

31. Pew Global Attitudes Project, *Views of a Changing World, June 2003* (Washington, D.C.: Pew Global Attitudes Project, 2003), 71–81 (http://pewglobal.org/reports/display.php?ReportID=185).

INTEREST ARTICULATION

Suppose an unjust or unfair law was being passed by the government—what could you do to express your dissatisfaction and try to stop the legislation? Or suppose you see a need that the government is not addressing—what could you do to encourage government action? These are the questions that often face us as citizens. What choices do we have for making our interests and needs known to policymakers?

People and social groups have some way to express their needs and demands to their government in almost every political system. This process, known as **interest articulation**, can take many forms. For example, a person might contact a city council member, or in a more traditional system, he or she might meet with the village head or tribal chieftain. Or, a group of people might work together on a common concern. In large, established political systems, formal interest groups are a primary means of promoting political interests.

As societies become internally more complex and the scope of government activity increases, the quantity and variety of ways to articulate public interests grow proportionately. People work together to address local and national needs, ranging from providing clean water in a village to passing national clean-water standards. Social movements involve the public in issues as diverse as protecting the rights of indigenous people in the Amazon to debating nuclear power. Formal, institutionalized interest groups develop to represent labor, farmers, businesses, and other social interests. Large numbers of interest groups work in capitals like London, Washington, D.C., and Tokyo. Today, Internet chatrooms and blogging provide another forum for expression. In countries with powerful local governments, interest groups are active at the provincial or local level as well.

This chapter considers the multiple ways in which people can express their interests in contemporary political systems. First, we discuss the means of interest articulation that are available to individuals. Then, we describe how formal interest groups and associations provide another means of interest articulation. For example, in most countries that allow them, labor unions, manufacturers' associations, farm groups, and associations of doctors, lawyers, engineers, and teachers represent these interests. In the end, most political systems have many different forms of interest articulation to determine what the public and social groups want from their government.

CITIZEN ACTION

One aspect of interest articulation involves what you might do as an individual citizen. People can make requests and demands for policies in various ways (Table 4.1).[1] Each of these forms of citizen action has different characteristics, as described in the table. The most common form of citizen participation is voting in an election. When elections are free and meaningful, they enable people to express their interests and to make a collective choice about the government's past progress and the future policies for the nation. Although elections select political elites, they often are a blunt policy tool because they involve many different issues; between elections, officeholders may stray from the voters' preferences.

People can also work with others in their community to address common needs, as when parents work to better the local schools or residents express their worries about how the community is developing.

TABLE 4.1

Articulating Interests
The forms of political participation vary in their scope and pressure on elites.

Form	Scope of Interests	Degree of Pressure on Elites
Voting, participation in elections	Broad, collective decision on government leaders and their programs	Modest pressure, but not policy-focused
Informal group	Collective action focused on a common interest	High pressure
Direct contact on personal matter	Normally deals with specific, personal problem	Low pressure
Direct contact on policy issue	Action on a government policy	Modest pressure
Protest activity	Highly expressive support for specific interests	High pressure
Political consumerism	Focused on specific issues, activities	High pressure

These activities are typically very policy-focused and exert direct pressure on decision-makers. Such group activity exists in both democratic and authoritarian systems, although nondemocracies may limit the methods of expression to those that do not openly confront authorities.

Some interest articulation involves direct contact with government, such as writing a letter to an elected official or to a government bureaucracy (see Box 4.1). Some direct contact involves personal issues, such as when a veteran writes to his legislator for help in getting benefits approved, or when a homeowner asks the council member to ensure her driveway is snow-plowed regularly. These forms of personal contact are common across political systems, including the authoritarian ones. Other direct contact involves broader political issues facing the government, such as campaigns to support or block new legislation. Direct contact on policy issues occurs primarily in democratic systems, where citizen input is broadly encouraged. However, even in autocratic nations, the public often finds ways to petition the government on policy matters.[2]

The expression of interests also may involve **protests** or other forms of contentious action. The spontaneous protest of outraged ghetto dwellers, the public protests that overthrew the communist governments of Eastern Europe, and the environmental actions of Greenpeace are all examples of how protest articulates policy interests. Protests and other direct actions tend to be high-pressure activities that can both mobilize the public and directly pressure elites; these activities can also be very focused in their policy content.

BOX 4.1

The *Shangfang* System

In 1949, the communist government in China created the *Shangfang* system, which allows individuals to petition the government formally to intervene on their behalf. This system was intended as a safety valve to allow disgruntled individuals to express their grievances, and as a method for the state to mobilize expression of support from the populace. The petitioners typically are concerned about personal problems or local issues, and this system allows them to bypass unresponsive local officials and petition Beijing. Sometimes, they even travel to the capital to present their petition in person. The use of *Shangfang* has ebbed and flowed over time, but it illustrates how even authoritarian governments seek input from their citizens. Experts estimate that the government in Beijing receives more than 10 million petitions, ranging from a complaint over an eviction notice to protests about the effects of the Three Gorges Dam. However, only a minuscule fraction of these petitions receive a government response, and sometimes local officials retaliate against the people who petittioned to a higher authority instead of coming to them.

Recent participation studies found that political consumerism—buying or boycotting a product for political reasons—is another active form of participation, at least in Western democracies.[3] Such participation allows individuals to protest the activities of a firm that pollutes or has unfair labor practices. For example, organized boycotts against child-labor practices have affected the sales and public images of many clothing manufacturers, and led to new public policies. Such efforts are very focused. If they become politically visible, they can have broader policy effects as well.

In summary, people can take many routes to express their interests, and each of these routes has particular characteristics associated with it.

HOW CITIZENS PARTICIPATE

The amount of citizen political participation varies widely according to the type of activity and the type of political system. Table 4.2 shows examples of the types of citizen participation in several of the nations examined in this book.

The most frequent forms of political participation revolve around elections: turning out to vote, trying to convince others how to vote, or working with political parties. Because elections are the most common form of public involvement in the political process, they are important forms of interest articulation. During elections, citizens speak their minds on current issues, attend meetings, contribute to campaigns, express their opinions to pollsters, and ultimately cast their ballots. At the same time, elections perform many other functions: aggregating political interests, recruiting political elites, and even socializing political values and preferences through the campaign process (see Chapter 2).

Among the democracies, the United States has rather low levels of national voting participation: both Western Europeans (with their long democratic experience) and several new democracies vote more frequently than Americans. However, as the table shows, Americans' low level of election turnout does not simply reflect apathy. Americans are relatively interested in politics and participate in other ways beyond elections.

Public efforts to express political interests and influence public policy extend beyond elections. Grassroots politics—people working together to address a common problem—is a very direct method for articulating political interests and attempting to influence policy. Alexis de Tocqueville considered such grassroots community action to be the foundation of democracy in America. Today, such activities are often identified with middle-class participation in affluent societies—such as parent–teacher association groups,

---

TABLE 4.2

How Are We Active?
People engage in a variety of political activities (percentage).

Type of Participation	United States	Britain	France	Germany	Japan	Russia	Mexico	Brazil	India	China	Iran
Voter turnout in most recent national elections	58	65	77	72	67	62	63	83	62	—	67
Interested in politics	59	44	38	62	64	39	34	49	44	65	46
Belong to environmental group	16	16	15	5	5	5	13	7	—	10	10
Signed a petition	70	68	67	50	60	8	21	56	29	6	—
Joined in a boycott	20	17	14	9	7	3	3	8	15	3	—
Participated in lawful protest demonstration	15	17	38	31	10	16	16	18	19	—	—

Sources: Election turnout data is percent of voting age public for most recent national legislative election from the International Institute for Elections and Democracy, downloaded from www.idea.org; 2005–2008 *World Values Survey* for other statistics. Some of the participation questions were not asked in each survey, and these missing items are noted by a dash in the table.

community associations, and public interest groups—but group activity occurs in almost any nation.[4] Indian villagers working together to build a communal latrine or to develop rural electricity and indigenous people protecting their land rights are other examples of community action. Table 4.2 presents membership in an environmental group as one example of public-interest group activity. About a sixth of the public in the United States, Britain, and France belong to an environmental group, but such citizen action is lower in less developed nations and new democracies.

Perhaps the most expressive and visible form of citizen action involves contentious actions, such as signing a petition, joining a boycott, or participating in protests. For instance, many environmentalists believe that direct actions—hanging an environmental banner from a polluting smokestack, staging a mass demonstration outside parliament, or boycotting polluters—effectively generate media attention and public interest in their cause. Political protests arise for quite different reasons. On the one hand, protest and direct action is often used by individuals and groups that feel they lack access to legitimate political channels. The mass demonstrations in Eastern Europe in the late 1980s and the public rallies and marches of black South Africans against apartheid illustrate protests as the last resort of the disadvantaged. On the other hand, peaceful protests are also increasingly used by the young and better-educated citizens in Western democracies. To many democratic citizens, protest is the continuation of "normal" politics by other means.

The majority of the public in most Western democracies say they have signed a petition, although such open disagreement with government policy is more limited in new democracies and autocratic states (see Table 4.2). In addition, about a sixth of Western publics say they have joined in a boycott or participated in a lawful protest. However, we again observe that protest activities are less frequent in developing societies, such as Mexico and Brazil. And the autocratic trends in Russia are suppressing popular dissent. Indeed, there is a general pattern for protest actually to increase with democratization, as governments become more tolerant of dissent and the rights of dissenters are protected.[5]

France is a nation where protests have become part of the tradition of politics. In the late 1960s, the French government nearly collapsed as a result of protests that began when university students stimulated a mass movement against the government. More recently, new policies to raise the retirement age to 62 generated massive protests in 2010, including "Project Escargot" in which truckers intentionally slowed traffic on the highways. In a typical year, Paris might experience protests by students, shopkeepers, farmers, homemakers, government employees, environmentalists, women's groups, and a host of other interest groups. Protest is almost a national political sport in France.

Citizen participation reflects the way that people use the opportunities existing within a political system. In nations with active political parties and competitive elections, many people participate in the electoral process. In nations where such activities are limited, people may turn to group-based activity or protest in order to express their preferences, but it is more likely that they are politically inactive. As we noted in Chapter 3, a participatory political culture is often a by-product of political modernization.

Cross-national research shows that better-educated and higher-social-status individuals are more likely to use the various opportunities for participation. These individuals tend to develop attitudes that encourage participation, such as feelings of efficacy and a sense of civic duty.[6] They also possess the personal resources and skills that are useful in becoming politically active when duty calls or a need arises. Skill and confidence are especially important for demanding activities, such as organizing new groups or becoming a leader in an organization. This inequality in participation is less for easier activities, such as voting. The tendency for the better-off to be politically active is more evident in societies (such as the United States) with weak party organizations, weak working-class groups (such as labor unions), and less party attention to lower-class interests. In nations with stronger working-class parties and labor unions, organizational networks encourage the participation of less affluent citizens.

Participation patterns are important for several reasons. For citizens to influence government policy, they first need to articulate their interests to the government. A wider choice of activities presumably increases the citizens' ability to express their interests and be heard. Moreover, the forms of action differ in their policy content and political pressure (see again Table 4.1). Finally, individuals differ in their level of political activities and the types of activities in which they participate. These differences in voice likely affect policy outputs if the government responds to public pressures. In other words, those who are more active in articulating their interests are more likely to have their interests addressed by policymakers.

INTEREST GROUPS

Interest articulation can also occur through the actions of groups that represent a set of people. In addition, interest groups can participate in the political process, serving on government advisory bodies and testifying at parliamentary hearings. Interest groups vary in structure, style, financing, and support base, and these differences may influence a nation's politics, its economics, and its social life. We begin by defining four types of interest groups: anomic, nonassociational, institutional, and associational.

Anomic Groups

Anomic groups are groups that suddenly form when many individuals react to an event that stimulates frustration, disappointment, or other strong emotions. They are flash affairs, rising and subsiding suddenly. Without previous organization or planning, frustrated people may suddenly take to the streets to vent their anger as news of a government action touches deep emotions or as a rumor of new injustice sweeps the community. Their actions may lead to violence, although not necessarily. Particularly where organized groups are absent or where they have failed to get adequate political representation, smoldering discontent may be sparked by an incident or by the emergence of a leader. It may then suddenly explode in relatively unpredictable and uncontrollable ways.

Some political systems, including both developed and developing nations, report a rather high frequency of violent and spontaneous anomic behavior.[7] Anger over the assassination of a popular political leader or another catastrophic event can also stimulate public outbursts. For instance, one commonly sees relatively spontaneous public demonstrations when one nation makes a hostile action toward another nation. Wildcat strikes (spontaneous strike actions by local workers, not organized actions by national unions), long a feature of the British trade union scene, also occur frequently in other European countries.

Sometimes, anomic groups are a subset of individuals drawn from a larger social grouping, such as a racial or ethnic group. For instance, in 1992, some residents in minority neighborhoods of Los Angeles rioted and looted following the acquittal of police officers accused of excessive violence in the beating of an African-American suspect. Similarly, in 2005 to 2006, protests broke out in many Muslim countries over the depiction of Mohammed in the Western press, producing deaths and mass violence. We treat these as anomic group actions because there is no structure or planning to the event, and the people involved disperse after the protest ends.

We must be cautious, however, about calling something an anomic political behavior when it really is the result of detailed planning by organized groups. For instance, the demonstrations against the World Trade Organization in Seattle in 1999 and Genoa in 2001 owed much to indignation but little to spontaneity (see Box 4.2).

Attacks on Globalization

BOX 4.2

In July 2001, tens of thousands of protestors arrived in Genoa to demonstrate at the G8 Summit Meeting. Hundreds of different groups came to protest at the meetings, and several of the more radical groups engaged in running battles with the police. Many of the most violent clashes involve the "Black Block." The Block is comprised of several loosely organized anarchist and radical groups, wearing trademark black clothing, black hoods, and gas masks. Confrontations with police often appeared choreographed in advance, coordinated by cell phones, and videotaped by sympathetic activists—and subsequently distributed on the Internet. Many other protest groups in Genoa were worried that the radical anarchist goals of the Block detracted attention from their policy concerns about the economic and social impacts of globalization. Similar violent protests occurred at the G8 summits in Germany in 2007 and Switzerland in 2009. The violence perpetrated by some groups overshadowed both the elected politicians at these summits and the policy goals of the nonviolent groups.

Nonassociational Groups

Like anomic groups, **nonassociational groups** rarely are well-organized, and their activity is episodic. They differ from anomic groups because they are based on common interests and identities of ethnicity, region, religion, occupation, or perhaps kinship. Because of these ties, nonassociational groups have more continuity than anomic groups. Subgroups within a large nonassociational group (such as an ethnic minority or workers) may act as an anomic group, as in the 1992 Los Angeles riots, the 2005 Paris immigrant riots, and the Middle East protests against the Danish cartoons of Mohammed in 2006. Throughout the world, ethnicity and religion, like occupation, are powerful identities that can stimulate collective activity.

Two kinds of nonassociational groups are especially interesting. One is a large group that is not formally organized, although its members may perceive common interests. Many ethnic, regional, and occupational groups fit into this category. The members share a common interest or need, but there is no formal group to represent their interests.

It can be very difficult to organize such groups because although members share a common problem, none of them will undertake the effort to organize other members because the individual costs outweigh the individual benefits. This is commonly known as the **collective action problem**.[8] If large collective benefits—for example, ending discriminatory legislation or cleaning up water pollution—are achieved, they are shared even by those who did not work, the so-called "free-riders." This pattern of people waiting for the rewards without sharing the cost or risk of action affects other types of groups as well. For instance, students who might benefit from lower tuition fees are typically underrepresented because they lack effective organizations to articulate their interests. Understanding the collective action problem helps us to see why some groups (including governments and revolutionary challengers) become organized and others do not, and under what circumstances the barriers to collective action are overcome.

A second type of nonassociational group is the small community economic group or ethnic subgroup whose members know each other personally. A small, face-to-face group has some important advantages and may be highly effective in some political situations. If its members are well-connected or its goals unpopular or illegal, the group may remain informal or even inconspicuous. Such groups may undertake various actions, such as engaging in work stoppages, circulating student petitions to demand better support and training, requesting that a bureaucrat continue a grain tariff to benefit landowners, or asking a tax collector for favored treatment to benefit relatives. As the last example suggests, personal interest articulation may often have more legitimacy and perpetuate itself by invoking group or personal ties.

Institutional Groups

Institutional groups are formal organizations that have other political or social functions in addition to interest articulation. Political parties, business corporations, legislatures, armies, bureaucracies, and churches often have separate political groups with special responsibility for representing a group's interests. Either as corporate bodies or as smaller groups within these bodies (legislative blocs, officer cliques, groups in the clergy, or ideological cliques in bureaucracies), institutional groups express the interests of their members. The influence of these interest groups is usually drawn from the strength of their primary organizational base—for instance, the size of their membership or their income. A group based on a governmental institution has direct access to policymakers.

In industrial democracies, bureaucratic and corporate interests use their resources and special information to affect policy. In the United States, for instance, the military industrial complex consists of the combination of the U.S. Department of Defense and defense industries that support military expenditures. Similarly, the farm lobby and the U.S. Department of Agriculture together often advocate agricultural policies. Political parties are among the most active institutional participants in the policy process of most democracies. In most societies, government bureaucracies do not simply react to pressures from the outside; they also can act as independent forces of interest representation.

Nonpolitical institutional groups can also participate in the political process. In Italy, for example, the Roman Catholic Church has exerted significant influence on the government. In electoral politics, the Church used to ask Catholics to vote against the communists. Less overtly, the Church has members of the clergy call on officeholders to express opinions on matters of concern to the Church. In Islamic countries, fundamentalist clergy pursue a similar role, prescribing what morals public policy should follow, actively lobbying governmental officials, and sometimes participating in the governing process.

In authoritarian regimes, which prohibit or at least control explicit political groups, institutional groups can still play a large role. Educational officials, party officials, jurists, factory managers, officers in the military services, and government bodies representing other social units had significant roles in interest articulation in communist regimes. In preindustrial societies, which usually have fewer associational groups and with limited popular support, military groups, corporations, party factions, and bureaucrats often play prominent political roles. Even where the military does not seize power directly, the possibility of such action often forces close government attention to military requests.

Associational Groups

Associational groups are formed explicitly to represent the interests of a particular group, such as trade unions, chambers of commerce, manufacturers' associations, and ethnic associations. These organizations have procedures for formulating interests and demands, and they usually employ a full-time professional staff. Associational groups are often very active in representing the interests of their members in the policy process. For instance, in recurring debates about health care in the United States, there is an enormous mobilization of pressure groups and lobbyists—from representatives of doctors and health-insurance organizations to consumer groups and the like—seeking to influence legislation.

Associational interest groups—where they are allowed to flourish—affect the development of other types of groups. Their organizational base gives them an advantage over nonassociational groups, and their tactics and goals are often recognized as legitimate in society. Labor unions, for example, are often central political actors because they represent the mass of the working class; in the same way, business associations often speak for the corporate interests of the nation.

A special subset of associational groups consists of citizens who are united not by a common economic or individual self-interest but by a common belief in a political ideology or a policy goal.[9] The environmental movement, many women's groups, human rights organizations, and other civic groups are examples of this kind of associational group. In some of these issue groups, the members may seldom interact directly and may not even share common social characteristics (such as employment or ethnicity), but are bound together by their support of a political organization, such as Greenpeace or Amnesty International. On the organizational side, many of these new social groups have fluid and dynamic organizations, with frequent turnover in both leadership and membership. On the

Jobs, Jobs, Jobs

Members of the International Labor Organization meet at a summit on the global jobs crisis.

© International Labour Organization

tactical side, they use a wide range of approaches, often discounting the value of partisan campaigning and conventional lobbying in favor of unconventional protests and direct actions.

Civic associations represent another way for citizens to articulate their policy goals by supporting groups that advocate their preferred policy positions. Such groups have proliferated in most advanced industrial democracies in the past generation, and they are now spreading to the developing world.

In summary, a social interest can manifest itself in many different groups. We can illustrate this point with examples of different groups that might involve members of the working class:

> *Anomic group:* a spontaneous group of working-class individuals living in the same neighborhood
>
> *Nonassociational group:* the working class as a collective
>
> *Institutional group:* the labor department within the government
>
> *Associational group:* a labor union

Distinguishing among the types of groups is important for several reasons. The nature of a group typically reflects the resources it can mobilize to support its political efforts. Perhaps one of the most important

resources is an institutional structure that will sustain political efforts until the government responds to the group's interests. The nature of a group also may signify the tactics it uses to gain political access. Finally, since the articulation of interest is the first step in policy influence, the nature of groups suggests which types of interests are more likely to get a hearing in the political system and which interests may be underrepresented.

CIVIL SOCIETY

Political analysts have devoted increasing attention to whether an extensive network of interest groups and public participation in these groups creates a **civil society**—a society in which people are involved in social and political interactions free of state control or regulation. Community groups, voluntary associations, and even religious groups—as well as access to free communication and information through the mass media and the Internet—are important parts of a civil society.[10] Participation in civil society groups can socialize individuals into the political skills and cooperative relations that are part of a well-functioning society. People learn how to organize, express their interests, and work with others to achieve common goals. They also learn that the political process itself is as important as the immediate results. Thus, a system of active associational groups can

Taking to the Streets

Pakistanis in Karachi, Pakistan, protest publication in Europe of offensive cartoons depicting Mohammed.

© Ilyas Dean/The Image Works

lessen the development of anomic or nonassociational activity. Group activity can help citizens to develop and clarify their own preferences, provide important information about political events, and articulate the interests of citizens more clearly and precisely than parties and elections.[11] Thus, an active public involved in various interest groups provides a fertile ground for the development of democratic politics.

As political and economic conditions become interdependent across nations, there is also increasing attention directed toward the development of a global civil society. Individuals and groups in one nation are connected to groups with similar concerns in other nations, and jointly reinforce their individual efforts. Environmental groups in the Western democracies, for example, assist environmental groups in developing nations with the expertise and organizational resources to address the issues facing their country. National groups meet at international conferences and policy forums, and the network of social relations, as well as Internet connections, extends across national borders.[12] This is another sign of how the international context of domestic politics is growing worldwide.

One problem facing the nations of Eastern Europe and other newly democratizing nations is building a rich associational group life in societies where the government had suppressed or controlled organized groups.[13] The Communist Party and the government bureaucracy dominated the nations of Eastern Europe for over forty years and prevented autonomous action. The process of building new, independent associational groups to articulate the interests of different citizens is under way and will be important to the democratic process. Similarly, many less economically developed nations need to create a civil society of associational groups to involve citizens in the political process and represent their interests if democratization is to succeed.

INTEREST-GROUP SYSTEMS

The relationship between interest groups and government policymaking institutions is another important feature of the political process. Different types of connections create different interest-group systems. All modern societies have large numbers of interest groups, but their relationships with government can follow different models. Interest-group systems are classified into three major groupings: pluralist, democratic corporatist, and controlled.[14]

Pluralist Interest-Group Systems

Pluralist interest-group systems have several features involving both how interests are organized and how they participate in the political process:

- Multiple groups may represent a single societal interest.
- Group membership is voluntary and limited.
- Groups often have a loose or decentralized organizational structure.
- There is a clear separation between interest groups and the government.

For instance, not only are there different groups for different social sectors (such as labor, business, and professional interests), but there may be many labor unions or business associations within each sector. These groups compete among themselves for membership and influence, and all simultaneously press their demands on the government. The United States is the best-known example of a strongly pluralist interest-group system; Canada and New Zealand are also cited as examples. Despite its greater labor-union membership (see Figure 4.1) and somewhat greater coordination of economic associations, Britain tends to fall on the pluralist side in most analyses, as do France and Japan.

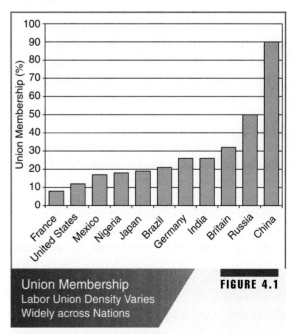

Union Membership
Labor Union Density Varies Widely across Nations

FIGURE 4.1

Source: International Labour Organization, UNION database (www.ilo.org); and International Labour Organization, *World Labour Report 1997–1998*, The Statistical Annex, Table 1.2 (www.ilo.org). The figure plots union membership as a percentage of wage and salary earners.

Democratic Neo-Corporatist Interest-Group Systems

Democratic **neo-corporatist interest-group systems** are characterized by a much more organized representation of interests:

- A single peak association normally represents each societal interest.
- Membership in the peak association is often compulsory and nearly universal.
- Peak associations are centrally organized and direct the actions of their members.
- Groups are often systematically involved in making and implementing policy.

For instance, in a neo-corporatist system, there may be a single peak association that represents all the major industrial interests; a pluralist system may have several different business groups that act autonomously. In addition, in a neo-corporatist system, peak associations are centrally organized, while groups in a pluralist system typically have decentralized organizational structures. The most thoroughly corporatist interest-group systems are in Austria, Finland, the Netherlands, Norway, and Sweden. These nations are characterized by a high level of union membership among the non-agricultural labor force, along with a highly centralized and united labor movement.

Equally important, interest groups such as labor unions in these systems often regularly and legitimately work with the government agencies and/or political parties as partners in negotiating solutions to policy problems. For instance, German labor unions have formal membership on many government commissions, have special access to policy administration, and are very influential through informal channels of influence. Thus, Germany is a close fit to the neo-corporatist model (see Chapter 10).

Mexico and Brazil are examples of another form of corporatist politics. Union membership is modest in both nations (see again Figure 4.1), although the trade unions and peasant associations are closely tied to political parties or religious interests. Usually, these groups mobilize support for the political parties or social institutions that dominate them, and they are closely tied to the state when their party is in power. This system is changing in both Mexico and Brazil, as democratization encourages the unions to become more politically independent and influential (see Chapters 14 and 15).

The best-studied democratic neo-corporatist arrangements involve economic problems. Democracies with business and labor peak associations that negotiate with each other and the government have had better records than more pluralist countries in sustaining employment, restraining inflation, and increasing social spending.[15] In addition, there is also evidence that neo-corporatist systems are more effective in implementing other public policies, such as environmental protection.[16]

In many advanced industrial societies, however, membership in labor unions has decreased and some bargaining patterns have become less centralized. Thus, some countries that have relied on neo-corporatist patterns have adapted this system to these new consequences and applied corporatism in new ways.[17] In contrast, several nations in Eastern Europe are attempting to develop more corporatist structures to nurture interest-group politics, but the system of autonomous interest groups remains underdeveloped. The experience with neo-corporatist models in developing nations is even more varied.[18] Nigeria and India illustrate a pattern common in other developing democracies. Interest groups, such as unions, are often not well-developed and have a limited mass membership. They are participants in the process, but without the mass membership or formal access that gives labor unions influence in established Western democracies of either the pluralist or corporatist model.

Controlled Interest-Group Systems

Finally, **controlled interest-group systems** follow a different pattern:

- There is a single group for each social sector.
- Membership is often compulsory.
- Each group is normally hierarchically organized.
- Groups are controlled by the government or its agents in order to mobilize support for government policy.

The last point is the most important: Groups exist to facilitate government control of society. The best examples are the traditional communist systems in which the party penetrates all levels of society and controls all the permitted associational groups. For instance, Figure 4.1 shows that 90 percent of wage earners in China belong to a union.[19] Unions and other interest associations are subordinated to the Communist Party, and they are only rarely permitted to articulate the interests of their members. Russia once followed this communist model, and the unions have large memberships as a result of this experience. Chapter 12 on Russia discusses how the unions are struggling to gain autonomy from the state and play an influential role in the postcommunist system. But they have made limited progress.

These nations limit interest articulation to leaders of institutional groups, who can use their positions in political institutions as a base for expressing their demands. Numerous institutional interest groups can also emerge in these societies, especially from parts of the party and bureaucracy, such as the military, as well as informal nonassociational groups.

ACCESS TO THE INFLUENTIAL

To be effective, interest groups must reach key policymakers through **channels of political access**. Otherwise, groups may express their members' interests yet fail to have an impact on policymakers. Political systems vary in the ways they respond to political interests. Interest groups vary in the tactics they use to gain access. Group tactics are partially shaped by the structure of policymaking, as well as by their own values and preferences.

There is a significant distinction between legitimate and constitutional channels of access (such as the mass media, parties, and legislatures) and illegitimate, coercive access channels. These two channels reflect the types of resources that groups can use to influence elites as well as the group's perceptions of which tactics will be most successful. Groups with substantial resources—money, members, or status—typically have an easier time working through legitimate constitutional channels. Groups with limited resources or legitimacy may feel they must act through coercive channels because they are not accepted by the political system. In democracies, groups tend toward legitimate channels because the system expects and allows group activity. In contrast, nondemocratic systems typically limit legitimate access, which might stimulate illegitimate or coercive activities.

Legitimate Access Channels

The legitimate channels of access can take many forms, and these often exist in both democratic and nondemocratic systems. For instance, personal connections are an important means of reaching political elites in all societies—the use of family, school, local, or other social ties. An excellent example is the information network among the British elite based on old school ties originating at Eton, Harrow, or other "public" schools, or at Oxford and Cambridge universities. Similarly, in Japan, many alumni of the University of Tokyo Law School hold top positions among the political and bureaucratic elites who interact because of these personal ties. Although personal connections are commonly used by nonassociational groups representing family or regional interests, they serve other groups as well. In modern nations, personal connections are usually cultivated with special care. In Washington, D.C., the business of advising interest groups and individuals on access to politicians is an increasingly lucrative profession (and increasingly a target of government regulation and potential corruption). These activities are often carried on by former officeholders, who use their personal governmental contacts for their lobbyist clients.

The **mass media**—television, radio, newspapers, and magazines—are another important access channel in democratic societies. The mass media and the Internet can mobilize support for interest-group efforts, leading to donations of time and money, and encouraging sympathizers to support the group. Many interest groups thus hire public-relations specialists, purchase direct advertising, and seek favorable attention in the media. Interest groups encourage media reports on their needs as well as coverage of their policy views. When a cause receives national media attention, the message to policymakers carries added weight if politicians know that millions of voters are interested in the issue. Moreover, groups believe that in an open society, "objective" news coverage has more credibility than sponsored messages.

The potential power of the media could be seen when the communist governments in Eastern Europe loosened control over the media in the late 1980s. This action gave a huge boost to democracy movements. For instance, when asked what caused the democratic revolution in Poland in the 1990s, Lech Walesa pointed to a television and said, "That did." Media reports on the failures in communist government policy and the contrasting lifestyles in the West undermined the legitimacy of the regimes. As democratic protests spread across Eastern Europe, stories of successful protests in other parts of the country, or in other countries, enhanced the confidence of demonstrators. Citizen protests encouraged by mass-media reports helped convince the ruling groups that their support had vanished.

Political parties are another important access point. Democratic political parties often rely on interest groups for financial and voter support, and act as representatives of these interests within government. In a nation like Germany, the various parts of the party organization, particularly parliamentary committees, are important channels for transmitting demands to the cabinet and the party in power. In some cases, other factors limit the role of parties as interest representatives. For instance, highly ideological parties, such as most communist parties, are more likely to control affiliated interest groups than to communicate the interest groups' demands. Decentralized party organizations, like those in the United States, may be less helpful than individual legislators in providing access.

Legislatures are a common target of interest-group activities (see Box 4.3). Standard lobbying tactics include making appearances before legislative committees and providing information to individual legislators. In the United States, political action committees raise campaign contributions for individual members of Congress and usually receive some political attention in exchange. In Britain and France, the strong party discipline in the legislature lessens the importance of individual members of Parliament (MPs) as access channels. In contrast, in the United States, the combination of loose party discipline and a decentralized legislative system makes the individual members of the Congress major targets of group efforts.

Government bureaucracies are another major access point in most political systems. Contacts with the bureaucratic agencies may be particularly important where the bureaucracy has policymaking authority or where interests are narrow and directly involve few citizens. A bureaucrat sympathetic to a group may try to respond to its demands by exercising administrative discretion without leaving bureaucratic channels. A government official may also give public consideration to an issue or frame an issue in a way that receives a sympathetic hearing by policymakers. The bureaucracy may be an especially important access point in nondemocratic systems because other legitimate channels of citizen access do not exist.

Government officials may consider protest demonstrations, strikes, and other forms of dramatic and direct pressure on government as legitimate or illegitimate tactics, depending on the political system. Protests may be either spontaneous actions of an anomic group or a planned use of unconventional channels by an organized group. In democratic societies, demonstrations often mobilize popular support—or electoral support—or media attention for the group's cause. On a regular basis, the Mall in Washington, D.C., or similar locations in

Lobbying Behind the Scenes

BOX 4.3

British beer companies use a variety of means to support their industry. For example, the industry contributed funds to Labour MPs who recently voted for longer opening hours for British pubs. They also provide travel support for MPs who are favorable to the industry. A group of MPs who support the industry formed the All-Party Parliamentary Beer Group (APBG). The group's announced goal is "to promote the wholesomeness and enjoyment of beer and the unique role of the pub in UK society." The parliamentary group campaigned to have beer taxes reduced, conducted hearings on whether the government overregulates British pubs, and supported the extension of pub hours. The group hosts a series of functions at Westminster, giving industry chiefs the opportunity to meet MPs and showcase their products. The parliamentary group also selects a "beer drinker of the year," who receives an award at their annual dinner. The parliamentary group receives direct financial support from breweries, and the secretary for the group is paid by the alcohol industry.

Visit the APBG Web site: www.publications.parliament.uk/pa/cm/cmallparty/register/memi184.htm.

other national capitals host groups protesting a wide variety of policy issues. In nondemocratic societies, such demonstrations are more hazardous and often represent more extreme dissatisfaction that cannot find voice through conventional channels of access.

Lawful demonstrations are another tactic of interest groups, especially those that do not have access or resources to influence policymakers through conventional channels. Protests are also a favored tactic of groups whose ideological commitments focus on challenging the established social and political order. Protests are increasingly used as a means of interest articulation by organized and accepted interests who feel that dramatic actions can heighten support for their cause. Protests can supplement other channels, especially in gaining the attention of the mass media in an age when television comes to every household. Thus, we find doctors in New Delhi, farmers in Japan, and "gray panthers" (the elderly) in Germany using a tactic that once was limited to the poor and minorities.[20]

Vote by Vote

Protesters hold a massive demonstration in front of Mexico's electoral court to demand a ballot-by-ballot recount of the disputed 2006 presidential election.

Eduardo Verdugo/AP Images

Coercive Access Channels and Tactics

Most scholars see the level of collective violence as closely associated with the character of a society and the circumstances in the nation. In his studies of civil strife, Ted Robert Gurr argued that feelings of relative deprivation motivate people to act aggressively.[21] These feelings can stimulate frustration, discontent, and anger—which may then lead to violence. People also may turn to violence if they believe it is justified and will lead to success. If they think that their government is illegitimate and that the cause of their discontent is justified, they will more readily turn to political violence. To this end, it is the responsibility of the government and its institutions to provide peaceful alternatives to violence as a means of change.

This general description of political violence should not overlook the differences among the types of violent political activities. A riot, for example, involves the spontaneous expression of collective anger and dissatisfaction by individuals. Though riots have long been dismissed as aberrant and irrational action by social riffraff, modern studies have shown that rioters vary greatly in their motivation, behavior, and social background.[22] Most riots seem to follow some fairly clear-cut patterns, such as confining destruction or violence to particular areas or targets. Relative deprivation appears to be a major cause of riots, but the release of the frustrations is not as aimless as is often supposed.

For instance, the 2005 riots in Paris were triggered by the accidental deaths of two teenagers, but most analysts see their deaths as only a proximate cause, a "spark" that ignited already volatile factors. Gangs of minority youth burned thousands of automobiles, damaged shops, and attacked police who attempted to quell the violence. The French president and then the Parliament declared a state of emergency in reaction to the violent protests, establishing a curfew and limiting civil liberties. Even though much of the mayhem seemed poorly related to effective political action, it was a cry for attention. Youth from immigrant families had high levels of unemployment and felt that social and economic discrimination was limiting their life chances. Even in a democracy, the government sometimes overlooks the needs of its own citizens and allows such frustrations to explode into violence.

While deprivation may help fuel the discontent, strikes and obstructions are typically carried out by well-organized associational or institutional groups.

For instance, a long series of violent protests against globalization involve highly organized activities among some of the more radical groups participating in the protests (see again Box 4.2).

Historically, labor unions used the general strike to pressure the government or employers on fundamental issues. The influence of strikes and obstructions has varied, however, depending on the legitimacy of the government and coercive pressure from other groups. A general strike after vote fraud in the 2004 Ukrainian elections produced a transition to a new democratic government, but student-inspired boycotts in Korea in the 1980s had only a modest impact on the government. Most spectacularly, the strikes, obstructions, and demonstrations in Eastern Europe in 1989 and 1990, like the earlier people's power movement in the Philippines, had massive success against regimes that had lost legitimacy.

Finally, radical groups sometimes use **political terror tactics**—including deliberate assassination, armed attacks on other groups or government officials, and mass bloodshed. The tragedies in Northern Ireland; the suicide bombings by Palestinians in Israel; and the attacks of jihadist terrorists in New York City, Madrid, London, Bali, and other cities demonstrate the use of such tactics. The use of terrorism typically reflects the desire of some group to change the rules of the political game or to destroy a political system, rather than to gain political access.

The use of political terror is more often likely to produce negative consequences rather than construct positive policy change. Massive deadly violence may destroy a democratic regime, leading to curtailment of civil rights or even military intervention when many people and leaders feel that any alternative is preferable to more violence. For example, democratically elected governments justified their suppression of democratic institutions in Peru in 1992 and India in 1975 (see Chapter 17) in response to the violent actions of terrorists. An authoritarian, repressive response often promises quick results against terrorists; however, small-group terrorism usually fails when confronted by united democratic leadership.[23] In a democratic society, violence often forfeits the sympathy that a group needs if its cause is to receive a responsive hearing. The current conflict between the West and jihadist terrorists has renewed the debate on how democratic governments should balance the need for security against the preservation of civil liberties.

Groups and Channels

In order to understand the formation of policies, we need to know which groups articulate interests, their policy preferences, and the channels of influence they use. Table 4.3 gives examples of legitimate and coercive interest articulation for different types of interest groups. Each case provides an example of the differences in legitimate access channels, such as informal meetings by Mexican business leaders lobbying their government to Greenpeace testifying before European Parliament committees. Similarly, coercive acts range from spontaneous outbursts by anomic groups to Hamas using terror tactics in Gaza. This framework also helps us to think about how a single interest group might pursue its goals through multiple channels,

---

TABLE 4.3

Examples of Interest Articulation
Interest groups can use either legitimate or coercive channels of action.

Types of Interest Groups	Channel of Action	
	Legitimate Channel	**Coercive Channel**
Anomic groups	Chinese workers stage impromptu strikes for better pay and working conditions	Iranians attack Danish embassy to protest cartoons depicting Mohammed
Nonassociational groups	Mexican business leaders discuss taxes with president	Minorities in France riot in 2005 over their social conditions
Institutional groups	U.S. Department of Agriculture advocates subsidies for honey production	Indonesian army supports democracy movement to overthrow Suharto regime
Associational groups	Greenpeace lobbies the European Parliament to ban genetically modified foods	Palestinian Hamas launches terror attacks on Israel

including protests, representation by institutional groups, and lobbying by associational groups. For instance, honeybee farmers in the United States have lobbied their representatives in Congress to maintain federal price supports, and they also use their allies in the U.S. Department of Agriculture to support their position (will honeybee protests be next?). This table presents examples from many nations in order to suggest the varied possibilities that exist in each nation.

INTEREST-GROUP DEVELOPMENT

One consequence of modernization is a widespread belief that the conditions of life can be altered through human action. Modernization normally involves education, urbanization, rapid growth in public communication, and improvement in the physical conditions of life. These changes are closely related to increases in political awareness, participation, and feelings of political competence. Such participant attitudes encourage more diverse and citizen-based interest articulation.

At the same time, modernization produces an increasing diversity of life conditions and a specialization of labor as people work in many types of jobs—a process that leads to the formation of large numbers of special interests. The interdependence of modern life, the exposure provided by mass communications, and a larger policy role of government further multiply political interests that are organized into different interest groups. Globalization processes have also increased the interactions between interest groups across nations, or between domestic groups and international actors.[24] Thus, the diversity of interest groups and their activities is another by-product of modernization.

Successful democratic development leads to the emergence of complex interest-group systems that express the needs of groups and individuals in the society. Yet this process is by no means automatic. The problems of organizing large groups for collective action are huge. Societies vary widely in the extent to which people engage in associational activity. The level of trust shared among members of a society is one factor influencing social group participation.[25] The resources and societal support available for collective action is another factor. However, modernization may weaken traditional structures in some societies and then fail to develop effective associational groups in their place because of restrictive social attitudes. A nation's ability to achieve either stability or democracy will be hindered as a result.

In other cases, authoritarian parties and bureaucracies may control associational groups and choke off the channels of political access. For nearly half a century, the communist governments of Eastern Europe suppressed autonomous interest groups. Eventually, the processes of economic modernization pressured these systems to allow more open organization and expression of political interests. In addition, social change expanded interest articulation activity and a need for associational groups to represent citizens' interests.

The development of organized interest groups should not, however, lead us to conclude that every group has equal standing. Using the American experience as an example, the articulation of interests is frequently biased toward the goals of the better-off, who are also often better organized.[26] It is frequently pointed out that the American Association of Retired Persons (AARP) is a highly effective group that is not counterbalanced by a "Young Taxpayers Group," and that the traditional labor-management competition leaves consumers underrepresented.

We might test the breadth of citizen representation by evaluating systems in terms of their inclusiveness: What proportion of the population is represented to what degree in national-level politics? South Africa under apartheid illustrates the extreme case where the majority was prevented outright from forming associational groups. In the Third World, competing interests in the capital rarely involve the interests of rural peasants; peasant organizations are sometimes brutally suppressed, while urban middle- and upper-class groups can petition authorities. It is no coincidence that the bias in group inclusion appears greatest where the gaps in income and education are widest. As noted above, pushed to the extreme, those excluded from the process may engage in anomic activity or resort to violence.[27] Even in less extreme cases, the presence of different levels of political awareness means that every interest-group system is somewhat biased. Democratization involves not only the provision of competitive elections but also the reduction of the bias in interest representation.

Another challenge faces the patterns of interest articulation and representation in advanced industrial democracies. There are claims that participation in associational groups is decreasing in the United States and perhaps in other established democracies.[28] For instance, memberships in labor unions and formal church engagement have steadily trended downward in most Western democracies over the past several decades. Some scholars argue that this trend represents a growing social isolation in developed nations, as people forsake social and political involvement for the comfort of a favorite chair and a favorite television program. However, other researchers argue that we are witnessing a change in how citizens organize and express their interests, such as through public-interest groups, Internet networks, and blogging.[29] Even in nations such as India and China, millions of people are now using the Internet to learn about politics and how they can articulate their interests.

What can be said for certain is that democratic politics rests on a participatory public that uses individual and group methods to express and represent its interests. Thus, developing an active social and political life is an important standard for measuring the political development of a nation.

REVIEW QUESTIONS

- How do the different forms of citizen action vary in their potential influence on policymakers?

- What are the main types of interest groups?

- How does a "civil society" differ from a noncivil society?

- What are the key differences among pluralist, neo-corporatist, and controlled interest-group systems?

- What are the consequences when an interest group works through legitimate channels of influence rather than coercive channels?

- If you studied interest articulation patterns in one of the nations in this book, could you build a table (like Table 4.3) showing examples of the types of groups and the channels they used?

KEY TERMS

anomic groups

associational groups

channels of political access

civil society

collective action problem

controlled interest-group systems

institutional groups

interest articulation

mass media

neo-corporatist interest-group systems

nonassociational groups

pluralist interest-group systems

political terror tactics

protests

SUGGESTED READINGS

Blais, Andre. *To Vote or Not to Vote: The Merits of Rational Choice Theory.* Pittsburgh, PA: University of Pittsburgh Press, 2000.

Dahl, Robert A. *Polyarchy: Participation and Opposition.* New Haven, CT: Yale University Press, 1971.

———. *Democracy and Its Critics.* New Haven, CT: Yale University Press, 1989.

Dalton, Russell J. *Citizen Politics: Public Opinion and Political Parties in Advanced Industrial Democracies,* 5th ed. Washington, D.C.: CQ Press, 2008.

Hirschman, Albert. *Exit, Voice, and Loyalty.* Cambridge, MA: Harvard University Press, 1970.

Howard, Marc Morjé. *The Weakness of Civil Society in Post-Communist Europe.* New York: Cambridge University Press, 2003.

Maloney, William, and Jan Van Deth. *Civil Society and Activism in Europe: Contextualizing Engagement and Political Orientations.* London: Routledge, 2010.

Norris, Pippa. *Democratic Phoenix: Reinventing Political Activism.* New York: Cambridge University Press, 2003.

Olson, Mancur. *The Logic of Collective Action.* Cambridge, MA: Harvard University Press, 1965.

Paxton, Pamela, and M. Hughes. *Women, Politics and Power: A Global Perspective.* London: Pine Forge Press, 2007.

Putnam, Robert. *Bowling Alone: The Collapse and Revival of American Community*. New York: Simon & Schuster, 2000.

Putnam, Robert D., ed. *Democracies in Flux: The Evolution of Social Capital in Contemporary Society*. Oxford: Oxford University Press, 2002.

Rootes, Christopher. *Environmental Movements: Local, National, and Global*. London: Frank Cass, 1999.

Shi, Tianjian. *Political Participation in Beijing*. Cambridge, MA: Harvard University Press, 1997.

Tarrow, Sidney. *The New Transnational Activism*. New York: Cambridge University Press, 2005.

Thomas, Clive. *Political Parties and Interest Groups: Shaping Democratic Governance*. Boulder, CO: Lynn Rienner, 2001.

Verba, Sidney, Norman H. Nie, and Jae-on Kim. *Participation and Political Equality*. Cambridge: Cambridge University Press, 1978.

Verba, Sidney, Kay Schlozman, and Henry Brady. *Voice and Equality*. Cambridge, MA: Harvard University Press, 1995.

Zurn, Michael, and Gregor Walter, eds. *Globalizing Interests: Pressure Groups and Denationalization*. Albany: State University of New York Press, 2005.

ENDNOTES

1. This framework draws on Sidney Verba, Norman N. Nie, and Jae-on Kim, *Participation and Political Equality* (New York: Cambridge University Press, 1978), Chapter 2.

2. See, for example, the range of activities of Beijing residents described in Tianjin Shi, *Political Participation in Beijing* (Cambridge, MA: Harvard University Press, 1997).

3. Michele Micheletti, Andreas Follesdal, and Dietlind Stolle, *Politics, Products, and Markets: Exploring Political Consumerism Past and Present* (Transaction Publishers, 2003).

4. Pippa Norris, *Democratic Phoenix: Reinventing Political Activism* (New York: Cambridge University Press, 2003); Verba, Nie, and Kim, *Participation and Political Equality*.

5. Russell Dalton, Alix van Sickle, and Steve Weldon, "The Individual-Institutional Nexus of Protest Behavior," *British Journal of Political Science* 40 (2010): 51–73.

6. See Verba, Nie, and Kim, *Participation and Political Equality*; Norris, *Democratic Phoenix*.

7. See the evidence in J. Craig Jenkins and Kurt Schock, "Political Process, International Dependence, and Mass Political Conflict: A Global Analysis of Protest and Rebellion, 1973–1978," *International Journal of Sociology* 33 (2004): 41–63.

8. Studies of these problems were stimulated by the now-classic work of Mancur Olson, *The Logic of Collective Action* (Cambridge, MA: Harvard University Press, 1965). See also Mark Lichbach, *The Rebel's Dilemma* (Ann Arbor: University of Michigan Press, 1994); Todd Sandler, ed., *Collective Action: Theory and Applications* (Ann Arbor: University of Michigan Press, 1992).

9. Christopher Rootes, ed., *Environmental Movements: Local, National, and Global* (London: Frank Cass, 1999); Amrita Basu, ed., *The Challenges of Local Feminism: Women's Movements in Global Perspective* (Boulder, CO: Westview, 1995).

10. Jean Cohen and A. Arato, *Civil Society and Political Theory* (Cambridge: Massachusetts Institute of Technology Press, 1992); M. Walzer, ed., *Toward a Global Civil Society* (Oxford: Berghahn Books, 1995).

11. See Table 4.1; John Pierce et al., *Citizens, Political Communication, and Interest Groups: Environmental Organizations in Canada and the United States* (Westport, CT: Praeger, 1992).

12. Sidney Tarrow, *The New Transnational Activism* (New York: Cambridge University Press, 2005); Margaret Keck and Kathryn Sikkink, *Activists beyond Borders: Advocacy Networks in International Politics* (Ithaca, NY: Cornell University Press, 1998).

13. Marc Morjé Howard, *The Weakness of Civil Society in Post-Communist Europe* (New York: Cambridge University Press, 2003); Russell Dalton, "Civil Society and Democracy," in *Citizens, Democracy, and Markets Around the Pacific Rim*, ed. Russell Dalton and Doh Chull Shin (Oxford: Oxford University Press, 2006).

14. Philippe Schmitter, "Interest Intermediation and Regime Governability," in *Organizing Interests in Western Europe*, ed. Suzanne Berger (New York: Cambridge University Press, 1981), Chapter 12; Arend Lijphart and Markus Crepaz, "Corporatism and Consensus Democracy in 18 Countries," *British Journal of Political Science* 21, no. 2 (April 1991): 235–46.

15. On the relative success of the corporatist systems in economic performance, see Miriam Golden, "The Dynamics of Trade Unionism and National Economic Performance," *American Political Science Review* 87, no. 2 (June 1993): 439–54; Arend Lijphart, Ronald Rogowski, and R. Kent Weaver, "Separation of Powers and Cleavage Management," in R. Kent Weaver and Bert A. Rockman, *Do Institutions Matter? Government Capabilities in the United States and Abroad* (Washington, D.C.: Brookings Institution, 1993), 302–44.

16. Lyle Scruggs, "Institutions and Environmental Performance in Seventeen Western Democracies," *British Journal of Political Science* 29 (1999): 1–31.

17. Oscar Molina and Martin Rhodes, "Corporatism: The Past, Present and Future of a Concept," *Annual Review of Political Science* 2 (2002): 305–31.

18. Howard Wiarda, ed. *Authoritarianism and Corporatism in Latin America—Revisited* (Gainesville: University Press of Florida, 2004); Julius E. Nyang'Oro and Timothy M. Shaw, *Corporatism in Africa: Comparative Analysis and Practice* (Boulder, CO: Westview Press, 1990).

19. We should also note that most Chinese work and live in rural areas and are not wage earners. The figure is based on the share of the labor force that receives a regular salary, which in China means urban workers. But India has a comparable labor structure, and many fewer Indian wage earners are unionized.

20. Norris, *Democratic Phoenix*.

21. T. Robert Gurr, *Why Men Rebel* (Princeton, NJ: Princeton University Press, 1970).

22. See Pippa Norris, Stefaan Walgrave, and Peter van Aelst, "Does Protest Signify Disaffection? Demonstrators in a Postindustrial Democracy," in *Political Disaffection in Contemporary Democracies*, ed. Mariano Torcal and Jose Ramón Montero (London: Routledge, 2006): 279–307.

23. On violence and democratic survival, see G. Bingham Powell, Jr., *Contemporary Democracies: Participation, Stability, and Violence* (Cambridge, MA: Harvard University Press, 1982), Chapter 8; see also the contributions to Juan J. Linz and Alfred Stepan, eds., *The Breakdown of Democratic Regimes* (Baltimore: Johns Hopkins University Press, 1978).

24. Michal Zurn and Gregor Walter, eds., *Globalizing Interests: Pressure Groups and Denationalization* (Albany: State University of New York Press, 2005); Keck and Sikkink, *Activists beyond Borders*.

25. Ronald Inglehart, *Culture Shift in Advanced Industrial Societies* (Princeton, NJ: Princeton University Press, 1990), 34–36.

26. Jeffrey M. Berry, *The Interest Group Society* (New York: Longman, 1997).

27. Many of these studies are reviewed by Mark I. Lichbach, "An Evaluation of 'Does Economic Inequality Breed Political Conflict' Studies," *World Politics* 41 (1989): 431–70. More recent references and analyses appear in T. Y. Wang et al., "Inequality and Political Violence Revisited," *American Political Science Review* 87, no. 4 (Dec. 1993): 979–93.

28. Robert Putnam, *Bowling Alone: The Collapse and Revival of American Community* (New York: Simon & Schuster, 2000); Robert Putnam, ed., *Democracies in Flux: The Evolution of Social Capital in Contemporary Society* (Oxford: Oxford University Press, 2002).

29. Cliff Zukin et al., *A New Engagement? Political Participation, Civic Life, and the Changing American Citizen* (New York: Oxford University Press, 2006); Russell Dalton, *The Good Citizen* (Washington, D.C.: CQ Press, 2007), Chapter 4.

INTEREST AGGREGATION AND POLITICAL PARTIES

Many voters want their governments to make decisions on the basis of a coherent policy program. For political decisions to be made this way, interests must not only be articulated, but also packaged into alternative visions or programs. **Interest aggregation** is the process by which political demands are combined into policy programs. For example, when politicians make economic policy, they often have to balance farmers' desires for higher crop prices, consumers' preferences for lower prices and taxes, and environmentalists' concerns about water pollution and pesticides. Who prevails in such balancing acts depends in part on political institutions, which is the subject of Chapter 6. But interest aggregation depends also on political skills and resources, such as votes, campaign funds, political offices, media access, or even armed force.

How interests are aggregated is a key feature of politics. The aggregation process determines which interests are heard and who is allowed to participate. Interest aggregation can help create a balanced government program out of competing policy goals, but it can also generate a bundle of compromises that satisfy no one. How stable and effective governments are depends on their success in interest aggregation.

Interest aggregation can occur in many ways. An elected leader or military dictator may have a considerable personal impact. Yet large states usually develop more specialized organizations for aggregating interests. Political parties are just such organizations, and they aggregate interests in democratic, as well as in many nondemocratic, systems. Each party (or its candidates) stands for a set of policies and tries to build a coalition of support for this program. In democracies, two or more parties compete to gain support for their alternative policy programs. In autocracies, the ruling party or institution may try to mobilize citizens' support for its

policies, but the process is frequently covert, controlled, and top-down rather than bottom-up. In other words, autocratic (authoritarian) parties mobilize interests to support the government rather than responding to demands by ordinary citizens or social interests.

It is important to remember that political parties may perform many different functions other than interest aggregation and that interests may be aggregated by many different structures. For instance, parties frequently shape the political culture as they strive to build support for their programs and candidates. Parties recruit voters and select candidates for office. They articulate interests of their own and transmit the demands of others. Governing parties are also involved in making public policy and overseeing its implementation and adjudication. Yet parties are particularly important structures of interest aggregation because of their distinctive role in mobilizing support for their policies and candidates. In this chapter, we compare the role of parties in interest aggregation to those of other structures.

PERSONAL INTEREST AGGREGATION

One way to bring political interests together in policy-making is through personal connections. Virtually all societies feature **patron–client networks**—structures in which a central officeholder, authority figure, or group provides benefits (patronage) to supporters in exchange for their loyalty. It was the defining principle of feudalism. The king and his lords, the lord and his knights, the knight and his serfs and tenants—all were bound by ties of personal dependence and loyalty. The American political machines of Boss Tweed of New York or Richard Daley, Sr., of Chicago were similarly bound together by patronage and loyalty. Personal networks are not confined to relationships cemented by patronage only. The president of the United States, for instance, usually has a circle of personal confidants, a "brain trust" or "kitchen cabinet," bound to their chief by ideological and policy propensities as well as by ties of friendship.

The patron–client network is so common in politics that it resembles the cell in biology or the atom in physics—the primitive structure out of which larger and more complicated political structures are composed. Students of politics in all countries report such networks. When interest aggregation is performed mainly within patron–client networks, it is difficult to mobilize political resources behind unified policies of rapid social change. This is because political decisions depend on ever-shifting agreements among many factional leaders (patrons) who all want to benefit. Patron–client politics thus typically means a static political system with little policy innovation.

Contemporary research on patron–client relationships was pioneered in studies of Asian politics, where this structure runs through the political processes of countries such as the Philippines, Japan, and India.[1] But parallels exist in Europe, the Middle East, Latin America, and most regions of the world. Patron–client relationships affect recruitment to political office, interest aggregation, policymaking, and policy implementation. Yet as Table 5.1 shows, patron–client networks are a particularly important means of aggregating political interests in poorer countries.

INSTITUTIONAL INTEREST AGGREGATION

In developing societies, as citizens become aware of larger collective interests and have the resources and skills to work for them, personal networks tend to be regulated, limited, and incorporated within broader organizations. Interest groups with powerful resources can easily cross the subtle line between interest articulation and aggregation. Associational groups (see Chapter 4) often support political contenders such as political parties. But they can occasionally wield sufficient resources to become contenders in their own right. For instance, the political power of the labor unions within the British Labour Party historically rested on their ability to develop coherent policy positions and mobilize their members (who were typically also party members) to support those positions. As we discussed in Chapter 4, corporatist interest-group systems empower both labor and business groups to become actively engaged in making economic policies. These arrangements include continuous political bargaining among organized labor, business interests, political parties, and government representatives. Such corporatist systems interconnect organizations that in other political systems play very different, often antagonistic, roles. Table 5.1 illustrates how associational groups tend to play a larger role in democracies that accept interest groups actively attempting to influence

Elections and Protest

Elections can stir strong feelings of joy or disappointment. Here, French protesters demonstrate against the election of President Nicolas Sarkozy in May 2007. The placard reads: "No to capitalism with a human face."

Jean Philippe Ksiazek/ AFP/Getty Images

	TABLE 5.1

Structures Performing Interest Aggregation in Selected Contemporary Nations

Parties are not alone.*

	Extensiveness of Interest Aggregation by Actor				
Country	**Patron–Client Networks**	**Associational Groups**	**Competitive Parties**	**Authoritarian Parties**	**Military Forces**
Brazil	Moderate	Moderate	Moderate	—	Moderate
Britain	Low	High	High	—	Low
China	Moderate	Low	—	High	High
France	Low	Moderate	High	—	Low
Germany	Low	High	High	—	Low
India	High	Moderate	Moderate	—	Low
Iran	High	Moderate	Low	—	Moderate
Japan	Moderate	High	High	—	Low
Mexico	Moderate	Moderate	Moderate	—	Low
Nigeria	High	Low	Moderate	—	Moderate
Russia	Moderate	Low	Moderate	—	Moderate
United States	Low	Moderate	High	—	Low

*Extensiveness of interest aggregation rated as low, moderate, or high. Rating refers to broad-level performance issue areas at different times. Blank (—) implies that such actors do not exist.

government policy, which is often where these groups have close ties with particular political parties.

Institutional groups, such as bureaucratic agencies and military factions, can also be important interest aggregators. Indeed, the bureaucracy performs this function in most societies. Although established primarily to implement public policy, the bureaucracy may negotiate with interest groups to identify their preferences or to mobilize their support. Government agencies may even be "captured" by interest groups and used to press their demands. Bureaucrats often cultivate client-support networks to expand their organizations or to enhance their power. Military organizations, with their special control of physical force, can also be powerful interest aggregators. We shall have more to say about their role later in this chapter.

COMPETITIVE PARTY SYSTEMS AND INTEREST AGGREGATION

In many contemporary political systems, parties are the primary structures of interest aggregation. Political parties are *groups or organizations that seek to place candidates in office under their label*. In any given society, there may be one party, two parties, or as many as ten or twenty. We refer to the number of parties, and the relationships among them, as properties of the **party system**. A major distinction runs between **competitive party systems**, in which parties primarily try to build electoral support, and noncompetitive or **authoritarian party systems**, in which parties seek to direct society. This distinction does not depend on the closeness of electoral victory, or on the number of parties. It depends instead on the ability of political parties to form freely and compete for citizen support, and on whether this competition for citizen support is the key to government control. Thus, a party system can be competitive even if one party wins an election resoundingly or even dominates several consecutive elections, as long as other parties are free to challenge its dominance at the polls.

The role of competitive parties in interest aggregation depends not only on the individual party but also on the structure of parties, electorates, electoral laws, and policymaking institutions. Typically, interest aggregation in a competitive party system occurs at several stages: within the individual parties, as the party chooses candidates and adopts policy proposals; through electoral competition; and after the election

BOX 5.1

Personalistic Parties

Political parties are typically formal organizations with officers, members, statutes, and official policy programs. Sometimes, however, parties can be much looser *personalistic* movements built around one political leader, or a small group of leaders. Personalistic parties are particularly common in new democracies. In Russia, for example, President Vladimir Putin (2000–2008) was able to form a party (United Russia) with a strong personal following. Even India and France have highly personalistic parties. In India, the Congress Party has been dominated by the families of its most important founders, Gandhi and Nehru. In France, most presidents have come out of the Gaullist movement, which has had many names but was dominated from the start by President Charles de Gaulle and later by some of his followers. Personalistic parties commonly do not have a very clear policy program. They are often susceptible to clientelistic politics and sometimes become vehicles for purely personal ambitions and rent-seeking.

Shmuel Flatto-Sharon offers an extreme example. Flatto-Sharon was a Polish-born businessman of Jewish background living in France. In 1977, he fled to Israel because the French authorities wanted to prosecute him for embezzling $60 million. To get immunity from prosecution and avoid extradition, he ran for election to the Knesset (the Israeli national assembly). He formed a party, which he ran as a one-man operation—it had no other candidates or officers. Flatto-Sharon refused to identify himself as left, right, or center. He appealed for Jewish solidarity, arguing that Israel should not allow him to be extradited. He also promised a free television set to all Israeli households (this was before television sets became inexpensive and commonplace) and subsidized apartments for young couples. And he promised to pay people who voted for him as "campaign workers." Remarkably, Flatto-Sharon won two parliamentary seats, even though as his party's only candidate he could not fill the second seat. In 1981, however, he lost his bid for reelection. He was later convicted of bribery for his vote-buying scheme and sent to jail in Israel, but never extradited to France.

Some personalistic parties seem to have no other purpose than to make fun of politics and politicians. In Denmark, comedian Jacob Haugaard several times ran for office as a candidate for the Association of Deliberate Work Avoiders. In 1994, he won election to the Danish Parliament. His election platform included demands for disability pensions for people who lack a sense of humor, tailwinds on all Danish bike paths, more generous Christmas presents, more renaissance furniture at IKEA, and more whales in Danish waters. Haugaard also promised his voters free beer, and he used the public funds his party received from the Danish government to fulfill this campaign commitment (he bought beer and hot dogs for his supporters after the election).

through bargaining and coalition-building with other parties in the legislature or executive.

Political parties have been around as long as there have been elections and representative assemblies, but modern democratic parties began developing in Europe and the Americas from about the mid-nineteenth century. They have since emerged in all societies that have adopted free and fair elections and democratic government. Parties differ in their purposes and organization. Some have elaborate policy platforms, whereas others are little more than vehicles for ambitious politicians to get elected (or even to enrich themselves). Some parties are highly structured mass organizations, whereas others are loose, *personalistic* groups dominated by their leaders (see Box 5.1).

The first parties were typically *internally created*; their founders were politicians who already held seats in the national assembly or other political offices. These parties were often committed to broad constitutional principles (such as republican government, universal suffrage, or separation of church and state), but otherwise they often had only loose policy programs and little organization outside the legislature. They often had colorful names that said little about their policies, such as Whigs and Tories in Britain, Whites ("Blancos") and Reds ("Colorados") in several Latin American countries, Hats and Caps in Sweden, or for that matter, Democrats and Republicans in the United States.

During the late nineteenth and early twentieth centuries, other types of parties emerged as the democratic countries industrialized and urbanized, and as an increasing number of adults gained the right to vote. The growth of the industrial working class led to the formation of socialist, social democratic, communist, and other workers' parties. Farming interests gained representation through agrarian parties, and other parties emerged to represent religious communities (such as Catholics or Hindus) or ethnic or linguistic minorities. In countries that were not independent, parties of national independence often became a dominant force. All of these parties were typically *externally created*—they organized outside parliament before they became a force inside that institution. They often had much stronger mass-membership organizations than their older competitors, and they often had (and continue to have) closer ties to specific interest groups. Thus, social democrats and communists tend to have strong ties to labor unions, agrarian parties to farmers' organizations, and many Christian Democratic parties (at least Catholic ones) to the Vatican and religious organizations.

Most of these parties still exist and continue to play a leading role. They have settled into stable *party families* of Social Democrats, Conservatives, Christian Democrats, Liberals, Nationalists, and others, which often maintain close contacts across national boundaries. The party systems of most established democracies show a great deal of stability, and many of the most important parties today were also the dominant parties a hundred years ago. Yet two important new types of parties have emerged in the past several decades, particularly in advanced industrial countries. "New left" or "Green" parties emerged in many countries in the 1960s and 1970s to champion international peace and disarmament, environmental protection, gender equality, and minority rights. They are often more supportive of alternative lifestyles than traditional working-class parties of the left (such as Social Democrats). The other important type of new party is the "populist right" party, such as the National Front in France. These parties tend to be critical of existing parties and political leaders, whom they see as elitist, corrupt, or out of touch. They are concerned with internal and external security and favor strict law-and-order policies, but criticize what they see as "politically correct" government interventionism in other policy areas. They dislike the distortions that welfare states sometimes create, such as policies that make it unattractive to work and easy to live off welfare benefits

(see Chapter 7). And they typically champion national sovereignty and citizenship rights and oppose large-scale immigration and international integration.

The party systems of most democratic countries reflect a mix of these various party families. But no two party systems are exactly alike, and not all party families are represented in all countries. The variations in party systems reflect differences in demographics, economic development, and political histories. They also depend on differences in electoral systems, as we shall discuss below.

Elections

In democracies, political parties live and die by their performance in elections. The act of voting, and thereby giving support to a political candidate, party, or policy proposal, is one of the simplest and most frequently performed political acts. Through voting, citizens can make a collective decision about their future leaders and public policies. Elections are one of the few devices through which diverse interests can be expressed equally and comprehensively.[2]

The simple act of voting can have profound implications for interest aggregation. Electoral outcomes directly or indirectly determine who manages the affairs of government and makes public policy. And parties generally fulfill their electoral promises when they gain control of government.[3] When leftist governments come to power in advanced industrial democracies, they tend to expand the size and ambitions of the government; conservative parties generally slow the growth of government programs and promote private enterprise. Parties that want radical change or have not recently been in office often find it difficult to implement their programs when they eventually come to power. When, for example, the German Greens came to power in 1998 as part of a coalition government, they had to modify their promise to shut down Germany's nuclear power plants immediately. Instead, they negotiated a phase-out over many years. And they had to accept German military involvement in the civil conflict in Kosovo, even though their program was critical of such military interventions. But by and large, parties try hard to implement their programs, and citizens can therefore influence interest aggregation and policy-making through their role in elections.

When they aggregate interests and make policy, party leaders are often caught between the demands of

BOX 5.2

The Iron Law of Oligarchy

Can political parties be the main vehicles of democratic representation if they do not govern themselves democratically? This has been a main concern among students of modern political parties. In 1911, young German sociologist Robert Michels published a study of the German Socialist Party in which he formulated the **"iron law of oligarchy,"** which states that all organizations tend toward oligarchy (rule by the few) rather than democracy. "Who says organization says oligarchy," Michels famously observed. He identified several forces that push organizations such as political parties toward oligarchy. One is the need for specialization and differentiation that exists in all large, modern organizations. A second cause of oligarchy lies in

the facts that most ordinary members do not have the time or resources to hold their leaders accountable and that they often crave strong leadership. A third reason is that parties foster leaders who live "off" politics rather than "for" politics. They exploit their leadership positions to advance their own ambitions for wealth or power, often to the detriment of their followers. (In contemporary terms, we would refer to such self-interested pursuit of power as *rent-seeking*.) Michels's study was particularly troubling because he found these tendencies even in a party, the German Socialist Party, with which he sympathized and that was considered particularly strongly committed to democratic ideals.

Source: Robert Michels, *Political Parties* (New York: Free Press, 1962).

their party activists and the voters. Party activists often want policies that are more radical than those that most voters prefer. And activists typically insist more vigorously that the party program should be implemented, whereas ordinary voters are often happier when governments compromise and listen to opinions outside their own parties. There is a broad and ongoing debate about the extent to which democracy requires political parties to be internally democratic (see Box 5.2). Advocates of participatory democracy strongly support this idea, as do parties such as the European Greens. On the other hand, the famous Austrian economist Joseph A. Schumpeter argued that vigorous competition *between* parties is what matters for a healthy democracy and that democracy *within* parties is irrelevant or even harmful.[4]

Elections often have other functions as well (see also Chapter 4). Autocrats often manipulate elections to legitimize their governments. Until 1990, voters in the Soviet Union were given only one candidate to vote for, and this person was always the nominee of the Communist Party. Voter participation was very high because the government pressured people to participate and express their symbolic support for the regime, not because the elections actually decided anything. Elections played a role in socializing and shaping citizens' attitudes, but had little to do with interest articulation or aggregation.[5]

In most democracies, citizens can freely choose whether to vote. Yet some countries require citizens to vote and impose penalties on those who do not. Voting choices reflect a mix of motivations.[6] Many citizens try to judge the parties' policy promises. For others, elections are a simple referendum on government performance. They vote to throw the rascals out if times are bad, and to reelect them if times are good. In other cases, elections can be dominated by the charisma of a strong leader or the incompetence of a weak one. In each case, however, elections aggregate these diverse concerns into a collective decision on the composition of the government.

Electoral Systems

The rules by which elections are conducted are among the most important structures that affect political parties. We refer to these rules as the **electoral system**. These rules determine who can vote, how to vote, and how votes are counted. The rules that determine how votes are converted into seats are especially important. The United States, Britain, and many countries influenced by Britain (such as India and Canada) are divided into a large number of election districts. In each district, the candidate who gains more votes than any other—a *plurality*—wins the election. This simple, **single-member district plurality (SMDP) election**

rule is often called "first past the post," a horse-racing term, because the winner need only finish ahead of any of the others but need not win a majority of the votes. This system seems obvious and natural to Americans, but it is rarely used in continental Europe or in Latin America. Another version of single-member district elections is the **majority runoff** (or **double-ballot**) system used in France and in presidential elections in Russia. Under this system, voting happens in two stages, normally separated by a couple of weeks. In the first round, it takes a majority of all votes (50 percent + one vote) to win. To win, then, a candidate has to earn not just more votes than any other candidate, but more votes than all other candidates combined. If there is no majority winner in the first round, only a smaller number of candidates (in French and Russian presidential elections, the top two) make it into the second round, in which whoever gets the largest number of votes (a plurality) is elected.

In contrast to the single-member district system, most democracies in Europe and Latin America use some form of **proportional representation (PR)** in multimember districts. In these systems, the country is divided into a few large districts, which may elect as many as twenty or more members. These districts are often the states or provinces that make up the country. In the Netherlands and Israel, the entire country is a single electoral district that elects more than a hundred representatives. The parties offer lists of candidates for the slots in each district. The number of representatives that a party wins depends on the overall proportion of the votes it receives, though no system is perfectly proportional. A party receiving 10 percent of the vote would be awarded approximately 10 percent of the legislative seats. Sometimes, parties must achieve a minimum threshold of votes, usually 3 to 5 percent nationally, to receive any seats at all. If so many parties compete that many of them fall below this threshold, many voters may be left unrepresented, as happened in Russia in 1995.

In order to compete effectively, parties must formulate appealing policy programs and nominate attractive candidates for office. They must anticipate the offerings of their competitors and the preferences of the voters. The procedures that parties use to develop policy positions vary greatly from country to country and from party to party. In the United States, the national party conventions held before each presidential election formalize the party's policy positions, both by adopting a party platform and by selecting a slate of candidates. In other countries, parties have more regular congresses, and centralized party organizations issue party programs (also known as *platforms* or *manifestos*).[7] Whatever the system, a successful program must both spell out policy positions that are popular with the voters and aggregate interests within the party.

Parties must also offer candidates for office. In the United States, voters directly select these candidates through **primary elections**. But primaries are an unusually open form of candidate selection. In most other countries with **single-member district (SMD)** elections, party officials select the candidates, either locally or nationally. In proportional representation elections, the party draws up a list of candidates for each district. In **closed-list PR systems**, the elected representatives are then simply drawn from the top of this list, in declining order, and ordinary voters have no say about their candidates. In **open-list systems**, in contrast, voters can give preference votes to individual candidates, and these votes determine which candidates will represent the party in that district. Besides adopting programs and selecting candidates, parties also attempt to publicize them and mobilize electoral support through rallies, media advertising, door-to-door campaigning, and other activities.

Patterns of Electoral Competition

In democratic party systems, the electoral system is a major determinant of the patterns of electoral competition. Two famous political science theories help us understand this connection: Duverger's Law and Downs's median voter result. **Duverger's Law**, which is named after the French political scientist Maurice Duverger, is one of the best-known theories in political science.[8] It states that there is a systematic relationship between electoral systems and party systems, so that plurality single-member district election systems tend to create **two-party systems** in the legislature, while proportional representation electoral systems generate multiparty systems. Duverger identified two mechanisms behind this regularity. He called them the *mechanical effect* and the *psychological effect*. The **mechanical effect** is to be found in the way that different electoral systems convert votes into seats. In single-member district systems, parties get no representation unless they finish first in at least one district.

Therefore, smaller parties that run second, third, or fourth across many districts receive little or no representation. In the 2010 election in Britain, for example, the Liberal Democratic Party (Britain's third-largest party) received 23 percent of the votes, but only 9 percent of the seats in the House of Commons. The **psychological effect** lies in the fact that both voters and candidates anticipate the mechanical effect. Therefore, voters do not throw their support behind "hopeless" parties and candidates. Instead, they may support their second-best (or even third-best) option in order to keep a party that they strongly dislike from winning. And knowing that the voters will not support them, minor party candidates are reluctant to run. Giving your support to a party or candidate that is not your first choice in order to avoid an even worse outcome is known as **strategic voting**. Duverger argued that strategic voting tends to work to the advantage of parties that are already large and to the disadvantage of small ones. In U.S. elections, it has been fairly common for third-party candidates to run well in the polls until close to the election date, when voters realize that these candidates are not going to win. Their support then often declines rapidly.

Anthony Downs examined the effects of the number of parties on their policy positions. He showed that in two-party systems in which the parties are competing along a left–right (or other) policy dimension and are interested only in winning elections, and where all voters choose the party closest to their policy preferences, the parties will moderate their policies so as to try to win the support of the median voter (the voter who is at the midpoint of the policy spectrum, with as many other voters to the right as to the left). Downs's contribution is known as the **median voter result**. According to this theory, two-party systems will exhibit a centrist pull or "convergence." In systems with only two parties, parties have to try to win a majority, so targeting the "center" of the electorate is critical. In PR systems with many political parties, however, no one group has much chance of winning a majority, and parties can survive with much less support. Therefore, there is not the same centrist pull, and parties may instead spread themselves out across the policy spectrum.[9]

Figure 5.1 offers a comparative "snapshot" of parties and voters in several democracies. It shows where party supporters in each country placed their party on a left-to-right scale in recent election surveys, with one identified as Left (or liberal, in the United States) and ten identified as Right (or conservative, in the United States). Note that the meanings of *left*, *right*, and *center* can vary across countries. The height of the columns above the scale shows what percentage of the voters supported each party. The two countries at the top of the figure, the United States and Britain, use SMDP electoral systems, whereas France uses a majority runoff system, Mexico and Japan mixed systems, and Germany and Brazil PR systems. According to Duverger, we should expect the United States and Britain to have only two major parties and the others more. Following Downs, we should expect the two-party systems to be centrist and clustered in policy space and the multiparty systems to be more dispersed.

By and large, Figure 5.1 supports the theories of both Duverger and Downs. In the countries at the top of the figure, especially in the United States, there are only two large parties. Moreover, the parties are fairly close to the center. Democrats are somewhat to the left and Republicans somewhat to the right, with a great deal of overlap. The left–right "gap" between the average party supporters, although larger than it was twenty years ago, is still fairly small. Although the Japanese system is more fluid, it too features two large and fairly similar dominant parties. In France, toward the bottom of the figure, there are many parties and a very large distance between the left-most party (the Communists) and right-most party (the National Front), and even between the two largest parties (Socialists and RPR). Germany falls between these more extreme cases. As Duverger would predict, Britain looks more like the United States, but the parties are farther apart. Mexico has shown that even systems with proportional representation and more than two parties (though only three significant ones) can have convergent and centrist electoral politics. Yet in the most recent years, the Mexican parties have seemed to pull apart and become less centrist. In Brazil, there are many parties and moderate left–right diversity; the largest party, Lula's Worker's Party on the left, won only 15 percent of the vote. Many of the small parties are not shown because the survey did not ask about them.

Table 5.2 presents additional information on the electoral and party systems of the twelve countries in this book. It displays data on the **effective number of parties** in each country. This measure takes into

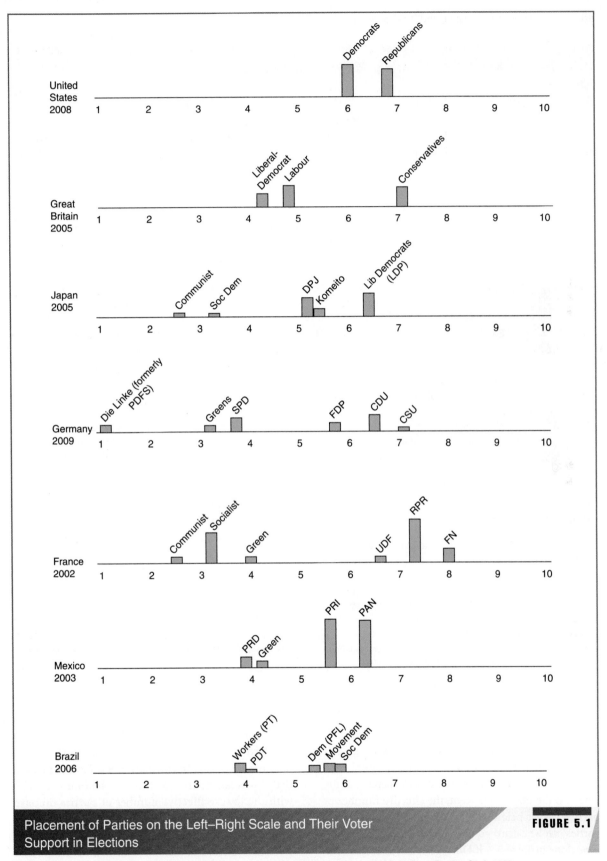

Placement of Parties on the Left–Right Scale and Their Voter Support in Elections

FIGURE 5.1

Source: The Comparative Study of Electoral Systems (www.cses.org), CSES Modules 2, 3; U.S. National Election Study 2008.

Elections and the Effective Number of Parties (Lower House of Legislature)
Rules matter.

TABLE 5.2

Country	Electoral System	Effective Number of Parties—Vote Shares	Effective Number of Parties—Seat Shares	How Are Individual Candidates Selected?
Brazil	PR open list	10.62	9.32	Candidate preference vote
Britain	SMD plurality	3.71*	2.57*	Nominated by local constituency association
China	No contested elections	No contested elections	No contested elections	No contested elections
France	SMD majority runoff	4.32	2.49	Nominated by local constituency association
Germany	Mixed system: SMD plurality + PR closed list	5.58**	4.83**	National party and state party conventions
India	SMD plurality	7.74	5.01	Nominated by local constituency association
Iran	MMD majority runoff	No data	No data	Must be approved by Council of Guardians
Japan	Mixed system: SMD plurality + PR closed list	3.15***	2.10***	National party
Mexico	Mixed system: SMD plurality + PR closed list	3.77	2.75	Nominated by local constituency association and national party
Nigeria	SMD plurality	2.62	2.34	Nominated by local constituency association
Russia	PR closed list	2.22	1.92	National party
United States	SMD plurality	2.09	1.94	Primary elections

Note: Data from the most recent national elections, as of May 10, 2010.

MMD = Multimember district

SMD = Single-member district

 PR = Proportional representation

*Calculated on the basis of 649 out of 650 seats due to postponement of the 2010 poll in the constituency of Thirsk and Malton.

**Calculated with CDU and CSU as separate parties.

***Based on total votes and total seats.

Sources: Arend Lijphart, *Patterns of Democracy: Government Forms and Performance in Thirty-Six Countries* (New Haven, CT: Yale University Press, 1999); www.ElectionGuide.org; www.Wikipedia.org.

account both the overall number of parties and their relative sizes. For example, if there are two parties and they are exactly the same size, the effective number of parties is 2.0. If, however, one party has 80 percent of the vote and the other 20 percent, the effective number of parties is just below 1.5.[10] The effective number of parties can be calculated for either votes or seats, as we have done in Table 5.2. If Duverger's Law is correct, the

effective number of parties should be lower in countries that have SMDP electoral systems than in those that have other systems (particularly PR). Table 5.2 shows that this is largely true, as three of the four countries with the lowest effective number of parties do have SMDP elections. At the same time, India is an exception; it has a large number of parties despite an SMDP electoral system. But a closer look at India shows that even though the country has many parties overall, most electoral districts feature only two serious parties.[11] Thus, India helps us understand one limitation of Duverger's Law, which is that while SMDP systems tend to sustain only two parties in each election district, these two parties need not be the same throughout the country.

Table 5.2 also gives us a measure of the mechanical effect in Duverger's Law, the consequences of the counting rules themselves. By comparing the effective number of parties among the voters (vote shares) with the effective number of parties in the national assembly (seat shares), we can see how much the electoral system helps the large parties and disfavors the small ones. This bias exists in all countries and electoral systems, as the numbers in the column for seat shares are always consistently lower than those in the column for vote shares. Duverger's Law suggests that this difference should be greater in "first-past-the-post" (SMDP) systems than elsewhere.

Competitive Parties in Government

If a competitive party wins control of the legislature and the executive branch, it will (if unified) be able to pass and implement its policies. Sometimes, this control emerges directly from the electoral process, as a single party wins a majority of the vote. But in many countries, the election laws help the largest party gain a governing majority even if it does not enjoy majority support among the voters. Thus, less than 50 percent of the vote may be converted into more than 50 percent of the legislative seats. Such "artificial" or "manufactured" legislative majorities have been the rule in countries with SMDP electoral systems, such as Britain.[12]

For example, from 1979 until 2010, either the Conservative Party or the Labour Party consistently won a majority of seats in the British House of Commons, even though neither party was ever supported by a majority of the voters in any of these elections. Margaret Thatcher's Conservative Party won a solid majority in the House of Commons in 1983 and 1987 with only about 42 percent of the vote. With almost exactly the same level of support, Tony Blair and the Labour Party won nearly two-thirds of the seats in 1997 and 2001. In 2005, Labour's share of the vote fell to about 35 percent, but the party still got a clear majority of the seats. In 2010, although they actually received a slightly larger share of the vote than Labour had in 2005, the Conservatives fell just short of a majority in the House of Commons. In all these elections, the 25 to 35 percent of the electorate supporting the smaller British parties received 10 percent or less of the parliamentary seats.

In other countries, multiparty elections do not yield single-party majorities, but party coalitions formed before the election may still offer the voters a direct choice of future governments. Before the election, a group of parties may join forces, agree to coordinate their election campaigns, or agree to govern together if they jointly win a parliamentary majority. When such coalitions form, as they have in many (but not all) elections in France and Germany, it is almost like a two-party system. Voters can clearly identify the potential governments and reward or punish the incumbents if they so choose. They thus have the ability to choose the direction of government policy through their party choice.

When elections do not create a majority party and there is no preelectoral coalition, the political parties and their leaders must negotiate a new government after the election. This is common in many multiparty parliamentary systems, such as the Netherlands and Italy.[13] In these nations, interests are not aggregated through elections because the election does not directly determine who governs. Instead, the aggregation of interests occurs in negotiations between different parties over control of the executive branch, most often after an election but also sometimes when an existing coalition breaks up (see also Chapter 6, specifically Figure 6.2).

The aggregation of interests at the executive rather than electoral level can have both costs and benefits. On the one hand, when elite party coalitions determine government policy, voters may feel that the government is not accountable to them. And because interest aggregation occurs among political elites, different elite coalitions can form on different issues. This can be confusing to citizens (and even informed observers). It may be difficult for voters to assign clear responsibility for government policy, and it may seem unfair that the electoral losers sometimes get to decide. This situation lessens the value of the vote as an instrument to shape future policy or to punish parties responsible for bad policy choices in the past.

On the other hand, there may be benefits for minority interests when all parties, not just the election

Elections Bring Change

Democratization means new political rights and, often, social change. Here, women line up to vote in Afghanistan's first democratic elections.

Caren Firouz/Reuters/Corbis

winners, are represented in policymaking. All citizens hold minority opinions on some issues, and some are in the minority on many issues. If even minority representatives can influence policy between elections, they may feel that they have more political protection. Finally, even governments that win a majority of votes typically do not have majority support for all of their policy proposals. So there may be benefits for the nation as a whole when even the winners have to negotiate the different parts of their programs. Such bargaining may even increase the likelihood that policies reflect different majorities on different issues. The value of elections as instruments of representation may increase when interests are aggregated within a government coalition, though the value of elections as instruments of accountability may diminish.[14]

Cooperation and Conflict in Competitive Party Systems

Competitive party systems can be classified by the number of parties as well as by the patterns of competition or cooperation among them. **Majoritarian two-party systems** either are dominated by just two parties, as in the United States, or have two dominant parties and election laws that usually create legislative majorities for one of them, as in Britain. In **majority-coalition systems,** parties establish preelectoral coalitions so that voters know which parties will attempt to work together to form a government. Germany and France have in most elections been in this category. Pure **multiparty systems** have election laws and party systems that virtually ensure that no single party wins a legislative majority and no tradition of preelection coalitions. Interest aggregation then depends on a coalition of parties bargaining and coming to agreement after the election.

The degree of antagonism or polarization among the parties is another important party system characteristic. In a **consensual party system**, the parties commanding most of the legislative seats are not too far apart on policies and have a reasonable amount of trust in each other and in the political system. These are typically party systems like those shown toward the top of Figure 5.1. Bargaining may be intense and politics exciting, but it seldom threatens the system itself. In a **conflictual party system**, the legislature is dominated by parties that are far apart on issues or are antagonistic toward each other and the political system, such as the Russian party system in the 1990s.

Some party systems have both consensual and conflictual features. The term **consociational** (or **accommodative**) refers to party systems in which political leaders seek to bridge intense social divisions through power-sharing, broad coalition governments, and decentralization of sensitive decisions to the separate social groups.[15] A consociational system can enable a deeply divided nation to find a way to peaceful democratic development. In Austria and Lebanon after World War II, mutually suspicious and hostile groups—the socialists and Catholics in Austria, and the Christians and Muslims in Lebanon—developed consociational arrangements that made stable government possible. Austria's accommodation occurred within a two-party system and Lebanon's among many small, personalistic religious parties. Austria's consociationalism was largely successful. After some twenty years of the consociational "Grand Coalition," in which both major parties held office together, these parties felt much less antagonistic and reverted to "normal" competition for office. The Lebanese experiment was less happy. After 1975, the country fell victim to civil war. South Africa also adopted consociational practices in its transition to democracy in the 1990s. Party leaders representing the white minority as well as different segments of the black majority negotiated power-sharing arrangements for a transitional period. The "Interim Constitution" guaranteed a share of power—cabinet posts—to all parties winning over 5 percent of the vote. Later, as the democratic order became more secure, this feature was abandoned.

Consociational practices thus offer deeply divided democracies hope but no guarantees of long-term stability. As Austria and South Africa show us, consociationalism may be especially suitable as a temporary solution after a period of intense conflict or turmoil. But consociationalism means that small groups of politicians make many important decisions behind closed doors. If these politicians are able to work together more constructively than their respective supporters, consociationalism can be a happy solution. If, however, the politicians are intransigent or self-interested, consociationalism may fail.

The number of parties does not always tell us much about their degree of antagonism. The United States and Britain are relatively consensual majoritarian party systems. They are not perfect two-party systems because minor parties exist in both countries, especially in Britain. In the United States, the degree of consensus changes from election to election because of the shifting programs of presidential candidates. Moreover, the looser cohesion of American parties and the frequency of divided government lead to post-election bargaining that is similar to consensual multiparty systems.

But not all majoritarian party systems are consensual. Austria between 1918 and 1934 was a conflictual majoritarian party system. Antagonism between the Socialist Party and the other parties was so intense that in the mid-1930s, it produced a brief civil war. The Austrian experience also illustrates how party systems can change. As we noted above, after World War II, the two major parties negotiated an elaborate coalition agreement of mutual power-sharing—checks and balances—to contain the country's conflicts. In recent years, Ukraine has been another example of a conflictual majoritarian party system.

Consensual multiparty systems are found in Scandinavia and the Netherlands, among other countries. France (1946–1958), Italy (1945–1992), and Weimar Germany (1919–1933), on the other hand, are historical examples of conflictual multiparty systems, with powerful communist parties on the left and conservative or fascist movements on the right. Cabinets had to form out of centrist movements, which were themselves divided on many issues. This resulted in instability, poor government performance, and loss of citizen confidence in democracy. These factors contributed to the collapse of the French Fourth Republic in 1958, to government instability and citizen alienation from politics in Italy by the 1990s, and to the overthrow of democracy in Weimar Germany.

New democracies, especially those divided by language or ethnicity, sometimes face similar challenges. Some of the emerging party systems in Central and Eastern Europe have fallen into the pattern of conflictual, multiparty competition. For instance, in the 1995 parliamentary elections in Russia, forty-three parties appeared on the ballot, and seven parties won representation in Parliament. But later elections greatly reduced the number of parties.

Thus, although the number of parties affects political stability, the degree of antagonism among parties is more important. Two-party systems are stable and effective, but they may be dangerous if society is too deeply divided. Multiparty systems consisting of relatively moderate parties can often offer stability and fairly effective performance, especially if the parties are willing to commit themselves to preelectoral coalitions. Pure multiparty systems without preelectoral coalitions are more prone to ineffectiveness, but some have worked well over long periods. Where social groups and parties are highly antagonistic, however, collapse and civil war are ever-present possibilities, regardless of the number of parties. When crises develop, the most critical factor is typically how committed party leaders are to working together to defend democracy.[16]

AUTHORITARIAN PARTY SYSTEMS

Authoritarian party systems can also aggregate interests. They develop policy proposals and mobilize support for them, but they do so in a completely different way from competitive party systems. In authoritarian party systems, aggregation takes place within the party or in interactions with business groups, unions, landowners, and institutional groups in the bureaucracy or military. Although there may be sham elections, the citizens have no real opportunity to shape aggregation by choosing between party alternatives.

Authoritarian party systems vary in the degree of top-down control within the party and the party's control over other groups in society. At one extreme is the **exclusive governing party**, which insists on almost total control over political resources. It recognizes no legitimate interest aggregation by groups within the party. Nor does it permit any free activity, much less opposition, from interest groups, citizens, or other government agencies. In its most extreme form, sometimes called *totalitarianism*, it penetrates the entire society and mobilizes support for policies developed at the top. Its policies are legitimated by a political ideology, such as communism or national socialism (Nazism) that claims to identify the true interests of the citizens, regardless of what the citizens themselves believe.[17] At the other extreme is the **inclusive governing party**, which recognizes and accepts at least some other groups and organizations, but may repress those that it sees as serious challenges to its own control.

Exclusive Governing Parties

In a purely totalitarian society, there is only one party with total top-down control of society, and no autonomous opposition parties or interest groups. Totalitarian single-party systems can be impressive vehicles of political mobilization. A clear ideology provides legitimacy and coherence, and the party penetrates and organizes society in the name of that ideology and in accordance with its policies. But totalitarianism is difficult to sustain. Although the ruling communist parties of the Soviet Union before 1985, of Eastern Europe before 1989, and of North Korea, Vietnam, and Cuba today resemble this model, few parties have long maintained such absolute control. China is an interesting mixed case. While the Chinese government has withdrawn from the direct administration of much of the economy, it does not recognize the legitimacy of any opposition groups. The ruling party permits, within bounds, some interest articulation by individuals, but not mass mobilization against government policy.[18]

Not all exclusive governing parties are totalitarian, however. Many leaders committed to massive social change—for example, national independence from colonialism—have used the exclusive governing party as a tool for mass mobilization. Such exclusive governing parties may experience more internal dissent than is commonly recognized. Within the party, groups may unite around such interests as their region or industry, or behind leaders of different policy factions. Beneath the supposedly united front, power struggles may erupt in times of crisis. Succession crises are particularly likely to generate such power struggles, as at the death of Stalin in the Soviet Union and Mao Zedong in China. Several times, the Chinese Communist Party has had to rely on the army, even on coalitions of regional army commanders, to sustain its control.

It is difficult to build an exclusive governing party as an agent for social transformation. The seduction of power regularly leads to rent-seeking or other abuses of power that are not checked by competitive democratic politics and that may distort the original party objectives. The exclusive governing parties in some African states also had limited capacity to control society. Furthermore, the loss of confidence in Marxist–Leninist ideology and in the Soviet model led all eight of the African regimes that had once invoked it to abandon that approach by the early 1990s.

As exclusive governing parties age, many enter a stage in which they maintain control but place less emphasis on mobilization. Some, such as North Korea, may degenerate into vehicles for personal rule and exploitation by the ruler's family and supporters.[19] Finally, as shown by the collapse of communism in the former Soviet Union and Eastern Europe, if and when the party leaders lose faith in the unifying ideology, it is difficult to maintain party coherence.

Inclusive Governing Parties

Among the preindustrial countries, especially those with notable ethnic and tribal divisions, the more successful authoritarian parties have been *inclusive*. These systems recognize the autonomy of social, cultural, and economic groups and try to incorporate them or bargain with them, rather than control and remake them. The more successful African one-party systems, such as in Kenya and Tanzania, have permitted aggregation around personalistic, factional, and ethnic groups within a decentralized party.

Inclusive party systems have sometimes been labeled *authoritarian corporatist systems*. Like the democratic corporatist systems (see Chapter 4), some of these systems encourage the formation of large, organized interest groups that can bargain with each other and the state. Unlike the democratic corporatist systems, however, these authoritarian systems place no power directly in the hands of the people. Authoritarian corporatist systems suppress independent protest and political activity outside of official channels. The party leaders permit only limited autonomous demands within the ranks of the party and by groups associated with it.

The inclusive authoritarian systems may permit substantial amounts of autonomous interest aggregation, which may take many forms. The party typically tries to gather various social groups under the general party umbrella and negotiate with outside groups and institutions. Some inclusive parties have attempted aggressive social change. Others have primarily been arenas for interest aggregation. Many inclusive party governments permit other parties to offer candidates in elections, as long as these opposition candidates have no real chance of winning. Indeed, one interesting feature of politics since about the 1980s, along with the increasing number of liberal democracies, has been the growth of **electoral authoritarianism**. This is where there is a facade of democracy providing "some space for political opposition, independent media, and social organizations that do not seriously criticize or challenge the regime."[20] The Mexican Partido Revolucionario Institucional (PRI) was long a successful example of an inclusive governing party featuring electoral authoritarianism (see Box 5.3).

The fact that some inclusive authoritarian parties have been impressively durable does not necessarily mean that they are strong or successful. In many countries, these parties coexist in uneasy and unstable coalitions with the armed forces and the civilian bureaucracy. In some countries, the party has become window dressing for a military regime or personal tyranny. Seldom have these parties been able to solve the economic or ethnic problems that face their countries.

These political systems were often created in a struggle against colonialism, and as colonialism becomes more distant, they may implode. As memories of the independence struggle fade and the leaders die off or retire, the ties of ideology and experience that hold these parties together weaken. These developments, in conjunction with the worldwide expansion of democracy, have led to a general loss of legitimacy for the single-party model. In some cases (as in Tanzania), they have adjusted by permitting real party competition. More frequently, they have resorted to electoral authoritarianism with varying degrees of manipulation to provide a veneer of domestic and international legitimacy. In more than a few cases, they have turned to naked coercion, with the military serving as final arbiter.

THE MILITARY AND INTEREST AGGREGATION

After independence, most Third World nations adopted at least formally democratic governments. But in many countries, these civilian governments lacked effectiveness and authority, which often led to their breakdown and replacement by **military governments**. The military had instruments of force and organizational capacity, and in the absence of a strong constitutional tradition, it was an effective contender for power. Even under civilian rule, the military had substantial political influence and often constituted a significant power contender. In Brazil, for example, the military played a crucial role in interest aggregation even under the civilian government prior to the coup of 1964. After that intervention, it was the dominant actor for the next twenty years. In many other countries, the military has long been a similarly important interest aggregator. Many Latin American countries had military governments on and off for much of the twentieth century, and Africa experienced a wave of military coups after its decolonization in the 1960s.

The military's virtual monopoly on coercive resources gives it great potential power. Thus, when aggregation fails in democratic or authoritarian party systems, the military may emerge by default as the only force able to maintain orderly government. The military may also intervene for more self-interested reasons, such as protecting its autonomy or budgets from civilian interference. And in many countries, military governments have served as a vehicle for ethnic politics.

About two-fifths of the world's nations have confronted military coup attempts at some time, and in about a third of the nations, these coups were at least partially successful in changing leaders or policy (see Box 5.4). Fewer than half of these coup attempts, however, focused on general political issues and public policy. Most coups seemed motivated by the professional interests of the military.

What happens after the military intervenes can vary. The soldiers may support the personal tyranny of a civilian president or a dominant party. Or, the armed forces may use their power to further institutional or ideological objectives. Military rulers may try to create military and/or bureaucratic versions of authoritarian corporatism, linking organized groups and the state bureaucracy with the military as final arbiter. They may undertake "defensive" modernization in alliance with business groups or even more radical modernization. Most Latin American versions of authoritarian corporatism have relied on a strong military component rather than a dominant authoritarian party.

The major limitation of the military in interest aggregation is that it is not designed for that function. The military is primarily organized to have an efficient command structure. It is not set up to aggregate internal differences, to build compromise, to mobilize popular support, or even to communicate with social groups outside the command hierarchy. Nor do military regimes have the legitimacy in the international community that elections provide. Thus, the military lacks many of the advantages held by elected party leaders. These internal limitations may be less serious when the military is dealing with common grievances or responding to abuses of power by unpopular politicians. The same limitations become a major problem, however, when a military government needs to stake

---

Mexico's PRI

BOX 5.3

One of the oldest and most inclusive authoritarian parties is the Partido Revolucionario Institucional (PRI) in Mexico. For more than fifty years, the PRI dominated the political process and gave other parties no realistic chances of winning elections. The PRI attained this dominance after President Lázaro Cárdenas turned it into a "big-tent" coalition in the 1930s. It also carefully controlled the counting of the ballots. The PRI incorporated many social groups, with separate sectors for labor, agrarian, and middle-class interests. The party dealt with its opponents in carefully designed ways. While some political dissidents were harassed and suppressed, others were deliberately enticed into the party. The party also gave informal recognition to political factions grouped behind such figures as former presidents. Various Mexican leaders mobilized their factions within the PRI and in other important groups not directly affiliated with it, such as big-business interests. Bargaining was particularly important every six years when the party had to choose a new presidential nominee, since the Mexican Constitution limits presidents to one term. This guaranteed some turnover of elites.

As a consequence of its elaborate schemes of governing, the PRI did not have to fear electoral competition, at least until the 1990s. Yet rising discontent made it increasingly difficult to aggregate interests through a single party. The urban and rural poor who had not shared in Mexico's growth joined with reformers to demand a more fully democratic system. An armed uprising of peasant guerrillas in early 1994 shocked the political establishment and led to promises of genuine democratic competition. Legislative elections in 1997 were more open than earlier contests, and ended the seventy-year rule of the PRI, which then lost the presidency to the National Action Party (PAN) in 2000. After that election, the PRI has quickly diminished as a political force, even though it still controls many state and local governments. In 2006, its candidate ran a distant third in Mexico's presidential election (see Chapter 14).

BOX 5.4

Trying to Make Democracy Work

Nigeria is in many ways typical of the rough road to democracy that many developing countries have traveled. After gaining its independence, Nigeria experienced brief periods of democratic government in the 1960s and again in the late 1970s. In both cases, the military quickly intervened and ousted governments that had become oppressive or ineffective. The military government that came to power in 1983 responded to the global democratization wave of the early 1990s by introducing measured reforms leading up to a presidential election in 1993. But the military kept strict control of the electoral process and disqualified politicians who had held office under previous civilian regimes (because they were considered to be tainted by corruption). Voters were left with a choice of only two parties, both created by the government. Voting turnout was low because many voters became cynical about the process. These doubts were confirmed when the military annulled the presidential election even before the results had been

announced, apparently because the "wrong" candidate was winning. General Sani Abacha then launched a coup which banned all political activity, dissolved the legislature, dismissed the elected governments in Nigeria's thirty-six states, and thus ended Nigeria's cautious experiment with elections. In 1998, President Abacha suddenly died of a heart attack, and the reform process began anew. In spring 1999, a presidential election was held. The victor was a former army general and president (1976–1979), Olusegun Obasanjo, who went on to implement democratic reforms. He was reelected four years later and stepped down in 2007 after his second term, as the constitution required. The new president that was chosen in the 2007 election later died in office and was replaced by his vice president. Thus, Nigeria has by now experienced its longest period of civilian government ever. But continuing ethnic and religious violence, corruption, and abuses of power have made Nigerian democracy fragile (see Chapter 18).

out its own course and mobilize support for it. For these reasons, military governments frequently prove unstable and are often forced to share power with other institutions or simply to withdraw from politics.

Recent surveys show little popular support for military government anywhere in the world. Perhaps because most citizens do not consider authoritarian rule legitimate, the military throughout the world is now more likely to dominate from behind the scenes than through direct rule. In such important Latin American countries as Argentina, Brazil, Chile, and Uruguay, military regimes have been replaced by competitive party regimes. The same thing has happened in a number of African countries, including Nigeria (see Chapter 18).

TRENDS IN INTEREST AGGREGATION

As we have previously noted, the democratic trend in the world gained momentum in the 1980s, when many Latin American countries democratized. This trend began accelerating in 1989 in Eastern Europe, with new pressures for democracy in the developing world also. By the late 1990s, for the first time in world

history, there were more free than unfree states. The collapse of communism in Europe and elsewhere was in large part responsible, but the number of military dictatorships also declined. The declining acceptance of authoritarian governments, as well as the withdrawal of Soviet support, contributed to this trend, especially in Africa. Many African nations moved toward a more democratic and free system during the 1990s. Yet a few authoritarian party systems with exclusive governing parties are still around, such as in China and Cuba. Most of the remaining unfree states are in the Middle East, Central Asia, and Africa. Many African nations still feature some variety of the "electoral authoritarianism" discussed earlier, with severe constraints on civil freedom and electoral opposition. A few remain unabashed authoritarian systems (as in Zimbabwe) or are mired in deadly civil war (as in Sudan and Somalia).

We cannot assume that democratization will continue relentlessly. Party politicians who seem unable to cope with economic and social problems often lose their legitimacy. Such is now the challenge facing many developing countries, especially in Africa. In many of these countries, competitive party systems exist, but citizens have very little trust in them and

The Army Takes Power

Onlookers cheer as members of a military junta speak to supporters in Niamey, Niger, Saturday, Feb. 20, 2010. Thousands of people rallied on the streets of Niger's capital in support of a military coup that ousted the West African nation's strongman president.

Rebecca Blackwell/AP Images

often consider them to be corrupt. And military coups have continued to occur, as in Thailand and Fiji in 2006 and Niger in 2010.

SIGNIFICANCE OF INTEREST AGGREGATION

How interests are aggregated is an important determinant of what a country's government does for and to its citizens. Successful public policy depends on effective interest aggregation. Interest aggregation narrows policy options so that the desires and demands of citizens are converted into a few policy alternatives. Many possible policies are eliminated in the process. Those that remain typically have the backing of significant sectors of society.

In democratic countries, competitive party systems narrow down and combine policy preferences. Through elections, voters throw their support behind some of these parties and thus shape party representation in the legislature. Even at the legislative stage, further consolidation and coalition-building take place. At some point, however, most policy options have been eliminated from consideration—either no party backed them or the parties supporting them fared badly in the elections.

In noncompetitive party systems, military governments, and monarchies, aggregation works differently, but with the similar effect of narrowing policy options.

On some issues, aggregation virtually determines policy, as when a military government or a faction of an authoritarian party can decide the government's program. In other cases, the legislative assembly, military council, or party politburo may contain several factions that must negotiate over policy.

Politics shapes its environment as well as reflecting it. Interest aggregation often alters the political culture. That is one reason why politics is so fascinating. Well-organized and well-led political parties might, at least for a while, be able to dominate politics and limit the strength of extremist groups in the legislature. Conversely, well-organized extremists might be able to appeal to the fears, envies, and prejudices of some groups and get their support at the polls, thus gaining more legislative strength in an otherwise consensual country.

Aggregation ultimately affects the government's adaptability and stability. Authoritarian interest aggregation tends to create political power structures that do not reflect popular opinion. In highly divided and conflict-ridden societies, rulers may portray such lack of representation as a virtue. Leaders of military coups often justify their overthrow of party governments by claiming to depolarize politics and rid the nation of conflict it cannot afford. Similarly, heads of authoritarian parties typically claim that their nation must concentrate all its energies and resources on common purposes and that party competition would be too polarizing.

In contrast, most proponents of democratic interest aggregation argue that the best hope for accommodating conflicting social and political interests lies in free and fair electoral competition, followed by negotiation among those groups that gain the voters' favor. Democracy thus leads policymakers to act as the people wish. In a polarized political culture, the division and uncertainty that interest aggregation implies may be seen as a high price to pay for citizen control. As the frequent instability in authoritarian governments indicates, however, it may be easier to do away with the appearance of polarization than with the reality. Competing demands may find their way to the surface anyway, and the citizens may end up with neither freedom and participation nor stability.

REVIEW QUESTIONS

- What structures other than political parties aggregate interests?

- What is Duverger's Law? Which two effects does it imply?

- What is the median voter result, and why does it pertain only to two-party systems?

- What are the differences between totalitarian parties and other single-party systems?

- Why do many countries turn to military governments, and why are military governments often short-lived?

KEY TERMS

accommodative party system

authoritarian party system

closed-list PR system

competitive party system

conflictual party system

consensual party system

consociational

double-ballot

Duverger's Law

effective number of parties

electoral authoritarianism

electoral system

exclusive governing party

inclusive governing party

institutional groups

interest aggregation

majoritarian two-party system

iron law of oligarchy

majority runoff

majority-coalition system

mechanical effect

median voter result

military governments

multiparty system

open-list PR system

party system

patron–client networks

primary elections

proportional representation (PR)

psychological effect

single-member district (SMD)

single-member district plurality (SMDP) election rule

strategic voting

two-party system

SUGGESTED READINGS

Bratton, Michael, and Nicolas van de Walle. *Democratic Experiments in Africa.* Cambridge: Cambridge University Press, 1997.

Cox, Gary W. *Making Votes Count: Strategic Coordination in the World's Electoral Systems.* Cambridge: Cambridge University Press, 1997.

Dalton, Russell J., and Martin P. Wattenberg. *Parties without Partisans: Political Change in Advanced Industrial Democracies.* New York: Oxford University Press, 2000.

Decalo, Samuel. *Coups and Army Rule in Africa,* 2nd ed. New Haven, CT: Yale University Press, 1990.

Downs, Anthony. *An Economic Theory of Democracy.* New York: Harper & Row, 1957.

Geddes, Barbara. "What Do We Know about Democratization after Twenty Years?" *Annual Reviews of Political Science* 2 (1999): 115–44.

Jackson, Robert H., and Carl G. Rosberg. *Personal Rule in Black Africa.* Berkeley: University of California Press, 1982.

Kitschelt, Herbert. *The Transformation of European Social Democracy.* New York: Cambridge University Press, 1994.

Laver, Michael, and Norman Schofield. *Multiparty Government.* New York: Oxford University Press, 1990.

Lijphart, Arend. *Electoral Systems and Party Systems.* New York: Oxford University Press, 1994.

———. *Patterns of Democracy: Government Forms and Performance in Thirty-Six Countries.* New Haven, CT: Yale University Press, 1999.

Linz, Juan J. *Totalitarian and Authoritarian Regimes.* Baltimore: Johns Hopkins University Press, 2002.

Michels, Robert. *Political Parties.* New York: Free Press, 1962.

Powell, G. Bingham, Jr. *Contemporary Democracies: Participation, Stability, and Violence.* Cambridge, MA: Harvard University Press, 1982.

———. *Elections as Instruments of Democracy.* New Haven, CT: Yale University Press, 2000.

Riker, William H. *Liberalism Against Populism.* San Francisco: W. H. Freeman, 1982.

Strøm, Kaare, Wolfgang C. Müller, and Torbjörn Bergman, eds. *Cabinets and Coalition Bargaining: The Democratic Life Cycle in Western Europe.* Oxford: Oxford University Press, 2008.

ENDNOTES

1. See, for example, Luis Roniger and Ayse Gunes-Ayata, eds., *Democracy, Clientelism, and Civil Society* (Boulder, CO: Lynne Rienner, 1994); S. Eisenstadt and L. Roniger, *Patrons, Clients, and Friends* (Cambridge: Cambridge University Press, 1984); Lucian W. Pye, *Asian Power and Politics* (Cambridge, MA: Harvard University Press, 1985); and Martin Shefter, "Patronage and Its Opponents," in *Political Parties and the State* (Princeton, NJ: Princeton University Press, 1994).

2. Unfortunately, elections cannot solve all the problems of aggregating interests fairly. For example, giving each citizen one vote does not take into account the varying intensities with which different people may hold their opinions. Moreover, economists and political scientists have found that when there are three or more alternatives in any decision, there is no fair way to aggregate votes to select a single, best outcome (a problem known as "Arrow's Paradox"). See Kenneth Arrow, *Social Choice and Individual Values* (New Haven, CT: Yale University Press, 1951). For an accessible discussion of some political implications, see William H. Riker, *Liberalism Against Populism* (San Francisco: W. H. Freeman, 1982); and Kenneth A. Shepsle, *Analyzing Politics: Rationality, Behavior, and Institutions* (New York: Norton, 2010), Second edition.

3. Hans-Dieter Klingemann, Richard Hofferbert, and Ian Budge, eds., *Parties, Policy, and Democracy* (Boulder, CO: Westview, 1995); Michael Gallagher, Michael Laver, and Peter Mair, *Representative Government in Western Europe*, 4th ed. (New York: McGraw-Hill, 2005); and Richard Rose, *Do Parties Make a Difference?* (Chatham, NJ: Chatham House, 1984), Chapter 5.

4. Joseph A. Schumpeter, *Capitalism, Socialism, and Democracy* (New York: Harper, 1943).

5. However, in China, semicompetitive elections for village leadership positions have in some areas brought the opinions of local leaders and ordinary citizens closer together. See Larry Diamond and Ramon H. Myers, eds., *Elections and Democracy in Greater China* (Oxford: Oxford University Press, 2001).

6. See Russell J. Dalton, *Citizen Politics: Public Opinion and Political Parties in Advanced Industrial Democracies*, 5th ed. (Washington, D.C.: Congressional Quarterly Press, 2008).

7. Ian Budge, David Robertson, and Derek Hearl, eds., *Ideology, Strategy, and Party Change: Spatial Analyses of Post-War Election Programmes in 19 Democracies* (New York: Cambridge University Press, 1987); Richard Katz and Peter Mair, eds., *How Parties Organize: Change and Adaptation in Party Organizations in Western Democracies* (Thousand Oaks, CA: Sage, 1994).

8. Maurice Duverger, *Political Parties: Their Organization and Activity in the Modern State*, trans. Barbara and Robert North (New York: Wiley, 1963). See also Gary W. Cox, *Making Votes Count* (Cambridge: Cambridge University Press, 1997).

9. Anthony Downs, *An Economic Theory of Democracy* (New York: Harper & Row, 1957).

10. The effective number of parties is calculated as follows: First, calculate the proportion of seats (or votes) held by each party. Square each of these proportions and then add them all up. Finally, divide 1 by the sum of all the squared proportions. See Markku Laakso and Rein Taagepera, "'Effective' Number of Parties: A Measure with Application to West Europe," *Comparative Political Studies* 12 (1979): 3–27.

11. Pradeep Chhibber and Kenneth Kollman, *The Formation of National Party Systems* (Princeton, NJ: Princeton University Press, 2004).

12. Douglas Rae, *The Political Consequences of Election Laws* (New Haven, CT: Yale University Press, 1967); and Arend Lijphart, *Electoral Systems and Party Systems: A Study of Twenty-Seven Democracies, 1945–1990* (Oxford: Oxford University Press, 1994).

13. On government coalitions, see especially Michael Laver and Norman Schofield, *Multiparty Government: The Politics of Coalition in Europe* (New York: Oxford University Press, 1990); and Kaare Strøm, Wolfgang C. Müller, and Torbjörn Bergman, eds., *Cabinets and Coalition Bargaining: The Democratic Life Cycle in Western Europe* (New York: Oxford University Press, 2008).

14. See G. Bingham Powell, Jr., *Elections as Instruments of Democracy* (New Haven, CT: Yale University Press, 2000), Chapters 5–10.

15. Arend Lijphart, *Democracy in Plural Societies* (New Haven, CT: Yale University Press, 1977); and Arend Lijphart, *Patterns of Democracy: Government Forms and Performance in Thirty-Six Countries* (New Haven, CT: Yale University Press, 1999).

16. Lijphart, *Patterns of Democracy*; G. Bingham Powell, Jr., *Contemporary Democracies: Participation, Stability, and Violence* (Cambridge, MA: Harvard University Press, 1982), Chapters 8 and 10; and Juan J. Linz and Alfred Stepan, eds., *The Breakdown of Democratic Regimes* (Baltimore: Johns Hopkins University Press, 1978).

17. Juan Linz, *Totalitarian and Authoritarian Regimes* (Boulder, CO: Lynne Rienner, 2000); Amos Perlmutter, *Modern Authoritarianism: A Comparative Institutional Analysis* (New Haven, CT: Yale University Press, 1981), especially 62–114.

18. Melanie Manion, "Politics in China," Chapter 13, this text; for the earlier period, see, for example, Franz Schurman, *Ideology*

and Organization in Communist China (Berkeley: University of California Press, 1966).

19. Juan Linz calls these "sultanistic" regimes; see *Totalitarian and Authoritarian Regimes*, 151–157; Houchang Chehabi and Juan Linz, eds., *Sultanistic Regimes* (Baltimore: Johns Hopkins

University Press, 1998); and Robert H. Jackson and Carl G. Rosberg, *Personal Rule in Black Africa* (Berkeley: University of California Press, 1982).

20. Larry Diamond, "Thinking about Hybrid Regimes," *Journal of Democracy* 13 (2002): 26; see also other articles in the same issue.

GOVERNMENT AND POLICYMAKING

In a social science class, you might have discussed how to form a government in a new nation. This is a theoretical exercise, but in fact dozens of nations have created new governing systems in the past few decades. Democratization led to new governing systems in postcommunist Europe and in the new democracies of East Asia and Latin America. Other nations have experienced major reforms in the institutions of government.

Policymaking is the pivotal stage in the political process, the point at which bills become law or edicts are issued by rulers. To understand public policy, we must know how decisions are made. Where is power effectively located in different political systems? What does it take to change public policy: a simple majority vote in the legislature or approval also by an independently elected executive? Or is it a decree issued by the military commanders or the party central committee? Or is it merely the whim of the personal dictator?

This chapter focuses on the structures of government—such as legislatures, chief executives, bureaucracies, and courts—and how these agencies enact public policies. While parties, interest groups, and other actors may actively articulate and aggregate interests, government officials do most of the actual initiation and formulation of policy proposals. Interest-group demands for tax relief or for the protection of endangered species cannot succeed unless they are transformed into policy by government officials according to some accepted decision rules. They cannot be effective until these policies are appropriately implemented by other officials.

Yet government action does not flow in one direction only. The interaction between government and citizens is a two-way process. It includes an upward flow of influence and demands from the society, as well as a downward flow of decisions from the government (refer back to Figure 2.2).

CONSTITUTIONS AND DECISION RULES

A constitution establishes the basic rules of decision-making, rights, and the distribution of authority in a political system. We sometimes use the term "constitution" to refer to a specific document laying out such principles—for example, the one adopted by the Founders of the United States in 1787. But a constitution need not be embodied in a single document. In fact, it rarely is. We should therefore think of a constitution as a set of rules and principles, whether it is a specific written document, a set of customs or practices, or, as is usually the case, both. Even a military or party dictatorship typically sets procedures for having decrees proposed, considered, and adopted.

Written constitutions are particularly important in political systems based on the *rule of law*. This means that government should take no action that has not been authorized by law and that citizens can be punished only for actions that violate the law. Under the rule of law, the constitution is the supreme body of laws.

A constitution thus contains a set of **decision rules**—the basic rules governing how decisions are made. Policymaking is the conversion of social interests and demands into authoritative public decisions.

Constitutions establish the rules by which this happens. They confer the power to propose policies on specific groups or institutions. They may give others the right to amend, reject, or approve such proposals, or to implement, police, or adjudicate them. They may specify how many resources are needed to make policies, as well as what these resources are.

Decision rules affect political activity because they determine what political resources are valuable in influencing decisions and how to acquire and use these resources. For example, in a federal and decentralized system such as Germany, a pressure group may lobby both the legislative and the executive branches, and it may have to be active both at the state and the federal levels (and also in the European Union). If decisions are made by decree from the commander of the armed forces or the central committee of a single-party state, groups will need to influence these crucial policymakers.

Different decision rules have different attractions. More inclusive rules about policymaking—such as those that require the cooperation of several institutions or the support of over 50 percent of voters—can protect against hasty decisions. They can also prevent decisions that disadvantage large minorities (perhaps close to half) of the voters. At the same time, more inclusive rules can give a minority the power to block proposals favored by a majority. The more inclusive the voting rules are (as the percentage to approve approaches unanimity), the less likely it is that any decision can be made at all. Less inclusive decision rules make it easier to reach a policy, but many interests may be ignored.

Both the government as a whole and its institutions have decision rules. Decision rules may be simple or complex and apply to different circumstances. For example, the U.S. Congress has many different decision rules that apply under different circumstances. Decision rules may be more or less formal and precise. Most legislatures have formal and precise decision rules, whereas cabinets at the head of the executive branch often have informal and flexible rules.

Within each branch of government or other political institution, numerous rules affect the policymaking process. In most modern assemblies, the decision rules about voting are *egalitarian* so that each member has the same voting power—simply speaking, one person, one vote. That is hardly ever true in government departments (ministries), however. Or in dictatorships.

There, decision-making is *hierarchical*. Everybody is supposed to defer to his or her superior. In a pure hierarchy, only the vote of the person at the very top counts. Such a decision rule makes it easy to respond quickly in a policymaking emergency, but few interests or ideas may be taken into account.

Even when decisions are made through equal voting, the inclusiveness of the decision rules still shapes the outcomes. Many institutions operate through simple majority voting: In a choice between two options, whichever option gets the larger number of votes wins. For example, the British House of Commons mainly uses the simple majority rule. Alternatively, more inclusive rules—such as "qualified" majorities of three-fifths, two-thirds, or even three-fourths—are sometimes required for particularly consequential decisions. The U.S. Constitution requires two-thirds majorities in both houses of Congress in order to amend the Constitution or override a presidential veto. The most inclusive voting rule is unanimity, which means that any one member can block any decision.

It is important that decision rules in a democracy be transparent and stable. If they are not, citizens will not know what to expect from government. That may erode political legitimacy and make people less willing to accept and support government actions. It may also lead to serious conflicts, and ultimately government may break down and issues be decided by force. Thomas Jefferson suggested the importance of having predictable decision rules in his introduction to the first *Manual of the House of Representatives*: "A bad set of rules is better than no rules at all."

Making Constitutions

Making a constitution is a fundamental political act; it creates or transforms decision rules. Most current constitutions were formed as the result of some break, often violent, with the past—war, revolution, or rebellion against colonial rule. New decision rules were made to accommodate new internal or external powers. Thus, the defeated powers and the successor states of World Wars I and II all adopted new constitutions or had new constitutions imposed on them.

Britain is unusual in having not a formal written constitution but only a long-accepted and highly developed set of customs and conventions, buttressed by important ordinary statutes. This reflects the British record of gradual, incremental, and (on the whole) peaceful political change. Nevertheless, the major changes in British decision rules—such as the shift of power from the Crown to Parliament in the seventeenth century—followed periods of civil war or unrest.

Perhaps the most significant exception to the association between disruptive upheavals and constitution creation is the peaceful development over the last fifty years of the constitution of the European Union, whose growing powers are altering the decision rules affecting about 501 million Europeans in twenty-seven countries. While there has been no violence associated with the formation and growth of the EU, its origins lie in the bitter lessons of World Wars I and II.

The decades since World War II have seen much constitutional experimentation. Not only the defeated powers, but many new states—such as India and Nigeria, which achieved independence with the breakup of colonial empires—introduced new political arrangements. Some developing nations, such as Nigeria, have subsequently changed their form of government several times. In the last two decades, the worldwide trend toward democracy, the end of the Cold War, and the dissolution of the Soviet Union produced a new round of constitutional design. The recent constitutional crafting in Eastern Europe, Russia, East Asia, and Africa has reignited old debates about the virtues and faults of different constitutional arrangements, or about the very wisdom of constitutional engineering.[1]

DEMOCRACY AND AUTHORITARIANISM

The most important distinction in policymaking is between democratic and authoritarian systems. **Democracy** means "government by the people." In small political systems, such as local communities, "the people" may share directly in debating, deciding, and implementing public policy. In large political systems, such as contemporary states, democracy must be achieved largely through indirect participation in policymaking. Policymaking power is delegated to officials chosen by the people.

Elections, competitive political parties, free mass media, and representative assemblies are political structures that make some degree of democracy, some "government by the people," possible in large political systems. Competitive elections give citizens a chance to shape policy through their selection and rejection of key policymakers. Such indirect democracy is not complete or ideal. Moreover, the democratic opportunities

in less economically developed societies are often meaningful to educated elites or to those living near the centers of government, but less relevant to the average citizen in the countryside. The more citizens are involved and the more influential their choices, the more democratic the system.

In **authoritarian regimes**, in contrast, the policymakers are chosen by military councils, hereditary families, dominant political parties, and the like. Citizens are either ignored or pressed into symbolic assent to the government's choices.

The basic decision rules of political systems—both democratic and authoritarian—differ along three important dimensions:

1. The separation of powers among different branches of government
2. The geographic distribution of authority between the central (national) government and lower levels, such as states, provinces, or municipalities
3. Limitations on government authority

We shall discuss these dimensions in order, beginning with the separation of authority between executive and legislative institutions.

SEPARATION OF GOVERNMENT POWERS

The theory of **separation of powers** between different institutions of government has a long and venerable history going back at least to the work of Locke and Montesquieu.[2] Separation of powers, they argued, prevents the injustices that might result from an unchecked executive or legislature. Madison and Hamilton elaborated this theory in *The Federalist*,[3] which described and defended the institutional arrangements proposed by the U.S. Constitutional Convention of 1787.

Political theorists often draw upon the two successful historical cases of representative democracy—Britain and the United States—to create the "classic" separation of powers theory. This theory argues that there are essentially two forms of representative democratic government: the presidential and the parliamentary.

The **democratic presidential regime** provides two separate agencies of government—the executive and the legislative—separately elected and authorized by the people (see Table 6.1, column 3). Each branch is elected for a fixed term, neither branch can unseat the

TABLE 6.1

Distinguishing Features of Parliamentary and Presidential Democracies

Parliamentary and presidential democracies differ in the selection and removal of the chief executive, as well as in the authority to legislate.

Distinguishing Features[a]	Parliamentary Democracies	Presidential Democracies
Title of chief executive	Prime minister (head of government)	President (head of state and government)
Selection of assembly	By citizens in competitive election	By citizens in competitive election
Selection of chief executive	By assembly after election or removal	By citizens in competitive election
Removal of chief executive before fixed term?	By assembly: (No) confidence vote	Fixed terms
Dismissal of assembly before fixed term?	Prime minister may call for early election[b]	Fixed terms
Authority to legislate	Assembly only	Assembly plus president (e.g., veto)
Party relations in assembly and executive	Same parties control both; cohesive party voting	Different party control possible; less cohesive party voting

[a]These define the pure parliamentary and presidential types; as discussed in the text, many constitutional systems, especially in Eastern Europe, "mix" the features of the two types.

[b]Some constitutional systems that are parliamentary in all other ways do not allow for early legislative elections. All parliamentary democracies provide for legislative elections after some maximum time (from three to five years) since the last election.

other by ordinary means, and each has specific powers under the constitution. Ultimate power to authorize legislation and approve budgets in these democracies resides with the legislature, whose relationships with the executive are then critical for concentration or dispersal of power. Different presidential regimes provide their presidents with various powers over government appointments and policymaking. For example, some presidents have the authority to veto legislation or to make policy by executive decree under some conditions.[4] In the United States, both the legislature and executive (Congress and the presidency) have large and significant roles in policymaking. In some other democratic presidential systems, such as Brazil, the president may have such a variety of constitutional powers (including the power to make laws through "emergency" decrees) that he or she can reduce the role of the legislature. But coordination between the separate institutions of executive and legislature must somehow be achieved to make policy.

Parliamentary regimes make the executive and legislative branches much more interdependent (see Table 6.1, column 2). First, only the legislative branch is directly elected. The prime minister and the cabinet (the collective leadership of the executive branch)

emerge from the legislature. The cabinet is chaired by the prime minister, who is the head of government and selects the other cabinet members.[5] Typically, neither branch has a fixed term of office. The cabinet can be voted out of office at any time, and most often this is true of the legislature (the parliament) as well.

The critical feature that makes this possible is the **confidence relationship** between the prime minister and the parliamentary majority. In a parliamentary system, the prime minister and the cabinet must at all times enjoy the confidence of the parliamentary majority. Whenever the parliamentary majority, for whatever reason, votes a lack of confidence, the prime minister and the cabinet members have to resign. At the same time, the prime minister typically has the power to dissolve parliament and call new elections at any time. The parliamentary majority's dismissal power and the prime minister's dissolution power make the two branches mutually interdependent. This structure induces agreement between them by forcing each branch to be acceptable to the other.

Prime ministers in parliamentary democracies lead precarious political lives. Unlike presidents in presidential systems, prime ministers can be voted out of office at any time, and for any reason, by a parliamentary majority. There are two ways this can happen. First, parliament may pass a motion expressing a lack of confidence in the prime minister—a no-confidence motion. This is typically introduced by the parliamentary opposition in the hope of bringing down the prime minister. Second, parliament may defeat a motion expressing confidence in the prime minister—a confidence motion. Confidence motions are normally introduced by prime ministers themselves.

The confidence vote can be a powerful weapon in the hands of the prime minister. It is typically attached to a bill the prime minister favors but the parliamentary majority does not. By attaching a confidence motion to the bill, the prime minister forces the members of parliament to choose between the bill and the fall of the cabinet. This can be a particularly painful choice for dissident members of the prime minister's own party. If they vote for the bill, they may bring down their own government and perhaps immediately have to face the voters, too (see Box 6.1). Therefore, the possibility of a confidence motion partially explains why party discipline tends to be stronger in parliamentary than in presidential systems.

Thus, parliamentary democracies do not experience the form of divided government that is common under presidentialism when the party that controls the presidency does not control the legislature. Instead, the chief executive (prime minister and cabinet) becomes the agent of the parliamentary majority. In most parliamentary systems, the cabinet consists largely of members of parliament. Conflicts between parliament and the executive are less likely to occur, and decision-making tends to be more efficient than under presidentialism. Since the same party (or parties) controls both branches of government, the cabinet tends to dominate policymaking, and the legislature may be less influential than under a presidential constitution.

Not all democracies fit neatly into the presidential or parliamentary category. Some, such as France, are often characterized as mixed, or "**semipresidential**." In these types, the president and the legislature are separately elected (as in presidential systems), but the president also has the power to dissolve the legislature (as in parliamentary systems). In these systems, the president may appoint the cabinet (as under presidentialism), but subject to dismissal by the legislature (as under parliamentarism). A variety of arrangements exist for such shared control. Their consequences are often sharply affected by which party or coalition controls the presidency and legislature. Many of the new constitutions of the emergent democracies of Eastern Europe and Asia are of this mixed type.

Reading across Figure 6.1, we see political systems classified by the separation of policymaking powers between executive and legislative institutions, from concentrated to dispersed. The vertical dimension of the table shows geographic division of power, which is discussed in the next section. In authoritarian governments (on the left of the figure), executive, legislative, and judicial power are typically concentrated. Two of the twelve countries discussed in this book—China

---

The Confidence Vote in Britain   **BOX 6.1**

British prime ministers can resort to the confidence motion in order to bring rebellious party members into line. Usually, the mere threat of a confidence motion is sufficient. But in 1993, Conservative Prime Minister John Major faced a parliamentary crisis over the ratification of the Maastricht Treaty, which expanded the powers of the European Union. Major had only a slim majority in the House of Commons. Many "Euro-skeptics" in his own party were opposed to the Maastricht Treaty. About twenty of these Conservative dissidents voted with the Opposition and helped defeat the Maastricht Treaty in the House of Commons.

Immediately after this embarrassing defeat, however, Major introduced a confidence motion on his Maastricht policy. He announced that if he lost this vote, he would dissolve the House of Commons and hold new elections. Many of the Conservative dissidents feared that their party would do poorly in such an election and that they might personally lose their seats. Major's confidence motion passed by a vote of 339 to 299, and the House of Commons approved the Maastricht Treaty.

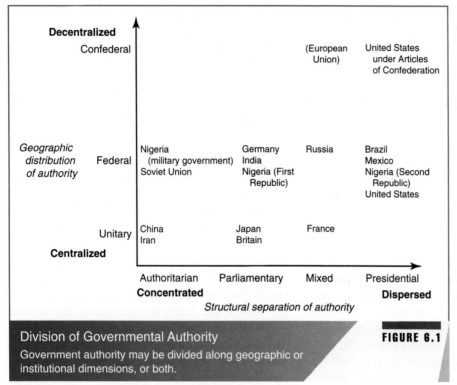

Division of Governmental Authority

Government authority may be divided along geographic or institutional dimensions, or both.

FIGURE 6.1

proportional representation can be quite stable when ideological conflict between the political parties remains moderate. Moreover, dominating parliamentary majorities, as in Northern Ireland until 1998, can sometimes threaten minority groups and intensify conflict.[6] In comparison with both versions of parliamentary government, the U.S. presidential system is often criticized for periodically producing divided government, which could result in stalemate or "gridlock."

The third wave of democratization reopened these parliamentary/presidential debates. Advocates of proportional parliamentarism argue that it provides a consensual framework in which different economic, ethnic, and religious groups can find representation and negotiate their differences. Parliamentary systems also have the flexibility to change governments between elections if the people disapprove of actions of the executive. Since many of the current transitional democracies are deeply divided, a parliamentary, proportional representation system may be particularly suitable. These same experts argue that presidentialism is more susceptible to social conflict and democratic breakdown. Under conditions of divided government, a confrontation between the two legitimately elected institutions representing the people can tear a political system apart. Or, a strong president can use executive powers to repress competition.

Other scholars point out the practical advantages of presidential systems with significant executive power.[7] Even in the domain of the former British empire (such as in Nigeria) and in most of Eastern Europe and the Soviet successor states, the constitutions provide for powerful presidents. Presidential regimes have dominated Latin America for more than a century. A 1993 referendum in Brazil reaffirmed its commitment to presidentialism. Presidentialism also

and Iran—have authoritarian governments not chosen in competitive elections. Britain, Germany, Japan, and India are parliamentary systems in which executive and legislative powers are concentrated in cabinets responsible to the popularly elected lower houses of parliament. At the extreme right of Figure 6.1 are pure presidential systems, such as Brazil, Mexico, and the United States. Nigeria seems to be in transition to a presidential democracy. In between are mixed systems, such as France and Russia, although the latter has become increasingly authoritarian (see Chapter 12).

In the debate over the best system of representative democracy, many political theorists traditionally favored the British-style parliamentary system. This version of parliamentarism—coupling plurality voting rules that usually create clear single-party majorities in parliament with a cabinet and prime minister responsible to parliament—can result in fairly stable governments responsible to the public will. Parliamentarism coupled with proportional representation—as in Germany and France between the two world wars—seemed more crisis-prone. Such crises occurred because large extremist political parties emerged and produced cabinet instability and even breakdown. However, the Scandinavian countries demonstrate that parliamentary systems with offers the citizens a more direct choice of chief executive, and it puts more effective checks on the power of the majority in the legislature.

GEOGRAPHIC DISTRIBUTION OF GOVERNMENT POWER

Another distinction between governmental structures is the geographic division of power: confederal systems at one extreme, unitary systems at the other extreme, and **federal systems** in the middle (see the vertical dimension of Figure 6.1.). The United States under the Articles of Confederation was confederal. Ultimate power rested with the states. The central government had authority over foreign affairs and defense but depended on financial and other support from the states. Under the Constitution of 1787, the U.S. government changed from confederal to federal, which is to say that both central and state governments had separate spheres of authority and the means to implement their power. Today, the United States, Germany, Russia, India, Nigeria, Mexico, and Brazil are federal systems in which central and local units each have autonomy in certain public policy spheres. Britain, France, China, Japan, and Iran are unitary systems with power and authority concentrated in the central government. Regional and local units have only limited powers specifically delegated to them by the central government, which may change or withdraw these powers at will.

Most of the world's states are unitary. In fact, only eighteen states are federal, or fewer than one in ten. Although the federal states are relatively few in number, they tend to be large and politically important. Thus, federal states account for more than one-third of the world's population and 41 percent of its land area. In general, the larger and the more diverse a state is, the more likely it is to be federal.

Analysts attribute several advantages to federalism. In culturally divided societies, it may help protect ethnic, linguistic, or religious minorities, particularly if they are geographically concentrated. It may serve as a check on overly ambitious rulers and thus protect markets and citizen freedoms. Moreover, federalism may allow subunits (such as states) to experiment with different policies. Governments may thus learn from the experiences of others. In addition, citizens may be free to "vote with their feet" and choose the policy environment that best fits their preferences.

While federalism promotes choice and diversity, it does so at the expense of equality. Federalism allows local governments to pursue different policies. One implication is that citizens may get different treatments and benefits from different local governments. Unitary governments may also be in a better position to redistribute resources from richer regions to poorer regions, if that is desirable.

In comparing confederal, federal, and unitary systems, we must distinguish between formal and actual distributions of power. In unitary systems, in spite of the formal concentration of authority at the center, regional and local units may acquire power that the central government rarely challenges. In federal systems, centralized party control may overcome apparent regional autonomy. Thus, the real differences between federal and unitary systems may be considerably less significant than their formal arrangements suggest.

Mexico is an example of the discrepancy between formal and actual federalism. Until recently, the PRI had centralized, authoritarian control in this formally federal system. Recent democratization in Mexico, with formerly opposition parties winning the presidency and many state governments, has produced some "real" federalism to go along with the formalities (see Chapter 14).

LIMITATIONS ON GOVERNMENT POWER

Unlike authoritarian regimes, democracies are characterized by some legal or customary limitation on the exercise of power. Systems in which the powers of government units are defined and limited by a written constitution, statutes, and custom are called **constitutional regimes**. Civil rights—such as the right to a fair trial and freedom to speak, petition, publish, and assemble—are protected against government interference except under specified circumstances.

The courts are crucial to the limitations on governmental power. As illustrated in Table 6.2, governments may be divided into those at one extreme in which the power to coerce citizens is relatively unlimited by the courts, and those at the other extreme in which the courts protect the rights of citizens and ensure that other parts of the government exercise their powers properly. The United States, Germany, and India are systems in which high courts rule on challenges that other units of government have

TABLE 6.2

Judicial Limitation of Governmental Authority

The power of judicial review of legislation is found in about half of the world's democracies, but it varies in effectiveness.

Unlimited		Limited
Nonindependent Courts	Independent Courts	Judicial Review
China	Britain	United States
Iran		India
Nigeria		Germany
		France
		Brazil
		Japan
		Russia

exceeded the powers allocated by the constitution. This practice of **judicial review** is authorized to various degrees in about half of the world's democracies. But judicial review is often weakened by lack of independence of the appointment or tenure of judges or by their ineffectiveness in overcoming executive power.

Some other constitutional regimes have independent courts that protect persons against the improper implementation of laws and regulations, but cannot legally overrule the assembly or the political executive. The citizens' substantive rights in these systems are protected by statute, custom, self-restraint, and political pressure—which are also essential to the effectiveness of courts even where judicial review is authorized. In authoritarian systems, policymakers do not usually allow courts to constrain their use and abuse of power, even where brave judges attempt to rule against them.[8]

Arend Lijphart characterizes only four of the thirty-six democratic systems he examines as having "strong" judicial review: Germany, India, the United States, and Canada after 1982.[9] The Supreme Court of India is most similar to the U.S. Supreme Court, having successfully declared many national laws and ordinances to be unconstitutional (see Chapter 17). The German Constitutional Court also significantly influences national and state policymaking through its rulings and through government's anticipation of those rulings.[10]

About a quarter of Lijphart's democracies had either strong or medium-strength judicial review. In France, Germany, and Brazil, new legislation may be

challenged in court by opposition members of parliament even before it takes effect, a process called "abstract" judicial review. Lijphart classified a little over half of his democracies as having "weak judicial review," with the powers of courts constrained by very limited constitutional authority (as in Sweden) or limited independence of government-appointed judges (as in Japan). In the remaining democracies, courts enjoyed no power of judicial review of legislation, although they may still protect individuals from government abuse not specifically authorized by law (see again Table 6.2).[11]

Many of the new democracies of Eastern Europe proclaimed judicial review in their constitutions, but it has proved harder to implement in practice. There have been striking successes in constraining governments in some countries, but failures in others.

In Nigeria, the courts long retained a striking degree of judicial independence under a succession of otherwise undemocratic military regimes. However, the courts were shown little respect under the Abacha regime of the mid-1990s, which established special military tribunals to prosecute its perceived enemies.

China, in contrast, after explicit rejection of any limits on "mass justice" from the late 1950s to the 1970s, has gradually attempted to introduce a very limited "rule by law." One recent reason is Chinese participation in the global economic system, which requires a legal basis for trade and investment. Chinese rulers see this as a way to encourage stability and economic growth and control corruption. However, the practice falls far short of the promise of limitation on governmental authority (see Chapter 13).

All written constitutions provide for amending procedures. Most framers of constitutions recognize that basic decision rules must be adaptable, because of potential ambiguities, inefficiencies, changes in citizen values, or unforeseen circumstances. If amendments are too easy to make, they may jeopardize important constitutional protections. Therefore, many constitutions provide that certain arrangements may not be amended (for example, the provision in the U.S. Constitution granting each state equal representation in the Senate).

Amending procedures vary widely, ranging from the complex to the simple. Perhaps the simplest case is that of the United Kingdom, where an ordinary parliamentary statute may alter the constitution. In some cases, constitutional amendments must be approved by a popular vote. The U.S. Constitution has the most difficult formal procedure.

In summary, constitutions may concentrate or disperse government power along several dimensions.[12] There are necessary trade-offs involved in making such constitutional choices. Probably no one who favors democracy and individual liberties would argue for extreme centralization of power in an omnipotent dictator, as in Thomas Hobbes's *Leviathan* (see Chapter 1). However, constitutional democracies that concentrate power to a somewhat lesser degree, such as the British system, have some important advantages. Their governments tend to be effective and efficient, and by relying on majority rule, they tend to treat all citizens equally. No small group can hold up a decision favored by a solid majority. In contrast, constitutions that disperse power, like more inclusive decision rules, have their own advantages. They are more likely to check potential abuses of power, such as the tyranny of a majority, and policies will tend to be stabler over time.

CHECKING THE TOP POLICYMAKERS

One challenge of government is to control the excesses of top political leaders. In many authoritarian systems, there is no legal and institutionalized way to remove the top political leaders if they become unpopular or overstep whatever bounds they may face. Moreover, authoritarian leaders can usually change or simply ignore the formal constitution when it restricts their desires. Democracies have various procedures for keeping the leaders in check, but the procedures vary among the types of systems. In parliamentary systems, chief executives can be removed virtually at any time through a vote of no confidence if they lose the support of a parliamentary majority. In Germany, for example, Social Democratic Party Chancellor Helmut Schmidt was ousted by Helmut Kohl of the Christian Democratic Party in October 1982.

Democratic presidential systems fall somewhere in between. Unlike prime ministers under parliamentary constitutions, presidents have fixed terms of office. Most presidential systems provide for the removal of presidents, but typically only if they are guilty of serious criminal or other wrongdoing. This procedure is called **impeachment**. Impeachment typically involves three components: (1) impeachable offenses are usually identified as presenting unusual danger to the public good or safety; (2) the penalty is removal from office (sometimes with separate criminal penalties); and (3)

impeachment cases are decided by the legislature but require more than ordinary majorities and may involve the judiciary in some way. The positive value of impeachment is that it provides a way of legally mobilizing political power against a threat to the constitutional or legal order. At the same time, the danger is that it can be used for mere partisan or personal goals.

In the U.S. system, impeachment procedures can be used against the incumbents in top offices, even the president (as in the cases of Presidents Nixon and Clinton), if their activities stray too far beyond legal bounds. No U.S. president has yet been convicted by the Senate and removed from office, although that fate has befallen other federal officials, such as judges.

Impeachment is associated with constitutions having powerful presidencies with fixed terms of office, such as those in the United States, Brazil, South Korea, and the Philippines (see Box 6.2). Impeachment rules have also been adopted in the constitutions of semipresidential regimes, such as Russia, and even in purely parliamentary regimes.

In the long run, the ultimate control of democratic order is periodic and competitive elections. This need to achieve and regularly renew their popular mandates is the fundamental device that leads politicians to respond to the needs and demands of citizens. It is deeply imperfect. It may be difficult to tell when elected officials are incompetent, deceitful, or just unlucky. The complexities of policymaking may baffle the attempt of even trained observers to assign responsibility for successes or failures. The multiplicity of political issues may leave citizens torn between their candidate choices. Or, none of the choices may seem very palatable. Yet, deeply imperfect as it is, this remarkable recruitment structure gives every citizen some influence on the policymaking process. For this reason, we consider the competitive election to be the most significant democratic structure.

ASSEMBLIES

Legislative **assemblies** have existed for thousands of years. Ancient Greece and Rome had them, for example. Indeed, the Roman Senate has given its name to modern assemblies in the United States and many other countries.

Almost all contemporary political systems have assemblies, variously called *senates*, *chambers*, *diets*, *houses*, and the like. Assemblies are also known as

BOX 6.2

Impeachment in Latin America

Brazil, Mexico, and many other Latin American nations with strong presidents have impeachment rules and traditions. Many are modeled on the U.S. Constitution. In Mexico, the president, the state governors, and federal judges are subject to impeachment. Brazil has an impeachment process similar to that of the United States, except that it takes a two-thirds vote in the lower house of the assembly to charge the president and other high civil officers with impeachable offenses.

A two-thirds vote is also required in the Senate to convict. The clause was invoked in 1992, when Brazil's president, Fernando Collor, was impeached on charges of large-scale corruption. He resigned before trial in the Senate. Impeachment procedures also forced presidents from office in Venezuela in 1993 and Paraguay in 1999. A slightly different procedure was used by the Congress in 1997 to declare the incumbent president of Ecuador mentally unfit.

Source: Anibal Perez-Linan, *Presidential Impeachment and the New Political Instability in Latin America* (New York: Cambridge University Press, 2007).

"legislatures" (regardless of what role they actually play in legislating) or as "parliaments" (mainly in parliamentary systems). Their formal approval is usually required for major public policies. They are generally elected by popular vote, and hence are at least formally accountable to the citizenry. Today, 186 countries have such governmental bodies. The almost universal adoption of legislative assemblies suggests that in the modern world, a legitimate government must formally include a representative popular component.

Assembly Structure

Assemblies vary in their size—from less than 100 to more than 1,000 members—and their organization. They may consist of one chamber (in which case they are called *unicameral*) or two chambers (*bicameral*). Most democracies, and some authoritarian systems, have bicameral (two-chamber) assemblies. Federal systems normally provide simultaneously for two forms of representation; often, representation in one chamber is based on population and representation in the second chamber is based on geographic units. Even in unitary systems (such as France or Japan), **bicameralism** is common, but the purpose of the second chamber is to provide a check on policymaking rather than to represent subnational units. The bicameral German parliament grew out of both federalism and the desire to separate the power of the federal government.

In most bicameral systems, one chamber is dominant, and the second (such as the Russian Council of the Federation or the French Senate) has more limited

powers that are often designed to protect regional interests. While representatives in the dominant chamber are popularly elected, those in the second chamber are sometimes chosen by the regional governments (as in Germany) or in other indirect ways. The prime minister in most parliamentary systems is responsible only to the more popularly elected chamber, which therefore has a more important position in policy-making than the second chamber. (See the discussion of the vote-of-confidence procedure earlier in this chapter and in Box 6.1.).

Assemblies also differ in their internal organization in ways that have major consequences for policymaking. There are two kinds of internal legislative organization: party groups and formal assembly subunits (presiding officers, committees, and the like). There is often an inverse relationship between the strength of parties and the strength of other subunits (such as committees): The stronger the parties are, the weaker the committees are, and vice versa. As in most parliamentary systems, British members of Parliament vote strictly along party lines much more consistently than members of the U.S. Congress. Because cabinets generally hold office only as long as they can command a parliamentary majority, deviating from the party line means risking the fall of the government and new elections.

In presidential systems, the president and the legislators are independently elected for fixed terms of office. Thus the fate of the executive is less directly tied up with voting on legislative measures. Moreover, the president and the legislative party leadership may offer conflicting messages to the president's party, leading to party divisions. For both reasons, party voting is less cohesive in presidential systems, depending also on whether the election rules foster competition within the parties.[13]

All assemblies have a committee structure—some organized arrangement that permits legislators to divide their labor and to specialize in particular issue areas. Without such committees, it would be impossible to handle the large flow of legislative business. However, the importance of committees varies.[14] In some legislatures—such as those in the United States, Japan, and Germany—committees are very influential. This is partially because they are highly specialized, have jurisdictions that match those of the executive departments, and have numerous staff resources. Strong committees tend to have a clear legislative division of labor that matches the executive branch, allowing for specialized oversight of executive activity. They are often arenas in which the opposition can be influential. British committees, by comparison, are much weaker since they have small staffs, are dominated by the governing party, and get appointed for one bill at a time. Hence, they cannot accumulate expertise in a particular policy area.

Assembly Functions

Assembly members deliberate, debate, and vote on policies that come before them. Most important policies and rules must be considered and at least formally approved by these bodies before they have the force of law. Assemblies typically also control public-spending decisions; budgeting is one of their major functions. In addition, some assemblies have important appointment powers, and some may serve as a court of appeals. Although laws typically need assembly approval, in most countries, legislation is actually formulated elsewhere, usually by the political executive and the upper levels of the bureaucracy.

When we compare the importance of assemblies as policymaking agencies, the U.S. Congress, which plays a very active role in the formulation and enactment of legislation, is at one extreme. The other extreme is represented by the National People's Congress of the People's Republic of China, which meets infrequently and does little more than listen to statements by party leaders and rubber-stamp decisions made elsewhere. Roughly midway between the two is the House of Commons in Britain. There, legislative proposals are sometimes initiated or modified by ordinary members of Parliament, but public policy is usually initiated and proposed by members of the Cabinet (who are, to be sure, chosen from the members of the parliamentary body). The typical assembly provides a deliberating forum, formally enacts legislation, and sometimes amends it.

Assemblies should not be viewed only as legislative bodies. All assemblies in democratic systems have an important relationship to legislation, but not necessarily a dominant role. Their political importance is based not just on this function but also on the great variety of other political functions they perform. Assemblies can play a major role in elite recruitment, especially in parliamentary systems, where prime ministers and cabinet members typically serve their apprenticeships in parliament. Legislative committee hearings and floor debates may be important sites for interest articulation and interest aggregation, especially if there is no cohesive majority party. Debates in assemblies can be a source of public information about politics and thus contribute to the socialization of citizens generally and elites in particular.

Representation: Mirroring and Representational Biases

Contemporary legislatures, especially in democratic systems, are valued particularly because they represent the citizens in the policymaking process. It is not obvious, however, what the ideal linkage between citizens and government officials should be. Some argue that government officials should mirror the characteristics of the citizens as far as possible. This principle, also known as *descriptive representation*, is held to be particularly important with respect to potentially conflictual divisions (such as race, class, ethnicity, gender, language, and perhaps age).

However, descriptive representation is not the only concern in recruiting public officials. The limits of mirroring were inadvertently expressed by a U.S. senator. In defending a U.S. Supreme Court nominee who was accused of mediocrity, the senator lamely contended, "[E]ven if he were mediocre, there are a lot of mediocre judges and people and lawyers. They are entitled to a little representation, aren't they?"[15] Most people would probably not agree that government officials should mirror the general population in their abilities to do their jobs. Instead, we generally want political elites to be the best possible *agents* for their constituents. In this view, government officials should be selected for their ability to serve the interests of the citizens, whether they share the voters' background characteristics or do not.

For politicians to be good agents, they need to have similar *preferences* to the citizens they represent *and* they need the appropriate *skills* to do their jobs. In democracies, political parties and elections are the most important mechanisms by which the preferences of citizens and the preferences (or at least commitments) of leaders are aligned.[16] As far as skills are concerned, political and governmental leadership—particularly in modern, technologically advanced societies—requires knowledge and skills that are hard to acquire except through education and training. Natural intelligence or experience may, to a limited degree, take the place of formal education.

Hence, it might be a good thing for government officials to be better informed, more intelligent, more experienced, and perhaps better educated than the people who they serve. Just as medical patients tend to look for the most capable physician rather than the one who is most like them, one could argue that citizens should look for the best qualified officeholder. In this view, selecting government officials, including representative policymakers, is like delegating to experts. It may be a hopeful sign that citizens in many modern democracies are increasingly willing to select leaders who do not share their background characteristics.

As in the case of so many other political choices, there is no obvious or perfect way to choose between mirroring and expert delegation. This is an old debate, and in many situations, it is necessary to make a trade-off between the two. Different offices may require different considerations. Most people would, for example, probably put a higher emphasis on mirroring in their local assembly than in a regulatory agency overseeing nuclear technology.

The bad news is that political elites, even democratically elected members of legislatures, hardly ever mirror the citizens they represent on any of the standard social characteristics. Even in democracies such as Britain and France, political leaders tend to be of higher social status, unusually well-educated, or upwardly mobile individuals from the lower classes. There are exceptions. In some countries, trade unions or leftist political parties may serve as channels of

political advancement for people with modest economic or educational backgrounds. These representatives acquire political skills and experience by holding offices in working-class organizations. During the long domination of the executive by the Norwegian Labor Party (1935–1981), none of its prime ministers had even completed secondary school. But these are rare and vanishing examples. In most contemporary states, the number of working-class people in high office is small and declining.

Women have traditionally been poorly represented in political leadership positions in most countries. However, the situation has changed significantly in the last thirty years. In 1980, women held about 10 percent of the parliamentary seats around the world. By 2010, that figure had nearly doubled, to 19 percent. Women have also held the chief executive office in a growing number of countries (see Box 6.3). Angela Merkel, for example, became chancellor of Germany in 2005 and was reelected in 2009.

But women's advancement has been uneven.[17] In many Northern European countries, such as Sweden, women by 2010 accounted for 40 percent or more of the legislators and a similar proportion of cabinet members. In Germany, Mexico, Britain, and China, women held over 20 percent of the legislative seats. But in Brazil and Nigeria, women still accounted for fewer than 10 percent. The proportion in Iran was only 3 percent.

Political elites also tend to be unrepresentative with respect to age. In many countries, legislators (much less chief executives) under age 40 are a rarity, whereas a large proportion of leading politicians are past normal retirement age. In many countries, university graduates—and often lawyers and civil servants in particular—are vastly overrepresented, whereas ethnic, linguistic, and religious minorities are often underrepresented. Representational biases are thus numerous and pervasive. And while women's representation is increasing, class biases are getting worse.

POLITICAL EXECUTIVES

In modern states, the executive branch is by far the largest, the most complex, and typically the most powerful branch of government. It is not easy to describe executives in simple ways, but it is sensible to start at the top. Governments typically have one or two **chief executives**, officials who sit at the very top of the often

Women as Chief Executives

BOX 6.3

From about 1970 on, women have gained chief executive office in a growing number of countries. Interestingly, many of the early leaders were from Asian and Middle Eastern countries, where women's roles in public life traditionally have been limited. Sinmavo Bandaranaike of Sri Lanka (1960–1965 and 1970–1977), Indira Gandhi of India (1966–1977 and 1980–1984), and Golda Meir of Israel (1969–1974) were among the pioneers. In the 1980s and 1990s, women also came to power in the Philippines, Pakistan, Bangladesh, and again in Sri Lanka. In Burma, Nobel Peace Prize winner Aung San Suu Kyi won the elections of 1990, but the military prevented her from taking office.

Women have recently made inroads in leadership positions in Europe and the Americas, though they are still few and far between in Africa. The first female leader in a major European country was Prime Minister Margaret Thatcher of Britain (1979–1990).

Her strong and decisive leadership made her one of Europe's most influential politicians in the 1980s. Women have come to power in other Western countries as well. Angela Merkel is now chancellor of Germany. In Norway, Gro Harlem Brundtland held the prime ministership for a total of about ten years between 1981 and 1996. In Latin America, female presidents have recently come to office in Argentina, Chile, and Costa Rica.

The career paths of Asian women leaders have tended to differ from those elsewhere. Many of the former have come from prominent political families, such as the Gandhi family in India and the Bhuttos in Pakistan. In several cases, they have been the widows or daughters of important political leaders. In Europe and Latin America, women leaders are more likely to have made independent political careers, and they can rely on stronger women's interest groups.

---

colossal executive branch. Such executives have various names, titles, duties, and powers. They are called *presidents*, *prime ministers*, *chancellors*, *secretaries general*, or even *leader* (in Iran). There are even a few kings who still have genuine power. Titles may mislead us as to what functions these officials perform, but they tend to be the main formulators and executors of public policy.

Structure of the Chief Executive

Democratic governments typically have either a single chief executive (in presidential systems) or a split chief executive of two offices: a largely ceremonial head of state (who represents the nation on formal occasions) and a more powerful head of government (who determines public policies). Table 6.3 distinguishes among executives according to the bases of their power to affect policymaking. In the left column, we see the chief executives in authoritarian systems, whose power ultimately rests on coercion. The middle and right columns show the chief executives in democratic countries. The middle column shows executives whose power rests primarily on their partisan influence in the legislature, which is the case of the prime ministers in

most parliamentary systems. The right column includes chief executives whose ability to influence legislation resides in powers directly granted them by the constitution, rather than partisan connection alone. Strong presidents may be able to veto legislation, for example, issue legal decrees, or introduce the budget. They usually have the power to appoint and dismiss members of the cabinet.

Reading down the table, we see the distinction between executives with effective power over policy, purely ceremonial roles, or both effective and ceremonial power. Political executives are effective only if they have genuine discretion in the enactment and implementation of laws and regulations, in budgetary matters, or in important government appointments. Where they do not have these powers, they are symbolic or ceremonial. In presidential systems, the ceremonial and effective roles are almost always held by the same person, the president, as we see in both authoritarian and democratic systems at the bottom of Table 6.3. In parliamentary democratic systems, and in some authoritarian systems, the two roles are separated between the "head of state," who is primarily a ceremonial official, and a "head of government," who makes and implements the decisions. The British, German,

	TABLE 6.3

Bases of Legislative Power of Chief Executives

Chief executives vary in the effectiveness and in the bases of their legislative powers.

Authoritarian	Democratic: Partisan Influence	Democratic: Constitutional Powers
	Effective	
General Secretary, China	British Prime Minister	
	French Prime Minister	
	German Chancellor	
	Indian Prime Minister	
	Japanese Prime Minister	
	(Russian Prime Minister)	
	Ceremonial	
Chinese President		British Queen or King
		German President
		Indian President
		Japanese Emperor
	Ceremonial and Effective	
Iranian Leader	French President	Brazilian President
		Mexican President
		Nigerian President
		Russian President
		U.S. President

Indian, and Japanese prime ministers appear in the second column at the top of the table, while their ceremonial counterparts appear at the center right.

These distinctions are not absolute. Some constitutions, such as the German constitution, give substantial formal powers to their prime ministers. At the same time, even largely ceremonial presidents can exert important influence if the parties are divided or by exercising special constitutional powers (or both, as has happened in India in the 1990s). Moreover, partisan influence in the legislature is useful even to the strongest democratic presidents. Still, it is usually easy to determine the primary sources of legislative power, even where the formal names may be misleading.

A few countries have both significant presidents and prime ministers. The balance of power between them depends on the constitutional powers of the president and on the partisan division in the legislature. In Russia, the constitutional powers of veto and decree of the president are very great, and expanded under recent authoritarian trends. Until recently, the prime minister has been mostly just another administrator, with little effective power. In France, however, the president's formal powers are much weaker; when the legislature is unified under opposition parties, it has elected a prime minister who has effectively dominated policymaking, greatly reducing the president's political influence.

In China, the chairman of the Communist Party is the most powerful political figure and the effective chief executive. The Chinese president is the head of state, which is a purely ceremonial role, without associated powers. However, in recent years, the same individual has held both offices, and also a key role as chairman of the party military commission. A separate premier, or head of government, is a largely administrative position.

Monarchies are much rarer at the beginning of the twenty-first century than they were at the beginning of the twentieth. Some monarchs, such as the king of Saudi Arabia and some other Arab monarchs, still exercise real power. Most contemporary monarchs,

Chief Executives

Chief executives, including the new U.S. president Barack Obama, and the German chancellor Angela Merkel, attend an April 2009 NATO summit with their defense ministers, foreign ministers, and NATO officials in Strasbourg, France.

Action Press-Pool/Getty Images

however, have little or no actual political influence. Monarchs like the British or Scandinavian royal families hold principally ceremonial and symbolic positions with limited political powers. They are living symbols of the state and nation and of their historical continuity. Britain's queen may bestow honors or appointments to the nobility with a stroke of her sword, but these are recommended by the prime minister. The Japanese monarchy has also traditionally been dignified and exalted, and played an important role as a national symbol. In contrast, the Scandinavian monarchies are more humdrum. Because members of these royal families occasionally use humbler means of transportation, these dynasties are sometimes called "bicycle monarchies." In republican democracies with parliamentary systems, presidents perform the functions that fall to kings and queens in parliamentary monarchies. Thus, German presidents give speeches on important anniversaries and designate prime ministers after elections or when a government has resigned.

A system that separates the ceremonial executive from the effective executive has a number of advantages. The ceremonial executive symbolizes unity and continuity and can be above politics. The U.S. presidency, which combines both effective and ceremonial functions, runs the risk that the president will use his ceremonial and symbolic authority to enhance his political power or that his involvement in politics may make him a less effective symbolic or unifying figure.

Recruitment of Chief Executives

Historically, finding effective and legitimate ways to select the individuals to fill the top policymaking roles has been critical to political order and stability. "Recruitment structures" are the means by which nations choose their top policymakers and executives. Table 6.4 shows the recruitment structures in the countries discussed in this book.

A major accomplishment of stable democracies is regulating the potential conflict involved in leadership succession and confining it to the mobilization of votes instead of weapons. The most familiar structures are the presidential and parliamentary forms of competitive party systems. In presidential systems, parties select candidates for nomination, and the electorate chooses among them. Russia and France have directly elected presidents but also give an important role to the prime minister, who is appointed by the president but can be removed by the legislature.

Mexico appears similar to other presidential systems. But for half a century, the PRI had such control over the electoral process that the voters merely ratified the party's presidential nominee. Until the remarkable July 2000 election, many voters remained skeptical that a non-PRI president could really come to power. As the table shows, Mexico now has a democratic presidential system, with parties nominating candidates and voters genuinely choosing among them, as in the very close election of 2006.

Bicycle Royalty

Crown Princess Victoria, heir to the Swedish throne, illustrates why the Scandinavian and Low Country monarchies are commonly referred to as "bicycle monarchies."

Jonas Esktrmer/Scanpix Sweden/Sipa Press

In both presidential and parliamentary democracies, the tenure of the chief executive is limited, directly or indirectly. In the presidential system, this is usually directly, through fixed terms of office for the chief executive. In the parliamentary system, there is a maximum term for the parliament, which then indirectly also limits the life of the cabinet, since the prime minister is accountable to the new parliamentary majority and can be removed by it.

Table 6.4 also illustrates the role of the noncompetitive party and the military organizations in China, the military in Nigeria, and nonelected religious elites in Iran. The important role played by political parties illustrates the great need to mobilize broad political support behind the selection of chief executives. The frequent appearance of parties also reflects, no doubt, the modern legitimacy of popular sovereignty: the promise that the rulers' actions will be in the interest of the ruled.

Authoritarian systems rarely have effective procedures for leadership succession. The more power is concentrated at the top, the riskier it is to transfer it from one person to the next. Very often, authoritarian leaders do not dare to relinquish their power, and leadership succession occurs only when they die or are overthrown. In communist regimes, the Communist Party selects the general secretary (or equivalent), who is the controlling executive force. Individual succession is not a simple matter. These systems do not limit the terms of incumbents, who are difficult to oust once they have consolidated their supporters into key party positions. Nonetheless, they always have to be aware of the possibility of a party coup of the type that ousted Nikita Khrushchev from the Soviet leadership in 1964. As a system, however, the Soviet leadership structure seemed quite stable until the dramatic 1991 coup attempt against Mikhail Gorbachev. Although he was briefly restored to power, the events surrounding the coup stripped the Soviet presidency of power, and legitimacy passed to the presidencies and legislatures of the fifteen constituent republics. Russia managed its first democratic transition surprisingly smoothly, from Boris Yeltsin to his chosen successor, Vladimir Putin, who was elected president in 2000. Putin arranged a less democratic transition in 2008, when Dmitrii Medvedev was elected president in an unfree election (see Chapter 12).

The poorer nations show substantially less stability, and the regimes usually have had less experience at surviving succession crises.[18] Nigeria experienced a succession of military coups and governments from 1966 until 1979, and then introduced a competitive presidential system, which was overthrown by a military coup shortly after its second election in 1983. The military government again moved toward civilian rule in the early 1990s, but then annulled the 1993 presidential election before the results were announced. The military rulers finally allowed a return to civilian rule in 1999, but the system has seemed fragile.

Military governments, stable or unstable, have also been common in Latin America and the Middle East, although they are now more likely to work with other groups or from behind the scenes (see Chapter 5). The Chinese Communist Party has remained in power for fifty years but has suffered several periods of internal strife, and the army has been involved in recruitment at all levels. India's democracy has been an exception to the rule among poorer nations. It has had

	TABLE 6.4

Recruitment of Chief Executive
Political parties of various kinds are involved in the recruitment of most chief executives.

Country	Chief Executive Structure	Recruitment Structures	How Often Has This Type of Government Survived Succession?[b]
Brazil	President	Party and voters	Often
Britain	Prime minister	Party, House of Commons, voters	Very often
China	Party secretary[a]	Party and military	Often
France	President/Prime minister	Party, (Assembly) voters	Often
Germany	Chancellor	Party, Bundestag, voters	Often
India	Prime minister	Party, Lok Sabha, voters	Often (one interruption)
Iran	Leader	Religious elites	Once
Japan	Prime minister	Party, Diet, voters	Often
Mexico	President	Party and voters	Twice
Nigeria	President	Military, party, voters	Twice
Russia	President	Party, president, voters	Twice
United States	President	Party and voters	Very often

[a]"Party secretary" refers to that position or to a similar one as head of party in a communist regime.
[b]"Often" means that at least three successions have taken place under that type of government.

a number of democratic successions with a single interruption (authoritarian emergency rule that postponed elections for several years) in the 1970s.

The Cabinet

In many political systems, the **cabinet** is the most important collective decision-making body. Its power can be particularly great in parliamentary systems, where its formation is closely linked to selection of the prime minister. It typically contains the leaders (often called "ministers") of all the major departments (sometimes called "ministries") of the executive branch. The cabinet meets frequently, often several times per week. It is typically led by the head of government: the president in presidential systems and the prime minister in parliamentary ones. In some parliamentary systems, the entire cabinet is collectively responsible to the legislature. The prime minister may be little more than "first among equals," especially under conditions of multiparty coalition governments. In other parliamentary systems, such as Germany, the constitution confers much more authority on the chief executive.[19]

How is the cabinet selected? In presidential systems, selecting cabinet members is typically a presidential prerogative, though sometimes (as with the U.S. Senate), the legislature has approval. The president can typically also dismiss cabinet members at will, whereas the legislature's ability to do so is most often severely limited.

In parliamentary systems, the process is very different, since the prime minister and the cabinet need to maintain the confidence of the parliamentary majority. Therefore, cabinet formation depends on the result of parliamentary elections and on the composition of parliament. If a competitive party wins a parliamentary majority by itself, it will (if unified) be able to form a cabinet of its own members and can then pass and implement its policies. Sometimes the election directly determines who controls the majority. This is always the case in pure two-party systems, where one party always has a parliamentary majority. It can also happen in multiparty systems, whenever one party gets more seats than all its competitors combined. The election laws play an important part in shaping legislative representation of the parties. The more parties there are, the less likely it is that one of them will have a majority on its own. When one party controls a parliamentary majority, the party almost always forms a *majority single-party cabinet* by itself.

In most multiparty countries, the typical election result is that no party has a parliamentary majority by itself. Most commonly under such circumstances, several parties (two, three, or more) join forces and form a *coalition cabinet* in which they are all represented. Sometimes, parties anticipate this need to form coalitions before the election. They may make a formal agreement

Pre-election Coalition in India

The government of India is headed by the United Progressive Alliance (UPA), a coalition formed by parties before the parliamentary election. The coalition is led by the Indian National Congress, whose president, Sonia Gandhi (shown here in the center of the photo, meeting with heads of other coalition partner parties), serves as the chairperson of the UPA.

Prakash Singh/AFP/Getty Images

with one another and inform the voters that they intend to govern together if they collectively get enough votes. The allied parties may thus encourage their voters to support the coalition partners' candidates where their own party's candidates seem weak and often take advantage of special provisions of voting laws. Many German and French governments have come to power in this fashion. (See the discussion of the German election of 2009 and the new CDU/FDP coalition in Chapter 10.) In such cases, the voters can have a direct voice in the choice of the future cabinet, much as they do in two-party systems. Voters are thus given a major role in choosing the direction of government policy.

If no party or preelection coalition wins control of the legislature through the election, parties may bargain after the election, or between elections, to form a new cabinet. In the Netherlands, such bargaining took four months after the 2003 election. However, only a few days were needed to form a coalition government of the Conservatives and Liberal Democrats after the British election in 2010 (see Chapter 8).

Whether bargaining takes place before or after the elections, the parties in parliamentary systems typically have many options concerning the composition of the cabinet. In some cases, a single party decides that it can form a minority cabinet alone, often because the other parties disagree too much among themselves to offer any alternative. Figure 6.2 illustrates these various possibilities. With a minority government, the parties in the cabinet must continually bargain with other parties to get policies adopted and even to remain in office. In majority coalitions, bargaining occurs primarily among coalition partners represented in the cabinet. In both of these circumstances, the power of the prime minister may depend on the bargains he or she can strike with leaders of other parties.

These complications illustrate two of the problems of combining parliamentary government with electoral systems of proportional representation. Such systems do not produce a single majority party, which does not give the voters a very clear choice about who will control the executive branch. Instead, the parties may determine this behind closed doors after the election. Sometimes, the results are paradoxical, as when parties that have just lost votes in the elections are able to negotiate their way into a governing coalition. The second problem is that multiparty cabinets are sometimes unstable. Italy, for example, has had on average more than one change of government per year since World War II. Yet such problems need not always emerge. In Germany, cabinets have been quite stable, and the voters have generally been given fairly clear options ahead of elections.

Functions of the Chief Executive

Typically, the chief executive is the most important structure in policymaking. The executive normally initiates new policies. Depending on the division of powers with the legislature and the partisan balance, the executive also has a substantial part in their adoption. In presidential systems, the president very often has veto powers. Thus the chief executive typically has both the first and the last word in policymaking. In parliamentary systems, on the other hand, the chief executive is less likely to be able to exercise a veto.

The political executive also oversees policy implementation and can hold subordinate officials accountable for their performance. The central decisions in a foreign policy crisis are generally made by the chief

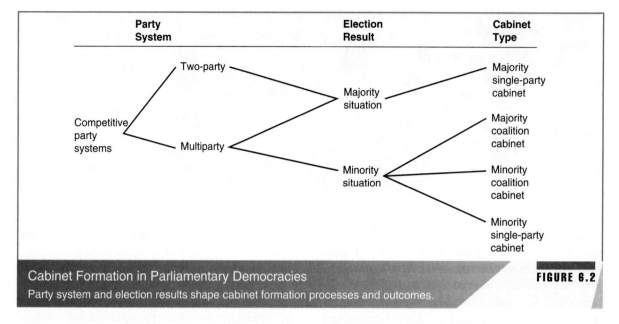

Party System	Election Result	Cabinet Type

Competitive party systems
- Two-party
- Multiparty

Majority situation
Minority situation

- Majority single-party cabinet
- Majority coalition cabinet
- Minority coalition cabinet
- Minority single-party cabinet

Cabinet Formation in Parliamentary Democracies   **FIGURE 6.2**

Party system and election results shape cabinet formation processes and outcomes.

executive. Political initiatives and new programs typically originate in the executive. A bureaucracy without an effective executive tends to implement past policies rather than initiate new ones. Without politically motivated ministers, bureaucracies tend toward inertia.

The decision of a president, prime minister, cabinet, or central party committee to pursue a new foreign or domestic policy is usually accompanied by structural adaptations—the appointment of a vigorous minister, the establishment of a special cabinet committee, and the like. Where the political executive is weak and divided, as in contemporary Italy (at least until recently), this dynamic force is missing. Initiative then passes to the bureaucracy, legislative committees, and powerful interest groups—and general needs, interests, and problems may be neglected. In a separation-of-powers system, when the presidency and the congress are controlled by different parties, even a strong president may be hampered in carrying out an effective policy. And if the president is hamstrung, the assembly can rarely fill the gap.

Chief executives also perform important system functions. Studies of childhood socialization show that the first political role perceived by children tends to be the chief political executive—the president, prime minister, or king or queen. In early childhood, the tendency is to identify the top political executive as a parent figure. As the child matures, he or she begins to differentiate political from other roles, as

well as to differentiate among various political roles (see Chapter 3). The conduct of the chief executive affects the trust and confidence that young people feel in the whole political system, and they carry that with them into adulthood. The role of the chief executive in recruitment is obviously important, appointing the cabinet and other officials. The political executive also plays a central role in communication, in explaining and building support for new policies or in improving performance in various sectors of the society and economy.

THE BUREAUCRACY

Modern societies are dominated by large organizations, and this applies to governments as well. **Bureaucracies,** by which we mean all the members of the executive branch below the top executives, are generally in charge of implementing government policy. The size of government bureaucracies increased over the course of the twentieth century. This is partly due to the expanding policy responsibilities and efforts of governments. It may also be partly due to the tendency for government agencies, once they have been established, to seek growth for its own sake. In reaction to this tendency, and as part of the concern about government inefficiencies, there has been a recent movement in many advanced democracies to reduce government budgets and to downsize the bureaucracy (see Chapter 7).

Structure of the Bureaucracy

The most important officials in bureaucracies are the experienced and expert personnel of the top **civil service**. The British "government" consists of approximately one hundred top executive positions of ministers, junior ministers, and parliamentary secretaries. This relatively small group of political policymakers oversees some 3,000 permanent members of the **higher civil service**. These civil servants spend their lives as an elite corps, moving about from ministry to ministry, watching governments come and go, and becoming increasingly important as policymakers as they rise in rank. Below the higher civil service is a huge body of more than half a million permanent public employees, ordinary civil servants, organized into about twenty government departments and a number of other agencies. The total number of British civil servants rose from 100,000 in 1900 to more than 700,000 in 1979; it declined under Conservative governments of the 1980s to 1990s and numbers about 500,000 today.

The importance of the permanent higher civil service is not unique to Britain. In France, too, the higher civil service is filled with powerful generalists who can bring long tenure, experience, and technical knowledge to their particular tasks. In the United States, many top positions in government agencies go to presidential appointees rather than to permanent civil servants, but there are permanent civil servants in the key positions just below the top appointees in all the cabinet departments. These people tend to be specialists—such as military officers, diplomats, doctors, scientists, economists, and engineers—who exert great influence on policy formulation and execution in their specialties. Below these specialists and administrators are the vast numbers of ordinary government employees—postal workers, teachers, welfare case agents, and so forth—who see that governmental policies are put into practice. In 2009, the United States had 21 million public employees of all kinds (federal, state, and local), or about 17 percent of the total labor force. In many European countries, that proportion is even higher, approaching a third of the labor force in Norway, Denmark, and Sweden.

Functions of the Bureaucracy

Bureaucracies have great significance in most contemporary societies. One reason is that the bureaucracy is almost alone in implementing and enforcing laws and regulations. In so doing, they may have quite a bit of discretion. Most modern legislation is general and can be effectively enforced only if administrative officials work out its detail and implementation. Policy implementation and enforcement usually depend on bureaucrats' interpretations and on the spirit and effectiveness with which they put policies into practice. But the power of bureaucracies is not restricted to their implementation and enforcement of rules made by others. In Chapters 4 and 5, we discussed how bureaucratic agencies may articulate and aggregate interests. Departments such as those for agriculture, labor, defense, welfare, and education may be among the most important voices of interest groups. Moreover, administrative agencies in modern political systems do a great deal of adjudication. Tax authorities, for example, routinely determine whether citizens have faithfully reported their income and paid their taxes, and these authorities assess penalties accordingly. While citizens may in principle be able to appeal such rulings to the courts, relatively few actually do. Finally, political elites, whether executives or legislators, base many of their decisions on the information they obtain from the public administration. Similarly, interest groups, political parties, the business elites, and the public depend on such information.

Bureaucracy and Performance

We commonly use the term "bureaucracy" to refer to all systems of public administration. Strictly speaking, however, *bureaucracy* refers to a particular way of organizing such agencies. According to the classical German sociologist Max Weber, bureaucracies have the following features:

1. Decision-making is based on fixed and official jurisdictions, rules, and regulations.
2. There are formal and specialized educational or training requirements for each position.
3. There is a hierarchical command structure: a firmly ordered system of superordination and subordination, in which information flows upward and decisions downward.
4. Decisions are made on the basis of standard operating procedures, which include extensive written records.
5. Officials hold career positions, are appointed and promoted on the basis of merit, and have protection against political interference, notably in the form of permanent job tenure.[20]

No organization is perfectly bureaucratic in this sense, but professional armies come reasonably close, as do tax revenue departments.

These features of bureaucracies have a number of desirable effects. They promote competence, consistency, fair treatment, and freedom from political manipulation. Imagine what life would be like without bureaucracies. Before the advent of modern bureaucracy, public officials were often a sorry lot. Some of them inherited their jobs; others got them through family or political connections. Yet others bought their posts and used them to enrich themselves, gain social status, or both. They often used their powers arbitrarily, to favor friends and neighbors, and to the disadvantage of others. Many devoted little time to their duties. No wonder, then, that public officials were often incompetent, uninterested in their jobs, corrupt, or all of the above. Given the lack of rules and records, aggrieved citizens typically had few recourses.

The negative connotation associated with the word "bureaucracy" suggests that such organizations have liabilities as well. Bureaucratic organizations can become stodgy, rule-bound, inflexible, and insensitive to the needs of their clients. In many cases, bureaucrats have few incentives to be innovative and efficient or even to work very hard. Although bureaucracies are supposed to be politically and ideologically neutral, they are often influenced by the dominant ideologies of the time, have conservative propensities, and pursue institutional interests of their own.[21] Many citizens are exasperated with bureaucracy and its propensities for inefficiency and lack of responsiveness. This frustration is reflected in popular cynicism as well as in periodic attempts to reform government.

Modern authoritarian systems discovered that the bureaucracy was an essential tool of government control. Thus, recruitment of the bureaucracy was part of a larger pattern of control. Bureaucratic selection in the former Soviet Union, as in China today, was controlled through a device called *nomenklatura*. Under this procedure, important positions were kept under the direct supervision of a party agency that had the final word on recruitment. Moreover, the party offered inducements to control the behavior of the chosen officials. These inducements made it difficult for any but the topmost officials to have much freedom of action. Soviet leaders used normative incentives (such as appeals to party, ideology, and national idealism), financial incentives (such as better salaries, access to finer food and clothing, better housing, and freedom to travel), and coercive control (such as reporting by police, party, and bureaucrats). They used demotion or imprisonment, even execution, as penalties. To avoid a coup by police or military forces, the varied layers of command and inducement structures were interwoven, so that no layer could act independently.

In democracies, assemblies and courts also help control the bureaucracy. Legislative committee hearings or judicial investigations may bring bureaucratic performance into line with political desires. Sweden invented the institution of the **ombudsman** to prevent bureaucrats from doing injury or injustice to individuals.[22] This invention has been copied by other states. In the Scandinavian countries, Britain, Germany, and elsewhere, ombudsmen now investigate citizen claims that they have suffered injury or damage as a result of government action. Ombudsmen typically have no power of their own but report to the legislature for remedial action. Their cases rarely lead to criminal conviction, but government officials often change their policies as a result of embarrassing publicity. Thus, ombudsmen offer a more expeditious and less costly procedure than court action. Among the extragovernmental forces that constrain bureaucracies are public opinion and the mass media, as well as interest groups of various kinds.

Controls on civil servants tend to be less effective outside the advanced industrial democracies. Authoritarian systems lack many potential controls, such as effective elected political executives and legislators, independent courts, free mass media, and interest groups. Therefore, authoritarian regimes are particularly prone to bureaucratic inefficiency and inertia. Moreover, in many developing nations, the mass media are neither independent nor influential, few citizens participate in politics, and lower-level government employees are poorly trained and paid—all conditions that encourage bribery, extortion, and bureaucratic mismanagement.[23]

Successful democracy requires that public policies made by national assemblies and chief executives be implemented fairly and effectively; democracy depends on the rule of law. When ruling parties demand kickbacks of public money from construction firms seeking public-works contracts, the democratic process is subverted by rent-seeking politicians (see Chapter 1, specifically Box 1.2). Similarly, when tax officials and border authorities take bribes to overlook tax deficiencies and customs violations, democratic law-making is undermined. Citizens who must bribe teachers to get education for their children or health officials to get immunizations are deprived of the benefits of democratic public policies. Such practices are all too common in the poorer nations of the world.

Failure of the rule of law is difficult to study systematically, but some comparative insight into corruption in public bureaucracies is provided by the surveys of perceptions of corruption on the part of businesspeople, academics, and analysts in different countries. These have been combined into the Corruption Perceptions Index, which rates about one hundred countries each year on a scale from 0 ("highly corrupt") to 10 ("highly clean"). Figure 6.3 shows on the vertical dimension the ratings for 2006 to 2009 of the twelve countries studied in this book. All the countries experience some levels of corruption. However, Figure 6.3 shows that corruption is very strongly associated with poverty and underdevelopment (see also Table 1.3).[24] The affluent democracies in our comparisons—Britain, Germany, the United States, France, and Japan (despite notorious individual corruption cases in each)—rated in the top half of the scale. Developing nations such as Brazil, China, India, and Mexico are substantially more corrupt, with scores in the lower range of the scale. Nigeria, despite some recent improvement, is still perceived as highly corrupt. Russia, plagued by many problems of its dual economic and political transitions, scores even worse. Russia is also more corrupt than we would expect from its middle-level income. Despite the theocratic nature of its regime, Iran is rated as one of the world's least transparent and most corrupt countries.

The ills of bureaucracy, including inefficiency and inertia, are pandemic. This is truly a dilemma because we are unlikely to invent any schemes for

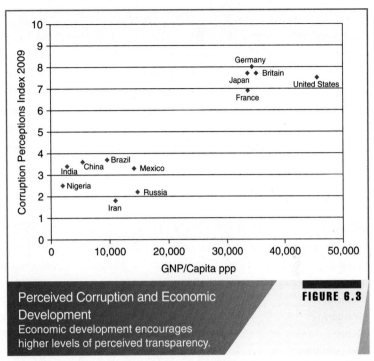

Perceived Corruption and Economic Development
Economic development encourages higher levels of perceived transparency.

FIGURE 6.3

Source: Economic development level from United Nations Development Program, *World Development Report 2009*, downloaded from www.undp.org, July 2010; Corruption Perceptions Index from Transparency International, downloaded from www.transparency.org on June 21, 2010.

carrying out large-scale social tasks without the organization, division of labor, and professionalism that bureaucracy provides. Its pathologies can only be mitigated. The art of modern political leadership consists of defining and communicating appropriate goals and policies, as well as getting them implemented by a massive and complex bureaucracy—how and when to press and coerce it, reorganize it, reward it, teach it, or be taught by it.

In summary, the structure of government does make a difference in the way the political process functions and in the strengths and weaknesses of the government. Some government structures are better at representing public preferences, while others are more effective in implementing policy. Some government structures allow for more debate and deliberation, while others are more decisive in making policy decisions. There is no perfect form of government, but there are clear differences in the types of interests that get represented, the methods of devising public policy, and the implementation of policy that flow from the organization of the government.

REVIEW QUESTIONS

- What are the advantages of more inclusive decision rules in making policies? What are the disadvantages?

- Why is the confidence relationship so important in parliamentary democracies?

- In what different ways can policymaking power be dispersed and limited by constitutional arrangements?

- What are the advantages and disadvantages of assembly representation that mirrors the characteristics of citizens?

- How are cabinets formed after national elections in parliamentary systems?

- Why are bureaucracies necessary but sometimes liabilities in policymaking?

KEY TERMS

assemblies
authoritarian regimes
bicameralism
bureaucracies
cabinet
chief executives
civil service
confidence relationship
constitutional regimes
decision rules
democracy
democratic presidential regime
federal systems
higher civil service
impeachment
judicial review
ombudsman
parliamentary regimes
policymaking
semipresidential
separation of powers

SUGGESTED READINGS

Carey, John M. *Legislative Voting and Accountability*. New York: Cambridge University Press, 2009.

Colomer, Josep M. *Political Institutions: Democracy and Social Choice*. New York: Oxford University Press, 2001.

Döring, Herbert, ed. *Parliaments and Majority Rule in Western Europe*. New York: St. Martin's Press, 1995.

Hicken, Allen. *Building Party Systems in Developing Democracies*. New York: Cambridge University Press, 2009.

Huber, John D. *Rationalizing Parliament*. Cambridge: Cambridge University Press, 1996.

Huber, John D., and Charles R. Shipan. *Deliberate Discretion? The Institutional Foundations of Bureaucratic Autonomy*. New York: Cambridge University Press, 2002.

Laver, Michael, and Norman Schofield. *Multiparty Government: The Politics of Coalition in Europe*. Ann Arbor: University of Michigan Press, 1998.

Lijphart, Arend. *Democracy in Plural Societies*. New Haven, CT: Yale University Press, 1977.

———. *Patterns of Democracy: Government Forms and Performance in Thirty-Six Countries*. New Haven, CT: Yale University Press, 1999.

Linz, Juan, and Arturo Valenzuela, eds. *The Failure of Presidential Democracy: Comparative Perspectives*. Baltimore: Johns Hopkins University Press, 1994.

Mainwaring, Scott, and Matthew Shugart, eds. *Presidentialism and Democracy in Latin America*. New York: Cambridge University Press, 1997.

North, Douglass. *Institutions, Institutional Change, and Economic Performance*. Cambridge: Cambridge University Press, 1990.

Perez-Linan, Anibal. *Presidential Impeachment and the New Political Instability in Latin America*. New York: Cambridge University Press, 2007.

Powell, G. Bingham, Jr. *Contemporary Democracies: Participation, Stability, and Violence*. Cambridge, MA: Harvard University Press, 1982.

Secondat, Charles de, Baron de Montesquieu. *The Spirit of the Laws*. London: Hafner, 1960.

Shugart, Matthew, and John Carey. *Presidents and Assemblies: Constitutional Design and Electoral Dynamics*. Cambridge: Cambridge University Press, 1992.

Stone-Sweet, Alec. *Governing with Judges: Constitutional Politics in Europe*. Oxford: Oxford University Press, 2002.

Strøm, Kaare. *Minority Government and Majority Rule*. Cambridge: Cambridge University Press, 1990.

Tsebelis, George. *Veto Players: How Political Institutions Work*. Princeton, NJ: Princeton University Press, 2002.

Weber, Max. "Bureaucracy," in *From Max Weber*, ed. H. H. Gerth and C. Wright Mills. New York: Oxford University Press, 1976, 196–244.

ENDNOTES

1. For a skeptical view of constitutional design, see James G. March and Johan P. Olsen, *Rediscovering Institutions: The Organizational Basis of Politics* (New York: Free Press, 1989), 171–72. For a more sanguine argument, see Giovanni Sartori, *Comparative Constitutional Engineering* (New York: New York University Press, 1995).

2. John Locke, *Two Treatises of Government*, ed. Peter Laslett (Cambridge: Cambridge University Press, 1960); and Charles de Secondat, Baron de Montesquieu, *The Spirit of the Laws* (London: Hafner, 1960).

3. *The Federalist: A Commentary on the Constitution of the United States* (Washington, D.C.: National Home Library Foundation, 1937).

4. On presidential decree powers, see John M. Carey and Matthew S. Shugart, *Executive Decree Authority* (New York: Cambridge University Press, 1998); for more general discussions of presidential powers, see Matthew S. Shugart and John M. Carey, *Presidents and Assemblies: Constitutional Design and Electoral Dynamics* (Cambridge: Cambridge University Press, 1992); and Scott Mainwaring and Matthew S. Shugart, eds., *Presidentialism and Democracy in Latin America* (New York: Cambridge University Press, 1997).

5. It is important to avoid confusion between the formal titles of government officials and the source of their selection and bases of their powers—which determine the type of political system. For example, Germany is a parliamentary system, whose executive is headed by a prime minister, although his official title is *chancellor*. The German head of state is a president, chosen by a federal convention, with little policymaking power. See also Table 6.3.

6. G. Bingham Powell, Jr., *Contemporary Democracies: Participation, Stability, and Violence* (Cambridge, MA: Harvard University Press, 1982); and Arend Lijphart, *Patterns of Democracy: Government Forms and Performance in Thirty-Six Countries* (New Haven, CT: Yale University Press, 1999). On Northern Ireland, see David McKittrick and David McVea, *Making Sense of the Troubles: The Story of the Conflict in Northern Ireland* (Chicago: Ivan R. Dee, 2002).

7. Donald Horowitz, "Comparing Democratic Systems," in *The Global Resurgence of Democracy*, ed. Larry Diamond and Mark F. Plattner (Baltimore: Johns Hopkins University Press, 1993), 127 ff. Also see Shugart and Carey, *Presidents and Assemblies*.

8. Gretchen Helmke and Frances Rosenbluth, "Regimes and the Rule of Law: Judicial Independence in Comparative Perspective," *Annual Review of Political Science* 12 (June 2009): 345–66.

9. Arend Lijphart, *Patterns of Democracy*, 226.

10. Georg Vanberg, *The Politics of Constitutional Review in Germany* (New York: Cambridge University Press, 2005). Also see Chapter 10.

11. Moreover, in Britain, as in France, Germany, and the twenty-four other members of the EU, the European Court of Justice provides some degree of judicial review to ensure that national laws and government activities are compatible with EU treaties and laws.

12. A major recent trend in the division and limitation of policymaking powers is the growth of independent central banks. Central banks, such as the Federal Reserve in the United States, regulate the supply of money and the interest rates, as well as many financial transactions for government and society. In most countries, such bank policy was long controlled by the chief executive as part of the government bureaucracy. But in the last twenty years, many countries have given their central banks substantial independence and set for them the primary task of using monetary policy to maintain price stability and limit inflation. Such independence reassures investors, domestic and foreign, and seems to constrain inflation, but it limits the economic policy alternatives of the chief executive and cabinet.

13. John Carey, *Legislative Voting and Accountability* (New York: Cambridge University Press, 2009).

14. For a survey of parliamentary committees in Europe, see Ingvar Mattson and Kaare Strøm, "Parliamentary Committees," in *Parliaments and Majority Rule in Western Europe*, ed. Herbert Döring (New York: St. Martin's Press, 1995), 249–307.

15. Senator Roman Houska quoted in *Time* magazine, March 30, 1970.

16. In multiparty systems, the process of building coalitions between executive and legislature also plays a role. See Gary Cox, *Making Votes Count* (New York: Cambridge University Press, 1997), Chapter 12, and G. Bingham Powell, Jr., *Elections as Instruments of Democracy* (New Haven, CT: Yale University Press, 2000). A substantial body of political science research has begun to explore how such congruence between voters, legislatures, and governments is created or disrupted.

17. Data from the Inter-Parliamentary Union. Downloaded from www.ipu.org on June 21, 2010.

18. Adam Przeworski et al., *Democracy and Development: Political Institutions and Well-Being in the World, 1950–1990* (New York: Cambridge University Press, 2000).

19. See the relevant chapters in Michael Laver and Kenneth A. Shepsle, *Cabinet Ministers and Parliamentary Government* (New York: Cambridge University Press, 1994).

20. See the discussion in Julien Freund, *The Sociology of Max Weber* (New York: Random House, 1969), 234–35.

21. See Joel Aberbach, Robert D. Putnam, and Bert A. Rockman, *Bureaucrats and Politicians in Western Democracies* (Cambridge, MA: Harvard University Press, 1981).

22. See Christopher Ansell and Jane Gingrich, "Reforming the Administrative State," in *Democracy Transformed*, ed. Bruce Cain, Russell Dalton, and Susan Scarrow (Oxford: Oxford University Press, 2003).

23. On the difficulties involved in reducing administrative corruption in developing countries, see Robert Klitgard, *Controlling Corruption* (Berkeley: University of California Press, 1989).

24. For a statistical analysis explaining scores on the Corruption Perceptions Index, see Daniel Triesman, "The Causes of Corruption: A Cross-National Study," *Journal of Public Economics* 76 (June 2000): 399–457, who suggests lower levels of economic development, shorter exposure to democracy, and federalism to be among the factors encouraging more perceived corruption. Also see Melanie Manion, *Corruption by Design: Building Clean Government in Mainland China and Hong Kong* (Cambridge, MA: Harvard University Press, 2004).

7

PUBLIC POLICY

Public policy consists of all the authoritative public decisions that governments make—the **outputs** of the political system. Policies or outputs are normally chosen for a purpose—they are meant to promote end results that we refer to as political **outcomes**. Different policies may be more or less efficient ways to reach the outcomes that policymakers want. But the values and goals of policymakers and citizens affect their evaluation of the political outcomes they actually reach. Since politicians and citizens often disagree over **political goods** and values, it is important to keep these goals in mind when we study public policy.

GOVERNMENT AND WHAT IT DOES

Governments do many things. Some things they do are timeless. In the days of the Roman Empire, defense against external and internal enemies was a major government responsibility. It continues to be so in most societies today. In other ways, governments today do things that were unthinkable in the past. For example, governments now regulate telecommunications and air traffic, policy areas that were unknown until the twentieth century.

Governments produce many goods and services, though exactly which ones vary a great deal from country to country. In most societies, governments provide law enforcement, roads, and postal services, and in many countries, they do much more. In socialist states and some other authoritarian states, governments own and operate most major industries and produce everything from military equipment to

such consumer goods as clothing and shoes. In a capitalist society, such as the United States, most consumer goods are produced in the private sector. In much of Europe, the governments have a larger role than in the United States, but far less than in a socialist system.

The range of government involvement varies not just among countries, but also among different economic sectors within the same country. For example, government agencies in the United States employ few of the people engaged in mining and manufacturing, but a much larger proportion of those working for the utilities that supply gas, water, and electrical power. Yet there is no society in which the government produces no goods or services, and conversely no state in which all industries are run by the government. Even in the former Soviet Union, part of the agricultural sector was private, as were many simple consumer services, such as babysitting.

Political Goals and Political Goods

To compare and evaluate public policy in different political systems, we need to consider the political goals that motivate different policies. Of course, as we discussed in Chapter 1, the policymakers in any political system may be self-interested, seeking rents rather than development, or exploiting divisions rather than building community. But particularly in democratic societies, politicians also have incentives to pursue political goals that seek to satisfy the values and aspirations of the citizens. We refer to these as "political goods."

TABLE 7.1

Political Goods

Difficult trade-offs, as well as constraints, may be involved in obtaining desirable goods.

Levels of Political Goods	Classes of Goods	Content and Examples
System level	System maintenance	The political system features regular, stable, and predictable decision-making processes.
	System adaptation	The political system is able to adapt to environmental change and challenges.
Process level	Participation in political inputs	The political system is open and responsive to many forms of political speech and action.
	Compliance and support	Citizens fulfill their obligations (e.g., military service and tax obligations) to the system and comply with public law and policy.
	Procedural justice	Legal and political procedures are orderly and fair (due process), and there is equality before the law.
	Effectiveness and efficiency	Political processes have their intended effects and are no more cumbersome, expensive, or intrusive than necessary.
Policy level	Welfare	Citizens have access to health care, learning, and economic and environmental goods, which the government seeks to distribute broadly.
	Security	The government provides safety of person and property, public order, and national security.
	Fairness	Government policy is not discriminatory and recognizes individuals from different ethnic, linguistic, or religious groups; both genders are respected; vulnerable or disadvantaged citizens are protected.
	Liberty	Citizens enjoy freedom from excessive regulation, protection of their privacy, and respect for their autonomy.

We can organize this framework of political goods around each of the three levels of analysis used in this book: system, process, and policy (see Table 7.1).

At the system level, a long tradition in political analysis emphasizes order, predictability, and stability. Citizens are most free and most able to act purposefully when their environment is stable, transparent, and predictable. We call these conditions *system goods*, since they reflect the functioning and effectiveness of the whole political system. While people generally want some measure of change and new opportunities, most prefer stability to abrupt and unforeseeable change. Political instability—constitutional breakdowns, frequent leadership changes, riots, demonstrations, and the like—upsets most people's plans and can cost lives and cause material destruction. Creating and sustaining a compatible political community, whose members share many values and respect differences when they disagree, helps support political stability. System goods address the regularity and

predictability with which political systems work, but also their ability to adapt to environmental challenges. Regularity and adaptability are typically somewhat in conflict.

Another category of goods is associated with the political process—citizen participation and free political competition. Democracy is good and authoritarianism is bad, according to this school of thought, because of the way citizens are treated in the process, and not because democracy might produce better economic or security results. Democratic procedures and various rights of due process, then, are process goods. Process goods include participation, compliance, and procedural justice. We value participation not merely as a means to responsive government, but for its own sake, since it enhances citizen competence and dignity. Procedural justice (trial by jury, *habeas corpus,* no cruel and unusual punishment, and fair and equal treatment) is another crucial process value, without which citizens would have much greater reasons to fear their governments. Procedural goods also include effectiveness and efficiency. We prefer political processes that actually deliver the desired results, and all else being equal, we especially prefer institutions that give us such outcomes at low cost and relatively quickly.

A third focus is on **policy goods**, such as economic welfare, quality of life, freedom, and personal security. Most people value policies that improve welfare, reduce inequalities, enhance public safety, enable people to live as they want, and clean up our environment. Yet well-meaning people do not always agree on which of these policy goods are most important. Political philosophers have long debated the content and importance of policies in the public interest. In different cultures and times, these goods have given priority to different needs and aspirations. But over the past two hundred years, a series of public documents from the U.S. Declaration of Independence to the UN Millennium Development Goals have expressed developing public support for expanded human rights. Box 7.1 shows the eight Millennium Development Goals that were officially supported by 189 nations at a summit in 2000. These were not meant to be all-inclusive, but they reflect a consensus on the meaning of improving the lives of citizens around the world. Eradicating extreme poverty, reducing mortality, combating disease, providing primary education, developing environmental sustainability, and promoting gender equality won this support and probably seem unobjectionable to most of us.

Although these eight goals were accepted by leaders of many nations, they conceal sharp differences—not only regarding their relative importance, but on the way they affect other values. For example, at a follow-up summit in 2005, a substantial controversy erupted over their relationship to birth-control policies and to national sovereignty. Yet these goals provide a starting point for identification of important policy goals that encompass our discussion in Chapters 1 and 2: the functions and purposes that governments serve and the challenges that confront them.

Even if we were to agree on the Millennium Development Goals, we would not necessarily know what weight to give to one goal when it conflicts with another, or what to do with policies that might help some groups at the expense of others. For example, how do we choose between enhancing one person's health care versus improving another person's educational opportunities? In such difficult cases, one criterion that most of us would agree upon is that government policy should be *fair*. The problem is that people often disagree over what is fair. In some situations, we believe that **fairness** requires all people to be treated

---

Millennium Development Goals

BOX 7.1

In 2000, the leaders of 147 nations and official representatives of many others attended the Millennium Summit at the United Nations Headquarters in New York City. At the end, 189 nations agreed to support the United Nations Millennium Declaration, which confirmed their intention to help the world's poorest nations improve the lives of their citizens by 2015. The Millennium Development Goals, a concrete series of targets, were derived from this declaration. Many other international organizations have also agreed to these goals. They include eight general goals and suggest specific indicators for monitoring progress in achieving them. The official list of Millennium Development Goals (MDGs) includes:

Goal 1. Eradicate extreme poverty and hunger.
Goal 2. Achieve universal primary education.
Goal 3. Promote gender equality and empower women.
Goal 4. Reduce child mortality.
Goal 5. Improve maternal health.
Goal 6. Combat HIV/AIDS, malaria, and other diseases.
Goal 7. Ensure environmental sustainability.
Goal 8. Develop a global partnership for development.

The Millennium Development Goals represent, at least in principle, a contemporary consensus on policy goals that could be considered policy goods.

Source: http://mdgs.un.org/unsd/mdg/

equally (as when family members attempt to divide a tempting pie). In other situations, fairness demands that individuals be treated according to performance (as when grades are given in a college course). In yet other situations, fairness means that people are treated according to their needs (for example, in cases of medical treatment). Thus, fairness can imply *equal treatment* in some cases, *just deserts* (reward in proportion to merit or contribution) in others, and *treatment according to need* in yet others. Different value systems, such as ideologies or religious systems, may even define fairness differently. Many **public policies**—for example, pension systems such as social security in the United States—rely on some combination of these criteria. The debate over these various conceptions of fairness is never settled.

A final policy regarded highly in Table 7.1 is *freedom*. As anarchists, libertarians, and other government skeptics would remind us, public policies should promote and protect freedom and basic human and political rights. If two policies are equally efficient and fair, we would prefer the one that better respects the rights and liberties of citizens. But even citizens in democratic societies do not always choose freedom over other political goods. For example, freedom of speech is a constitutional guarantee, but many people want to prohibit speech that is insulting, blasphemous, or offensive.

Liberty is sometimes viewed only as freedom from governmental regulation and harassment. Yet even private individuals and organizations may violate the liberty and privacy of others. In such cases, government intervention may enhance liberty. Much legislation against racial segregation and discrimination generally has been impelled by this purpose. Liberty to act, organize, obtain information, and protest is an indispensable part of effective political participation. Nor is it irrelevant to social, political, and economic fairness. Prior to the breakdown of communism in Eastern Europe and the Soviet Union, it was a common view that these communist countries were trading liberty for equality. In contrast, capitalism was said to trade off equality for liberty. However, the collapse of communism uncovered the extent of corruption and privilege in communist societies. While they had surely traded off liberty for a basic security of employment, it was not clear that the communists had otherwise gained much in the way of equality.

Table 7.1 draws on our three-level analysis of political systems to present a checklist of political

goods that are widely valued in contemporary societies. There is no simple way to say which value should prevail when they conflict. In fact, different preferences among such values as freedom, fairness, and efficiency set different cultures, parties, and political philosophies apart. One society or group of citizens may value fairness over liberty; another may make the opposite choice, as in Patrick Henry's famous exclamation, "Give me liberty or give me death!"

This chapter focuses on the third category in Table 7.1—policy goods. We first describe the varieties of activities that governments perform, such as extracting resources to support the government in the various means of providing policy goods. Then we focus on the four policy goods outlined in the table: welfare, security, fairness, and liberty.

PUBLIC POLICY OUTPUTS

One aspect of public policy is the outputs of government activities, or different instruments of policy. We can compare the actions that governments may take to accomplish their policy purposes under four headings:

1. **Extraction** of resources—money, goods, persons, and services—from the domestic and international environments
2. **Distribution**—of money, goods, and services—to citizens, residents, and clients of the state
3. **Regulation** of human behavior—the use of compulsion and inducement to bring about desired behavior
4. **Symbolic outputs**—used to exhort citizens to engage in desired forms of behavior, build community, or celebrate exemplary conduct (see Chapter 1).

Political systems have different policy action profiles. Some governments distribute a great deal of goods and services but regulate little. Elsewhere, the government may be heavily engaged in regulation but may rely on the private sector to produce most goods and services. In the next sections, we discuss these four types of policy outputs, beginning with extraction.

Extraction

Before governments can spend, they must have ways to collect money and other resources. All political systems *extract* resources from their environments and inhabitants. When societies go to war, for example, young people (typically men) may be called on to fight. Anthropologists estimate that in some hunter-gatherer societies, such obligations have been so onerous that about half of all males have died in warfare. (Thomas Hobbes would not have been surprised.) Such direct extraction of services is found in many modern states in the form of compulsory military service, jury duty, or compulsory labor imposed on those convicted of crime.

The most common form of resource extraction is taxation. *Taxation* is the government's extraction of money or goods from members of a political system for which they receive no immediate or direct benefit. A related form of extraction is "social contribution," or "social insurance" revenues, which are typically held as special funds targeted to be spent on social protection benefits, such as old age pensions (social security). Revenue policies are designed to meet many different objectives, which sometimes conflict. On the one hand, governments often want to collect as much revenue as possible to finance various public services. On the other hand, governments do not want to kill the goose that lays the golden egg. The more that governments tax their citizens, the less incentive people and businesses have to increase their income. If the tax burden becomes too great, they may try to evade taxes or even leave the country altogether.

Another common trade-off in extraction policies is between efficiency and equity. *Efficiency* means collecting the most revenue possible at the lowest cost to economic production. *Equity* means taxing so that no one is unfairly burdened, and particularly those who have the least are spared. In most societies, the tax and spending systems redistribute wealth in favor of the less well-off. Therefore, income taxes are generally progressive, which means that citizens with greater incomes pay at higher rates than those who earn less. However, highly progressive taxes can reduce the incentives for high earners to work and invest, and thus lessen the incentives for economic growth. Therefore, such taxes are often inefficient.

Personal and corporate income taxes, property taxes, and taxes on capital gains are called **direct taxes**, since they are directly levied on persons and corporations. If you pay a tax bill at the end of the year, or have taxes withheld in your paycheck, you are paying taxes directly. Payroll taxes tend to hit the middle class and those in the labor force, since the wealthy tend to get a larger share of their income from dividends, interest, and capital gains, and retirees from pensions. High taxes on wages can also hurt employment or drive businesses into the "underground economy," in which they do not report their incomes or expenditures. **Indirect taxes** include sales taxes, value-added taxes, excise taxes, and customs duties. These are commonly

Protesting Taxes

French farmers protest taxes and a fall in agricultural prices by driving tractors through the Place de la République in Paris on April 27, 2010.

Benoit Tessier/Reuters/Landov

included in the prices of goods and services that consumers buy. The redistributive effects of indirect taxes depend on who pays them. Since the poor spend more of their income on food and clothing, sales (or value-added) taxes can be regressive (which means that the poor pay relatively more than the rich), so many nations have a lower tax rate on necessities. In contrast, indirect taxes on luxury goods may be progressive, since the poor rarely purchase luxury items like fine jewelry. Countries with weak administrative capacities often prefer indirect taxes. Particularly where financial record-keeping is imprecise, indirect taxes are easier to collect. In addition, indirect taxes tend to rise with inflation or as the costs of products increase, which provides a natural source of increasing government revenue.

Besides redistribution and efficiency, tax policies often promote such values as charity, energy conservation, or home ownership. For example, many countries stimulate home ownership by making mortgage interest payments tax-deductible. Several European nations have a large gasoline tax to reduce energy consumption and encourage the sale of energy-efficient automobiles. In France, 70 percent of the cost of gasoline is for government taxes, which raises the price to about $7 a gallon.

Given the many difficult issues involving taxation, and the inevitable public resistance to high taxes, it might seem a blessing if a government could receive income windfalls from other sources. Countries with large reserves of oil or other valuable natural resources are often in this situation. Many oil-producing countries, such as Iran, Russia, and Nigeria, can tap their natural resource reserves and sell them at a large profit in the international market. Yet when the riches from easily obtained natural resources are a large share of a government's income, the consequences can be far from an unmitigated blessing. A large political science literature focuses on the problems of so-called "**rentier states**," which derive much of their revenue from the "rents" of selling oil and other natural resources.[1] This literature often refers to a "resource curse" impeding development and democracy when the economy is distorted by oil windfalls.

Why should oil or diamonds or copper constitute a "curse" when they can finance public policies without burdening citizens with taxes?[2] One explanation suggests that windfall resource profits can make governments independent from their citizens. As Samuel Huntington put it, "Oil revenues . . . reduce the need for the government to solicit the acquiescence of its subjects to taxation. The lower the level of taxation, the less reason for the public to demand representation."[3] And if politicians do not feel such demands from their citizens, they may be less likely to behave accountably. Direct resource-based revenues also may enable authoritarian rulers to pay off citizens through patronage (e.g., subsidized goods, services, and loans) without yielding political power to them. Or, the easy money of the rentier state may be a tempting target for predatory authoritarians who use these funds to repress society while taking the profits for themselves. Although the resource curse is common wisdom in studies of less economically developed economies, the windfall income can soften the intensity of redistributive conflict in very unequal societies and have positive consequences for democracy.[4] Nor do such windfalls seem problematic in already economically developed democracies, such as Norway.

Figure 7.1 shows the general government revenues as a percentage of **gross domestic product (GDP)**, the total value of goods and services produced by a country's residents in a year. (In Brazil, India, and Mexico, the figure shows only central government revenue; state and local taxes can increase the total revenue by a third or more.) For the average country, about a quarter of the GDP is extracted by the government, but in some countries, the proportion is much higher. Most of the more developed democracies rely primarily on taxes and social contributions for government revenues. In Germany and France, the social contributions are nearly as large as the taxes.

Figure 7.1, however, shows that some governments also get substantial revenues from nontax and noncontribution sources (the third columns), such as administrative fees, rents, and income from business enterprises that they run. In Iran, a classic "rentier state" (see Chapter 16), nontax income provides over two-thirds of the government's revenues. Russia is also rich in oil and other natural resources, and it relies heavily on nontax income. If we had data on Nigeria, it would probably show a similar picture. China also relies on nontax sources from government-owned enterprises, a carryover from its socialist past despite its marketization of much of the economy. Democracy has had a hard time in all these countries, although dependence on nontax revenues is not the only reason.

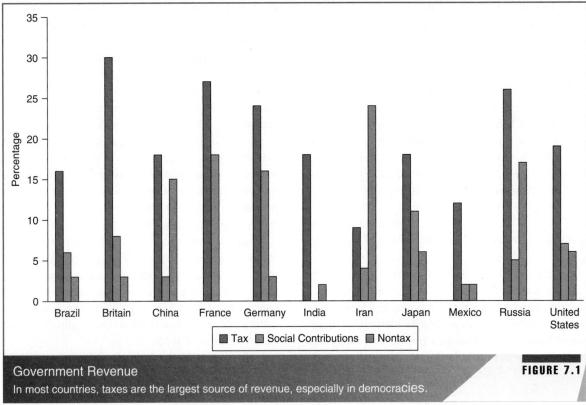

Government Revenue

In most countries, taxes are the largest source of revenue, especially in democracies.

FIGURE 7.1

Source: International Monetary Fund, downloaded from www2.imfstatistics.org/GFS on June 4, 2010, Table W4.

The tax profiles of different countries vary both in their overall tax burdens and in their reliance on different types of taxes. Sweden has the highest tax rates overall, as it extracts more than 50 percent of its GDP in taxes. France and Russia are in the 45-percent range. Britain and Germany are among the advanced industrial societies that collect about 40 percent of GDP, while the United States and Japan extract about 30 percent. These two countries depend more on direct income taxes than on sales or consumption taxes. Outside the economically developed areas, government revenue rarely exceeds 25 percent of GDP. The central government revenue of India is about 15 percent. For the states that are highly dependent on natural-resource windfalls, these proportions can fluctuate sharply with the price of their export commodities, which can create additional problems for government and for development.

In the long run, governments cannot spend more money than they raise. If governments fail to balance their books and instead run budget deficits, they have to borrow money. This creates debt that future generations of taxpayers have to pay off. Even rich governments are notoriously bad at balancing their books, and many run budget deficits year after year. In 2004, nineteen of the twenty-eight (highly developed) Organization for Economic Co-operation and Development (OECD) countries ran budget deficits, and the average deficit was equal to 3.5 percent of GDP. The United States briefly balanced its budget in the late 1990s, but then slid back into fiscal imbalance. When Germany, France, and many other European countries decided to adopt a common currency, the euro, they also committed themselves to keeping their national deficits smaller than 3 percent of GDP. In practice, however, they have often broken that promise. Since the financial crisis of 2008 and 2009, most of these countries have borrowed massively to finance emergency spending to combat the worldwide recession, greatly increasing their national debts.

Recently, in some European countries, especially Greece, the combination of massive, long-standing deficits and the more recent pressures of the global financial crisis threatened the country's ability to meet its future financial obligations. Despite a large aid package promised by other Euro countries in exchange for Greece's drastically cutting its spending, the debt crisis threatened the financial stability of all the European countries. The 2008 and 2009 economic crisis has produced similar economic strains on the governments of many developing nations. It is a measure of the globalization of trade and financial capital flows that this economic crisis rapidly created difficult budgetary choices in countries throughout the world as economies contracted, unemployment rose, and revenues faltered.

Distributive Policy Profiles

Distributive policies include transfers of money, goods, services, honors, and opportunities to individuals and groups in the society. Distributive policies generally consume more government resources and employ more government officials than anything else that modern governments do. Distributive policies include support for infrastructure, agriculture, and various other industries, but the most common form of distributive policies are social-welfare programs.

The first modern welfare state programs were introduced in Germany in the 1880s. In response to rapid industrialization and urbanization, the German government offered social-insurance programs that protected workers against unemployment, accidents, sickness, and poverty during old age. During the twentieth century, and particularly from the Great Depression of the 1930s until the 1970s, most industrialized states adopted, and greatly expanded, such welfare state policies. Over time, welfare state policies expanded to include broader health-care programs, disability benefits, public education, housing subsidies, child and childcare benefits, pensions, and other distributive policies. As developing countries become wealthier, they also tend to spend more of their resources on welfare programs. In Mexico, for example, the last three presidents have each launched a major social-welfare initiative. In Brazil, the *Bolsa Familia* program is the world's largest conditional cash-transfer program and a flagship of President Lula's administration. The program reaches a quarter of the Brazilian population and is especially targeted at eradicating hunger (see Chapter 15).

Welfare policies typically combine a social-insurance system and a program of social redistribution. It is partly paternalistic (forcing people to put away money for their old age and potential illnesses) and in part Robin Hood (taking from the rich and giving to the poor). The balance between these two functions depends on which programs a particular country emphasizes and on how it finances them. Thus, not all welfare programs are alike. Even among the advanced industrial countries, some welfare states are larger than others or offer different benefits. All the wealthier nations try to assist the aged, the disabled, and the unemployed. However, differences in expenditures reflect the priorities of citizens and their governments, social and economic conditions (such as a country's age distribution and unemployment levels), and historical experiences.[5] Countries that have more frequently elected social democratic governments, rather than conservative ones, generally have larger welfare states.

Figure 7.2 reports overall governmental expenditures as a percentage of GDP, followed by the percentages spent on health, education, and social protection (such as unemployment benefits and pensions for the elderly). Clearly, both the magnitude and profile of government expenditures depend heavily on a nation's economic development. In the developed world, countries are spending a third to half of their GDP on government. Among the countries shown here, Japan has the smallest government sector in the developed world and France the largest. Government spending in Russia accounts for 43 percent of GDP; in China and Iran, it is about a third. Government spending is a smaller fraction of GDP in most of the other countries, although Brazil, India, and Mexico only provide statistics for the central governments.

Developed countries generally allocate the majority of their government expenditures to health, education, and social protection. France, Germany, and Japan spend more than two-thirds of their budgets in these areas, compared with about one-half in the United States. The U.S. model stresses equality of opportunity through public education, making a greater and earlier effort in this area than did most European nations. Americans began spending on social protection programs later, and, as shown in Figure 7.2, still does less in these areas. This may reflect the U.S. heritage as a nation of immigrants, many of whom arrived poor and have been expected to prosper by their own efforts.

Sadly, as the figure illustrates, the countries that need them most, such as India, have the least to spend on education and health. Public health expenditures in

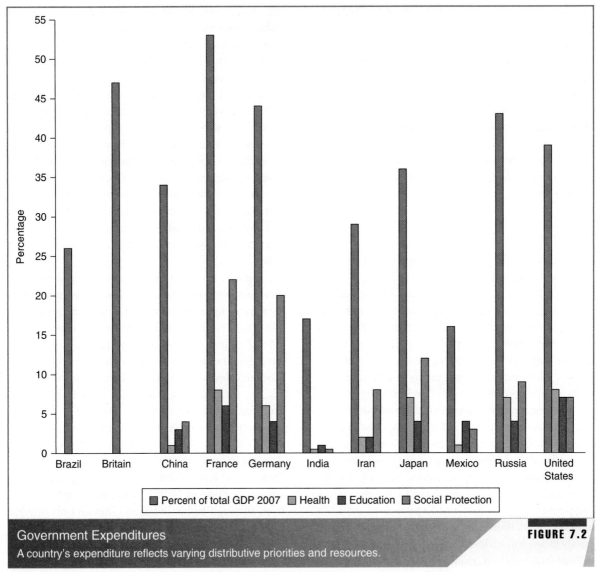

Government Expenditures

FIGURE 7.2

A country's expenditure reflects varying distributive priorities and resources.

Source: International Monetary Fund, downloaded from www2.imfstatistics.org/GFS on June 4, 2010, Table W6.

our developed countries, such as the United States, France, Germany, and Japan are $2,000 to $3,000 per capita. In the poorest countries, health spending in absolute dollars is miniscule—$15 per person in Nigeria and $21 per person in India. These spending numbers are generated by varying public policy efforts, as shown in Figure 7.2, and even more by the enormous variations in income created by developed economies (countries also rely on their private sector to varying degrees to finance health spending). Poor nations, with limited budgets and many pressing demands, lack the resources for health and education. Social protection expenditure in poor nations also

tends to be low. Resources are scarce, and shorter life expectancies and high birth rates mean that there are comparatively few older people. Also, many people live in the rural areas, where unemployment is less easily observed and where the aged and the infirm typically receive some care through the extended family; these services go unreported in our statistics.

National security spending follows a different pattern. Particularly among less-developed countries, spending varies as much with the international environment as with overall economic means. Some states that are locked in tense international confrontations make extraordinary defense efforts. India, Iran, and the United States spend more than 10 percent of their government outlays (2 to 5 percent of GDP) on defense. Because of its worldwide security commitments and large economy, the United States is by far the heaviest military spender in absolute terms.

Challenges to the Welfare State Welfare states have many beneficial consequences. The Western European countries that pioneered these programs have virtually eradicated dire poverty, and they have created a much more "level playing field" for their citizens. Crime rates tend to be low in countries with extensive welfare states, and most of the programs are popular with ordinary citizens. Yet the welfare state is also expensive. As total government expenditures have grown to around half of GDP in many industrial democracies, this has created political opposition to high taxes and deficits. One of the most serious problems is the generational deficit that these policies are creating. Welfare programs are committing entitlements that will fall on future generations (your generation) to pay. At the same time that senior citizens qualify for greater pension benefits and health-care costs are rising rapidly, the ranks of the elderly are swelling relative to those in the workforce. Thus, the ratio of those outside the workforce (because they are too young or too old) to those in the working-age population is increasing rapidly in Europe and Japan. A smaller number of working people in future

years will have to pay higher taxes just to support existing health and welfare programs.[6]

In addition, some welfare state policies give citizens fewer incentives to work. Norway and Sweden are among the leading countries in the world in life expectancy and public health statistics. Yet workers in these countries are on sick leave about twice as often as workers elsewhere in Europe, and record numbers of these Scandinavians are on permanent disability pensions. This is partly because of generous sick-leave benefits and partly because it is easy to qualify for disability benefits. But these policies are costly and reduce incentives to work.

These problems with the welfare state have stirred efforts to prevent further increases in spending obligations (entitlements) and to contain the costs of those already in effect. Thus, the gradual expansion of welfare benefits that characterized most of the twentieth century in the developed countries can no longer be taken for granted.

Regulation

Regulation is the exercise of political control over the behavior of individuals and groups in the society. Most contemporary governments have a large regulatory role. Our civilization and amenities depend on regulation. As we discussed in Chapter 1, social-contract

Receiving Distributions

Indian school children are served government sponsored free midday meals at a government primary school in Hyderabad, India, June 23, 2010.

Mahesh Kumar A/AP Images

theorists such as Hobbes and Locke maintain that regulation can facilitate many beneficial activities. Economic production and commerce, for example, rely on government regulation to establish and protect property rights and to enforce contracts. There need to be rules to keep traffic moving smoothly on the freeways, in the air, and on the airwaves. Citizens and consumers often demand protections against fraud, manipulation, and obnoxious externalities, such as toxic waste and pollution. And governments are increasingly involved in setting product standards, particularly for pharmaceuticals and food, to make sure that these products are safe. Governments also regulate to shield their citizens, and often particularly children and women, from physical and other abuse. However, regulation can create an opportunity for government officials to extract bribes from citizens (see Box 7.2).

In the developed democracies, government regulation has proliferated enormously over the last century. Industrialization and urbanization have caused problems in traffic, health, and public order. Industrial growth has also generated concerns about industrial safety, labor exploitation, and pollution. Moreover, the growth of science and the belief that humanity can harness and control nature have led to increased demands for government action. Globalization has created increased pressures to regulate the international flows of capital, trade, and people. Finally, changes in citizen values have led to demands for new kinds of regulation. Immigration policy, safety standards for offshore oil drilling, and banking regulation have become major policy disputes. At the same time, however, at least most Western societies have lessened their regulation of birth control, abortion, divorce, blasphemy, obscenity, and sexual conduct.

Governments regulate the lives of their citizens in many ways. Although we often associate regulation with legal means, there are other ways to regulate. Governments may control behavior by offering material or financial inducements or by persuasion or moral exhortation. For example, many governments try to reduce tobacco use by a combination of methods: bans on smoking, tobacco sales, or advertising; sales ("sin") taxes; and information campaigns to convince people of the hazards of smoking.

Even though there are many similarities in regulative policies across the world, states still differ substantially in their policy profiles. Patterns of regulation vary not only with industrialization and urbanization,

---

BOX 7.2

Regulation and Development

In the advanced industrial countries of North America, Japan, and Western Europe, regulation has grown enormously along with their industrial and postindustrial economies. It is easy to think, therefore, that there is more regulation in wealthy countries than in poor ones. But this is not always true. In fact, low-income countries sometimes regulate more than rich ones. This is particularly true of regulations of business entry and competition. In many less-developed countries, it is cumbersome and time-consuming, for example, to get the permits necessary to start a new business. Such regulations often mainly serve to create *rents* that government officials can exploit for their own benefit (see Chapter 1). They protect existing businesses by giving them monopolies or other protections. Many politicians expect the businesspeople who benefit from these regulations (often their family members, friends, or business associates) to show their gratitude through kickbacks and other favors. Or, business owners pay off politicians or civil servants to get around onerous regulations or to avoid long delays in handling their applications. Overregulation of this kind tends to hurt economic productivity and keep out foreign investment.

The Peruvian economist Hernando de Soto reports a sobering experience with abusive government regulation. As an experiment, he registered a small clothing factory in Lima, Peru, and decided in advance not to pay bribes. While he was waiting for his business to be registered, government officials asked him for bribes no fewer than ten times. Twice he broke his own rule and paid the bribe so that he would not be forced to give up his experiment. After ten months, his factory was finally registered. In New York, a similar procedure takes four hours.

Source: World Bank, *World Development Report 2005*, Chapter 5; William Easterly, *The Elusive Quest for Growth: The Economists' Adventures and Misadventures in the Tropics* (Cambridge: Massachusetts Institute of Technology Press, 2001), 233.

but also with cultural and ideological values. For example, population-control policies in China (Chapter 13) and Islamic dress-code policies in Iran (Chapter 16) illustrate the varieties of ways in which governments can regulate their societies. Table 7.2 shows the degree to which different countries try to control their economic markets. (This measure is intended to include "market-unfriendly" policies such as price controls or inadequate bank supervision, as well as excessive regulation of foreign trade and business development.) Although the capitalist democracies, such as Britain, the United States, Germany, France, and Japan tend to be the friendliest to market competition, the nondemocracies vary greatly in their government regulatory profiles. China is far more open than Iran, and in these policies rather similar to India. Public-policy studies describe regulatory differences among political systems by asking what aspects of human behavior are regulated, what social groups

are regulated, and what sanctions are used to pressure people to comply.

Although all modern states use sanctions, they vary in their goals and strategies. Yet one aspect of regulation is particularly important politically: government control over political participation and communication. Table 7.2 also shows freedom of the press, which is heavily shaped by the legal and political environment. Recall from earlier chapters that democracy requires political competition. As we might expect, the authoritarian systems control the press much more severely than their democratic counterparts. China, Iran, and Russia are ranked as "unfree" in their press freedom scores and are shown at the bottom of the table. A recent Freedom House study of Internet regulation in fifteen countries also showed the extensive efforts at controlling access and content of the Internet in China and Iran, while Brazil and Britain allowed their citizens relatively uncontrolled access. Authoritarian governments often suppress political competition by prohibiting party organization, voluntary associations, and political communication. All too often, they repress political opponents through imprisonment, disappearances, and torture. Studies of governmental repression have found that government abuses of physical integrity rights of citizens were best explained by nondemocratic political institutions and conditions of war and social disorder.[7] A lower level of economic development also encourages a weaker human-rights record.

Community Building and Symbolic Outputs

A fourth type of output is symbolic policies. Political leaders often make appeals to the courage, wisdom, and magnanimity embodied in the nation's past; or appeals to values and ideologies, such as equality, liberty, community, democracy, communism, liberalism, or religious tradition; or promises of future accomplishment and rewards. Political leaders appeal to such values for different reasons—for example, to win elections or to push their own pet projects. At the same time, many symbolic appeals and policies are trying to build community, such as by boosting people's national identity, civic pride, or trust in government.

Symbolic outputs also try to enhance other aspects of performance: to make people pay their taxes more readily and honestly; comply with the law more faithfully; or accept sacrifice, danger, and hardship.

TABLE 7.2

Controlling Markets and the Press

Governments vary in their use of regulatory policy to control the economy and communication.

Country	Regulation of Markets	Regulation of Press
Brazil	42	42
Britain	2	18
China	54	84
France	13	22
Germany	9	16
India	53	35
Iran	97	85
Japan	14	21
Mexico	35	55
Nigeria	70	53
Russia	69	78
United States	7	17

Note: Market regulation is a World Bank measure of "incidence of market-unfriendly policies, such as price controls or inadequate bank supervision, as well as perceptions of the burdens imposed by excessive regulation in areas such as foreign trade and business development" (from www.worldbank.org/governance/wgi/) on a 0-to-100 scale. Press freedom rating also on a 0-to-100 scale, where 100 is least free, downloaded from www.freedomhouse.org on July 9, 2010.

Such appeals may be especially important in times of crisis. Some of the most magnificent examples are the speeches of Pericles in the Athenian Assembly during the Peloponnesian War, Franklin D. Roosevelt in the depths of the Great Depression, or Winston Churchill during Britain's darkest hours in World War II. Symbolic policies are important even in less extreme circumstances. Public buildings, plazas, monuments, holiday parades, and civic and patriotic indoctrination in schools all attempt to contribute to a popular sense of governmental legitimacy and its willingness to comply with public policy.

DOMESTIC POLICY OUTCOMES

While we can describe different government policy activities in the previous section, their consequences in providing actual policy goods are not always clear. How do extractive, distributive, regulative, and symbolic policies affect the lives of people? Unexpected economic, international, or social events may frustrate the purpose of political leaders. Thus, a tax rebate to stimulate the economy may be nullified by a rise in the price of oil. Increases in health expenditures may have no effect because of unexpected epidemics or rising health

costs, or health services may not reach those most in need. Sometimes, policies have unintended and undesirable consequences, as when the introduction of benefits for troubled social groups leads others to simulate the same troubles to get the same favors. Consequently, to estimate the effectiveness of public policy, we have to examine actual policy outcomes as well as governmental policies and their implementation.

Welfare Outcomes

We begin by comparing different measures of public welfare across our set of nations. Welfare can involve the living standards of the average citizen, but also the other social conditions that affect quality of life and life chances.

The first column of Table 7.3 reports a measure of economic well-being or lack thereof: the share of the population living on less than $2 per day. The severe problems of Nigeria and India are particularly notable: the vast majority of those populations live on less than $2 a day. Clearly, this measure of welfare is closely related to the general level of economic development of the society, although inequality of income also plays a role (refer back to Table 1.3). Governments in most poorer countries are trying to encourage economic

TABLE 7.3

Welfare Outcomes

Economic development helps sustain basic material and health amenities, but also creates potential for environmental damages.

Country	Population below $2 per Day PPP (%), ca. 2007	Rural Population Access to Safe Water (%), 2006	Access to Sanitation (%) 2006	Carbon Dioxide Emissions, metric tons/capita, 2006
Brazil	12.7	58	77	1.9
Britain	—	100	—	9.4
China	36.3	81	65	4.7
France	—	100	—	6.2
Germany	—	100	100	9.8
India	75.6	86	28	1.4
Iran	8.0	—	—	6.7
Japan	—	100	100	10.0
Mexico	8.2	85	81	4.2
Nigeria	83.9	30	30	0.7
Russia	2.0	88	87	11.0
United States	—	94	100	19.0

Source: World Bank, *World Development Indicators* (downloaded June 6, 2010, from http://data.worldbank.org/indicator/).

development with the help of international organizations and donors, but sustained growth is hard to achieve. Eradication of extreme poverty is the number-one goal in the United Nations Millennium Development goals list (see Box 7.1).

The next two columns report the availability of two critical public facilities: safe water in rural areas, and sanitation. While most of the people of the developed world have access to safe water, this is true for less than half of the rural populations of many less-advantaged countries. And often, a majority of those populations live in rural areas. In Nigeria, for example, only 30 percent of the large rural population had access to safe water in 2006. Less than a third of the Nigerian and Indian populations overall have access to improved sanitation facilities, which are a major factor in disease prevention. Comparing the performance in China to Nigeria and India, and even rural Brazil, we can see that government policies can to some extent overcome the barriers of low economic development.

The last column in Table 7.3 shows one of the negative outcomes of higher economic development: pollution. Carbon-dioxide emissions per capita, which are a major contributor to air pollution and to global warming, are much higher in developed economies. The worst record is created by the most industrialized country, the United States, followed (distantly) by Russia, Japan, Germany, and Britain. Russia produces many more emissions than we might expect for its development level. These countries have all introduced measures to regulate pollution, but they are lagging far behind need. Carbon-dioxide emissions are not a problem so far in Nigeria, India, or Brazil. But China and Iran are closing in on the more industrialized countries. China's huge population and rapid growth make its pollution a serious threat, both to its own population and the global population. Because of their dual needs for economic growth and pollution control, these countries face hard regulatory policy choices (see Chapter 13).

Health outcomes also figure largely in the Millennium Development Goals (Box 7.1). Table 7.4 shows that the average developed nation has about 3 physicians per 1,000 people, compared with 1.3 in the developing world. In Nigeria, there are only 0.3 doctors in 1,000 people. The country has a high birth rate, but almost one out of ten infants fails to survive the first year of life. Nigerians have a life expectancy at birth of just forty-eight years (compared with seventy-eight to eighty-three years in advanced industrial countries). Nigeria demonstrates the ills of poverty, as do figures for India, which are also quite grim. But some poorer countries cope more successfully than others. Consider the difference between two

Health Outcomes

TABLE 7.4

Government efforts can help combat the problems of low economic development for citizens' health.

Country	Physicians per 1,000 Citizens, 2009	Life Expectancy at Birth, 2008	Infant Mortality per 1,000 Live Births, 2008	Fertility Rate, 2007
Brazil	1.2	72	18	1.9
Britain	2.3	78	5	1.9
China	1.4	73	18	1.8
France	3.4	82	3	2.0
Germany	3.4	80	4	1.4
India	0.6	64	52	2.7
Iran	0.9	71	27	1.8
Japan	2.1	83	3	1.3
Mexico	2.0	75	15	2.1
Nigeria	0.3	48	96	5.7
Russia	4.3	68	12	1.5
United States	2.6	78	7	2.1

Source: World Health Statistics 2009, downloaded June 7, 2010, from www.who.int/whosis/whostat/2009.

low-income nations: China and India. The Chinese average life expectancy is seventy-three years and their infant mortality is 18 per 1,000 live births, while the Indian life expectancy is sixty-four years and their infant mortality is 52 per 1,000. China has nearly three times as many physicians as India relative to its population. Fortunately, health conditions are improving in most of the poor countries, including India.

While the incidence of infant mortality and malnutrition is much lower in advanced economies, these problems are still serious among the poor in advanced industrial countries such as the United States. The United States spends the largest proportion of its GDP on health care (approximately 15 percent, of which about half is from the public sector) of any country. At the same time, however, in 2008, the United States had a somewhat higher infant death rate than Japan and Western Europe due to more widespread poverty, drug abuse, and unequal access to health care (which new policies are attempting to change). As Table 7.4 shows, Japan has an exceptional health record. It has the longest life expectancy and the lowest infant mortality rate among all the study countries in this book.

However, its low fertility rate means a declining population. (With no net migration, a fertility rate of approximately 2.1 is needed to produce a steady-state population.)

Education is another vital policy outcome, also stressed in the Millennium Development Goals. It provides individuals with skills and resources that enable them to be engaged in the political process; these skills shape their life chances in establishing a career and improving their personal conditions. Education is also necessary for successful economic development and all that means for many other welfare outcomes. Table 7.5 provides a picture of educational and information attainment. In most industrial democracies, high school education is mandatory and college education is commonplace. At the high end in educational outcomes, France, Germany, Japan, and Britain have virtually all of their primary and secondary school-aged children in schools, and about half of the college-aged population is in some form of advanced education. In the United States, college education is even more common. Nigeria requires only children from ages six to

Education, Equality, and Information

TABLE 7.5

Education efforts, gender policies, and development shape information access and inequality.

Country	Gross Percentage of Relevant Age Group Enrolled, Tertiary, 2007	Percentage Fifteen Years and Above Illiterate, Male/ Female, 2007	Ratio of Female to Male Earned Income, 2007	Personal Computers per 100 Inhabitants, 2008	Internet Users per 100 Inhabitants, 2008
Brazil	30	10/10	0.60	16	38
Britain	58	—	0.67	80	76
China	22	3/10	0.68	6	22
France	55	—	0.61	65	68
Germany	49	—	0.59	66	75
India	14	23/45	0.32	3	5
Iran	30	13/23	0.32	11	32
Japan	58	—	0.45	—	75
Mexico	26	6/9	0.42	14	22
Nigeria	10	20/36	0.42	1	16
Russia	75	1/1	0.64	13	32
United States	82	—	0.62	81	76

Source: World Bank, *World Development Indicators* (downloaded June 7, 2010, from http://data.worldbank.org/indicator/); also, for female inequality, United Nations Human Development Report 2009 (downloaded June 7, 2010, from http://hdr.unpd.org/en/reports/global/hdr2009).

twelve to attend school and has only 10 percent of the appropriate age cohort in tertiary education, by far the poorest record of these countries. India's figure is 14 percent.

The payoff of development and education is clearly reflected in literacy rates: 20 to 23 percent of adult men and 36 to 45 percent of adult women in Nigeria and India are unable to read or write. Yet China has less than 10 percent illiteracy.

Table 7.5 also highlights access to information technologies, such as the Internet and personal computers. As shown, many more people access the Internet in wealthy and well-educated countries, such as Japan, than in the developing world. Yet even in poorer countries, communications have become much easier. Television has become widely available even in countries at modest development levels (e.g., Brazil and Mexico). Internet use is growing very rapidly. Nearly a quarter of the population in China and Mexico report having access to the Internet, as do about a third in Iran and Brazil. Despite the efforts of authoritarian governments in countries such as Iran and China to control Internet use (see Chapters 16 and 13, as well as the discussion of regulatory policies above), information potential is remarkable. In the developed countries, most adults and many children have cell phones, and even in India and Nigeria, there is already a cell phone for about every three people. The advent of cell phones has made it much easier to connect the rural population in developing countries where there are often very few landlines. Personal computers, however, are much rarer outside the advanced industrial economies. Compared with people in Brazil and Mexico, people in the United States are five times more likely to own a personal computer.

Table 7.5 reveals the sobering difficulties of trying to change societies, even in an area such as literacy, where modern technologies are available. It is hard for a poor country to spend a high percentage of its GDP on education, because it must then make sacrifices elsewhere. And the effects are limited if much of the country's productive effort has to go into feeding a rapidly growing population. No matter how large the educational effort may be, it does not translate into much per child, because the resource base is small and the population is growing rapidly. Moreover, since most older people are illiterate, the net effect on literacy is slow. And in many poorer countries, their best-educated young people often leave the country to take jobs in the big cities of the rich countries.

Fairness Outcomes

Fairness was one of the welfare outcomes discussed in the framework of Table 7.1 on policy goods. Concepts of fairness vary by culture and ideology. Despite these differences, promoting gender equality and empowering women appear on the Millennium Development Goals that were endorsed by so many nations (see again Box 7.1). Column 2 in Table 7.5 shows that women in developing countries often lag behind in literacy. Culture and policy also affect the male/female differences, as we see in comparing gender differences in Brazil and Iran, for example. The discrepancy between male and female literacy rates tells us something of the status of women and the achievement of fairness by gender. Column 3 provides additional insight by showing us the ratio of female to male earned incomes. Differences in the types of jobs in which they are employed and pay discrimination mean that women only earn about two-thirds of the income of men even in the most equal countries—which are China and Britain. Clearly, achievement of gender fairness has far to go everywhere. At the bottom of the scale, in Iran and India, women earn only one-third the income of men.

Faced with poverty, disease, and the absence of a social safety net, parents in poor countries traditionally want to have many children to ensure that some survive and can support them in old age. In large families, mothers usually have few opportunities to educate themselves or hold jobs outside the home (but see Boxes 7.3 and 7.4). Modernizing the status of women generally makes them better informed and more capable of making choices that lead to a stabler and healthier population. As women are educated and/or enter the labor force, they recognize the advantages of smaller families and become more aware of the importance of education and adequate health care. The important place of gender equality and empowering women in the Millennium Development Goals reflects these implications for other aspects of welfare as well as fairness itself (also refer back to Box 1.4).

Fairness in the treatment of minority ethnic, racial, and religious groups is also an issue in many countries. Although democracies are generally less abusive of minorities than are authoritarian systems, democratic majorities can often cruelly ignore their own standards of fairness in treating minority groups. The Minorities at Risk project tracks the status of 282 minority groups using expert informants. The records of our twelve large nations showed that in ten nations, at least one minority group was subject to "significant poverty and underrepresentation due to prevailing social practices by dominant groups" (www.cidcm. umd.edu/mar). Public policies either deliberately contributed to the problem or were inadequate to overcome discriminatory practices. Such minority groups included Afro-Brazilians in Brazil, Corsicans in France, scheduled tribes in India, Mayans in Mexico, Chechens in Russia, and Native Americans in the United States.

Often, unfair treatment of minorities is closely related to the problem of rural poverty. While there are many causes of the inequality between city and countryside in basic health facilities and income, government policy can contribute. In many African states, for example, the rulers tend to favor the urban population because they want the country to modernize and industrialize. Sometimes, politicians also worry that a starving urban population might riot and bring down the government. For these reasons, governments tend to keep food prices artificially low, which hurts farmers. Governments also tend to prefer targeted government agricultural programs (often subsidies), which help particular groups of farmers (often wealthy ones). Such targeted programs help governments gain political supporters but are often wasteful. Even in democratic countries where the majority of voters are poor farmers, government policies often do little for them. Many voters do not trust politicians who promise to deliver broad public goods (such as health care and education), but instead support candidates who promise targeted private goods (such as jobs and subsidies). Thus, even spending on schools becomes a way to create jobs rather than to educate children. In India, teachers' salaries account for 96 percent of recurrent expenditures in primary education. Even so, teacher absenteeism is rampant. When inspectors made unannounced visits to rural schools, about two-thirds of the teachers were absent.[8]

Of course, great income inequality of all kinds violates most standards of fairness. One of the problems of economic development is that the middle stages of development are often associated with new concentrations of wealth and greater gaps between the newly prosperous, usually urban, middle class and those left behind. Indeed, the hope that new democratic governments would lead to greater equality has historically been one of the driving forces in democratization. Yet even in the wealthiest democracies today, the wealthiest 10 percent of the population earns as much as the poorest 40 percent (refer back to Table 1.4). In the

---

Microcredit   BOX 7.3

One of the greatest obstacles to economic growth in many poor areas is the difficulty of obtaining credit. In advanced industrial countries, property owners (for example, farmers or homeowners) typically have a recognized title to their property. If they want to invest to expand their business or start a new one, they can borrow against this collateral. People in poor countries rarely have this opportunity, and it is especially difficult for poor farmers and women to obtain loans. As a result, they often cannot get the funds they need to tide them over during hard times or to take advantage of promising business opportunities.

Muhammad Yunus, a U.S.-educated professor of economics, noticed these problems in his native country of Bangladesh. In 1974, he began extending small loans to poor people to help them out of these circumstances. His first loan amounted to $27 from his own pockets, which he lent to forty-two people, including a woman who made bamboo furniture, which she sold to support herself and her family. In 1976, Yunus founded Grameen Bank to make loans to poor Bangladeshis. The bank has since given out more than $5 billion in loans. To secure its loans, the bank sets up a system of "solidarity groups," which meet on a weekly basis and support each other's efforts. As of May 2006, Grameen Bank had almost 7 million borrowers, 97 percent of whom were women. Their repayment rate is 98 percent. In 2006, Muhammad Yunus and the Grameen Bank received the Nobel Peace Prize for these efforts to help poor people improve their lives.

BOX 7.4

Women and the Informal Economy

Parmila is an Indian widow in her thirties with two young children. Although she comes from a wealthy family, her husband's death forced her to take various part-time jobs. She collects wood from local forests, dries it, and then twice a week walks five miles to sell it at a local market. In the winter (November to January), she works on farms dehusking rice. She gets to keep some of the rice she produces. Outside of the rainy season, she also works as a laborer on a construction site, where her boss pays her about half of the Indian minimum wage. Parmila's total income is very low by Western standards, but it is enough to allow her to send her two children to school. Parmila does not ask for sympathy or for financial support from her relatives. "Even in times of acute crisis, I held my nerves and did not give in to circumstances," she says. "My God has always stood with me."

Women make up an increasing share of the world's workers. In most non-Islamic countries, they now make up 40 percent or more of the labor force. But in many parts of the world, most women work in the informal economy, where their work is often poorly paid. It commonly also escapes taxation and regulation. In India and in many African countries, for example, more than four out of five women who work outside of agriculture are in the informal economy. Many women choose such jobs voluntarily. They may do childcare for others or produce arts and crafts, often for local consumption. These jobs may be attractive because they can be performed at home while the women also take care of their own children or relatives. But many women also work in the informal sector because they face discrimination elsewhere. And some are enticed or forced into exhausting, dangerous, or degrading work in sweatshops or in the sex industry. While the informal economy can offer job flexibility, it can also be a place where there is little protection against abusive working conditions.

Source: William Easterly, *The Elusive Quest for Growth: The Economists' Adventures and Misadventures in the Tropics* (Cambridge: Massachusetts Institute of Technology Press, 2001), 45.

United States, the gap between rich and poor is substantially larger. This gap between rich and poor continues to be a particular problem in middle-level countries like Brazil and Mexico, where the gap is much greater (as we saw in Table 1.4.). On the one hand, social and economic conditions, such as levels of literacy, occupational skills, and land-holding, are derived from historic development experiences and continue to feed income inequality. On the other hand, government policies play an important role through the progressiveness or regressiveness of revenue policies and the redistributiveness of welfare policies. There is a great deal of debate about this gap—how great the injustice it does to the poor, to what extent it is justified by the incentives it provides for individual efforts or by established property rights, and the degree to which it should be eased by the welfare state.

Liberty and Freedom Outcomes

One of the prime objectives of good government is to provide for the freedom and liberty of its citizens. Even if there is a popular myth that authoritarian governments help make societies more efficient, the goal of government is to empower its citizens so that they can control their own lives. We can measure individual liberty and freedom outcomes in several ways.

Table 7.6 shows political experts' ratings of the political-rights and civil-liberties scores for the countries included in this book. *Political rights* refers to citizen opportunities to participate in the choice of political leaders—voting rights, the right to run for office, and the like. *Civil liberties* refers to protections in such areas as freedom of speech, press, assembly, and religion, as well as to procedural rights, such as trial by a jury of peers and bans on arbitrary or cruel treatment. The levels of liberties reflect the outcomes of government policies, especially regulatory policies, but are also affected by social and economic conditions, such as prosperity, inequality, and crime, in the societies. The affluent democratic countries all have positive ratings for both political and civil rights. India, Brazil, and Mexico, which have improved significantly in recent years, follow next. At the other extreme, China, Iran, and most recently Russia substantially suppress both political rights and civil liberties. China

Country	Political Rights	Civil Liberties	Economic Freedom
Brazil	2	2	5.6
Britain	1	1	7.7
China	7	6	5.1
France	1	1	6.4
Germany	1	1	7.1
India	2	3	5.4
Iran	6	6	4.3
Japan	1	2	7.3
Mexico	2	3	6.8
Nigeria	5	4	5.7
Russia	6	5	5.0
United States	1	1	7.8

TABLE 7.6

Political and Economic Rights and Liberties, 2009

Political rights, civil liberties, and economic freedom are strongly associated.

Note: Expert ratings of political rights and civil liberties for each country on 1 (highest) to 7 (lowest) scale. Economic freedom scored on summary scale from 0 (low) to 10 (high).

Source: Freedom House Web site, www.freedomhouse.org (downloaded June 10, 2010); 2010 Index of Economic Freedom, product of the Heritage Foundation and the *Wall Street Journal*, www.heritage.org (downloaded June 10, 2010).

in particular has tried to control the media comprehensively (see Table 7.1) and sets few limits on government regulation vis-à-vis the individual. Nigeria is rated in the middle.

These rankings, of course, vary over time. Rights and liberties in the United States have improved since the civil rights movement of the 1960s. Nigeria's military governments of the 1990s were repressive and frequently brutal; political rights and civil liberties have improved there since power was turned over to an elected civilian president in 1999, but remain fragile. Nigeria was downgraded substantially after observers reported massive vote-rigging and fraud in the (disputed) 2007 presidential and gubernatorial elections.

There is a strong correlation between political and civil rights. No country that scores high on participatory rights also scores very low on civil liberties, and no country low on participatory rights is high on civil

liberties. This suggests a strong relationship between popular participation and the rule of law and equitable procedure. Studies of governmental repression have also found that limitations on government abuses of physical integrity rights of citizens were best explained by democratic political institutions and conditions of peace and social order. Authoritarian states and those involved in internal or international war were the most frequent violators of personal integrity.

Table 7.6 also reports the level of economic freedom in each country. It is not always true that countries that are politically free also foster economic freedom, or vice versa. For example, Mexico shows substantially more economic freedom than Brazil or India, although its political freedom ratings are similar. And even though Britain and France score the same on political rights and liberties, Britain has a higher level of economic freedom. On the whole, though, political and economic freedoms tend to go together.

Domestic Security Outcomes

As Thomas Hobbes would have reminded us, maintaining domestic law and order and protecting persons and property are among the most basic government responsibilities. Without them, the conduct of personal, economic, and civic life are impossible. It is therefore worrisome that until recently, crime rates were on the increase in many advanced industrial countries as well as in the developing world. For example, in the United States, the crime rate increased by almost 15 percent between 1982 and 1991. In France, the 1990 incidence of crimes against persons and property was almost twice that of 1975. In Russia, the crime rate doubled between 1985 and 1993 as the moral and legal order collapsed.

High crime rates are primarily a problem of the larger urban areas where much of the population of modern countries resides. The causes of urban crime are complex. Rapidly increasing migration into the major cities, from the domestic countryside or from poorer foreign countries, increases diversity and often conflict. The pace of urbanization is particularly explosive in many developing countries, such as Brazil and Nigeria, where there are severe problems of poverty and infrastructure. The newly arrived city-dwellers often find themselves uprooted from their cultures, unwelcome, without a job, and living in squalor far apart from their families and traditional communities. Also, inequality of income and wealth, unemployment, and drug abuse lie behind this general decline in public order and safety. Increased globalization of crime, especially in drugs and human trafficking, has also played its part.

Figure 7.3 presents figures on the number of homicides per 100,000 inhabitants for the nations in this book. Brazil has the most homicides per 100,000 inhabitants. Its murder rate is almost five times as high as that in the United States. Russia and Mexico also have considerably higher murder rates than the United States. Iran and India have rates about half those of the United States, while the other industrialized nations have rates that are a small fraction of the U.S. numbers. China and Nigeria report similarly low murder rates. Yet crime rates have recently come down significantly in the United States and some other countries. The number of murders per 100,000 inhabitants in the United States peaked at 9.4 in 1994 and declined to 5.2 in 2008.

There are several reasons that crime rates might decrease. One is economic conditions, with crime rates decreasing when the economy is strong. A second reason is stricter law enforcement. This is partially reflected in the number of police officers relative to total population, which ranges from 1 police officer for every 350 persons in the United States to 1 in 820 in India and 1 in 1,140 in Nigeria. In the United States, both federal and state governments have also sought to reduce crime by increasing the length of imprisonment. A third cause of lower crime rates has been a decrease in the number of youth at the age at which most crimes are committed. Yet as the fifteen-to-twenty-five-year-old male population in the United States is now on the rise and youth unemployment has risen sharply with the recession of 2008 and 2009, violent crime may increase once again.

An even greater threat to personal security than private crime can be intense domestic political conflict culminating in civil war. In recent years, much of the world's media focus has been on conflicts in the Middle East, but conflicts in Africa have in fact been more

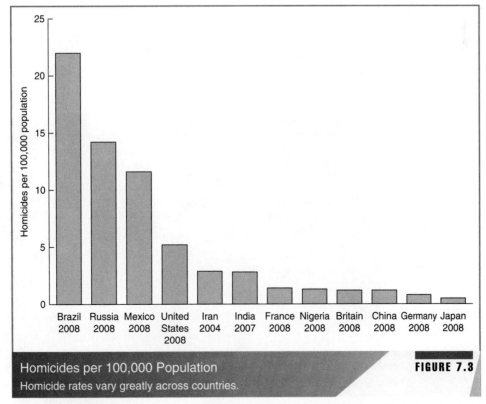

Homicides per 100,000 Population
Homicide rates vary greatly across countries.

FIGURE 7.3

Source: United Nations Office on Drugs and Crime, downloaded from www.unodc.org/unodc/en/data-and-analysis/homicide.html on June 14, 2010.

frequent and devastating. Many African countries, newly independent from about 1960, but with borders arbitrarily drawn by colonial powers, have serious problems of national cohesion and have suffered from chronic civil war. Large-scale civil war in Nigeria (1967 to 1970) cost perhaps a million lives, and more sporadic conflict continues to the present time.

The Uppsala Conflict Data Project reports 128 armed worldwide conflicts (defined as involving at least twenty-five battle deaths) from 1989 through 2008. In 2008, there were thirty-six ongoing conflicts, of which five (in Afghanistan, Iraq, Pakistan, Somalia, and Sri Lanka) involved more than 1,000 deaths.[9] All but one was a civil war occurring within state boundaries, although several were internationalized in that foreign powers were also involved. In every year since the end of World War II in 1945, there have been more civil wars than interstate conflicts (wars between countries), and civil wars have also caused more casualties than interstate wars.

There are many reasons for the high incidence of civil war. Some are related to ethnic or religious conflicts. But others seem mainly due to struggles between warlords over lootable resources, such as diamonds, gold, or oil. External actors—such as the UN, the United States, NATO, or strong regional powers—can sometimes help end civil wars, but in some cases (such as Angola), civil wars have been prolonged because

foreign powers have been engaged on both sides of the conflict.

The UN in the post–Cold War world has intervened in some of these conflicts by providing peacekeeping missions when the parties to conflicts are ready to accept these mediations. As of July 2010, there were sixteen peacekeeping missions in various parts of the world. More rarely, the UN intervenes as a peacemaker, as in Bosnia and later in neighboring Kosovo in the 1990s, or when the peacekeeping mission in Sierra Leone (West Africa) was converted into a peacemaking effort. The UN's effectiveness in controlling domestic and international collective violence depends on consensus among the great powers.

INTERNATIONAL OUTCOMES

Most states engage in a great variety of international activities. Such economic, diplomatic, military, and informational activities may result in prosperity or depression, war or peace, secularization or the spread of particular beliefs.[10] The phenomenon known as *globalization* has increasingly demanded more economic, social, and political involvement by ever more states. National economies have become more dependent on international trade and capital flows, creating intense pressures from those advantaged by trade to

International Peacekeepers

Police and troops from a U.N. peacekeeping force carry a victim of a school collapse on November 7, 2008, in Pétionville, Haiti.

Thony Belizaire/AFP/Getty Images

ease restrictions and those hurt by international competition to increase barriers. These conflicting demands can be a major source of internal conflict.[11] Moreover, a major economic setback in one part of the world, such as the financial credit crisis in the developed nations in 2008 and 2009, ripples though many distant countries. Crippled industrialized economies import fewer goods, hitting the producing countries in turn. Increasingly, countries need coordinated political action to regulate capital flows and encourage trade. The very interdependence that globalization creates can threaten damage to all if key countries break off their involvement, as happened during the 1930s.

Environmental damage, too, flows beyond the boundaries of individual countries, as in the threat that cumulative atmospheric emissions pose to global climate stability. The social side of globalization has also expanded. Personal contacts and information flows, including television and Internet use, have increased, as has the presence of cultural (and economic) symbols such as McDonald's. These have brought pressures to respect international standards of personal integrity and gender equality (see Chapter 3). However, while individuals may benefit greatly from the opportunities that the Internet or McDonald's offer, these exposures may also threaten traditional values. Issues such as controlling immigration loom large in many countries.

Table 7.7 shows the KOF index of globalization, which tracks a wide variety of economic, social, and political measures. Countries with higher globalization scores have more trade and foreign direct investment relative to their GDP and lower import barriers. On the social globalization dimension, they also have more international telephone traffic and letters, more Internet users, and more memberships in international organizations. We see that globalization has increased in most countries during the last thirty-five years, especially since 1990. China, which was once at the lowest levels of globalization, expanded its global exposure—economic, social, and political—into the middle ranks, from 15 on a 100-point scale in 1970 to 63 in 2007. India and Brazil, too, have exploded onto the global stage, as has Russia since the breakup of the Soviet Union. At the same time, countries like France, Germany, Britain, and the United States, beginning from a much more globalized base, have further expanded their involvement in the global flows of trade, capital, and information, reaching scores in the 70 to 80 range. Of the countries in our set, by far the

TABLE 7.7

Change in the Index of Globalization, 1970–2007

Globalization has been increasing across the world, but government policies can affect the rate and level.

Country	1970	1980	1990	2000	2007
Brazil	37	43	44	58	60
Britain	57	67	73	82	80
China	15	20	35	54	63
France	58	65	75	86	86
Germany	47	58	61	84	84
India	24	25	29	44	51
Iran	25	27	22	35	37
Japan	35	43	48	61	68
Mexico	43	45	52	60	61
Nigeria	27	38	40	49	56
Russia	—	—	39	63	69
United States	60	65	71	78	79

The KOF index of globalization, a 0-to-100 scale, is composed of economic, social, and political elements.

Source: Axel Dreher, "Does Globalization Affect Growth? Evidence from a New Index of Globalization," *Applied Economics* 38, no. 10 (2006):1091–110, downloaded June 11, 2010, from http://globalization.kof.ethz.ch/.

most resistant to globalization has been Iran, which since the Islamic Revolution in 1979 has tried to maintain its general economic and social isolation. So, while globalization exerts powerful incentives for economic and social integration, government policies can powerfully promote or constrain it.

The most costly outcome of the interaction among nations is warfare. Table 7.8 reports the numbers of deaths from international and internal collective violence for our twelve study countries for almost the entire twentieth century (1900 to 1995). The figures are mostly civilian and military deaths from interstate warfare, but they also include the slaughter of civilians in the efforts to implement communism in the Soviet Union, the holocaust of European Jews under the German Nazis (Hitler's National Socialist Party), many "ethnic cleansing" episodes in Europe and Africa, and civil wars in all parts of the world.

Over the long haul, the deadly costs of international warfare have gradually escalated. Civilian deaths caused by war increased even more rapidly than military ones.

TABLE 7.8

Deaths from Collective Civilian–Military Violence, 1900–1995
Citizens in some nations paid a terrible price for the international conflicts of the twentieth century.

Country	Civilian Deaths	Military Deaths	Unspecified Deaths	Total Deaths
Brazil	—	1,000	2,000	3,000
Britain	131,000	1,350,000	—	1,481,000
China	4,047,000	2,671,000	818,000	7,536,000
France	490,000	1,830,000	—	2,320,000
Germany	2,232,000	7,150,000	—	9,382,000
India	889,000	71,000	37,000	997,000
Iran	120,000	468,000	1,000	589,000
Japan	510,000	1,502,000	—	2,012,000
Mexico	125,000	125,000	10,000	260,000
Nigeria	1,005,000	1,000,000	6,000	2,011,000
USSR/Russia	12,028,000	11,901,000	96,000	24,025,000
United States	—	524,000	—	524,000
TOTALS	21,577,000	28,593,000	970,000	51,140,000

Source: Adapted from Ruth Leger Sivard, "Wars and War Related Deaths, 1900–1995," *World Military and Social Expenditures 1996* (Washington, D.C.: World Priorities, 1996), 18–19. U.S. deaths add Korean and Vietnam war totals, from U.S. Department of State figures, to Sivard report of World War I and II deaths.

In the last decades of the twentieth century, more than three-quarters of the war deaths were civilian.[12]

Table 7.8 shows that the people of USSR/Russia, by a margin of more than two to one, were the most numerous victims of the tormented history of the twentieth century. The enormous Russian casualties during World War I destroyed the czarist regime. Its collapse was followed by the 1917 Bolshevik Revolution, the Civil War (1918 to 1921), and Stalin's Great Terror (particularly in the 1930s), each of which cost the lives of millions. Soviet suffering climaxed in World War II with a total of 17 million civilian and military dead. All told, the USSR/Russia suffered more than 24 million civilian and military deaths in the wars and political horrors of the twentieth century.

Germany suffered the second-largest number of deaths from twentieth-century collective violence. More than 3 million deaths, mostly military, occurred in World War I. In World War II, Germany suffered almost 5 million military and another 1.75 million civilian deaths. Other countries with huge losses include China (7 to 8 million) and Japan, whose more than 2 million deaths include half a million civilians, notably many

residents of Hiroshima and Nagasaki. French and British sufferings were of roughly similar magnitude.

After World War II, the most devastating conflicts have occurred in the Third World. The partition of formerly British India into India, Pakistan, and Bangladesh has been associated with numerous deadly conflicts within and among the three countries. Some 2 million lives, mostly civilian, have been lost. The end of the Cold War around 1990 witnessed a wave of instability and conflict in Eastern Europe and Central Asia. The breakup of the Soviet Union and Yugoslavia resulted in bloody border wars and secession conflicts (for example, in Bosnia and Kosovo in the former Yugoslavia, and Chechnya in Russia). These conflicts brought another wave of ethnic slaughter, religious clashes, and struggles for power among different warlords. But since 1992, the number of wars and casualties has gradually declined. And although recent years have seen horrific acts of terrorism, its annual human toll has not changed much. Some students of international conflict see hope in what they call the "democratic peace," the fact that democratic countries hardly ever fight wars against one another. As more countries become democratic, will the world also become more peaceful? International warfare, which would be even more terrible if nuclear powers were involved, is potentially the greatest threat to human security.

THE COMPLEXITY OF POLICY CHOICE

One of the hard facts about political goods is that we cannot always have them simultaneously. A political system often has to trade off one value to obtain another. Spending funds on education is giving up the opportunity to spend them on welfare, or to leave them in the hands of those who earned them. Politicians also have to decide how much to invest for the future rather than spend today (for example, when they determine future retirement benefits). Even more difficult are the trade-offs between security and liberty. Extreme liberty, as Hobbes would tell us, would give us a highly insecure world where the strong might bully the weak and where collective action would be difficult. Yet without liberty, security may be little more than servitude or imprisonment. The trade-offs between political goods are not the same under all circumstances. Sometimes, increasing liberty will also increase security (for example, because riots against censorship will end). And under some conditions,

investment in education will be paid back many times in health and welfare, because trained citizens can better care for themselves and work more productively. These are positive trade-offs. But often you "cannot have your cake and eat it too." One of the important tasks of social science is to discover the conditions under which positive and negative trade-offs occur.

Political science has no way of converting units of liberty into units of safety or welfare. And we can never calculate the value of a political outcome gained at the cost of human life. Political decision-makers often have to make such conversions, but as political scientists, we can only point to value judgments that they are willing to make. The weight given to various goods differs across cultures and contexts. A religious faith or a political ideology may tell us how one value should be traded against another and thus offer an orderly basis for choice. Such schemes may be invaluable for those pressed into action in the terrible circumstances of war, revolution, and famine. When people do not share these underlying schemes and values, there may be serious conflicts. Sadly, there is no ideology, just as there is no political science, that can solve all these problems objectively. However, governments should provide a means for the people to decide for themselves, because this may be the only acceptable resolution of complex policy choices.

REVIEW QUESTIONS

- What explains the growth of the welfare state?
- What are the advantages and disadvantages of different types of taxes?
- Why may a "windfall" of natural resources make it more difficult to introduce or sustain democracy?
- Do some governments tend to promote political rights and others civil rights, or do civil and political rights tend to go together?

- How is the welfare outcome for women changing in developing countries today?
- Why does globalization give rise to internal conflict within nations?
- What sorts of armed conflicts are most common in today's world, and what problems do they cause?

KEY TERMS

direct taxes
distribution
extraction
fairness

gross domestic product
    (GDP)
indirect taxes
outcomes

outputs
policy goods
political goods
public policies

regulation
rentier states
symbolic outputs

SUGGESTED READINGS

Bates, Robert H. *When Things Fell Apart: State Failure in Late-Century Africa.* New York: Cambridge University Press, 2008.

Boix, Carles. *Political Parties, Growth, and Equality: Conservative and Social Democratic Economic Strategies in the World Economy.* New York: Cambridge University Press, 1998.

Castles, Francis G., ed. *The Comparative History of Public Policy.* Cambridge: Polity Press, 1989.

Dahl, Robert. *Democracy and Its Critics.* New Haven, CT: Yale University Press, 1989.

Easterly, William. *The Elusive Quest for Growth: The Economists' Adventures and Misadventures in the Tropics.* Cambridge: Massachusetts Institute of Technology Press, 2001.

Flora, Peter, and Arnold Heidenheimer. *The Development of Welfare States in Europe and America.* New Brunswick, NJ: Transaction Books, 1981.

Franzese, Robert. *Macroeconomic Policies of Developed Democracies.* New York: Cambridge University Press, 2002.

Gourevitch, Peter. *Politics in Hard Times.* Ithaca, NY: Cornell University Press, 1986.

Halperin, Morton H., Joseph T. Siegle, and Michael M. Weinstein. *The Democracy Advantage: How Democracies Promote Prosperity and Peace.* New York: Routledge, 2010.

Lijphart, Arend. *Patterns of Democracy: Government Forms and Performance in Thirty-Six Countries.* New Haven, CT: Yale University Press, 1999.

Persson, Torsten, and Guido Tabellini. *The Economic Effects of Constitutions.* Cambridge: Massachusetts Institute of Technology Press, 2003.

Putnam, Robert. *Making Democracy Work: Civic Traditions in Modern Italy.* Princeton, NJ: Princeton University Press, 1993.

Rogowski, Ronald. *Commerce and Coalitions: How Trade Affects Domestic Political Alignments.* Princeton, NJ: Princeton University Press, 1989.

Tsebelis, George. *Veto Players: An Introduction to Institutional Analysis.* Princeton, NJ: Princeton University Press, 2002.

Wilensky, Harold. *Rich Democracies: Political Economy, Public Policy, and Performance.* Berkeley: University of California Press, 2002.

ENDNOTES

1. This literature seems to have originated in studies of the Middle East. See the reviews in Michael L. Ross, "Does Oil Hinder Democracy?" *World Politics* 53 (2001): 325–61 and Thad Dunning, *Crude Democracy: Natural Resource Wealth and Political Regimes* (New York: Cambridge University Press, 2008). Also see Kiren A. Chaudhry, *The Price of Wealth: Economies and Institutions in the Middle East* (Ithaca, NY: Cornell University Press, 1997).

2. See especially Ross, "Does Oil Hinder Democracy?" who sketches multiple causal mechanisms proposed in the literature.

3. Samuel P. Huntington, *The Third Wave: Democratization in the Late Twentieth Century* (Norman: University of Oklahoma, 1991), 65.

4. Dunning, *Crude Democracy.*

5. See, for example, Carles Boix, *Political Parties, Growth, and Equality: Conservative and Social Democratic Economic Strategies in the World Economy* (New York: Cambridge University Press, 1998); Robert Franzese, *Macroeconomic Policies of Developed Democracies* (New York: Cambridge University Press, 2002); Shin-Goo Kang and G. Bingham Powell Jr., "Representation and Policy Responsiveness," *Journal of Politics* 72 (October 2010): 1014–1028; Michael D. McDonald and Ian Budge, *Elections, Parties, Democracy: Conferring the Median Mandate* (New York: Oxford University Press, 2005); Harold Wilensky, *Rich Democracies: Political Economy, Public Policy, and Performance* (Berkeley: University of California Press, 2002).

6. Laurence J. Kotlikoff and Scott Burns, *The Coming Generational Storm: What You Need to Know about America's Economic Future* (Cambridge: Massachusetts Institute of Technology Press, 2004).

7. Steven C. Poe and C. Neal Tate, "Repression of Human Rights to Personal Integrity in the 1980s: A Global Analysis," *American Political Science Review* 88, no. 4 (December 1994): 853–72; also see Christian Davenport, *State Repression and the Democratic Peace* (Cambridge: Cambridge University Press, 2007).

8. Robert H. Bates, *Markets and States in Tropical Africa* (Berkeley: University of California Press, 1981); Philip Keefer and Stuti Khemani, "Why Do the Poor Receive Poor Services?" *Economic and Political Weekly* 28 (February 2004): 935–43; World Bank, *World Development Report, 2002* "Building Institutions for Markets" (A World Bank Publication), 31–32.

9. See Lotta Harbom and Peter Wallensteen, "Armed Conflict, 1946–2008," *Journal of Peace Research* 46, no. 4 (2009): 577–87.

10. Peter Gourevitch, in his book *Politics in Hard Times* (Ithaca, NY: Cornell University Press, 1986), analyzes the policy responses of five Western industrial nations—Britain, France, Germany, Sweden, and the United States—to the three world depressions of 1870–1890, 1930–1940, and 1975–1985. Gourevitch shows how these crises affected business, labor, and agriculture differently in each country; consequences for political structure and policy varied greatly. Thus, the world

depression of the 1930s resulted in a conservative reaction in Britain (the formation of a "National" government), a moderate left reaction in the United States (the "New Deal"), a polarization and paralysis of public policy in France ("Immobilisme"), a moderate social democratic reaction in Sweden, and a radical right-and-left polarization in Germany, leading to a breakdown of democracy and the emergence of National Socialism. While the causes of World War II were complex, the pacifism of Britain, the demoralization and defeatism in France, the isolationism of the United States, and the nihilism and aggression of Germany were all fed by the devastating worldwide economic depression of the 1930s.

11. See especially Ronald Rogowski, *Commerce and Coalitions: How Trade Affects Domestic Political Alignments* (Princeton, NJ: Princeton University Press, 1989).

12. Ruth Leger Sivard, *World Military and Social Indicators* (Washington, D.C.: World Priorities, 1993), 20.

N

ATLANTIC
OCEAN

North
Sea

SCOTLAND

Wick

Inverness

Aberdeen

Glasgow Edinburgh

NORTHERN
IRELAND Belfast

Irish Sea

Tyne

NORTH

NORTH
WEST Leeds

Liverpool Manchester
Sheffield
Mersey

EAST
MIDLANDS

Norwich

EAST
ANGLIA

WALES WEST Birmingham
MIDLANDS

Severn

SOUTH
EAST

Thames

Cardiff London

SOUTH WEST Portsmouth

Plymouth

English Channel

BRITAIN

0   100   200   300 Miles

0   100   200   300 Kilometers

POLITICS IN BRITAIN

Richard Rose

Country Bio

UNITED KINGDOM

Population
61.8 million

Territory
94,525 square miles

Year of Independence
From twelfth century

Year of Current Constitution
Unwritten; partly statutes, partly common law and practice

Head of State
Queen Elizabeth II

Head of Government
Prime Minister David Cameron

Language
English; plus about 600,000 who regularly speak Welsh and about 60,000 who speak Gaelic; plus immigrants speaking languages of the Indian subcontinent and elsewhere

Religion
Nominal identification in census: Church of England 26.1 million, Roman Catholic 5.7 million, Presbyterian 2.6 million, Methodist 1.3 million, other Christian 2.6 million, Muslim 1.5 million, Hindu 500,000, Sikh 330,000, Jewish 260,000, other 300,000, no religion 8.6 million, no reply 4.4 million

In a world of new democracies, Britain is different because it is an old democracy. Its political system has been evolving for more than 800 years. In medieval times, the king of England claimed to rule France and Ireland, too. While the claim to rule France was abandoned in the fifteenth century, sovereignty was gained over Wales and Scotland. The government of the **United Kingdom** was created in 1801 by merging England, Scotland, Wales, and Ireland under the authority of Parliament in London.

Unlike new democracies, Britain did not become a democracy overnight. It became a democracy by evolution rather than revolution. Democratization was a slow process. The rule of law was established in the seventeenth century, the accountability of the executive to Parliament was established by the eighteenth century, and national political parties organized in the nineteenth century. Even though competitive elections had been held for more than a century, the right of every adult man and woman to vote was not recognized until the twentieth century.

The influence of British government can be found in places as far-flung as Australia, Canada, India, and the United States. Just as Alexis de Tocqueville travelled to America in 1831 looking for the secrets of democracy, so we can examine Britain for secrets of stable representative government. Yet the limitations of the British model are shown by the failure to transplant its institutions to countries gaining independence from the British Empire, and even more by the failure of institutions that have worked in England to bring political stability in Northern Ireland.

The evolution of democracy in Britain contrasts with a European history of countries switching between democratic and undemocratic forms of government. Whereas the oldest British people have lived in the same political system all their lives, the oldest Germans have lived under four or five constitutions, two democratic and two or three undemocratic.

At no point in history did representatives of the British people meet to decide what kind of government they would like to have, as happened in America at the end of the eighteenth century, and as has happened many times in France. There is no agreement among political scientists about when England developed a modern system of government.[1] The most reasonable judgment is that this occurred during the very long reign of Queen Victoria from 1837 to 1901, when institutions were created or adapted to cope with the problems of a society that was increasingly urban, literate, industrial, and critical of unreformed institutions. However, the creation of a modern system of government does not get rid of the problems of governing.

POLICY CHALLENGES FACING THE BRITISH GOVERNMENT

The general election of 2010 has faced British party leaders with their biggest political challenge in more than half a century. Normally, the party with the most votes gains an absolute majority of seats in the House of Commons. It can thereby take control of the chief offices of government, the prime ministership and Cabinet. However, in 2010, no party won the 326 seats needed to have a majority of MPs with seats in the House of Commons. The **Conservative Party** under the leadership of David Cameron came first with 307 seats, the outgoing Labour government of Gordon Brown trailed in second place with 258 seats, and the **Liberal Democratic Party** led by Nick Clegg came third with 57 seats.

After losing three successive elections, the Conservative leadership was desperate to gain office. After half a century of Liberal leaders claiming that they wanted their party to become a party of government, a hung Parliament (that is, a House of Commons in which no party had an absolute majority) gave the Liberals an opportunity to gain office. Following a week of intense negotiations, the Conservative and Liberal Democratic parties formed the country's first coalition government since that led by Winston Churchill in 1940 to fight World War II.

The coalition government's chief offices are divided between Conservative David Cameron as **prime minister** and Liberal Democratic leader Nick Clegg as deputy prime minister (see Box 8.1). Conservative MPs head most government departments

---

Two Faces at the Top of Government   **BOX 8.1**

While a government can have only one head, the Conservative and Liberal Democratic coalition has two faces at the top: David Cameron, the Conservative prime minister, and Nick Clegg, the Liberal Democratic deputy prime minister.

Both party leaders are youthful; each was forty-three years old on assuming the highest offices in government and neither had held high office before. Both have been full-time politicians since leaving university.

Cameron started as a young assistant to a Conservative Cabinet minister and was then a lobbyist. He won the leadership on the grounds that he was not associated publicly with the electoral defeats of his predecessors and could present himself as a centrist, post-Thatcherite Conservative. In opposition, Cameron's strategy was to make the party electable by moving it to the political center. He endorsed measures to improve the environment, accepted liberal policies on gay and minority rights, and endorsed such popular programs as the National Health Service. Cameron silenced Thatcherite critics by claiming that the alternative to changing the party was a fourth election defeat.

Clegg, a polylingual supporter of the EU, was an assistant to a Conservative in the European Commission in Brussels. Because of his views on Europe, he joined the Liberal Democratic Party and served a term as a Member of the European Parliament before becoming a British MP in 2005. Unlike some of his Liberal Democratic colleagues, he was never a member of the Labour Party, nor has he identified himself with the left of center, as have most of his predecessors as party leader.

See: Peter Snowdon, *Back from the Brink* (London: Harper Press, 2010); Paul Marshall and David Laws, eds., *The Orange Book: Reclaiming Liberalism* (London: Profile Books, 2004).

with a Liberal Democrat as their deputy, but Liberal Democrats are in charge of major departments concerned with the environment, business, and the economy. A German-style coalition compact recorded agreement on policies; it involved concessions by both parties.

The first challenge facing the government is to keep the coalition together. Some Conservatives were unhappy that their leader did not try to form a minority government that held onto office by avoiding controversial legislation and relied on divisions among its opponents to remain in office. Many Conservatives oppose EU measures, whereas Liberal Democrats are strong supporters of greater British integration into the EU. Some Liberal Democrats were unhappy because they consider their policies closer to the **Labour Party** on, for example, which programs to cut and which taxes to increase in order to deal with the massive budget deficit that the coalition inherited from its Labour predecessor.

The coalition partners agreed to disagree about what kind of electoral system should be used at the next national election. The Conservatives favor keeping the existing first-past-the-post system, in which the candidate with the most votes in a constituency, whether less or more than half, becomes its MP. The

Liberal Democrats have favored the introduction of proportional representation as a fairer system, and incidentally, one which would more than double their number of MPs. Coalition leaders have agreed to hold a referendum in May 2011 offering voters the choice between the first-past-the-post system and the alternative vote, in which voters list their second and third preferences for an MP and these votes may be transferred to ensure that the winner has the support of at least half of the constituency's voters. The coalition has also agreed to reduce the number of MPs and to fix the term of Parliament to five years, except in unusual circumstances, rather than allowing the prime minister of the day to call a national vote sooner if he or she thinks election victory is likely.

Traditionally, experts interpreted the doctrine of the sovereignty of Parliament to mean that the government can do whatever it wants as long as it has the backing of a majority in the House of Commons. However, many problems facing British government are "intermestic," because globalization is blurring the traditional distinction between international and domestic problems. While a coalition agreement can be managed in London, effective economic, national security, and trade policies involve the cooperation of national governments and intergovernmental institutions scattered from Berlin

Two People, Two Party Leaders, One Coalition Government

An election result with no party winning a majority of seats has resulted in party leaders who campaigned against each other sharing power as prime minister (David Cameron, Conservative) and deputy prime minister (Nick Clegg, Liberal Democrat).

David Bebber/AFP/Getty Images/Newscom

and Brussels to Washington and Asia. Whatever their party, Britain's governors accept the inevitability of globalization. Many top ministers spend as much as one day a week at meetings in other countries.

Globalization challenges the country's governors to answer the question, "Where does Britain belong?" Traditionally, the answer has been that Britain is a major world power having close ties with Commonwealth countries, the United States, and Europe.

The British Empire was transformed into the Commonwealth, a free association of fifty-three sovereign states with members on every continent, after World War II. The independent status of its chief members is shown by the absence of the word *British* from the name of the Commonwealth. Its members range from Antigua and Australia to India, Pakistan, and Zambia. Commonwealth countries differ from each other in wealth, culture, and their commitment to democracy. The Commonwealth has no military or economic power and its diplomatic influence is slight. When it sought to put pressure on the dictatorship of Robert Mugabe in Zimbabwe, Zimbabwe left the Commonwealth.

Every British prime minister claims a special relationship with the United States. The traditional view,

dating back to the time of Winston Churchill and Franklin D. Roosevelt, was "America provides the brawn and we provide the brains." However, the number of countries with which America has a special relationship keeps expanding, whereas British prime ministers have not built equally strong relationships with other countries. After the end of the Cold War, the emergence of the United States as a unique global force has made the relationship more attractive to Britain but less relevant to Washington. When President George W. Bush formed a "coalition of the willing" to attack Iraq in 2003, Prime Minister Tony Blair was eager to participate in the war. Subsequent official reviews of the decision have questioned his evidence and whether his actions were in Britain's own interests.

An all-party House of Commons committee concluded that the idea of a special relationship should be abandoned as misleading and that the United Kingdom should be "less deferential and more willing to say no to the U.S. on those issues where the two countries' interests and values diverge." A majority of the British public also rejects the idea of a special relationship with the United States while endorsing cooperation on specific issues where there are common interests.[2]

The Mother of Parliaments

Parliament has met in London by the River Thames for more than seven hundred years, and the clock tower of Big Ben is famous as a symbol of democracy in Canada and Australia as well as in Europe.

Maksym Gorpenyuk/ Shutterstock

The coalition government is under pressure to undertake a fundamental review of Britain's overall commitments abroad. The war in Afghanistan has revealed the cost in human life of budget cuts that left British soldiers short of protective equipment. Simultaneously, the Royal Navy and Royal Air Force want more money for aircraft carriers, nuclear submarines, and planes. This goes against the coalition government's priority for cutting spending to reduce the country's budget deficit.

After rejecting becoming a founding member of the European Community in 1957, Britain joined it in 1973. The EU now has the power to impose regulations affecting British business, spending decisions in such fields as agriculture, and Acts of Parliament. Government ministers spend an increasing amount of their time negotiating with other countries of the EU on everything from political fundamentals to whether British beer should be served in metric units or by the traditional measure of a British pint. The Channel Tunnel makes the rail link to Paris shorter than that to the North of England or Scotland. Manufacturers such as the Ford Motor Company link their plants in Britain with factories across Western Europe, just as Ford links factories across American states.

One theory is that Britain could increase its influence in Washington and further afield by becoming a leading member of the EU. However, Britain has always had a limited commitment, seeing the EU as an important market but rejecting proposals to strengthen its supranational powers. The Conservative Party is divided between those who are skeptical of the benefits it brings and a hard core that wishes Britain, like Norway, were not an EU member state. Liberal Democrats are very pro-EU, and the Labour Party tends to evaluate EU measures in terms of its party interest. The coalition government has submitted a bill to Parliament requiring a national referendum to be held on any further changes in EU treaties.

In small countries, which have always recognized the influence of bigger neighbors, exchanging nominal sovereignty to participate in the EU presents no problems. However, it is a shock to Britons who pride themselves on being a leader in world affairs, rather than just another partner in an international coalition. However, many British opinion leaders now think that the country should play a smaller role in world affairs. In this era of globalization, it is not possible for Britain to become a small and prosperous country. The effective choice today is between Britain

being a big, prosperous country or a big country that is not prosperous.

Government influences the market through taxing and spending policies, interest rates, and policies that are designed to stimulate growth and reduce unemployment. Increasingly, what happens to the British economy is also influenced by what happens elsewhere in the EU and on other continents too, because Britain imports much of its food and raw materials and pays for them by exporting manufactured goods, tourism, and the "invisible" services of international banks and financial institutions. The British pound sterling (£) is an international currency, but speeches by the prime minister and head of the Treasury do not determine its international value. This is decided in foreign exchange markets in which currency speculators play a significant role. Since 1997, the value of the British pound in exchange for the dollar has ranged from above $2.50 to less than $1.25. In 2010, the value of the pound fluctuated around $1.50. In the decade before the global financial crisis, the British economy grew by two-fifths and its growth rate was higher than the average for the EU and was similar to that of the United States.

When the 2008 global financial crisis erupted, a number of major British banks faced the threat of bankruptcy; the government hurriedly took ownership in a number of banks and pumped hundreds of billions of pounds of credit into the banking system to prevent its collapse. However, the cost of bailing out the banks, added to the cost of Labour government spending commitments designed with an eye on the 2010 election, resulting in a public sector deficit equivalent to more than 10 percent of gross domestic product. For every three pounds that are raised in taxes, the government spends almost four pounds.

The coalition government faces a double challenge: to reduce the size of the government's deficit and to stimulate a return to economic growth. When the coalition took office, the rate of growth was only 1 percent. There are built-in pressures to increase public expenditure, because an aging population requires more health care, longer life increases the cost of pensions, an educated population demands better education for their children, and a more prosperous society wants a better environment.

There is no agreement among professional economists or among coalition partners about how or whether all its desired economic goals can be achieved within the life of the coalition government. Most Conservatives want to give priority to spending cuts,

A Stronghold of Financial Capitalism

The financial institutions of the city of London, such as the London Stock Exchange, pictured here, are a major source of earnings for the British economy when times are good and of losses when times are bad.

Bloomberg/Getty Images

while most Liberals are prepared to maintain higher spending financed by higher taxes. In an emergency budget introduced in June 2010, the coalition government imposed major cuts in public expenditure and in public employment. It said mismanagement by Labour predecessors was the reason for doing so. However, during the life of a Parliament, it cannot evade the blame if the economy remains troubled, just as it will take the credit if economic conditions improve.

THE ENVIRONMENT OF POLITICS: ONE CROWN BUT FIVE NATIONS

The Queen of England is the best-known monarch in the world, yet there is no such thing as an English state. In international law, the state is the United Kingdom of Great Britain and Northern Ireland. Great Britain is divided into England, Scotland, and Wales. The most distinctive feature of **Wales** is that one-quarter speak an old Celtic language, Welsh, as well as English. **Scotland**, once an independent kingdom, has been an integral part of Britain since 1707. However, the Scots have separate legal, religious, and educational institutions. The fourth part of the United Kingdom, **Northern Ireland**, consists of six counties of Ulster (note that Ulster has nine counties, three of which are in the Republic of Ireland). The remainder of Ireland rebelled against the Crown in 1916 and established a separate Irish state in Dublin in 1921. The current

boundaries of the United Kingdom, colloquially known as *Britain*, were fixed in 1921.

The United Kingdom is a unitary state because there is a single source of authority, the British Parliament. However, the institutions of government are not uniform throughout the Kingdom. In the minds of its citizens, it is a multinational state, for people differ in how they describe themselves (see Table 8.1). In England, people often describe themselves as English or British without considering the different meanings of these terms. This does not happen elsewhere in the United Kingdom. In Scotland, almost three-quarters see themselves as Scots. In Wales, two-thirds identify as Welsh. In Northern Ireland, people divide into three groups, some seeing themselves as British, some as Irish, and others as Ulster.

Historically, Scotland and Wales have been governed by British Cabinet ministers accountable to Parliament. After decades of campaigning by nationalist parties seeking independence, in 1997, the Labour government endorsed **devolution**; an Act of Parliament gave responsibilities for policy to elected assemblies in Scotland and in Wales, and they came into being in 1999. The revenue of both assemblies comes from Westminster. It is assigned by a formula relating it to public expenditure on comparable policies in England.

The Scottish Parliament in Edinburgh has powers to legislate, to decide its own budget, and to initiate a variety of policies. Elections to the 129-seat Parliament mix the traditional British first-past-the-post electoral

	TABLE 8.1

National Identities
Identities of people vary by nation.

	Region of Residence			
	England	**Scotland**	**Wales**	**Northern Ireland**
British	52%	24%	26%	37%
English, Scots, Welsh, Irish	37%	72%	65%	26%
Other, don't know	11%	4%	9%	37%*

*Includes 29% identifying as Ulster.
Sources: Calculated from British Social Attitudes survey, June–September 2008 (*n* = 4,486) and Northern Ireland Life and Times Survey, October 2008–February 2009 (*n* = 1,216).

system and proportional representation. After the 1999 and 2003 elections, the Labour Party in Scotland formed a government in coalition with the Liberal Party. At the May 2007 Scottish election, the unpopularity of the British Labour Party gave the Scottish National Party (SNP) a margin of one seat over Labour, forty-seven seats to forty-six. The remaining seats were divided between the Conservatives (seventeen), Liberal Democrats (sixteen), and others (three).

Under the leadership of Alex Salmond as First Minister, the SNP established a minority government. Its first aim was to demonstrate that the SNP was not just a protest party but a party capable of governing as well as or better than British parties. Its second aim was to promote a referendum on independence for Scotland. The three Opposition parties reacted by establishing a commission to recommend increases in powers devolved to Scotland, subject to approval by the British government in London. At the May 2011 election of the Scottish Parliament, the Labour Party seeks to regain office. If it does, it will face a different situation than before, since it will not be the junior partner of a Labour government in London but trying to wriggle free of domination by a Conservative-led government in London while also opposing the Nationalist claim that this would be best achieved through Scottish independence.

The Welsh Assembly in Cardiff has powers over a variety of local and regional services and its activities are conducted in English and in Welsh. However, it does not have the power to enact legislation. It is elected by a mixed first-past-the-post and PR ballot. Labour has consistently been the biggest party at each election, but has difficulty in winning a majority of Assembly seats. After the May 2007 Assembly election, Labour held twenty-six seats; Plaid Cymru (the Welsh

Language Party), fourteen; the Conservative Party, twelve; Liberals, six; and others, two. Labour and Plaid Cymru together formed a coalition government, which is possible because Plaid Cymru does not demand independence as the Scottish Nationalists do. The May 2011 Welsh election will decide the composition of a new coalition or minority government.

Northern Ireland is the most un-English part of the United Kingdom. Formally, it is a secular polity, but differences between Protestants and Catholics about national identity dominate its politics. Protestants, comprising about three-fifths of the population, want to remain part of the United Kingdom. Until 1972, the Protestant majority governed through a home-rule Parliament at Stormont, a suburb of Belfast. Many of the Catholic minority did not support this regime, wanting to leave the United Kingdom and join the Republic of Ireland, which claims that Northern Ireland should be part of the Republic.

After Catholics launched protests against discrimination in 1968, demonstrations turned to violence in 1969. The illegal **Irish Republican Army (IRA)** was revived and in 1971 began a military campaign to remove Northern Ireland from the United Kingdom. Protestants organized illegal armed forces in response. In 1972, the British government abolished the Stormont Parliament, placing government in the hands of a Northern Ireland Office under a British Cabinet minister. Political violence has killed more than 3,700 people since the troubles began in 1969. After adjusting for population differences, this is equivalent to about 150,000 deaths in Britain or almost 750,000 political killings in the United States.

In 1985, the British government took the unprecedented step of inviting the Dublin-based government of the Republic of Ireland to participate in institutions affecting the governance of part of the United Kingdom. A stable settlement requires the support of paramilitary organizations as well as political parties on both sides of the political divide. In 1994, the IRA announced a cessation of its military activity, and Sinn Fein, the party political wing of the Irish Republican movement, agreed to talks. Protestant paramilitary forces also announced a cessation of activities. On Good Friday, 1998, an agreement was reached for an elected power-sharing executive and cross-border institutions involving both Dublin and Belfast. Contrary to the practice of government at Westminster, power-sharing means that whatever the outcome of a Northern Ireland election, government must be a coalition of parties representing both the pro-British Protestant majority and the pro-Irish Republic Catholic minority. This has been described as "a unique form of devolution—involuntary coalition."[3]

An election to the Northern Ireland Assembly in 2007 gave the Democratic Unionist Party led by Dr. Ian Paisley thirty-six seats; Republican Sinn Fein, twenty-seven seats; the Ulster Unionist Party, eighteen seats; the pro-Irish Social Democratic and Labour Party, sixteen seats; the cross-religious Alliance Party, seven seats; and others, four seats. After intensive negotiations in which London and Dublin offered incentives to Irish Republicans and put pressure on Ulster Unionists, a coalition government was formed with Dr. Ian Paisley, an outspoken Unionist and Protestant, as First Minister, and Martin McGuinness, a Sinn Fein politician who had been active in the IRA, as Deputy First Minister, plus representatives of the Ulster Unionist Party and the Social Democratic and Labour Party. On Paisley's retirement, Peter Robinson became the Democratic Unionist party leader and First Minister.

While there is no agreement about national identity within Britain, there is no doubt about which nationality is the most numerous. England dominates the United Kingdom. It accounts for 84 percent of the UK population against 8 percent in Scotland, 5 percent in Wales, and 3 percent in Northern Ireland. In earlier editions of this book, this chapter has been called "Politics in England" because, as Tony Blair once said, "Sovereignty rests with me, as an English MP, and that's the way it will stay."[4] However, changes in the institutions of the United Kingdom have begun to affect politics in England. For example, in the 2005 British general election, the Conservative Party won the most votes in England but the Labour Party, thanks to its dominance in Scotland and Wales, won the most votes in the United Kingdom and a majority in the British Parliament. In 2010, the Conservative Party won an absolute majority of seats in England as well as having a big lead in votes there.

A Multiracial Britain

Throughout the centuries, England has received a relatively small but noteworthy number of immigrants from other parts of Europe. The Queen herself is descended from a titled family that came from Hanover, Germany, to assume the English throne in 1714. Until the outbreak of anti-German sentiment in World War I, the surname of the royal family was Saxe-Coburg-Gotha. By royal proclamation, King George V changed the family name to Windsor in 1917.

The worldwide British Empire was multiracial and so is the Commonwealth. Since the late 1950s, job-seekers from the West Indies, Pakistan, India, Africa, and other parts of the Commonwealth have settled in Britain. Hundreds of thousands of people from Australia, Canada, the United States, and the EU flow in and out of Britain as students or as workers. A strong British economy attracts temporary workers from Eastern European countries of the EU. Public opinion has opposed unlimited immigration and both Labour and Conservative governments have passed laws trying to limit the number of immigrants. However, these laws contain many exceptions.

Political disturbances around the world have resulted in an increasing number of immigrants who claim asylum as political refugees from troubled areas in the Balkans, the Middle East, and Africa. Some have valid credentials as refugees, whereas others have arrived with false papers or make claims to asylum that courts have not upheld. In response to popular concern, the government has tried to make deportation of illegal immigrants easier. However, the government has admitted that there are hundreds of thousands of illegal immigrants in Britain.

The minority ethnic population of the United Kingdom has risen from 74,000 in 1951 to 4.6 million in the latest census, almost 8 percent of the UK population. All together, almost half of the minority category comes from the Indian subcontinent, a quarter are black people from the Caribbean or Africa, one in seven are of mixed British and minority origin, and the remainder are from many different countries.

Younger Generation is the Most Multi-Racial Generation

Schools and street scenes in big cities show that Britain is now a multiracial society.

Universal Images Group/
Diverse Images/Getty Images

Official statistics define the minority population by the one characteristic that they have in common—they are not white. Because persons placed in this catchall category have neither culture nor religion in common, there is a further subdivision by race and ethnicity. West Indians speak English as their native language and have a Christian tradition, but this is often not the case for black Africans. Ethnic minorities from India, Pakistan, and Bangladesh are divided between Hindus, Muslims, and Sikhs, and most speak English as a second language. Chinese from Hong Kong have a distinctive culture. In addition, there are gender differences. There is a tendency for immigrant women not to speak English as well as male immigrants, and this is particularly the case for immigrants from Pakistan and Bangladesh.

With the passage of time, the ethnic minority population is becoming increasingly British-born and British-educated. This raises an important issue: What is the position of British-born offspring of immigrants? Whatever their country of origin, they differ in how they see themselves: 64 percent of Caribbean origin identify themselves as British, as do more than three-fifths of Pakistanis, Indians, and Bangladeshis, and two-fifths of Chinese. However, some offspring of immigrants have rejected integration. A coordinated terrorist attack in London on July 7, 2005, killing more than fifty people, was organized by British-born offspring of Pakistani immigrants who had been converted to jihadism at British mosques. British-born jihadists

have been able to receive training in Pakistan and neighboring Afghanistan. The government has greatly increased police powers, justifying shoot-to-kill policies even when people wrongly suspected of being terrorists are the victims.

In response to terrorist attacks, the government has shifted from promoting multiculturalism to stressing the integration of immigrant families into the British way of life. The government seeks to promote a sense of Britishness among immigrants, giving lessons about rights and obligations of citizens to immigrants wanting British passports. British-born offspring of immigrants automatically gain citizenship. Whether they choose to adopt British ways is much influenced by family and ethnic background.

Many immigrants and their offspring are being integrated into electoral politics, since residential concentration makes their votes important in some parliamentary constituencies, where candidates from different immigrant groups may compete with each other. A disproportionate number of minority ethnic people have voted Labour. There are now hundreds of elected minority ethnic councilors in local government. The twenty-six ethnic Conservative and Labour MPs in the Commons today come from diverse backgrounds—India, Pakistan, the West Indies, Ghana, and Aden—and include three Muslim women. A white backlash against immigration organized by the British National Party has not received much electoral support. At the 2010 election, the party won only 1.9 percent of the popular vote.

THE LEGACY OF HISTORY

The legacy of the past limits current choices, and Britain has a very long past. The continuity of England's political institutions through the centuries is remarkable. Prince Charles, the heir to an ancient Crown, pilots jet airplanes, and a medieval-named Chancellor of the Exchequer pilots the British economy through the deep waters of the international economy. Yet symbols of continuity often mask great changes in English life. Parliament was once a supporter of royal authority. Today, it is primarily an electoral college deciding which party is in charge of government.

The 1940 to 1945 wartime coalition government laid foundations for the introduction of a welfare state led by Winston Churchill. The victory of the Labour Party at the 1945 general election established a comprehensive National Health Service and took many major industries into state ownership. Between 1951 and 1964, Conservative governments led by Winston Churchill, Sir Anthony Eden, and Harold Macmillan maintained a consensus about the mixed economy welfare state. Economic growth, full employment, and low inflation led to an era of consumer prosperity, and there was the beginning of a big expansion of free university education. After thirteen years of Conservative government, the Labour Party under Harold Wilson won the 1964 election campaigning with the vague activist slogan, "Let's go with Labour." New names were given to government department offices, but behind their doors, many officials went through the same routines as before. The economy did not grow as predicted. In 1967, the government was forced to devalue the pound and seek a loan from the International Monetary Fund. Labour lost the 1970 election.

The major achievement of Edward Heath's 1970 to 1974 Conservative government was to make Britain a member of the EU. In trying to limit unprecedented inflation by controlling wages, Heath risked his authority in a confrontation with the left-wing-led National Union of Mineworkers, which struck for higher wages in what was then the state-owned coal industry. When Heath called the "Who Governs?" election in February 1974, the vote of both the Conservative and Labour parties fell. Labour formed a minority government with Harold Wilson as prime

minister, and he won a bare majority at a second election held in October. Inflation, rising unemployment, and a contraction in the economy undermined Labour's platform. James Callaghan succeeded Wilson as prime minister in 1976, and the economy deteriorated. A loan from the International Monetary Fund was followed by the Labour government's adopting monetarist policies in an attempt to curb inflation.

When Margaret Thatcher won the 1979 election as leader of the Conservative Party, she became the first female prime minister of a major European country. Uniquely among modern British prime ministers, Margaret Thatcher gave her name to a political ideology emphasizing the value of letting people make decisions in the market rather than relying on government to promote their well-being (see Box 8.2.).

While proclaiming the virtues of the market and attacking big government, Thatcher did not court electoral defeat by imposing radical spending cuts on popular social programs. Thatcherite policies did not win favor among the electorate. On the tenth anniversary of Thatcher's tenure as prime minister, an opinion poll asked whether people approved of "the Thatcher revolution." Less than one-third said they did.[5]

Divisions among opponents enabled Thatcher to lead her party to three successive election victories. Militant left-wing activists seized control of the Labour Party, and in 1981, four former Labour Cabinet ministers formed a centrist Social Democratic Party (SDP) in an alliance with the Liberal Party. The Labour Party's 1983 election manifesto was described as the longest suicide note in history. After Thatcher's third successive election victory in 1987, the SDP leadership merged with the Liberals to form the Liberal Democratic Party.

During her third term of office, Thatcher became very unpopular in opinion polls. In autumn 1990, disgruntled Conservative Members of Parliament forced a ballot for the party leadership that caused her to resign. Conservative MPs elected a relatively unknown John Major as party leader, and he thereby became prime minister. In 1992, Major won an unprecedented fourth consecutive term for the Conservative government. However, a few months afterward, his economic policy, based on a strong British pound, crashed under pressure from foreign speculators. The Major government maintained such Thatcherite policies as the **privatization** of the coal mines and railways, but sniping from Conservative ranks and the rise of a reinvigorated Opposition undermined Major's authority.

BOX 8.2

The Meaning of "Thatcherism"

Among British prime ministers, Margaret Thatcher has been unique in giving her name to a political ideology, **Thatcherism**. Her central conviction was that the market offered a cure for the country's economic difficulties. She had more in common with the market-oriented outlook of President Ronald Reagan than with the mixed-economy welfare state philosophy of her Conservative as well as Labour predecessors.

In economic policy, the Thatcher administration experienced both successes and frustrations. Her anti-inflation policies succeeded, but unemployment increased. Industrial relations acts gave union members the right to elect their leaders and vote on whether to hold a strike. State-owned industries and municipally owned council houses were sold to private owners. What were described as "businesslike" methods were introduced into managing everything from hospitals to museums.

As long as it was in her hands, Thatcher believed in strong government. In foreign policy, she was a formidable proponent of what she saw as Britain's national interest in dealings with the EU and in alliance with President Ronald Reagan. The 1982 Argentine invasion of the Falkland Islands, a remote British colony in the South Atlantic, led to a brief and victorious war there. Thatcher was also quick to assert her personal authority against colleagues in the Cabinet and against civil servants. The autonomy of local government was curbed and a property tax on houses was replaced by a poll tax on each adult.

Following her departure from office, Conservatives divided between Thatcherites, who sought to push market-oriented and anti-EU measures further, and those who believed that the time had come to maintain the status quo. David Cameron gained office in 2010 by avoiding association with Thatcherism.

See: Margaret Thatcher, *The Downing Street Years* (New York: HarperCollins, 1993); Dennis Kavanagh, *The Reordering of British Politics* (Oxford: Oxford University Press, 1997); Richard Vinen, *Thatcher's Britain* (London: Simon and Schuster, 2009).

In 1994, Tony Blair was elected Labour leader because he did *not* talk or look like an ordinary Labour Party member. Instead of being from a poor background, he was educated at boarding school, he studied law at Oxford, and his parents were Conservatives. To show that he rejected socialist values, he sought to relabel the party as the **New Labour Party** and proclaimed a vague Third Way philosophy modeled on that of President Bill Clinton. He pledged a pragmatic government that would do "what works" and appealed to the voters to "trust him." The strategy was electorally successful (see Box 8.3).

In his first term of office, Blair and his Chancellor of the Exchequer, Gordon Brown, sought media publicity to demonstrate that Labour was good at governing. Blair appointed many media-oriented political advisors with little or no prior experience of working in government. Five years after becoming prime minister, Blair recognized the limits of a media-oriented strategy: "In opposition, announcement is the reality. For the first period in government, there was a tendency to believe this is the case. It isn't. The announcement is only the intention."[6]

The Blair government implemented Labour's long-standing program of constitutional reforms, including the devolution of powers to elected assemblies in Scotland and Wales and creation of a power-sharing government in Northern Ireland. Major laws protecting individual human rights were adopted. However, in the wake of terrorist attacks, the government sought to limit human rights in ways that drew protests from civil liberties groups. Blair welcomed such criticism as proof of his toughness.

In 2005, Labour again won a majority of seats in the House of Commons, making Tony Blair Britain's second-longest-serving prime minister in more than a century. Since a prime minister does not have a fixed term of office, when Blair's popularity fell in the opinion polls, he came under pressure from his long-serving and jealous heir apparent, Gordon Brown, to retire rather than fight a fourth election. Blair resigned in June 2007.

The Labour Party unanimously elected Gordon Brown as its leader on the basis of his record as the Chancellor of the Exchequer during a period when the economy grew, inflation was low, and unemployment

BOX 8.3

The Electoral Success of Tony Blair

Tony Blair became leader of the Labour Party with the goal of winning elections. To make the party electable, he abandoned its traditional commitments to the trade unions and to socialist values. The strategy accomplished an unprecedented series of three straight Labour wins in three straight general elections. However, the Labour share of the vote declined from 43 percent in 1997 to 41 percent in 2001 and then to 35 percent in 2005.

As prime minister, Blair sought to make his office the focus of attention. A high priority was given to media publicity, where a sound bite or a clever phrase is sufficient. Political advisors used the prime minister's authority to push government ministers and civil servants to produce good headlines.

Blair promoted policies to change the delivery of state-financed health and education services by introducing more market mechanisms intended to increase efficiency and give citizens a degree of choice. The Chancellor of the Exchequer, Gordon Brown, played a key role, too, in allocating public expenditure. Many doctors, teachers, and public employees were demoralized or angered by these measures; for example, in 2006, university teachers staged their first nationwide strike.

In international affairs, Blair's chief initiative was to bond not only with Democratic president Bill Clinton but also with Republican president George W. Bush in support of the Iraq War. Since he left office, when his popularity was falling and Gordon Brown was pressing to take over, he has had a successful career in consultancies and lecture fees.

See: Simon Jenkins, *Thatcher and Sons* (London: Allen Lane, 2006); Terrence A. Casey, ed., *The Blair Legacy* (New York: Palgrave, 2009); Peter Mandelson, *The Third Man* (New York: Harper Collins, 2010).

fell. Brown boasted that he had ended the economic cycle of "boom and bust." His critics charged him with trying to run an expensive Swedish-style welfare state without imposing the taxes necessary to finance it. Brown's hesitancy in making and explaining decisions, combined with a reserved personality, led to his approval rating in the polls falling as low as Blair at his worst. Labour critics fed stories of his faults to the media and Lord Peter Mandelson, a Cabinet colleague, privately described the relationship between Blair and Brown as "dysfunctional."

The world economic crisis and the subsequent plunge in the government's finances raised questions about Brown's achievements at the Exchequer. In May 2010, he led his party to defeat; Labour's 29 percent share of the popular vote was its second lowest since 1918. The new leader of the Labour Party, Ed Miliband, elected in September 2010, has the task of explaining to traditional Labour voters and ex-Labour voters where the party now stands. The position the Labour Party takes in opposition depends, in the words of a former Labour Cabinet minister, on whether the Conservative-Liberal Democratic coalition government "embeds a status quo it wouldn't have created" (that is, the New Labour legacy) and on "whether the country would welcome that with relief or be thirsty for greater change."[7]

THE STRUCTURE OF GOVERNMENT

In Britain, the term *government* is used in many senses. People may speak of the *Queen's government* to emphasize enduring and nonpartisan features; they may refer to a *Labour government* or *Conservative government* to emphasize partisanship, or to *David Cameron's government* to stress a personal feature. The departments headed by Cabinet ministers advised by senior civil servants are referred to collectively as **Whitehall**, after the London street in which many major government departments are located. **Downing Street**, where the prime minister works, is a short street off Whitehall. **Parliament**—that is, the popularly elected House of Commons and the nonelected House of Lords—is at one end of Whitehall. The term *Parliament* is often used as another way of referring to the House of Commons. Together, all of these institutions are often referred to as **Westminster**, after the district in London in which the principal offices of British government are located. With devolution, institutions are found in Scotland, Wales, and Northern Ireland, too (see Figure 8.1).

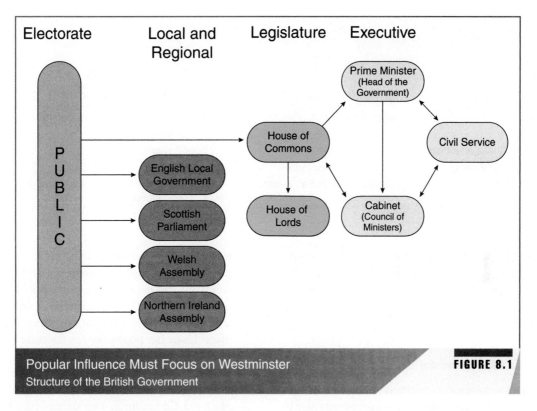

Electorate   Local and   Legislature   Executive
              Regional

Popular Influence Must Focus on Westminster
Structure of the British Government

FIGURE 8.1

Descriptions of a government often start with its constitution. However, Britain has never had a written constitution. In the words of a constitutional lawyer, J. A. G. Griffith, "The Constitution is what happens."[8] The **unwritten constitution** is a jumble of Acts of Parliament, judicial pronouncements, customs, and conventions that make up the rules of the political game. The vagueness of the constitution makes it flexible, a point that political leaders such as Margaret Thatcher and Tony Blair have exploited to increase their own power. Comparing the written U.S. Constitution and the unwritten British constitution emphasizes how few are the constraints of an unwritten constitution (see Table 8.2). Whereas amendments to the U.S. Constitution must receive the endorsement of well over half the states and members of Congress, the unwritten constitution can be changed by a majority vote in Parliament or by the government of the day acting in an unprecedented manner.

The U.S. Constitution gives the Supreme Court the final power to decide what the government may or may not do. By contrast, in Britain, the final authority is Parliament, where the government of the day commands a majority of votes. Courts do not have the power to declare an Act of Parliament unconstitutional;

judges simply ask whether the executive acts within its authorized powers. Many statutes delegate broad discretion to a Cabinet minister or to public authority. Even if the courts rule that the government has improperly exercised its authority, the effect of such a judgment can be annulled by a subsequent Act of Parliament retroactively authorizing an action.

The Bill of Rights in the U.S. Constitution allows anyone to turn to the courts for the protection of their personal rights. Instead of giving written guarantees to citizens, the rights of British people are meant to be secured by trustworthy governors. An individual who believes his or her personal rights infringed must seek redress through the courts by invoking the European Convention of Human Rights and the 1998 British Human Rights Act, adopted in emulation of it.

The **Crown** is the abstract concept that Britain uses in place of the continental European conception of the state. It combines dignified parts of the constitution, which sanctify authority by tradition and myth, with efficient parts, which carry out the work of government. The Queen is only a ceremonial head of state. The public reaction to the accidental death of Princess Diana was a media event but not a political event like the assassination of President Kennedy.

British and American Constitutions Comparing an unwritten and a written constitution.		**TABLE 8.2**
	Britain (unwritten)	**United States (written)**
Origin	Medieval customs	1787 Constitutional Convention
Form	Unwritten, vague	Written, precise
Final constitutional authority	Majority in Parliament	Supreme Court
Bill of individual rights	Borrowed from Europe	Yes
Amendment	Ordinary vote in Parliament; unprecedented action by government	More than majority vote in Congress, states
Policy relevance	Low	High

Queen Elizabeth II does not influence the actions of what is described as Her Majesty's Government. The Queen is expected to respect the will of Parliament, as communicated to her by the leader of the majority in Parliament, the prime minister.

What the Prime Minister Says and Does

Leading a government is a political rather than a managerial task. The preeminence of the prime minister is ambiguous, and this is especially so in a coalition government (see Box 8.4). A politician at the apex of government is remote from what is happening on the ground. The more responsibilities attributed to the prime minister, the less time there is to devote to any one task. Like a president, a prime minister is the prisoner of the law of "first things first." The imperatives of the prime minister are as follows.

- *Winning elections.* A prime minister may be self-interested, but he or she is not self-employed. To become prime minister, a politician must first be elected leader of his or her party. The only election that a prime minister must win is that of party leader. Seven prime ministers since 1945—Winston Churchill, Anthony Eden, Harold Macmillan, Alec Douglas-Home, James Callaghan, John Major, and Gordon Brown—initially entered Downing Street during the middle of a Parliament rather than after a national election. In the eighteen elections since 1945, the prime minister of the day has ten times led the governing party to victory and eight times to defeat.
- *Campaigning through the media.* A prime minister does not need to attract publicity; it is thrust upon

him or her by the curiosity of television and newspaper reporters. Media eminence is a double-edged sword, for bad news puts the prime minister in an unfavorable light. The personality of a prime minister remains relatively constant, but during a term of office, his or her popularity can fluctuate by more than 45 percentage points in public opinion polls.[9]
- *Patronage.* To remain prime minister, a politician must keep the confidence of a party, or in the case of David Cameron, of two parties (the Liberal Democrats as well as Conservatives). Potential critics can be silenced by appointing a quarter of MPs to posts as government ministers, who sit on front bench seats in the House of Commons. MPs not appointed to a post are backbenchers; many ingratiate themselves with their party leader in hopes of becoming a government minister. In dispensing patronage, a prime minister can use any of four different criteria: (1) personal loyalty (rewarding friends); (2) co-option (silencing critics by giving them an office so that they are committed to support the government); (3) representativeness (for example, appointing a woman or someone from Scotland or Wales); and (4) competence in giving direction to a government department.
- *Parliamentary performance.* The prime minister appears in the House of Commons weekly for half an hour of questions from MPs, engaging in rapid-fire repartee with a highly partisan audience. Unprotected by a speechwriter's script, the prime minister must show that he or she is a good advocate of government policy or suffer a reduction in confidence. By being in the Commons and participating in votes there, the prime minister is able to judge the mood of the governing party.

■ *Making and balancing policies.* As head of the British government, the prime minister deals with heads of other governments around the world; this makes foreign affairs a special responsibility of Downing Street. When there are conflicts between international and domestic policy priorities, the prime minister is the one person who can strike a balance between pressures from the world "out there" and pressures from the domestic electorate. The prime minister also makes policy by striking a balance between ministers who want to spend more money to increase their popularity and a Treasury minister who wants to cut taxes in order to boost his or her popularity.

In a coalition government, the role of deputy prime minister is also important; Nick Clegg leads the Liberal Democratic Party, on whose support the prime minister depends for a parliamentary majority. In the formation of the coalition, Clegg bargained for a significant amount of patronage. The coalition pact involved compromises that balanced competing demands from each party as well as having policy commitments on which they agree (see Box 8.4). The extent to which Clegg is able to secure substantial media attention will depend on the issue at hand. His strategy for the Liberal Democrats doing well at the next general election is not oriented toward television appearances; he wants to change the electoral system to remove the handicaps under which it has suffered.

While the formal powers of the office remain constant, individual prime ministers have differed in their electoral success (see Figure 8.2), how they view their job, and their impact on government. Clement Attlee, Labour prime minister from 1945 to 1951, was an unassertive spokesperson for the lowest common denominator of views within a Cabinet consisting of very experienced Labour politicians. When an aging Winston Churchill succeeded Attlee in 1951, he concentrated on foreign affairs and took little interest in domestic policy; the same was true of his successor, Anthony Eden. Harold Macmillan intervened strategically on a

---

BOX 8.4

Keeping a Coalition Together

A coalition government gives new meaning to the doctrine of collective responsibility. Coalition ministers who competed against each other at the 2010 election are expected to support each other in the Commons and to refrain from briefing the media against each other. Equally important, they are expected to persuade backbench Conservative and Liberal Democratic MPs to vote for compromises necessary to maintain the coalition, even if these compromises sometimes depart from previously endorsed party policies.

The formation of the Con-Lib coalition was preceded by bargaining about issues that were likely to provoke disagreement between the two parties. The result was a thirty-six-page coalition pact recording the compromises reached. In addition, the pact listed issues on which public differences of opinion could be expressed, such as electoral reform.

Policymaking and coalition building starts in government departments. In the majority, the minister in charge and his or her deputy are from different parties. Thus, before a departmental position can be established on issues where the parties tend to differ, the departmental ministers must agree between themselves. If there is a disagreement between departments, it may be handled in the conventional way through Cabinet committees. However, if interdepartmental differences reflect partisan differences, competing claims of the coalition partners must be reviewed by the Conservative and Liberal Democratic leaders in order to maintain the unity of the coalition.

When a Commons vote is an issue of confidence in the government, both Conservative and Liberal Democratic MPs are expected to unite to keep it in office. However, political confrontation makes news, and journalists are always looking for signs of disagreement to publicize. Backbench Conservative and Liberal Democratic MPs are not bound by collective Cabinet responsibility. They may criticize a coalition policy when they dislike a compromise. In addition, all-party committees of MPs can hold hearings that reveal divisions within the coalition.

See: www.cabinetoffice.gov.uk/jked9a'409088/p0fg_coalition.pdf, accessed June 29, 2010. David Laws, *22 Days in May* (London: Biteback, 2010).

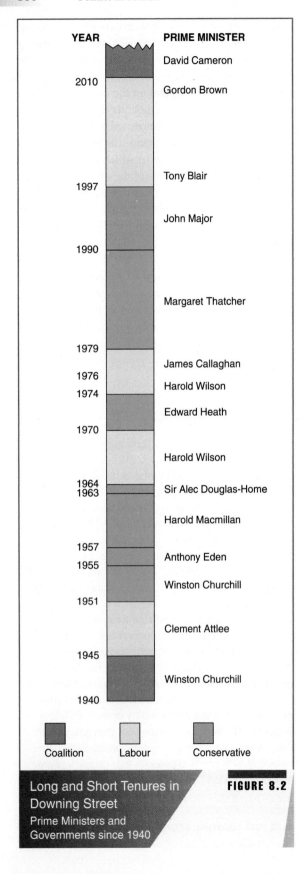

YEAR | **PRIME MINISTER**

David Cameron

2010

Gordon Brown

1997

Tony Blair

John Major

1990

Margaret Thatcher

1979

1976　James Callaghan

1974　Harold Wilson

Edward Heath

1970

Harold Wilson

1964
1963　Sir Alec Douglas-Home

Harold Macmillan

1957

1955　Anthony Eden

Winston Churchill

1951

Clement Attlee

1945

Winston Churchill

1940

Coalition　Labour　Conservative

Long and Short Tenures in Downing Street
Prime Ministers and Governments since 1940

FIGURE 8.2

limited number of domestic and international issues while giving ministers great scope on everyday matters. Alec Douglas-Home was weak because he lacked knowledge of economic affairs, the chief problem during his administration.

Both Harold Wilson and Edward Heath were initially committed to an activist definition of the prime minister's job. However, Wilson's major initiatives in economic policy were unsuccessful, and in 1974, the electorate rejected Heath's direction of the economy. Wilson won office again by promising to replace confrontation between management and unions with political conciliation. James Callaghan, who succeeded Wilson in 1976, also emphasized consensus, but economic crises continued.

Margaret Thatcher had strong views about many major policies; associates gave her the nickname "Tina" because of her motto: There Is No Alternative. Thatcher was prepared to push her views against the wishes of Cabinet colleagues and civil service advisors. In the end, her "bossiness" caused a revolt of Cabinet colleagues that helped bring about her downfall. Her former colleagues welcomed John Major as a consensus replacement of a domineering Thatcher. However, his conciliatory manner was often interpreted as a sign of weakness. Sniping from ministers led Major to refer to his Cabinet colleagues as "bastards."

Tony Blair carried into the prime ministership the priority he gave in Opposition to attracting support from middle-class voters and business, and he paid little attention to traditional Labour activists and trade union officials. Cabinet ministers were supposed to support his strategy on pain of losing favor with Downing Street. While in charge of the Treasury, Gordon Brown used its power of the purse to influence Cabinet colleagues and to build up a coterie of supporters who would help him hasten Tony Blair's retirement and his own succession. After a brief honeymoon with public opinion, Prime Minister Brown fell out of favor and Labour ministers briefed the media about the need for changing the party's leadership to prevent defeat at the next election. Brown's critics were unwilling to mount an open challenge to his position, which is difficult to do under the party rules. When Brown lost the 2010 election, he immediately resigned.

Tony Blair's personalistic leadership led to claims that Britain now has a presidential system of government. However, by comparison with a U.S. president, a British prime minister has less formal authority and less security of office (see Table 8.3).

	TABLE 8.3

Prime Minister and President
Comparing the power of and processes for choosing a prime minister and a president.

	Britain (prime minister)	**United States (president)**
Media visibility	High	High
Route to top	Parliament	Governor, senator
Chosen by	Party vote	State primaries and caucuses
Elected by	Parliament	National election
Term of office	Flexible, insecure	Four years, secure
Constitution	Unitary	Federal
Domestic influence	High	So-so
International role	Semi-independent	Superpower
Checks	Informal	Congress, Supreme Court

Source: Adapted from Richard Rose, *The Prime Minister in a Shrinking World* (Boston: Polity Press, 2001), 242.

The president is directly elected for a fixed four-year term. A prime minister is chosen by his or her party for an indefinite term and is thus vulnerable to losing office if confidence wanes. The president is the undoubted leader of the federal executive branch and can dismiss Cabinet appointees with little fear of the consequences; by contrast, senior colleagues of a prime minister are potential rivals for leadership and may be kept in Cabinet to prevent them from challenging him or her. With the support of the Cabinet and governing party, a prime minister can be far more confident than a president that major legislative proposals will be enacted into law, since the president is without authority over Congress. By contrast, the prime minister is at the apex of a unitary government, with powers not limited by the courts or by a written constitution.[10]

Coalition government introduces another distinction, for the role of the deputy prime minister is much more important than that of the American vice president. Nick Clegg is the leader of a party on whose votes the prime minister and the majority of Cabinet ministers depend for their jobs. Thus, when disagreements arise, David Cameron must bargain with his deputy rather than give orders to him.

The Cabinet and Cabinet Ministers

The **Cabinet** consists of senior ministers appointed by the prime minister; they must be either members of the House of Commons or of the House of Lords. As MPs as well as ministers, they contribute to what Walter Bagehot described as "the close union, the nearly complete fusion of the executive and legislative powers."[11]

Historically, the Cabinet has been the forum in which the prime minister brought together leading members of the governing party, many with competing departmental interests and personal ambitions, to ensure agreement about major government policies. A half century ago, there were usually two Cabinet meetings a week, and many took several hours to arrive at a political consensus. Tony Blair reduced the frequency of meetings to less than once a week and cut their average length to under an hour. Coalition government has revived the need for the Cabinet to meet.

The convention of Cabinet responsibility requires that all Cabinet ministers give public support to or at least refrain from public criticism of what the government is doing, even if they have opposed a policy in private. A minister unwilling to share responsibility has been expected to resign office. However, ministers almost always prefer to complain in private or leak their views to the press rather than resign.

Cabinet ministers remain important as department heads, for most decisions of government are made within departments, and departments are responsible for overseeing all the services of government, most of which are delivered by public agencies subordinate to and distant from Whitehall. Whitehall departments differ greatly from each other. The coalition Cabinet formed in May 2010 had the following departments:

- *External affairs*: Foreign and Commonwealth Affairs; Defense; International Development
- *Economic affairs*: Treasury; Business, Innovation, and Skills; Energy and Climate Change; Transport
- *Legal and constitutional issues*: Justice and Lord Chancellor; Home Office and Women's Affairs
- *Social services*: Culture, Media, and Sport
- *Territorial*: Environment, Food, and Rural Affairs; Communities and Local Government; Northern Ireland office; Scotland office; Wales office
- *Managing government business*: Lord President of the Council and deputy prime minister; leader of the House of Commons; chief whip in the House of Commons; leader of the House of Lords

For example, the Department of Business, Innovation, and Skills supervises a larger staff than the Treasury. However, because of the importance of the Treasury's responsibility for taxation and public expenditure, it has more senior civil servants. The Business Department's staff has a dispersed variety of concerns, including the competitiveness of industry, trade, employment, and university education. The Treasury concentrates on one big task: the management of the economy. The job of the Chancellor of the Exchequer is more important politically, insofar as economic performance affects the governing party's electoral fate. But the head of the Department of Business, Vince Cable, is the Liberal Democratic Party's leading figure on economic affairs, and as a former Labour Party activist, his political background differs from that of the Conservative Chancellor.

Cabinet ministers are willing to go along silently with their colleagues' proposals in exchange for endorsement of their own measures. However, ministers often have to compete for scarce resources, making conflict inevitable between departments. Regardless of party, the Defense and Education ministers press for increased spending, while Treasury ministers oppose such moves. Cabinet ministers sometimes resolve their differences in Cabinet committees including all ministers whose departments are most affected by an issue.

A minister has many roles: initiating policies, selecting among alternatives brought forward from within the department, or avoiding a difficult or unpopular decision. A minister is responsible for actions taken by thousands of civil servants nominally acting on the minister's behalf and must answer for agencies to which Whitehall is increasingly contracting out responsibility for delivering public services. In addition, a minister is a department's ambassador to the world outside, including Downing Street, Parliament, the mass media, and interest groups. Not least, Cabinet ministers are individuals with ambitions to rise in politics. The typical minister is not an expert in a subject but an expert in politics. This skill has particular importance when MPs in two coalition parties must be asked to support what the minister is doing.

The Civil Service

Government could continue for months without new legislation, but it would collapse overnight if hundreds of thousands of civil servants stopped administering laws and delivering public services that had been authorized by Acts of Parliaments. The largest number of civil servants are clerical staff with little discretion; they carry out routine activities of a large bureaucracy. Only if these duties are executed satisfactorily can ministers have the time and opportunity to make new policies.

The most important group of civil servants is the smallest: the few hundred higher civil servants who advise ministers and oversee work of their departments. Top British civil servants deny they are politicians because of the partisan connotations of the term. However, their work is political because they are involved in formulating and advising on policies. A publication seeking to recruit bright graduates for the higher civil service declares, "You will be involved from the outset in matters of major policy or resource allocation and, under the guidance of experienced administrators, encouraged to put forward your own constructive ideas and to take responsible decisions."

Top civil servants are not apolitical; they are bipartisan, being ready to work for whichever party wins an election. High-level civil servants are expected to be able to think like politicians, anticipating what their minister would want and objections that would be raised by Parliament, interest groups, and the media. Civil servants like working for a political heavyweight who can carry the department's cause to victory in interdepartmental battles.

The relationship between ministers and higher civil servants is critical. A busy politician does not have time to go into details; he or she wants a brief that can catch a headline or squash criticism. Ministers expect higher civil servants to be responsive to their political views and to give advice consistent with their outlook and that of the governing party or the coalition. Civil servants like working for a minister who has clear views on policy, but they dislike it when a minister grabs a headline by expressing views that will get the department into trouble later because they are impractical. In the words of a senior civil servant, "Just because ministers say to do something does not mean that we can ignore reality."[12]

Both ministers and senior civil servants have been prepared to mislead Parliament and the public. When accused in court of telling a lie about the British government's efforts to suppress an embarrassing memoir by an ex–intelligence officer, the then-head of the civil service, Robert Armstrong, described the government's statements as "a misleading impression, not a lie. It was being economical with the truth."

The appointment of political advisors from outside Whitehall has caused difficulties with civil servants. The advisors are loyal to their minister and to the governing party. While experienced in dealing with personalities in the governing party and the media, they have no experience with Whitehall. When departmental policies attract criticism, some ministers now blame civil servants rather than take responsibility themselves. The head of the trade union of higher civil servants has argued, "There is a danger of descending into a search for scapegoats when problems emerge."[13]

The Thatcher government introduced a new phenomenon in Whitehall: a prime minister who believed civil servants were inferior to businesspeople because they did not have to "earn" their living—that is, make a profit. *Management* was made the buzzword in Whitehall, and it has continued under each of Thatcher's successors. Departments are now supposed to be run in a businesslike fashion, achieving value for money so that the government could profit politically by avoiding tax increases to pay for its spending priorities. Parts of government departments were "hived off" to form separate public agencies, with their own accounts and performance targets. However, when an agency's task is politically sensitive, such as the marking of national school examinations,

the education minister cannot avoid blame if there are major errors in delivering examination marks to pupils.

The coalition government has Conservative and Liberal advisors for its ministries. It has also called on outside experts to head task forces and has created bodies to offer expert information. For example, the team of economists at the Office of Budget Responsibility is expected to produce an independent forecast of the state of the economy before the government announces its annual budget.

The Role of Parliament

The House of Commons is a rectangular room in which the majority of MPs supporting the government sit on one side and Opposition MPs sit facing them. The government's state of mind is summed up in the words of a Labour Cabinet minister who declared, "It's carrying democracy too far if you don't know the result of the vote before the meeting."[14] In the great majority of House of Commons votes, MPs vote along party lines. The Opposition cannot expect to alter major government decisions because it lacks a majority of votes in the Commons. For the life of a Parliament, it accepts the frustrations going with its minority status because it hopes to win a majority at the next election.

The government expects to get its way because its ministers are the leading politicians in the parliamentary majority. If a bill or a motion is identified as a vote of confidence in the government, defeat risks the government having to resign and call a general election. The leaders of the Conservative and Liberal coalition formed in 2010 have sought to alter this assumption so that a general election will only be called if both the coalition partners want this to happen.

Whitehall departments draft bills that are presented to Parliament, and few amendments to legislation are carried without government approval. Laws are described as Acts of Parliament, but it would be more accurate if they were stamped "Made in Whitehall." In addition, the government rather than Parliament sets the budget for government programs. The weakness of Parliament is in marked contrast to the U.S. Congress, where each house controls its own proceedings independent of the White House. A U.S. president may *ask* Congress to enact a bill, but cannot compel a favorable vote.

The first function of the Commons is to weigh political reputations. MPs continually assess their colleagues as ministers, potential ministers, and coalition partners. A minister may win a formal vote of confidence but lose status if his or her arguments are demolished in debate. They continually assess their leader as a person who will lead them to victory or defeat at the next election.

Second, backbench MPs can demand that the government do something about an issue and force a minister to explain and defend what he or she is responsible for. The party whip is expected to listen to the views of dissatisfied backbench MPs and to convey their concerns to ministers. In the corridors, dining rooms, and committees of the Commons, backbenchers can tell ministers what they think is wrong with government policy. If the government is unpopular and MPs feel threatened with losing their seats, they will be aggressive in demanding that something be done.

Publicizing issues is a third function of Parliament. MPs can use their position to call the media's attention to issues and to themselves. Television cameras are now in Parliament, and a quick-witted MP can provide the media with sound bites.

Fourth, MPs can examine how Whitehall departments administer public policies. An MP may write to a minister about a departmental responsibility affecting a constituent or interest group. MPs can request the parliamentary commissioner for administration (also known as the *ombudsman*, after the Scandinavian original) to investigate complaints about maladministration. Committees scrutinize administration and policy, interviewing civil servants and ministers. However, as a committee moves from discussing details to discussing issues of government policy, it raises a question of confidence in the government; this can divide a committee along party lines, with MPs in the governing party in the majority.

A newly elected MP contemplating his or her role as one among 650 members of the House of Commons is faced with many choices. An MP may decide to be a party loyalist, voting as the leadership decides without participating in deliberations about policy. The MP who wishes more attention can make a mark by brilliance in debate, by acting as an acknowledged representative of an interest group, or in a nonpartisan way—for example, as a wit. An MP is expected to speak for constituency interests, but constituents accept that their MP will not vote against party policy if it is in conflict with local interests. The only role that an MP rarely undertakes is that of lawmaker.

To keep the published salary of MPs from rising, they receive very generous expense allowances, including amounts for the upkeep of a second home, since many divide their time between London and their constituency outside London. The expense claims were not audited until after the press published evidence that MPs were claiming expenses for everything from cleaning the moat around their country house to remodeling a London flat that was quickly sold for a profit of tens of thousands of pounds. Hundreds of MPs paid back some expenses rather than defend their claims, and a few have been indicted on charges of criminal fraud. New rules now restrict expenses and open them to public scrutiny.

Backbench MPs perennially demand changes to make their jobs more interesting and to give them more influence. However, the power to make major changes rests with the government rather than the House of Commons. Whatever criticisms MPs make of Parliament while in opposition, once they are in government, party leaders have an interest in maintaining arrangements that greatly limit the power of Parliament to influence or stop what ministers do.

Among modern Parliaments, the House of Lords is unique because it was initially composed of hereditary peers, supplemented by lords appointed for life. However, in 1999, the Labour government abolished the right of all but ninety-two hereditary peers to sit in the House of Lords. Today, a large majority of its members are life peers who have received a title later in life for achievement in one or another public sphere, for having been government ministers without a seat in the House of Commons, or for being prominent financial donors to a party.

No party has a majority of seats in the House of Lords, and more than one-quarter of its members are cross-benchers who do not identify with any party. The government often introduces relatively noncontroversial legislation in the Lords, and it uses the Lords as a revising chamber to amend bills. Members of the Lords can raise party political issues or issues that cut across party lines, such as problems of the fishing industry or pornography. The Lords cannot veto legislation, but it can and does amend or delay the passage of some government bills.

Although all parties accept the need for some kind of second chamber to revise legislation, there is no agreement about how it should be composed or what its powers should be. In 2007, a majority of MPs voted in favor of a completely elected House of Lords, and the coalition government has affirmed its desire to move toward an elected upper chamber. However, the last thing the government of the day wants is a reform that gives the upper chamber enough electoral legitimacy to challenge government legislation.

The Courts and Abuses of Power

The creation of a Supreme Court as the highest judicial authority in the United Kingdom in 2009 replaced the centuries-old practice of the highest court operating as a committee of the House of Lords. The court consists of a president and eleven justices appointed by a panel of lawyers. Its chief function is to serve as the final court of appeal on points of law in cases initially heard by courts in England, Wales, and Northern Ireland. It also hears some cases from Scotland, which maintains a separate legal system, although its laws are usually much the same.

Although the new British Supreme Court has the same name as the highest court in the United States, its powers are much more limited. It can nullify government actions if they are deemed to exceed powers granted by an Act of Parliament, but it cannot declare an Act of Parliament unconstitutional. Governments often include clauses in Acts that give ministers broad discretionary powers. Parliament remains the supreme authority, deciding what government can and cannot do. In practice, when the government is under attack, it can usually rely on its own MPs to close ranks in its defense.

Britain's membership in the EU offers additional channels for judicial influence. The United Kingdom is now bound to act within laws and directives laid down by the EU. British judges can use EU standards when evaluating government actions, and plaintiffs can challenge British government actions at the European Court of Justice. The 1998 Human Rights Act of the Westminster Parliament allows citizens to ask British courts to enforce rights conferred by the European Convention on Human Rights.

There is tension between the principle that the elected government of the day should do what it thinks best and the judges' view that government should act in accord with the rule of law, whether it be an Act of Parliament or an obligation in a European treaty that the British government has endorsed. When judges have handed down decisions that ministers do not like, ministers have publicly attacked them. Judges have replied by declaring that they should not be attacked for enforcing the law; if the government does not like it, they say, it should pass a new Act of Parliament or alter a European law.

In constitutional theory, Parliament can hold prime ministers accountable for abuses of power by the government. In practice, Parliament is an ineffective check on abuses of executive power, because the executive consists of the leaders of the majority in Parliament. When the government is under attack, MPs in the governing party tend to close ranks in its defense. The government can use this shield to protect itself from charges of abusing its power.

Whitehall practices that abuse powers have been protected from parliamentary scrutiny by legislation on **official secrecy**. This legislation treats information as a scarce commodity that should not be given out freely. The Whitehall view is that "The need to know still dominates the right to know."[15] A Freedom of Information Act has reduced but has not ended the executive's power to keep secret the exchange of views within the Whitehall network. Information about policy deliberations in departments is often deemed to be not in the "public" interest to disclose, for it can make government appear uncertain or divided. The introduction of a coalition government is loosening up these restrictions, since there is now a need to consult more widely and openly among ministers and MPs in two parties. This makes unauthorized leaks to the media more likely.

Terrorist activities challenge conventional norms about individual rights and the collective interests of the state. The Labour government's proposals for reducing the rights of suspected terrorists have been condemned by Conservative and Liberal parties as creating the risk of a "siege" or "authoritarian" society.[16] At times, British government forces have dealt with the violence of the Irish Republican Army and illegal armed Protestant groups by "bending" the law, including fabricating evidence to produce convictions that courts have subsequently overturned. However, the government is slow to admit it has erred. For example, it took thirty-eight years before it admitted that the British Army's killing of thirteen Irish demonstrators in Londonderry in 1972 was totally unjustified. In response to jihadist terrorist bombs in London in 2005, the police have been ready to use harsh measures against suspects, including shoot-to-kill responses when arresting suspects.

Occasional abuses of executive power raise problems for civil servants who believe that their job is not only to serve the elected government of the day, but also to maintain the integrity of government. This has led civil servants at times to leak official documents with the intention of preventing government from carrying out a policy that the leaker believes to be unethical or inadvisable (see Box 8.5).

Government as a Network

The ship of state has only one tiller, but whenever a major policy decision comes up, many hands reach out to steer it. Policymaking involves a network of prime minister, ministers, leading civil servants, and political advisors, all of whom share in what has been described as the "village life" of Whitehall.[17] However, the growth of government has increased specialization so that policymakers see less and less of each other. For a given issue, a relatively small number of people are involved in the *core executive* group that makes a decision. However, the people in decision-making networks are a floating population; the core network is

not the same for transport and agriculture, or for health and defense.

The prime minister is the single most important person in government. Since there is no written constitution, a determined prime minister can challenge the status quo and turn government to fresh ends. But to say that the prime minister makes the most important decisions and less important decisions are left to departmental ministers leads to the question, "What is an important decision?" Decisions on issues in which the prime minister is not involved, such as social security, are more numerous, require more money, and affect more lives than most decisions made at Downing Street. Scarcity of time is a major limitation on the influence of the prime minister. In the words of one Downing Street official, "It's like skating over an enormous globe of thin ice. You have to keep moving fast all the time."[18] In a coalition government, major decisions cannot be made by a single politician because they require interparty agreement.

Within each department, the permanent secretary, its highest-ranking civil servant, usually has much more knowledge of a department's problems than does a transitory Cabinet minister. Political advisors brought into a department to put the best spin on what their minister does know less about the department's work than its career civil servants. However, they have the political advantage of knowing the minister better.

BOX 8.5

Conflicting Loyalties among Civil Servants

The inability of Parliament to hold the government of the day accountable for palpable misdeeds disturbs senior civil servants who know what is going on and risk becoming accessories before the fact if they assist ministers in producing statements that mislead Parliament.

In one well-publicized case, a Ministry of Defense official, Clive Ponting, leaked to the House of Commons evidence that questioned the accuracy of government statements about the conduct of the Falklands War. He was indicted and tried for violating the Official Secrets Act. The judge asked the jury to

think about the issue this way: "Can it then be in the interests of the state to go against the policy of the government of the day?" The jury concluded that it could be; Ponting was acquitted.

Most senior civil servants are unwilling to become whistle-blowers and jeopardize their own careers by voicing doubts about what ministers do. Inquiries after major mistakes can show that these mistakes have occurred because ministers have refused to listen to cautions from civil servants or misrepresented their views. This was notably so in Tony Blair's justification of going to war in Iraq.

See: Graham Wilson and Anthony Barker, "Whitehall's Disobedient Servants? Senior Officials' Potential Resistance to Ministers in British Government Departments," *British Journal of Political Science* 27, no. 2 (1997): 223–46.

POLITICAL CULTURE AND LEGITIMACY

Political culture refers to values and beliefs about how the country ought to be governed. For example, there is a consensus that Britain ought to have a government accountable to a popularly elected parliament. This view is held not only by the major parties but also by the parties that demand independence, such as the Scottish National Party.

The values of the political culture impose limitations on what government *can* do and what it *must* do. Regardless of party preference, the great majority of British people today believe that government ought to provide education, health services, and social security. Cultural norms about freedom of speech prevent censorship of criticism, and liberal laws about sexual relations and abortion allow great freedom of choice in sexual matters.

Today, the most significant limits on the scope of public policy are practical and political. Public expenditure on popular policies such as the health service is limited by the extent to which the economy grows and the reluctance of government to raise more money for health care by increasing taxes or by imposing some charges for its use, as is done in continental European countries.

The **trusteeship theory of government** assumes that leaders ought to take the initiative in deciding what is collectively in the public interest. This theory is summarized in the epigram, "The government's job is to govern." The trusteeship doctrine is always popular with the majority party because it justifies doing whatever the government wishes. The opposition party rejects this theory because it is not in office.

The **collectivist theory of government** sees government as balancing the competing demands of collective groups in society. From this perspective, parties and interest groups advocating group or class interests are more authoritative than individual voters.[19] Traditional Conservatives emphasize harmony between different classes in society, each with its own responsibilities and rewards. For socialists, group politics has been about promoting working class and trade union interests. With changes in British society, party leaders have distanced themselves from close identification with collective interests as they realize that votes are cast by individuals rather than by business firms or trade unions.

The **individualist theory of government** postulates that political parties should represent people rather than group interests. In the 1980s, Margaret Thatcher proclaimed that personal welfare should be the responsibility of each individual rather than of the state. She went so far as to declare, "There is no such thing as society." David Cameron has amended this view by emphasizing the importance of what he calls a big society, that is, a set of institutions bigger and broader than the state. Liberal Democrats put emphasis on individual freedom from government enforcement of social norms.

The legitimacy of government is seen by the readiness of the British people to conform to basic obligations such as paying taxes and cooperating with public officials. However, British people make many specific criticisms about government. Citizens have become distrustful of many political institutions in reaction to changing standards of elite behavior, such as MPs making excessive claims for expenses and Cabinet ministers seeking to besmirch the reputation of colleagues with whom they compete.

Less than one in five Britons trusts political parties that seek their support, and even fewer trust the press, which claims to represent the voice of the people. The press and television are trusted by less than one-third of the population. Barely one in three expresses trust in Parliament as a whole. Civil society organizations such as churches and trade unions likewise have the trust of less than half of the population. The most trusted public institutions today are those that maintain authority, including the armed forces, the police, and the courts (see Figure 8.3).

Dissatisfaction with government policies can stimulate popular protest, but the legitimacy of government means that protest is normally kept within lawful bounds. The World Values Survey finds that nearly every Briton says they might sign a petition, and half might participate in a lawful demonstration, but only one-sixth consider participating in an illegal occupation of a building or factory. The readiness of groups in Northern Ireland to use guns and bombs for political ends makes it the most "un-British" part of the United Kingdom.

The legitimacy accorded to British government is not the result of economic calculations about whether parliamentary democracy "pays" best, as rational-choice theories propose. During the depression of the

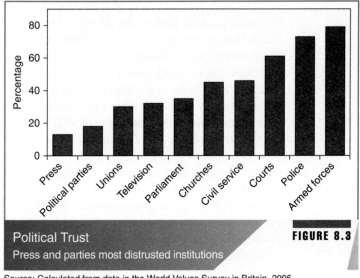

Political Trust
Press and parties most distrusted institutions

FIGURE 8.3

Source: Calculated from data in the World Values Survey in Britain, 2005.

1930s, Communist and Fascist parties received only derisory votes in Britain, while their support was great in Germany and Italy. Likewise, inflation and unemployment in the 1970s and 1980s did not stimulate extremist politics.

The symbols of a common past, such as the monarchy, are sometimes cited as major determinants of legitimacy. But surveys of public opinion show that the Queen has little political significance; her popularity derives from the fact that she is nonpolitical. The popularity of a monarch is a consequence, not a cause, of political legitimacy. In Northern Ireland, where the minority denies the legitimacy of British government, the Queen is a symbol of divisions between British Unionists and Irish Republicans who reject the Crown. Habit and tradition appear to be the chief explanations for the persisting legitimacy of British government. A survey asking people why they support the government found that the most popular reason was, "It's the best form of government we know."

Authority is not perfect or trouble-free. Winston Churchill made this point when he told the House of Commons:

> No one pretends that democracy is perfect or all wise. Indeed, it has been said that democracy is the worst form of government, except all those other forms that have been tried from time to time.[20]

In the words of the English writer E. M. Forster, people give "two cheers for democracy."

POLITICAL SOCIALIZATION

Socialization influences the political division between those who participate in politics and those who do not. The family's influence comes first chronologically; political attitudes learned within the family become intertwined with primary family loyalties. However, social change means that the views parents transmit to their children may not be relevant by the time their offspring have become forty to fifty years old. For example, a religious identification learned in childhood may no longer have a political relevance, for in contemporary Britain, whether one is a Christian or a Muslim tends to be more relevant than whether one was raised as a member of the Church of England or as a Roman Catholic.

Family and Gender

A child may not know what the Labour, Conservative, or Liberal Democratic Party stand for, but if it is the party of Mom and Dad, this can be enough to create a youthful identification with a party. However, the influence of family on voting is limited, because a third do not know how one or both of their parents usually voted, or else their parents voted for different parties. Among those who report knowing which party both parents supported, just over half vote as their parents have. In the electorate as a whole, only 35 percent say that they know how both parents voted and that they vote for the same party.[21]

Children learn different social roles according to gender, yet as adult citizens, men and women have the same legal right to vote and participate in politics. Men and women tend to have similar political attitudes. For example, more than half of women and half of men favor capital punishment, and a substantial minority in each group oppose it. At each general election, the votes of women are divided in much the same way as the votes of men (see Table 8.4).

Gender differences do lead to differences in political participation, however. Two-thirds of local government councilors are men; one-third are women. Women make up almost half the employees in the civil service but are concentrated in lower-level clerical jobs;

Social Differences in Voting

TABLE 8.4

In a multiparty system, no party has majority support in any social group.

	Conservative	Labour	Liberal Democrat	Other
Gender				
Women	38%	28%	22%	12%
Men	36%	31%	26%	8%
Age				
18–24	30%	31%	30%	9%
25–54	34%	30%	27%	9%
55–64	38%	28%	23%	12%
65 and over	44%	31%	16%	9%
Social Class				
Middle, professional	44%	23%	27%	7%
Lower middle	40%	28%	24%	9%
Skilled manual	33%	33%	19%	15%
Unskilled manual	32%	35%	13%	20%

Source: Ipsos MORI, *How Britain Voted in 2010* (www.ipsos-mori.com/researchpublications/researcharchive/poll.aspx?oItemId=2613); analysis of all who said they were absolutely certain to vote or had already voted, interviewed March 5–May 19, 2010 (*n* = 5,927).

Conservative, Labour, and Liberal Democratic Parties.

Education is strongly related to active participation in politics. The more education a person has, the greater his or her chances of climbing the political career ladder. One-third of MPs went to fee-paying private schools. University graduates make up nine-tenths of the members of the House of Commons. The expansion of universities has broken the traditional dominance of Oxford and Cambridge; only one-quarter of MPs went to these two institutions. The concentration of university graduates in top jobs is a sign of a meritocracy, in which persons qualified by education have replaced an aristocracy based on birth and family.

women hold about one-third of the top appointments in the civil service. In 2010, a total of 142 women were elected to the House of Commons; it remains more than three-quarters male. The coalition Cabinet has four women ministers.

Education

The majority of the population was once considered fit for only a minimum level of education, but the minimum level has steadily risen. In today's electorate, the oldest voters left school at the age of fourteen and the median voter by the age of seventeen. Only a small percentage of young persons attend "public" schools, that is, fee-paying schools, which are actually private. Whereas half a century ago Britain had few universities, today more than two-fifths of young persons enter postsecondary institutions. However, many of the new institutions created in the past two decades lack the facilities of established research universities.

The stratification of English education used to imply that the more education a person had, the more likely a person was to be Conservative. This is no longer the case. People with a university degree or its equivalent now divide their votes between the

Class

Historically, party competition has been interpreted in **class** terms; the Conservative Party has been described as a middle-class party, and Labour as a working-class party. Class is relatively important in England because of the absence of major divisions in race, religion, or language, as are found in the United States, Canada, or Northern Ireland.

Occupation has been the most commonly used indicator of class. Manual workers are usually described as the working class and nonmanual workers as the middle class. Changes in the economy have led to a reduction in manual jobs and an increase in middle-class jobs. Today, many occupations such as computer technician have an indeterminate social status. When British people are asked about belonging to a class, 57 percent reject placing themselves in either the middle or the working class.

The relationship between class and party has become limited. No party now wins as much as half the vote of middle-class or of skilled or unskilled manual workers (see Table 8.4). Due to the cross-class appeal of parties, less than two-fifths of voters now conform to the stereotypes of middle-class Conservatives or working-class Labour voters.

Most Britons have a mixture of middle-class and working-class attributes. Socioeconomic experiences other than occupation often influence voting. At each level of the class structure, people who belong to trade unions are more likely to vote Labour than Conservative. Housing creates neighborhoods with political relevance. People who live in municipally built council houses tend to vote Labour, while Conservatives do relatively well among homeowners, who are now a big majority of the electorate.

Media

The mass media's emphasis on what is happening today makes it an agency for resocializing people. Today, the upper class no longer commands deference, and celebrities prominent in sports, rock music, or making money are better known than most MPs and many Cabinet ministers. Moreover, the Internet provides people with alternative sources of information and opinion, and most Britons old enough to vote are able to find information there.

The British press is sharply divided into a few quality papers (such as *The Times*, *The Guardian*, *The Daily Telegraph*, *The Independent*, and *The Financial Times*) that carry news and comment at an intellectual level higher than American newspapers, and mass-circulation tabloids that concentrate on trivia and trash (such as *The Sun* and the *Daily Mirror*). *The Economist* is the best-known weekly periodical for politics and for economics; it circulates worldwide. Most papers tend to lean toward one party. However, if the party that they normally support becomes very unpopular, they tend to lean toward a party that has risen in popularity.

In the aggressive pursuit of news and audiences, journalists are prepared to grab attention by making the government of the day look bad, and television interviewers can gain celebrity by insulting MPs and ministers on the air. A majority of MPs think that the media is to blame for popular cynicism about politicians and parties. However, opinion polls find that a majority of the electorate thinks that the conduct of politicians is just as much to blame for cynicism about politics as is the conduct of the media.

Television is the primary source of political news. Historically, radio and television were a monopoly of the British Broadcasting Corporation (BBC), which sought to educate its audience and was respectful of politicians. There are now many television channels and a great variety of radio stations competing for audiences. Current-affairs programs seek audiences by exposing the failings of government. The law forbids selling advertising to politicians, parties, or political causes.

The government of the day controls the license renewals of broadcasting companies, and it sets the annual fee that every viewer must pay for noncommercial BBC programs, currently about $210 a year. Broadcasters try to avoid favoring one party, because over time, control of government (and with it the power to make decisions that affect broadcasting revenue and licenses) is likely to shift between parties.

Use of the Internet and other new media of communication by a majority of Britons has opened up a wide variety of sources of information to the public. Government agencies, Parliament, and the Prime Minister's Office provide substantial details about their activities and policies. Political parties produce electronic "mail shots" to targeted audiences, and MPs' hard drives overflow with communications from constituents and interest groups. Politicians are also vulnerable to having opinions expressed in informal e-mails leaked to the press.

Since political socialization is a lifetime learning process, the loyalties of voters are shaped by an accumulation of influences over many decades. Today, there are still some members of the electorate who were old enough to vote for or against Winston Churchill when he led the Conservative Party. In 2010, the youngest voters had not been born until after Margaret Thatcher retired as leader of the Conservative Party. At the next British general election, more than half the electorate will have cast their initial vote at the 1997 election or subsequently.

POLITICAL PARTICIPATION

An election is the one opportunity people have to influence government directly. Every citizen aged eighteen or over is eligible to vote. Local government officials register voters, and the list is revised annually, ensuring that nearly everyone eligible to vote is actually registered. Turnout at general elections has fallen from a high of 84 percent in the closely fought 1950 election to as low as 59 percent. In 2010, the closeness of the election increased turnout; it rose to 65 percent. However, only half those who vote say they feel close to a political party.

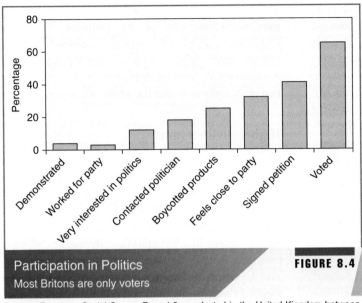

Participation in Politics
Most Britons are only voters

FIGURE 8.4

Source: European Social Survey Round 3, conducted in the United Kingdom between September 5, 2006, and January 14, 2007 (*n* = 2,319).

In addition to voting, there are many ways in which Britons participate in politics. Two-fifths have signed a petition on a public issue. One-quarter say that politics has affected their shopping by causing them to boycott a product. In the course of a year, almost one-fifth say that they have contacted a politician about a matter that concerns them. One in eight describe themselves as very interested in politics (see Figure 8.4).

Party workers are a very small minority of the electorate; Britons are much more inclined to participate in voluntary associations that they regard as nonpolitical, or nonparty, such as Oxfam, which is concerned with reducing world poverty. The concentration of the media in central London means that a political demonstration there in which ten thousand people participate will get national coverage. However, those participating are less than one-tenth of 1 percent of the electorate (see Figure 8.4).

POLITICAL RECRUITMENT

We can view recruitment into politics deductively or inductively. The deductive approach defines the job to be done and individuals are recruited with skills appropriate to the task; this practice is favored by management consultants. Alternatively, we can inductively examine the influences that lead people into politics and ask: Given their skills and motives, what can such people do? The constraints of history and institutions make the inductive approach more realistic.

The most important political roles in Britain are those of Cabinet minister, higher civil servant, partisan political advisor, and intermittent public persons analogous to Washington insiders. Each group has its own recruitment pattern. To become a Cabinet minister, an individual must first be elected to Parliament. Shortly after leaving university, ambitious politicians often become assistants to politicians and then "graduate" to lobbyist or journalist, then to parliamentary candidate for a constituency that their party normally wins. Individuals enter the civil service shortly after leaving university by passing a highly competitive entrance examination; promotion is based on achievement and approval by seniors. Intermittent public persons gain access to ministers and civil servants because of the knowledge and position that they have gained by making a career outside party politics.

In all political roles, starting early on a political career is usually a precondition of success, because it takes time to build up the skills and contacts necessary to become a major political actor. Geography is a second major influence on recruitment. Ministers, higher civil servants, and other public persons spend their working lives in London. A change at Downing Street does not bring in policymakers from a different part of the country, as can happen in the White House when a president from Chicago succeeds a president from Texas. Since London is atypical of the cities and towns in which most British people live, there is a gap between the everyday lives of policymakers and the majority on whose behalf they act.

MPs and Cabinet Ministers

For a person ambitious to be a Cabinet minister, becoming an MP is the necessary first step. Nomination as a parliamentary candidate is in the hands of local party committees. A candidate does not have to be resident in the constituency in which he or she is nominated. Hence, it is possible for a young person to go straight from university to a job in the House of Commons or party headquarters, and then look around the country for nomination for a winnable seat, a process that usually takes years. Once selected for a constituency in which his or her party has a big majority, the MP can then expect to be reelected routinely for a decade or more.

After entering the House of Commons, an MP seeks to be noticed. Some ways of doing so—for example, grabbing headlines by questioning the wisdom of the party leadership—make it difficult to gain promotion to ministerial rank. Other approaches assist promotion, such as successfully attacking opposition leaders in debate or being well-informed about a politically important topic, or showing loyalty to the party leader.

Experience in the Commons does not prepare an individual for the work of a minister. An MP's chief concerns are dealing with people and talking about what government ought to do. A minister must also be able to handle paperwork, relate political generalities to specific technical problems facing his or her department, and make hard decisions when all the alternatives are unpopular.

The restriction of ministerial posts to MPs prevents a nationwide canvass for appointees. A prime minister must distribute about a hundred jobs among approximately two hundred MPs in the governing party who are experienced in Parliament and have not ruled themselves out of consideration on grounds of parliamentary inexperience, old age, political extremism, personal unreliability, or lack of interest in office. An MP has a better than even chance of a junior ministerial appointment if he or she serves three terms in Parliament. A few people who have special skills or the confidence of the prime minister can be given ministerial appointments without becoming an MP; they are given a seat in the House of Lords.

A minister learns on the job. Usually, an MP is first given a junior post as a Parliamentary Under Secretary and then promoted to Minister of State before becoming a full member of the Cabinet. In the process, an individual is likely to be shuffled from one department to another, having to learn new subject matter with each shift between departments. The average minister can expect to stay in a particular job for about two years, and never knows when the accidents of politics—a death or an unexpected resignation—will lead to a transfer to another department. The rate of ministerial turnover in Britain is one of the highest in Europe. The minister who gets a new job as the result of a reshuffle usually arrives at a department with no previous experience of its problems. Anthony Crosland, an able Labour minister, reckoned: "It takes you six months to get your head properly above water, a year to get the general drift of most of the field, and two years really to master the whole of a department."[22]

Higher Civil Servants

Whereas MPs come and go from ministerial office, civil servants can be in Whitehall for the whole of their working lives. Higher civil servants are recruited without specific professional qualifications or training. They are meant to be the "best and the brightest"— a requirement that has traditionally meant getting a prestigious degree in history, literature, or languages. The Fulton Committee on the Civil Service recommended that recruits should have "relevant" specialist knowledge, but members could not decide what kind of knowledge was relevant to the work of government.[23] The Civil Service Commission tests candidates for their ability to summarize lengthy prose papers, to resolve a problem by fitting specific facts to general regulations, to draw inferences from a simple table of social statistics, and to perform well in group discussions about problems of government.

Because bright civil service entrants lack specialized skills and need decades to reach the highest posts, socialization by senior civil servants is especially important. The process makes for continuity, since the head of the civil service usually started there as a young official under a head who had himself entered the civil service many decades before.

In the course of a career, civil servants become specialists in the difficult task of managing ministers and government business. As the television series *Yes, Minister* shows, they are adept at saying "yes" to a Cabinet minister when they mean "perhaps" and saying "up to a point" when they really mean "no." Increasingly, ministers have tended to discourage civil servants from pointing out obstacles in the way of what government wants to do; they seek people offering "can do" advice from outside the civil service.

Political Advisors

Most advisors are party-political; their job is to mobilize political support for the government and for the Cabinet minister for whom they work. Because their background is in party politics and the media, such advisors bring to Whitehall skills that civil servants often lack and that their ministers value. But because they have no prior experience of the civil service, they are often unaware of its conventions and legal obligations. Some tricks used by political appointees to put a desirable spin on what the government is doing can backfire, causing public controversy and even their dismissal.

In addition, experts in a given subject area, such as environmental pollution or cloning, can act as political advisors. Even if inexperienced in the ways of Whitehall, they can contribute specialist knowledge that is often lacking in government departments, and they can be supporters of the governing party, too.

Most leaders of institutions such as universities, banks, churches, and trade unions do not think of themselves as politicians and have not stood for public office. They are principally concerned with their own organization. But when government actions impinge on their work, they become involved in politics, offering ministers advice and criticism. They are thus intermittent public persons.

Selective Recruitment

Nothing could be more selective than an election that results in one person becoming prime minister of a country. Yet nothing is more representative, because an election is the one occasion when every adult can participate in politics with equal effect.

Traditionally, political leaders had high social status and wealth before gaining political office. Aristocrats, business people, or trade union leaders can no longer expect to translate their high standing in other fields into an important political position. Today, politics is a full-time occupation. As careers become more specialized, professional politicians become increasingly distant from other spheres of British life.

The greater the scope of activities defined as political, the greater the number of people actively involved in government. Government influence has forced company directors, television executives, and university heads to become involved in politics and public policy. Leadership in organizations outside Whitehall gives such individuals freedom to act independently of government, but the interdependence of public and private institutions, whether for-profit or nonprofit, is now so great that sooner or later they meet in discussions about the public interest.

ORGANIZING GROUP INTERESTS

Civil society institutions have existed in Britain for more than a century. Their leaders regularly discuss specific policies with public officials in expectation that this will put pressure on government to do what they argue is in the public interest as well as their own group's interest.

The scope of group demands varies enormously from the narrow concerns of an association for the blind to the encompassing economic policies of organizations representing business or trade unions. Groups also differ in the nature of their interests; some are concerned with material objectives, whereas others advocate for single causes such as reducing violence on television or race relations.

The Confederation of British Industries is the chief representative organization of British business. As its name implies, its membership is large and varied. The Institute of Directors represents individuals at the top of large and small businesses. The heads of the biggest businesses usually have direct contacts with Whitehall and with ministers, whatever their party, because of the importance of their activities for the British economy and for its place in the international economy. For example, the dividends of BP (British Petroleum) have been a major source of income for British investors, most of the oil it drills is outside the United Kingdom, and when things go wrong, as in the Gulf of Mexico, it can create diplomatic problems. The construction industry has access to government because home-building is important for the national economy, and Whitehall's tight control over land use influences where houses can be built.

The chief labor organization is the Trades Union Congress (TUC); its members are trade unions that represent many different types of workers, some white-collar and some blue-collar. Most member unions of the TUC are affiliated with the Labour Party, and some leading trade unionists have been Communists or Maoists. None is a supporter of the Conservative or Liberal Democratic parties.

Changes in employment patterns have eroded union membership, and union members are disproportionately older workers. Today, less than one-quarter of the labor force belongs to a trade union.

Over the years, the membership of trade unions has shifted from manual workers in such industries as coal and railways to white-collar workers such as teachers and health-service employees. Less than one in six private sector workers belongs to a trade union. By contrast, more than half of the public sector workers are union members. Elected representatives control their wages, and strikes or go-slow actions by teachers, hospital workers, or other public employees can cause political embarrassment to the government.

Britain has many voluntary and charitable associations, from clubs of football team supporters to the Automobile Association. It is also home to a number of internationally active nongovernmental organizations such as Oxfam, dealing with problems of poor countries, and Amnesty International, concerned with political prisoners. The latter organizations try to bring pressure not only on Westminster but also on organizations such as the World Bank and on repressive governments around the world.

Unlike political parties, interest groups do not seek influence by contesting elections; they want to influence policies regardless of which party wins. Nonetheless, there are ties between interest groups and political parties. Trade unions have been institutionally part of the Labour Party since its foundation in 1900 and are the major source of party funds. The connection between business associations and the Conservatives is not formal, but the party's traditional commitment to private enterprise is congenial to business. Notwithstanding common interests, both trade unions and business groups demonstrate their autonomy by criticizing their partisan ally if it acts against the group's interest.

Party politicians seek to distance themselves from interest groups. Conservatives know that they can only win an election by winning the votes of ordinary citizens as well as prosperous businesspeople. Tony Blair sought to make the Labour government appear business-friendly and reaped large cash donations from very wealthy businessmen. However, this led union leaders to attack his government as unsympathetic, and a few small unions have left the Labour Party.

To lobby successfully, interest groups must be able to identify those officials most important in making public policy. When asked to rank the most influential offices and institutions, interest-group officials named the prime minister first by a long distance; Cabinet ministers came second, the media third, and senior civil servants fourth. Less than 1 percent thought MPs outside the ministerial ranks were of primary importance.[24] However, interest groups do not expect to spend a great deal of time in Downing Street. Most of their contacts are with officials in government departments concerned with issues of little public concern but of immediate interest to the group.

What Interest Groups Want

Most interest groups pursue three major goals: the sympathetic administration of established policies, information about government policies, and influencing policymaking and implementation. Whitehall departments are happy to consult with interest groups that provide information about what is happening outside Whitehall, cooperation in administering and implementing policies, and support for government initiatives. As long as the needs of Whitehall and interest groups are complementary, they can bargain as professionals sharing common concerns. Both sides are ready to arrive at a negotiated agreement.

The more committed members are to an interest group's goals, the more confidently leaders can speak for a united membership. Consumers are more difficult to organize because they have no social contacts with other people who buy what they buy. Drivers of Ford cars are a category rather than a social group. Changes in the economy, in class structure, and in the lifestyles of generations have resulted in a decline in the "dense" social capital networks of coal mining villages and textile mill towns.

Individuals usually have a multiplicity of identities that are often in conflict—for example, as workers desiring higher wages and as consumers wanting lower prices. The spread of mass consumption and decline in trade union membership has altered the balance between these priorities. As a trade union leader has recognized, "Our members are consumers too."[25]

Group members who care about an issue can disagree too about what their leaders ought to do. Even if an interest group is internally united, its demands may be counteracted by opposing demands from other groups. In economic policy, ministers can play off producers against consumers or business against unions to increase their scope for choice and present their policies as "something-for-everybody" compromises.

The more a group's values are consistent with the cultural norms of society as a whole, the easier it is to equate its interest with the public interest. But in an open society such as Britain, the claims of one group to speak for the public interest can easily be challenged by competing groups. The **centralization** of authority in British government means that interest groups must treat as given the political values and priorities of the government of the day.

Insider interest groups usually have values in harmony with every party. Insiders advance their case in quiet negotiations with Whitehall departments. Their demands tend to be restricted to what is politically possible in the short term, given the values and commitments of the government of the day.[26] **Outsider interest groups** are unable to negotiate because their demands are inconsistent with the party in power. Outsider groups without any influence in Whitehall often campaign through the media. To television viewers, their demonstrations appear as evidence of their importance; in fact, they are often signs of a lack of political influence. Green interest groups face the dilemma of either campaigning for fundamental change in hopes that eventually Whitehall departments will turn their way, or becoming insiders working within the system to improve the environment to some extent, but not as much as some ecologists would like.

Keeping Interest Groups at a Distance

Whitehall civil servants find it administratively convenient to deal with united interest groups that can implement agreements. For a generation after World War II, ministers endorsed the corporatist philosophy of bringing together business, trade unions, and political representatives in tripartite institutions to discuss such controversial issues as inflation and unemployment. Corporatist bargaining assumed a consensus on political priorities and goals and that each group's leaders could deliver the cooperation of those they claimed to represent. In practice, neither Labour nor Conservative governments were able to maintain a consensus. Nor were interest-group leaders able to deliver their nominal followers. By 1979, unemployment and inflation were both out of control.

The Thatcher administration demonstrated that a government firmly committed to distinctive values can ignore group demands and lay down its own pattern of policy. It did so by dealing at arm's length with both trade unions and business groups. Instead of consulting with interest groups, it practiced state-distancing, keeping the government out of everyday marketplace activities such as wage-bargaining, pricing, and investment.

A state-distancing strategy emphasizes the use of legislation to achieve goals, since no interest group can defy an Act of Parliament. Laws have reduced the capacity of trade unions to frustrate government policies through industrial action. The sale of state-owned industries has removed government from immediate responsibility for the operation of major industries, and Labour Chancellor Gordon Brown gave the Bank of England responsibility for monetary policy.

State-distancing places less reliance on negotiations with interest groups and more on the authority of government. Business and labor are free to carry on as they like—but only within the pattern imposed by government legislation and policy. Most unions and some business leaders do not like being "outside the loop" when government makes decisions. Education and health-service interest groups like it even less, because they depend on public funds for their revenue.

PARTY SYSTEM AND ELECTORAL CHOICE

British government is party government. The candidates on the ballot in each parliamentary constituency are nominated by party members, and the party leaders are chosen by the vote of their MPs and party members. The prime minister is not popularly elected, but gains office by being the leader of the party with the most MPs.

A Multiplicity of Choices

A general election must occur at least once every five years. The coalition government favors changing the law to have elections occurred at a fixed date, starting in 2015, while making allowance for an earlier contest if the government loses the confidence of a clear majority of MPs. This would replace the long-established practice of the prime minister's being able to call an election sooner if he or she thinks this is politically more favorable.

An election offers a voter a very simple choice between candidates competing to represent one of the 650 constituencies into which the House of Commons is divided. Within each constituency, the winner is the candidate who is **first past the post** with a plurality of votes, even if this is less than half the total vote. In 2010, the winner in one English constituency received only 29 percent of the total vote, and in most constituencies, the victor had a plurality but not an absolute majority of the vote. The winner nationally is the party gaining the most MPs. In 1951 and in February 1974, the party winning the most votes nationally did not win the most seats; the runner-up party in the popular vote formed the government.

Between 1945 and 1970, Britain had a two-party system; the Conservative and Labour parties together took an average of 91 percent of the popular vote and in 1951 took 97 percent (see Figure 8.5). The Liberals had difficulty fielding candidates in a majority of constituencies and even more difficulty in winning votes and seats. Support for the two largest parties was evenly balanced; Labour won four elections and the Conservatives won four.

The decline in the attractiveness of the class-based Labour and Conservative parties gave other parties an opportunity to gain support. A **multiparty system** emerged in the elections of 1974. The Liberals won nearly one-fifth of the vote, and Nationalists did well in Scotland, Wales, and Northern Ireland. Together, the Conservative and Labour parties took

only 75 percent of the vote. The Liberal Democrat and Nationalist parties have maintained their strength. The number of parties in the system today depends on the measure used.

- The number of parties competing for votes varies from three to five in different parts of the United Kingdom. In England, three parties—Labour, Conservatives, and Liberal Democrats—compete for votes (and in 2010, four, as the anti-EU United Kingdom Independence Party fought in most seats, too). In Scotland and Wales, there are normally four parties, and the Scottish National and Plaid Cymru (Welsh Nationalist) parties also elect MPs. In Northern Ireland, at least five parties contest seats, two representing Unionist and Protestant voters, two Irish Republican and Catholic voters, and the weakest a cross-religious Alliance of voters.

- The two largest parties do not monopolize votes. In the 2010 election, the biggest parties together won less than two-thirds of the popular vote (see Table 8.5). No party has won half the popular vote since 1935. In recognition of this, the 2010 televised election debates gave equal attention to Labour Prime Minister Gordon Brown,

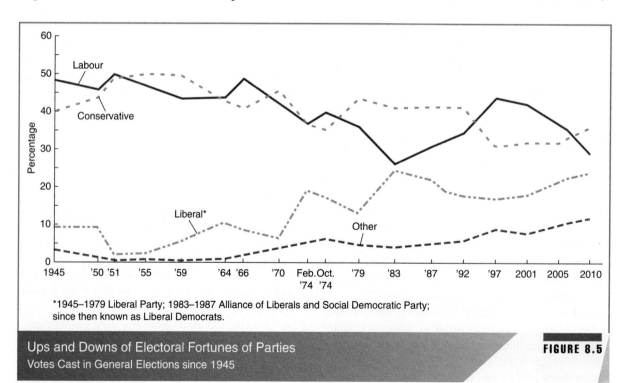

*1945–1979 Liberal Party; 1983–1987 Alliance of Liberals and Social Democratic Party; since then known as Liberal Democrats.

Ups and Downs of Electoral Fortunes of Parties
Votes Cast in General Elections since 1945

FIGURE 8.5

	England	Scotland	Wales	Northern Ireland	United Kingdom
The 2010 Election Party vote percentages by nation in 2010.					**TABLE 8.5**
Conservative	39.5%	16.7%	26.1%	—	36.0%
Labour	28.1%	42.0%	36.3%	—	29.0%
Liberal Democratic	24.2%	18.9%	20.1%	—	23.0%
Nationalists*	—	19.9%	11.3%	89.3%	—
Others	8.2%	2.4%	6.2%	10.8%	11.9%

*Scottish National Party, Plaid Cymru (Wales), and in Northern Ireland the Alliance party, the Democratic Union and Ulster Unionist parties, and pro–Irish Republic Sinn Fein and the Social Democratic and Labour Party.

Source: General Election 2010: Preliminary Analysis. House of Commons Library Research Paper 10/36.

Conservative leader David Cameron, and Liberal Democratic leader Nicholas Clegg.

- The two largest parties in the House of Commons are often not the two leading parties at the constituency level. At the 2010 election, in more than one-quarter of constituencies, one or both of the two front-running parties was neither Labour nor Conservative.
- More than half a dozen parties consistently win seats in the House of Commons. In 2010, so-called "third" parties won more than one-eighth of the seats in the Commons.
- Significant shifts in voting usually do not involve individuals moving between the Labour and Conservative parties but rather in and out of the ranks of abstainers or between the Liberal Democrats and the two largest parties. Nationalist parties in Scotland, Wales, and Northern Ireland win seats because they concentrate their candidates in one part of the United Kingdom.

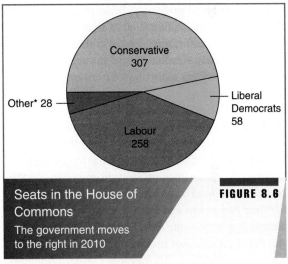

Seats in the House of Commons
The government moves to the right in 2010

FIGURE 8.6

*Includes six Scottish Nationalists, three Welsh Plaid Cymru, eight Northern Ireland Democratic Unionists, five Sinn Fein, three Northern Ireland Social Democratic and Labour, one Green, and two others.

Source: General Election 2010: Preliminary Analysis. House of Commons Library Research Paper 10/36.

The distribution of seats in the House of Commons is different from the distribution of the share of votes. In 2010, the Conservative Party won 47 percent of MPs with 36 percent of the vote, and the Labour Party won 40 percent of the seats in the House of Commons with 29 percent of the popular vote (see Figures 8.5 and 8.6). The Liberal Democrats gained just under 9 percent of MPs with 23 percent of the popular vote.

In 2009 the election of British Members of the European Parliament (MEPs) was held with a proportional representation ballot, and it occurred when the Labour government was very unpopular. The anti-EU

United Kingdom Independence Party came second in the popular vote, and the anti-immigrant British National Party and the Green Party also elected MEPs. However, when the choice in the following year was about who governs Britain, only the Green Party was able to win a single seat at Westminster.

Defenders of the first-past-the-post electoral system argue that proportionality is not a goal in itself. It is justified because it usually places responsibility for government in the hands of a single party. This justification is used in the United States, where the president can be described as representing all the people, whether he wins just over half or just under half the popular vote. In countries using proportional representation, coalition or minority governments are the norm. When a coalition is necessary, a party finishing third in the popular vote usually determines who governs by joining in a formal or informal coalition with one or the other of the two largest parties.

The strongest advocates of proportional representation are the Liberal Democrats. In a proportional representation system, the Liberal Democrat vote in 2010 would have given it 150 seats, more than double what it actually received. The coalition government is committed to holding a referendum in May 2011 on whether the plurality first-past-the-post system should be maintained or replaced by the alternative vote (AV) system. The AV system asks voters to indicate their order of preference between candidates. If the front-running candidate lacks an absolute majority, the candidates finishing lowest in the constituency are progressively eliminated and the second preferences of their voters redistributed until one candidate gets a majority.

In elections that do not affect the composition of the Westminster Parliament, a variety of electoral systems are in use.[27] All British members of the European Parliament are elected by proportional representation, and this has been true of electing members of the Northern Ireland Assembly for four decades. The Scottish Parliament and Welsh Assembly use a mixed electoral system: some representatives are elected by the first-past-the-post method and some by proportional representation. The mayor of Greater London is elected by the alternative vote, ensuring that the winner is the first or second choice of more than half the voters.[28]

Political parties are often referred to as "machines," but this description is very misleading, for parties cannot mechanically manufacture votes. Nor can a political party be commanded like an army. Parties are like universities; they are inherently decentralized, and people belong to them for a variety of motives. Thus, party officials have to work hard to keep together three different parts of the party: those who vote for it, the minority active in its constituency associations, and the party in Parliament. If the party has a majority in Parliament, there is a fourth group: the party in government. Whether the party leader is the prime minister or the leader of the Opposition, he or she must maintain the confidence of all parts of the party or risk ejection as leader.[29]

The headquarters of each party provides more or less routine organizational and publicity services to constituency parties and to the party in Parliament. Each party has an annual conference to debate policy and to vote on some policy resolutions. Constituency parties are nationally significant because each selects its own parliamentary candidate. The **decentralization** of the selection process has allowed the choice of parliamentary candidates with a wide variety of political outlooks and abilities. Under Tony Blair, the Labour Party introduced more central direction in choosing candidates. Doing so was justified on the grounds of securing more female MPs, and this has happened.

The Liberal Democrats have a small central organization and have built up the party by winning council seats at local government elections and at parliamentary elections targeting seats where the party is strong locally. This strategy has paid off; it has almost trebled its number of MPs from twenty in 1992 to fifty-eight in 2010, while its share of the popular vote has scarcely altered.

Party Images and Appeals

While the terminology of "left" and "right" is part of the language of elite politicians, it is rejected by the great majority of British voters. When asked to place themselves on a left/right scale, the median voter chooses the central position, and only a tenth place themselves on the far left or far right. Consequently, parties that veer toward either extreme risk losing votes. Tony Blair won elections for Labour because he avoided left-wing rhetoric and policies, and David Cameron led the Conservatives to victory by moving the party toward the center of British politics.

A large majority of the public named economic problems as a major issue at the 2010 general election. Second in importance were issues related to race relations and immigration. A quarter of the electorate also expressed concerns about crime, and the health service was important to a quarter of the voters. Foreign-policy issues were of limited concern. When public opinion is examined across a variety of issues, such as inflation, protecting the environment, spending money on the health service, and trade union legislation, a majority of Conservative, Labour, and Liberal Democratic voters tend to agree. Big divisions in contemporary British politics often cut across party lines. Any attempt to impute a coherent ideology to a political party is doomed to failure, for institutions cannot think and are not organized to debate philosophy.

Instead of campaigning in ideological terms or by appealing to collectivist economic interests, parties increasingly stress consensual goals, such as promoting prosperity and fighting crime. They compete in terms of which party or party leader can best be trusted to do what people want, or whether it is time for a change because one party has been in office for a long time. The titles of election manifestos are virtually interchangeable between the parties. In 2010, manifestos had such titles as "A Future Fair for All," "An Invitation to Join the Government of Britain," and "Change That Works for You."[30]

Much of the legislation introduced by the government is meant to be so popular that the Opposition dare not vote against the bill's principle. For every government bill that the Opposition votes against on principle in the House of Commons, up to three are adopted with interparty agreement.[31] MPs who rebel against their party whip are usually so extreme and insufficient in number that government bills are not threatened with defeat.

Most policies of government are not set out in its party manifesto; they are inherited from predecessors of the same or a different party. When the Thatcher administration entered office in 1979, it inherited hundreds of programs enacted by preceding governments, including some on the statute books since 1760.[32] It repealed some programs inherited from its predecessors—and it repealed some of its own programs that were quickly recognized as mistakes. When Margaret Thatcher left office, two-thirds of the programs for which the government was responsible had been enacted by her predecessors.

The freedom of action of the governing party is limited by constraints embedded in the obligations of office. Once in office, ministers find that all the laws enacted by their predecessors must be enforced, even if the government of the day would not have enacted them. A newly elected government also inherits many commitments to foreign countries and to the EU. As a former Conservative minister said of his Labour successors, "They inherited our problems and our remedies."[33]

CENTRALIZED AUTHORITY AND DECENTRALIZED DELIVERY OF POLICIES

In a unitary state, political authority is centralized. Decisions made by central government are binding on all public agencies through Acts of Parliament and regulations prepared in Whitehall. In addition, Whitehall controls taxation and public expenditure to a degree unusual among other member states of the EU, where coalition government and federalism encourage decentralization.

Centralization is justified as the best way to achieve **territorial justice**—that is, public services being at the same standard throughout the United Kingdom. For example, schools in inner cities and rural areas should have the same resources as schools in prosperous suburbs. This can be achieved only if tax revenues collected by central government are redistributed from wealthy to poor parts of the country. In addition, ministers emphasize that they are accountable to a national electorate of tens of millions of people, whereas local councilors are only accountable to those who vote in their ward. Instead of small being beautiful, a big, nationwide electorate is assumed to be better. The statement "Local councillors are not necessarily political animals; we could manage without them" was made by a left-wing law professor.[34]

For ordinary individuals, the actions of government are tangible only when services are delivered locally at a school, at a doctor's office, or in rubbish collection at their doorstep. However, Whitehall departments usually do not deliver policies themselves. Most public goods and services are delivered by agencies headquartered outside Whitehall. Moreover, five-sixths of public employees work for non-Whitehall agencies.[35] Thus, making and delivering public policies involves *intra*governmental politics.

Whitehall

Running the "Whitehall obstacle race" is the first step in intragovernmental politics. Most new policies must take into account the effects of existing policies in a crowded policy "space." Before a bill can be put to Parliament, the Cabinet minister sponsoring it must negotiate with ministers in other departments about how the new measure will affect existing programs

England: an Urban Country with Lots of Green Fields

Although three-quarters of the residents of the United Kingdom live in cities or suburbs, strict planning laws have left most of the landmass of the country open countryside including greenbelts around cities to preserve countryside and villages.

Soundsnaps/Shutterstock

and the terms of cooperation between departments to implement it. Negotiations are time-consuming. Often, a department will begin work on a new initiative under one minister and complete it under another or even under a different party in power.

Because of Treasury control of public expenditure, before a bill can be put to Parliament, the Treasury must authorize the additional expenditure required, because increased spending implies increased taxation. Ministers in charge of spending departments dislike constant Treasury reminders that there are strict cash limits on what they can spend. In the words of a veteran Treasury official, "the Treasury stands for reality."[36]

A minister anxious to gain attention by introducing a popular bill in Parliament cannot do so on his or her own. Approval must be gained from those concerned with the government as a whole. Criticism by the opposition party is less of a concern than attacks from MPs within the government's ranks. In a single-party government, approval to important measures may be needed from the prime minister and from Cabinet colleagues on matters of lesser importance. The coalition government adds a new dimension; there are committees representing both the Conservative and Liberal Democrat leaders to check that legislation is acceptable to both parties in government.

Once a bill becomes a law, there are many reasons why ministers do not want to be in charge of delivering services. Ministers may wish to avoid charges of political interference, allow for flexibility in the market, lend an aura of impartiality to quasi-judicial activities, allow qualified professionals to regulate technical matters, or remove controversial activities from Whitehall. The prime minister prefers to focus upon the glamorous "high" politics of foreign affairs and economic management. However, since "low-level" services remain important to most voters' lives, ministers are under pressure to do something—or at least *say* something—in response to media demands, for example when there is evidence of declining standards in schools, lengthening lines for hospital admission, and an increase of crime on the streets.

Devolution to Elected Officials

Local government councilors are elected, but within England, local government is subordinate to central government. Westminster has the power to write or rewrite the laws that determine what locally elected governments do and spend, or even to abolish local authorities and create new units of government with different boundaries. Both Conservative and Labour governments have used these powers. Changes in local government boundaries have reflected a never-ending search to find a balance between efficiency (assumed to correlate with fewer councils delivering services to more people spread over a wider geographical area) and responsiveness (assumed to require more councils, each with a smaller territory and fewer people).

Local council elections are fought on party lines. In the days of the two-party system, many cities were solidly Labour for a generation or more, while leafy suburbs and agricultural counties were overwhelmingly Conservative. The Liberal Democrats now win many seats in local elections and, when no party has a majority, introduce coalition government into town halls. However, being a councilor is usually a part-time job.

The Blair government introduced the direct election of the mayor of Greater London, citing New York and Chicago as positive examples. However, it refused to give London the independence in taxing and spending that American local government enjoys.[37] The office is a political platform that attracts media attention. London's first mayor, a left-wing independent, and its second, a Conservative eccentric, have used their legitimacy as elected officials to challenge the views of government at Westminster.

Local government is usually divided into two tiers of county and district councils, each with responsibility for some local services. The proliferation of public–private initiatives and special-purpose agencies has reduced the services for which local government is exclusively responsible. Today, there is a jumble of more or less local institutions delivering such public services as education, police protection, garbage collection, housing, and cemeteries (see Box 8.6). Collectively, local institutions account for about a fifth of total public expenditure.

Grants of money from central government are the largest source of local government revenue. There is no local income tax or sales tax, since the central government does not want to give local authorities the degree of fiscal independence that American local government has. The Thatcher government replaced the local property tax with a poll tax on every adult resident of a local authority, believing it would make voters more aware of the costs of local government. In practice, the tax produced a political backlash and was replaced by a community charge (tax) on houses and business real estate, which central government tends to control.[38] The problem of how to fund services that local government delivers remains a contentious issue.

Devolution to Scotland, Wales, and Northern Ireland is an extreme form of decentralization. The Scottish government, accountable to a parliament in Edinburgh, has the right to enact legislation about a large range of services—such as education, health, and roads—of direct concern to individuals and communities in Scotland. It is also responsible for determining spending priorities within the limits set by its block grant of money from the British Treasury. With the Scottish National Party in government, it has political incentives to challenge the authority of Westminster; the Welsh Assembly has administrative

---

BOX 8.6

Delivering Public Services on the Doorstep

Education is an example of how different institutions relate in complex ways. It is authorized by an Act of Parliament and principally financed by central government. Two Cabinet ministers divide responsibility; one is responsible for schools and the other for universities. The delivery of primary and secondary education is the responsibility of classroom teachers who are immediately accountable to the head of their school and not to Parliament. Dissatisfaction with the management of schools by local government has led Whitehall to establish city academies, secondary schools independent of local government but dependent on Whitehall for funding.

Increasingly, central government seeks to monitor the performance of schools in nationwide examinations and set targets that teachers and pupils are expected to achieve. But since the Whitehall department responsible for schools employs only 1 percent of the people working in education, success depends on actions taken by others. Conservative Minister of Education Lord Hailsham contrasted his position with that of being a minister of defense. In the latter, "You say to one person 'come' and he cometh and another 'go' and he goeth"; with the former, "You say to one man 'come' and he cometh not, and another 'go' and he stays where he is."[39]

See: Richard Rose, "The Growth of Government Organizations," in *Organizing Government, Governing Organizations*, ed. C. Campbell and B. G. Peters (Pittsburgh, PA: University of Pittsburgh Press, 1988), 99–128.

discretion, but has not gained legislative or taxing powers. Northern Ireland is exceptional because the key service is police and security, which was kept under the control of British ministers until agreement was achieved under a power-sharing government that included participants active in organizing its decades of civil war.

Nonelected Institutions

Executive agencies are headed by nonelected officials responsible for delivering many major public services. The biggest, the National Health Service (NHS), is not one organization but a multiplicity of separate institutions with separate budgets, such as hospitals and doctors' offices. Access to the National Health Service is free of charge to every citizen, but health care is not costless. Public money is allocated to hospitals and to doctors and dentists who must work within guidelines and targets established centrally. Because central government picks up the bill, the Treasury, as the monopoly purchaser, regularly seeks to cut costs in providing increasingly expensive health care.

Public demand for more and better health care has increased with the aging of the population and the development of new forms of medical treatment. The government's rationing of supply has sometimes involved months of waiting before a person can see a medical specialist or have a nonemergency hospital operation. British government has sought to deal with this problem by administrative changes intended to increase efficiency; that is, keeping total expenditure relatively constant by cutting the cost of individual services while expanding the total number supplied. It has not adopted the practice common in most EU countries of asking patients to pay a limited part of the cost of seeing a doctor or getting hospital treatment.

British government sponsors more than a thousand **quasi-autonomous nongovernmental organizations** ("**quangos**"). All are created by an Act of Parliament or by an executive decision; their heads are appointed by a Cabinet minister and public money can be appropriated to finance their activities. When things go wrong with quangos delivering public services, Parliament has difficulty in assigning responsibility. The coalition has sought to reduce the number of quangos on the grounds that they blur responsibility for decision-making.

Advisory committees draw on the expertise of individuals and organizations involved in programs for which Whitehall departments are responsible. For example, ministry officials dealing with agriculture can turn to advisory committees for detailed information about farming practices. Because they have no executive powers, advisory committees usually cost very little to run. Representatives of interest groups are glad to serve because this gives them privileged access to Whitehall and an opportunity to influence policies in which they are directly interested.

Administrative tribunals are quasi-judicial bodies that make expert judgments in such fields as medical negligence or handle a large number of small claims, such as disputes about whether the rent set for a rent-controlled flat is fair. Ministers may use tribunals to avoid involvement in politically controversial issues, such as decisions about deporting immigrants. Tribunals normally work much more quickly and cheaply than the courts. However, the quasi-judicial role of tribunals has created a demand for independent auditing of their procedures to ensure that they are fair to all sides. The task of supervising some seventy tribunals is in the hands of a quango, the Council on Tribunals.

Turning to the Market

The 1945 to 1951 Labour government turned away from the market because its socialist leaders believed that government planning was better able to promote economic growth and full employment. It nationalized many basic industries, such as electricity, gas, coal, the railways, and airlines. State ownership meant that industries did not have to run at a profit; some consistently made money while others consistently lost money and required big subsidies. Government ownership politicized wage negotiations and investment decisions. The Thatcher government promoted privatization by selling shares of nationalized industries on the stock market. Selling council houses to tenants at prices well below their market value was popular with tenants. Industries needing large public subsidies to maintain public services, such as the railways, have continued to receive subsidies after privatization.

Privatization has been justified on grounds of economic efficiency (the market is better than civil servants in determining investment, production, and prices); political ideology (the power of government is reduced); service (private enterprise is more consumer-oriented than civil servants); and short-term financial gain (the sale of public assets can provide billions in revenue for government). Although the Labour Party initially opposed privatization, it quickly realized it would be electorally disastrous to take back privatized council houses and shares that people had bought at bargain prices.

Since many privatized industries affect the public interest, new regulatory agencies have been established to monitor telephones, gas, electricity, broadcasting, and water. Where there is a substantial element of monopoly in an industry, the government regulatory agency seeks to promote competition and often has the power to fix price increases at a lower rate than inflation. Even when government no longer owns an industry, when things go wrong, government ministers cannot ignore what has happened. An extreme example of government intervention occurred when several fatal accidents occurred on railway track maintained by a privatized transport company. The Blair government took it back into public ownership.

From Trust to Contract

Historically, the British civil service has relied on trust in delivering policies. British civil servants are much less rule-bound than their German counterparts and less threatened with being dragged into court than are American officials. Intragovernmental relations between Whitehall departments and representatives of local authorities arrived at consensual understandings upheld by all sides on the basis of trust as well as law. However, the Thatcher government preferred to use law and its control of finance to constrain local government and promote competition by establishing new agencies or contracting for public services with private sector companies. The New Labour government intensified the use of targets to be met by agencies receiving public money. The coalition government talks about decentralization but this can only be achieved on terms set by central government.

Trust has been replaced by contracts with agencies delivering such everyday services as automobile licenses and patents. In addition, the government has sought to keep capital expenditure from visibly increasing public debt through private finance initiatives. Banks and other profit-making companies loan money to build facilities that will be leased by government agencies or even operated by profit-making companies. The theory is that government can obtain the greatest value for money by buying services from the private sector, ranging from operating staff canteens in government offices to running prisons. However, the government's experience with cost overruns and failure to meet targets for expensive information-technology services shows that either the market cannot supply what government needs, civil servants do not know how to purchase and manage contracts for services costing hundreds of millions of pounds, or both.

Government by contract faces political limits because a departmental minister must answer to Parliament when something goes wrong. The Prison Service is a textbook example. It was established as an executive agency separate from Whitehall in 1993 to bring in private management in order to reduce unit costs in the face of rising "demand" for prisons due to changes in crime rates and sentencing policies. However, when prisoners escaped and other problems erupted, the responsible Cabinet minister blamed the business executive brought in to head the Prison Service. The Prison Service head replied by attacking the minister's refusal to live up to the terms of the contract agreed upon between them.

The proliferation of many agencies, each with a distinctive and narrow responsibility for a limited number of policies, tends to fragment government. For example, parents may have to deal with half a dozen different agencies to secure all the public services to which they are entitled for their children. Tony Blair promoted "joined up" government, linking the provision of related services so that they could more easily be received by individual citizens. To many public agencies, this looked like a device to increase Downing Street's power. In fact, it demonstrated the limited ability of a few people in Downing Street to determine what is done by millions of people delivering public services.

The Contingency of Influence

The theory of British government is centralist; all roads lead to Downing Street, where the prime minister and the Chancellor of the Exchequer have their homes and offices. The Foreign Office and the Treasury are only a few steps away. In practice, policymaking occurs in many buildings, some within Whitehall and others far from London. Those involved can be divided horizontally between ministries and executive agencies, and vertically between central government, local authorities, and other nondepartmental bodies that deliver particular public services.

Influence is contingent; it varies with the problem at hand. Decisions about war and peace are made in Downing Street by the highest-ranking political and military officials. In the Iraq War, Tony Blair's media advisor was also heavily involved. By contrast, decisions about whether a particular piece of land should be used for housing are normally made by local authorities far from London.

The Conservative and Liberal Democratic coalition has sought to reduce differences by having ministers from both parties serve within most government departments. However, most political decisions involve two or more government agencies. Therefore, discussion and bargaining between government departments is required before decisions can be implemented. The making of policy is constrained by disputes within government much more than by differences between the governing party and its opponents. Many tentacles of the octopus of government work against each other, as public agencies often differ in their definition of the public interest. For example, the Treasury wants to keep taxes down while the Ministry of Defense wants more money to buy expensive equipment.

While the center of central government has been pressing harder on other public agencies, Whitehall itself has been losing influence because of its obligations in the EU. The Single Europe Act promotes British exports, but it also increases the scope for EU decisions to regulate the British economy. Whitehall has adopted a variety of strategies in its EU negotiations, including noncooperation and public dispute. Ironically, these are just the tactics that local government and other agencies use when they disagree with Whitehall.

WHY PUBLIC POLICY MATTERS

However a citizen votes, she or he does not need to look far to see the outputs of government. If there is a school-aged child or a pensioner in the house, the benefits to the family are continuous and visible. If a person is ill, the care provided by doctors and hospitals are important outputs of public policy; so too are police protection and tight controls of land use in order to maintain greenbelts.

To produce the benefits of public policy, government relies on three major resources: laws, money, and personnel. Most policies involve a combination of all three resources, but they do not do so equally. Policies regulating individual behavior, such as marriage and divorce, are law-intensive; measures that pay benefits to millions of people, such as social security, are money-intensive; and public services such as health care are labor-intensive.

Laws are the unique resource of government, for private enterprises cannot enact binding laws, and contracts are only effective if they can be enforced by courts. The British executive centralizes the power to draft laws and regulations that are usually approved without substantial amendment by Parliament. Moreover, many laws give ministers significant discretion in administration. For example, an employer may be required to provide "reasonable" toilet facilities rather than having all features of lavatories specified down to the size and height of a toilet seat.

Public employees are needed to administer laws and deliver major services. The top civil servants who work in Whitehall are few. The number of people officially counted as civil servants and public employees has been reduced by privatization. Nonetheless, more than a fifth of the entire British labor force directly depends on public spending for their jobs. The single biggest public employer is the NHS.

To meet the costs of public policy, British government collects up to two-fifths of the gross national product in taxation. Income tax accounts for 27 percent of tax revenue; the top rate of taxation is 50 percent on incomes over about $210,000 a year. Social security taxes are paid by deductions from wages and additional contributions of employers; these account for an additional 18 percent of revenue. Since there are no state or local income taxes, a well-to-do British person can pay taxes on income at a rate not much more than an American subject to federal, state, and local taxation in New York City.

Taxes on consumption are important, too. There is a value-added tax of 20 percent on the sale of almost all goods and services. Gasoline, cigarettes, and alcohol are taxed very heavily, too. Taxes on consumption in total account for about one-quarter of all tax revenue.

Since profits fluctuate from year to year, the government prefers businesses to pay taxes through Value Added Tax and on their total wages bill through the employer's contribution to social security. Taxes on the profits of corporations provide under a tenth of total tax revenue. Additional revenue comes from "stealth" taxes that ordinary citizens rarely notice and from taxes that do cause complaints, such as the council tax on houses. The government also raises money by taking a big cut from the National Lottery.

Social security programs are the most costly government policies; they account for one-third of total public expenditure (see Figure 8.7). They are also the most popular, transferring money from government to more than 10 million older people receiving pensions, in addition to millions of invalids, the unemployed, women on maternity leave, and poor people needing to supplement their limited incomes. Spending on health claims almost one-fifth of the public budget, and education one-seventh. Together, these three social welfare programs account for two-thirds of total public expenditure. Next in total spending are the classic responsibilities of government—defense and payment of interest on the national debt.

Since there is no item in the public budget labeled as "waste," any government wanting to make a big cut in public spending must squeeze existing programs—and big savings can be made only by squeezing popular programs. When Margaret Thatcher entered office in 1979, the public divided into three almost equal groups: those wanting to spend more and tax more, those in favor of

cutting taxes even if it meant a reduction in public services, and a group wanting to leave things as they were. Thatcher's campaign to cut taxes and public spending initially produced a reaction in favor of public expenditure. During the New Labour government that followed, the pendulum swung back to an almost equal division between those who wanted to cut taxes and spending and those wanting to increase both, with the median group wanting to keep both as they were. Within weeks of taking office in 2010, the coalition government introduced substantial spending cuts. It said the need to do so was the fault of the big budget deficit left behind by the outgoing Labour government. Labour responded by charging that cutbacks in public spending would stifle economic growth, thus reducing tax revenue and increasing the government's deficit.

POLICY OUTCOMES IN SOCIETY

In an open society such as Britain, social conditions reflect the interaction of public policies, the national and international economy, the not-for-profit institutions of civil society, and the choices that individuals and households make. Thus, the term *welfare state* is misleading. Total welfare in society is the sum of a "welfare mix," combining actions of government, the market, and the nonmonetized production of welfare in the household.[40]

Although commentators on British society often bemoan the country's economic decline relative to the United States and leading continental European countries, ordinary people do not compare their lives with those of people in other countries. The most important comparison is with their own past. Evaluating change across time shows great improvements in the living conditions of most people compared with their parents or grandparents. The longer the time span, the greater the improvement. Furthermore, in the production of such political "goods" as freedom from the state, confidence in the honesty of public officials, and administrative flexibility, British government has been an international leader. The great majority of people are proud of the achievements of Britain and would not want to be citizens of any other country.

Maintaining order within the United Kingdom is a unique responsibility of Westminster. In Northern Ireland, Whitehall has created a power-sharing government after a quarter century of negotiations with

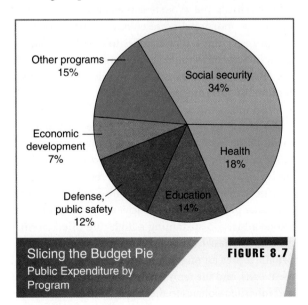

Other programs
15%

Social security
34%

Economic development
7%

Health
18%

Defense, public safety
12%

Education
14%

Slicing the Budget Pie
Public Expenditure by Program

FIGURE 8.7

Irish Republicans and armed Protestant groups about giving up violence. Since terrorist attacks by jihadists began in London in 2005, the British government has pursued a multiplicity of measures in an attempt to identify, isolate, and, as appropriate, arrest and jail those planning violence. One strategy has been to encourage moderate Muslim groups to engage in "self-policing" of their communities. Another has been to maintain surveillance on individuals and groups voicing fanatical opinions, including the endorsement of violence. A third has been to use extraordinary police powers to arrest and interrogate suspects.

In each of the past six decades, the British economy has grown. Compounding a small annual rate of growth over many decades cumulatively results in a big rise in living standards. Per capita national income has doubled in the lifetime of the median voter. Many consumer goods that were once thought of as luxuries, such as owning a car or one's own home or enjoying holidays abroad, are now mass-consumption goods. In addition, products unknown a few decades ago such as home computers and mobile phones are now commonplace.

Poverty can be found in Britain; the extent depends on the definition used. If poverty is defined in relative terms, such as having less than half the average wage, then about 10 percent of Britons are living in relative poverty. If poverty is defined as being trapped at a low income level for many years, then less than 4 percent are long-term poor.

In the past half century, small annual changes have compounded into cumulatively big changes over the generations. Infant mortality has declined by more than four-fifths since 1951. Life expectancy for men and for women has risen by twelve years. A gender gap remains, as women on average live five years longer than men. The postwar expansion of schools has significantly raised the quantity of education available. Classes are smaller in size, more than two-fifths of British youths go on to some form of further education, and many attend universities that did not exist in 1960. More than two-thirds of families now own their own home, and nine-tenths report satisfaction with their housing.

The outputs of public policy play a significant part in the everyday lives of Britons, and the benefits received are especially important for low-income families. During the year, the average family makes use of at least two major social programs. Everyone makes major use of publicly financed health and education services. Children at school and patients seeing a doctor do not think of themselves as participating in politics. Yet the services received are paid for by government and supervised by public officials. Social benefits such as free education, health care, and the guarantee of an income in old age are seen by many people as nonpolitical, and they do not want an election outcome to result in radical changes in familiar social policies.

When people are asked to evaluate their lives, they are most satisfied with their families, friends, homes, and jobs, while having just an average level of satisfaction with public services.[41] Public policies are evaluated differently. When opinion polls annually ask what people think next year will be like for themselves and their families, nine-tenths of the time, a majority say they expect the coming year to be all right for themselves, even when many expect economic difficulties for the country as a whole.

Satisfaction with the present goes along with acceptance of the principle of political change. However, there is no agreement about what direction change should take. Deputy Prime Minister and Liberal Democratic Party leader Nick Clegg introduced a set of electoral reforms, claiming that Britain is a "fractured democracy" because a party's share of MPs is not proportional to its share of votes. However, Prime Minister and Conservative Party leader David Cameron opposes abandoning the first-past-the-post electoral system, and some advocates of electoral reform criticize the AV system as an inadequate substitute for proportional representation. Party leaders at Westminster think that changes to devolved institutions in Scotland should strengthen its integration in the British political system, while the Scottish Nationalist government wants a weakening of ties and Scottish independence.

There is broad agreement about the need to make the British economy more competitive in a global economy. But even when goals are agreed on, such as achieving economic growth and reducing unemployment, there are differences of opinion about the particular policy that can best achieve the goal, and previous failures in sustaining a high rate of economic growth emphasize the difficulty of doing so. Politics in Britain is thus an ongoing debate about the direction, the means, and the tempo of adapting old institutions and inherited policies to the twenty-first century.

REVIEW QUESTIONS

- How would you describe the unwritten constitution of Britain?

- What are the similarities and differences between being a president and being a prime minister?

- What are the nations of the United Kingdom, and how are they governed?

- What are the continents and countries with which Britain has the closest links?

- How would you describe the different parties that have seats in the House of Commons?

- What are the arguments for and against the use of the first-past-the-post electoral system in Britain?

- What policies claim the largest portion of public expenditures, and why?

- What are the main challenges facing the coalition government elected in the 2010 general election?

KEY TERMS

Cabinet
centralization
class
collectivist theory of government
Conservative Party
Crown
decentralization
devolution
Downing Street

first past the post
individualist theory of government
insider interest groups
Irish Republican Army (IRA)
Labour Party
Liberal Democratic Party
multiparty system
New Labour Party

Northern Ireland
official secrecy
outsider interest groups
Parliament
prime minister
privatization
quasi-autonomous nongovernmental organization (quangos)
Scotland

territorial justice
Thatcherism
trusteeship theory of government
United Kingdom
unwritten constitution
Wales
Westminster
Whitehall

INTERNET RESOURCES

Site of British government departments: www.direct.gov.uk.

Site of the House of Commons and of the House of Lords: www.parliament.uk.

Prime Minister's site: www.pm.gov.uk.

Comprehensive coverage of UK and global news: www.bbc.co.uk/news.

Commentaries on current proposals to reform government: www.ucl.ac.uk/constitution-unit.

Reports of public opinion polls: http://ukpollingreport.co.uk/blog.

Official site of the Political Studies Association, the professional body of British political scientists: www.psa.ac.uk.

SUGGESTED READINGS

Allen, Nicholas, and John Bartle, eds. *Britain at the Polls 2010*. London: Sage Publications, 2010.

Bache, Ian, and Andrew Jordan, eds. *The Europeanization of British Politics*. Basingstoke, England: Palgrave Macmillan, 2006.

Butler, D. E., and Geraint Butler. *British Political Facts since 1979*. Basingstoke, England: Palgrave Macmillan, 2006.

Campbell, Rosie. *Gender and Voting Behaviour in Britain*. Colchester, England: ECPR Press, 2006.

Clarke, Harold D., David Sanders, Marianne C. Stewart, and Paul F. Whiteley. *Performance Politics and the British Voter*. New York: Cambridge University Press, 2009.

Flinders, Matthew. *Delegated Governance and the British State: Walking without Order*. Oxford: Oxford University Press, 2008.

Geddes and Tonge, Jonathan, eds., Britain Votes 2010. Oxford: Oxford University Press, 2010.

Constitutional Futures Revisited: Britain's Constitution to 2020. Basingstoke: Palgrave Macmillan.

Ingle, Stephen. *The British Party System*, 4th ed. London: Routledge, 2008.

Jordan, Grant, and William A. Maloney. *Democracy and Interest Groups.* Basingstoke, England: Palgrave Macmillan, 2007.

Jowell, Jeffrey, and Dawn Oliver, eds. *The Changing Constitution*, 6th ed. Oxford: Oxford University Press, 2007.

McGarvey, Neil, and Paul Cairney. *Scottish Politics: An Introduction.* Basingstoke, England: Palgrave Macmillan, 2008.

Page, Edward C., and Bill Jenkins. *Policy Bureaucracy: Government with a Cast of Thousands.* Oxford: Oxford University Press, 2005.

Park, Alison, ed. *British Social Attitudes Survey: The 27th Report.* Thousand Oaks, CA: Sage, 2010.

Pattie, Charles, Patrick Seyd, and Paul Whiteley. *Citizenship in Britain.* New York: Cambridge University Press, 2004.

Rallings, Colin, and Michael Thrasher. *British Electoral Facts, 1832–2006.* Aldershot, England: Ashgate, 2007.

Rose, Richard. *The Prime Minister in a Shrinking World.* Boston: Polity Press, 2001.

Rose, Richard, and Phillip L. Davies. *Inheritance in Public Policy: Change without Choice in Britain.* New Haven, CT: Yale University Press, 1994.

Seldon, Anthony, Peter Seldon, and Daniel Collings. *Blair Unbound.* New York: Simon and Schuster, 2007.

Social Trends. London: Stationery Office, annual.

Whitaker's Almanack. London: J. Whitaker, annual.

Wilson, David, and Chris Game. *Local Government in the United Kingdom*, 5th ed. Basingstoke, England: Palgrave Macmillan, 2011.

ENDNOTES

1. See Richard Rose, "England: A Traditionally Modern Political Culture," in *Political Culture and Political Development*, ed. Lucian W. Pye and Sidney Verba (Princeton, NJ: Princeton University Press, 1965), 83–129.

2. House of Commons Foreign Affairs Committee, Global Security: UK–US Relations, Chatham House, *British Attitudes towards the UK's International Priorities* (London: Royal Institute of International Affairs, 2010), 77.

3. The opinion of Sir Nigel Hamilton, former head of the Northern Ireland Civil Service, quoted in *Public Service Magazine,* February–March 2009, 27.

4. John Kampfner and David Wighton, "Reeling in Scotland to Bring England in Step," *Financial Times*, April 5, 1997.

5. Cf. Andrew Dilnot and Paul Johnson, eds., *Election Briefing 1997* (London: Institute for Fiscal Studies, Commentary 60, 1997), 2.

6. Quoted in Krishna Guha, "Labour Escapes from Its Bloody Tower," *Financial Times,* August 24, 2002.

7. James Purnell, "Labour's Brush with Death Has Left Us in Shock," *The Times* (London), May 17, 2010.

8. Quoted in Peter Hennessy, "Raw Politics Decide Procedure in Whitehall," *New Statesman* (London), October 24, 1986, 10.

9. See Richard Rose, *The Prime Minister in a Shrinking World* (Boston: Polity Press, 2001), Figure 6.1.

10. For transatlantic comparisons of presidents and prime ministers, see Richard Rose, "Giving Direction to Government in Comparative Perspective," in *The Executive Branch*, ed. Joel Aberbach and Mark A. Peterson (New York: Oxford University Press, 2005), 72–99.

11. Walter Bagehot, *The English Constitution* (London: World's Classics, 1955), 9.

12. Quoted in David Leppard, "ID Cards Doomed, Say Officials," *Sunday Times* (London), July 9, 2006. See also an interview with Sir Robin Butler, "How Not to Run a Country," *The Spectator* (London), December 11, 2004.

13. Quoted in "Whitehall Remains Closed to Outsiders and Needs Radical Change, Report Says," *The Times* (London).

14. Eric Varley, quoted in A. Michie and S. Hoggart, *The Pact* (London: Quartet Books, 1978), 13.

15. Cf. Colin Bennett, "From the Dark to the Light: The Open Government Debate in Britain," *Journal of Public Policy* 5, no. 2 (1985): 209; italics in the original.

16. The words of former Conservative prime minister John Major, "The Threat to Liberty Is Graver than Terrorism," *The Times* (London), June 6, 2008.

17. Hugh Heclo and Aaron Wildavsky, *The Private Government of Public Money* (London: Macmillan, 1974).

18. Bernard Ingham, press secretary to Margaret Thatcher, quoted in R. Rose, "British Government: The Job at the Top," in *Presidents and Prime Ministers*, ed. R. Rose and E. Suleiman (Washington, D.C.: American Enterprise Institute, 1980), 43.

19. See Samuel H. Beer, *Modern British Politics*, 3rd ed. (London: Faber and Faber, 1982).

20. House of Commons, *Hansard* (London: Her Majesty's Stationery Office, November 11, 1947), col. 206.

21. See Richard Rose and Ian McAllister, *The Loyalties of Voters* (Newbury Park, CA: Sage, 1990), Chapter 3.

22. Quoted in Maurice Kogan, *The Politics of Education* (Harmondsworth, England: Penguin, 1971), 135.

23. See the report of the Fulton Committee, The Civil Service (London: Her Majesty's Stationery Office, 1968, Cmnd. 3638), vol. 1, 27ff, and Appendix E, especially 162.

24. Rob Baggott, "The Measurement of Change in Pressure Group Politics," *Talking Politics* 5, no. 1 (p. 19, 1992).

25. Sir Ken Jackson, quoted by Krishna Guha, "Engineers and Electricians Turn Away from Moderate Traditions," *Financial Times,* July 19, 2002.

26. See W. A. Maloney, G. Jordan, and A. M. McLaughlin, "Interest Groups and Public Policy: The Insider/Outsider Model Revisited," *Journal of Public Policy* 14, no. 1 (1994): 17–38.

27. See Ministry of Justice, *The Governance of Britain: Review of Voting Systems* (London: Stationery Office, Cm. 7304, 2008).

28. For details, see Ministry of Justice, *The Governance of Britain.*

29. See the Symposium on Electing and Ejecting British Party Leaders, *Representation* 46, no. 1 (2010): 69–117.

30. The Labour Party used the first title, the Conservative Party the second, and the Liberal Democrats the third.

31. For details, see Denis Van Mechelen and Richard Rose, *Patterns of Parliamentary Legislation* (Aldershot, England: Gower, 1986), Table 5.2, and more generally, Richard Rose, *Do Parties Make a Difference?* (Chatham, NJ: Chatham House, 1984).

32. Richard Rose and Phillip L. Davies, *Inheritance in Public Policy: Change without Choice in Britain* (New Haven, CT: Yale University Press, 1994), 28.

33. Reginald Maudling, quoted in David Butler and Michael Pinto-Duschinsky, *The British General Election of 1970* (London: Macmillan, 1971), 62.

34. J. A. G. Griffith, *Central Departments and Local Authorities* (London: George Allen and Unwin, 1966), 542. Cf. Simon Jenkins, *Accountable to None: The Tory Nationalization of Britain* (Harmondsworth, England: Penguin, 1996).

35. See *Better Government Services: Executive Agencies in the 21st Century* (London: Office of Public Service Reforms and the Treasury, 2002).

36. Sir Leo Pliatzky, quoted in Peter Hennessy, "The Guilt of the Treasury 1000," *New Statesman*, January 23, 1987.

37. See Paul Peterson, "The American Mayor: Elections and Institutions," *Parliamentary Affairs* 53, no. 4 (2000): 667–79.

38. David Butler, Andrew Adonis, and Tony Travers, *Failure in British Government: The Politics of the Poll Tax* (Oxford: Oxford University Press, 1994).

39. Lord Hailsham, quoted in Kogan, *The Politics of Education*, 31.

40. See Richard Rose, "The Dynamics of the Welfare Mix in Britain," in *The Welfare State East and West*, ed. Richard Rose and Rei Shiratori (New York: Oxford University Press, 1986), 80–106.

41. See Richard Rose and Kenneth Newton, *Evaluating the Quality of Society and Public Services* (Dublin: European Foundation for the Improvement of Living and Working Conditions, 2010) and Robert Anderson, Branislav Mikuliç, Greet Vermeylen, Maija Lyly-Yrjanainen, and Valentina Zigante, *Second European Quality of Life Survey: Overview* (Dublin: European Foundation for the Improvement of Living and Working Conditions, 2009).

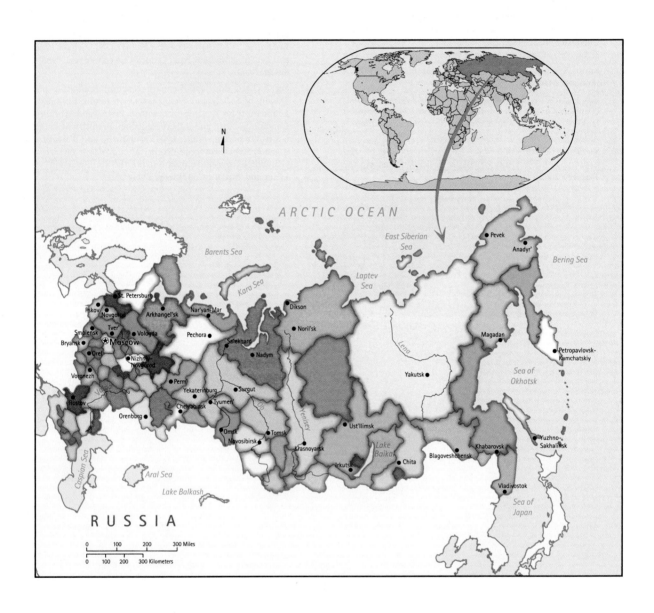

POLITICS IN RUSSIA

Thomas F. Remington

Country Bio

Population
142.2 million

Territory
6,593,000 square miles

Year of Independence
1991

Year of Current Constitution
1993

Head of State
President Dmitrii Anatol'evich Medvedev

Head of Government
Premier Vladimir Vladimirovich Putin

Languages
Russian, other languages of ethnic nationalities

Religion
Russian Orthodox 70–80%, other Christian 1–2%, Muslim 14–15%, Buddhist 0.6%, Jewish 0.3%, other or nonreligious 5–15%

RUSSIA

ENSURING CONTINUITY OF POWER

On May 7, 2008, **Dmitrii Anatol'evich Medvedev** took the oath of office as president of the Russian Federation. The solemn ceremony—attended by his predecessor, Vladimir Putin, and the Russian Orthodox Patriarch of Russia, Alexii II—signaled that the leadership was united around the choice of the new president. In Ukraine, Georgia, Armenia, and other states in the former Soviet Union, the succession from one president to another has sometimes triggered a struggle for power among contending political forces, leading to popular uprisings with unpredictable outcomes.[1] The Russian authorities were determined not to allow a similar disruption in the transfer of power from one president to the next.

The succession was smooth, but hardly democratic. Although a presidential election had been held on March 2, every detail was closely controlled so that no serious challenge to Medvedev could arise. Once Putin had chosen Medvedev to succeed him, the Kremlin took no chances on the outcome. The state-controlled mass media, regional governors, big business, and the election commission all fell in line. The manipulated election process demonstrated to the world and to any would-be opponents that Medvedev was backed by a united front of all the authorities.

Adding to the display of continuity was the fact that Vladimir Putin himself stayed on in power as prime minister. Medvedev's first act as newly inaugurated president was to name Putin as head of government. This neat arrangement—Putin made Medvedev his successor, Medvedev kept Putin in power—solved several problems. Putin's exceptional popularity among the public and the authorities' fear of a destabilizing split among the ruling elite made it desirable to find a postpresidency role for Putin that would ensure continuity in policy and instant acceptance of the new president by the political elite. At the same time, the authorities deemed it important to observe the niceties of constitutional law, which require that a president serve no more than two consecutive terms. Putin's move therefore allowed the leadership to comply with the constitution while retaining a final say over policy.

The new "tandem" leadership arrangement created some uncertainty in elite circles about who was really in charge (see Box 9.1). With time, Medvedev has expanded the sphere of his influence by announcing major new policy initiatives and replacing senior government officials, but he has not altered any of the basic policies or institutional arrangements established when Putin was president. Most Russians believe that Medvedev is basically continuing Putin's policies.[2] However, as the next presidential election—scheduled for 2012—draws closer, it is possible that competition between Medvedev and Putin will grow, particularly if Medvedev chooses to run again for president.

The peculiarity of the situation arises from the gap between the formal constitutional rules and the informal understandings that guide the exercise of power. Russia's constitution provides both for a directly elected president, who is head of state, and a prime minister, who heads the government. The prime minister is chosen by the president but must enjoy the confidence of parliament. But Russia has never had successful experience with the sharing of power between two leaders. As former Russian president Boris Yeltsin once put it, "In Russia, only one person can be number one." For most of the period since Russia's present-day constitution has been in force, the president has been the clearly dominant political figure, while the prime minister has mainly been responsible for managing the economy and carrying out the president's commands. However, Putin accumulated a great deal of power during his tenure as president, using such classic power-consolidation tactics as rewarding supporters with lucrative posts in ministries and state corporations. He maintained impressively high public support, in large part thanks to the economy's robust performance

---

BOX 9.1

The Putin–Medvedev Tandem

The tandem leadership of Vladimir Putin as prime minister and Dmitrii Medvedev as president invites constant speculation about their relationship. Is Putin still running Russia, with Medvedev a mere decorative appendage? A power struggle between them could have destabilizing consequences for the country as the political elites divide into opposing factions.

Putin is Medvedev's senior by thirteen years. Their association began in 1990, when Putin started work in the mayor's office in St. Petersburg and made Medvedev his legal advisor. In 1996, Putin moved to Moscow to take a job in Yeltsin's presidential administration. Here his career took off. In July 1998, Yeltsin named Putin head of the FSB, and in March 1999, secretary of the Security Council as well. In August 1999, President Yeltsin appointed him prime minister. Thanks in part to his decisive handling of the federal military operation in Chechnia, Putin's popularity ratings rose quickly. On December 31, 1999, Yeltsin resigned, automatically making Putin acting president. Putin went on to run for the presidency and, on March 26, 2000, he won with an outright majority of the votes in the first round. He was reelected president in March 2004 by a wide margin.

In 1999, Putin brought Medvedev to Moscow. Medvedev ran Putin's successful presidential election campaign, and after Putin was inaugurated as president, Putin made Medvedev deputy chief of staff in the presidential administration. In 2003, Putin appointed him head of the presidential administration. In 2005, probably with a view to grooming him as a possible successor, Putin named Medvedev first deputy prime minister. In late 2007, Putin declared that Medvedev was his choice for president but that he intended to stay on in some position of responsibility. Immediately upon being inaugurated as president, Medvedev named Putin his prime minister.

Putin and Medvedev project different public personas. Putin cultivates an image of a tough, decisive, down-to-earth leader. Although uncomfortable with the give-and-take of public politics, he is skillful at explaining complex issues in clear and plain language. Medvedev, in contrast, projects a cultivated, scholarly demeanor. His public statements are much more unequivocal than Putin about the need for democratic and market-oriented reform.

So far, the two have maintained a remarkably harmonious relationship as president and prime minister based on their twenty years of association. As President Medvedev noted in an interview with a French newspaper, he and Putin have an effective "working alliance."

until 2008. He retained his power and popularity when he moved to head the government and continued to dominate the decision-making process in most spheres of policy, regardless of the formal lines of authority. Still, as president, Dmitrii Medvedev has considerable institutional prerogatives and has sought to use them to consolidate his own base of power. As a result, under the "tandem" arrangement of Medvedev and Putin, it is often unclear which of them has the predominant power to set policy in any given issue area. So far, the arrangement has worked harmoniously, but the breakout of an open rivalry between the two would split the political elite and destabilize the regime.

CURRENT POLICY CHALLENGES

Within months of Medvedev's inauguration, Russia's economy succumbed to the severe worldwide financial crash that began in summer 2008. Up to that point, Russia had enjoyed a decade of steady economic growth. As a major world exporter of oil and gas and other natural resources, Russia benefited from the sharp rise in world energy and commodity prices in the 2000s: real incomes tripled from 2000 to 2008. The decade of recovery followed a harsh decade of economic contraction and social dislocation resulting from the painful transition from the socialist economic system to a market-oriented capitalist system. Russia benefited from opening its economy up to the world as capital investment entered the country and raw-materials exports created immense incomes. But globalization had a steep downside when the worldwide financial crash struck in 2008. Capital fled the country (the stock market lost two-thirds of its value in less than one year), and its highly indebted firms struggled to meet their obligations. As world oil and gas prices tumbled to one-third of their peak level, Russian budget revenues plummeted and the federal budget fell into a deep deficit. Consumer demand dropped, hurting Russia's manufacturers. Russia's economy contracted more than that of any other major power; its GDP fell almost 8 percent in 2009 alone and began to recover slowly only in 2010. Financial reserves that the government had set aside during the boom years of the 2000s spared the country many of the worst effects of the recession. The government was able to pump hundreds of billions of rubles into failing banks, industrial enterprises, unemployment benefits, and pensions. As a result, many Russians were shielded from poverty,

and the country was spared the massive financial instability that broke out in other heavily indebted states that lacked Russia's deep reserves.

President Medvedev has attempted to spell out the implications of the crisis for Russia. He has repeatedly pointed out that Russia must overcome its reliance on exports of natural resources to maintain its growth, and instead must modernize and diversify its economy. But neither Medvedev nor other Russian leaders have effective policy instruments for bringing about such a huge change in the country's basic economic structure. This reflects a recurring dilemma in Russian history: Major reform requires an enormous and sustained exercise of power by the country's political leaders to overcome the resistance of administrative and social groups to change. To accomplish their ends, modernizing rulers have traditionally centralized power, thereby weakening the incentives for initiative outside the state that could drive sustained growth and initiative in society.

Both Putin and Medvedev have spoken frankly about the dangers of the "resource curse" for Russia. That is the idea that in countries relying on windfall revenues from natural resources, the leaders avoid investing in the skills and knowledge of the population, as a result of which the societies wind up with lower levels of economic and political development than in resource-poor countries. In September 2009, President Medvedev denounced Russia's current economic structure as "primitive" for its dependence on natural-resource production, its "chronic corruption, the outdated habit of relying on the state to solve our problems, on foreign countries, on some sort of 'all-powerful doctrine,' on anything and everything except on ourselves." He noted that "the energy efficiency and labor productivity of most of our enterprises are shamefully low" and added that the real tragedy was that most owners, managers, and state officials do not appear to be particularly worried about the situation.[3]

Medvedev and Putin have also frankly acknowledged the grim demographic facts: Russia's population has been shrinking as a result of the excess of deaths over births, and the economy is increasingly dependent on migrant labor from China, Central Asia, and elsewhere. Inequality across regions and social groups is rising. A recent National Human Development Report written by a team of Russian experts noted that some regions of Russia live at a level of human development comparable to that of Central Europe, while others are closer to an African level.[4]

But while Russian leaders have admitted the gravity of the problems the country faces, they have been unable to break through the obstacles standing in the way of solving them. Three in particular have proven to be stumbling blocks: the resistance by state officials to any reforms that weaken their power; the vast physical size of the country, which impedes efforts to forge coalitions in society around broad common interests in support of significant reform; and the legacy of the Soviet development model, which concentrated resources in giant state-owned enterprises—often located in remote, harsh regions—that are nearly impossible to convert into competitive capitalist firms viable in a global marketplace. Taken together, these factors stack the deck against modernizing and democratizing reforms.

HISTORICAL LEGACIES

The Tsarist Regime

The Russian state traces its origins to the princely state that arose around Kiev (today the capital of independent Ukraine) in the ninth century. For nearly a thousand years, the Russian state was autocratic, ruled by a hereditary monarch whose power was unlimited by any constitutional constraints. Only in the first decade of the twentieth century did the Russian tsar agree to grant a constitution calling for an elected legislature—and even then, the tsar soon dissolved the legislature and arbitrarily revised the constitution.

In addition to autocracy, the historical legacy of Russian statehood includes lasting strains of absolutism, patrimonialism, and Orthodox Christianity. *Absolutism* means that the tsar aspired to wield absolute power over the subjects of the realm. *Patrimonialism* refers to the idea that the ruler treated his realm as property that he owned, rather than as a society with its own legitimate rights and interests.[5] This concept of power continues to influence state rulers today. Finally, the tsarist state identified itself with the *Russian Orthodox Church*. In Russia, the Orthodox Church ties itself closely to the state, considering itself a national church. Traditionally, it has exhorted its adherents to show loyalty and obedience to the state in worldly matters, in return for which it enjoyed a monopoly of spiritual power as Russia's state church. This legacy is still manifest in the present-day rulers'

efforts to associate themselves with the heritage of the church and in many Russians' impulse to identify their state with a higher spiritual mission.

Absolutism, patrimonialism, and orthodoxy have been recurring elements of Russian political culture. But alternative motifs have been influential as well. At some points in Russian history, the country's rulers have sought to modernize its economy and society. Russia imported Western practices in technology, law, state organization, and education in order to make the state competitive with other great powers. Modernizing rulers had a powerful impact on Russian society, bringing it closer to West European models. The imperative of building Russia's military and economic potential was all the more pressing because of Russia's constant expansion through conquest and annexation of neighboring territories and its ever-present need to defend its borders. The state's role in controlling and mobilizing society rose with the need to govern a vast territory. By the end of the seventeenth century, Russia was territorially the largest state in the world. But for most of its history, Russia's imperial reach exceeded its actual grasp.

Compared with other major powers of Europe, Russia's economic institutions remained backward well into the twentieth century. However, the trajectory of its development, especially in the nineteenth century, was toward that of a modern industrial society. By the time the tsarist order fell in 1917, Russia had a large industrial sector, although it was concentrated in a few cities. The middle class was greatly outnumbered by the vast and impoverished peasantry and the radicalized industrial working class. As a result, the social basis for a peaceful democratic transition was too weak to prevent the Communists from seizing power in 1917.

The thousand-year tsarist era left a contradictory legacy. The tsars attempted to legitimate their absolute power by appealing to tradition, empire, and divine right. They treated law as an instrument of rule, rather than a source of authority. The doctrines that rulers should be accountable to the ruled and that sovereignty resides in the will of the people were alien to Russian state tradition. Throughout Russian history, state and society have been more distant from each other than in Western societies. Rulers and populace regarded one another with mistrust. This gap has been overcome at times of great national trials, such as World War II. Russia celebrated victory in that war as a triumphant demonstration of the unity of state and people. But Russia's political traditions also include a yearning for equality, solidarity, and community, as well as for moral purity and sympathy for the downtrodden. And throughout the Russian heritage runs a deep strain of pride in the greatness of the country and the endurance of its people.

The Communist Revolution and the Soviet Order

The tsarist regime proved unable to meet the overwhelming demands of national mobilization in World War I. Tsar Nicholas II abdicated in February 1917 (March 1917, by the Western calendar). He was replaced by a short-lived provisional government, which, in turn, fell when the Russian Communists—Bolsheviks, as they called themselves—took power in October 1917 (November, by the Western calendar). Their aim was to create a socialist society in Russia and, eventually, to spread revolutionary socialism throughout the world. Socialism, the Russian Communist Party believed, meant a society without private ownership of the means of production, one where the state owned and controlled all important economic assets and where political power was exercised in the name of the working people. **Vladimir Ilyich Lenin** was the leader of the Russian Communist Party and the first head of the Soviet Russian government. (Figure 9.1 lists the Soviet and post-Soviet leaders since 1917.)

Under Lenin's system of rule, the Communist Party controlled all levels of government. At each level of the territorial hierarchy of the country, full-time Communist Party officials supervised government. At the top, final power to decide policy rested in the Communist Party of the Soviet Union (CPSU) Politburo. Under **Joseph Stalin**, who took power after Lenin's death in 1924, power was even further centralized. Stalin instituted a totalitarian regime intent on building up Russia's industrial and military might. The state survived the terrible test of World War II, but the combined cost of war and terror under Stalin was staggering: The war is estimated to have cost the country some 26 million lives, and terror, as the secret police sent many millions of people to labor camps on suspicion of opposing the regime, millions more.

The institutions of rule that Stalin left behind when he died in 1953 eventually crippled the Soviet

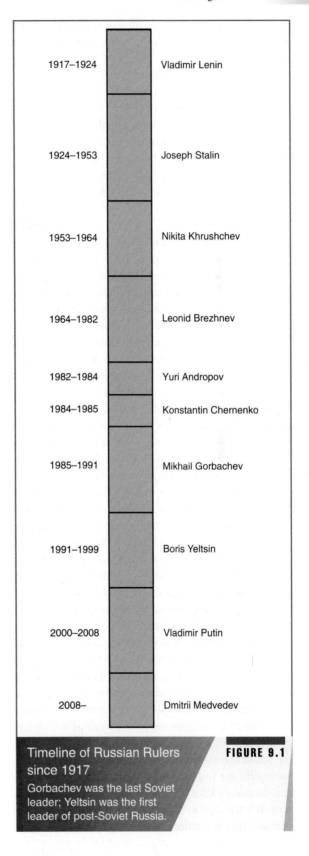

1917–1924	Vladimir Lenin
1924–1953	Joseph Stalin
1953–1964	Nikita Khrushchev
1964–1982	Leonid Brezhnev
1982–1984	Yuri Andropov
1984–1985	Konstantin Chernenko
1985–1991	Mikhail Gorbachev
1991–1999	Boris Yeltsin
2000–2008	Vladimir Putin
2008–	Dmitrii Medvedev

Timeline of Russian Rulers since 1917   **FIGURE 9.1**

Gorbachev was the last Soviet leader; Yeltsin was the first leader of post-Soviet Russia.

state. They included personalistic rule, insecurity for rulers and ruled alike, heavy reliance on the secret police, and a militarized economy. None of Stalin's successors could reform the system without undermining Communist rule itself. Stalin's immediate successor, Nikita Khrushchev, loosened some of the harsh controls and reduced the level of political repression, but was unable to accomplish fundamental reform. His successor, Leonid Brezhnev, abandoned the impulse for reform and instead concentrated on consolidating power. As a result, the political system and economy stagnated, and the fundamental weaknesses of the system mounted.

The problem of the late Soviet system was that, as vast as the state's powers were, their use was frustrated by bureaucratic immobilism. Overcentralization undermined the leaders' actual power to enact significant policy change—or even to recognize when serious policy change was needed. The center's ability to coordinate bureaucratic agencies in order to execute its initiatives was frequently undermined by tacit resistance to the center's orders by officials at lower levels. Bureaucratic officials were generally more devoted to protecting and advancing their own personal and career interests than to serving the public interest. The political system of the Soviet Union grew top-heavy, unresponsive, and corrupt. The regime had more than enough power to crush any political opposition. However, it was unable to modernize the economy or improve living standards for the population. By the early 1980s, the economy had stopped growing, and the country was unable to compete militarily or economically with the West.

After the deaths of three elderly leaders—Brezhnev, Andropov, and Chernenko—in quick succession in 1982, 1984, and 1985, the ruling party Politburo turned to a vigorous reformer named **Mikhail Gorbachev** to lead the country. Gorbachev quickly grasped the levers of power that the system granted the general secretary. He moved both to strengthen his own political base and to carry out a program of reform.[6] Emphasizing the need for greater openness—**glasnost'**—in society, Gorbachev stressed that the ultimate test of the party's effectiveness lay in improving the economic well-being of the country and its people. Gorbachev not only called for political democratization, he also legalized private enterprise for individual and cooperative businesses and encouraged them to fill the many gaps in the economy left by the inefficiency of the state sector. He declared that the entire economic system needed to be

overhauled, a program he called **perestroika**, or restructuring. *Perestroika* referred to introducing elements of market competition and management flexibility while preserving state ownership in most sectors of the economy. Gorbachev made major concessions to the United States in the sphere of arms control, which resulted in a treaty that, for the first time in history, called for the destruction of entire classes of nuclear missiles.

Frustrated by the lack of success of his economic reforms, Gorbachev turned to democratization in order to mobilize popular pressure for reform. In 1989 and 1990, Gorbachev's plan for competitive elections and a working parliament was realized as elections were held and new deputies were elected at the center and in every region and locality. He welcomed the explosion of new, unlicensed associations that sprang up, and when nearly half a million coal miners went on strike in the summer of 1989, Gorbachev declared himself sympathetic to their demands.

Gorbachev's radicalism received its most dramatic confirmation through the astonishing developments of 1989 in Eastern Europe. All the regimes making up the Communist Bloc collapsed and gave way to multiparty parliamentary regimes in virtually bloodless popular revolutions. The Soviet Union stood by and supported the revolutions. The overnight dismantling of communism in Eastern Europe meant that the elaborate structure of party ties, police cooperation, economic trade, and military alliance that had developed with Eastern Europe after World War II vanished. Divided Germany was allowed to reunite.

In the Soviet Union itself, the Communist Party faced a critical loss of authority. The newly elected governments of the national republics making up the Soviet state one by one declared that they were sovereign. The three Baltic republics declared their intention to secede from the union. Between 1989 and 1990, throughout the Soviet Union and Eastern Europe, Communist Party rule crumbled.

Political Institutions of the Transition Period: Demise of the Soviet Union

Gorbachev's reforms had consequences he did not intend. The 1990 elections of deputies to the supreme soviets in all fifteen republics and to local soviets stimulated popular nationalist and democratic movements in most republics. In the core republic of Russia itself, Gorbachev's rival, Boris Yeltsin, was elected chairman of the Russian Supreme Soviet in June 1990. As chief of state in the Russian Republic, Yeltsin was well-positioned to challenge Gorbachev for preeminence.

Yeltsin's rise forced Gorbachev to alter his strategy. Beginning in March 1991, Gorbachev sought terms for a new federal or confederal union that would be acceptable to Yeltsin and the Russian leadership, as well as to the leaders of the other republics. In April 1991, he reached an agreement on the outlines of a new treaty of union with nine of the fifteen republics, including Russia. A weak central government would manage basic coordinating functions. But the republics would gain the power to control the economies of their territories.

Gorbachev had underestimated the strength of his opposition. On August 19, 1991, a conspiracy of senior officials placed Gorbachev under house arrest and seized power. In response, thousands of citizens in Moscow and St. Petersburg rallied to protest the coup attempt. Yeltsin, who avoided being arrested by the coup leaders, led the protests in Moscow. The coup collapsed on the third day, but Gorbachev's power had been fatally weakened.

Neither the union nor the Russian power structures heeded his commands. Through the fall of 1991, the Russian government took over the union government, ministry by ministry. In December, Yeltsin and the leaders of Ukraine and Belarus formally declared the Union of Soviet Socialist Republics dissolved. On December 25, 1991, Gorbachev resigned as president and turned the powers of his office over to Boris Yeltsin. On New Year's Day, 1992, the Soviet flag was hauled down over the Kremlin, and the white, blue, and red flag of independent Russia was raised in its place.

Political Institutions of the Transition Period: Russia 1990–1993

Boris Yeltsin was elected president of the Russian Federation in June 1991. Unlike Gorbachev, Yeltsin was elected in a direct, competitive election, which gave him a considerable advantage in mobilizing public support against Gorbachev and the central Soviet Union government (see Box 9.2).

BOX 9.2

Boris Yeltsin: Russia's First President

Boris Yeltsin, born in 1931, graduated from the Urals Polytechnical Institute in 1955 with a diploma in civil engineering and worked for a long time in construction. From 1976 to 1985, he served as first secretary of the Sverdlovsk *oblast* (provincial) Communist Party organization.

Early in 1986, Yeltsin became first secretary of the Moscow city party organization, but he was removed in November 1987 for speaking out against Mikhail Gorbachev. Positioning himself as a victim of the party establishment, Yeltsin made a remarkable political comeback. In the 1989 elections to the Congress of People's Deputies, he won a Moscow at-large seat with almost 90 percent of the vote. The following year, he was elected to the Russian republic's parliament with over 80 percent of the vote. He was then elected its chairman in June 1990. In 1991, he was elected president of Russia. Thus, he had won three major races in three successive years. He was reelected president in 1996 in a dramatic, come-from-behind race against the leader of the Communist Party.

Yeltsin's last years in office were notable for his lengthy spells of illness and for the carousel of prime ministerial appointments. The entourage of family members and advisors around him seemed to exercise undue influence over him. Yet, infirm as he was, he judged that Russia's interests and his own would be safe in Vladimir Putin's hands. Yeltsin's resignation speech was full of contrition for his failure to bring a better life to Russians. After retiring, Yeltsin stayed out of the public eye. He died of heart failure on April 23, 2007, and was buried in Moscow with full honors.

Yeltsin's legacy is mixed. He was most effective when engaged in political battle, whether he was fighting for supremacy against Gorbachev or fighting against the Communists. Impulsive and undisciplined, he was gifted with exceptionally keen political intuition. He regarded economic reform as an instrument in his political war with the Communist opposition and used privatization to make it impossible for any future rulers to return to state socialism. Imperious and willful, he also regarded the adoption of the 1993 constitution as a major achievement and willingly accepted the limits on his presidential power that it imposed.

Like Gorbachev before him, Yeltsin demanded extraordinary powers from parliament to cope with the country's economic problems. Following the August 1991 coup attempt, parliament granted him emergency decree powers to cope with the economic crisis. Yeltsin formed a government led by a group of young, Western-oriented reformers determined to carry out a decisive economic transformation. The new government's economic program took effect on January 2, 1992. Their first results were felt immediately as prices skyrocketed. Quickly, many politicians began to distance themselves from the program; even Yeltsin's vice president denounced the program as "economic genocide." Through 1992, opposition to the reforms grew stronger and more intransigent. Increasingly, the political confrontation between Yeltsin and the reformers on the one side and the opposition to radical economic reform on the other became centered in the two branches of government. President Yeltsin demanded broad powers to carry out the reforms, but parliament refused to go along. In March 1993, an opposition motion to remove the president through impeachment nearly passed in the parliament.

On September 21, 1993, Yeltsin decreed the parliament dissolved and called for elections for a new parliament. Yeltsin's enemies barricaded themselves inside the parliament building. After a ten-day standoff, the dissidents joined with some loosely organized paramilitary units outside the building and attacked the Moscow mayor's offices. They even called on their followers to "seize the Kremlin." Finally, the army agreed to back Yeltsin and suppress the uprising by force, shelling the parliament building in the process.

The violence of October 1993 cast a long shadow over subsequent events. Yeltsin's decree meant that national elections were to be held for a legislature that did not constitutionally exist, since the new constitution establishing these institutions was to be voted on in a referendum held in parallel with the parliamentary elections. The Duma election and referendum were held in December 1993, and the constitution was approved. For all the turmoil surrounding its adoption, the formal institutions established under the constitution adopted in December 1993 have remained in place ever since.[7]

THE CONTEMPORARY CONSTITUTIONAL ORDER

The Presidency

Yeltsin's constitution combined elements of presidentialism and parliamentarism. (See Figure 9.2 for a schematic overview of the Russian constitutional structure.) Although it provided for the separation of the executive, legislative, and judicial branches, and for a federal division of power between the central and regional levels of government, it made the president by far the strongest institution in the state. The president is directly elected for a six-year term and may not serve more than two consecutive terms. The president names the prime minister to head the government. The government must have the confidence of parliament to remain in power. Although the constitution does not call the president the head of the executive branch, he is so in fact by virtue of his power to appoint the prime minister and the rest of the government and his right to issue **presidential decrees** with the force of law. (The decree power is somewhat limited in that decrees may not violate existing law and can be superseded by legislation.)

Over the years since the constitution was approved, some informal practices have come to govern the exercise of central power. For example, the president and government divide executive responsibility. The government, headed by the prime minister, is primarily responsible for economic and social policy. The president directly oversees the ministries and other bodies directly concerned with coercion, law enforcement, and state security—the "power ministries." These include the Foreign Ministry, Defense Ministry, Ministry of Internal Affairs (which controls the regular police and security troops), Federal Security Service (FSB—formerly the KGB), and several other security and intelligence agencies. The president and his staff set overall policy in the foreign and domestic domains, and the government develops the specific proposals and rules carrying out this policy. In practice, the government answers to the president, not parliament. The government's base of support is the president, rather than a particular coalition of parties in parliament. This arrangement has continued under the duo of President Medvedev and Prime Minister Putin.

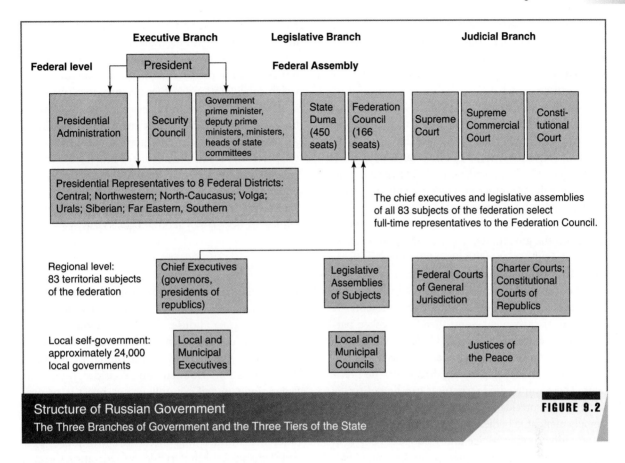

Structure of Russian Government
The Three Branches of Government and the Three Tiers of the State

FIGURE 9.2

Despite the pronounced presidential tilt to the system, the parliament does have some potential for independent action. Its ability to exercise its rights, however, depends on the composition of political forces represented in parliament and the cohesiveness of the majority. Parliament's approval is required for any bill to become law. The State Duma (the lower house of parliament) must confirm the president's nominee for prime minister. If, after three successive votes, the Duma refuses to confirm the nomination, the president must dissolve the Duma and call new elections. Likewise, the Duma may vote to deny confidence in the government. If a motion of no confidence carries twice, the president must either dissolve parliament or dismiss the government. During Yeltsin's tenure as president, the Duma was able to block some of Yeltsin's legislative initiatives. Since 2003, however, it has largely been a rubber stamp. The constitution allows for a variety of types of relationships among the president, government, and parliament, depending on the degree to which the president dominates the political system.

In addition to these powers, the president has a number of other formal and informal powers in his constitutional capacity as "head of state," "guarantor of the constitution," and commander-in-chief of the armed forces. He oversees a large presidential administration, which supervises the federal government and keeps tabs on regional governments. Informally, the administration also manages relations with the parliament, the courts, big business, the media, political parties, and major interest groups.

The president also oversees many official and quasi-official supervisory and advisory commissions, which he creates and directs using his decree power. One is the **Security Council**, chaired by the president. Besides the president, the Security Council consists of a permanent secretary, the heads of the power ministries and other security-related agencies, the prime minister, and the chairs of the two chambers of parliament. Its powers are broad but shadowy. Putin used it to formulate policy proposals not only in matters of foreign and defense policy, but also on selected issues having to do with the organization of the executive branch.

Another prominent advisory body is the **State Council**, which comprises the heads of the regional governments and thus parallels the Federation Council. Still another is the **Public Chamber**, which is made up of 126 members from selected civic, professional, artistic, and other nongovernmental organizations (NGOs). Its purpose is to deliberate on matters of public policy, make recommendations to parliament and the government on pending policy issues, and link civil society with the state. Like the State Council, it is a quasi-parliamentary deliberative body that the president can consult at will. All three bodies duplicate some of the deliberative and representative functions of parliament—and therefore weaken parliament's role. They illustrate the tendency, under both Yeltsin and Putin, for the president to create and dissolve new structures answering directly to the president. These improvised structures can be politically useful for the president as counterweights to constitutionally mandated bodies (such as parliament), as well as providing policy advice and feedback. They help ensure that the president is always the dominant institution in the political system, but they undermine the authority of other constitutional structures such as parliament.

The Government

The *government* refers to the senior echelon of leadership in the executive branch and consists of the prime minister, a number of deputy prime ministers, and the heads of ministries and state agencies. It is charged with formulating the main lines of national policy (especially in the economic and social realms) and overseeing their implementation. (The president oversees the formulation and execution of foreign and national-security policy.) In this respect, the government corresponds to the Cabinet in Western parliamentary systems. But in contrast to most parliamentary systems, the makeup of the Russian government is not directly determined by the party composition of the parliament. Indeed, there is scarcely any relationship between the distribution of party forces in the Duma and the political balance of the government.

Nearly all members of the government are career managers and administrators, rather than party politicians. Overall, the government is not a party government, but reflects the president's calculations about how to weigh considerations such as personal loyalty, professional competence, and the relative strength of major bureaucratic factions in selecting Cabinet ministers. Although there is recurrent discussion of the idea that the party that forms the majority in the Duma should have the right to name the head of the government, no president has been willing to agree to institute this arrangement—no doubt out of fear that it would reduce his freedom of action in governing.

The Parliament

The parliament—called the Federal Assembly—is bicameral. The lower house is called the **State Duma** and the upper house the **Federation Council**. Legislation originates in the Duma. As Figure 9.3 shows, upon passage in the State Duma, a bill goes to the Federation Council for consideration. The Federation Council can only pass it, reject it, or propose the formation of an agreement commission (consisting of members of both houses) to iron out differences. If the Duma rejects the upper house's proposed changes, it can override the Federation Council by a two-thirds vote and send the bill directly to the president for his signature.

When the bill has cleared parliament, it goes to the president. If the president refuses to sign the bill, it returns to the Duma. The Duma may pass an amended version by a simple absolute majority, or it may override the president's veto, for which a two-thirds vote is required. The Federation Council must then also approve the bill by a simple majority if the president's amendments are accepted or by a two-thirds vote if it chooses to override the president. On rare occasions—and never since 2000—the Duma has overridden the president's veto; it has overridden the Federation Council more frequently. In other cases, the Duma has passed bills rejected by the president after accepting the president's proposed amendments. Under President Yeltsin, opposition parties, particularly Communists and nationalists, held the majority in the Duma. But usually parliament and the president worked to head off major confrontations.

The Duma's 450 members are elected through proportional representation (PR) in a single national

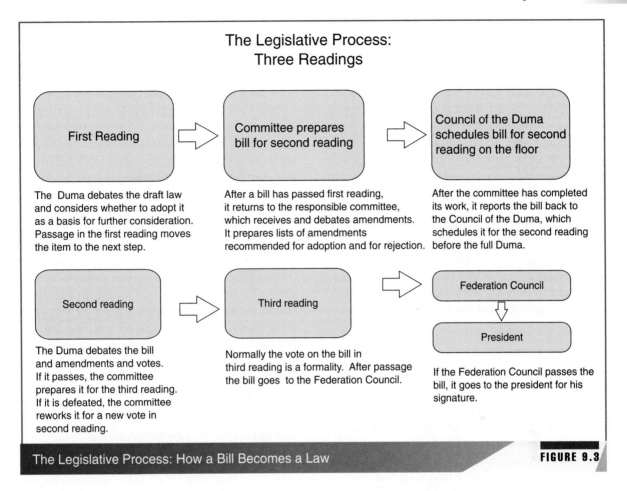

The Legislative Process: Three Readings

First Reading

The Duma debates the draft law and considers whether to adopt it as a basis for further consideration. Passage in the first reading moves the item to the next step.

Committee prepares bill for second reading

After a bill has passed first reading, it returns to the responsible committee, which receives and debates amendments. It prepares lists of amendments recommended for adoption and for rejection.

Council of the Duma schedules bill for second reading on the floor

After the committee has completed its work, it reports the bill back to the Council of the Duma, which schedules it for the second reading before the full Duma.

Second reading

The Duma debates the bill and amendments and votes. If it passes, the committee prepares it for the third reading. If it is defeated, the committee reworks it for a new vote in second reading.

Third reading

Normally the vote on the bill in third reading is a formality. After passage the bill goes to the Federation Council.

Federation Council

President

If the Federation Council passes the bill, it goes to the president for his signature.

The Legislative Process: How a Bill Becomes a Law   **FIGURE 9.3**

electoral district. A party receiving at least 7 percent of the vote on the party-list ballot is entitled to as many of the party-list seats in the Duma as its share of the party-list vote. As in other PR systems, votes cast for parties that fail to clear the barrier are redistributed to winning parties.[8]

The parties clearing the 7 percent threshold form their own factions in the Duma. According to newly amended Duma rules, deputies may not switch faction membership (those who leave or are expelled lose their seats). Faction leaders are represented in the governing body of the Duma, the Council of the Duma. Factions are the main site of political discussion in the Duma and give members a channel for proposing bills to the chamber.

Since the December 2003 elections, the Kremlin has enjoyed the support of a commanding majority in the Duma, where the **United Russia** party holds two-thirds of the seats. United Russia also holds twenty-six of the thirty-two committee chairmanships and eight

of the eleven seats of the Council of the Duma, which is the steering body for the chamber. Since United Russia deputies vote with a high degree of discipline, the Duma consistently delivers the president solid legislative majorities. Other factions have very little opportunity to influence the agenda, let alone the outcomes of legislative deliberations. Therefore, United Russia's control over the agenda and voting has turned the Duma into a rubber stamp for the executive branch.

Each deputy is a member of one of thirty-two standing committees. Bills submitted to the Duma are assigned to committees according to their subject matter. The committees collect and review proposed amendments before reporting out the bills for votes by the full chamber with the committee's recommendations.

The Federation Council is designed as an instrument of federalism in that (as in the U.S. Senate) every constituent unit of the federation is represented by two representatives. Thus, the populations of small territories are greatly overrepresented compared with more populous regions. The Federation Council has important powers. Besides acting on bills passed by the lower house, it approves presidential nominees for high courts, such as the Supreme Court and the Constitutional Court. It must approve presidential decrees declaring martial law or a state of emergency and any acts altering the boundaries of territorial units. It must consider any legislation dealing with taxes, budget, financial policy, treaties, customs, and declarations of war.

The procedure for selecting members to the Federation Council has been changed several times. Currently, they are formally named by the governor and regional legislature of each territorial subject from among elected deputies of a local or regional legislative assembly. In practice, the appointments are made in close consultation with the Kremlin.

Executive–Legislative Relations

Relations between president and parliament during the 1990s were often stormy. The first two Dumas, elected in 1993 and in 1995, were dominated by the Communist and other leftist factions hostile to President Yeltsin and the policies of his government. This was particularly true in areas of economic policy and privatization. On other issues, such as matters concerning federal relations, the Duma and president often reached agreement—sometimes over the opposition of the Federation Council, whose members fought to protect regional prerogatives.

The 1999 election produced a Duma with a pro-government majority. President Putin and his government formed a reliable base of support in the Duma for their legislative initiatives by building a coalition of four centrist political factions. The 2003 election gave the president a still wider margin of support in the Duma and an overwhelming majority for the United Russia party—which means that the president does not need to expend much effort in bargaining with the Duma to win its support for his policies. The Fifth Duma, elected in December 2007, is also dominated by the United Russia party and has continued to give its loyal support to the Medvedev–Putin team.

The level of voting discipline within the majority party is similar to that in a Westminster-style parliament (i.e., a parliament modeled on the British Parliament). So is the practice of reliably supporting the government's initiatives. In reality, the relationship between the Duma and the government is quite different. In a Westminster-type setting, parliament and government have mutually offsetting powers. If a government loses its majority in parliament, it must face the voters in a new election. Majority members of parliament would prefer to hold onto their seats as long as possible and vote for the government's proposals so as to avoid a parliamentary dissolution and new election. By the same token, the government is normally unwilling to face a revolt on the floor of parliament and the possible loss of its majority. Thus, the government and the majority party need each other. In Russia, the parliamentary deputies have almost no political resources outside the party, and the presidential administration and government control the United Russia party—the majority party cannot counterbalance the executive. A deputy who defies party discipline can be expelled and has very few alternatives. In the future, though, a major shift in the alignment of political forces in society could lead to a different relationship between executive and legislative power.

The Judiciary and Law Enforcement

The major institutional actors in the legal system are the procuracy, the courts (judiciary), and the bar. Each has undergone substantial change in the post-Communist period.

The Procuracy Russia's legal system traditionally vested a great deal of power in the **procuracy**, which was considered to be the most prestigious branch of the legal system. The procuracy is comparable to the system of federal and state prosecuting attorneys in the United States, but it has wider-ranging responsibilities and is organized as a centralized hierarchy headed by the procurator-general. The procuracy is charged with fighting crime, corruption, and abuses of power in the bureaucracy. It seeks to ensure that all state officials and public organizations observe the law. It investigates criminal charges and prosecutes cases in court. The procuracy has traditionally been the principal check on abuses of power by state officials. But it is inadequately equipped to meet the sweeping responsibilities assigned to it because of the difficulty of effectively supervising the vast state bureaucracy. Although the procuracy is nominally independent of the executive, the president names the procurator-general (subject to confirmation by the Federation Council) and informally supervises any politically significant cases.

The Judiciary In contrast to the influence that the procuracy has traditionally wielded in Russia, the bench has been relatively weak. Trial judges are usually the least-experienced and lowest-paid members of the legal profession—and the most vulnerable to external political and administrative pressure. In a few instances, judges have been murdered when they attempted to take on organized crime. Many judges have left their positions to take higher-paying jobs in other branches of the legal profession, and caseloads have risen substantially.

State officials pay lip service to the principle of judicial independence, but often violate it in practice by pressuring judges to render particular judgments in politically sensitive matters. At the same time, many reforms since the end of Communism are intended to make the administration of justice more effective, and some increase the rights of defendants in criminal cases. For example, in the 1990s, trial by jury in major criminal cases was introduced in several regions on an experimental basis and since then has spread throughout the country in serious criminal cases. The goal of adopting the jury system was to put the prosecution and the defense on an equal footing in the courtroom and to make the judge a neutral arbiter between them. The goal is to give the defendant a fairer chance in court. In a number of high-profile cases, juries have acquitted defendants when they found the procuracy's case unconvincing.

The Russian judiciary is a unitary hierarchy. All courts of general jurisdiction are federal courts. There are also other specialized types of courts in addition to federal courts of general jurisdiction—among them, the commercial courts, the constitutional courts of ethnic republics, the local municipal courts (equivalent to justices of the peace), and the military courts. Most criminal trials are held in district and city courts of general jurisdiction, which have original jurisdiction in most criminal proceedings. Higher-level courts, including regional and republic-level courts, hear appeals from lower courts and have original jurisdiction in certain cases. At the pinnacle of the hierarchy of courts of general jurisdiction is the Russian Supreme Court, which hears cases referred from lower courts and also issues instructions to lower courts on judicial matters. The Supreme Court does not have the power to challenge the constitutionality of laws and other official actions of legislative and executive bodies. The constitution assigns that power to the Constitutional Court. Under the constitution, the judges of the Supreme Court are nominated by the president and confirmed by the Federation Council.

There is a similar hierarchy of courts hearing cases arising from civil disputes between firms or between firms and the government called **commercial courts (*arbitrazhnye sudy*)**. Like the Supreme Court, the Supreme Commercial Court is both the highest appellate court for its system of courts and the source of instruction and direction to lower commercial courts. As with the Supreme Court, the judges of the Supreme Commercial Court are nominated by the president and confirmed by the Federation Council. In recent years, the Supreme Commercial Court has handed down a number of major decisions that clarify the rules of the economic marketplace.

The Ministry of Justice oversees the court system and provides for its material and administrative needs. Its influence over the legal system is limited, however, because it lacks any direct authority over the procuracy.

The Bar Change of another sort has been occurring among those members of the legal profession who represent individual citizens and organizations in both criminal and civil matters: advocates (*advokaty*). They are comparable to barristers in Great Britain and litigating attorneys in the United States. Their role has expanded considerably with the spread of the market economy. They have long enjoyed some autonomy through their self-governing associations, through which they elect officers and govern admission of new practitioners. In the past, their ability to use their rights was limited, but in recent years, their opportunities have risen markedly. Private law firms are proliferating. The profession is attractive for the opportunities it provides to earn high incomes. A number of lawyers have become celebrities by taking on high-profile cases.

The Constitutional Court

One of the most important reforms in post-Communist Russia's legal system has been the establishment of a court for constitutional review of the official acts of government. The **Constitutional Court** has authority to interpret the constitution in a variety of areas. It has ruled on several ambiguous questions relating to parliamentary procedure. It has overturned some laws passed by national republics within Russia and has struck down several provisions of the Russian Criminal Code that limited individual rights. Generally, in disputes between individuals and state authorities, the court finds in favor of individuals, thus reaffirming the sphere of individual legal rights. It has consistently upheld the sovereignty of the federal constitution over regional governments.

The most important challenge for the court, however, is the huge domain of presidential authority. The court has been reluctant to challenge the president. One of its first and most important decisions concerned a challenge brought by a group of Communist parliamentarians to President Yeltsin's decrees launching the war in Chechnia. The court ruled that the president had the authority to wage the war through the use of his constitutional power to issue decrees with the force of law. In other, less highly charged issues, the court established legal limits to the president's authority. Since Putin took office in 2000, however, the court has taken care to avoid crossing the president. Nevertheless, even the possibility that it might exert a measure of independent political influence led Putin to move the seat of the court to St. Petersburg in 2008. This may have been intended as a means to distance the court from the tight web of governing bodies located in Moscow and thus to marginalize it politically.

Central Government and the Regions

Following the breakup of the Soviet Union, many Russians feared that Russia would also dissolve into a patchwork of independent fiefdoms. Certainly, Russia's territorial integrity was subjected to serious strains. Under President Yeltsin, the central government granted wide autonomy to regional governments in return for political support. Yeltsin went so far as to sign a series of bilateral treaties with individual regions to codify the respective rights and responsibilities of the federal government and the given regional governments. Under Putin, however, the pendulum of federal policy swung back sharply toward centralization.

The demographic factor is one reason that Russia did not break up. Eighty percent of Russia's population

is ethnically Russian. None of its ethnic minorities accounts for more than 4 percent of the total (the Tatars form the largest of the ethnic minorities). Rebuilding national community in post-Soviet Russia has been helped by Russia's thousand-year history of statehood. Yet until 1991, Russia was never constituted as a nation-state: Under the tsars it was a multinational empire, and under Soviet rule it was nominally a federal union of socialist republics. State policy toward nationality has also varied over the centuries. In some periods, Russia recognized a variety of self-governing ethnic-national communities and tolerated cultural differences among them. In other periods, the state pressured non-Russian groups to assimilate to Russian culture.

Russia was formally established as a federal republic under the Soviet regime. In contrast to the Soviet Union, of which it was the largest component, only some of Russia's constituent members were ethnic-national territories.[9] The rest were pure administrative subdivisions, populated mainly by Russians. The non-Russian ethnic-national territories were classified by size and status into autonomous republics, autonomous provinces, and national districts. In many of them, the indigenous ethnic group constituted a minority of the population. As of 2010, Russia comprises eighty-three constituent territorial units, officially termed "subjects of the federation." They represent six different types of units. Republics, autonomous districts (all but one of them located within other units), and the one autonomous *oblast* give formal political representation to ethnic minorities; *oblasts* (provinces), *krais* (territories), and two cities of federal status (Moscow and St. Petersburg) are treated as ordinary administrative subdivisions with no special constitutional status.

One of the centralizing measures President Putin pursued is the merger of smaller ethnic territories into larger surrounding units. In most of these cases, the smaller ethnic district was impoverished and hoped for better living standards by becoming part of a consolidated territory. The mergers also reduced the patronage rights and political voice that came with an ethnic district's status as a constituent unit of the federation.[10]

The ethnic republics jealously guard their special status. From 1990 to 1992, all the republics adopted declarations of sovereignty, and two made attempts to declare full or partial independence from Russia. Only one, however, the Chechen Republic (**Chechnia**), resorted to arms to back up its claim. Chechnia is one of a belt of predominantly Muslim ethnic republics in the mountainous region of the North Caucasus, between the Black and Caspian seas. Chechnia's president declared independence from Russia in 1991, an act Russia refused to recognize but did not initially attempt to overturn by force. When negotiations failed, however, in December 1994, Russian forces attacked the republic directly, subjecting its capital city, Groznyi, to devastating bombardment. This forced tens of thousands of Chechen and Russian residents to flee and led to a protracted, destructive war. Fighting ceased in the summer of 1996, but resumed in 1999. Federal forces had established control over most parts of Chechnia by early 2000, but Chechen guerrillas continue to carry out ambushes and suicide attacks against federal units.

In the mid-1990s, a radical fundamentalist form of Islam replaced national independence as the guiding ideology of the Chechen rebel movement. The guerrillas have resorted to terrorist attacks, including suicide terrorism, against civilian targets both in the North Caucasus region and in Moscow. One of the most shocking of these incidents was the seizure of a school in the town of Beslan, near Chechnia, in September 2004 (see Box 9.3). The brutal methods used by federal forces to suppress the uprising have fueled continuing hatred on the part of many Chechens against the federal government, which, in turn, facilitates recruitment by the terrorists. With time, order has been restored under the sometimes brutal rule of Ramzan Kadyrov, and much of Groznyi has been rebuilt. Attacks and reprisals continue to occur occasionally, however. And throughout the North Caucasus region, unemployment and social dislocation are severe, creating a favorable milieu for religious radicalism and violence.

Chechnia, fortunately, was an exceptional case. In the other twenty ethnic republics, Moscow reached an accommodation granting the republics a certain amount of autonomy in return for acceptance of Russia's sovereign power. All twenty-one ethnic republics have the constitutional right to determine

---

BOX 9.3

Beslan

September 1 is the first day of school each year throughout Russia. Children, accompanied by their parents, often come to school bringing flowers to their teachers. A group organized by the Chechen warlord Shamil Basaev chose September 1, 2004, to carry out a horrific attack. A group of heavily armed militants stormed a school in the town of Beslan, located in the republic of North Ossetia, next door to Chechnia. They took over a thousand schoolchildren, parents, and teachers hostage. The terrorists crowded the captives into the school gymnasium, which they filled with explosives to prevent any rescue attempt. The terrorists refused to allow water and food to be brought into the school. Negotiations over the release of the hostages failed.

On the third day of the siege, something triggered the detonation of one of the bombs inside the school. In the chaos that followed, many of the children and adults rushed to escape. The terrorists fired at them. Federal forces stormed the school, trying to rescue the escaping hostages and to kill the terrorists. Many of the bombs planted by the terrorists exploded. Ultimately, about 350 of the hostages died, along with most of the terrorists.

The media covered the events extensively. The Beslan tragedy had an impact on Russian national consciousness comparable to that of September 11 in the United States. While there had been a number of previous attacks tied to Chechen terrorists, none had cost so many innocent lives.

Putin claimed that the terrorists were part of an international terrorist movement aimed ultimately at the dismemberment of Russia itself and avoided linking the incident to Russian policy in Chechnia. In response to the crisis, Putin called for measures to reinforce national security. He also demanded increased centralization of executive power, including an end to the direct election of governors. Most observers assumed that Putin had wanted to make these changes anyway and that the Beslan tragedy simply gave him a political opening to enact them. Beslan was a tragic indication that the insurgency that began in Chechnia was spreading throughout the North Caucasus region.

their own form of state power as long as their decisions do not contradict federal law. All twenty-one have established presidencies. In many cases, the republic presidents have constructed personal power bases around appeals to ethnic solidarity and the cultural autonomy of the indigenous nationality. They have often used this power to establish personalistic dictatorships in their regions.

President Putin made clear his intention to reassert the federal government's authority over the regions. Putin's decree of May 13, 2000, which created seven new "federal districts," was one of several steps in this direction.[11] He appointed a special presidential representative to each district who monitors the actions of the regional governments within that district. This reform sought to strengthen central control over the activity of federal bodies in the regions. In the past, local branches of federal agencies had often fallen under the influence of powerful governors.

Still another important measure was the abolition of direct popular election of governors, including the presidents of the ethnic republics. Before 2005, regional chief executives were chosen by direct popular election. Since 2005, however, the president nominates a candidate to the regional legislature, which then approves the nomination (no legislature has dared to oppose a presidential appointment). Many Russians supported this change, believing that the institution of local elections had been discredited by corruption and fraud and that elections were more often determined by the influence of wealthy insiders than by public opinion. Critics of the reform accused Putin of creating a hypercentralized, authoritarian system of rule. Putin clearly hoped that appointed governors would be more accountable and effective, but past experience suggests that centralizing power by itself is unlikely to improve governance in the regions in the absence of other mechanisms for monitoring government performance and for enforcing the law.

Below the tier of regional governments are units that are supposed to enjoy the right of self-government—municipalities and other local government units. Under new legislation, the right of local self-government has been expanded to a much larger set of units—such as urban and rural districts and small settlements—raising the total number of local self-governing units to 24,000. In principle, local self-government is supposed to permit substantial policymaking autonomy in the spheres of housing, utilities, and social services (and to reduce the

federal government's burden in providing such services). However, the new legislation provides no fixed, independent sources of revenue for these local entities. They thus depend for the great majority of their budget revenues on the regional governments. For their part, the regional governments resist allowing local governments to exercise any significant powers of their own. In many cases, the mayors of the capital cities of regions are political rivals of the governors of the regions. Moscow and St. Petersburg are exceptional cases because they have the status of federal territorial subjects, like republics and regions. Elsewhere, city governments must bargain with their superior regional governments for shares of power. Moreover, the centralizing trend of the 2000s has extended to local government as an increasing number of localities have replaced elected mayors with appointed ones or city managers.

Russia's post-Communist constitutional arrangements are still evolving. The political system allows considerable room for the arbitrary exercise of power and the evisceration of democracy. Both Yeltsin and Putin interpreted their presidential mandates broadly, and although President Medvedev repeatedly calls for adherence to the rule of law, he has also continued the practice of relying heavily on informal powers. Executives at lower levels, particularly in the regions, take similarly expansive views of their powers. But while Russia remains a long way from the ideal of the rule of law, the post-Communist regime has allowed far more open competition and consultation among organized social groups than did the Communist regime. The limits of allowable debate and criticism are far wider than in the Soviet era, and there is far more open articulation and aggregation of interests.

The constitutional arrangements originally established after the end of the Communist regime are likely to evolve further over the long run, depending on the balance of power in state and society. If President Medvedev is successful in bringing about liberalization in the economy and political system as part of his drive to modernize the country, the dispersion of power in civil society will gradually bring about greater formal constraints on state power and greater respect for the formal constitutional rules. But a change of leadership, or a spell of economic recovery fueled by high world oil prices, could easily stifle the impulse for political reform.

Under Vladimir Putin, Russia's system of rule became a hybrid regime that includes elements of democracy within a largely authoritarian framework. In this system, elections are held regularly, and opposition forces are allowed a small, marginal role. The ruling authorities decide how much freedom to allow opposition groups to organize and campaign, and they exercise substantial control over television and radio, although allowing much greater freedom to the print and Internet media. Business is given wide sway to pursue its economic interests, but may not finance a political challenge to the authorities. Civil society organizations can offer policy proposals for debate. But elections are not a means for deciding who governs; the ruling authorities rarely allow elections to produce unplanned results. Moreover, corruption is rampant, and the state bureaucracy remains inefficient and poorly controlled. The centralization of power in the 2000s has been much more effective at pushing political opposition to the sidelines than at giving the authorities an independent means of controlling the bureaucracy.

Yeltsin and Putin used presidential power very differently without changing the formal rules of the constitution. Yeltsin ruled erratically and impulsively, but he respected certain limits on his power: He did not suppress media criticism, and he tolerated political opposition.[12] Faced with an opposition-led parliament, Yeltsin was willing to compromise with his opponents to enact legislation. However, Yeltsin grew dependent on a small group of favored **oligarchs** (business magnates with strong connections to government) for support and allowed them to accumulate massive fortunes and corrupt influence. Likewise, Yeltsin allowed regional bosses to flout federal authority with impunity because he found it less costly to accommodate them than to fight them. The loss of state capacity under Yeltsin illustrates one danger of an overcentralized political system. When the president does not effectively command the powers of the office, power drifts to other centers of authority.

Putin's presidency illustrates the opposite danger. When Putin took over, he undertook to reverse the breakdown of political control and responsibility in the state. Although publicly he called for a system based on respect for the rule of law, he restored authoritarian methods of rule. And although Dmitrii Medvedev often refers to freedom and democracy as necessary for Russia, the actual changes he has introduced to its political system are extremely modest.

RUSSIAN POLITICAL CULTURE IN THE POST-SOVIET PERIOD

Russian political culture is the product of centuries of autocratic rule, rapid but uneven improvement of educational and living standards in the twentieth century, and rising exposure to Western standards of political life. The resulting contemporary political culture is a contradictory bundle of values: A sturdy core of belief in democratic values is accompanied by a firm belief in the importance of a strong state together with deep mistrust of most actual state institutions. In a 2005 survey, 66 percent of Russians agreed that "Russia needs democracy," but 45 percent said that the kind of democracy Russia needs is "a completely special kind corresponding to Russian specifics."[13] A survey shortly before the December 2007 election found that almost two-thirds of the public did not believe the elections would be free or fair; yet a majority believed that their lives would improve thanks to the elections.[14] Asked whether they believed they could have any influence on policy decisions in the country, 83 percent said no.[15] But two-thirds of voters thought that democratic elections are at least somewhat important to the country, and a majority said that as president, Dmitrii Medvedev would pursue policies that would strengthen democracy.[16] Can such contradictory beliefs about democracy be reconciled?

We must remember that Russians judge democracy and other forms of government according to their ability to make the Russian state more effective at providing stability, order, and security. Many Russians cannot forgive Gorbachev and Yeltsin for pursuing policies that led to the breakup of the Soviet state, widespread poverty, the amassing of great wealth by a few individuals using unscrupulous methods, and the loss of status as a great world power. Some even believe that the ideals of democracy and the market economy represented misguided or malicious efforts to remold Russia along Western lines. The restoration of the state's power and prestige, therefore, is a criterion for judging the worth of democracy.

Democracy is also judged by its ability to benefit individuals materially. Asked in a recent survey what freedoms were most important to them *personally*, over half the respondents named the "freedom to be protected by the state in case of illness, loss of work, or poverty" and the "freedom to purchase what I want" as the most important; freedoms such as the right to vote for competing political parties or to participate in political demonstrations were named by only 13 percent and 10 percent, respectively.[17] In addition, 46 percent named the freedom to choose their job as being important to them personally, but only 30 percent named freedom of religion as personally important, while 38 percent named the freedom to acquire property such as real estate and a car as important.

This pragmatic view of democracy helps explain why many Russians praise Putin for strengthening democracy and praise Medvedev for continuing his policies. Far from seeing "freedom" and "order" as necessary enemies, many recognize that freedom is possible only in an ordered society. But if forced to choose *between* freedom and order, Russians divide rather evenly. For example, in an international survey, 47 percent of Russians (compared with 40 percent internationally) said that stability and peace are more important concerns than freedom of the press, whereas 39 percent (versus 56 percent globally) gave priority to press freedom.[18]

We can understand these competing influences on Russian political culture when we consider the long-term forces shaping it, as well as the impact of recent history.

The reforms of the late 1980s and early 1990s raised expectations that Russia would enjoy a significant rise in living standards once it got rid of communism. The sharp fall in living standards that followed the collapse of the old regime dispelled any notion that changing the political and economic systems could turn the country around overnight.

However, the decade of economic recovery and political stability after 1999 erased much of the nostalgia for the old Soviet order and increased optimism. In December 2007, 40 percent of Russians reported that they were looking ahead to 2008 with optimism; a year before, only 30 percent expressed optimism about the coming year.[19] More people were willing to look back and say that the radical reforms of the economy beginning in 1992 brought greater good than harm.[20] And 61 percent were willing to say that it was a good thing that Russia became independent of the Soviet Union. Ten years before, only 27 percent thought so.[21] On the other hand, the devastating economic crisis beginning in 2008 weakened the sense of confidence most people were feeling about the future. A June 2010 survey found that almost three quarters of the population saw the current economic situation as a crisis and 11 percent saw it as "catastrophic."[22]

One reason Russians take a conditional view of the value of democratic rights is the widespread belief that political order is fragile, a view that the authorities have worked hard to keep alive. Russians have long been taught that a weakening of the internal cohesion of the state invites predation from outside powers, and many episodes of Russian history bear out this belief. The Putin leadership pointed to the popular uprisings in Ukraine, Georgia, and elsewhere not as signs of a democratic spirit in the face of attempted election fraud by local strongmen, but as proof that outside powers (such as the U.S. Central Intelligence Agency) were fomenting unrest in order to overthrow the legitimate state authorities. Asked what they consider the main internal threat facing Russia today, Russians expressed fear about political instability connected with political succession (16 percent), struggle among competing factions in power (12 percent), loss of control by the central government over the regions (9 percent), separatism in the North Caucasus (4 percent), and loss of control over the regions in the Far East located near China (4 percent).[23]

Surveys also show that citizens have little faith in most present-day political institutions, although, as Figure 9.4 shows, they have a good deal of confidence in the president and government. Confidence in elective bodies such as the parliament is low, and in the law enforcement and security organs it is even lower, while it is higher in local and regional government and higher still in the Orthodox Church. The great majority of Russians believe that they are not protected from arbitrary treatment by the state; only a quarter of the population say that they feel any sense of protection from abuse at the hands of the police, courts, tax authorities, and other state structures.[24]

Still, although Russians placed more faith in Putin and Medvedev than in other political institutions, they also recognized the value of some constitutional constraints on presidential power. Few Russians thought that power should transfer with Putin from the presidency to the prime ministership; two-thirds preferred maintaining a system of "strong presidential power."[25] Nor did most Russians want to see presidential power increased.[26] As Figure 9.5 shows, Russians believe by a wide margin that there should be a political opposition to the authorities. Russians exhibit a strong sense of skepticism about and mistrust of most institutions of the state; yet by a two-to-one margin, most Russians believe they cannot solve their problems without it.[27]

of society. They also feel powerless to affect state policy. Little wonder that a leader such as Putin, who is associated with the restoration of order and predictability, can command such widespread support despite the general mistrust Russians have for their political institutions.

Surveys also reveal considerable continuity with the past in support of the idea that the state should ensure society's prosperity and the citizens' material security. More so than residents of Western Europe or the United States, Russians believe that the state is responsible for providing a just moral and social order, with justice being understood more as social equality than as equality before the law. This pattern reflects the lasting influence of traditional conceptions of state and society on Russian political culture.

Political culture is also shaped by slower-acting but more lasting influences, including the succession of generations, rising educational levels, and urbanization. These are mutually reinforcing changes as new generations of young people are exposed to fundamentally different influences than those to which their parents were exposed.

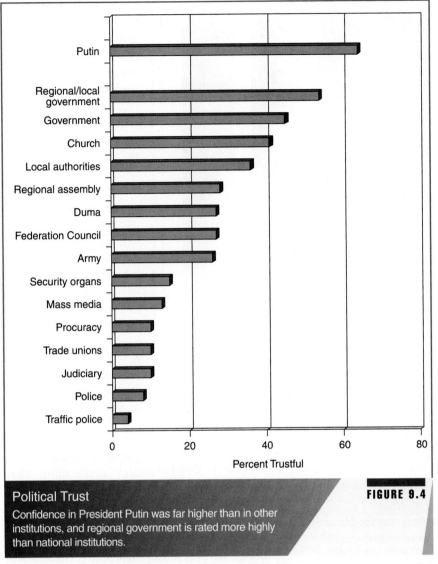

Political Trust

Confidence in President Putin was far higher than in other institutions, and regional government is rated more highly than national institutions.

FIGURE 9.4

Sources: Putin trust: Fond obshchestvennogo mneniia, July 2008. Retrieved July 11, 2008, from http://bd. fom.ru/report/map/projects/dominant/dom0826/d082621#Abs3. All other items: Fund for Public Opinion, May 2007. Retrieved July 11, 2008, from http://bd.fom.ru/report/cat/power/pow_rei/d071901.

Most accept that the state requires firm guidance by a capable president, and they give Putin credit for having restored order and purpose to the state. Therefore, although there continues to be a strong foundation of support for democratic values, that support is contingent on whether these values will help hold the country together or pull it apart.

The political culture thus combines contradictory elements. Russians do value democratic rights, but experience has taught them that under the banner of democracy, politicians can abuse their power to the detriment of the integrity of the state and the well-being

Political Socialization

The Soviet regime devoted enormous effort to political indoctrination and propaganda. The regime controlled the content of school curricula, mass media, popular culture, political education, and nearly every other channel by which values and attitudes were

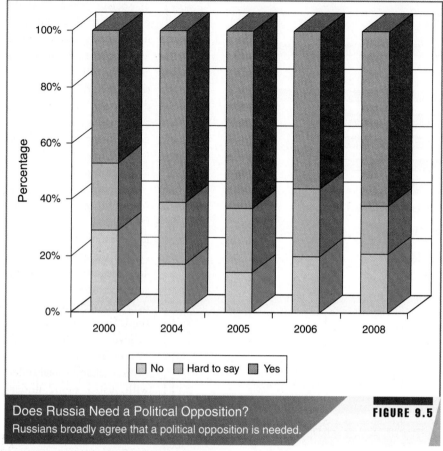

Does Russia Need a Political Opposition?
Russians broadly agree that a political opposition is needed.

FIGURE 9.5

Note: Percentages are percentages of those responding.
Source: Levada Center, "Politicheskaia oppozitsiia v Rossii," July 2008. Retrieved July 11, 2008, from www.levada.ru/press/2008073102.html.

overt political control over the formation of attitudes and values. In place of the idea of the class struggle and the international solidarity of the working class, textbooks stress love for the Russian national heritage. Historical figures who in the Communist era were honored as heroes of the struggle of ordinary people against feudal or capitalist masters are now held up as great representatives of Russia's national culture.[28] Schoolbooks and mass media place heavy emphasis on loyalty to Russia as a state. This theme underlies Russia's effort to create a new sense of national community within the country's post-Soviet state boundaries.

The authorities have also turned to the Orthodox Church as an aid in political socialization. They regard the Church as a valuable ally in building patriotic loyalty, national pride, and a framework of ethical values. The Church, in turn, seeks to protect its traditional status as Russia's state church, enabling it to block other Christian denominations from proselytizing in Russia. There has been an ongoing debate over whether to make Russian Orthodoxy the foundation for ethics instruction in the schools. As of spring 2010, for example, a new course was introduced into the curriculum of nineteen regions. All fourth- and fifth-graders must take a course on "the fundamentals of religious culture and ethics," but their families may choose among several different versions of the course, each using a different textbook. Options include textbooks based on Orthodox Christian, Muslim, Buddhist, or Jewish beliefs, as well as one oriented to secular ethics. According to the Ministry of Education, by far the largest number of requests came in for the secular ethics book—only 20 percent of families

formed. The heart of Soviet doctrine was the Marxist belief that the way in which a society organizes economic production—feudalism, capitalism, socialism, and so forth—determines the structure of values and beliefs prevalent in the society. The idea was that the ruling class in each society determines the basic ideology of the society. Therefore, Soviet propaganda and indoctrination emphasized that Soviet citizens were part of a worldwide working-class movement to overthrow capitalism and replace it with socialism, in which there would be no private property. Needing to knit together a highly diverse multinational state, the Soviet regime downplayed national feeling and replaced it with a sense of patriotic loyalty to the Soviet state and to the working class's interests in the worldwide class struggle.

Today the ideological content of Russian education has changed significantly, and there is much less requested the Orthodox Christian version. The Orthodox Church, however, disputes the government's figures.[29]

The Church's rising influence in the schools has prompted a backlash among many intellectuals, who protest that teaching religion in the schools violates the constitutional provision that Russia is a secular state. But many people, whether religious or not, deplore the decay of morals in society and the relentless rise of consumerism and materialism as Russia opens itself to the global capitalist system. They see the Church, with its long history of partnership with the state, as a way of restoring traditional moral values in society.

In the 1990s, the regime generally respected media freedom. Private businesses bought many formerly state-owned media outlets or created new ones, and a wide range of expression of news and opinion was available. Under Putin, the authorities moved to set limits on the media (particularly television), but they did not institute an elaborate political socialization system such as the Soviet state employed. Nevertheless, the authorities have used the media to build support for their foreign and domestic policies. The overall political line under Putin and Medvedev has been that Russia is rejecting totalitarian communism on the one hand and unbridled oligarchic capitalism on the other, and is restoring continuity with the best traditions of Russia's political history. Both, however, have repeatedly insisted that Russia must make use of democracy and capitalism, although in its own way.

The media system is stratified. Television reaches almost everyone and is by far the most important source of news for the population. Accordingly, it is subjected to the tightest political control by the authorities, who give the editors of the main broadcast programs regular guidance on what to cover and what not to cover. Print and online media are allowed much more freedom, but they reach a far smaller audience, so they are of less immediate concern to the authorities.[30] Aware of the stultifying effects of the old Soviet system of ideological control over communications, the authorities' strategy is defensive, in that they want to prevent organized groups from challenging their claim to power rather than being overtly ideological.

Russian political socialization is therefore much less subject to direct state control than it was in the Soviet era; and even then, awareness of the political and economic standards of the outside world filtered into the consciousness of the Soviet population. Today's authorities want to use schools and communications media to build loyalty to the state and its leaders, confidence in the future, and acceptance of a centralized regime, while at the same time spurring Russians to modernize the economy. At the same time, they want to prevent the media from being an arena of open political contestation.

POLITICAL PARTICIPATION

In Russia, there is much less direct political participation (such as voting, canvassing for a candidate, or collecting signatures for a petition) than in Western democracies, as well as less indirect participation (such as holding membership in civic groups and voluntary associations). Democracy requires both forms of participation. Participation in civic life builds social capital—reciprocal bonds of trust and obligation among citizens that facilitate collective action. Where social capital is abundant, people treat one another as equals rather than as members of social hierarchies. They are more willing to cooperate in ways that benefit the society and improve the quality of government by sharing the burden of making government accountable and effective.[31] People are more willing to pay their taxes, so government has more revenue to spend on public goods—and less ability and less incentive to divert it into politicians' pockets. The success of capitalism and democratic government rests on citizens' ability to cooperate for the common good.

In Russia, however, social capital has historically been scarce, compared with West European societies, and participation in civic activity has been extremely limited. Moreover, state and society have generally been separated by mutual mistrust and suspicion. State authorities have usually stood outside and above society, extracting what resources they needed from society but not cultivating ties of obligation to it. The Communist regime further depleted the stock of social capital by coopting associations useful for the state and repressing those that threatened its interests. Therefore, social capital not only in Russia but also throughout the former Communist Bloc is significantly lower than in other parts of the world.[32]

The weakness of intermediate associations linking political elites to ordinary citizens widens the felt distance between state and society. Thus, although Russians turn out to vote in elections in relatively high numbers, participation in organized forms of political activity is low. Opinion polls show that most people believe that their involvement in political activity is futile, and they have little confidence that they can influence government policy through their participation. Although there was an intense surge in political involvement in the late 1980s and early 1990s, when controls over political expression and association were lifted, it ebbed substantially.

Membership in voluntary associations in contemporary Russia is extremely low. According to survey data, 91 percent of the population does not belong to any sports or recreational club, literary or other cultural group, political party, local housing association, or charitable organization. About 9 percent report attending church at least once a month, and about 20 percent say that they are members of trade unions. Attending religious services and being a member of a trade union are very passive forms of participation in public life. Yet even when these and other types of participation are taken into account, almost 60 percent of the population still is outside any voluntary public associations.[33] For example, today some 87 percent of Russian Orthodox believers are not members of a congregation, going to church only occasionally.[34]

This is not to say that Russian citizens are *psychologically* disengaged from public life or that they are socially isolated. Half of the Russian adult population reports reading national newspapers "regularly" or "sometimes," and almost everyone watches national television "regularly" (81 percent). Sixty-nine percent read local newspapers "regularly" or "sometimes." Sixty-six percent discuss the problems of the country with friends "regularly" or "sometimes," and 48 percent say that people ask them their opinions about what is happening in the country. A similar percentage of people discuss the problems of their city with friends.[35] Russians do vote in high proportions in national elections—higher in fact than do their American counterparts.[36]

Moreover, Russians prize their right *not* to participate in politics. Today's low levels of political participation are a reflection of the low degree of confidence in political institutions and the widespread view that ordinary individuals have little influence over government. In the 2003 Duma elections, 4.7 percent of the voters expressed their dissatisfaction with the array of choices offered by checking the box marked "against all" on the party-list ballot.[37] But the authorities worried that this was too attractive a means of expressing disaffection and eliminated the option from later elections.

Elite Recruitment

Elite recruitment refers to the institutional processes in a society by which people gain access to positions of influence and responsibility. Elite recruitment is closely tied to political participation because it is through participation in community activity that people take on leadership roles, learn civic skills (such as organization and persuasion), develop networks of friends and supporters, and become interested in pursuing political careers.

In the Soviet regime, the link between participation and elite recruitment was highly formalized. The Communist Party recruited the population into a variety of officially sponsored organizations, such as the Communist Party, youth leagues, trade unions, and women's associations. Through such organizations, the regime identified potential leaders and gave them experience in organizing group activity. The party reserved the right to approve appointments to any positions that carried high administrative responsibility or that were likely to affect the formation of public attitudes. The system for recruiting, training, and appointing individuals for positions of leadership and responsibility in the regime was called the **nomenklatura** system. Those individuals who were approved for the positions on *nomenklatura* lists were informally called "the *nomenklatura.*" Many citizens regarded them as the ruling class in Soviet society.

The democratizing reforms of the late 1980s and early 1990s made two important changes to the process of elite recruitment. First, the old *nomenklatura* system crumbled along with other Communist Party controls over society. Second, although most members of the old ruling elites adapted themselves to the new circumstances and stayed on in various official capacities, the wave of new informal organizations and popular elections brought many new people into elite positions. Today, the contemporary Russian political elite consists of a mixture of career types: those who worked their way up through the state bureaucracy and those who entered politics through other channels, such as elective politics or business.

President Medvedev and Prime Minister Putin Confer at the Kremlin

Formally, the prime minister reports to the president, but the actual lines of accountability are unclear under the tandem leadership of Putin and Medvedev.

Ria Novosti/Kremlin Pool/epa/Corbis

Today, some of the old Soviet institutional mechanisms for recruitment are being restored. In the Communist regime, the party maintained schools to train political leaders, where rising officials received a combination of management education and political indoctrination. Today, most of those schools serve a similar function as academies for training civil servants and are overseen by the presidential administration. The authorities are working to systematize the selection and training of officials in order to ensure that a competent and politically reliable cadre is available for recruitment, not only to state bureaucratic positions but even for management positions in major firms.[38]

There are two major differences between elite recruitment in the Communist regime and that in the present. The *nomenklatura* system of the Soviet regime ensured that in every walk of life, those who held positions of power and responsibility were approved by the party. They thus formed different sections of a single political elite and owed their positions to their political loyalty and usefulness. Today, however, there are multiple elites (political, business, professional, cultural, etc.), reflecting the greater degree of pluralism in post-Soviet society.

Second, there are multiple channels for recruitment to today's *political* elite. Many of its members come from positions in the federal and regional executive agencies. Putin relied heavily on the police (the regular police and the security services) and the military as sources of personnel for his senior-level appointments.[39] He also turned to colleagues with whom he had worked closely in St. Petersburg in the 1990s. This pattern of close patron–client relations, where a rising politician brings members of his "team" with him each time he moves up the career ladder, is a common feature of elite recruitment in Russia. One effect is to generate competition between rival groups of clients, sometimes called "clans." In Russia's case, there has been persistent behind-the-scenes rivalry between two such clans, both composed of associates of Putin. One is close to the security services, while the other, with a slightly more liberal cast, is made up of trained lawyers. When Putin chose Medvedev as his anointed successor, it was seen as a serious blow against the first group.

The Soviet elite recruitment system produced many of today's successful businesspeople as old-guard bureaucrats discovered ways to cash in on their political contacts and get rich quickly. Money from the Communist Party found its way into the establishment of many new business ventures. Insiders took advantage of their contacts to obtain business licenses, office space, and exclusive contracts with little difficulty. Some bought (at bargain basement prices) controlling interests in state firms that were undergoing privatization; a few years later, these insiders became millionaires.

Today's business elite is closely tied to the state, both because state officials keep business on a short leash and because business provides material and political benefits to officials. In some cases, bureaucratic factions form around particular enterprises and industries, such as the oil or gas industry. Businesses need licenses, permits, contracts, exemptions, and other benefits from government. Political officials, in turn, need financial contributions to their campaigns, political support, favorable media coverage, and other benefits that business can provide. In the 1990s, the close and collusive relations between many businesses and government officials nurtured widespread corruption and the meteoric rise of a small group of business tycoons, or oligarchs. They took advantage of their links to Yeltsin's administration to acquire control of some of Russia's most valuable companies. The prominence of the newly rich fed a public backlash that made it politically viable for Putin to suppress some of them and destroy their business empires by police methods. And in many cases, the state takeover of private firms ended up concentrating wealth and power in the hands of well-connected state officials (often from the security services), who have treated the firms as private fiefdoms rather than increasing their productivity or accountability.

INTEREST ARTICULATION: BETWEEN STATISM AND PLURALISM

The political and economic changes of the last two decades in Russia have had a powerful impact on the way social interests are organized. A diverse spectrum of interest associations has developed. The pattern of interest articulation, however, reflects the powerful impact of state control over society as well as the sharp disparities in wealth and power that formed during the transition period. A few organizations have considerable influence in policymaking, while other groups have little.

The Communist regime did not tolerate the open pursuit of any interests except those authorized by the state. Interest organizations—such as trade unions, youth groups, professional societies, and the like—were closely supervised by the Communist Party. Glasnost' upset this statist model of interest articulation by setting off an explosion of political expression. This, in turn, prompted new groups to form and to make political demands. It is hard today to imagine how profound the impact of glasnost' was on Soviet society. Almost overnight, it opened the floodgates to a

growing stream of startling facts, ideas, disclosures, reappraisals, and scandals. In loosening the party's controls over communication sufficiently to encourage people to speak and write freely and openly, the regime also relinquished the controls that would have enabled it to rein in political expression when it went too far.

As people voiced their deep-felt demands and grievances, others recognized that they shared the same beliefs and values and made common cause with them, sometimes forming new, unofficial organizations. Therefore, one result of glasnost' was a wave of participation in "informal"—that is, unlicensed and uncontrolled—public associations. When the authorities tried to limit or prohibit such groups, they generated still more frustration and protest. Associations of all sorts formed, including ultranationalists who wanted to restore tsarism and nationalist movements in many republics. The explosion of the nuclear reactor at Chernobyl in 1986 had a tremendous impact in stimulating the formation of environmental protest, linked closely to nationalist sentiment in Belarus and Ukraine.[40]

The elimination of the state's monopoly on productive property resulted in the formation of new interests, among them those with a stake in the market economy. Now groups can form to represent a diversity of interests, compete for access to influence and resources, and define their own agendas. The Justice Ministry estimates that there are nearly half a million NGOs, although probably no more than a quarter of them are active at any given time.[41]

In some cases, NGOs are the successors of recognized associations of the old regime, such as official trade unions. Often, these groups cling to their inherited organizational assets and continue to seek "insider" access to the state. Other groups sprang up during the glasnost' period or later, but must cooperate with local authorities in order to gain access to meeting places and media attention.

There were elements of corporatism in the state's relations with interest groups under Putin because of the regime's preference for dealing directly with controllable umbrella organizations representing particular segments of society. An example is the formation of the Public Chamber to create a state-approved platform for the activity of selected NGOs. Operating within the limits set by the regime, the Public Chamber has been able to serve to some extent as a channel of communication between the public and the authorities. Similar chambers have been created in many regions. Overall, however, the pattern of interest group activity is more pluralist than corporatist because in most cases interest associations are too numerous, too weak internally, and too competitive for corporatism to succeed. But under Putin, interest articulation did become more statist as the regime gradually increased political controls on nongovernmental associations.

A law enacted at the beginning of 2006 imposed new restrictions on NGOs, making it easier for the authorities to deny them registration and to shut them down. At the same time, the authorities warned that foreign intelligence services were sponsoring Russian NGOs for the purposes of intelligence-gathering and subversion. The political atmosphere for NGOs became considerably chillier.

Let us consider three examples of associational groups: the **Russian Union of Industrialists and Entrepreneurs (RUIE)**, the **League of Committees of Soldiers' Mothers**, and the **Federation of Independent Trade Unions of Russia (FITUR)**. They illustrate different strategies for organization and influence and different relationships to the state.

The Russian Union of Industrialists and Entrepreneurs

Most former state-owned industrial firms are now wholly or partly privately owned. Most industrial firms participate in a competitive market (and increasingly globalized) economic environment. Under the socialist regime, managers were told to fulfill the plan regardless of cost or quality. Profit was not a relevant consideration.[42] Now most managers seek to maximize profits and increase the value of their firms. Although many still demand subsidies and protection from the state, an increasing number want an environment where laws and contracts are enforced by the state, regulation is reasonable and honest, taxes are fair (and low), and barriers to foreign trade are minimized. These changes are visible in the political interests of the association that represents the interests of big business in Russia, the RUIE. The RUIE is the single most powerful organized interest group in Russia. Its membership comprises both the old state industrial firms (now mostly private or quasi-private) and new private firms and conglomerates.

In the early 1990s, the RUIE's lobbying efforts were aimed at winning continued state support of industrial firms, but with time, the RUIE has become the leading voice of big business in the market system. The RUIE helps broker agreements between business and labor, and it is a source of policy advice for government and parliament. All the major industrial firms—including those of the oligarchs—belong to the RUIE and do much of their lobbying through it. Of course, on matters that concern individual firms, those businesses still seek to influence policy on their own.

Over time, the RUIE's role has changed, according to the opportunities and limits set by the state authorities. It has expanded its in-house capacity for working with the government in drafting legislation. On a number of policy issues, such as tax law, pension policy, bankruptcy legislation, regulation of the securities market, and the terms of Russia's entry to the WTO, the RUIE has been active and influential. For the most part, it works behind the scenes to lobby for its interests, but occasionally, if it feels its voice has been ignored, it applies pressure more publicly.

Yet the limits of the RUIE's power as the collective voice of big business are clear. When the Putin regime began its campaign to destroy the Yukos oil firm starting in July 2003 (see Box 9.4), the RUIE confined itself to mild expressions of concern. Its members, evidently fearful of crossing Putin, chose not to defend Yukos's head, Mikhail Khodorkovsky, or to protest the use of police methods to destroy one of Russia's largest oil companies. Instead, they promised to meet their tax obligations and to do more to help the country fight poverty. Perhaps if big business had taken a strong, united stand, it could have influenced state policy. But the desire by each individual firm to maintain friendly relations with the government, and the fear of government reprisals, undercut big business's capacity for collective action.

The League of Committees of Soldiers' Mothers

The Soviet regime sponsored several official women's organizations, but these mainly served propaganda purposes. During the glasnost' period, a number of unofficial women's organizations sprang up. One such group was the Committee of Soldiers' Mothers. It formed in the spring of 1989, when some 300 women in Moscow rallied to protest the end of student deferments from military conscription. Their protest came

BOX 9.4

Mikhail Khodorkovsky and the Yukos Affair

One of the most widely publicized episodes of the Putin era was the state takeover of the powerful private oil company, Yukos, and the criminal prosecution of its head, Mikhail Khodorkovsky. At the time of his arrest in October 2003, Khodorkovsky was the wealthiest of Russia's new post-Communist magnates. His career began in the late 1980s when he started a bank. Later he acquired—at a bargain-basement price—80 percent of the shares of the Yukos oil company when the government privatized it. At first, Khodorkovsky sought to squeeze maximum profit from the firm by stripping its assets. Soon, his business strategy changed, and he began to invest in the firm's productive capacity. He made Yukos the most dynamic of Russia's oil companies. As he improved the efficiency and transparency of the firm, the share prices rose and, with them, Khodorkovsky's own net worth. At its peak in 2002, the company's assets were estimated at about $20 billion, of which Khodorkovsky owned nearly $8 billion.

Seeking to improve his public image, Khodorkovsky created a foundation and launched several charitable initiatives. He became active in Russian politics, helping to fund political parties and sponsoring the election campaigns of several Duma deputies. Critics accused him of wanting to control parliament and even of wanting to change the constitution to turn it into a parliamentary system. There was talk that he intended to seek the presidency.

By spring 2003, the Putin administration decided that Khodorkovsky and Yukos had grown too independent. Several top figures in Yukos and associated companies were arrested and charged with fraud, embezzlement, tax evasion, and even murder. In December 2003, the government began issuing claims against the company for billions of dollars in back taxes and froze the company's bank accounts as collateral against the claims. When Yukos failed to pay the full tax bill, the government seized its main production subsidiary and auctioned it off to a firm that, three days later, sold it to Russia's only state-owned oil company, Rosneft'. In October 2003, Khodorkovsky was arrested and charged with fraud and tax evasion. He was sentenced to nine years' imprisonment and sent to a prison camp in Siberia. In 2006, the last remnants of the company were forced into bankruptcy. In 2008, the authorities pressed a new set of charges that added another six years to his sentence.

Whatever the regime's motives—political, economic, or both—the Yukos affair shows that the authorities are willing to manipulate the legal system for political purposes when it suits them and that the fight to redistribute control of Russia's natural resource assets remains a driving force in politics.

---

on the heels of Gorbachev's withdrawal of Soviet forces from the decade-long war in Afghanistan, where over 13,000 Soviet troops were killed. In response to the actions by the Soldiers' Mothers, Gorbachev agreed to restore student deferments. Since then, the Soldiers' Mothers' movement has grown, with local branches forming in hundreds of cities and joining together in the League of Committees of Soldiers' Mothers. Their focus remains centered on the problems of military service. The league presses the military to end the brutal hazing of recruits, which results in the deaths (in many cases by suicide) of hundreds of soldiers each year. The league also advises young men on how to avoid being conscripted.[43]

The onset of large-scale hostilities in Chechnia in 1994 through 1996 and 1999 through 2000 stimulated a new burst of activity by the league. It helped families locate soldiers who were missing in action or captured by the Chechen rebel forces. It sent missions to Chechnia to negotiate for the release of prisoners and to provide proper burial for the dead. It collected information about the actual scale of the war and of its casualties. It also continued to lobby for decent treatment of recruits. Through the 1990s, it became one of the most sizeable and respected civic groups in Russia. It can call on a network of thousands of active volunteers for its work. One of the movement's greatest assets is its members' moral authority as mothers defending the interests of their children. This stance makes it hard for their opponents to paint them as unpatriotic.

The league plays both a public political role (for instance, it lobbied to liberalize the law on alternative civil service for conscientious objectors, and it fights for an end to the brutality in the treatment of

Former Yukos Head Mikhail Khodorkovsky is Led under Guard to Court

Mikhail Khodorkovsky, head of the Yukos oil company, was imprisoned when the Putin administration decided that he and his company had grown too independent.

Alexander Zemlianichenko/ AP Images

servicemen[44]) and a role as service provider. Much of its effort is spent on helping soldiers and their families deal with their problems.

Like many NGOs, the League of Committees of Soldiers' Mothers cultivates ties with counterpart organizations abroad, and it has won international recognition for its work. For some groups, such ties are a source of dependence, as organizations compensate for the lack of mass membership with aid and know-how from counterpart organizations abroad. However, the league enjoys a stable base of public support in Russia. Its international ties have also probably helped protect the group in the face of the sometimes hostile attitude of the authorities.

The Federation of Independent Trade Unions of Russia

The FITUR is the successor of the official trade-union federation under the Soviet regime. Unlike the RUIE, however, it has poorly adapted itself to the post-Communist environment, even though it inherited substantial organizational resources from the old Soviet trade-union organization. In the Soviet era, virtually every employed person belonged to a trade union. All branch and regional trade-union organizations were part of a single labor federation, called the All-Union Central Council of Trade Unions. With the breakdown

of the old regime, some of the member unions became independent, while other unions sprang up as independent bodies representing the interests of particular groups of workers. Nonetheless, the nucleus of the old official trade-union organization survived in the form of the FITUR. It remains by far the largest trade-union federation in Russia. Around 95 percent of all organized workers belong to unions that are, at least formally, members of the FITUR. The independent unions are much smaller. By comparison with big business, however, the labor movement is fragmented, weak, and unable to mobilize workers effectively for collective action. The workers of as many as half of all enterprises do not belong to any union at all.[45]

The FITUR inherited valuable real-estate assets from its Soviet-era predecessor organization, including thousands of office buildings and hotels. It also inherited the right to collect workers' contributions for the state social insurance fund. Control of this fund enabled the official trade unions to acquire enormous amounts of income-generating property over the years. These assets and income streams give leaders of the official unions considerable advantages in competing for members. But the FITUR no longer has centralized control over its regional and branch members. In the 1993 and 1995 parliamentary elections, for instance, member unions formed their own political alliances with parties. Thus, internal disunity is another major reason for the relative weakness of the FITUR as an organization. Much of its effort is expended in fighting independent unions to win a monopoly on representing workers in collective bargaining with employers, rather than in joining with other unions to defend the interests of workers generally.[46]

The ineffectiveness of the FITUR is also illustrated by the tepid response of organized labor to the severe deterioration in labor and social conditions in the 1990s. Unemployment rose to some 13 percent (very high, given that it was essentially unknown under the Communist regime), and even among employed workers, wage arrears were widespread. Surveys found that in any given year in the 1990s, three-quarters of all workers received their wages late at least once.[47] There were strikes, but far fewer than might have been expected, given how dire the economic situation was. Again, during the recession of 2008 and 2009, when unemployment rose to over 10 percent, there was very little protest. There were a small number of strikes, particularly at foreign-owned plants (where the authorities are more willing to allow workers to strike), but the numbers were very small: In all of 2008, there were only four officially registered strikes and only one in 2009.[48]

Why are unions so weak? One reason is that workers depend on the enterprises where they work for a variety of social benefits that are administered through the enterprise, such as housing, recreation facilities, and medical and childcare services.[49] Another, however, is the close relationship between the leadership of the FITUR and government authorities. Unwilling to forfeit the goodwill of those in power, trade union leaders are reluctant to mount protests against them. As a result, workers generally feel unrepresented by their unions.[50] While this situation would seem to favor the interests of business and the state, in fact, senior state leaders express frustration at how poorly organized the FITUR is; it means that neither business nor the state has a credible negotiating partner in dealing with issues concerning labor. As a result, the state fears the prospect that in a crisis, labor grievances could spread and become explosive, destabilizing the state.

New Sectors of Interest

In Russia, many new associations have formed around the interests of new categories of actors. Bankers, political consultants, realtors, judges, attorneys, auditors, and numerous other professional and occupational groups have formed associations to seek favorable policies or set professional standards. Environmental groups, women's organizations, human-rights activists, and many other cause-oriented groups have organized. Most of these operate in a particular locality, but a few have national scope. One of the most publicized movements is that of automobile owners, who have formed organizations in several cities to protest the abuse of privileges by VIPs (such as using flashing blue lights on top of their cars to cut through traffic jams).

The rules of the game for interest articulation changed sharply after the Soviet regime fell. There is much more open bargaining over the details of policy, although organizations need to operate within limits set by the authorities. Still, tens of thousands of non-state associations compete to voice their interests through the mass media, the parliament, and the government. And in a variety of issue areas, public pressure and quiet lobbying articulated through interest groups does influence public policy.

PARTIES AND THE AGGREGATION OF INTERESTS

Interest aggregation refers to the process by which the demands of various groups of a society are pooled to form programmatic options for government. Although other institutions also aggregate interests, in most countries, political parties are the quintessential structure performing this vital task. How well parties aggregate interests, define choices for voters, and hold politicians accountable is of critical importance to democracy.

Although Russia's party system in the 1990s was fluid and fragmented, a clear structure has emerged in the 2000s, in which the United Russia party dominates while other parties are marginal. In the 1990s, there was considerable turnover in the parties from one election to the next. Voters had little sense of attachment to parties and more often associated them with particular politicians' personalities than with specific ideological stances. Most parties had very weak roots in society, although parties guided the work of the State Duma through their parliamentary factions.[51]

Russia's party system underwent a major transformation in the 2000s. The authorities have succeeded in creating a single party that dominates elections. Russians term such a party a **party of power**, indicating that the party serves the collective interests of those holding office. For them, it is a vehicle for career advancement, while for the voters, it is the electoral face of the state. In the 1990s, there were several short-lived attempts to form parties of power, but in the 2000s, the United Russia party has become *the* unquestioned party of power. At the same time, the political authorities also exercise influence over other parties in varying degrees, determining what political role each may play. Parties that refuse to play by the regime's rules find it virtually impossible to operate. The president and government use United Russia and other parties to secure their control over the State Duma and regional legislatures, to channel political competition into safe outlets, and to manage the careers of ambitious politicians.

Elections and Party Development

Table 9.1 indicates the official results of the party-list voting in the 1993, 1995, 1999, 2003, and 2007 elections. The table groups parties into five categories that have characterized party identities since the early 1990s: *democratic* (those espousing liberal democratic

Party-List Vote in Duma Elections since 1993   TABLE 9.1

Support for United Russia has grown at the expense of support for democratic, Communist, and nationalist parties.

Party	1993	1995	1999	2003	2007
Democratic Parties					
Russia's Choice	15.5	3.9	—	—	—
Union of Rightist Forces (SPS)	—	—	8.5	4.0	0.9
Yabloko	7.8	6.8	5.9	4.3	1.5
Party of Russian Unity and Concord (PRES)	6.7	—	—	—	—
Democratic Party of Russia (DPR)	5.5	—	—	0.2	0.1
Centrist Parties					
Women of Russia	8.1	4.6	2.0	—	—
Civic Union[a]	1.9	1.6	—	—	—
Parties of Power					
Our Home Is Russia	—	10.1	1.2	—	—
Fatherland—All Russia (OVR)	—	—	13.3	—	—
Unity/United Russia[b]	—	—	23.3	38.2	64.3
A Just Russia	—	—	—	—	7.7
Nationalist Parties					
Liberal Democratic Party of Russia (LDPR)[c]	22.9	11.2	5.9	11.6	8.1
Congress of Russian Communities (KRO)[d]	—	4.3	0.6	—	—
Motherland (Rodina)	—	—	—	9.2	—
Leftist Parties					
Communist Party of the Russian Federation (CPRF)	12.4	22.3	24.2	12.8	11.5
Agrarian Party	7.9	3.8	—	3.6	2.3
Other parties failing to meet 5% threshold	10.9	26.8	12.5	11.1	2.1
Against all[e]	4.3	2.8	3.3	4.7	—

[a]In 1995, the same alliance renamed itself the Bloc of Trade Unionists and Industrialists.

[b]In 2003, Unity changed its name to United Russia, following a merger with the Fatherland party.

[c]In 1999, the LDPR party list was called the Zhirinovsky bloc.

[d]In 1999, this party was called Congress of Russian Communities and Yuri Boldyrev Movement.

[e]In 2007, the "Against all" option was not available.

Source: Compiled by author from reports of Central Electoral Commission. See http://cikrf.ru.

principles); *leftist* (those advocating socialist and statist values); *centrist* (those mixing leftist and liberal democratic appeals); *nationalist* (those highlighting ethnic nationalism, patriotism, and imperialism); and *parties of power*.

Figure 9.6 shows how the election results translated into the distribution of seats in the Duma to various party factions following the 2003 and 2007 elections. Note how the spectrum of parliamentary parties has dwindled as United Russia has come to occupy a dominant position. It has been aided by some strategic engineering of the electoral system that has included tightening the rules for party registration, raising the threshold for representation from 5 percent to 7 percent, switching to an all-PR Duma, and prohibiting deputies from leaving their factions without losing their seats. Above all, the increasing use of electoral fraud to ensure overwhelming victories for United Russia has padded its margin. In the nearly twenty years since contested elections first were held, the party system has evolved from being one with many weakly supported parties to an authoritarian dominant party system.[52]

From the Multiparty System to the Dominant Party Regime

The multiparty system arose with the elections under Gorbachev to the reformed Soviet and Russian Republic parliaments. Democratically oriented politicians coalesced to defeat Communist Party officials in the 1989 and 1990 elections and, once elected, formed legislative caucuses in parliament. There they fought with Communist, nationalist, and agrarian groups. These parliamentary factions became the nuclei of political parties in the parliamentary election of December 1993.

Polarization and the Party System Elections in the late 1980s and early 1990s were aligned around two poles: one associated with Yeltsin and the forces pushing for democracy and a market economy, and the other fighting to preserve the old system based on state ownership and control of the economy. Other parties positioned themselves in relation to these poles. For instance, Vladimir Zhirinovsky's nationalistic **Liberal Democratic Party of Russia (LDPR)** claimed to offer an alternative to both the democrats and the Communists, appealing to xenophobia, authoritarianism, and the nostalgia for empire. The party's unexpectedly strong showing in the 1993 election was a signal of widespread popular discontent with the Yeltsin economic reforms.

The main anchor of the left (statist and socialist) pole of the spectrum has been the Communists (**Communist Party of the Russian Federation**, or **CPRF**), who are the heirs of the old ruling Communist Party of the Soviet Union and who espouse a mixture of Communist and nationalist principles.

On the pro-market and pro-democracy side of the spectrum have been several parties whose fortunes have fallen dramatically since the 1990s. One of these is *Yabloko*. Yabloko has consistently defended

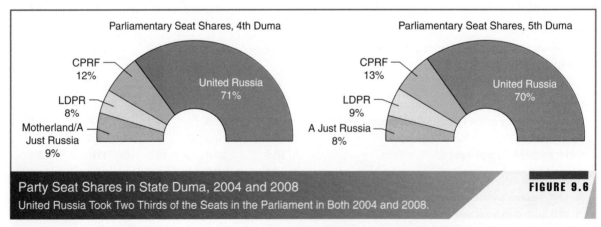

Parliamentary Seat Shares, 4th Duma

CPRF 12%
LDPR 8%
Motherland/A Just Russia 9%
United Russia 71%

Parliamentary Seat Shares, 5th Duma

CPRF 13%
LDPR 9%
A Just Russia 8%
United Russia 70%

Party Seat Shares in State Duma, 2004 and 2008
United Russia Took Two Thirds of the Seats in the Parliament in Both 2004 and 2008.

FIGURE 9.6

Notes: Figures taken as of May 2004 and January 2008. Percentages shift with time as members change factional affiliations. Note that United Russia was the result of a merger of the Fatherland Party and Unity and that A Just Russia formed in 2006 from the merger of Motherland, the Pensioners' Party, and the Party of Life.

Source: Compiled by author from reports of State Duma.

democratic principles and a social democratic policy in the economy, and has opposed some of the policies pursued by Yeltsin and Putin that have sought to dismantle most of the old state supports and controls in the economy. It is no longer represented in the Duma because it has failed to attract enough votes to clear the 7-percent threshold.

Elections in the early to mid-1990s reflected the polarization between democrats and Communists, but also tended to produce a fragmented field of parties. In the 1993 and 1995 Duma elections, neither pro-democracy parties nor Communists won a clear majority, although democrats were in the minority, while Communists, nationalists, and their allies had a majority of seats. Except for a few parties (the CPRF, the LDPR, and Yabloko), most parties had shallow roots and tended to spring up shortly before elections. Many sought to avoid taking a clear programmatic stance, instead claiming to be "centrists" and pragmatists who would steer between the opposing poles of the democrats and Communists.

Presidential elections have not tended to stimulate party development as much as parliamentary elections have because they have revolved more around the personalities of the candidates. When Boris Yeltsin ran for reelection in 1996, he started out with an approval rating in the single digits (and even considered canceling the election at one point), but he ultimately rallied his strength and succeeded in persuading voters that the election was about a choice between him and a return to Communism. Yeltsin's displays of vigor during the campaign, his lavish promises to voters, and his domination of the media all contributed to a surge in popularity and a victory over Gennadii Ziuganov, his Communist rival (see Table 9.2).[53] The campaign took its toll on Yeltsin, however. Soon afterward he had major heart surgery, and for much of his second term, he was in poor health.

Building the Party of Power The 1999 election was dominated by the question of who would succeed Yeltsin as president. Many federal and regional office-holders wanted to rally around a new "party of power" in order to protect their jobs. A group of backroom Kremlin strategists formed a movement called Unity in the late summer of 1999. They wanted to create an electoral bloc that state officials throughout the country could rally around in the race for the Duma. They also intended it to serve as a political vehicle for

TABLE 9.2

Presidential Election, 1996
Yeltsin edged out the Communist candidate in the first round and then won decisively in the second round.

	First Round (June 16, 1996) (%)	Second Round (July 3, 1996) (%)
Boris Yeltsin	35.2	53.8
Gennadii Ziuganov	32.0	40.3
Alexander Lebed'	14.5	—
Grigorii Yavlinskii	7.3	—
Vladimir Zhirinovsky	5.7	—
Svyatoslav Fedorov	0.9	—
Mikhail Gorbachev	0.5	—
Martin Shakkum	0.3	—
Yurii Vlasov	0.2	—
Vladimir Bryntsalov	0.1	—
Aman Tuleev	0.0	—
Against all candidates	1.5	4.8

Vladimir Putin, whom Yeltsin had just named prime minister and anointed as his successor. Conveniently for Putin, within days of Unity's formation and Putin's appointment, Chechen rebels launched raids into the neighboring region of Dagestan. Bombings of apartment buildings—officially blamed on Chechen terrorists—also occurred in Moscow and other cities. Putin's decisive handling of the military operations against the Chechen guerrillas gave him and the Unity movement a major boost in popularity. Unity, which had not even existed until late August, won 23 percent of the party-list vote in December.

The presidential election of 2000 occurred ahead of schedule due to President Yeltsin's early resignation. Under the constitution, the prime minister automatically succeeds the president if the president leaves office early, but new elections must be held within three months. Accordingly, the presidential election was scheduled for March 26, 2000. The early election gave the front-runner and incumbent, Putin, an advantage because he could capitalize on his popularity and the country's desire for continuity. Putin ran the Russian equivalent of a "rose garden" campaign, preferring to be seen handling the normal daily business of a president, rather than going out on the hustings and asking for people's votes. He counted on

TABLE 9.3

Russian Presidential Elections in the 2000s

Putin and Medvedev won in the first round by wide margins in each race.

	2000	2004	2008
Vladimir Putin	52.9	71.3	—
Gennadii Ziuganov (CPRF)	29.2	—	17.7
Vladimir Zhirinovsky (LDPR)	2.7	—	9.3
Grigorii Yavlinskii (Yabloko)	5.8	—	—
Nikolai Kharitonov (CPRF)	—	13.7	—
Dmitrii Medvedev	—	—	70.2
Andrei Bogdanov (DPR)	—	—	1.3
Other	6.5	10.7	—
Against all candidates	1.8	3.4	—

Legend: CPRF: Communist Party of the Russian Federation; LDPR: Liberal Democratic Party of Russia; DPR: Democratic Party of Russia

Note: The "Against all candidates" option was not available on the 2008 ballot.

the support of officeholders at all levels, a media campaign that presented a "presidential" image to the voters, and the voters' fear that change would only make life worse. His rivals, moreover, were weak. Several prominent politicians prudently chose not to run against him. Putin's strategy worked brilliantly: He won an outright majority in the first round (see Table 9.3).

The 2003 and 2004 Elections Under Putin, the ideological divide between Communists and democrats that had marked the transition era disappeared. The political arena was dominated by the president and his supporters. The loyal pro-Putin party, Unity, was renamed United Russia after it absorbed a rival party, Fatherland (headed by Moscow mayor Yuri Luzhkov). United Russia soon acquired a near-monopoly in the party spectrum, squeezing other parties to the margins. A series of changes in the electoral law made it increasingly difficult for all but a few parties to compete in elections, while the regime mounted a major effort to pressure regional governors and big business to back United Russia.

The Kremlin's success in making United Russia the dominant party was demonstrated vividly in the 2003 parliamentary election. United Russia won 38 percent of the party-list vote and wound up with two-thirds of the seats in the Duma. The Communists suffered a

severe blow, losing almost half their vote share, and the democrats did even worse. For the first time, none of the democratic parties won seats on the party-list vote. The result underscored Putin's drive to eliminate any meaningful political opposition. Such an impressive showing for United Russia assured Putin's reelection as president. The March 2004 race was a landslide. Putin won easily with 71.3 percent of the vote, while his Communist rival received less than 14 percent of the vote (see again Table 9.3). European observers commented that the elections were "well administered" but hardly constituted "a genuine democratic contest," in view of the president's overwhelming control of media coverage of the race and the absence of genuine competition.[54]

United Russia's dominance was confirmed in the 2007 Duma election. Shortly before the election, Putin declared that he would head the party's list (though he said he would not join the party and he did not intend to take his Duma seat).[55] This indicated that Putin intended to use the party as a basis for his power even after he left the presidency. Even though the presidential administration created a second party of power (called A Just Russia) as a mechanism to siphon off some votes on the left side of the spectrum and to offer an alternative outlet for some politicians who could not be accommodated in United Russia, United Russia's overwhelming success was never in doubt, and it went on to win 64.3 percent of the vote. The authorities used a variety of methods to manipulate the election, ranging from grossly unequal access to the media for the parties to outright falsification of results in many regions (in some districts, the reported vote for United Russia was greater than 100 percent of the registered voters).[56]

Similarly, the authorities took no chances in the 2008 presidential election. Again, they violated numerous provisions of the law in order to guarantee the desired outcome—for example, by disqualifying potentially serious opposition candidates, pouring large resources from the state budget into Medvedev's campaign, giving Medvedev disproportionate media coverage, and ignoring challenges brought by opposition groups and election-rights NGOs over violations of the election law. Medvedev would probably have won in any case, but the large-scale manipulation of the election signaled to voters and opponents alike that the authorities were in complete control of the succession. The authorities managed the outcome so successfully that Medvedev officially won over 70 percent

Vladimir Putin Addresses the State Duma

Recent elections to the Duma have been manipulated by Russian authorities in order to eliminate meaningful political opposition.

Natalia Kolesnikova/AFP/Getty Images

of the vote—about 1 percentage point below Putin's reported margin in 2004 (see again Table 9.3).

The establishment of the dominant party regime has changed the way parties represent different social groups. In the 1990s, there were some systematic links between particular social groups and particular parties. For instance, younger and better-educated voters tended to support the democratic parties, while older and less-educated voters supported Communist and nationalist parties. But as the United Russia party has gained dominance, it has appealed to all parts of the society. As a result, social structure has become less and less significant as an influence on voting, while voters' attitudes toward the authorities in general and toward Putin in particular have become the most important predictor of voting preferences.

Table 9.4 indicates that United Russia draws its support broadly from all parts of society, although it draws more support from women than from men and from among older voters than youth. It is strongly identified in the public mind with Putin (note that 21 percent of those who do not have confidence in Putin voted for the Communists). The challenge for United Russia in the future will be to establish a basis of support that goes beyond simply its identification with Putin. Putin and other officials have warned the party that it cannot hope to stay on the Kremlin's life-support system forever—though they are unwilling to cut it loose.

For other parties, the 2007 and 2008 elections confirmed the new reality that United Russia is likely to enjoy a dominant position for years to come. Other parties have been relegated to playing a small, marginal role in national politics and concentrating their efforts on winning seats in regional parliaments.

THE POLITICS OF ECONOMIC REFORM

The Dual Transition

Russia's post-Communist transition was wrenching because the country had to remake both its *political* and its *economic* institutions following the end of Communism. The move to a market economy created opportunities for some—and hardships for many more. Democratization opened the political system to the influence of groups that could organize to press for exclusive economic benefits for themselves. Many people who had modest but secure livelihoods under the Soviet regime were ruined by inflation and unemployment when the planned economy broke down. A smaller number took advantage of opportunities for entrepreneurship or exploited their connections with government to amass sizeable fortunes. One reason Vladimir Putin was so popular was that people gave him credit for restoring growth and prosperity to the economy and cracking down on some of the tycoons who had amassed great fortunes by dubious means.

TABLE 9.4

Social Support for Parliamentary Parties, Duma Elections, 2007

United Russia draws evenly from most sections of the population, but its support from women is substantially stronger than from among men.

	Total sample	UR	CPRF	SR	LDPR	APR	SPS	Yabloko	Other party or cast invalid ballot	Hard to say, do not remember	Did not vote
As share of sample	100	41	7	5	5	1	1	1	0	4	39
Sex:											
Male	46	33	8	3	7	1	1	1	0	4	46
Female	54	48	6	6	3	1	1	0	0	3	35
Age:											
18–35 years old	37	36	2	2	7	1	0	0	0	3	52
36–54 years old	36	40	7	6	4	1	1	1	0	4	40
55 or older	28	49	13	8	2	1	1	1	1	4	24
Education:											
Less than secondary education	12	50	7	4	3	1	0	0	0	2	35
Complete secondary education	35	38	6	4	6	1	0	0	0	4	45
Specialized secondary education	35	41	6	5	4	1	1	1	0	4	41
Higher education	18	40	9	7	5	1	1	2	1	4	34
Income:											
Less than 2,500 rubles/month	16	44	7	4	6	0	0	0	1	3	38
2,501–4,500 rubles	29	48	8	6	4	1	0	0	0	4	33
Greater than 4,500 rubles	26	39	6	5	4	1	1	1	2	2	41
Residence:											
Moscow	8	28	7	6	3	1	3	2	0	4	50
Other megapolis	12	38	6	7	5	1	0	1	0	1	42
Large city	16	36	6	6	5	1	0	0	0	3	46
Small city	38	41	7	4	5	1	1	0	0	4	41
Village	26	49	7	4	4	1	0	0	0	4	35
Trust Putin:											
Fully	68	51	4	4	3	1	0	0	0	3	37
Partly	21	23	12	7	8	0	1	1	1	5	47
Do not trust	8	3	21	5	10	2	2	2	2	3	53

Note: Read figures across rows. For instance, men comprised 46% of the sample. 33% of men voted for United Russia; 8% voted for the Communist Party of the Russian Federation; 46% did not vote.

Legend:
UR: United Russia
CPRF: Communist Party of the Russian Federation
SR: A Just Russia
LDPR: Liberal Democratic Party of Russia
APR: Agrarian Party of Russia
SPS: League of Right Forces
Source: Figures taken from Web site of Fond "Obshchestvennogo mneniia." Published December 13, 2010. Survey conducted immediately after Duma election, n = 1,500.
http://bd.fom.ru/report/map/d074922.
Accessed June 29, 2010.

Stabilization Russia pursued two major sets of economic reforms in the early 1990s: macroeconomic stabilization and privatization. Stabilization, which in Russia came to be called **shock therapy**, is a program intended to stop a country's financial meltdown. This required a painful dose of fiscal and monetary discipline by slashing government spending and squeezing the money supply. Structural reform of this kind always lowers the standard of living for some groups of the population in the short run.

Initially, many expected that the greatest enemies of stabilization would be persons whose living standards suffered as a result of the higher prices and lower incomes, such as pensioners and workers in state enterprises. In practice, however, those who benefited from the early steps to open the economy and privatize state assets proved to be the greatest obstacles to further reform because they exploited their privileged access to the authorities to lock in their own gains and to oppose any subsequent measures to expand competition. Among these were officials who acquired ownership rights to monopoly enterprises and then worked to shut out potential competitors from their markets, state officials who benefited from collecting "fees" to issue licenses to importers and exporters or permits for doing business, and entrepreneurs whose firms dominated the market in their industry.[57] A fully competitive market system, with a level playing field for all players, would have posed a threat to their ability to profit from their privileged positions.

From Communism to Capitalism Communist systems differed from other authoritarian regimes in ways that made their economic transitions more difficult. This was particularly true for the Soviet Union and its successor states. For one, the economic growth model followed by Stalin and his successors concentrated much production in large enterprises. This meant that many local governments were entirely dependent on the economic health of a single employer. The heavy commitment of resources to military production in the Soviet Union further complicated the task of reform in Russia, as does the country's vast size. Rebuilding the decaying infrastructure of a country as large as Russia is staggeringly expensive.

The economic stabilization program began on January 2, 1992, when the government abolished most controls on prices, raised taxes, and cut government spending sharply. Almost immediately, opposition to the new program began to form. Economists and politicians took sides. The shock-therapy program was an easy target for criticism, even though there was no consensus among critics about what the alternative should be. It became commonplace to say that the program was "all shock and no therapy."

By cutting government spending, letting prices rise, and raising taxes, the stabilization program sought to create incentives for producers to increase output and find new niches in the marketplaces. But Russian producers did not initially respond by raising productivity. As a result, society suffered from a sharp, sudden loss in purchasing power. People went hungry, bank savings vanished, and the economy fell into a protracted slump. Firms that were politically connected were able to survive by winning cheap credits and production orders from the government, which dampened any incentive for improving productivity. Desperate to raise operating revenues, the government borrowed heavily from the International Monetary Fund (IMF) and issued treasury bonds at ruinously high interest rates. IMF loans came with strings attached—the government pledged to cut spending further and step up tax collections as a condition of accepting IMF assistance, which fueled the depression further. Communists and nationalists got a rise out of audiences by depicting the government as the puppet of a malevolent, imperialist West.

Privatization Stabilization was followed shortly afterward by the mass **privatization** of state firms. In contrast to the shock-therapy program, privatization enjoyed considerable public support, at least at first. Privatization transfers legal title of state firms to private owners. Under the right conditions, private ownership of productive assets is usually more efficient for society as a whole than is state ownership because in a competitive environment, owners are motivated by an incentive to maximize their property's ability to produce a return. Under the privatization program, every Russian citizen received a voucher with a face value of 10,000 rubles (around $30 at the time). People were free to buy and sell vouchers, but they could be used only to acquire shares of stock in privatized enterprises or shares of mutual funds investing in privatized enterprises. The program sought to ensure that everyone became a property owner instantly. Politically, the program aimed to build support for the economic reforms by giving citizens a stake in the outcome of the market transition. Economically, the government hoped that privatization would eventually spur increases in productivity by creating meaningful property rights. Beginning in October 1992, the program distributed 148 million privatization vouchers to citizens. By June 30, 1994, when the program ended, 140 million vouchers had been exchanged for stock out of the 148 million originally distributed. Some 40 million citizens were, in theory, share owners. But these shares were often of no value because they paid no dividends and shareholders exercised no voting rights in the companies.

The next phase of privatization auctioned off most remaining shares of state enterprises for cash. This phase was marked by a series of scandalous sweetheart deals in which banks owned by a small number of Russia's wealthiest tycoons wound up with title to some of Russia's most lucrative oil, gas, and metallurgy firms for bargain-basement prices. The most notorious of these arrangements became known as the **loans for shares** scheme. It was devised in 1995 by a small group of business magnates with strong connections to government, who persuaded Yeltsin to auction off management rights to controlling packages of shares in several major state-owned companies in return for loans to the government. If the government failed to repay the loans in a year's time, the shares would revert to the banks that made the loans. The government, as expected, defaulted on the loans, letting a small number of oligarchs acquire ownership of some of Russia's most valuable companies.[58]

Consequences of Privatization On paper, privatization was a huge success. By 1996, privatized firms produced about 90 percent of industrial output, and about two-thirds of all large and medium-sized enterprises had been privatized.[59] In fact, however, the actual transfer of ownership rights was far less impressive than it appeared. For one thing, the dominant pattern was for managers to acquire large shareholdings of the firms they ran. As a result, management of many firms did not change. Moreover, many nominally private firms continued to be closely tied to state support, such as cheap state-subsidized loans and credits.[60]

The program allowed a great many unscrupulous wheeler-dealers to prey on the public through a variety of financial schemes. Some investment funds promised truly incredible rates of return. Many people lost their savings by investing in funds that went bankrupt or turned out to be simple pyramid schemes. The Russian government lacked the capacity to protect the investors. Privatization was carried out before the institutional framework of a market economy was in place. Markets for stocks, bonds, and commodities were small in scale and weakly regulated. The legal foundation for a market economy has gradually emerged, but only after much of the economy was already privatized. For much of the 1990s, the lack of liquidity in the economy meant that enterprises failed to pay their wages and taxes on time, trading with one another using barter.

The government fell into an unsustainable debt trap. Unable to meet its obligations, it grew increasingly dependent on loans. As lenders became ever more certain that the government could not make good on its obligations, they demanded ever higher interest rates, deepening the trap. Ultimately, the bubble burst. In August 1998, the government declared a moratorium on its debts and let the ruble's value collapse against the dollar. Overnight, the ruble lost two-thirds of its value and credit dried up.[61] The government bonds held by investors were almost worthless. The effects of the crash rippled through the economy. The sharp devaluation of the ruble made exports more competitive and gave an impetus to domestic producers, but also significantly lowered people's living standards.

As Table 9.5 shows, economic output in Russia fell for a decade before beginning to recover in 1999. The recovery was not due to a structural reform of the economy. There has not been a substantial overhaul of the banking system or of the way industry is managed. As a result, the economy was particularly vulnerable to a worldwide financial and economic crisis because it remained dependent on exports of natural resources: Oil and gas make up a quarter of Russian GDP. The rise in the world prices for oil and gas in the 2000s and the sharp drop in the value of the ruble brought a decade of steady growth from 1999 to 2008. As the economy revived, enterprises were able to pay off arrears in back wages and taxes. In turn, these taxes allowed government to meet its own obligations, thereby allowing consumer demand for industry's products to rise, and so on. Living standards rose for all sections of the population and in most parts of the country.

The leaders have expressed satisfaction with the favorable trends in the economy, but warn that they

TABLE 9.5

Russian Annual GDP Growth and Price Inflation Rates, 1991–2009
Russia enjoyed sustained growth for most of the 2000s, after a dismal decade in the 1990s, but 2009 saw a sharp contraction.

	1991	1992	1993	1994	1995	1996	1997	1998	1999	2000	2001	2002	2003	2004	2005	2006	2007	2008	2009
GDP	−5	−14.5	−8.7	−12.6	−4.3	−6	0.4	−11.6	3.2	7.6	5	4	7.3	7.1	6.4	7.4	8.1	5.6	−7.9
Inflation	138	2323	844	202	131	21.8	11	84.4	36.5	20.2	18.6	15.1	12	11.7	10.9	9	11.9	13.3	8.8

Note: GDP is measured in constant market prices. Inflation is measured as the percentage change in the consumer price index from December of one year to December of the next.

Source: Press reports of Russian State Statistical Service (www.gks.ru).

are not sufficient to achieve sustained and balanced development. Both Putin and Medvedev have called for reducing the economy's reliance on natural resource exports and increasing its capacity for innovation. Medvedev has called for a large-scale program of modernization of the economy, one feature of which is a massive state-funded effort to create a Russian version of "Silicon Valley" outside Moscow— a city devoted to high-tech research and development and innovative start-up firms. He has attempted to interest Russian and international investors in the project. Whether it will have the intended transformative effect on the economy remains to be seen.

Social Conditions Living standards fell sharply during the 1990s. A small minority became wealthy, and some households improved their lot modestly. Most people, however, suffered a net decline in living standards as a result of unemployment, lagging income, and nonpayment of wages and pensions.

Income inequality grew sharply both during the period of economic decline in the 1990s and again during the period of economic recovery in the 2000s. This has been caused by many factors. In the 1990s, it was the result of the lag of wage increases behind price inflation, the sharp rise in unemployment, the deterioration of the pension and other social assistance systems, and the concentration of vast wealth in the hands of a small number of people. In the 2000s, poverty has decreased significantly, along with unemployment, and pension levels have risen. Yet inequality continues to rise as a result of large disparities in wage levels (two workers in the same occupation and in the same region might have widely different wages, depending on where they work); the extremely high earnings of managers in industries such as energy and finance; and the Putin regime's shift to a flat (13-percent)

income tax and abolition of estate taxes. As a result of both government policy and current economic trends, therefore, economic prosperity is benefiting those at the upper end of the income distribution much more than it is those at the lower end. This helps explain the sharp rise in the number of Russian billionaires. According to *Forbes* magazine's list, the number of billionaires in Russia shot up from 60 to 110 between 2007 and 2008.[62] But the financial crisis hit them hard; on average, they lost something like half their wealth in the 2008 financial crash.[63]

One commonly used measure of inequality is the Gini index, which is an aggregate measure of the total deviation from perfect equality in the distribution of wealth or income. In Russia, the Gini index nearly doubled during the early 1990s, rising from 26 in 1987 through 1990 to 48 in 1993 and 1994. Inequality in Russia was higher than in any other post-Communist country except for Kyrgyzstan.[64] As the economy began to recover and poverty fell, the Gini index declined slightly, to just under 40, before creeping back up in the late 2000s to over 42 (close to the level of income inequality in the United States). In 2009, the richest tenth of the population in Russia received over sixteen times as much income as did the poorest tenth, up from fourteen times in 2002. The actual level of income inequality is probably considerably greater than the official figure because of the large scale of unreported, "off-book" income due to tax evasion.

The continuing rise in inequality and the absence of a growing middle class constitute a matter of some concern to Russian leaders. In his address to the State Council on February 8, 2008, President Putin declared that the current level of income inequality was "absolutely unacceptable" and should be reduced to more moderate levels; he called for measures that would bring about an expansion of the middle class.

Its share of the population, he declared, should reach 60 or even 70 percent by 2020.[65]

An especially disturbing dimension of the social effects of transition has been the erosion of public health. Although public health had deteriorated in the late Communist period, the decline worsened after the regime changed. Mortality rates have risen sharply, especially among males. Life expectancy for males in Russia is at a level comparable to that in poor and developing countries. At present, life expectancy at birth for males is just over sixty-two years and for females seventy-four years. The disparity between male and female mortality is generally attributed to the higher rates of abuse of alcohol and tobacco among men. Other demographic indicators are equally grim. Prime Minister Fradkov told a Cabinet meeting in July 2006 that only 30 percent of newborn children "can be described as healthy" and that "there are more than 500,000 disabled children in need of various forms of treatment, and also some 730,000 orphans or abandoned children."[66] Rates of incidence of HIV and other infectious diseases, murders, suicides, drug addiction, and alcoholism are rising.

Russia's leaders consider the demographic crisis to pose a grave threat to the country's national security, both because of the growing shortage of labor in some regions (experts believe that there are 8 to 10 million illegal immigrants in Russia) and because of the army's inability to recruit enough healthy young men. On average, each year Russia's population declines by about three-quarters of a million people due to the excess of deaths over births. Demographers estimate that Russia's population could fall by over one-third by 2050. In his 2006 message to parliament, President Putin called for a series of measures to raise birthrates, reduce mortality, and stimulate immigration.

Setting the country on a path of self-sustaining economic growth, where workers and investors are confident in their legal rights, requires a complete overhaul of the relationship of the state to the economy. The Soviet state used central planning to direct enterprises on what to produce and how to use resources. Much of the economy was geared to heavy industry and defense production, and government ministries directly administered each branch of the economy. The post-Communist state must have an entirely different relationship to the economy in order to stimulate growth. It must set clear rules for economic activity, regulate markets, enforce the law, supply public goods and services, and promote competition. Shifting the structure of the state bureaucracy and the attitudes of state officials has been a Herculean task.

We can get some idea of the legacy of the Communist system in the way the state was intertwined with the economy by looking at the structure of the state budget. Figure 9.7 shows the breakdown of spending for the 2010 federal budget. Total spending was set at 8.8 trillion rubles, or about $282 billion. The share spent on national defense (at 8 percent) probably understates the actual amount, although it is equaled by spending on national security and law enforcement. The shares of spending on general administration (12 percent) and subsidies to various federal and regional funds (42 percent) are high, compared with other countries, and indicate how substantial the central government's role is in state and society. The share of spending on social welfare—most of which goes for pensions—at 3.7 percent is low by comparative standards.

The government also recognizes that the oil- and gas-fueled budget surpluses pose a serious danger of creating inflationary pressures in the economy. For this reason, like some other oil-rich states, Russia has created a "stabilization fund" that removes some of the revenues generated by high world energy prices from circulation and uses them to pay off external debt. In 2007, the government divided the stabilization fund into two portions, one called the *reserve fund*, to be used in the event of a serious fall in government revenues, and the other called a *national welfare fund*, to be used mainly to shore up the pension system. These funds became crucial in enabling Russia's government to cover its deficits as its revenues dropped and its social-spending obligations rose when the 2008 financial crisis struck. The government drew down both heavily in order to increase spending on pensions and unemployment benefits.

TOWARD THE RULE OF LAW?

The Law-Governed State

One of the most important goals of Gorbachev's reforms was to make the Soviet Union a **law-governed state (*pravovoe gosudarstvo*)**, rather than one in which state bodies and the Communist Party exercised power arbitrarily. Since 1991, the Russian leaders have asserted that the state must respect the primacy of law over politics—even when they took actions grossly violating the constitution. The difficulty in placing law above politics

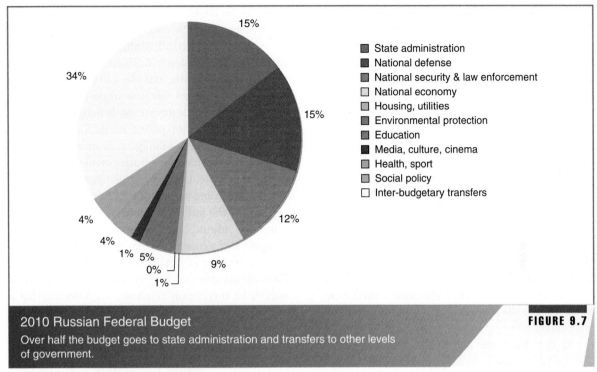

2010 Russian Federal Budget
Over half the budget goes to state administration and transfers to other levels of government.

FIGURE 9.7

Source: Russian Ministry of Finance, www.minfin.ru.

testifies to the lingering legacy of the old regime's abuse of the legal system. Presidents Putin and Medvedev have repeatedly declared their commitment to the principle of the rule of law, even when their actions have flagrantly infringed on the independence of the judiciary.

The struggle for the rule of law began well before Gorbachev. After Stalin died, his successors ended mass terror and took significant steps to reduce the use of law for political repression. Still, throughout the late Soviet era, the Communist Party and the KGB often used legal procedures to give the mantle of legal legitimacy to acts of political repression. Although the prosecution of political dissidents has ended, the use of the legal system for political purposes by state authorities continues. Reforms in the 1990s took some steps toward making the judiciary independent of the authorities, but in the 2000s, political control over the legal system has increased.

Obstacles to the Rule of Law

Movement toward the rule of law continues to be hampered by the abuse of legal institutions by the political authorities and by endemic corruption in state and society.

In the post-Soviet state, the security police continue to operate autonomously. In the Soviet period, the agency with principal responsibility for maintaining domestic security was the KGB (State Security Committee). The KGB exercised wide powers, including responsibility for both domestic and foreign intelligence. Since 1991, its functions have been split up among several agencies. The main domestic security agency is the FSB. Although the structure and mission of the security agencies have changed, they have never undergone a thorough purge of personnel. No member of or collaborator with the Soviet-era security services has been prosecuted for violating citizens' rights. There has been no review of officials' records for past collaboration with the secret police. This is one of several ways in which post-Soviet Russia has still not put its Communist past behind it.

The security police are regarded as one of the more professionally competent and uncorrupted state agencies. However, despite being assigned new tasks, such as fighting international narcotics trafficking and terrorism, they still demonstrate a Soviet-style preoccupation with policing the country's political life. For example, they have proposed legislation giving them broad powers to shut down Internet providers and media outlets for publishing "extremist" content. Many Soviet-era police practices have been revived.

President Putin also resumed the Soviet-era practice of using the legal system to suppress potential political opposition. An example is the series of legal maneuvers taken against the owners of independent media in the early 2000s. These included police harassment and criminal prosecution, as well as civil actions such as bankruptcy proceedings. For example, the owners of two television companies were forced to divest themselves of their media holdings and transfer ownership to companies loyal to the administration. As a result, Russia's two relatively autonomous national television companies lost their political independence, one respected liberal newspaper was shut down, and the entire media establishment was sent a strong signal that it would be wise to avoid crossing the current administration. Today, only a small number of print media have retained a measure of political independence.[67]

In the 1990s, the bankruptcy laws were often used by businesses to drive rivals into bankruptcy in order to take them over; today, state companies use civil and criminal laws for the same purpose—to force a private company to sell out at a bargain price so that it can then be taken over and its assets stripped. These forced hostile takeovers are called *reiderstvo* (raiding).

Corruption Another obstacle to the rule of law is endemic corruption. Corruption increased substantially after the Soviet period. It is widespread both in everyday life and in dealings with the state. A survey in May 2010 found that 55 percent of respondents agreed with the statement that "everyone who deals with officials gives bribes," although 79 percent of the respondents had not paid a bribe themselves in the last twelve months.[68] Transparency International's Corruption Perceptions Index ranks Russia 146th out of 190 countries in the pervasiveness of corruption (1st means the least corrupt country; 190th is the most corrupt). Experts estimate that the total volume of corrupt transactions in the economy exceeds the total value of the state budget.[69] Law-enforcement (especially the traffic police), health-care, education, and government-registration offices are considered the worst offenders.

President Medvedev has declared fighting corruption to be a top priority of his administration, forcing officials to publish declarations of their income and property. So far, however, most observers believe that his drive has had little effect in reducing corruption.

Corruption is hardly unique to Russia or to the former Communist world. However, it is especially widespread in Russia and the other former Soviet states. Corruption on this scale imposes a severe drag on economic development, both because it diverts resources away from public needs and because it undermines people's willingness to invest in productive activity.[70] Moreover, much corruption is tied to organized crime, which bribes government officials for protection and drives out legal businesses. The corruption of the police and courts ensures that many crimes go unpunished and forces legal businesses to compete in the corruption market with illegal ones.

Corruption in Russia has deep roots, and many Russians assume that it is ineradicable. Comparative studies of corruption demonstrate, however, that a culture of corruption can be changed by changing the expectations of the public and the government.[71] The key is for the political leadership to make a serious effort to combat corruption and to back up this commitment with institutional reform and sustained attention to the problem.

Since the early 1990s, there have been a number of reforms, such as the adoption of trial by jury and the creation of the Constitutional Court, that have the potential to strengthen the judiciary's independence from both political pressure and corruption. However, the authorities' habitual use of the procuracy and the courts for political purposes and the powerfully corrosive effect of corruption continue to subvert the integrity of the legal system. In the long run, movement toward the rule of law will require that power be sufficiently dispersed among groups and organizations in the state and society so that neither private nor state interests are powerful enough to subordinate the law to their own purposes.

RUSSIA AND THE INTERNATIONAL COMMUNITY

Russia's thousand-year history of expansion, war, and state domination of society has left behind a legacy of autocratic rule and a preoccupation with defending national borders. The collapse of the Soviet regime required Russia to rebuild its political institutions, economic system, national identity, and relations with the

Chechnia's Leader Kadyrov Giving an Address

Ramzan Kadyrov, president of Chechnia, has been credited for bringing some stability to the region but has also been accused of human-rights violations.

RIA Novosti/TopFoto/The Image Works

outside world. During the Soviet period, state propaganda used the image of an international struggle between capitalism and socialism to justify its repressive control over society and its enormous military establishment. Now the country's leaders recognize that only through strong ties with the world economy can Russia hope to prosper. Yet they also want to maintain strong controls over the political system in order to preserve stability and prevent threats to their power.

Gorbachev, Yeltsin, Putin, and Medvedev all asserted that the integration of Russia into the community of developed democracies is strategically important for Russia. Gorbachev was willing to allow Communist regimes to fall throughout Eastern Europe for the sake of improved relations with the West. Yeltsin accepted the admission of East European states into NATO as a necessary condition for close relations with the United States and Europe. Putin repeatedly emphasized that he regarded Russia's admission to the WTO as critical for Russia's long-term economic success. Following the September 11, 2001, terrorist attacks on the United States, Putin immediately telephoned U.S. president George W. Bush to offer his support. Putin clearly saw an advantage for Russia in aligning itself with the United States against Islamic terrorism, which it identified as an immediate threat to its own security. Putin cited Russia's own war in Chechnia as part of the global struggle against Islamist terrorists.

At the same time, Russia has not accepted the constraints of international law. It has expanded its military presence in several former Soviet republics, pressuring them to become satellites of Russia. In August 2008, it launched a well-prepared military invasion of independent, pro-Western Georgia after Georgia attempted to use force to take back control over a Russia-backed breakaway region, South Ossetia. The overwhelming Russian response was clearly intended to subjugate Georgia to Russia's interest in preserving a buffer of subordinate states in the territory of the former Soviet Union.

Likewise, in its brutal military campaigns in Chechnia from 1994 to 1996 and then again from 1999 to 2006, Russia refused to allow international human-rights organizations to monitor Russian practices, which included mass bombardment of civilian areas. In 2007, Russia resumed the Cold War–era practice of sending its strategic bombers on long-distance missions over the Atlantic, Pacific, and Arctic oceans to demonstrate the global reach of its military power. As its economic and military power has revived, Russia has attempted to establish itself as a counterweight to American power and to rebuild Russian influence in the former Soviet region.

Russia's quasi-imperial behavior in parts of the former Soviet Union and its refusal to be bound by democratic principles have kept it from becoming fully integrated into the international community. Yet it is far more open than it was under Soviet rule, and its leaders recognize that they cannot retreat into isolation and autarky. They are also aware of the grave vulnerabilities Russia faces—its declining population, aging infrastructure, dependence on immigrant labor, and overreliance on natural resources for state revenues. Thus, while they seek to be a hegemonic power in the territory of the former Soviet Union, they also do not want to resurrect Russia's role as the United States' enemy in the bipolar world; they would prefer that Russia be one of several major powers in a multipolar world.

Russia's vast territory, weak government capacity, and tradition of state domination over society make it likely that the primary objective of its leaders for the foreseeable future will be to strengthen the state, in both its internal and its international dimensions. The end of the Communist regime and the dissolution of the Soviet Union damaged the state's capacity to enforce the laws, protect its citizens, and provide basic social services. Favorable economic conditions in the 2000s enabled the state to rebuild its power at home and abroad, but the crisis of 2008 and 2009 revealed Russia's susceptibility to trends in international financial and energy markets. In the long run, self-sustaining economic development will require the rule of law and effective institutions for articulating and aggregating social interests. The viability of Russia's post-Communist state will ultimately depend on how responsive and adaptive its institutions are to the demands of Russia's citizens in a globalized and interdependent world.

REVIEW QUESTIONS

- What is the formal relationship between president and prime minister in Russia? What determines the actual powers wielded by each?

- What effects did the constitutional struggles of 1992 and 1993 have on the features of the 1993 constitution?

- How did President Putin go about strengthening the power of the central government vis-à-vis regional governments? What were his reasons for shifting the balance of power in this way?

- What are the main similarities and differences between the channels of elite recruitment under the Soviet system and today?

- Most Russians evaluate the pre-Gorbachev Soviet system favorably, yet would prefer not to bring it back. How would you explain this apparent contradiction?

- Why has United Russia been so successful as a "party of power"?

- What are the main obstacles to the rule of law in Russia? What changes in the political system would be required to overcome them?

KEY TERMS

Chechnia
commercial courts (*arbitrazhnye sudy*)
Communist Party of the Russian Federation (CPRF)
Constitutional Court
Federation Council
Federation of Independent Trade Unions of Russia (FITUR)
glasnost'
Gorbachev, Mikhail
law-governed state (*pravovoe gosudarstvo*)
League of Committees of Soldiers' Mothers
Lenin, Vladimir Ilyich
Liberal Democratic Party of Russia (LDPR)
loans for shares
Medvedev, Dmitrii Anatol'evich
nomenklatura
oligarchs
party of power
perestroika
presidential decrees
privatization
procuracy
Public Chamber
Russian Union of Industrialists and Entrepreneurs (RUIE)
Security Council
shock therapy
Stalin, Joseph
State Council
State Duma
United Russia

SUGGESTED READINGS

Aslund, Anders. *Russia's Capitalist Revolution: Why Market Reform Succeeded and Democracy Failed.* Washington, D.C.: Peterson Institute for International Economics, 2007.

Baker, Peter, and Susan Glasser. *Kremlin Rising: Vladimir Putin's Russia and the End of Revolution.* New York: Scribner, 2005.

Breslauer, George W. *Gorbachev and Yeltsin as Leaders.* Cambridge: Cambridge University Press, 2002.

Colton, Timothy J. *Yeltsin: A Life.* New York: Basic Books, 2008.

Fish, M. Stephen. *Democracy Derailed in Russia: The Failure of Open Politics.* Cambridge: Cambridge University Press, 2005.

Hale, Henry. *Why Not Parties in Russia? Democracy, Federalism, and the State.* Cambridge: Cambridge University Press, 2006.

Hellman, Joel S. "Winners Take All: The Politics of Partial Reform in Postcommunist Transitions," *World Politics* 50, no. 1 (1998): 203–34.

Hill, Fiona, and Clifford Gaddy. *The Siberian Curse: How Communist Planners Left Russia Out in the Cold.* Washington, D.C.: Brookings Institution, 2003.

McFaul, Michael. *Russia's Unfinished Revolution: Political Change from Gorbachev to Putin.* Ithaca, NY: Cornell University Press, 2001.

Rose, Richard, William Mishler, and Neil Munro. *Russia Transformed: Developing Popular Support for a New Regime.* Cambridge: Cambridge University Press, 2006.

Sakwa, Richard. *Putin: Russia's Choice.* London: Routledge, 2004.

Shleifer, Andrei, and Daniel Treisman. *Without a Map: Political Tactics and Economic Reform in Russia.* Cambridge: Massachusetts Institute of Technology Press, 2000.

INTERNET RESOURCES

The main institutions of the federal government—the president, the parliament, and the government: **www.gov.ru/index.html** (most of the content accessible through this site is in Russian, but some resources are in English).

An e-mail newsletter containing news stories and commentary: **www.cdi.org/russia/johnson**.

A wide range of political resources: **www.politicalresources.net/russia.htm**.

The University of Pittsburgh's links to resources on Russia: **www.ucis.pitt.edu/reesweb**.

A joint Internet project by a team of Russians and Americans: **www.friends-partners.org**.

The *Moscow Times* is an English-language daily newspaper primarily for expatriates: **www.themoscowtimes.com**.

The University of Strathclyde's Center for the Study of Public Policy provides public opinion and electoral information from Russia: **www.RussiaVotes.org**.

ENDNOTES

1. Hale, Henry E. "Regime Cycles: Democracy, Autocracy, and Revolution in Post-Soviet Eurasia," *World Politics* 58 (2005): 133–65.

2. Viktor Khamraev, "U rossiian rastut simpatii k prezidentu," *Kommersant*, June 1, 2010.

3. President Dmitrii Medvedev, "Rossiia, vpered! [Go, Russia!]," as published on the presidential Web site, http://kremlin.ru, on September 10, 2009.

4. UN Development Programme, Russia, *National Human Development Report, Russian Federation 2006/2007: Russia's Regions: Goals, Challenges, Achievements* (Moscow: United Nations Development Programme, 2007), 8.

5. Richard Pipes, *Russia Under the Old Regime*, 2nd ed. (New York: Penguin Books, 1995).

6. Archie Brown, *The Gorbachev Factor* (New York: Oxford University Press, 1996).

7. In 2008, the constitution was amended at President Medvedev's request to extend the president's term of office from four years to six, and that of the Duma from four years to five. Both amendments only take effect after the 2011 and 2012 election cycle. These are the only amendments to have been made so far to the constitution.

8. Before 2007, the Duma comprised two sets of members, 225 elected in single-member districts and 225 elected from party lists using a 5-percent threshold. Most observers agreed that purpose of eliminating single-member district seats was to weaken the influence of local interests on Duma deputies, further centralizing power in the executive.

9. On nationality policy in the Soviet Union, see Terry Martin, *The Affirmative Action Empire: Nations and Nationalism in the Soviet Union, 1923–1939* (Ithaca, NY: Cornell University Press, 2001).

10. J. Paul Goode, "The Push for Regional Enlargement in Putin's Russia," *Post-Soviet Affairs* 20, no. 3 (July–September 2004): 219–57.

11. Recently, President Medvedev created an eighth federal district to deal specifically with the problems of the North Caucasus region.

12. Timothy J. Colton, *Yeltsin: A Life* (New York: Basic Books, 2008).

13. From a survey conducted by the widely respected Levada Center in June 2005.

14. Brian Whitmore, "RFE/RL Poll Finds Russians Skeptical about Elections, Hopeful for Future," *RFE/RL Newsline,* November 16, 2007.

15. L. D. Gudkov, B. V. Dubin, and Yu A. Levada, *Problema v segodniashnei Rossii: Razmyshleniia nad rezul'tatami sotsiologicheskogo issledovaniia* (Moscow: Fond Liberal'naia missiia, 2007), 136.

16. Whitmore, "RFE/RL Poll"; *RFE/RL Newsline,* March 14, 2008.

17. Levada.ru, May 26, 2010, www.levada.ru/press/2010052618. html.

18. Reported in Polit.ru, December 10, 2007; full report in BBC World Service Poll, "World Divided on Press Freedom," www.globescan.com/news_archives/bbc75. Thirteen other countries from the developed and developing worlds were surveyed.

19. *RFE/RL Newsline,* December 28, 2007.

20. Retrieved January 11, 2008, from Polit.ru.

21. *Nezavisimaia gazeta,* June 11, 2008.

22. Anastasiia Bashkatova, "Ekonomicheskie ministry pochemu-to ne vyzyvaiut doveriia," *Nezavisimaia gazeta,* June 10, 2010.

23. Levada Center, www.levada.ru/press/2008020800.html.

24. Polit.ru, June 25, 2010. Interestingly, those most likely to report that they feel protected from arbitrary treatment are women, individuals with lower educational levels, and those with low incomes.

25. *RFE/RL Newsline,* March 31, 2008.

26. *RFE/RL Newsline,* September 18, 2007.

27. *RFE/RL Newsline,* October 3, 2007.

28. Elena Lisovskaya and Vyacheslav Karpov, "New Ideologies in Postcommunist Russian Textbooks," *Comparative Education Review* 43, no. 4 (1999): 522–32.

29. "Shkol'niki Rossii predpochli izuchat' svetskuiu etiku," *Vedomosti,* February 24, 2010; Polit.ru, March 26, 2010.

30. On television, see Ellen Mickiewicz, *Television, Power, and the Public in Russia* (Cambridge: Cambridge University Press, 2008); on the regime's media policies more generally, see Sarah Oates, "The Neo-Soviet Model of the Media," *Europe-Asia Studies* 59, no. 8 (2007): 1279–97; on the Internet, see Marcus Alexander, "The Internet and Democratization: The Development of Russian Internet Policy," *Demokratizatsiiya* 12 (2004): 607–27.

31. Robert D. Putnam, *Making Democracy Work: Civic Traditions in Modern Italy* (Princeton, NJ: Princeton University Press, 1993).

32. Marc Morje Howard, *The Weakness of Civil Society in Post-Communist Europe* (Cambridge: Cambridge University Press, 2003).

33. Richard Rose and Neil Munro, *Elections Without Order: Russia's Challenge to Vladimir Putin* (Cambridge: Cambridge University Press, 2002), 224–25; Richard Rose, *Getting Things Done with Social Capital: New Russia Barometer VII* (Glasgow: Center for the Study of Public Policy, University of Strathclyde, 1998), 32–33.

34. Emil' Pain, "Ot vlasti avtoriteta k vlasti normy," *Nezavisimaia gazeta,* May 20, 2008.

35. Rose, *Getting Things Done.*

36. Turnout for the 2008 presidential election was reportedly 69.8 percent. In the United States, turnout of the voting-age population for the presidential election in 2008 was 56.8 percent.

37. A reform sponsored by President Putin and the United Russia Party has moved to eliminate the "Against all" option from future elections. Although the goal is to force voters to support one of the given parties, many observers—including the chairman of the Central Election Commission—warn that this change will reduce electoral turnout.

38. Eugene Huskey, *Nomenklatura Lite? The Cadres Reserve (Kadrovyi reserv) in Russian Public Administration* (NCEEER Working Paper) (Washington, D.C.: National Council for Eurasian and East European Research, 2003).

39. Olga Kryshtanovskaya and Stephen White, "Putin's Militocracy," *Post-Soviet Affairs* 19, no. 4 (2003): 289–306.

40. Jane I. Dawson, *Eco-Nationalism: Anti-Nuclear Activism and National Identity in Russia, Lithuania, and Ukraine* (Durham, NC: Duke University Press, 1996).

41. *RFE/RL Newsline,* April 18, 2006.

42. In a system where all prices were set by the state, there was no meaningful measure of profit in any case. Indeed, relative prices were profoundly distorted by the cumulative effect of decades of central planning. The absence of accurate measures of economic costs is one of the major reasons that Russia's economy continues to be so slow to restructure.

43. Article 59 of the constitution provides that young men of conscription age who are conscientious objectors to war may do alternative service, rather than being called up to army service. Legislation specifying how this right may be exercised finally passed in 2002.

44. The chairwoman of Soldiers' Mothers recently estimated that some 3,500 servicemen lose their lives each year as a result of "various accidents and suicides." *RFE/RL Newsline,* February 14, 2008.

45. Polit.ru, June 18, 2009.

46. The FITUR reached a Faustian bargain with the government over the terms of a new labor relations code, which was adopted in 2001. Under the new legislation, employers no longer have to obtain the consent of the unions to lay off workers. But collective bargaining will be between the largest union at each enterprise and the management unless the workers have agreed on which union will represent them. Thus, the new labor code favors the FITUR at the expense of the smaller independent unions.

47. Richard Rose, *New Russia Barometer VI: After the Presidential Election* (Studies in Public Policy no. 272) (Glasgow: Center for the Study of Public Policy, University of Strathclyde, 1996), 6; and Rose, *Getting Things Done,* 15.

48. Unofficial estimates indicated that there were about sixty actual strikes in 2008 and about a hundred in 2009. Sergei Kulikov and Mikhail Sergeev, "Rossii grozit protestnoe obostrenie," *Nezavisimaia gazeta,* February 18, 2010.

49. Linda J. Cook, *Labor and Liberalization: Trade Unions in the New Russia* (New York: Twentieth Century Fund Press, 1997), 76–77.

50. A recent survey in Nizhnii Novgorod found that 81 percent of workers said their interests were either not protected at all or protected insufficiently; 85 percent did not consider themselves members of a trade union, but 58 percent said they desired to belong to a union that would actually defend their interests. Ol'ga Morozova, "Profsoiuzy ne pomogaiut," Vedomosti.ru, July 8, 2008.

51. Two recent books detail the obstacles to the formation of a stable competitive party system: Henry Hale, *Why Not Parties in Russia?* (Cambridge: Cambridge University Press, 2006);

and Regina Smyth, *Candidate Strategies and Electoral Competition in the Russian Federation: Democracy Without Foundation* (Cambridge: Cambridge University Press, 2006).

52. Ora John Reuter and Thomas F. Remington, "Dominant Party Regimes and the Commitment Problem: The Case of United Russia," *Comparative Political Studies* 42, no. 4 (2009): 501–26.

53. Stephen White, Richard Rose, and Ian McAllister, *How Russia Votes* (Chatham, NJ: Chatham House, 1997), 241–70.

54. Quoted from a press release of the election observer mission of the Organization for Security and Cooperation in Europe, posted to its Web site immediately following the election, as reported by *RFE/RL Newsline,* March 15, 2004.

55. In all, 108 candidates on the United Party list declined to take their seats in parliament. Such candidates were used as "loco-motives"—they were used to attract votes, but had no inten-tion of serving in the Duma once the party won.

56. On the scale of fraud in recent Russian elections, see Mikhail Myagkov, Peter C. Ordeshook, and Dmitri Shakin, *The Forensics of Election Fraud: Russia and Ukraine* (Cambridge: Cambridge University Press, 2009).

57. Joel S. Hellman, "Winners Take All: The Politics of Partial Reform in Postcommunist Transitions," *World Politics* 50, no. 1 (1998): 203–34.

58. An excellent account of the "loans for shares" program, based on interviews with many of the participants, is Chrystia Freeland, *Sale of the Century: Russia's Wild Ride from Communism to Capitalism* (New York: Crown, 2000), 169–89.

59. Joseph R. Blasi, Maya Kroumova, and Douglas Kruse, *Kremlin Capitalism: Privatizing the Russian Economy* (Ithaca, NY: Cornell University Press, 1997), 50.

60. Blasi, Kroumova, and Kruse, *Kremlin Capitalism;* Michael McFaul, "State Power, Institutional Change, and the Politics of Privatization in Russia," *World Politics* 47 (1995): 210–43.

61. Thane Gustafson, *Capitalism Russian-Style* (Cambridge: Cambridge University Press, 1999), 2–3, 94–95.

62. Nikolaus von Twickel, "Rich Get Richer as Poor Get Poorer," *Moscow Times,* August 8, 2008.

63. Philip P. Pan, "Russian Elite Looks to Kremlin for Aid as Wealth Evaporates," *Washington Post*, October 17, 2008.

64. World Bank, *Transition: The First Ten Years—Analysis and Lessons for Eastern Europe and the Former Soviet Union* (Washington, D.C.: World Bank, 2002), 9.

65. Quoted from Vladimir Putin's address to an expanded session of the State Council, February 8, 2008, "On the Strategy of Development of Russia to 2020," http://president.kremlin.ru/text/appears/2008/02/159528.shtml.

66. *RFE/RL Newsline,* July 20, 2006.

67. For the most part, the Internet remains uncensored. But nearly all television and radio broadcast companies are sub-ject to close political supervision.

68. Polit.ru, May 13, 2010.

69. Polit.ru, November 17, 2009.

70. Joel S. Hellman, Geraint Jones, and Daniel Kaufmann, *'Seize the State, Seize the Day': State Capture, Corruption, and Influence in Transition* (Policy Research Working Paper no. 2444) (Washington, D.C.: World Bank Institute, September 2000).

71. Susan Rose-Ackerman, *Corruption and Government: Causes, Consequences and Reform* (Cambridge: Cambridge University Press, 1999), 159–74.

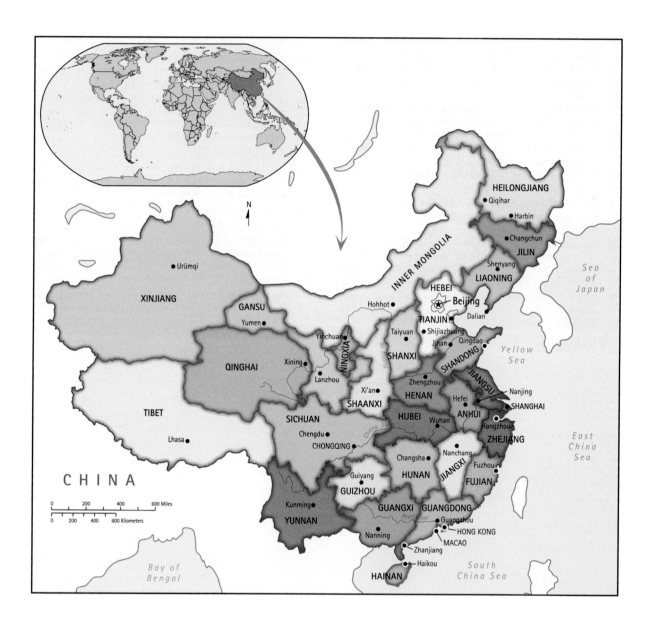

POLITICS IN CHINA

Melanie Manion

Country Bio

CHINA

Population
1,330 million

Territory
3,705,386 square miles

Year of PRC Inauguration
1949

Year of Current Constitution
1982 (amended in 1988, 1993, 1999, 2004)

Head of Party and State
Hu Jintao

Head of Government
Wen Jiabao

Languages
Standard Chinese or Mandarin (Putonghua, based on the Beijing dialect), Yue (Cantonese), Wu (Shanghaiese), Minbei (Fuzhou), Minnan (Hokkien-Taiwanese), Xiang, Gan, Hakka dialects, minority languages

Religion
Daoist (Taoist), Buddhist, Muslim 2–3%, Christian 1% (est.) (note: officially atheist)

On October 1, 1949, **Mao Zedong**, the peasant revolutionary who had led the Chinese communists in war against the Japanese and in civil war, pronounced a basic communist victory, proclaimed a new regime, and promised a new era for China. From the centuries-old Gate of Heavenly Peace in Beijing, Mao formally inaugurated the People's Republic of China (PRC). For nearly three decades after, until his death in 1976, Mao was the chief architect and agitator for a comprehensive project of revolutionary transformation designed to lead a largely backward agrarian people to modernization, prosperity, and (ultimately) communist utopia. A few years after Mao's death, his successors officially and publicly rejected most of the premises, strategies, and outcomes of this revolutionary project, essentially declaring it a failure. They launched a new era of reform, ongoing today. Economic reform in post-Mao China is nearly as radical and dramatic as the revolutions that toppled most of the world's communist regimes in 1989 and 1990. The resulting transformation is awesome.

Without publicly abandoning the ultimate goal of communism, Mao's successors have defined their current quest mainly in pragmatic economic terms, rather than utopian ideological terms. They have identified economic growth as the nation's highest priority and the Communist Party's main assignment. To achieve this objective, the communist party-state has largely retreated from thirty years of direct administration of the economy. Openly acknowledging the superiority of the capitalist experience, Chinese reformers are promoting a "**socialist market economy**," with a place for foreign investors, private entrepreneurs, and stock markets. More than anything else, Chinese leaders have staked their legitimacy on the performance of this new economy.

While embracing economic markets, Chinese leaders have repeatedly rejected political pluralism. The communist party-state was in clear evidence in Beijing on June 4, 1989, when the People's Liberation Army employed its tanks and machine guns to clear the streets and main public square of thousands of protesters. The regime tolerates no open challenge to the Communist Party's monopoly on political power.

For most of the 1.3 billion ordinary Chinese, political reform is mainly reflected in a new official acceptance of a private sphere and a new official tolerance of political apathy. Compared with the Maoist years, when a taste for the music of Beethoven signified dangerous "bourgeois decadence," much less in daily life today is considered political. Moreover, under the new regime, ordinary citizens need not necessarily demonstrate active support for official policies and the political system—so long as they do not engage in active opposition. Chinese leaders have not charted a road toward liberal democracy—at least not purposefully. Instead, the political system has become merely authoritarian in its limited reach, rather than pervasively totalitarian.

Yet post-Mao reform is more than the retreat of the state from the economy and the imposition of fewer demands on citizens politically. A project of institutionalization is underway in China to create an infrastructure promoting more transparency, stability, and responsiveness. In large part, this is to encourage investment and innovation, to support the goal of economic growth. At the same time, Mao's successors are also committed to political institutionalization for political reasons: to safeguard against the arbitrary dictatorship and disruptive politics of the Maoist past. The effort has included better-crafted laws and a new legality, more assertive representative assemblies, and popularly elected grassroots leaders.

Much of China's transformation in the past three decades is only partly a direct result of the various policies that constitute reform. It is at least as much a by-product of these policies. Reform has set in motion processes of economic, political, and social change that appear now largely beyond the control of leaders at the political center. Consider a few examples. Eased restrictions on population movement have created a "floating population" of some 140 million internal migrants from the countryside, seeking work outside their home counties, many of them unregistered urban squatters, all of them reflecting a new relationship between state authority, social welfare, and market opportunity. Local governments, empowered by a new fiscal federalism, pursue local economic growth with less and less heed to central guidelines. Growth in individual wealth and a telecommunications revolution have produced an astonishing 420 million Internet users in China, linking Chinese to one another and to the outside world in ways that are nearly impossible to control.

CURRENT POLICY CHALLENGES

China's current policy challenges arise very significantly from its economic successes in the past three decades. Beginning in 1978, Chinese leaders agreed to be judged mainly by their ability to foster economic growth and deliver a better material life for Chinese citizens. China's development has in fact been impressive. Its economy has grown at a rate of nearly 10 percent per year since 1980, a record of sustained growth comparable only to Japan and Korea in the latter half of the twentieth century. In terms of purchasing power parity, China is now the world's second-largest economy (after the United States). In 2006, it overtook Japan as the world's biggest holder of foreign-exchange reserves. Indeed, aided by massive government intervention, China emerged from the 2008 and 2009 global economic crisis more powerful than ever. This has fostered a new confidence: Premier Wen Jiabao criticized the United States for economic mismanagement, and senior Chinese bank officials questioned the reserve currency status of the U.S. dollar.

Economic success over the past three decades has not been costless. It has provided more opportunities to pursue private gain, legally and also illegally through the abuse of public office. Despite decades of anticorruption efforts, year after year, ordinary citizens tell pollsters that corruption is one of China's most serious problems. In the cities, Chinese poke fun at the perceived insincerity of the anticorruption reforms: "not daring *not* to fight corruption, not daring to fight corruption seriously." In the countryside, villagers rise up to protest abuses of power by "local emperors" imposing illegal fees and excessive taxes.

In recent years, the requisition, rezoning, and sale of agricultural land by local governments has provoked rural riots, usually suppressed with great violence. Land is not privately owned, but rather contracted for agricultural use by Chinese farmers. Local governments have seized on more lucrative opportunities for land use provided by real-estate and industrial development. Farmers tend to be poorly compensated in these instances of eminent domain for local economic development (and local government profit). Top Chinese leaders have condemned these actions, not least of all because arable land is already scarce.

The growing wealth gap fuels the perceptions of official abuse. In the 1980s and 1990s, Chinese policymakers promoted a policy that "some get rich first."

One result has been rapidly rising inequality. Urban household incomes are three times as high as rural incomes; within the cities, migrant workers without official resident status lack access to basic social welfare. Poorer Chinese deeply resent the newly conspicuous economic inequalities of the socialist market economy. As the wealth gap has exploded within a single generation, it has great potential to ignite social instability. An estimated 128,000 "public disturbances" erupted in 2008. Land takings, economic distress, and political corruption provoked much of this unrest.

Chinese leaders are today in the process of a major transition to a new generation of leaders, which will unfold fully in 2012. Xi Jinping and Li Keqiang, likely successors to top Communist Party leader Hu Jintao and government Premier Wen Jiabao, are already playing an active role in policymaking. The least ideologically dogmatic generation of leaders ever to rule modern China will be replaced in 2012 by a more educated, diverse, and less technocratic "fifth generation."

China has thoroughly abandoned the strictures of communist ideology, has experienced an awesome economic revolution, and is taking its place as an important world power. Yet unlike most other communist regimes, which toppled in the face of popular uprisings, China has experienced no second political revolution. Today, it is still a communist party-state. Chinese policymakers have promoted limited liberalization, sometimes as an antidote to corruption at the grassroots. While they have opened up political processes to more diversified inputs, they have also firmly suppressed organized challenges to the Communist Party. A handful of leaders at the very top still monopolize the authority to choose what sorts of inputs from what sorts of groups are acceptable, and the decision rules are not always transparent.

Strikingly little remains of Mao's grand revolutionary schemes. Viewed from the perspective of the 1970s, the magnitude and pace of change in China in the past three decades are practically unimaginable. Chinese politics today is "post-Mao" politics in the sense that there is a new regime, not simply a change of leaders—and, given its dynamics, there appears to be no turning back. Of course, without a grasp of China's rich political history, it is not only impossible to appreciate what has (and has not) changed, but also impossible to understand the crucial context of post-Mao reform: what has been rejected.

HISTORICAL SETTING

Chinese civilization emerged more than six thousand years ago. As a polity, imperial China was the longest-lived major system of governance in world history, enduring as a centralized state ruled with little change in political philosophy or bureaucratic organization for more than two millennia until the fall of the Qing, the last dynasty, in 1911.[1]

Traditional China was governed by an emperor and a unique bureaucracy of scholar-officials at the capital and in the localities, who gained their positions meritocratically through examinations that tested knowledge of the Confucian classics. Anyone was eligible to participate in the examinations, but successful performance required a classical education, usually through a private tutor, not available to most ordinary Chinese. **Confucianism** was basically a conservative philosophy. It conceived of society and the polity in terms of an ordered hierarchy of harmonious relationships. At the top of the hierarchy was the emperor, who maintained social order through his conduct as a moral exemplar. Confucianism blurred the distinction between state and society: It saw harmony (not conflict) as the natural social order, resulting from the virtuous emperor's example of correct conduct. Loyalty to the emperor was the highest principle in the hierarchy of relationships entailing mutual obligations throughout society.

Imperial Order to the Founding of the PRC

This remarkable imperial order began to crumble in the mid-nineteenth century, when Qing rulers proved unable to uphold their political authority and maintain territorial integrity in the presence of large-scale domestic rebellion and foreign economic and military encroachment. The republic founded in 1912 did not restore order or sovereignty to China, but effectively collapsed within a few years, as dozens of Chinese regional warlords ruling with personal armies competed for control of territory.[2] Nearly four decades of political upheaval and continuous warfare ensued, as the Chinese sought solutions to the problems of governance that had brought down the Qing.

The dominant problems were the struggle for national sovereignty and the struggle for peasant livelihood. The former involved two sorts of claims: cession of Chinese territory in treaties imposed forcibly by Western powers beginning in the nineteenth century and outright military invasion and occupation by the Japanese in the 1930s. As for the Chinese peasantry, poverty in the countryside due to socioeconomic conditions of exorbitant taxes, high rents, and usurious credit was aggravated by frequent floods and droughts, which usually brought ruin.

These two struggles were played out in the context of a competition to unify the country. By the 1920s, the **Nationalist Party** and army had emerged as the most prominent political and military force in the country. The Nationalists had their strongest social base in the urban areas; in the countryside, they were mainly dependent on the support of the landlord class. This largely explains Nationalist reluctance to implement land and social reforms to resolve the problems of Chinese peasants. Peasant poverty was exacerbated by absentee landlordism and the replacement of ties of mutual obligation with economic ties enforced by managing agents. Land distribution was not part of the Nationalist agenda, nor were tax controls or provision of cheap credit effectively implemented.

Between 1924 and 1927, the Nationalists allied with the communists in a battle to eliminate regional warlords and to unify China. By the late 1920s, the Nationalists had practically realized this aim. In 1927, they broke their alliance with the communists in a violent massacre that reduced the Communist Party from nearly 58,000 to 10,000 members. The break inaugurated a new civil war that lasted a decade.

By contrast with the Nationalists, the intellectual revolutionaries who founded the **Chinese Communist Party** in 1921 were unlikely contenders for power. The rise and eventual victory of the communists owe much to historic opportunities in the 1930s and 1940s. These opportunities were available for other forces to exploit too, but the communists exploited them best.[3] Mao Zedong emerged as leader of the communists in the mid-1930s, consolidating his leadership in the early 1940s.[4]

After the Nationalist attack in 1927, many communists retreated to the countryside. Mao had already reported on the spontaneous impulse for radical social change among the peasantry and had proposed a revolutionary strategy different from that suggested by communist theory or Russian experience. Mao rejected the idea that the Chinese communists could win power through a revolution of the small urban working class in China. Instead, he argued, a communist victory could be achieved only by providing leadership for a nascent rural revolution and building a guerrilla Red Army to surround the cities with the countryside. From a base in southeastern China, Mao and other communists implemented a program of political education and social change, including land redistribution. In 1934, a major Nationalist offensive forced them on a strategic retreat, the historic Long March, that ended at the caves of Yan'an in China's northwest, where Mao and his communist forces, their numbers literally decimated, established their headquarters. From Yan'an, they built on the strategy of rural revolution to develop support further in the countryside.

The second indispensable component in communist victory was the 1937 Japanese invasion of central China, beyond territory in the northeast that the Japanese had occupied since 1931.[5] Mao seized the strategic initiative to call for a truce in the civil war so that Chinese could unite to resist Japanese aggression. Nationalist leaders were initially wary. This combination of Nationalist reluctance and strong anti-Japanese sentiment in the cities and countryside earned the communists enormous popularity as the true nationalist resistance to foreign aggression. From 1937 to 1945, the communists grew in force from 40,000 to more than a million. Japanese defeat in World War II ended the alliance between Nationalists and communists. A new civil war began.[6] In four years, the communists won victory, as peasant revolutionaries and Chinese nationalists, and the Nationalists were forced to retreat to the island of Taiwan in 1949. Once in power, they turned their energies to the construction of socialism.

History of the PRC

The history of the PRC can be divided into three major periods. In the first, between 1949 and 1957, the Chinese emulated the experience of the first and most powerful communist state, the Soviet Union. The second period began in 1958, when the Chinese introduced their own model of revolutionary development. Except for a few years at the beginning of the 1960s, this Maoist model prevailed until Mao's death in 1976. A short transitional period ensued, during which immediate problems of policy orientation and leadership succession were resolved with the arrest and trial of key radical leaders. In December 1978, the third period, a new era of reform, ongoing today, was inaugurated with a Central Committee declaration favoring learning from practical experience and rejecting the ideological constraints of Maoism—or any theory.[7] **Deng Xiaoping,** China's new "paramount leader," charted and presided over the reforms. In the same sense that Chinese politics in the two decades ending in 1976 are appropriately characterized as the Maoist years, the last two decades of the twentieth century belong most to Deng—despite important differences in the power of these two leaders and how they wielded it.

Learning from the Soviet Union The Chinese communists had won power largely by ignoring Soviet advice. Once in power, however, they looked to the Soviet Union for a plan to build socialism. They concluded a treaty of friendship and alliance in 1950. Soviet financial aid to China in the 1950s was not large. Aid was mainly given in a massive technology transfer—over 12,000 Soviet engineers and technicians were sent to work in China, over 6,000 Chinese studied in Soviet universities, and tens of thousands more studied in Soviet factories on short-term training courses. With this Soviet assistance, the Chinese developed heavy industry, establishing a centralized bureaucracy of planning agencies and industrial ministries to manage the economy according to five-year plans. They nationalized private industry. In the early 1950s, they sent communists down to the grassroots to instigate and organize land reform, a violent "class struggle." Each peasant household was classified according to land holdings, and land seized from landlords was redistributed to poor peasants, the majority of the peasantry.[8] Agricultural collectivization followed. This process was also essentially coercive, especially in its later stages, but not as violent as land reform.

This period did feature some Maoist strategies, especially in political participation and socialization. The Chinese implemented many policies by mobilizing the masses in intensive campaigns, with essentially compulsory participation. For the Chinese communists, potential regime opponents—such as intellectuals and capitalists—were capable of being politically transformed through practices such as "thought reform." Communist leaders were sufficiently confident about the results of political education and regime accomplishments to invite nonparty intellectuals to voice criticism in the Hundred Flowers Campaign in 1957. When criticism was harsh, revealing weak support for the communist system, the leaders quickly reversed themselves. They launched an Anti-Rightist Campaign, which discovered more "poisonous weeds" than "blooming flowers." About a half million people, many of them intellectuals, were persecuted as "rightists" in a campaign that effectively silenced political opposition for twenty years.[9] Mass campaigns, political education, and political labeling were all coercive measures that resulted in the persecution of millions. To some extent, this coercion had a characteristic Maoist (and Confucian) element: Fundamentally, it rejected the Stalinist version of political purge as physical liquidation, because it viewed the individual as malleable and ultimately educable. Yet "enemies of the people" were not spared; 1 to 3 million landlords and "counterrevolutionaries" were persecuted to death in the early 1950s alone.

Frictions in relations with the Soviet Union increased throughout the 1950s, resulting in the withdrawal of aid and advisors and a Sino-Soviet split that shocked the world in 1960. Major irritants included Soviet reluctance to support efforts to "liberate" Taiwan, Soviet unwillingness to aid China's nuclear development, and a relaxation of Soviet hostility toward the United States. At about the same time, Mao was reconsidering his view of the Soviet model of development and developing his own radical model of building communism.

Great Leap Forward The first five-year plan had invested in heavy industry, not agriculture. Following the Soviet model, central planners had not diverted resources from industry to promote agricultural growth. In 1958, Mao proposed a strategy of simultaneous development of industry and agriculture to be achieved in two ways: (1) the labor-intensive mass mobilization of peasants to increase agricultural output by building irrigation facilities, and (2) the organization of primitive production processes to give inputs to agriculture (such as small chemical fertilizer plants and primitive steel furnaces to make tools) without taking resources from industry. A crucial element of Mao's solution was an increase in the size of the collective farms. In order to build irrigation facilities, local communist officials needed to control a labor force of large numbers of peasants, larger than the current collectives that grouped together a few hundred households. By combining several collectives into one gigantic farm, Mao hoped to realize economies of scale. In 1958, with prodding from above, the people's commutes were born, grouping together thousands of households in one unit of economic and political organization managed by Communist Party officials.

The Maoist model was not simply an economic development strategy. It was fundamentally a political campaign, a point exemplified in the main slogan of the **Great Leap Forward**: "politics in command."[10] The Great Leap Forward abandoned most material rewards for moral incentives. By 1958, in Mao's view, Chinese peasants had demonstrated tremendous enthusiasm and were ready to leap into communism, if properly mobilized by local leaders. In the politically charged climate, economic expertise was denigrated and caution criticized as lack of faith in the masses. Leaders in Beijing set output targets high, demanding that local leaders believe in the ability of the Chinese people to accomplish miracles. By implication, failure to achieve high targets could be due only to poor leadership. A dangerous vicious cycle was set in motion: Local leaders competed to demonstrate their political correctness; when communes failed to meet targets set in Beijing, local leaders calculated output imaginatively to report that targets had been met or exceeded; production results were increasingly exaggerated as reports went to higher and higher levels; the response from Beijing to the falsely reported leap in output was a further leap in targets.

In 1958, dislocation associated with forming the communes and peasant mobilization to help meet high steel-output targets by making steel in primitive furnaces was so great that the autumn harvest was not all gathered. That year, too, a false belief in excess production led to reduction in areas sown in grain. Even with reduced acreage, peasant contributions to agricultural labor were decreasing due to physical exhaustion, weak material rewards, and the abolition of private plots (and, in some cases, private property for complete communization). In 1959, when top Chinese leaders met to consider these problems, the minister of national defense criticized radicalism in policy implementation. In response, Mao accused the minister of factionalism, turned the meeting into a referendum on his leadership, and challenged others to dare to attack the Leap's radical principles.

The meeting was a terrible turning point. With political correctness reasserted, radicalism returned. Moreover, just as the 1957 Anti-Rightist Campaign had silenced opposition outside the party, Mao's 1959 accusations and threats effectively silenced opposition

in the top echelons of party leadership.[11] That same year, large parts of China suffered from severe drought, others from severe flooding, in one of the worst natural disasters experienced in decades.

Retreat from the Leap Over the next three years, the famine cost an estimated 27 million lives.[12] China retreated from Maoist radicalism. Mao retreated from day-to-day management of public affairs, but continued in his position as Communist Party chairman. In the early 1960s, the communes ceased to be relevant to agricultural production. Instead, peasant households contracted with the state for production, selling the surplus in newly established free markets. In industry, there was a renewed reliance on material incentives, technical expertise, and profitability as the standard to judge performance. The education system emphasized the creation of a knowledgeable and highly skilled corps of managers and leaders. Policy processes took into account advice by experts, rather than reliance on mass miracles.

Cultural Revolution By the mid-1960s, Mao had further developed his radical critique of the Soviet model and extended it to the Chinese experience. In China, Mao saw a "new class" of economic managers and political officials, privileged by elitist policies that increased social antagonisms. In 1966, Mao argued that many communist leaders were corrupt "capitalist roaders" who opposed socialism and must be thrown out of power. He launched the Great Proletarian Cultural Revolution, yet another exercise in radical excess. The **Cultural Revolution** was simultaneously a power struggle, an ideological battle, and a mass campaign to transform culture. Compared with the Great Leap Forward, its impact on the Chinese economy was minor; its impact on society was devastating.

For Mao, the enemy of socialism was within the Communist Party. Unable to rely on the party to correct its mistakes, Mao instructed secondary school and university students to overturn "bourgeois culture" and "bombard the headquarters." The Communist Party became effectively powerless as an organization. For the first time since 1949, Chinese were free to organize politically. Unconstrained by the party, Chinese engaged in political action legitimated by their own interpretations of Mao Zedong Thought. Students formed radical Red Guard groups to criticize and persecute victims, often chosen quite

Cult of Mao in the Cultural Revolution

Defense Minister Lin Biao sits beside Chairman Mao Zedong and Premier Zhou Enlai during the Cultural Revolution. PLA soldiers wave the *Little Red Book* of quotations from Chairman Mao, a reflection of the cult of Mao that Lin helped to build.

SV-Bilderdienst/The Image Works

arbitrarily or for reasons more personal than political. In schools, factories, and government agencies, those in power were criticized and persecuted. Persecution was frequently physical. It was not uncommon for victims to be held in makeshift prisons, forced to do harsh manual labor, and subjected to violent public "struggle sessions" to force them to confess their crimes. Many were "struggled" to death, and many others committed suicide. Factional fighting was inevitable, as rival Red Guard groups fought for power, each faction claiming true representation of Mao Zedong Thought.[13]

In 1967, the country was near anarchy. The schools had been shut down; most party and government offices no longer functioned; transportation and communications were severely disrupted; factional struggles were increasingly violent contests, some of them armed confrontations. Having unleashed social conflict, Mao had been able to manipulate it—but not to control it. Mao called on the army to restore order, a process that began in 1969.

The 1970s were years of more moderate conflict, mostly played out as a struggle at the apex of power rather than in society generally. Radical leaders (including Mao's wife) who had risen to power in the Cultural Revolution supported a continuation of radical policies. Other leaders, reinstated by Mao to balance the power of the radicals, supported policies of economic modernization. The conflict was ongoing at the time of Mao's death in 1976. Within two years, the economic modernizers had won. China embarked on a new course of reform, different from anything in the experience of any communist system.

SOCIAL CONDITIONS

Chinese society has changed in various ways since the communists came to power. These changes include social structural transformations engineered by the regime, especially in the early decades. This section focuses on basic features that make up the social environment for Chinese politics that have not undergone fundamental transformation but have changed only in degree, if at all.

First among these is China's huge population. When the communists came to power in 1949, China's population was 540 million. Today, China remains the world's most populous country, with a population of

1.3 billion. As in the 1950s, most Chinese live in the countryside, but the proportion has shrunk dramatically with economic reform. Less than 20 percent of Chinese lived in cities when reform began in the late 1970s, but de facto relaxation of rural to urban migration restrictions liberated the underemployed farming population to seek work in cities. Rural industrialization and the growth of towns also changed the situation. By 2010, nearly as many Chinese lived in cities as in the countryside.

The second basic feature involves geography. Although China is the world's second-largest country in area, the population is concentrated in the eastern third of the land. This is largely because only about a quarter of China's land is arable. Population growth and reduction in cultivated area have greatly exacerbated the land shortage. Despite efforts to preserve arable land for farming, China's leaders have been unable to reverse the reduction in cultivated area. In part, this is a result of agricultural decollectivization and a return to household farming: Land is used for property borders, burial grounds, and bigger houses. In recent years, local government land requisitions for lucrative residential and industrial development have further reduced arable land and provoked much rural unrest.

The third feature is that China is a multiethnic state. About 92 percent of Chinese are ethnically Han, but there are fifty-five recognized **ethnic minorities**, ranging in number from a few thousand to more than 16 million. Although minorities make up only a fairly small proportion of China's population, areas in which minorities live comprise more than 60 percent of China's territory, and much of this is in strategically important border regions.[14] This includes Tibet (bordering India) and Xinjiang (bordering three new post-Soviet states), which have experienced fairly continuous minority unrest over the decades. The Chinese have maintained large armed forces in these areas to quell secessionist efforts.

Finally, Han Chinese share the same Chinese written language, a unifying force in China for more than two millennia, practically defining what it is to be Chinese. The same written language is spoken in many different dialects, however, often making communication difficult. Mandarin, based on the dialect of the Beijing locality, is the official language promoted by the communist regime through the education system and mass media.

STRUCTURE OF THE PARTY-STATE

From top to bottom, Chinese politics has changed noticeably since the Maoist period. Yet the essential form of the Chinese political system retains an organizational design borrowed decades ago from the Soviet Union and developed nearly a century ago in Russia by Lenin—the design of the communist **party-state**.

Design Features

Lenin viewed political legitimacy in ways that justify a monopoly of power by a communist party elite that is not popularly elected. He believed that ordinary citizens do not understand their own real interests and that larger interests of society are not best advanced by aggregating interests that citizens articulate. According to Lenin, as ordinary citizens typically lack revolutionary consciousness and knowledge of communist theory, they are incapable of making the correct choices that will lead from capitalism to socialism and toward communism—a utopia characterized by a high level of economic prosperity, an absence of social conflict, and a minimal role for government. Lenin proposed a solution to this problem: a political party and political system built on the principles of guardianship and hierarchy.[15] To these two principles, Chinese leaders added the idea of the mass line, formulated by Mao in the 1940s. Guardianship and hierarchy define the communist party-state. The mass line adds another dimension, which moderates guardianship.

Guardianship describes the main relationship between the Communist Party and society. The party bases its claim to legitimate rule not on representation of the expressed preferences of a majority but on representation of the "historical best interests" of all the people. In theory, as most ordinary citizens do not know their best interests, society is best led by an elite vanguard party with a superior understanding of the historical laws of development. The Communist Party is therefore an exclusive organization—in China, membership is about 6 percent of the population—not a mass political party with membership open to all. The notion of Communist Party leadership is explicitly set forth in the constitution, as is some version of the notion of dictatorship. The constitution describes the political system as a socialist state under the "people's democratic dictatorship." As the Communist Party is the only organization with the politically correct knowledge to lead society, it is the authoritative arbiter of the interests of the people. In effect, dictatorship in the name of the people is Communist Party dictatorship. Party leaders today are more informed of public opinion than in the past, but there is no place in the Chinese political system (or in Leninist theory) for organized opposition to Communist Party leadership.

Chinese Communist Party guardianship is, in theory, informed by the practice of the mass line. The party leads, but its leadership is not isolated from the opinions and preferences of the mass public. The degree to which mass preferences actually find expression in public policy depends on their fit with larger goals determined by party leaders. Party leaders at all levels (but especially at the grassroots) are supposed to maintain a close relationship with ordinary citizens so that the party organization can transform the "scattered and unsystematic ideas" of the masses into "correct ideas" and propagate them "until the masses embrace them as their own." In this way, policy is supposed to flow "from the masses to the masses."[16]

Party Organization The Communist Party is organized around a hierarchy of party congresses and committees extending from the top of the system down to the grassroots. Lower party organizations are subordinate to higher party organizations, and individual party members are subordinate to the party as an organization. Inner-party rules for decision-making are based on the Leninist principle of **democratic centralism.**

In democratic centralism, *democracy* refers mainly to consultation. It requires that party leaders provide opportunities for discussion, criticism, and proposals in party organizations (often including lower party organizations) as part of the normal process of deciding important issues or making policy.

Centralism requires unified discipline throughout the party: top-level official party decisions are binding on party organizations and members. Centralism is never sacrificed to democracy. Party members are allowed to hold personal views contrary to party decisions and to voice them through proper party channels, but they are not free to act in ways that promote these views. According to the Communist Party constitution, the formation of "factions" or any sort of "small group activity" within the party is a punishable violation of organizational discipline. Communist

Party hierarchy and the requirement that party members observe party discipline are designed as organizational guarantees that the party, in exercising leadership over society, acts as a unified force, responsive to the leadership of the highest level of party organization.

Ideology is today both less prominent and less coherent in Chinese politics than it was in the past. The principles of guardianship, hierarchy, and the mass line are not inconsequential abstractions, however. They have concrete practical implications, evident throughout the Chinese political system. Change in the system is evident too, of course, both as a product and by-product of policies of reform in the past two decades. Yet while the political reforms of recent decades are not trivial, they do not add up to fundamental systemic change. For now, as in the past, the design of the communist party-state is a fair model of the organization of political power in China.

Two Hierarchies, with Party Leadership The design of the communist party-state is perhaps most evident in the organization of power in two hierarchies of political structures, illustrated in Figure 10.1. Government structures are more or less duplicated at each level of the political system by Communist Party structures. In principle, there is a division of labor between party and government structures. In practice, the two often perform similar functions, with party structures and party officials exercising leadership over parallel government structures and government officials.

Both party and government structures have changed since 1949. The description in the following section focuses on the system that emerged in the reform era.

Government Structures

At the political center in Beijing, the key government structures are the **National People's Congress (NPC)**, which is China's legislature, and the **State Council**, which exercises executive functions. Under the State Council are government ministries and commissions, which have ranged in number from thirty-two to one hundred since 1949. Below the political center, government structures extend downward in a four-tiered hierarchy consisting of 31 provinces, 333 large cities, 2,859 counties and smaller cities, and 40,814 townships and towns. The provincial level includes four

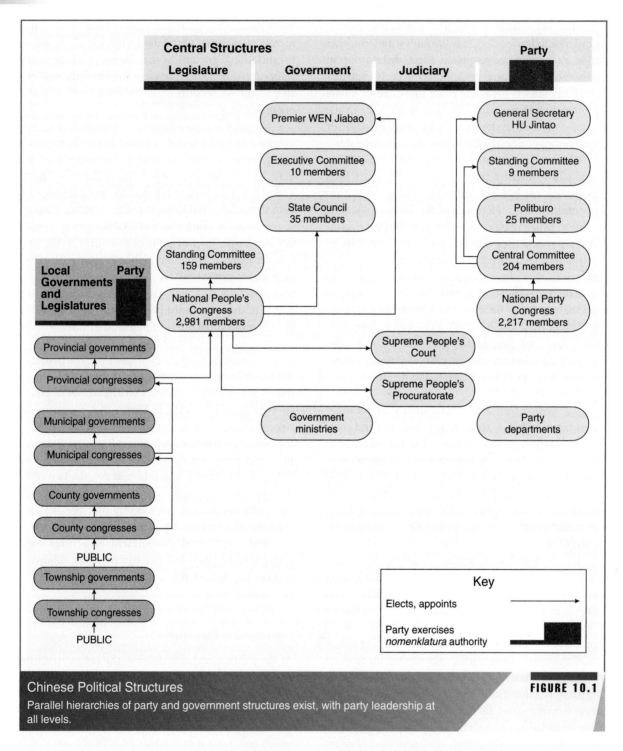

Chinese Political Structures

Parallel hierarchies of party and government structures exist, with party leadership at all levels.

FIGURE 10.1

megacities (Beijing, Shanghai, Tianjin, and Chongqing). Local people's congresses, local governments, and government departments are found at all levels. As shown in Figure 10.1, Chinese voters elect delegates to township and county people's congresses only; municipal, provincial, and national congress delegates are elected by congresses one level down. At all levels, congress delegates elect their governments. Villages and urban neighborhoods elect self-governing grassroots organizations, not part of the formal government hierarchy.

National People's Congress According to the constitution, the highest organization of state authority is the NPC.[17] The NPC and its permanent body, the NPC Standing Committee, exercise legislative functions. NPC delegates are elected for five-year terms by delegates in provincial-level congresses and the armed forces. Normally, NPC delegates assemble once annually for a plenary session of about two weeks. The number and composition of delegates are prescribed by law, but the NPC has always been huge. In 1986, the law set a ceiling of 3,000 delegates, which is about the number elected to each congress since 1983. Urban Chinese were overrepresented (by a ratio of eight to one, later changed to four to one) until a 2010 law gave rural residents equal representation in congresses at all levels.

Formally, the NPC has extensive powers, including amendment of the constitution, passage and amendment of legislation, approval of economic plans and government work reports, and appointment of top state and government leaders. For most of the year, when the NPC is not in session, its Standing Committee of about 150 members, who reside in Beijing and meet regularly throughout the year, serves as the working legislative assembly. The 1982 constitution considerably strengthened the role of the NPC Standing Committee. It now exercises all but the most formal powers of the NPC and prepares the agenda for the annual NPC plenary sessions, when the full NPC typically ratifies its interim legislative actions.

Is the NPC (and its Standing Committee) a "rubber-stamp" assembly? For the Maoist years, the answer is clearly yes. In recent decades, however, the NPC has become more assertive, and its Standing Committee has assumed a greater role in lawmaking. This is part of the political reform undertaken in response to the extreme institutional nihilism of the Cultural Revolution. NPC assertiveness is evident in an increase in delegate motions (by an order of magnitude) and, more significantly, in dissenting votes. The practice of unanimous approval, once automatic, has ended, sometimes with embarrassing results.

The full NPC cannot be expected to function routinely as a credible legislature because it is too large and meets too infrequently and briefly. More important is the lawmaking role of the less cumbersome NPC Standing Committee. In the early 1980s, many party and government elders retired from important positions in central and provincial administration to the NPC Standing Committee. Instead of retreating from political life, these elders used the Standing Committee as a channel for political influence. Their enhanced role was institutionalized with the establishment of a Legislative Affairs Committee (with significant staff) and nine permanent specialized legislative committees to consider draft legislation. With these changes, the NPC (and its Standing Committee) can no longer be dismissed as a rubber stamp. The legislature remains institutionally weak, however, for two main reasons (discussed later in this chapter): the practice of executive-led government (which does not distinguish the Chinese system from parliamentary systems in other countries) and the practice of Communist Party leadership (which is more fundamental).

State Council In lawmaking, the State Council is the center of government activity, although this role too is newly enhanced.[18] The State Council is composed of the premier, who is head of government, and his cabinet of vice-premiers, state councilors, ministers, auditor general, and secretary general (currently thirty-five members, all formally nominated by the premier and appointed by the NPC). In 2003, Wen Jiabao became premier. The State Council has an Executive Committee, which meets twice weekly, with members reporting on work in their assigned portfolios. As in parliamentary systems, the bulk of legislation is drafted by specialized ministries and commissions under the direction of the cabinet. Also, however, as most Chinese laws are drafted in general and imprecise language, they require detailed "implementing regulations" to have any effect. These regulations are typically drafted by State Council ministries (under the direction of the newly reestablished State Council Legislation Bureau) and promulgated by the ministries or State Council without consideration by the NPC or its Standing Committee.

Communist Party Leadership The Communist Party exercises direct leadership over government and legislative functions in a variety of ways. Before the NPC assembles, party leaders convene a meeting of all delegates who are members of the Communist Party (about 70 percent of NPC delegates). At these meetings, leaders discuss the NPC agenda and offer "hopes" of the party leaders for the forthcoming session, including suggestions about the tone (how open or restrained NPC debate should be, for example). Also, NPC powers of appointment are effectively nullified by party control over candidate nomination and little to no electoral choice. For example, although the NPC formally appoints the president, vice president, premier, and cabinet members, there has never been more than one nominee for these positions, and candidate nomination is decided at the party meeting convened before the NPC assembles.

As to lawmaking, Communist Party leaders have veto power over all legislation of consequence. The system of party review of legislation that emerged in the early 1990s rejects party micromanagement of the State Council or NPC Standing Committee work. Nonetheless, all important laws, constitutional amendments, and political laws submitted to the NPC or its Standing Committee must have prior approval by the party center. In short, the Chinese system is executive-led government, but with an important difference: leadership by the Communist Party.

The president of the PRC is head of state. This is a purely ceremonial office, held by **Hu Jintao**. Hu is also head of the Communist Party organization and of the Central Military Commission, in which leadership of military forces is formally vested. The commission was established as a government structure only in 1982, but its Communist Party counterpart functioned long before then and remains in existence, with the same membership in party and government structures.

Judiciary Judicial authority rests with the Supreme People's Court at the center and with local people's courts below. Formally, the Supreme People's Court is responsible to the NPC. Courts at lower levels are responsible to the people's congresses at their respective levels and also take direction from courts above them.

The Supreme People's Procuratorate, restored in 1978 after decades of neglect, is the central prosecutorial agency. It sits at the top of a hierarchy of procuratorates extending down to the county level, each formally responsible to a local people's congress and each also under the direction of the procuratorate above. The Supreme People's Procuratorate is responsible to the NPC.

Procuratorates act as a bridge between public-security agencies and the courts. They supervise criminal investigations, approve arrests, and prosecute cases. Beginning in the mid-1980s, the most important role of the procuratorates has been investigation and prosecution of corruption. In each new congress session, the NPC appoints the chief justice of the Supreme People's Court and the chief procurator.

Party Structures

At the political center in Beijing, the key party structures are the National Party Congress and its Central Committee, the Politburo, and the Politburo Standing Committee. In addition, party departments are organized under a secretariat. Below the center, down to the township level, are local party congresses and local party committees.

National Party Congress As in the government hierarchy, while the formal power of Communist Party structures is directly proportional to size, actual impact on policy is inversely proportional to size. The Communist Party constitution vests supreme authority in the **National Party Congress**, but this structure is too big and meets too infrequently to play a significant role in political decision-making. The Central Committee determines the number of congress delegates and the procedures for their election. Since 1949, National Party Congresses have ranged in size from 1,000 to 2,000 delegates, with recent congresses at about 2,000 delegates. In the past, the congresses met irregularly, but party constitutions since 1969 have stipulated that congresses are normally convened at five-year intervals. This has been more or less the practice since 1969 and has been strictly observed in the post-Mao years, as shown in Table 10.1.

National Party Congress sessions are short, about a week or two at most. A main function is to ratify important changes in broad policy orientation already decided by more important smaller party structures. Although party congresses yield no surprises, these changes receive their highest formal endorsement at the party congresses. Therefore, the sessions have the public appearance of major historic events. A second function of the National Party Congress is to elect the **Central Committee**, which exercises the powers of the congress between sessions. Official candidates for Central Committee membership are determined by the Politburo before the congress meets. According to the 1982 party constitution, elections to the Central Committee are by secret ballot, and wide deliberation and discussion of candidates precedes them. Of course, centralism prevails; elections rarely offer choice (or much choice) among candidates.

TABLE 10.1

Chinese Communist Party Congresses and Growth of Party Membership, 1921–2007

Today, about 6 percent of Chinese are members of the elite CCP.

Congress	Year	Party Members
First	1921	More than 50
Second	1922	123
Third	1923	432
Fourth	1925	950
Fifth	1927	57,900[a]
Sixth	1928	40,000
Seventh	1945	1.2 million
Founding of the PRC, 1949		
Eighth	1956	11 million
Ninth	1969	22 million
Tenth	1973	28 million
Eleventh	1977	35 million
Twelfth	1982	40 million
Thirteenth	1987	46 million
Fourteenth	1992	51 million
Fifteenth	1997	58 million
Sixteenth	2002	66 million
Seventeenth	2007	74 million

[a]Communist Party membership dropped from 57,900 to 10,000 after April 1927, when the Nationalists broke the "united front" with the communists in a massacre that decimated communist forces and ignited civil war.

Source: *Beijing Review* 41, no. 8 (1998): 22; *Peoples Daily*, September 2, 2002, and June 19, 2006; *Xinhua*, July 2, 2008.

Central Committee The Central Committee is the Chinese political elite, broadly defined; it is a collection of the most powerful several hundred political leaders in the country. All Central Committee members hold some major substantive position of leadership, as ministers in the central state bureaucracy or provincial party leaders, for example. Membership on the Central Committee reflects this political power; it does not confer it. In this sense, the Central Committee is less important intrinsically as a political structure than extrinsically, for the different sorts of interests and constituencies represented by its members. The next party congress, which meets in 2012, will elect a new "fifth generation" of political leaders to the Central Committee (see Box 10.1); a generational change in the Politburo will also occur.

Although the Central Committee does not initiate policy, changes in policy or leaders at the political center must be approved by it. This is done fairly routinely at plenary sessions now convened at least annually. Party leaders at the top rely on the bureaucratic and regional elites on the Central Committee to ensure that the "party line" is realized in practice. Central Committee membership brings these elites into the process as participants and, in effect, guarantors; in endorsing party policy, members also take on responsibility for its realization.

Politburo The Central Committee elects the **Politburo**, the Politburo Standing Committee, and the party general secretary—all of whom are also Central Committee members. These leaders are at the very apex of the political system. The composition of these

BOX 10.1

The "Fifth Generation" of Chinese Leaders

Top party and government chiefs Hu Jintao and Premier Wen Jiabao, along with more than half of the Politburo and its Standing Committee, will retire in 2012 to make way for a "fifth generation" of Chinese leaders. This generation is typified by the provincial party and government chiefs who gained their offices at the Seventeenth Party Congress in 2007. Their experience differs from "fourth-generation" leaders in a number of ways. Hu, Wen, and their cohort are mainly technocrats born in the 1940s, who studied engineering in college before the Cultural Revolution. By contrast, many in the fifth generation majored in economics, politics, business, or law as undergraduates. Many hold graduate degrees, often through part-time study. Most spent their formative years during the Cultural Revolution, part of the "lost generation" who missed out on the opportunity for high-school education. It is impossible to know how these experiences have prepared this generation for power, but it is reasonable to speculate that they will differ from the current cohort of top leaders in Beijing, already the least dogmatic to accede to top offices in Chinese politics.

structures is determined by party leaders before the party congress, and elections are mainly ceremonial, featuring no candidate choice. The Politburo is the top political elite, usually no more than two dozen leaders, most of whom have responsibility for overseeing policymaking in some issue area. Its inner circle is the Politburo Standing Committee, typically no more than a half-dozen leaders, who meet about once weekly, in meetings convened and chaired by the party general secretary. Members of the Politburo and its Standing Committee are the core political decision-makers in China, presiding over a process that concentrates great power at the top.

Top Leader and the Succession Problem Since the abolition of the position of party chairman in 1982, the top party leader is the general secretary, a position held by Hu Jintao since 2002. The change in terminology reflects the effort to promote collective leadership, a reaction against norms of past years when Mao presided as nearly all-powerful chairman of the party until his death in 1976.

In communist systems, the death of the top leader creates a succession crisis; there is no formal or generally acknowledged position of second-in-command and no regularized mechanism to choose a new top leader. Mao's death ushered in a power struggle at the top, won by Deng and his fellow modernizers. Deng, already in his seventies at the time of Mao's death, chose to eschew top formal leadership of party or government in the interest of resolving the problem of succession.

In the late 1970s, Communist Party elders who had formerly held important positions of power were reinstated after years of forced retirement during the Cultural Revolution. Within a few years, however, many of them retired (or semiretired) to the "second line," to serve as advisors and involve themselves only in major policy issues or broad strategy.

At the very top, a half-dozen elders, all senior communist revolutionaries in their eighties or nineties, continued to play key roles in decision-making and to occupy formal positions of leadership, although not the top party or government positions. The best example, of course, was "paramount leader" Deng himself. Deng never held the top formal position of leadership in party or government, although he was on the Politburo Standing Committee until 1987 and chaired the Central Military Commission until 1989.

Just below this very small group at the top, elders retired to advisory positions on a Central Advisory Commission, set up in 1982. Other elders "retired" to formal positions on the NPC. Younger leaders were promoted to the top positions on the "first line" to allow them to develop their own bases of support and authority with the support of their elder patrons.

This arrangement did not provide a solution to the succession problem, however. In principle, elders on the second line used their prestige and informal power to support younger leaders in top executive positions. In practice, younger leaders on the first line, in the effort to establish their own authority, sometimes adopted positions at odds with the views of elder patrons. Friction with party elders resulted in two purges of top party executives in the 1980s: Hu Yaobang was dismissed as party general secretary in 1987, and his successor, Zhao Ziyang, was dismissed in 1989 (see Figure 10.2). The situation today is different; by the mid-1990s, most of the elders at the very top, including Deng, had "gone to see Marx," and the Central Advisory Commission had been dismantled, having served its purpose of easing leaders into retirement. After a dozen years as party secretary and beneficiary of Deng's support until Deng's death in 1997, Jiang Zemin stepped down in 2002, lending his support to Hu Jintao.

Party Bureaucracy The party has its own set of bureaucratic structures, managed by the Secretariat. The Secretariat provides staff support for the Politburo, transforming Politburo decisions into instructions for subordinate party departments. Compared with their government counterparts, party departments are fewer in number and have more broadly defined areas of competence.

Party Dominance

Party and government structures from top to bottom are staffed by more than 40 million officials on state salaries. One important mechanism of party leadership, described earlier in this chapter, is the structural arrangement: the duplication of political structures and the dominance of party structures and leaders over government structures and leaders. The Chinese Communist Party exercises leadership in political structures in other ways, too. Among the most important are overlapping directorships, "party core groups," party membership penetration, and the *nomenklatura* system.

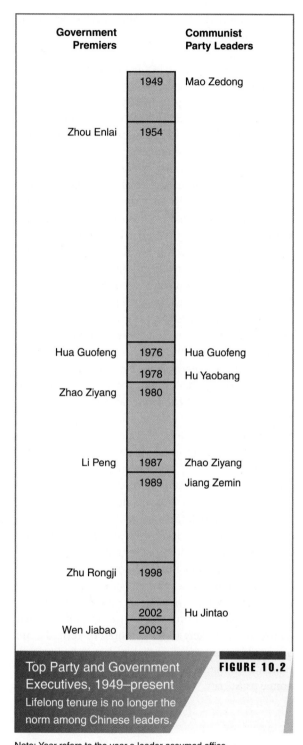

Government Premiers		Communist Party Leaders
	1949	Mao Zedong
Zhou Enlai	1954	
Hua Guofeng	1976	Hua Guofeng
	1978	Hu Yaobang
Zhao Ziyang	1980	
Li Peng	1987	Zhao Ziyang
	1989	Jiang Zemin
Zhu Rongji	1998	
	2002	Hu Jintao
Wen Jiabao	2003	

Top Party and Government Executives, 1949–present   **FIGURE 10.2**

Lifelong tenure is no longer the norm among Chinese leaders.

Note: Year refers to the year a leader assumed office.

Nomenklatura System The **nomenklatura** system is the most important mechanism by which the Communist Party exerts control over officials. In some sense, it is the linchpin of the political system. It refers to the management of all party and government officials in positions of even moderate importance by party committees. Party committees exercise authority over all major personnel decisions (such as appointment, promotion, transfer, and removal from office). Management authority is organized hierarchically and specified in lists of official positions. Any official in a position of even moderate importance is on such a list.[19]

Party committees, through their organization departments, directly manage all officials in positions one level down in the hierarchy. At the top of the system, the Politburo exercises direct management authority over all officials at the provincial level in the territorial hierarchy and at the ministerial level in the bureaucratic hierarchy—about 7,000 officials in all (including the entire NPC Standing Committee, for example).

The extension of management authority downward in a hierarchy of dyadic relationships that are known to officials has important implications. Party leaders have a means of ensuring that the real "boss" of every important official is the superior party committee—and ultimately the Central Committee and its Politburo. In looking ahead to career advancement, then, even officials who owe their positions formally to elections must look upward to "selectorates" of party committees rather than only (if at all) downward to electorates of congress delegates and ordinary citizens. Otherwise, they will not be promoted.

Party Membership Another means by which the Communist Party exercises leadership over officials is in party membership penetration in political structures. The vast majority of officials in political structures (including government structures and positions filled by elections) are Communist Party members. At their places of work, officials are members of party committees, general branches, or branches located in a hierarchy of basic-level party organizations. They meet regularly to participate in party "organizational life," which is quite apart from their professional work. They are obliged to observe the inner-party discipline of democratic centralism. The routine activities of party branches in government offices are supervised by departments specially assigned to ensure that the

Communist Party remains an active force in government structures. Because the party monopolizes opportunities to get along and ahead in the Chinese political system, the organizational hierarchy and party discipline designed to guarantee unified party leadership over society also promote party leadership in political structures.

Party Core Groups Separate from the basic-level party organizations that bring party members in all workplaces under the Communist Party hierarchy are party core groups, formed in government structures only and composed of a handful of party members who hold the most senior positions.[20] The head of the party core group is normally also the head of the structure (for example, government ministers typically head party core groups of their respective ministries). Party core groups are appointed by the party committees one level up, and they answer to these party committees. While basic-level party organizations are mechanisms to promote unity and discipline under party leadership within political structures overall, party core groups are mechanisms to promote party leadership over leaders in their government host structures. Between 1987 and 1988, the system of party core groups was formally abolished (and many were actually dismantled) as part of a brief reform effort to separate party and government functions. Party core groups were quickly revived in 1989, however, after the purge of Zhao Ziyang, the leader most closely associated with the reform.

Overlapping Directorships Finally, the structural distinctions illustrated in Figure 10.1 mask some overlap of directorates in party and government structures. Hu Jintao is concurrently head of state, head of the party, and chairman of the Central Military Commission of both government and party. The practice of "wearing two hats" (party and government) has always been common. Premier Wen Jiabao, as a member of the Politburo Standing Committee, is also at the apex of party power. Wu Bangguo, who chairs the NPC Standing Committee, is also a member of the Politburo Standing Committee. Overlapping directorships were much more extensive in the past than they are now. Membership of local party committees and their parallel governments used to be indistinguishable. In the 1980s, overlapping directorships were retained at the political center but were practically eliminated at lower

levels. There is some evidence that they are returning, partly to reduce local state expenditures.

Elite Recruitment Some key features of elite recruitment emerge from the discussion earlier in this chapter. First, membership in the Communist Party is a prerequisite for political elite status. Over the decades, the party has changed its focus of recruitment in society, reflecting larger changes in policy orientation. In the 1950s, for example, the party recruited most intensely among industrial workers to build a more traditional Communist Party from a largely peasant base. In the Cultural Revolution of the 1960s and 1970s, radical leftist standards dominated—and recruitment was directed toward those with less education and fewer connections. Since 1980, the party has focused its recruitment effort on intellectuals, professionals, and even private entrepreneurs—all social groups identified as important for China's development as a prosperous nation (see Box 10.2).

Second, the party not only controls accessibility to this fundamental prerequisite for elite status, but also possesses a powerful organizational mechanism to recruit and promote elites: the *nomenklatura* system. Both appointed and elected leaders are vetted for office, level by level, so leaders are ultimately accountable to party committees at higher levels. Beijing has not relinquished this key power, despite significant economic decentralization in recent decades.

What determines who gets along and ahead in the current Chinese political system? That is, what criteria have leaders at higher levels viewed as most important for promotion? While much is made of the role of informal politics in China, economic performance is the most important determinant of elite promotion.[21] Leaders in localities with higher economic growth or revenue contributions to the center during their tenure are less likely to be demoted or retired from office. This is not surprising, as leaders in Beijing have staked their claim to legitimacy on delivering economic prosperity.

Rule by Law

The principle of "rule of law" is traditionally associated with liberal democratic ideals. It implies a particular relationship between individuals and the state, the essence of which is protection of individual rights by limitations on arbitrary state power. Such limitations

BOX 10.2

"Red Capitalists"

In the mid-1980s, many party and government officials plunged into the private-sector economy, shedding their offices but not their Communist Party membership. With little fanfare, the party also began to recruit private entrepreneurs as new members—a practice that reflected the party's commitment to economic growth, but met strong opposition from many as an abandonment of basic communist tenets. How could millionaire exploiters represent Chinese workers and peasants? When private entrepreneurs lent their support to protesters in 1989, leaders imposed a ban on their recruitment into the party. More than a decade later, in 2000, party leader Jiang Zemin introduced a convoluted new formula to justify welcoming

them back: the "three represents," added in 2004 to China's constitution. In this formula, the party does not simply represent workers and peasants, but represents the developmental needs of the advanced social productive forces, the promotion of advanced culture, and the fundamental interests of the greatest majority of the people. In 2001, on the party's eightieth anniversary, Jiang proposed lifting the ban on recruitment of private entrepreneurs into the party. His proposal was soon implemented. Today, one-third of private entrepreneurs are party members. Even though "red capitalists" still account for only a very small proportion of party members, their inclusion reflects a highly significant policy.

---

are enshrined in the law and in legal institutions. This notion makes no sense in traditional communist ideology; law is a weapon of the state to use in exercising dictatorship. In 1978, however, Chinese leaders began to revive and develop important ideas and institutions of legality that had flourished for a brief period in the 1950s. The new Chinese legality acknowledges **rule by law**.[22] Briefly, this means (1) there are laws, and (2) all are equally subject to them. As the second principle is often violated, this may seem a trivial advance. It is not. The ongoing effort to establish rule by law in China has already changed in important ways how the Chinese act and think.

Socialist Legality The initial Chinese experiment with "socialist legality" began with the promulgation of the first constitution in 1954 and ended in 1957 with the Anti-Rightist Movement. Legalistic perspectives were rejected as examples of "bourgeois rightist" thinking. Legal scholars and legal professionals were criticized and labeled as "rightists." Work on development of criminal law stopped. Legal training and legal scholarship practically ceased. Defense lawyers disappeared from the legal process. Party committees took direct control of legal proceedings. The abandonment of law reached a peak during the Cultural Revolution, when violent "class struggle" and "mass justice" substituted for any regularized procedures to resolve social conflicts. This degree of radical lawlessness was not

characteristic of the entire Maoist period, but a general official hostility to law prevailed from the late 1950s.

Legal Reform Legal reform began in 1978. The legal system, barely functioning at the time, required urgent action for a number of reasons. First, there was an immediate need to establish legitimacy by righting past wrongs; investigating and reversing verdicts of dubious legality issued during the Cultural Revolution were a high priority. Second, Deng Xiaoping and other leaders wanted not only to restore public order and stability after years of chaos and uncertainty but also to express their commitment to system-building as a substitute for arbitrary political rule. Finally and not least of all, Chinese leaders hoped that the new legality would encourage economic investment and growth by promoting predictability—through transparent rules and impartial rule adjudication.

Rule by law requires laws. Nearly thirty years after the founding of the PRC, there was no criminal law. In 1978, Chinese leaders appointed committees of legal specialists to pick up work set aside for decades and to draft criminal codes for immediate promulgation. In 1979, the NPC passed the first criminal law and criminal procedure law. In the years that followed, as government agencies issued interim regulations that amended and clarified the hastily drafted laws, the NPC Legislative Affairs Committee worked on legal revisions. In 1996 and 1997, the NPC passed substantially amended and more precise versions of the laws. The 1997 amended criminal law takes into account changes in the Chinese economy that have created opportunities for economic crimes almost unimaginable in 1979 (such as insider securities trading). It abolishes the vaguely defined crimes of "counterrevolution." The 1996 amended criminal procedure law grants the accused the right to seek counsel (a right rejected in the 1950s) at an early stage of legal proceedings.

Rule by law implies equality before the law. This idea stands in sharp contrast to both the politicized view of law in communist ideology and routine practices in the Maoist years. In 1978, the NPC restored the procuratorates, which had been abolished in the 1960s. A new important role of procuratorates in the 1980s and 1990s became the investigation and prosecution of official crimes, for which procuratorates have full independent responsibility, according to law. Chinese leaders have regularly and prominently voiced a commitment to equality before the law, stating that officials who abuse public office and violate laws must be punished. Equality before the law, labeled "bourgeois" in the 1950s, is featured in the 1982 constitution—which also, for the first time, subjects the Communist Party (not only party members) to the authority of the law. At the same time, as described later in this chapter, there has been an explosion of corruption in recent years. In practice, the Communist Party, through its political-legal committees and its system of discipline inspection committees, routinely protects officials from equality before the law in cases involving abuses of power.

At the end of the 1970s, most Chinese were ignorant of laws and mistrustful of legal channels, a reasonable position when politics routinely superseded law. In the 1980s, the authorities launched a number of campaigns to educate ordinary citizens about the content of important laws and about certain ideas, such as equality before the law. Developing legal norms when legality has been actively denounced (not merely neglected) for decades has been difficult. Yet ordinary Chinese do use law to pursue their interests. One indicator of the effect of the legal education effort is the growth in lawsuits against government agencies and officials under the administrative litigation law. The number of such lawsuits processed in the legal system has increased steadily since passage of the law in 1989.

Criticism of Legal Practices Legal reform has provoked criticism of Chinese law and legal practices outside China.[23] Three examples illustrate. First, Chinese criminal law stipulates the death penalty in "serious circumstances" of smuggling, rape, theft, bribery, trafficking in women and children, and corruption. In periodic intensive efforts to "strike hard" at crime, the authorities have resorted widely to capital punishment. Critics argue that capital punishment is excessively harsh for these crimes. Second, by design, criminal proceedings are inquisitorial (not adversarial), focused on determination of punishment (not guilt). As cases are prosecuted only after sufficient evidence has been collected to demonstrate guilt, most prosecutions result in guilty verdicts. The right to seek counsel at an early stage of proceedings is recognized in the law, but the requirement is only that a public defender be assigned no later than ten days before trial. By that time, the case has been prepared for prosecution and usually a confession (for which the law promises leniency) has already been obtained. This practice of "verdict first, trial second" has been questioned and debated inside China and criticized outside China. Finally, despite abolition of specifically political crimes of counterrevolution, the Chinese authorities acknowledge "several thousand" political prisoners. While human-rights groups estimate the number to be much larger, all critics view the situation as essentially inconsistent with the new law.

Nonetheless, the new legality has produced significant change. Today more than ever before, the Chinese state is more constrained by laws, while Chinese citizens are freer from political arbitrariness because of laws. Abuse of authority is acted on differently from before. Ordinary citizens use the law as a political weapon against perceived injustice because the regime has invested heavily in the new legality. The official effort to build rule by law, by making law salient, has produced a basis for "rightful resistance" to hold the regime accountable to its own proclaimed standards.

POLITICAL SOCIALIZATION

One result of the economic policy of opening up to the outside is that Chinese leaders today cannot control information as in the Maoist years.[24]

Mass Media

Ordinary Chinese are now routinely exposed to news and opinions about public affairs in their country through access to Hong Kong (which maintains relatively free and critical mass media) and the outside world in newspapers, books, radio and television broadcasts, and the Internet. Moreover, Chinese connect with one another to transmit information as never before through blogs, bulletin boards, e-mail, telephone, and text messages. China imported its first mobile-phone facilities in 1987; today, 277 million of 420 million Internet users in China connect through their mobile phones. The Chinese authorities recognize the importance of the Internet to economic modernization, but also view it as a threat to their rule. The Communist Party Propaganda Department and State Council Information Office direct the world's most extensive system to control, censor, and monitor material considered politically subversive. Internet news is still mainly official news; news media are required to use the official Xinhua news agency as their news source. Despite great relaxation of media controls, certain topics remain taboo (multiparty competition, urban protests, and labor strikes, for example). In this way, the Internet allows the regime to spread its official message more effectively. The Chinese **Great Firewall** for Internet censorship blocks content by preventing Internet Protocol (IP) addresses from being routed through standard firewall and proxy servers at Internet gateways. As the government controls the domestic networks that connect service providers to international networks, it can block access to sites and delete Web pages considered subversive. Tens of thousands of "cyber-cops" selectively block foreign news sites and terminate domestic sites that publicize politically sensitive information. For example, the authorities quickly blocked any use of the phrase "empty chair" when it appeared in numerous Chinese blogs as an expression of solidarity with 2010 Nobel Peace Prize winner Liu Xiaobo, imprisoned for political dissidence and represented at the ceremonies in Oslo by an empty chair. Of course, total control is counterproductive (see Box 10.3). Internet users circumvent official blockages through proxy servers based outside China and by slightly altering Chinese characters to refer to political events and activities.

Education System

The new content and style of political socialization are clearly evident in the education system. Mao's successors inherited an educational system designed to build communist values—and fundamentally at odds with the priority of economic growth. During the Cultural Revolution, high-school graduates were sent to factories or farms to acquire work experience and learn from the masses. University entrance examinations were replaced with recommendations by grassroots leaders, focusing on revolutionary political credentials. With

---

Chinese Internet Censorship and Google

BOX 10.3

The Chinese government has issued dozens of documents regulating Internet content, but no official master list of taboo subjects has been made public. Instead, businesses interpret regulations and gauge the political environment as they censor and self-censor. Operating in this regulatory context, Google.cn, the Google search engine based in China until 2010, routinely filtered its content. Appearing at the bottom of each page of censored results on Google.cn was a notice informing readers that some information is hidden from them because of strictures from the Chinese authorities. In January 2010, Google announced it was no longer willing to filter its content; instead, it would attempt to negotiate a legal, unfiltered search engine. Failing that, it would close down its China operations. At the announcement, Chinese expressed their grief at the loss by laying flowers at the door of Google's Beijing offices; although the search engine's market share of 33 percent lagged far behind that of its Chinese competitor, Baidu, Google censored less than did Baidu; access to English-language periodicals was particularly valuable to Chinese researchers. In March 2010, with no Chinese flexibility on requirements to observe existing law, Google shut down its mainland offices to establish an unfiltered Google.cn in Hong Kong. Today, the Chinese Great Firewall regularly blocks searches of politically sensitive topics on Google.cn from within China.

420 Million Chinese "Netizens"

Cyber cafés are popular with urban Chinese youth. Even with some 50,000 cyberpolice, it is impossible to monitor Internet activity fully.

Greg Baker/AP Images

the persecution of scholars and denigration of expert knowledge in the universities, the content of university education was redesigned to include more politics in every specialization. Graduates were more "red" than expert. An entire decade was lost. The generation that missed out on an education during this decade is known today as the "lost generation."

Today, with the return of the university entrance examinations and huge numbers of Chinese studying in foreign universities, the respect for expertise is thoroughly restored. Indeed, in fall 2006, on instructions from top party and government departments, colleges across the country reduced the seven compulsory courses on political ideology and party history to four in the first major curricular change in twenty-five years.

POLITICAL CULTURE

Older and middle-aged Chinese have experienced not only the radicalism of the Maoist years, but also more than two decades of "reform and opening" to the outside world. Young Chinese have only the personal experience of the relatively open post-Mao years, including the decade of the 1990s that saw the "third wave" of democratization, with the triumph of democracy in nearly every communist country. Surely, recent changes both inside and outside China have left their imprint on the way Chinese view their government and their relationship to political authorities.

Because Maoist-era leaders regarded social science with great suspicion, we have no good baseline of public opinion data by which to assess change over time in the beliefs of ordinary Chinese. We can say something about the Chinese political culture today, however, based on survey research in China, including surveys organized and conducted by political scientists based in the United States. What is the orientation toward politics of ordinary Chinese? In particular, to what extent do the beliefs of Chinese seem conducive to political change in the direction of further democratization?

Political Knowledge

An important building block for democracy is a citizenry knowledgeable about politics and interested in public affairs, able to monitor the performance of representatives and leaders. Most ordinary Chinese follow public affairs at least weekly, mainly through radio or television programs and somewhat less through newspapers, but politics is not something that is a regular topic of discussion in China. A majority say they *never* talk about politics with others, a stark reflection of lack of active interest.

Political knowledge and interest are not uniformly distributed in China, of course. A more active knowledge and interest are seen among men, the more highly educated, and Chinese with higher incomes, which is not so different from what we observe in other countries. Not surprisingly, Chinese in Beijing are much more interested in politics than Chinese overall; in fact, they discuss politics very frequently. Yet even if we consider the situation of Chinese overall, which includes the relatively less knowledgeable and less interested rural population, political knowledge in China today is higher than in Italy in the early 1960s and political discourse higher than in Italy or Mexico in the early 1960s.[25]

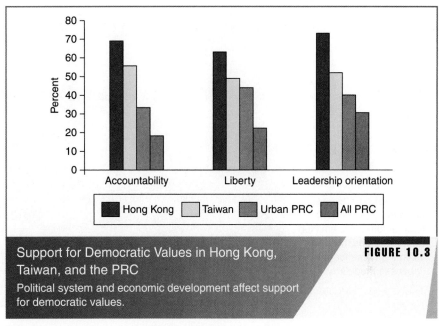

FIGURE 10.3

Support for Democratic Values in Hong Kong, Taiwan, and the PRC

Political system and economic development affect support for democratic values.

Percent expressing *disagreement* with statements below.

Accountability: "Top government officials are like the heads of a big family. We should follow all their decisions on national issues."

Liberty: "The government should have the power to decide which opinions (perspectives) are to be circulated in a society and which are not."

Leadership orientation: "We can leave everything to morally upright leaders."

Source: Yun-han Chu and Yu-tzung Chang, "Culture Shift and Regime Legitimacy: Comparing Mainland China, Taiwan, and Hong Kong," in *Chinese Political Culture, 1989–2000*, ed. Shiping Hua (Armonk, NY: M. E. Sharpe, 2001), 332–33. Based on surveys conducted in 1993 and 1994.

Political Values

Perhaps the most interesting perspective on contemporary Chinese political culture is a comparative one that considers its fate across three different Chinese political systems. An extraordinary survey of a representative sample of Chinese in mainland China, Hong Kong, and Taiwan conducted in 1993 and 1994 provides this perspective and helps to sort out different influences of traditional culture, political system, and socioeconomic development.[26] Figure 10.3 compares responses of ordinary Chinese in the PRC, Hong Kong, and Taiwan to questions about political relationships. Two questions tap orientations to popular accountability and political liberty. Another frames relationships in traditional Confucian terms of virtuous leadership. Altogether, these questions probe Chinese support for values commonly associated with liberal democracy. The responses reveal a fairly consistent, easily interpretable, and striking pattern.

First, there seems to be a strong impact due to political system. A majority of Chinese in the PRC reject every democratic value, and support for democratic values is generally lowest in the PRC. This is not surprising. By the early 1990s, when this survey was conducted, Taiwan's process of democratization was well underway. Hong Kong, while still under British colonial rule, had enjoyed significant civil liberties for decades and was taking initial steps to increase electoral competition.

Second, the influence of non-Chinese political socialization is evident. The traditional Confucian orientation to the moral state is least evident in Hong Kong; nearly three-fourths of Hong Kong Chinese reject the view that everything should be left up to virtuous leaders. By contrast, this view finds strong support in the PRC. Chinese in Taiwan are somewhere in the middle, perhaps reflecting rule by a Chinese government but a society long open to outside influences.

Third, and perhaps most interesting of all for speculation about support for democratization in the PRC, the responses show an impact of socioeconomic development. This is most evident in a comparison of responses in the PRC overall with those in urban China only. Urban Chinese are much more supportive of democratic values than are mainland Chinese generally.

Surveys conducted in the PRC nearly ten years later update this perspective on Chinese democratic

Big City Traffic, Big City Highways

China is no longer a bicycle nation. Chinese-designed and manufactured automobiles emit ten to twenty times more pollution than American or Japanese models.

Justin Guariglia/The Image Works

values. Although Chinese overwhelmingly support the abstract idea of democracy, 60 to 70 percent fear negative effects of some democratic practices (interest groups and a multiparty system, for example). Economic growth, social stability, and national strength are viewed as top priorities; political rights are assigned lower priority. Indeed, there is fairly high satisfaction with Chinese "socialist democracy" in this century. As above, some comparative leverage is useful; across generations, the cohorts born in the reform era are much more prodemocratic than those born before the 1980s cohort, and each successive reform-era cohort is more prodemocratic than the preceding one.[27] By about 2020, Chinese society will be dominated by the more democratic values of these cohorts.

POLITICAL PARTICIPATION

In the communist party-state, political participation, interest articulation, and interest aggregation differ from the processes normally found in liberal democratic systems. The source of difference is, of course, different conceptions of the relationship between leaders and citizens; the notion of guardianship is fundamentally incompatible with liberal democratic notions of representation. The Communist Party organization claims to represent the interests of all society. It rejects political parties other than itself as unnecessary and

unacceptable. While there has been change in political processes in recent decades, the "officially acceptable" forms of political participation, interest articulation, and interest aggregation in the Chinese political system continue to reflect the relationship of guardianship between party and society. This section discusses political participation; the next section explores interest articulation and aggregation.

Changes in the Rules

An important aspect of political reform undertaken after Mao's death in 1976 has been the redefinition of what constitutes "officially acceptable" political participation in the Chinese system. Guidelines for the new political participation are evident in three categories of rule changes that have routinized participation and reduced its burden for ordinary Chinese. The changes reflect an official reaction against the disruption that characterized mass participation in the Maoist years (especially during the Cultural Revolution), an official assumption that economic growth is predicated on order and stability, and an official recognition that changes in economic relationships require adjustments in political relationships.

The first category of rule changes involves political participation, which has become essentially optional for ordinary Chinese since the early 1980s. In the first thirty years of communist rule, for a broad range of political activities, failure to participate was considered tantamount to opposition to the communist regime. Today, politics intrudes far less in the lives of ordinary Chinese. The scope and demands of politics have shrunk. The single most important measure signifying this change is the official removal, in 1979, of all class and political labels. After thirty years, the Chinese are no longer formally identified by class background or past "political mistakes." Not only does politics no longer dominate daily life, but in the diminished sphere of political activities, political apathy is no longer risky for ordinary Chinese.

The second category has been the assiduous avoidance by the regime of rousing the mass public to realize policy objectives. In the Maoist years, by contrast, the quintessential form of political participation was the **mass mobilization campaign**—intensive, large-scale, disruptive group action implemented by grassroots leaders. The Great Leap Forward launched in 1958 and the Cultural Revolution launched in 1966 were essentially mass campaigns, on a gargantuan scale. Typically in mass campaigns, grassroots party leaders, responding to signals from the political center, roused ordinary Chinese to achieve regime goals of various sorts, often aimed at identified categories of enemies—such as "counterrevolutionaries" in 1950 and 1951; the "landlord class" in 1950 through 1952; the "rightists" in 1957; and the "unclean cadres" in 1962 and 1963. Mass-campaign methods were adopted for nonpolitical objectives too, such as the ill-conceived and ecologically harmful effort to eradicate "four pests" (sparrows, rats, flies, and mosquitoes) in 1956. Participation in campaigns was virtually compulsory. Only three years after Mao's death, Chinese leaders issued an official rejection of mass campaigns as a mode of political participation. Many leaders who emerged at the top echelons of power in the late 1970s had themselves been victims of persecution in the Cultural Revolution. The social disorder of campaigns was rejected as antithetical to the new priority of economic growth.

The third category is the rejection of mass mobilization as the dominant mode of political participation. Chinese leaders have instead encouraged ordinary citizens to express their opinions and participate in politics through a variety of regular official channels, some new, others newly revived: offices to receive complaints, centers and telephone hotlines to report abuses of power, and letters to newspaper editors, for example.[28] Not least of all, the authorities

have introduced important reforms in elections. As a consequence, political participation in China is varied and extensive in scope. Table 10.2 shows findings from a survey conducted in Beijing in the 1980s and 1990s. Beijing is surely the most highly politicized city in all of China, but the extent of citizen participation in a wide range of activities is nonetheless remarkable, not at all the picture of Maoist mobilization.

Elections and an electoral connection between citizens and leaders are integral to liberal democratic conceptions of representation. For this reason, governments and NGOs in liberal democracies have paid close attention to electoral reforms in China.

Local Congress Elections

Elections to local people's congresses in the Maoist years were political rituals, featuring no candidate choice and no secret ballot. Voters directly elected deputies to township-level congresses only; at higher levels, deputies were elected by congresses at the level immediately below. Such elections served as vehicles of regime legitimation, popular education, and political socialization, but they did not really allow ordinary citizens to choose representatives.

In 1979, a new election law introduced direct election of deputies to county-level congresses, mandated secret ballots rather than public displays of support, and required the number of candidates to be one and a half times the number of deputies to be elected.

Although local Communist Party organizations continue to play a key leadership role in election committees, essentially vetting candidates, not all candidates can win under current rules. Some officially nominated candidates lose elections. Indeed, some candidates officially designated for government office lose elections. A growing number of candidates who are not Communist Party members have competed and won in elections. A smaller number of government executives nominated by deputies are not official candidates and win without official endorsement.[29] An electoral victory signifies some degree of popular support, while losing signifies a problematic relationship with the mass public. At a minimum, the new rules are a means for the Communist Party organization to gauge popular views about local officials, diversify the pool from which leaders are recruited, and monitor local leaders. To be sure, the new rules have not produced radical change. Nor can such an

TABLE 10.2		
Political Participation in Beijing (percent reporting having participated in political act)		
Significant numbers of Chinese participate politically in officially acceptable ways.		
Political Act	**1988**	**1996**
Voting for deputies in local congress elections	71.5	81.0
Contacting leaders of workplace	51.2	54.2
Complaining through bureaucratic hierarchy	43.0	47.5
Voting for leaders in workplace	34.8	16.1
Complaining through trade unions	18.9	24.4
Using connections (*guanxi*)	15.5	16.6
Complaining through political organizations	15.0	17.7
Slowing down on the job	12.6	9.3
Writing letters to government officials	12.5	15.3
Persuading others to attend campaign meetings for congress deputies	8.9	13.0
Complaining through congress deputies	8.6	14.1
Persuading others to attend campaign or briefing meetings at workplace	7.7	5.4
Organizing others to fight against leaders	7.6	3.0
Writing letters to newspaper editors	6.8	8.3
Persuading others to vote for certain leaders in workplace elections	5.7	3.5
Whipping up public opinion against workplace leaders	5.1	1.7
Persuading others to vote for certain deputies in congress elections	4.7	8.0
Giving gifts in exchange for help	4.6	8.0
Persuading others to boycott unfair workplace elections	4.6	2.9
Reporting to complaint bureaus	4.0	8.1
Persuading others to boycott unfair congress elections	3.7	6.8
Bringing cases to court	1.2	4.5
Participating in strikes	0.9	2.6
Participating in demonstrations	0.4	1.4

Source: Tianjian Shi, "Mass Political Behavior in Beijing," in *The Paradox of China's Post-Mao Reforms*, ed. Merle Goldman and Roderick MacFarquhar (Cambridge, MA: Harvard University Press, 1999), 155.

outcome be expected without further change in rules; no platform of opposition to the Communist Party is permissible.

Village Committees

China also now has nearly two decades of experience with rural grassroots democratization, formally approved in November 1987 when the NPC, after over a year of debate, passed a provisional version of the Organic Law on Village Committees. A final revised version was passed in November 1998. The law defines **village committees** as "autonomous mass organizations of self-government," popularly elected in elections featuring choice among candidates for three-year terms and accountable to a village council comprised of all adult villagers.

The introduction of popularly elected village committees in 1987 was designed to strengthen state capacity to govern in the aftermath of agricultural decollectivization. In the early 1980s, the people's communes had been dismantled and replaced with township governments. Land and other production inputs were divided among peasant households to manage on their own, free markets were opened, most obligatory sales to the state were abolished, and private entrepreneurship was promoted.[30] The results of these reforms were successful by most economic standards, but disastrous in their consequences for rural leadership. As villagers gained greater economic initiative and autonomy, the power of the Chinese party-state to exact compliance was enormously weakened. By the mid-1980s, village leadership had seriously atrophied. Leaders were enriching themselves at the expense of the community, and villagers were resisting their efforts to implement unpopular policies. Violent conflicts between villagers and village leaders had become common. The revitalization of village committees in 1987 was designed to make the countryside more governable by increasing accountability. Presumably, villagers would be more responsive to leaders elected from below rather than those imposed from above as before.

In 1998, when the NPC affirmed the experience of village elections, most villages had undergone at least three rounds of elections, with enormous local variation in implementation. In many villages, the village Communist Party branch controlled candidate nomination, there was no candidate choice for the key position of village committee director, and voting irregularities were common. Even in villages that made serious progress—with genuinely competitive elections, widespread popular participation in candidate nomination, and scrupulous attention to voting procedure—real managerial authority often resided not with the popularly elected village committee but with the village Communist Party branch. Even today, too little is known to generalize about overall progress in village elections, its determinants, or its consequences.[31] Certainly, to the degree that the practices of grassroots democracy acquire the force of routine and expectations accumulate, however slowly, among nearly 625 million Chinese in more than 600,000 villages, political participation in the countryside will change profoundly.

"Unacceptable" Political Participation

More dramatic than the reforms that have redefined officially acceptable political participation has been the political action of ordinary Chinese in city streets and squares beginning in the late 1970s. With strikes, marches, posters, petitions, and occupation of public spaces, ordinary citizens have acted as if political reform comprehended or condoned mass political action and public disorder. The official record suggests the contrary, however.

In 1980, the right to post "big-character posters" (usually criticisms of leaders, written by individuals or groups and posted on walls), introduced during the Cultural Revolution, was removed from the Chinese constitution. In 1982, the constitutional right to strike was rescinded. As for mass protests, the official view

was made clear in 1979 with the introduction of the "four fundamental principles" that political participation must uphold: (1) the socialist road, (2) Marxism–Leninism–Mao Zedong Thought, (3) the people's democratic dictatorship, and (4) the leadership of the Communist Party. Of these principles, only the last is necessary to restrict political participation effectively, as the content of the first three has become what party leaders make of it. Participants (especially organizers) face real risks of physical harm and criminal punishment. Why, then, did ordinary citizens engage in mass protests with increasing frequency in the 1970s and 1980s? Why did urban worker and peasant unrest increase in the 1980s and 1990s?

Different sorts of "officially unacceptable" political participation have different explanations, but none can be explained without reference to the post-Mao reforms. On the one hand, economic reforms have produced some socially unacceptable outcomes: more (and more visible) inflation, unemployment, crime, and corruption, for example. Rural unrest has typically been triggered by local corruption and exaction of excessive (often illegal) taxes and fees. Urban unrest—strikes, slowdowns, and demonstrations—has increased too, as state enterprises struggle to survive in the socialist market economy. A number of enterprises have been closed down; many have engaged in massive layoffs; others have been unable to pay bonuses and pensions. For the first time since 1949, many urban Chinese have been living on fixed incomes, no incomes, or unpredictable incomes as the cost of living increases.

Protesters and Reformers

In 1989, a different sort of urban unrest captured the attention of the world news media and, consequently, of the world. The demonstration that brought a million people to Tiananmen Square was the third major political protest movement since Mao's death. The first was in 1978 and 1979, the second in 1986 and 1987. All three were officially unacceptable, all were linked in some important way to official reforms and reformers, and all ended in failure for mass protesters (and resulted in setbacks to official reforms, too).[32]

Despite links between protesters and official reformers, the post-Mao movements were not mass mobilization campaigns. As they were not explicitly initiated by the regime, once underway they could not be easily stopped with an official pronouncement from the political center. Instead, the authorities turned to coercive force wielded by the police, the armed police, and ultimately the army to terminate the protests with violence.

Protests are officially unacceptable mainly because of their form of expression. The official consensus since December 1978 has been that the most important priority for China is economic growth, with social order and stability as prerequisites for growth. Mass protests are distinctly disorderly. Further, as a form of political participation, mass protests are a symptom of regime failure in two senses. By turning to the streets to articulate their demands, protesters demonstrate that official channels for expressing critical views are not working and that they do not believe the Communist Party's claim that it can correct its own mistakes. Further, protesters are clearly not alienated from politics. While they reject official channels of participation, they are not politically apathetic; indeed, they articulate explicitly political demands despite serious risks and the difficulty associated with organizing outside the system. In short, political protests signify that mass political participation can neither be contained within official channels nor deterred with a better material life.

For the most part, despite some radical elements, the protests have not been blatantly antisystem in their demands. This does not appear to be merely strategic. Rather, the protests are something of a rowdy mass counterpart to the official socialist reform movement, exerting more pressure for more reform, and (while officially unacceptable) often linked with elite reformers.

In the **Democracy Movement** of 1978 and 1979, Deng Xiaoping publicly approved many of the demands posted on Democracy Wall and published in unofficial journals, which called for a "reversal of verdicts" on individuals and political events. The demands were an integral part of the pressure for reform that surrounded the meetings of top leaders in late 1978, allowing elite reformers to argue for major changes in policy and political orientation. The poster campaign and unofficial journals were tolerated. To be sure, when a bold dissident named Wei Jingsheng demanded a "fifth modernization," by which he meant democracy of a sort never envisaged by the communists, the Chinese authorities promptly sentenced him to a fifteen-year prison term (ostensibly for revealing state secrets) and introduced the "four fundamental principles" to establish the parameters of acceptable debate[33] (see Box 10.4).

When the Communist Party congress convened in late 1987, party leader Zhao Ziyang acknowledged conflicts of interest in society at the current time. The years 1988 and 1989 were high points for political liberalization. The political criticism expressed in Tiananmen Square in 1989 largely echoed public views of elite reformers in the party and government. From the perspective of communist authorities, the real danger in 1989 was not the content of mass

---

Wei Jingsheng and the "Fifth Modernization"   BOX 10.4

In late 1978, in an atmosphere of great change that included official "reversals of verdicts" of the Cultural Revolution, many Chinese began to gather regularly at a large wall close to Beijing's Tiananmen Square to post, read, and discuss political posters. One of the boldest posters to appear on Democracy Wall was an essay by Wei Jingsheng. It argued that the ambitious new program to modernize agriculture, industry, national defense, and science and technology could not succeed without a "fifth modernization"—democracy. Wei wrote: "The hated old political system has not changed. Are not the people justified in seizing power from the overlords?" Wei published even more critical essays in his unofficial journal *Explorations*, one of more than fifty such journals circulating at the time. In March 1979, he posted an attack on Deng Xiaoping, asking: "Do we want democracy or new dictatorship?" Wei was tried and convicted of "counterrevolutionary crimes" and "leaking state secrets" to foreigners. Some fifteen years later, Wei was released from prison, only to be rearrested for dissident activities. In 1997, after years of pressure from human-rights groups and governments outside China, China's most famous political dissident was released and exiled to the United States, where he continues to criticize the Chinese authorities.

demands but the organizational challenge: Students and workers organized their own unions, independent of the party, to represent their interests.

The challenge was exacerbated by an open break in elite ranks when Zhao Ziyang voiced his support for the protesters and declared his opposition to martial law. Other party and government leaders and retired elders, including Deng Xiaoping—many of whom had been victims of power seizures by youths in the Cultural Revolution—viewed the problem as a basic struggle for the survival of the system and their own positions. The movement was violently and decisively crushed with tanks and machine guns in the **Tiananmen massacre** of June 4, 1989.[34]

All three protests ended in defeat for the participants: prison for the main protest organizers in 1979, expulsion from the Communist Party for intellectual leaders in 1987, and prison or violent death for hundreds in 1989. The defeats extended beyond the mass protest movement to encompass setbacks to the official reform movement, too. When demands for reform moved to the city streets, more conservative leaders attributed the social disorder to an excessively rapid pace of reform. The result was a slower pace or postponement of reforms. Twice, the highest party leader was dismissed from office as a result of the mass protests (Hu Yaobang in 1987 and Zhao Ziyang in 1989), and the official reform movement lost its strongest proponent.

INTEREST ARTICULATION AND AGGREGATION

Most ordinary citizens engage in interest articulation without interest aggregation. This takes the form of personal contacts to articulate individual concerns about the effects of policies on their lives. Much of this interest articulation takes place at the workplace. For the most part, the function of interest aggregation is monopolized by the Communist Party, although the party's role in interest aggregation is being diluted and the methods it employs have also evolved.

Organizations under Party Leadership

Under the formal leadership of the Communist Party are eight "satellite parties," a legacy of the communist pre-1949 strategy of provisional cooperation with noncommunist democratic parties.[35] These parties have no real role in policymaking, but they are represented (with prominent nonparty individuals) in the Chinese People's Political Consultative Conference. In 1989, the Central Committee proposed greater cooperation with the noncommunist parties by regular consultation with their leaders on major policies—or at least a stronger effort to inform the parties of Communist Party policies. Of course, this proposal referred only to the eight officially tolerated parties. In 1998, the authorities arrested, tried, and imprisoned a veteran of the 1978 to 1979 Democracy Movement

Facing Down the Tanks in June 1989

In 1989, ordinary Chinese participated in the largest spontaneous protest movement the communists had ever faced. A lone protester shows defiance of regime violence in his intransigent confrontation with a Chinese tank.

Jeff Widener/AP Images

who attempted to register a fledgling China Democracy Party.

The other older formal organizations that aggregate like interests in the Chinese political system are the "mass organizations," extensions of the Communist Party into society, nationwide in scope and organized hierarchically. The All-China Federation of Trade Unions and the Women's Federation remain active and important mass organizations today. Mass organizations are led by Communist Party officials, who are specially assigned to these positions and who take direction from party committees. The main function of these organizations is not to aggregate and represent group interests for consideration in the policymaking process but to facilitate propagation of party policy to the relevant groups. Essentially, mass organizations represent the interests of the Communist Party to the organized "interest groups" it dominates, not vice versa.

NGOs and GONGOs

A very different set of associations emerged in the late 1980s with official encouragement. These "social organizations," over 450,000 in number (and millions more unregistered), range widely in form and focus. In form, they include genuine NGOs and government-organized nongovernmental organizations (**GONGO**s). Some GONGOs are essentially front organizations for government agencies, set up to take advantage of the interest of foreign governments and international NGOs to support the emergence of Chinese civil society. Other GONGOs have strong and mutually beneficial relationships with NGOs, acting as a bridge to government agencies. In focus, GONGOs and especially NGOs cover a wide range of interests and activities.

Among the most interesting GONGOs are the business associations set up to organize firms: the Self-Employed Laborers Association, the Private Enterprises Association, and the Federation of Industry and Commerce. The Federation of Industry and Commerce, which organizes the largest Chinese firms, has independent resources that have permitted it to create a separate organizational network (chambers of commerce), a national newspaper, and a financial institution to provide credit to members.

Among NGOs, the roughly 2,000 organizations that focus on environmental issues are at the vanguard of NGO activity.[36] The largest, best-funded, and best-organized environmental NGOs focus primarily on species and nature conservation and environmental education. With strong support from the media, these NGOs often work with central authorities to expose and counter local government failure to implement environmental laws and policies. One environmental NGO trains lawyers to engage in enforcement of laws, educates judges about the issues, and litigates environmental cases.

Individual environmental activists have also organized to influence political decisions. A good example is the independent publication of *Yangtze! Yangtze!*, a collection of papers by scientists and environmentalists critical of the world's biggest and most controversial hydroelectric project, the Three Gorges Dam. The study was released in early 1989 with the aim of influencing the widely publicized NPC vote to approve dam construction. Although it failed to halt approval, nearly a third of NPC delegates voted against the project or abstained—prompting the government to postpone dam construction until the mid-1990s.

Considering the "Leninist organizational predisposition" to thwart organizational plurality, the encouragement of NGO emergence and activity in the Chinese context seems puzzling.[37] It is explained by the closure of many state enterprises and the downsizing of government at all levels, in the 1980s and 1990s, creating a need for the growth of social organizations to take on some former government functions, especially social-welfare functions. Essentially, this change shifts the burden from government to society. The 1998 plan to downsize the central government bureaucracy explicitly noted that many functions "appropriated by government" must be "given back" to society and managed by new social associations. This plan opened the political space for the emergence of NGOs. The authorities also recognize that NGOs can help the center monitor local government policy implementation; this is the role that environmental NGOs have played most prominently, for example.

For the most part, NGO activity is in fact well within the parameters of officially acceptable political participation. Most groups do not seek autonomy from the state, but rather seek "embeddedness" within the state. To be autonomous is to be outside the system and relatively powerless, unable to exercise influence. In sum, for the most part, the emerging Chinese civil society aggregates and articulates its interests without challenging the state.

To be sure, the authorities have taken measures to guarantee that NGOs work with (not against) them. An elaborate set of regulations requires social organizations to affiliate with a sponsor that is responsible for their activity, to register with the government, and to have sufficient funding and membership. The regulations also prohibit the coexistence of more than one organization with the same substantive focus at the national level or in any particular locality. This preserves the monopoly of the official mass organizations to represent the interests of women and workers, for example.

In practice, however, it is simply impossible really to control NGO activity; some NGOs register as businesses, others thrive as Internet-based virtual organizations, and government sponsors cannot monitor the organizations registered as their affiliates. For example, the All-China Women's Federation is responsible for more than 3,000 social organizations dealing with women's issues. In this context, Chinese NGOs can be expected to continue to grow.

It is important to note that one significant social group lacks a legitimate organizational channel (even a mass organization) that aggregates its interests: farmers. To the extent that Chinese farmers engage in collective action to articulate their interests, it is largely through petitions and protests.

POLICYMAKING AND IMPLEMENTATION

Today, it is inconceivable that a scheme such as the Great Leap Forward could be launched and implemented as it was in the 1950s. Controversial policies are no longer adopted at the whim of a single leader, experts play a significant role in policy formulation, experimentation in selected localities precedes widespread implementation, and local authorities no longer slavishly sacrifice local development goals to meet unrealistic campaign targets dictated by the center.

The single most important difference distinguishing policy processes of the 1950s from those of the 1990s and after, however, is the recent greater reliance on consultation and consensus-building among a wider range of bureaucratic, local, and economic players. This change is partly due to economic reforms that provide increased opportunities and incentives for players to devote resources to projects outside the state plan rather than to state-mandated projects. In discussing policy processes, the Chinese often refer to the following expression: "The top has its policy measures; the bottom has its countermeasures." Having renounced campaigns and purges, policymakers at the

top have instead worked to forge agreements with a variety of players at the political center and in the localities so that policies adopted are implemented, not ignored or radically reshaped in the course of implementation. At the apex of the system, consultation has become even more important, because no leader possesses either the experience or the personal prestige of a Mao Zedong or a Deng Xiaoping.

The political structures described at the beginning of this chapter are essential points of reference for the description of policymaking and policy implementation here. However, key features of policy processes are not well illustrated by consideration of these formal structures alone. As elaborated below, the formal distinction between party and government structures is less relevant than it appears; at least one key structure does not appear on formal organizational charts, and authority is more fragmented and less well-bounded than formal structure suggests.

Policymaking

Policymaking in China today is less concentrated and more institutionalized than ever before. It involves three sets of institutional players: the party, the government, and the legislature, shown in Figure 10.4. It is also useful to distinguish three tiers in the policymaking process. Different party, government, and legislative structures at different tiers interact at different stages of the process. Moreover, a number of individual players overlap, appearing in more than one set of institutions. This section traces the process by which major policies emerge and are eventually formalized as laws. It is worth noting, however, that many important policy decisions do not go through the legislature at all. For example, the State Council has the power to issue administrative regulations, decisions, instructions, orders, and measures to local governments; central government ministries issue their own departmental regulations, clarifications, and responses to respective local government departments; and the Communist Party Politburo and individual party departments have their own separate systems of regulations, decisions, instructions, orders, and measures issued to counterparts in the localities and lower levels of the party bureaucracy.

Three Tiers in Policymaking At the very top tier are the leaders at the apex of the party—in the Politburo and its Standing Committee. The party generalists at

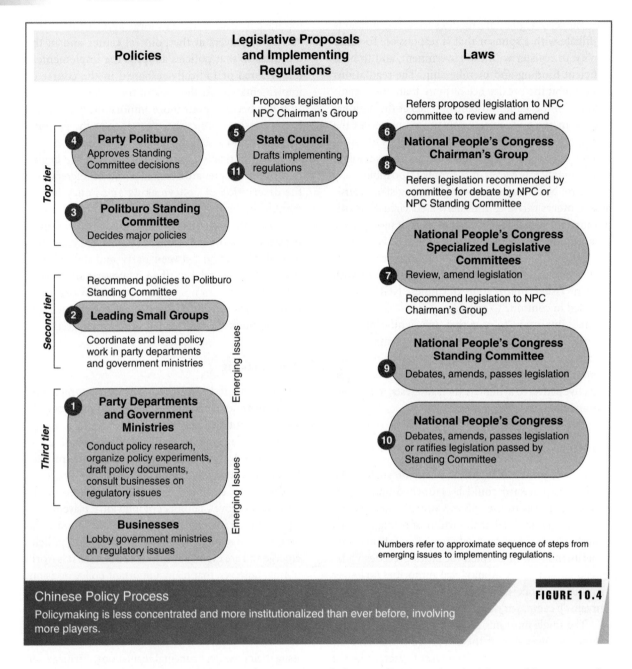

Chinese Policy Process

Policymaking is less concentrated and more institutionalized than ever before, involving more players.

FIGURE 10.4

this tier are each typically responsible for at least one broad policy area. As a group, they make all major policy decisions. Formally, the Politburo has the ultimate authority to determine major policies, but it probably meets in plenary session only about once monthly for a morning to ratify policies already approved by the Politburo Standing Committee. It is useful to recall here that the leaders at the top of the party hierarchy include not only party leaders but also the prime minister and the NPC chairman. Overlapping directorships

help coordinate major decision-making across the three sets of institutions.

The most thorough consideration of policy options and shaping of policy decisions occur at the second tier—within **leading small groups (LSGs)**, which are defined by broad policy areas.[38] LSGs are headed by leaders at the top tier of the party, although deputy heads are likely to be outside the top tier. LSGs have sweeping mandates to preside over policy research, formulation of policy proposals, sponsorship of policy experiments in the localities, and drafting of policy documents. LSGs bring together all the senior officials with responsibility for different aspects of a policy area.[39] They exercise leadership as policies emerge onto an initial agenda, and they make specific recommendations to the Politburo Standing Committee once policies are ready to move onto the legislative agenda. They are a crucial coordinating mechanism in the policymaking process, linking top decision-makers to bureaucracies and bridging institutional systems.

Coordinating mechanisms are particularly important to policymaking in the Chinese system because authority is formally structured so as to require the cooperation of many bureaucratic units, nested in separate chains of authority. The fragmentation of formal authority and its resolution by formal and informal coordinating mechanisms at the top of the system have led some scholars to characterize the Chinese system as one of **fragmented authoritarianism**.[40]

In what ways is formal authority fragmented? The best example is the system of dual subordination. On the one hand, authority is organized in systems of vertical bureaucracies in hierarchies that extend from ministries at the center to lower-level departments in the localities. Each ministry under the State Council is at the top of a hierarchy of subordinate departments that exist at the provincial, county, and township levels of government. On the other hand, the central ministry and subordinate departments are all government departments and, as such, are subordinate to their respective governments, too. The Chinese refer to the two structural arrangements as "lines" and "pieces." Authoritative communications are channeled from top to bottom (vertically, in lines) and also from governments to their departments (horizontally, in pieces). The two sorts of authority come together only at the center, at the level of the State Council. Simply put, then, all local government departments have two bosses in their formal authority relationships—not to mention their relationships with party departments in the same issue area and party committees with *nomenklatura* authority over them. In Chinese terminology, there are "too many mothers-in-law." This structure of formal authority routinely creates blockages in policy processes. Many policy issues cannot be resolved at lower levels but must be pushed up to a sufficiently high level, such as an LSG, that spans many authority structures and can overcome bureaucratic impasses below.

Below leading small groups, at the third tier, are the relevant party departments and government ministries. As LSGs have little staff of their own, the research centers and staff in departments and ministries at the third tier do the actual work of gathering information and drafting policy documents. Increasingly, with a high proportion of policy related to economic matters, government ministries play a key role—but at this tier, it is the specific policy area that determines which bureaucratic players are most involved.

From Agenda-Setting to Implementing Regulations
There are five main stages in policymaking and lawmaking: agenda setting; interagency review; Politburo approval; NPC review, debate, and passage; and the drafting of implementing regulations.[41] The two stages that have the most impact on substance are interagency review and drafting of implementing regulations. The State Council dominates both these stages.

LSGs provide leadership and coordination among party departments and government ministries, from which draft proposals emerge. Leaders of departments and ministries are continuously considering relevant policy issues and waiting for (or creating) opportunities to push proposals onto the agenda. A draft proposal is on the agenda when it is assigned to interagency review.

Interagency review is usually a very prolonged process, still at the third tier, initially involving only the most relevant ministries but gradually incorporating a wider group of departments, localities, and other players. At some point, either the State Council Legislation Bureau or the Legislative Affairs Work Committee approves a drafting group for the law. The last phase of interagency review is opinion solicitation. By then, most of the law's content has already been decided.

For policies that will involve passage of legislation, after interagency review, a draft proposal is included on the Legislation Bureau's or Legislative Affairs Work Committee's annual legislative plan. Politburo approval precedes NPC passage of any major piece of political, economic, or administrative legislation, although this practice is not formally required in any legal document.

Officially, legislation may be proposed by the State Council, its ministries, or groups of NPC delegates. Not surprisingly, in this quasi-parliamentary system, the overwhelming majority of legislation is proposed by the State Council and its ministries at the third tier. Although it is unusual for laws to pass through NPC review without amendment, a bill approved in principle by the Politburo is not normally opposed in the NPC.

The NPC review stage begins with referral (by the NPC Chairmen's Group) of the draft legislation to a specialized legislative NPC standing committee for review and amendment. The structure that links party and legislative institutions at this stage is the NPC Standing Committee party group. After draft legislation is recommended by an NPC legislative committee, the party group (acting officially through the NPC Chairmen's Group) decides whether the draft will be debated in the NPC Standing Committee or the full NPC. It is common for the NPC Standing Committee to debate and revise draft legislation many times before voting on passage. When draft legislation encounters significant opposition in the NPC, a vote is usually postponed to avoid a public show of opposition.

After a law is passed, implementing regulations are drawn up, usually by the State Council Legislation Bureau. Implementing regulations transform laws into language that can be applied by local governments and subordinate departments throughout the country. Through implementing regulations, the State Council regains design control over policy before releasing it for implementation.

Policy Implementation

Although the state has partially retreated from direct control over many aspects of the economy, politics, and society in recent decades, the proportion of decisions affecting all three spheres that is made at the political center in China remains higher than that in liberal democracies. Considering this scope, the fragmented structure of authority, and the size and regional diversity of the country, policymakers are seriously constrained in their efforts to elicit effective policy implementation, despite the recent trend toward greater consultation and consensus-building to bring relevant departments and localities into the policy process at an earlier stage.

Despite problems and their consequences for unsuccessful policy implementation, the Chinese authorities have achieved impressive policy success in two areas designated as vitally important for the country's development: promoting economic growth and controlling population growth. They have been less successful in another policy area: environmental protection. These examples of policy performance are discussed at length later in this chapter. Here, the focus is on general issues in policy implementation.

Monitoring The major issue of policy implementation is the monitoring problem, especially serious in China because of the constraints noted earlier.[42] How do China's policymakers ensure that central-level decisions are translated into actions at lower levels? Central authorities have a very limited capacity to monitor the many aspects of the economy, politics, and society affected by their policies. To cope, they adopt fairly simplistic performance indicators. Not only are these problematic as accurate measures of compliance, they can also produce unanticipated results. Additionally, policymakers rely mainly on departments and localities, which have their own particular interests to pursue, for much of the information on which to base evaluations of performance. Leaders at the political center have attempted in recent years to develop channels of information independent of ministries and local governments. The National Bureau of Statistics has been given more resources and responsibilities to gather and compile information relevant to policymaking and assessment of policy performance. Research institutes and public opinion polls have also played a greater role in channeling different sorts of information to leaders at the political center. The State Auditing Administration and the Ministry of Supervision, both newly established in recent years, are designed to improve central capacity to measure and monitor implementation. Nonetheless, central authorities are unable to verify most reports independently. As a result, information is routinely distorted to make policy implementers appear compliant. Policymakers appear to take this bias into consideration when assessing implementation.

Policy Priorities As policymakers routinely communicate multiple (and conflicting) policy objectives downward through several channels, local authorities must arrive at a reasonable ordering of policy priorities. In deciding priorities, local objectives as well as the apparent priorities of the political center are considered. Local governments and parallel party committees are multitask agencies. Policy priorities communicated in documents channeled down from Beijing in the functionally specialized line hierarchies of government may not be treated as policy priorities by local governments. Policies appear more likely to be implemented in conformity with central directives when signals from the center indicate that top leaders have reached a consensus among themselves and are paying attention. This sort of signal is generally communicated through documents issued by executive organizations (not simply central ministries) of the Communist Party (not simply the government). Party executives may also signal their attention to the implementation of policy issues by speaking at work conferences convened to assess progress in particular areas or establishing an ad hoc LSG to manage a particular policy problem.

Adapting Policy to Local Conditions Chinese politics presents no electoral incentives for top leaders to line up public policy with the expressed preferences of special interest groups or ordinary voters. To be sure, policymakers consult the players they view as relevant to policy outcomes. Yet with restrictions on investigation or criticism by the mass media and the prohibition on organized opposition groups, policymakers face relatively little routine outside pressure in formulating policies. Despite increased consultation of players below the top tiers, the policymaking process is relatively closed compared with liberal democracies. In a structural context that limits widespread input and provides no electoral connection to policymakers at the top, reshaping policy in the course of policy implementation is often the most effective way for officials to influence policy outcomes.

Corruption

Economic reform has produced unprecedented growth and prosperity, but also the conditions for new forms of **corruption.** Since the early 1980s, the economy, no longer centrally planned but not fully marketized, has provided opportunities for officials to gain privately from abuse of their control over resources, contracts, and permissions. On the one hand, the new opportunities for corruption may have eased resistance by officials with the most to lose from economic reform. On the other, abuse of public office

to pursue private gain has grown in scope, scale, volume, and severity to become one of the gravest challenges facing the regime, even threatening the Chinese armed forces.[43] In public-opinion polls conducted over the years, Chinese citizens consistently view corruption as a serious social problem, often the most serious problem. The huge 1989 mass protests, as much about corruption as about democracy, reflected and aired this view.

Chinese leaders are alarmed about corruption, recognizing the threat to regime legitimacy and political stability. Since 1982, they have waged a nearly continuous corruption-control effort. While corrupt officials have been prosecuted and punished, the battle against corruption suffers from a basic contradiction between Communist Party leadership and rule by law in China. In principle, as described earlier, equality before the law is a core component of the new legality. In practice, the Chinese legal system has not been used to full effect to control corruption. An important obstacle is a structural one, reflecting a more basic political obstacle. In 1978, party leaders reinstated discipline inspection committees, specialized departments subordinate to party committees at each level of the party hierarchy. Discipline inspection committees investigate misconduct and enforce ethical and political standards for party members. As the preponderance of officials are party members, discipline inspection committees investigate corruption. Regulations require the transfer of criminal cases to procuratorates, but party investigations and party punishments generally precede criminal investigations. Procuratorates routinely encounter obstacles in their efforts to prosecute such cases, not only because officials call up networks of cronies for support but also because successful prosecution is botched when officials have sufficient time to destroy evidence. In principle, the system holds Communist Party members to a higher standard of conduct than ordinary citizens. In practice, exemption from prosecution and substitution of disciplinary action for criminal punishment are very common for officials (but not for ordinary citizens). Public cynicism about corruption control is understandable. In the instances that high-ranking officials are removed from office and sentenced through the legal system, many interpret it as the outcome of a political power struggle.

The problem of corruption and corruption control reflects a basic contradiction between the principles of Communist Party leadership and rule by law. If law is supreme, the party is subordinate to law and under supervision by procuratorates and courts, not vice versa. So long as party leaders cannot commit to supervision by an impartial legal system, the building of a legal infrastructure will not amount to rule by law. Yet to commit to such supervision calls into question party leadership and the foundations of the communist party-state.

POLICY PERFORMANCE

In late 1978, China's leaders defined economic growth as the most important policy priority for decades to come. Despite disagreement about the appropriate pace and scope of economic reform, there has been consensus on a broad strategy of retreat from direct state intervention. The Chinese state has been achieving more by directly controlling less. This strategy has applied not only to economic goals but also to most other policy goals in the reform era. This includes environmental protection, which is less well-suited to such a strategy. The important exception has been population control, which Chinese leaders identified as a major policy priority in the late 1970s. The one-child family policy introduced in 1978 features the Chinese state in a more directly interventionist role in population control than ever before.

This section examines the performance of policies of economic reform, environmental protection, and compulsory family planning, focusing on the role of the state in achieving policy goals.

Economic Growth

Although the Chinese have moved only slowly on political reforms, they have been bold in economic reforms. Since 1978, Chinese leaders have staked their political legitimacy on economic growth, more than anything else. For the most part, the gamble has succeeded. Chinese economic growth, illustrated in Table 10.3, has averaged just under 10 percent per year since 1980, including a robust 9 percent in 2009, notwithstanding the financial crisis. Real per capita income has also grown, to more than $1,700 in 2009, or nearly $6,000 in purchasing power parity (PPP).

	GDP (billion yuan)	GDP per Capita (yuan)
TABLE 10.3		
Economic Performance, 1980–2009 (in constant yuan)		
Chinese economic growth has averaged about 10 percent per year in the reform era.		
1980	452	460
1985	898.9	853
1990	1,859.8	1,634
1995	5,749.5	4,854
2000	8,825.4	7,086
2005	18,232.1	14,025
2009	US$4,191 billion	US$1,701 ($6,600 PPP)

Sources: State Council Information Office, China Internet Information Center, http://www.china.org.cn; National Bureau of Statistics of China, *Statistical Communique*, February 28, 2006, www.stats.gov.cn; 2009 GDP figure is calculated from Wen Jiabao, *Report on the Work of the Government*, March 5, 2010; 2009 GDP per capita figure is from Central Intelligence Agency, *World Factbook*, www.cia.gov/cia/publications/factbook/.

China is still a developing country, but it is the world's second-largest economy in PPP terms. Economic reform has been a remarkable success story. It has been achieved through three major strategies: opening up the economy to the world outside, marketizing the economy, and devolving authority downward to create incentives for local governments, enterprises, households, and individuals to pursue their own economic advancement.

In the late 1970s, Chinese leaders rejected the economic autarky of Maoist "self-reliance," instead opening up the country to foreign trade and investment. China has become a major trading economy. Its trade balance has allowed it to amass the world's largest foreign-exchange reserves, including $895 billion in U.S. Treasury securities in 2010. It has also created frictions with the United States and some other trading partners. Foreign-invested firms are responsible for much of China's exports, reflecting the country's appeal—through preferential policies, cheap labor, and a potentially huge market—as a destination for foreign direct investment (FDI).

Post-Mao leaders inherited a centrally planned economy, organized according to a Stalinist model borrowed from the Soviet Union in the 1950s. They did not initially set out with a stated goal or program to create a socialist market economy. Indeed, the goal to create a market system was not officially affirmed until 1993. Rather, economic reform proceeded incrementally, in a process often described as "crossing the river by groping for stones." Initially, some top party leaders envisaged only a small secondary role for the market economy, as a "bird in a cage" of the planned economy. By the mid-1990s, however, the Chinese economy had basically "grown out" of the plan.[44] In 1998, the Chinese approved a "shareholding system" that is essentially privatization, thinly disguised to maintain ideological orthodoxy.

A key economic reform strategy has been decentralization. Leaders in Beijing have devolved authority to empower local governments, enterprises, households, and individuals. Agricultural decollectivization in the early 1980s was the first such reform, replacing collective farming with household farming. Individual entrepreneurs emerged at about the same time, engaging in small-scale production or providing services (such as transportation of commodities to markets) long ignored under central planning. Existing rural enterprises were allowed to expand into practically any product line, rather than being restricted to "serving agriculture," as before. Most of these industries were organized as "collective enterprises," with formal ownership by the township or village community and with strong direct involvement of local government in management. These small-scale township and village enterprises (TVEs) proved themselves adaptable to the demands of the new market environment. They drove much of China's rapid growth in the 1980s and into the 1990s. Fiscal arrangements negotiated in the mid-1980s also favored local governments, at the expense of the center; in a renegotiation in the mid-1990s, the central government gained back some revenues, but without removing incentives for local economic initiative.

The reform of the state-owned enterprise (SOE) system began in the mid-1980s. Initial reforms created incentives to boost production by replacing government appropriation of all SOE profits with a system of taxing profits—allowing SOEs to retain a portion of profits. Of course, until prices reflected scarcity, the incentives remained weak. More important,

SOEs employed (and employ) a very high proportion of urban workers. This effectively put SOEs on a "soft budget constraint": As local governments feared worker unrest, unprofitable SOEs did not fear bankruptcy; they could count on state banks to bail them out. In 1993, the Chinese authorities announced that one-third of SOEs were loss-making and one-third barely breaking even. In 1994, the Company Law was passed to provide a legal framework for corporatization. A strategy of "targeting the large, releasing the small" emerged: Beijing continued to nurture about 1,000 large SOEs, encouraging them to form giant conglomerates, assisting them with loans but imposing greater financial discipline; the smaller SOEs were left to confront market forces and reorganize themselves through mergers, takeovers, conversion into shareholding companies, or outright closure. After more than a decade of corporatization and reorganization, with increasing privatization through conversion to shareholding and greater political toleration of SOE closures and sales, including sales to foreign partners, SOEs account for a mere 3 percent of all enterprises (but more than 40 percent of enterprise assets) today.

The global financial crisis of 2008 and 2009 exposed the vulnerabilities of the Chinese economic model: excessive dependence on investment (which is less stable than consumption) and export demand (which is dependent on foreign consumption). At the same time, the decisive response of Chinese policymakers to the crisis revealed the advantages of concentrated political power: In November 2008, only weeks after statistics had revealed the severity of economic slowdown, Chinese leaders announced a $585 billion stimulus package focused on infrastructure investment. More important, credit from state-owned banks worked its way through to the real economy by the beginning of 2009, leading an economic recovery as early as March 2009. China's effective response stabilized the economy—and stabilized the global economy.

The Chinese response to the global financial crisis must be characterized as hugely successful. It was also pragmatic; considering the speed and severity of the economic decline, only an increase in investment could pump money into the economy quickly enough to offset crisis. Yet the stimulus is also costly in the longer term.[45] It has reversed the steady government retreat from economic intervention. It will also undoubtedly increase the number of nonperforming loans due to hasty investment decisions promoted by local governments eager to have projects approved. Most important of all, the investment boost of the stimulus did little to address the fundamental economic problem of low household consumption. Without the safety net of the socialist economy, Chinese households continue to anticipate future needs and save "too much."

Environmental Degradation

China's rapid economic growth has resulted in serious environmental damage. Environmental pollution and degradation have increased at a rate that outpaces the capacity of the Chinese state to protect the environment.[46] TVEs contribute more than half of pollutants of all kinds, dumping their untreated waste directly into rivers and streams and relying heavily on coal for energy. Use of coal, a major source of air pollution but a vital contributor to energy supply (see Box 10.5), has doubled since the economic reforms. Water scarcity poses a major challenge; prices do not reflect scarcity because most water is directed toward agriculture for irrigation, and local governments fear rural unrest will erupt with meaningful water-price increases. Integration into the global economy has made China a global market for resource-intensive goods, such as paper and furniture—producing a massive drop in forest coverage with increases in logging by Chinese and multinational businesses. China has also become a

destination of choice for some of the world's most environmentally damaging industries.

Environmental economists at the World Bank and other organizations estimate the cost to the Chinese economy of environmental degradation and resource scarcity at 8 to 12 percent of GDP annually. This includes health and productivity losses associated with air-pollution and water-scarcity costs in lost industrial output. Even so, through the mid-1990s, leaders and the Chinese media continued to articulate the principle of "first development, then environment." The ideal of sustainable development, prominent in official rhetoric today, was incorporated into the economic planning process only in 1992.

Over the past decade, China has erected a legal and bureaucratic infrastructure of environmental protection. In 1984, the State Council established a central government department responsible for environmental matters; in 1989, the NPC adopted an environmental protection law; and in 1993, a specialized legislative environmental protection and natural resources committee was established in the NPC.

Nonetheless, in the policymaking process, the environmental bureaucracy is weak in negotiations with the many ministries with developmental priorities. The problem is even more serious at the local level. The laws that emerge tend to be too diluted and general to provide useful guidelines for enforcement.

The Chinese tally a great number of enforcement successes over the past decade: the resolution of more than 75,000 environmental law violation cases, the

---

Shutting Down 5,000 Coal Mines

BOX 10.5

China depends on coal for more than 65 percent of its growing energy needs, but in 2005, the central government ordered more than 5,000 coal mines shut down. China's mines are the most dangerous in the world; in that year alone, nearly 6,000 Chinese coal miners died in mining accidents, almost 80 percent of the world's total mining fatalities. The mines ordered closed were both unsafe and illegal. Many were lucrative small-scale mines, managed as TVEs. Others were privately

owned, often with local officials holding private (strictly illegal) shares. Mine managers routinely flout safety standards, taking local government acquiescence for granted. The miners generally resign themselves to the high risks, because mining pays better than alternative employment in agriculture. In such conditions, despite laws, orders, and rhetoric on industrial safety, dangerous mines will continue to operate. Undoubtedly, they include many mines shut down in 2005.

Environmental Degradation

The policy of "first development, then environment" has taken a heavy toll. Pollution far outpaces the government's capacity for environmental protection.

Fang xinwu/Color China Photo/AP Images

closure of more than 16,000 enterprises for illegal discharge of pollutants, and the issuance of more than 10,000 warnings to environment polluters.[47] Yet the devolution of authority to local governments, a strategy that unlocked economic growth, constitutes a fundamental obstacle to enforcement.

Although local environmental protection bureaus (EPBs) are nominally accountable to both the State Environmental Protection Agency (SEPA) in Beijing and their local governments, they depend on local governments for their growth and survival—budgets, career advancement, staff size, and allocation of resources such as vehicles and office buildings. Local government developmental priorities practically always dominate efforts to enforce environmental standards, especially when enterprises are collective enterprises or firms with a large number of workers. Pollution-discharge fees are routinely not collected (or not fully collected), and legal

requirements to improve pollution-control capacity are routinely waived. The 2006 policy decision to consider environmental-protection performance, including energy use, in evaluating local governments may have some impact, but its importance is unlikely to trump economic growth in the near future.

Environmental protection is also underfunded. The five-year plan adopted in March 2006 budgeted 1.6 percent of GDP for environmental protection—an increase over past years but nonetheless an amount that Chinese scientists believe is well below what is needed to produce notable improvements.

Population Control

While reducing state intervention to promote economic growth, policymakers have increased their intervention involving a new policy priority: population control. For most of the Maoist years, population planning was not actively promoted. In 1978, with the population close to a billion and amid rising concern about meeting economic goals and ensuring basic livelihood, employment opportunities, and social-security support at the current rate of population growth, China's leaders declared population control a major policy priority. State-sponsored family planning was added to the constitution, and an ideal family size of one child was endorsed as national policy. According to this policy, most couples are required to stop childbearing after one or two births. Married couples in urban areas, with few exceptions, are restricted to one child. In rural areas, married couples are subject to rules that differ across provinces. In some provinces, two children are normally permitted; in others, only one child is permitted; in most provinces, a second child is permitted only if the first is a girl.

One-Child Family Policy The **one-child family policy** is inherently difficult to implement in China, particularly in the countryside, where nearly 50 percent of Chinese live.[48] There, the population is relatively poorly educated and has poor access to public health facilities—circumstances that do not facilitate an effective family-planning program. Traditional views about the family prevail; as in most agrarian societies, big families and many sons are viewed as ideal. Moreover, in China, a married daughter joins the household of her husband, while a married son remains in the household to support aging parents. Decollectivization and the return to household farming in the early 1980s enhanced the value of sons compared to daughters, for their labor power. The dismantling of the commune system has also left the state less able to monitor compliance, just as the new economic independence of peasants has left the state less able to enforce compliance. Finally, population control involves the state as the dominant decision-maker in choices that are traditionally viewed, in China as elsewhere, as private family matters.

Despite the inherent difficulties, the Chinese have curbed population growth dramatically, as is illustrated in Figure 10.5. A population structure normally resembles a pyramid; with relatively unchanged rates of births and deaths, the proportion of population from top to bottom is progressively bigger. The population pyramid in Figure 10.5 deviates from this form in a few places. The first, located at about the middle of the pyramid, reflects fewer births as well as differentially more deaths among the young in the disaster following the Great Leap Forward, in the cohort aged fifty to fifty-four in 2010. The second, evident beginning with the cohort aged thirty to thirty-four in 2010, reflects the impact of family-planning policies introduced in the 1970s. Variation in policy emphasis by leaders at the political center is reflected in variation in number of births beginning in the mid-1970s. Implementation of the one-child family policy began in 1979. In 1983, responding to concerns at the political center, implementation became more coercive. From 1984 through the late 1980s, the policy was relaxed and implementation in the countryside faltered due to difficulties associated with decollectivization. Births rose immediately. Currently, rural married couples are permitted to have a second child if their first is a girl, is disabled, or dies. In the cities, when married couples are both only children, they may have two children. Family-planning policies do not apply to minority nationalities.

Policy Implementation Policy implementation has taken a number of forms: a legal requirement of late marriage, a requirement of insertion of an intrauterine device after a first birth, and a requirement of sterilization of one partner after a second birth. There are incentives to sign a one-child family certificate after the first birth, including priority in entrance to schools and funding for health fees for the child. Fines are imposed on the family for policy violations. Birth-planning workers at the grassroots are given birth quotas from higher levels, which they allocate on the basis of family circumstances. From the perspective of leaders at the political center, abortion is a sign of failure, not success, in policy implementation. At the grassroots, from the perspective of birth-planning workers, however, the obvious fact is that abortions do not add above-plan births. Undeniably, birth-planning workers have incentives to encourage abortions and face few disincentives for doing so.

Perverse Outcomes In recent years, policymakers have expressed concern about a perverse result of compulsory family planning: the shortage of young girls, compared

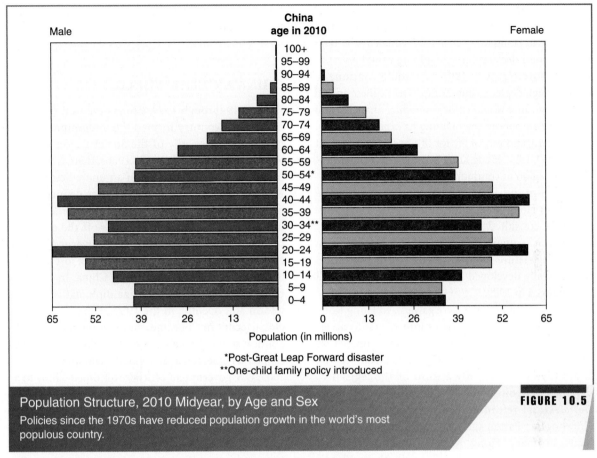

China age in 2010

Male | Female

100+	
95–99	
90–94	
85–89	
80–84	
75–79	
70–74	
65–69	
60–64	
55–59	
50–54*	
45–49	
40–44	
35–39	
30–34**	
25–29	
20–24	
15–19	
10–14	
5–9	
0–4	

65 52 39 26 13 0   0 13 26 39 52 65

Population (in millions)

*Post-Great Leap Forward disaster
**One-child family policy introduced

Population Structure, 2010 Midyear, by Age and Sex

FIGURE 10.5

Policies since the 1970s have reduced population growth in the world's most populous country.

Source: U.S. Census Bureau, International Data Base, www.census.gov/ipc/www/idb/country.php.

with boys. Recent figures show imbalance in the sex ratio, with the ratio of males to females at birth continually rising since the 1980s. The normal range worldwide is 103 to 107 males born for every 100 females; in China, that ratio was 120 in 2010.

The shortage of girls reflects the traditional Chinese preference for male children in the context of compulsory family planning. Traditional practices of female infanticide as well as abandonment and severe neglect of girls beyond infancy have led to excess female infant mortality. Not least of all, missing girls are increasingly the result of sex-selective abortion, made possible with the widespread use of ultrasound technology in the early 1980s.

China's success in reducing population growth has strong supporters and detractors outside the country. The official Chinese response to criticism from human-rights advocates has focused on "economic rights" that the government argues

would be denied to all Chinese in the decades to come if population growth is not brought under control.

HONG KONG

In 1842 and 1860, the island of **Hong Kong** and adjacent territory on the Chinese mainland were ceded by treaty to Britain in perpetuity. In 1898, more adjacent territory was ceded in a ninety-nine-year lease. These cessions were largely the outcome of British victory in wars fought to impose trade on China. For nearly a century, Hong Kong (including the adjacent territories) was a British colony, ruled by a governor appointed in London. Hong Kong flourished economically, with a disciplined labor force of Chinese immigrants, a free-market economy, and a government commitment to rule of law and civil liberties—but not an elected government.

In 1984, the Chinese communist authorities elaborated the principle of "**one country, two systems**," applicable to Hong Kong after 1997. China and Britain signed a joint declaration: Hong Kong would revert to Chinese sovereignty in 1997, but would continue to enjoy "a high degree of autonomy." The Chinese agreed that Hong Kong would enjoy economic, financial, and monetary autonomy, maintaining its capitalist system, legal system, and way of life for fifty years. At midnight on June 30, 1997, Hong Kong became a special administrative region of communist-ruled China.

The British had made little effort to democratize politics in Hong Kong through the 1980s. The governor had consulted business elites and other key constituencies on policy affairs, but there had been no elected legislature or government. Nor had political parties really developed in such an environment. All this changed in 1989.

The Tiananmen massacre galvanized Hong Kong Chinese and British expatriates into efforts to accelerate the pace of political democratization before 1997. In 1991, in the first direct elections to the Legislative Council, only a third of the legislative deputies were directly elected. In 1995, a controversial electoral-reform bill introduced by Governor Christopher Patten guided elections: for the first time, ordinary Hong Kong citizens elected all deputies in the Legislative Council. Hong Kong's most liberal democratic parties won overwhelmingly in geographic voting districts. Openly pro-Beijing forces did poorly.

Communist authorities rejected the elections and the legislature as violations of the Basic Law, Hong Kong's miniconstitution passed in China's NPC in 1990. They supervised selection of a chief executive and provisional legislature in 1996. At the moment of the historic handover, this chief executive and provisional legislature officially replaced the governor and the legislature elected in 1995.

Since the handover, Beijing authorities have been less heavy-handed than feared. Hong Kong today enjoys most of the same civil liberties as under British rule. Human-rights organizations and prodemocracy organizations that monitor and support progress in the PRC have bases in Hong Kong. Hong Kong newspapers provide information about politics in the PRC and are critical in ways not permitted on the mainland. Chinese communist authorities hope that success in implementing "one country, two systems" in Hong Kong will woo Taiwan back to the PRC too.

CHINA AND THE WORLD

From 1949 through 1979, China's political status as a communist country formed the underpinning of its global role: as an ally of the Soviet Union until the Sino-Soviet split in the early 1960s, then as a nuclear power under the leadership of an unpredictable Mao. Relations with the United States were defined largely by declaration of an American interest in the security of **Taiwan**, a mere hundred miles off the east coast of the Chinese mainland and governed by the Nationalists since 1945. In 1971, Taiwan lost its membership in the United Nations to China. In 1979, the United States recognized China diplomatically. With reform and opening in the 1980s, China's role in the global economy became more important than its political status. China's accession to the WTO in 2001 capped its emergence as a global economic player. In 2005, U.S. government officials welcomed China to an anticipated new role as a "responsible stakeholder" in the international system.

China has surely disappointed the United States and other Western powers as a global diplomatic player. China is the only country that could possibly influence an unpredictable nuclear North Korea, but it has done little more than set up the six-party talks in 2003. On the UN Security Council, it has voted for sanctions against North Korea and Iran for nuclear proliferation, but only after negotiating compromises so that sanctions are much weakened. China's need for raw materials (such as oil) certainly affect its diplomatic position on Iran; at the same time, Chinese leaders do not see Iran as a threat, do not believe sanctions are effective, and suspect a Western agenda of regime-change underlies sanctions efforts.[49]

China today projects a more confident nationalism than ever before. This confidence reflects the country's high growth rates in the global economic recession and Chinese perceptions of the decline of the United States as a global superpower and its replacement by a multipolar global system in which China has more influence. Addressing international concerns about the bounds of its assertive new nationalism, Chinese leaders point out that they have used significant force outside their borders only twice since the communists came to power—in short wars against India in 1962 and Vietnam in 1979. They insist that China in its new role as a global player is merely defending its "core interests" and national dignity.[50]

CHINA'S POLITICAL FUTURE

Two main themes have run through this study of Chinese politics today. First, despite very significant economic liberalization and a nascent political institutionalization, Chinese politics takes place within the boundaries of what is still essentially a communist party-state. Second, the dramatic changes sweeping the Chinese economy, polity, and society, many of which now seem beyond the control of political leaders, are as much a by-product of reform as a direct product of reform policies. The first theme cautions against liberal democratic optimism when considering China's political future. The second reminds us that the script of the political future will not be written by Chinese communist leaders alone.

In this new century, China must confront a number of key issues that will significantly determine its development. Can structures and processes that bolster and foster economic growth safeguard against the threat of more significant political liberalization and eventual democratization—which remain unacceptable to the Chinese authorities?

Around the world, political change in recent decades has created an age of democratization—the result, in many countries, of revolutions that toppled communist regimes older than the Chinese regime. Will the "third wave" of world democratization reach China early in the twenty-first century?

Certainly, liberal democratic ideals and practices are quite alien to Chinese culture. Chinese history provides no examples of democratic rule, and the Chinese cultural tradition expresses no concerns to protect individuals by checking state power. Past experience and cultural tradition, then, offer little encouragement to those looking for the seeds of democratization in China.

Yet authoritarianism has not survived intact with economic modernization in many East Asian countries that have a similar lack of historical and cultural foundations for democracy. To be sure, even with continued economic growth, China will differ from these countries for many years to come. It will be bifurcated in its development: middle-class prosperity is emerging in the big cities and coastal regions, but Chinese in the countryside will remain relatively poor for some time.

With reform, for most ordinary Chinese, the party has demanded less and delivered more in recent decades. Unlike communist parties that gained (and held) power with the aid of Soviet troops and tanks, the Chinese Communist Party has indigenous and nationalist roots. Barring a major economic crisis, it is less likely to collapse in the face of the sort of mass discontent that toppled communist regimes in Eastern Europe. More likely, in the medium term at least, the party will continue to transform China in the years to come and to transform itself in order to continue to rule.

REVIEW QUESTIONS

- How does the Chinese Communist Party exercise leadership through governance structures?

- Legal reform is a key priority in political change in China since the 1980s. How successful has it been in meeting key challenges?

- How is political life for ordinary Chinese different today, compared to the Maoist era?

- What policy decisions account for Chinese economic growth in the past three decades?

- Why is population control especially difficult to achieve in China? How and how well has the government measured up to the challenge?

- China is better able than ever before to take up its responsibilities as a global player, but its performance has been mixed. Explain.

KEY TERMS

Central Committee	fragmented authoritarianism	mass mobilization campaign	party-state
Chinese Communist Party	GONGOs	National Party Congress	Politburo
Confucianism	Great Firewall	National People's Congress (NPC)	rule by law
corruption	Great Leap Forward	Nationalist Party	socialist market economy
Cultural Revolution	Hong Kong	*nomenklatura* system	State Council
Democracy Movement	Hu Jintao	one-child family policy	Taiwan (Republic of China)
democratic centralism	leading small groups (LSGs)	one country, two systems	Tiananmen massacre
Deng Xiaoping	Mao Zedong		village committees
ethnic minorities			

SUGGESTED READINGS

Bianco, Lucien. *Origins of the Chinese Revolution, 1915–1949.* Stanford, CA: Stanford University Press, 1971.

Chang, Jung. *Wild Swans: Three Daughters of China.* New York: Anchor, 1991.

Economy, Elizabeth C. *The River Runs Black: The Environmental Challenge to China's Future.* Ithaca, NY: Cornell University Press, 2004.

Gries, Peter Hays, and Stanley Rosen, eds. *Chinese Politics: State, Society and the Market.* London: Routledge, 2010.

Lieberthal, Kenneth. *Governing China: From Revolution through Reform*, 2nd ed. New York: Norton, 2004.

Nathan, Andrew J. *Chinese Democracy.* Berkeley: University of California Press, 1986.

Spence, Jonathan D. *The Search for Modern China.* New York: Norton, 1990.

Weston, Timothy B., and Lionel Jensen, eds. *China Beyond the Headlines.* Lanham, MD: Rowman & Littlefield, 2000.

Wong, Jan. *Red China Blues.* Sydney: Doubleday, 1996.

INTERNET RESOURCES

China Internet Information Center, State Council Information Office. Authorized Web site of Chinese government, link to National People's Congress. Access to government White Papers, news, statistical data: **www.china.org.cn/english.**

National Bureau of Statistics. Official monthly and yearly statistics, including downloadable Excel files: **www.stats.gov.cn/english/.**

China Daily. News from China directed toward external readership: **www.chinadaily.com.cn.**

People's Daily. Official newspaper of Communist Party of China: **http://english.peopledaily.com.cn/.**

South China Morning Post. News about Hong Kong and mainland China, from Hong Kong: **www.scmp.com.**

Contemporary China bibliography, Professor Lynn White, Princeton University: **www.princeton.edu/~lynn/chinabib.pdf.**

United States–China Business Council. Analysis and advocacy of policy issues of interest to U.S. corporations engaged in business relations with China: **www.uschina.org.**

ENDNOTES

1. For a good, very readable discussion of Chinese history beginning with the late Ming (seventeenth century) and extending into the 1980s, see Jonathan D. Spence, *The Search for Modern China* (New York: Norton, 1990). Other good historical overviews include Charles O. Hucker, *China's Imperial Past: An Introduction to Chinese History and Culture* (Stanford, CA: Stanford University Press, 1975), and Immanuel C. Y. Hsu, *The Rise of Modern China*, 5th ed. (New York: Oxford University Press, 1995).

2. See Hsi-sheng Chi, *Warlord Politics in China, 1916–1928* (Stanford, CA: Stanford University Press, 1976), and Edward A. McCord, *The Power of the Gun: The Emergence of Modern Chinese Warlordism* (Berkeley: University of California Press, 1993).

3. See especially Lucien Bianco, *Origins of the Chinese Revolution, 1915–1949* (Stanford, CA: Stanford University Press, 1971). See also Benjamin Schwartz, *Chinese Communism and the Rise of Mao* (Cambridge, MA: Harvard University Press, 1951).

4. The classic political biography of Mao is Edgar Snow, *Red Star Over China* (New York: Grove Press, 1968). Of the many excellent studies by Stuart R. Schram, see especially *The Political Thought of Mao Tse-tung*, rev. ed. (New York: Praeger, 1969), *The Thought of Mao Tse-tung* (Cambridge: Cambridge University Press, 1989), and his biography of Mao, *Mao Tse-tung*, rev. ed. (Harmondsworth, UK: Penguin, 1967). After Mao's death, scholars appraised Mao and his legacy from a variety of perspectives in Dick Wilson, ed., *Mao Tse-tung in the Scales of History: A Preliminary Assessment* (Cambridge: Cambridge University Press, 1977).

5. See Chalmers A. Johnson, *Peasant Nationalism and Communist Power: The Emergence of Revolutionary China* (Stanford, CA: Stanford University Press, 1962).

6. See Suzanne Pepper, *Civil War in China: The Political Struggle, 1945–1949* (Berkeley: University of California Press, 1978).

7. For a good selection of essays offering a comprehensive overview of PRC history, see Roderick MacFarquhar, ed., *The Politics of China: The Eras of Mao and Deng*, 2nd ed. (Cambridge: Cambridge University Press, 1997). Other good discussions of post-Mao history are found in Richard Baum, *Burying Mao: Chinese Politics in the Age of Deng Xiaoping* (Princeton, NJ: Princeton University Press, 1994), and Harry Harding, *China's Second Revolution: Reform after Mao* (Washington, D.C.: Brookings Institution, 1987). Good discussions of particular topics of reform are found in Merle Goldman and Roderick MacFarquhar, eds., *The Paradox of China's Post-Mao Reforms* (Cambridge, MA: Harvard University Press, 1999).

8. The classic account is by William Hinton, who observed land reform before 1949 in *Fanshen: A Documentary of Revolution in a Chinese Village* (New York: Viking, 1966).

9. Roderick MacFarquhar, ed., *The Hundred Flowers Campaign and the Chinese Intellectuals* (New York: Praeger, 1960); and Fu-sheng Mu, *The Wilting of the Hundred Flowers Movement: Free Thought in China Today* (London: Heinemann, 1962).

10. See Dali L. Yang, *Calamity and Reform in China: State, Rural Society, and Institutional Change since the Great Leap Famine* (Stanford, CA: Stanford University Press, 1996).

11. See Frederick C. Teiwes, *Politics and Purges in China: Rectification and the Decline of Party Norms, 1950–1965* (Armonk, NY: M. E. Sharpe, 1979); and Frederick C. Teiwes, *Leadership, Legitimacy, and Conflict in China: From a Charismatic Mao to the Politics of Succession* (Armonk, NY: M. E. Sharpe, 1984).

12. See Jasper Becker, *Hungry Ghosts: Mao's Secret Famine* (New York: Free Press, 1996).

13. Some of the best accounts of the Cultural Revolution are biographical or autobiographical. See, for example, Gordon A. Bennett and Ronald N. Montaperto, *Red Guard: The Political Biography of Dai Hsiao-ai* (Garden City, NY: Doubleday, 1971); Jung Chang, *Wild Swans: Three Daughters of China* (New York: Anchor, 1991); Yuan Gao, *Born Red: Chronicle of the Cultural Revolution* (Stanford, CA: Stanford University Press, 1987); Liang Heng and Judith Shapiro, *Son of the Revolution* (New York: Knopf, 1983); Anne F. Thurston, *Enemies of the People: The Ordeal of the Intellectuals in China's Great Cultural Revolution* (Cambridge, MA: Harvard University Press, 1988); Daiyun Yue and Carolyn Wakeman, *To the Storm: The Odyssey of a Revolutionary Chinese Woman* (Berkeley: University of California Press, 1985); and Nien Cheng, *Life and Death in Shanghai* (New York: Grove Press, 1986).

14. See Dru C. Gladney, *Muslim Chinese: Ethnic Nationalism in the People's Republic* (Cambridge, MA: Council on East Asian Studies, Harvard University, 1991); and Stevan Harrell, ed., *Cultural Encounters on China's Ethnic Frontiers* (Seattle: University of Washington Press, 1995).

15. An excellent discussion of guardianship is found in Robert A. Dahl, *Democracy and Its Critics* (New Haven, CT: Yale University Press, 1989), Chapter 4. On Leninism in general, see especially Alfred G. Meyer, *Leninism* (Cambridge, MA: Harvard University Press, 1957).

16. Mao Zedong, "Some Questions Concerning Methods of Leadership," in *Selected Works of Mao Tse-tung*, vol. 3 (Peking: Foreign Languages Press, 1965), 117–22.

17. On the changing role of the NPC, see Murray Scot Tanner, *The Politics of Lawmaking in Post-Mao China: Institutions, Processes, and Democratic Prospects* (New York: Oxford University Press, 1999); and "Breaking the Vicious Cycles: The Emergence of China's National People's Congress," *Problems of Post-Communism* 45, no. 3 (1998): 29–47. For a historical perspective, see Kevin J. O'Brien, *Reform without Liberalization: China's National People's Congress and the Politics of Institutional Change* (Cambridge: Cambridge University Press, 1990).

18. See Murray Scot Tanner, "How a Bill Becomes a Law in China: Stages and Processes of Lawmaking," *China Quarterly* 141 (1995): 39–64.

19. See Melanie Manion, "The Cadre Management System, Post-Mao: The Appointment, Promotion, Transfer, and Removal of Party and State Leaders," *China Quarterly* 102 (1985): 203–33; John P. Burns, *The Chinese Communist Party's Nomenklatura System* (Armonk, NY: M. E. Sharpe, 1989); and "Strengthening Central CCP Control of Leadership Selection: The 1990 Nomenklatura," *China Quarterly* 138 (1994): 458–91.

20. See Hsiao Pen, "Separating the Party from the Government," in *Decision-Making in Deng's China: Perspectives from Insiders*, ed. Carol Lee Hamrin and Suisheng Zhao (Armonk, NY: M. E. Sharpe, 1995), 153–68.

21. See Zhiyue Bo, *Chinese Provincial Leaders: Economic Performance and Political Mobility Since 1949* (Armonk, NY: M. E. Sharpe, 2002). For an earlier discussion of elite recruitment and mobility, based on case studies, see David M. Lampton, *Paths to Power: Elite Mobility in Contemporary China* (Ann Arbor: Center for Chinese Studies, University of Michigan, 1986).

22. For an overview of the change, see Richard Baum, "Modernization and Legal Reform in Post-Mao China: The Rebirth of Socialist Legality," *Studies in Comparative Communism* 19, no. 2 (1986): 69–103. For notions underlying the change, see Carlos W. H. Lo, "Deng Xiaoping's Ideas on Law: China on the Threshold of a Legal Order," *Asian Survey* 32, no. 7 (1992): 649–65. For a description of the law in practice in post-Mao China, see James V. Feinerman, "Economic and Legal Reform in China, 1978–91," *Problems of Communism* 40, no. 5 (1991): 62–75; Pitman B. Potter, ed., *Domestic Law Reforms in Post-Mao China* (Armonk, NY: M. E. Sharpe, 1994); "The Chinese Legal System: Continuing Commitment to the Primacy of State Power," *China Quarterly* 159 (1999): 673–83; and Stanley B. Lubman, *Bird in a Cage: Legal Reform in China After Mao* (Stanford, CA: Stanford University Press, 1999).

23. See, for example, Donald C. Clarke and James V. Feinerman, "Antagonistic Contradictions: Criminal Law and Human Rights in China," *China Quarterly* 141 (1995): 135–54.

24. See the account of "thought work" in Daniel Lynch, *After the Propaganda State: Media, Politics, and "Thought Work" in Reformed China* (Stanford, CA: Stanford University Press, 1999).

25. See Tianjian Shi, "Cultural Values and Democracy in the People's Republic of China," *China Quarterly* 162 (2000): 540–59; and Yang Zhong, Jie Chen, and John Scheb, "Mass Political Culture in Beijing: Findings From Two Public Opinion Surveys," *Asian Survey* 38, no. 8 (1998): 763–83. For a comparative perspective, see Gabriel A. Almond and Sidney Verba, *Civic Culture: Political Attitudes and Democracy in Five Nations* (Princeton, NJ: Princeton University Press, 1963).

26. Yun-han Chu and Yu-tzung Chang, "Culture Shift and Regime Legitimacy: Comparing Mainland China, Taiwan, and Hong Kong," in *Chinese Political Culture, 1989–2000*, ed. Shiping Hua (Armonk, NY: M. E. Sharpe, 2001), 320–47. See also Tianjian Shi, "Cultural Values and Political Trust: A Comparison of the People's Republic of China and Taiwan," *Comparative Politics* 33, no. 4 (2001): 401–19.

27. For discussion of this and other relevant issues arising from the China portion of the 2001 World Values Survey and 2002 East Asia Barometer, see Zhengxu Wang, "Public Support for Democracy in China," *Journal of Contemporary China* 16, no. 53 (2007): 561–79; and Tianjian Shi and Diqing Lou, "Subjective Evaluations of Changes in Civil Liberties and Political Rights in China," *Journal of Contemporary China* 19, no. 63 (2010): 175–99.

28. See the excellent discussion of forms of political participation in Tianjian Shi, *Political Participation in Beijing* (Cambridge, MA: Harvard University Press, 1997), Chapter 2.

29. On the Maoist period, see James R. Townsend, *Political Participation in Communist China* (Berkeley: University of California Press, 1967). On post-Mao elections, see Andrew Nathan, *Chinese Democracy* (Berkeley: University of California Press, 1985); Robert E. Bedeski, "China's 1979 Election Law and Its Implementation," *Electoral Studies* 5, no. 2 (1986): 153–65; Barrett L. McCormick, *Political Reform in Post-Mao China* (Berkeley: University of California Press, 1990); J. Bruce Jacobs, "Elections in China," *Australian Journal of Chinese Affairs* 25 (1991): 171–200; and Melanie Manion, "Chinese Democratization in Perspective: Electorates and Selectorates at the Township Level. Report from the Field," *China Quarterly* 163 (2000): 133–51.

30. On rural decollectivization, see especially Daniel Kelliher, *Peasant Power in China: The Era of Rural Reform, 1979–1989* (New Haven, CT: Yale University Press, 1992); and Kate Xiao Zhou, *How the Farmers Changed China: Power of the People* (Boulder, CO: Westview Press, 1996).

31. See Melanie Manion, "The Electoral Connection in the Chinese Countryside," *American Political Science Review* 90, no. 4 (1996): 736–48; Tianjian Shi, "Economic Development and Village Elections in Rural China," *Journal of Contemporary China* 8, no. 22 (1999): 433–35; Anne F. Thurston, *Muddling toward Democracy: Political Change in Grassroots China* (Washington, D.C.: United States Institute of Peace, 1999); and Lianjiang Li, "Elections and Popular Resistance in Rural China," *China Information* 16, no. 1 (2002): 89–107.

32. On protest movements in the 1970s and 1980s, see especially Nathan, *Chinese Democracy*; Jeffrey N. Wasserstrom and Elizabeth J. Perry, eds., *Popular Protest and Political Culture in Modern China: Learning From 1989* (Boulder, CO: Westview, 1992); and Gregor Benton and Alan Hunter, *Wild Lily, Prairie Fire: China's Road to Democracy, 1942–1989* (Princeton, NJ: Princeton University Press, 1995).

33. James D. Seymour, ed., *The Fifth Modernization* (Stanfordville, NY: Human Rights Publishing Group, 1980).

34. On the 1989 protests, see Michel Oksenberg, Lawrence R. Sullivan, and Marc Lambert, eds., *Beijing Spring, 1989: Confrontation and Conflict, The Basic Documents* (Armonk, NY: M. E. Sharpe, 1990); Han Minzhu and Hua Sheng, eds., *Cries for Democracy: Writings and Speeches From the 1989 Chinese Democracy Movement* (Princeton, NJ: Princeton University Press, 1990); Tony Saich, ed., *The Chinese People's Movement: Perspectives on Spring 1989* (Armonk, NY: M. E. Sharpe, 1990); Jonathan Unger, ed., *The Pro-Democracy Protest in China: Reports From the Provinces* (Sydney: Allen & Unwin, 1991); and Craig Calhoun, *Neither Gods Nor Emperors: Students and the Struggle for Democracy in China* (Berkeley: University of California Press, 1995).

35. See James D. Seymour, *China's Satellite Parties* (Armonk, NY: M. E. Sharpe, 1987).

36. See Fengshi Wu, *New Partners or Old Brothers? GONGOs in Transnational Environmental Advocacy in China*, China Environmental Series, no. 5 (Washington, D.C.: Woodrow Wilson Center Press, 2002); and Elizabeth C. Economy, *The River Runs Black: The Environmental Challenge to China's Future* (Ithaca, NY: Cornell University Press, 2004), 129–76.

37. For good discussions of NGOs and their relationship to the state, see especially Tony Saich, "Negotiating the State: The Development of Social Organizations in China," *China Quarterly* 161 (2000): 124–41; and Bruce Dickson, *Red Capitalists in China: The Party, Private Entrepreneurs, and Prospects for Political Change* (Cambridge: Cambridge University Press, 2003), 1–28.

38. The most thorough description and thoughtful analysis of leading small groups is by Carol Lee Hamrin, "The Party Leadership System," in *Bureaucracy, Politics, and Decision Making in Post-Mao China*, ed. Kenneth G. Lieberthal and David M. Lampton (Berkeley: University of California Press, 1992), 95–124. See also David M. Lampton, ed., *The Making of Chinese Foreign and Security Policy in the Era of Reform* (Stanford, CA: Stanford University Press, 2001), especially the contribution by Lu Ning, "The Central Leadership, Supraministry Coordinating Bodies, State Council Ministries, and Party Departments," 39–60.

39. These areas are defined in very comprehensive terms, such as party affairs, national security and military issues, foreign affairs, legal issues, personnel, finance, and the economy.

40. See Kenneth Lieberthal and Michel Oksenberg, *Policy Making in China: Leaders, Structures, and Processes* (Princeton, NJ: Princeton University Press, 1988).

41. See Tanner, "How a Bill Becomes a Law," 39–64; and Tanner, *The Politics of Lawmaking in Post-Mao China*.

42. See David M. Lampton, ed., *Policy Implementation in Post-Mao China* (Berkeley: University of California Press, 1987); and Yasheng Huang, "Administrative Monitoring in China," *China Quarterly* 143 (1995): 828–43.

43. See especially Ting Gong, "Forms and Characteristics of China's Corruption in the 1990s: Change with Continuity," *Communist and Post-Communist Studies* 30, no. 3 (1997): 277–88; Xiaobo Lu, "Booty Socialism, Bureau-preneurs, and the State in Transition," *Comparative Politics* 32, no. 3 (2000): 273–94; Yan Sun, "Reform, State, and Corruption: Is Corruption Less Destructive in China than in Russia?"

Comparative Politics 32, no. 1 (1999): 1–20; and James Mulvenon, *Soldiers of Fortune: The Rise and Fall of the Chinese Military-Business Complex, 1978–1998* (Armonk, NY: M. E. Sharpe, 2001).

44. See Barry Naughton, *Growing Out of the Plan: Chinese Economic Reform, 1978–1993* (Cambridge: Cambridge University Press, 1996).

45. See especially Barry Naughton, "Understanding the Chinese Stimulus Package," *China Leadership Monitor* 28 (2009): 1–12, and "China's Emergence from Economic Crisis," *China Leadership Monitor* 29 (2009): 1–10.

46. Two excellent recent sources on the environment are Elizabeth C. Economy, *The River Runs Black: The Environmental Challenge to China's Future* (Ithaca, NY: Cornell University Press, 2004); and Kristen A. Day, ed., *China's Environment and the Challenge of Sustainable Development* (Armonk, NY: M. E. Sharpe, 2005).

47. State Council Information Office, "Environmental Protection in China (1996–2005)," White Paper on the Environment, 2006.

48. See Susan Greenhalgh, Zhu Chuzhu, and Li Nan, "Restraining Population Growth in Three Chinese Villages, 1988–93," *Population and Development Review* 20, no. 2 (1994): 365–95.

49. Francois Godement, "A Global China Policy," *European Council on Foreign Relations Policy Brief* 22 (2010): 1–10.

50. See Michael D. Swaine, "Perceptions of an Assertive China," *China Leadership Monitor* 32 (2010): 1–18.

POLITICS IN MEXICO

Wayne A. Cornelius and Jeffrey A. Weldon

Country Bio

MEXICO

Population
108.6 million

Territory
761,602 square miles

Year of Independence
1810

Year of Current Constitution
1917

Head of State
President Felipe Calderón Hinojosa

Head of Government
President Felipe Calderón Hinojosa

Languages
Spanish, Mayan, Nahuatl, Zapotec, and many
other regional, indigenous languages

Religions
Nominally Roman Catholic 88%, Protestant 7%

It is election night. Friends and family gather around televisions to watch the returns as computer-generated graphics showing vote trends flash on and off the screen. Mirroring the final preelection surveys, exit-poll results show a presidential race that is too close to call. A few hours after the polls close, both major candidates appear on television to claim victory. More than a month passes, but the election outcome remains in doubt. Millions of votes are recounted. Election officials are accused of incompetence and bias in the vote-counting. It is up to the lawyers and the courts to determine who will be the country's next president. More than two months after the election, the court finally declares a winner.

What is striking about this picture is that it occurred not in the United States (2000, Bush vs. Gore), but in Mexico (2006, Calderón vs. López Obrador). For more than six decades, the outcomes of Mexican presidential elections had been known the moment that the ruling **Partido Revolucionario Institucional (PRI)** announced its nominee. Since the hotly contested but fraud-ridden presidential election of 1988, however, Mexico has experienced a remarkable passage from a political system in which systematic

manipulation of elections by the ruling party was condoned by senior political leaders and cynically accepted by the general public to one in which government respect for voters' preferences is expected—indeed, demanded. This and other key elements of modern democratic politics have become routinized in Mexico.

Recurrent economic crises (1976–1977, 1982–1989, and 1994–1996) were among the most powerful catalysts for this revolution in citizen expectations. The vast majority of Mexicans suffered severe economic pain during these decades, directly attributable to government mismanagement of the national economy. Millions of jobs were lost, real wages were stagnant or declining in all but a few years of the period, savings and businesses were decimated by inflation and currency devaluations, and government benefits for the middle and lower classes were slashed in the austerity budgets necessitated by the economic crises. These economic shocks set the stage for massive anti-PRI voting that eventually broke the party's seventy-one-year hold on national executive power in 2000. But by 2008, a severe global recession was dragging down Mexico's economy and testing the resilience of "opposition" rule.

CURRENT POLICY CHALLENGES

Mexico had entered the twenty-first century with huge social and economic problems: an economy that produces far too few jobs to accommodate the young people entering the labor market each year; an educational system sorely in need of modernization; a growing impoverished population, with close to half of all Mexicans still living below the official poverty line; a highly unequal distribution of income; a huge developmental gap between the affluent, urbanized, economically modern Northern states and the poor, rural, heavily indigenous South; acute environmental problems that damage the health of both rural and urban dwellers; and a criminal-justice system that barely functions, routinely violates the human rights of citizens, and is heavily corrupted by drug trafficking. The PRI lost its grip on the Mexican political system in large part because it had failed to deal effectively with these problems. The democratic "opposition," now in power, has been able to manage them with only marginal success.

Several emerging economic policy challenges will be no less daunting. As a developing country, Mexico has to deal more directly with the global economic system; it must play catch-up with its international trade partners and competitors. The rise of China as a key competitor in global markets has had a particularly strong impact on Mexico. China has displaced Mexico as the second-largest exporter of manufactured goods to the **North American Free Trade Agreement** (**NAFTA**) market, and Chinese producers offer stiff competition to many Mexican firms within their domestic market. Mexico must modernize its agricultural sector to allow it to survive competition from the United States and Canada, where subsidies and more efficient methods make agricultural goods cheaper. This vulnerable sector was further challenged when trade barriers were eliminated completely under NAFTA in 2008.

Mexico needs to replace its antiquated and inefficient labor law with new statutes that both protect workers and encourage job creation. It must renovate the energy sector—oil, electricity, and natural gas—either by increasing government spending or by allowing more private or foreign investment, which would require controversial constitutional amendments. An unfamiliar demographic problem is beginning to emerge—an aging population—and the Mexican people must soon bolster the funding of private and government-sponsored pension plans. Finally, the government must expand the tax base to provide the resources needed to address all of these challenges.

On the political front, additional changes in electoral rules are needed to close loopholes concerning the financing of campaigns to make it more difficult for elected officials to use government resources to promote their party's candidates and to allow the immediate reelection of legislators, which would make them more responsive and accountable to their constituents. But in terms of consolidating a fully democratic system, these refinements may be less important than the rapidly spreading belief that alternation in power among Mexico's main parties, at all levels of governance, is both desirable and achievable. In the national elections of July 2010, PRI candidates won a majority of the state governorships being contested, but a center-right/center-left coalition won three states—Oaxaca, Puebla, and Sinaloa—previously held only by the PRI. The prospect of additional, successful left–right coalition candidates in 2011 and 2012—a presidential election year—to block the PRI's return to national power has injected a new source of dynamism and uncertainty into Mexico's electoral politics.

Mexico's politics are also being influenced powerfully by the government's campaign against drug trafficking, which since 2006 has become the single most salient public issue. The 2010 national elections were the first that Mexico's drug lords made a sustained effort to disrupt. They sought to do so by intimidating poll-watchers, depressing voter turnout, and assassinating a gubernatorial candidate less than a week before election day. Since 2006, when President Calderón called out the military to wage all-out war on narco-traffickers who posed a national security threat and had compromised countless public officials and police, Mexico has been gripped by pervasive, drug-related violence. From December 2006 through December 2010, nearly 30,000 Mexicans died in such violence, including innocent victims as well as narco-traffickers eliminated by their rivals in the industry.

But most voters in July 2010 seemed determined to deny the traffickers a victory. They showed up at the polls, even in the most dangerous parts of the country, and punished candidates who were perceived as having ties with drug trafficking. In short, most Mexicans seem to have concluded that it is time to get on with the business of modern democracy.

HISTORICAL PERSPECTIVES

Colonialism and Church–State Relations

Long before Hernán Cortés landed in 1519 and began the Spanish conquest of Mexico, its territory was inhabited by numerous indigenous civilizations. Of these, the Mayans on the Yucatán peninsula and the Toltecs on the central plateau had developed the most complex political and economic organizations. Both of these civilizations had disintegrated, however, before the Spaniards arrived. Smaller indigenous societies were decimated by diseases introduced by the invaders or were vanquished by the sword. Subsequent grants of land and native labor by the Spanish Crown to the colonists further isolated the rural native population and deepened their exploitation.

The combined effects of attrition, intermarriage, and cultural penetration of native regions have drastically reduced the proportion of Mexico's population culturally identified as indigenous. According to 2005 census figures, 7.5 percent of the nation's population speak a native language.[1] The indigenous minority has been persistently marginal to the national economy and political system. Today, the indigenous population is heavily concentrated in rural communities that the government classifies as the country's most economically depressed and service-deprived, located primarily in the Southeast and the center of the country. The indigenous population is an especially troubling reminder of the millions of people who have been left behind by uneven development in twentieth-century Mexico.

The importance of Spain's colonies in the New World lay in their ability to provide the Crown with vital resources to fuel the Spanish economy. Mexico's mines provided gold and silver in abundance until the wars of independence began in 1810. After independence, Mexico continued to export these ores, supplemented in subsequent eras by hemp, cotton, textiles, oil, and winter vegetables.

Since the Spanish conquest, the Roman Catholic Church has been an institution of enduring power in Mexico. Priests joined the Spanish invaders in an evangelical mission to convert the natives to Catholicism, and individual priests have continued to play important roles in national history. For example, Father Miguel Hidalgo y Costilla helped launch Mexico's War of Independence in 1810, and Father José María Morelos y Pavón replaced Hidalgo as spiritual and military leader of the independence movement when the Crown executed Hidalgo in 1811.

During Mexico's postindependence period, institutional antagonisms between the Church and the central government have occasionally flared into open confrontations on such issues as Church wealth, educational policy, the content of public school textbooks, and political activism by the Church. The Constitutions of 1857 and 1917 formally established the separation of church and state and defined their respective domains. Constitutional provisions dramatically reduced the Church's power and wealth by nationalizing its property, including church buildings and large agricultural landholdings. Government efforts during the 1920s to enforce these constitutional provisions led to a civil insurrection that caused 100,000 combatant deaths, uncounted civilian casualties, and economic devastation in a large part of central Mexico. The settlement of this "Cristero rebellion" established, once and for all, the Church's subordination to the state, in return for which the government relaxed its restrictions on Church activities in nonpolitical arenas.

This accord inaugurated a long period of relative tranquility in church–state relations, during which the government and the Church ignored many of the anticlerical provisions of the 1917 Constitution (such as the prohibition on Church involvement in education). The central Church hierarchy—among the most conservative in Latin America—seethed at anticlerical and socially liberal policies (such as divorce, birth control, and the tolerance of the growth of evangelical movements), yet cooperated with the government on a variety of other issues, and the Church posed no threat to the ruling party's hegemony.

Revolution and Its Aftermath

The nationwide civil conflict that erupted in Mexico in 1910 is often referred to as the first of the great "social revolutions" that shook the world early in the twentieth century. Mexico's upheaval, however, originated within the country's ruling class. The revolution did not begin as a spontaneous uprising of the common people against the entrenched dictator, Porfirio Díaz, nor against the local bosses and landowners who exploited them. Even though hundreds of thousands of workers and peasants ultimately participated in the civil strife, most of the revolutionary leadership came from the younger generation of middle- and upper-class

Mexicans who had become disenchanted with three and a half decades of increasingly heavy-handed rule by the aging dictator and his clique. These disgruntled members of the elite saw their future opportunities for economic and political mobility blocked by the closed group surrounding Díaz.

Led by Francisco I. Madero, whose family had close ties with the ruling group, these liberal middle-class reformers were committed to opening up the political system and creating new opportunities for themselves within a capitalist economy whose basic features they did not challenge. They did not seek to destroy the established order. Instead, they sought to make it work more in their own interest, rather than that of the foreign capitalists who dominated key sectors of Mexico's economy during the Porfirian dictatorship.

Of course, some serious grievances had accumulated among workers and peasants. Once the rebellion against Díaz got underway, leaders who appealed to the disadvantaged masses pressed their claims against the central government. Emiliano Zapata led a movement of peasants in the state of Morelos; they were bent on regaining the land they had lost to the rural aristocracy by subterfuge during the Porfiriato. In the north, Pancho Villa led an army of jobless workers, small landowners, and cattle hands, whose main interest was steady employment. As various revolutionary leaders contended for control of the central government, the political order that had been created and enforced by Díaz disintegrated into warlordism—powerful regional gangs led by revolutionary *caudillos* (political-military strongmen) who aspired more to increasing their personal wealth and social status than to leading a genuine social revolution.

The first decade of the revolution produced a new, remarkably progressive constitution, replacing the Constitution of 1857. The Constitution of 1917 established the principle of state control over all natural resources, subordination of the Church to the state, the government's right to redistribute land, and rights for labor that had not yet been secured even by the labor movement in the United States. Even so, nearly two decades passed before most of these constitutional provisions began to be implemented.

During the 1920s, the central government set out to eliminate or undermine the most powerful and independent-minded regional *caudillos* by coopting the local power brokers, known as **caciques**. These local political bosses became, in effect, appendages of the central government, supporting its policies and maintaining control over the population in their communities. By the end of this period, leaders with genuine popular followings (like Zapata and Villa) had been assassinated and control had been seized by a new postrevolutionary elite bent on demobilizing the masses and establishing the hegemony of the central government. The rural aristocracy of the Porfiriato had been weakened but not eliminated; its heirs still controlled large concentrations of property and other forms of wealth in many parts of the country.

The Cárdenas Upheaval

Elite control was maintained during the 1930s, but this was nevertheless an era of massive social and political upheaval in Mexico. During the presidency of Lázaro Cárdenas (1934–1940), peasants and urban workers succeeded for the first time in pressing their claims for land and higher wages; in fact, Cárdenas actively encouraged them to do so. The result was an unprecedented wave of strikes, protest demonstrations, and petitions for breaking up large rural estates.

Most disputes between labor and management during this period were settled, under government pressure, in favor of the workers. The Cárdenas administration also redistributed more than twice as much land as that expropriated by all of Cárdenas's predecessors since 1915, when Mexico's land reform program was formally initiated. By 1940, the country's land tenure system had been fundamentally altered, breaking the traditional domination of the large haciendas and creating a large sector of small peasant farmers (*ejidatarios*)—more than 1.5 million of them—who had received plots of land under the agrarian reform program. Even Mexico's foreign relations were disrupted in 1938 when the Cárdenas government nationalized oil companies that had been operating in Mexico under U.S. and British ownership.

Mexican intellectuals frequently refer to 1938 as the high-water mark of the Mexican revolution as measured by social progress; they characterize the period since then as a retrogression. Certainly, the distributive and especially the redistributive performance of the Mexican government declined sharply in the decades that followed, and the worker and peasant organizations formed during the Cárdenas era atrophied and became less and less likely to contest either the will of the government or the interests of Mexico's private economic elites. De facto reconcentration of landholdings and other forms of wealth occurred as the state provided increasingly generous support to the country's new commercial, industrial, and financial elites during a period of rapid industrialization.

The Cárdenas era fundamentally reshaped Mexico's political institutions. The presidency became the primary institution of the political system, with sweeping powers exercised during a constitutionally limited six-year term with no possibility of reelection, the military was removed from overt political competition and transformed into one of several institutional pillars of the regime, and an elaborate network of government-sponsored peasant and labor organizations provided a mass base for the official political party and performed a variety of political and economic control functions, using a multilayered system of patronage and clientelism.

By 1940, a much larger proportion of the Mexican population was nominally included in the national political system, mostly by their membership in peasant and labor organizations created by Cárdenas. No real democratization of the system resulted from this vast expansion of "political participation," however. Although working-class groups did have more control over their representatives in the government-sponsored organizations than over their former masters on the haciendas and in the factories, their influence over public policy and government priorities after Cárdenas was minimal and highly indirect.

The Era of Hegemonic Party Rule

The political system shaped by Lázaro Cárdenas proved remarkably durable. From 1940 until the late 1980s, Mexico's official party–government apparatus was the most stable regime in Latin America (see Box 11.1). It

had a well-earned reputation for resilience, adaptability to new circumstances, a high level of agreement within the ruling elite on basic rules of political competition, and a seemingly unlimited capacity to coopt dissidents, both within and outside of the ruling party.

With the fall of the Communist Party of the Soviet Union in 1991, the PRI became the world's longest continuously ruling political party. Since 1929, when the "official" party was founded, both political assassination and armed rebellion had been rejected as routes to the presidency by all contenders for power. A handful of disappointed aspirants to the ruling party's presidential nomination mounted candidacies outside the party (in the elections of 1929, 1940, 1946, 1952, and 1988), but even the most broadly supported of these breakaway movements were successfully contained through government-engineered vote fraud and intimidation.

In the early 1970s, concerns had been raised about the stability of the system, after the bloody repression of a student protest movement in Mexico City by President Gustavo Díaz Ordaz on the eve of the 1968 Olympic Games. The student massacre marked the opening of a "dirty war" in which the army and police forces are believed to have executed, without trial, more than seven hundred alleged enemies of the state. Many analysts at that time suggested that Mexico was entering a period of institutional crisis, requiring fundamental reforms in both political arrangements and economic development strategy.

The discovery of massive oil and natural-gas resources during the late 1970s gave the incumbent regime a new lease on life. Continued support of the masses and the elites was purchased with an apparently limitless supply of petro-pesos, even without major structural reforms. The government's room to maneuver was abruptly erased by the collapse of the oil boom in August 1982, owing to a combination of

---

BOX 11.1

Mexican Presidents and Their Parties since 1940

1940–1946	Manuel Avila Camacho (PRI)	**1976–1982**	José López Portillo (PRI)
1946–1952	Miguel Alemán (PRI)	**1982–1988**	Miguel de la Madrid (PRI)
1952–1958	Adolfo Ruiz Cortines (PRI)	**1988–1994**	Carlos Salinas de Gortari (PRI)
1958–1964	Adolfo López Mateos (PRI)	**1994–2000**	Ernesto Zedillo (PRI)
1964–1970	Gustavo Díaz Ordaz (PRI)	**2000–2006**	Vicente Fox (PAN)
1970–1976	Luis Echeverría (PRI)	**2006–2012**	Felipe Calderón (PAN)

adverse international economic circumstances (falling oil prices, rising interest rates, recession in the United States) and fiscally irresponsible domestic policies. Real wages and living standards for the vast majority of Mexicans plummeted, and the government committed itself to a socially painful restructuring of the economy, including a drastic shrinkage of the sector owned and managed by the government itself.

The economic crisis of the 1980s placed enormous stress on Mexico's political system. In the July 1988 national elections, the PRI suffered unprecedented reverses in both the presidential and congressional races. The vote share officially attributed to Carlos Salinas was more than 20 percent below that of PRI presidential candidate Miguel de la Madrid in the 1982 election. Ex-PRIista Cuauhtémoc Cárdenas, son of the much-revered former President Lázaro Cárdenas, heading a hastily assembled coalition of minor leftist and nationalist parties, was officially credited with 31.1 percent of the presidential vote— far more than any previous opposition candidate but probably much less than he would actually have received if the vote count had been honest.[2] A diminished PRI delegation still controlled the Congress, but the president's party had lost the two-thirds majority needed to approve constitutional amendments.

Carlos Salinas breathed new life into the creaking PRI apparatus. His brand of strong presidential leadership and his accomplishments—especially the toppling of corrupt labor union bosses, a sharp reduction in inflation, and the National Solidarity Program, a new-style antipoverty and public works program that increased government responsiveness to lower-class needs—sufficed to rebuild electoral support for the PRI and to paper over the cracks within the ruling political elite. Salinas opened the Mexican economy to foreign trade and investment and privatized hundreds of inefficient state-owned companies. While political liberalization had proceeded slowly and unevenly under Salinas, far behind the pace of his sweeping free-market economic reforms, Mexico appeared to be coasting inexorably toward a transfer of power to yet another PRI national government in 1994.

The illusion of proximate economic modernity and political inevitability was shattered on New Year's Day 1994 by a "postmodern" peasant revolt in Chiapas, Mexico's most underdeveloped and politically backward state. An estimated 2,000 primitively armed but well-disciplined indigenous rebels seized control of four isolated municipalities and declared war on the central government—something that had not happened since 1938. Their demands for social justice and democracy resonated throughout Mexico, long after the initial skirmishes with the Mexican army had claimed at least 145 lives and a cease-fire had been negotiated. Suddenly, middle- and upper-class Mexicans, as well as foreign governments and investors, were reminded of the persistence of political repression, human-rights violations, extreme poverty, and inequality in Mexico. The impoverished natives who took up arms against the state in Chiapas symbolized the many millions of Mexicans who had been left behind in the drive for economic modernity and internationalism.

Less than three months after the Chiapas rebellion erupted, President Salinas's hand-picked successor, Luis Donaldo Colosio, was assassinated while campaigning in Tijuana. With a last great exertion of presidential will, Carlos Salinas imposed on the PRI another hand-picked successor, economist-technocrat Ernesto Zedillo, to replace the slain Colosio. In August 1994, in a high-turnout election that was judged by most independent observers at the time to be the cleanest in Mexico's postrevolutionary history, the opposition parties were soundly defeated. Not only did the PRI retain control of the presidency (albeit with just a plurality of 48.8 percent of the total votes cast), it also maintained an ample majority in the federal Congress.[3]

The End of PRI Dominance

The appearance of restored stability created by the ruling party's impressive performance in the August 1994 elections was short-lived. In December 1994, a militarily insignificant renewal of the Zapatista rebels' activities in Chiapas, followed immediately by a sustained speculative attack on the overvalued peso by short-term foreign and domestic investors, opened a Pandora's box of economic and political troubles. What began as a currency and financial liquidity crisis quickly evolved into a massive capital flight and a deep recession.

By the late 1990s, the PRI once again appeared to be in a state of accelerated decomposition. Divisions within the party were deeper than at any time since the mid-1930s. The results of the 1997 elections for Congress were a stunning setback for the PRI, which lost 112 of 300 single-member districts. For the first time since 1929, the PRI had to surrender control of the Chamber of Deputies (the lower house of Congress) to a coalition of four opposition parties. The PRI also lost its two-thirds majority in the Senate, which is needed to approve constitutional amendments.

In the 2000 election, voters were furious at having been deceived twice by their government, first during the oil boom era of 1977 through 1981 and then during the Salinas presidency (1988–1994), periods when the government created an illusion of prosperity and boundless future economic gains. For the first time in seventy-one years, the voters soundly rejected the presidential candidate of the PRI, turning to Vicente Fox, a maverick former-Coca-Cola-executive-turned-politician who ran under the banner of **Partido Acción Nacional (PAN)**. With the defeat of its presidential candidate in 2000, the PRI lost control of the vast patronage resources of the central government, which were crucial to keeping it in power for more than seven decades.

The presidential election of 2006 featured three strong candidates and a highly divided electorate. Roberto Madrazo, the PRI's president (2002–2005), became the leading candidate for that party's 2006 presidential nomination. However, not all PRIistas favored Madrazo. Four candidates ran against him in an August 2005 first-round "primary," which consisted of a series of public-opinion polls. The former governor of the state of Mexico emerged as the winner, but he was forced to withdraw after media reports revealed that he had acquired a suspiciously large fortune in real estate. Madrazo quickly gained the PRI nomination in a virtually uncontested primary election.

Felipe Calderón was an underdog to become the PAN's 2006 candidate. Santiago Creel, the interior minister in the Fox administration, had been the front-runner since 2001. The PAN scheduled three regional primaries, with the rule that the candidate who won the most votes across the three primaries would win the nomination. The race turned out to be more competitive

Contested Presidential Election Brings Losing Candidate's Supporters into the Streets
López Obrador's supporters demonstrate in Mexico City's Zócalo (central plaza), August 2006.

Imelda Medina/epa/Corbis

BOX 11.2

Felipe Calderón: Mexico's Current President

Felipe Calderón's biography is a blend of "traditional politician" experiences with those of the modern Mexican technocrat who makes much of his career within the federal bureaucracy. He earned master's degrees in economics and public administration, the latter degree from Harvard University's Kennedy School of Government.

He was twice elected to a seat in Congress and once to the legislative body of Mexico City. Calderón also served as national chairman of his party, the PAN. He later served as director of BANOBRAS, a federal development bank, and as Secretary of Energy in President Vicente Fox's cabinet.

than expected. Calderón surprised nearly everyone by winning all three (see Box 11.2).

The **Partido de la Revolución Democrática (PRD)**'s candidate, Andrés Manuel López Obrador—the mayor of Mexico City from 2000 to 2005—began campaigning in fall 2005 with a considerable lead; Calderón started out in third place in most polls. In 2004, the federal attorney general's office began investigating López Obrador, who was accused of violating a court order arising from a land-use dispute in Mexico City. Because he was an elected official, he had the benefit of immunity from prosecution, and a ruling by the federal Chamber of Deputies was required to remove that immunity. After the attorney general formally sought an indictment against López Obrador, the chamber voted to remove his immunity (the PRI and the PAN voted in favor and the PRD against). People who are under indictment or are serving sentences after convictions are ineligible to run for federal office, so the removal of his immunity made López Obrador ineligible to run for president. His supporters claimed that the true rationale for the indictment was to remove the leading candidate from the presidential race. His opponents claimed that the charges were genuine and demonstrated his lack of respect for the separation of powers and the rule of law.

Responding to mounting domestic and international criticism of the López Obrador indictment, President Fox fired the attorney general and dismissed the charges against the mayor. This episode increased the popularity of López Obrador, who portrayed himself as the victim of a conspiracy organized by the Fox government, the PAN, the PRI, and the private sector. He returned to his job as Mexico City mayor, resigning a few months later to run for president. From that point, López Obrador maintained a lead in the presidential trial heats all the way through April 2006.

After beating Madrazo in a nationally televised debate, Calderón overtook López Obrador in most polls, with the PRI's Madrazo in third place. After a second debate and an extraordinarily negative campaign, Calderón and López Obrador were tied in all of the polls. On Election Day, July 2, 2006, the race was so close that both López Obrador and Calderón claimed victory. On July 5, the formal count of the votes began in each of the 300 electoral districts. The next day, the Federal Electoral Institute (IFE) announced that Calderón had won by 0.58 percent, or about 244,000 votes out of nearly 42 million cast (see Table 11.1). López Obrador immediately claimed that there had been electoral fraud, orchestrated by the PAN, the PRI, the Federal Electoral Institute, and the business community. To pressure the electoral tribunal to order a complete recount, the PRD launched a civil disobedience campaign in Mexico City. Thousands of protesters set up tents along the principal boulevard and the Zócalo (the central plaza), blocking all traffic in the heart of Mexico City. The partial recount and the subsequent nullification of some disputed precincts shifted only about 14,000 votes to López Obrador. Calderón's victory was certified by the electoral tribunal in early September. Nonetheless, López Obrador refused to recognize the "spurious president," and in November 2006 inaugurated himself as "the legitimate president of Mexico" before 100,000 of his supporters in the heart of Mexico City. He vowed to lead "years of resistance" throughout the country and to pressure the Calderón government into adopting his legislative proposals, including measures for breaking up business monopolies and creating a universal health care system.

The election results divided Mexico in two, with the PAN winning most of the Northern states (except Zacatecas and Baja California Sur, both governed by the PRD). The PRD won every state to the south,

TABLE 11.1

2006 Presidential Election Results

The election produced a highly contested, razor-thin victory for PAN's candidate, while PRI's candidate finished a distant third.

Candidate	Votes	% of Valid Votes
Felipe Calderón (PAN)	15,019,300	36.70
Andrés Manuel López Obrador (PRD-PT-Convergencia)	14,767,438	36.09
Roberto Madrazo (PRI-PVEM)	9,302,801	22.73
Patricia Mercado (PASC)	1,129,737	2.76
Roberto Campa (Nueva Alianza)	401,932	0.98
Nonregistered candidates	298,018	0.73
Invalid votes	937,735	
Total votes	**41,856,961**	**100.00**

Source: Instituto Federal Electoral (www.ife.org.mx), 2006 (official district counts, including voters abroad).

except Yucatán (governed by the PAN) and Puebla (where the PRI governor was under the clouds of scandal). Calderón and López Obrador each won sixteen states. Madrazo, incredibly, won not a single state.

After its disastrous, third-place finish in the 2006 presidential election, and with its delegation in Congress reduced to about a fifth of the lower chamber, the PRI seemed to be retreating into its regional strongholds. However, in subsequent gubernatorial elections, the PRI recovered states that it had previously lost to the opposition (see Table 11.2). By 2010, the PRI was well-positioned to retake the presidency in 2012, fueled by a stagnant economy and public disapproval of President Calderón's aggressive, violence-producing war against drug traffickers.

POLITICAL CULTURE

Most of what we know empirically about Mexican political culture is based on research completed during the period of sustained economic growth and virtually unchallenged one-party rule in Mexico, from 1940 through the mid-1970s. The portrait of Mexican political culture that emerges from these studies can be summarized as follows: Mexicans are highly supportive of the political institutions that evolved from the Mexican Revolution, and they endorse the democratic principles embodied in the Constitution of 1917. However, they are critical of government performance, especially in creating jobs, reducing social and economic inequality, fighting crime, and delivering basic public services. Most government bureaucrats and

politicians are viewed as distant, elitist, and self-serving, if not corrupt. Mexicans traditionally have been pessimistic about their ability to affect election outcomes, anticipating fraud and regarding attendance at campaign rallies and voting as ritualistic activities.

On the surface, this combination of attitudes and beliefs seems contradictory. How could Mexicans support a political system that they see as unresponsive or capricious at best, in which they are mere "subjects" rather than true participants? Historically, popular support for the Mexican political system derived from three sources: the revolutionary origins of the regime, the government's role in promoting economic growth, and its performance in distributing concrete, material benefits to a substantial proportion of the Mexican population since the Cárdenas era. Each of these traditional sources of support has been undermined to some extent since 1976.

The official interpretation of the 1910 revolution stressed symbols (or myths), such as social justice, democracy, the need for national unity, and the popular origins of the current regime. The government's identification with these symbols was constantly reinforced by the mass media, public schools, and the mass organizations affiliated with the official party. Over the years, the party's electoral appeals were explicitly designed to link its candidates with agrarian reform and other revered ideals of the revolution, with national heroes like Emiliano Zapata and Lázaro Cárdenas, and with the national flag. (The PRI emblem conveniently has the same colors, in the same arrangement.) However, President Salinas broke decisively with so many tenets of "revolutionary ideology"

Partisan Control of Mexican States — Parties now alternate in power at the state level.		TABLE 11.2
States not lost by the PRI	**States won by the PAN and held by the PAN**	**States won by the PRD and held by the PRD**
Campeche	Aguascalientes	Baja California Sur
Coahuila	Baja California	Chiapas
Colima	Guanajuato	Distrito Federal
Durango	Jalisco	Guerrero*
Hidalgo	Morelos	Michoacán
México	Sonora*	Zacatecas
Oaxaca		
Puebla		
	States won by the PAN and recovered by the PRI	**State won by the PRD and taken by the PAN**
Quintana Roo	Chihuahua	Tlaxcala
Sinaloa	Nayarit	
Tabasco	Nuevo León	
Tamaulipas	Querétaro	
Veracruz	San Luis Potosí	
	Yucatán	

*States still in first term of opposition control.

(strict church–state separation, land reform, economic nationalism, etc.) that the PRI's claim to the revolutionary mantle became tenuous. Indeed, since the late 1980s, that mantle has been claimed by the PRD.

Relatively few Mexicans based their support for the system primarily on its revolutionary origins or symbolic outputs, however. For most sectors of the population, symbols were supplemented with particularistic material rewards: plots of land or titles to land that had been occupied illegally, schools, low-cost medical care, agricultural crop price supports, government-subsidized food and other consumer goods, and public-sector jobs. For more than forty years, the personal receipt of some material "favor" from the official party–government apparatus, or the hope that such benefits might be received in the future, ensured fairly high levels of mass support for the system.

Even now, Mexicans' concept of democracy emphasizes economic and social outputs rather than procedural liberties, and the electoral strategies of all parties reflect this element of political culture.[4] For example, in the 2006 election, many voters were attracted to PRD candidate López Obrador by his performance as Mexico City mayor, delivering high-visibility public works and monthly payments to senior citizens. PAN candidate Felipe Calderón promised to reduce social inequality through a major expansion of Oportunidades, a federal welfare program already benefiting 5 million low-income families. While not on a par with traditional vote-buying by the PRI—trading specific material payoffs for votes at the individual level—such campaign strategies clearly resonate with an electorate whose concept of democracy is still largely distributive.

Despite their growing distrust of key political institutions (especially Congress and the political parties), a plurality of Mexicans have remained "system loyalists." For example, while they may be frustrated by interparty bickering within Congress, most Mexicans do not view their national legislature as obstructing unduly the ability of the president to accomplish his objectives. As shown in Table 11.3, Mexicans in 2008 were less likely to view Congress as obstructionist than citizens of all but three other Latin American countries (Brazil, Bolivia, and Chile).

TABLE 11.3

Does the National Legislature Obstruct the Power of the President?[1]

Mexicans do not see Congress as obstructionist compared to other Latin American nations.

Country	National average
Argentina	39.9
Belize	39.0
Honduras	37.9
Nicaragua	37.7
Haiti	36.5
Paraguay	32.8
Jamaica	31.6
Uruguay	30.4
Dominican Rep.	29.7
El Salvador	28.1
Guatemala	27.1
Panama	26.4
Peru	25.8
Ecuador	24.8
Colombia	24.2
Costa Rica	23.8
Mexico	23.0
Brazil	21.3
Bolivia	20.8
Chile	17.1

[1]The survey question was: "To what extent does the National Legislature obstruct the power of the President?" Responses were given on a scale of 1 to 7, where 1 meant "not at all" and 7 meant "a lot." These responses were then recoded on a scale of 0 to 100 to facilitate comparison across questions and survey waves. A national probability sample was surveyed in each country. Nonresponse was 14.8 percent for the sample as a whole.

Source: Latin American Public Opinion Project, Vanderbilt University, *AmericasBarometer Insights* 26 (2009).

Nevertheless, most Mexicans today do not hesitate to criticize the way in which local, state, and national government function, and many more feel free to demonstrate their dissatisfaction by voting to throw the rascals out.

Historically, most Mexicans tolerated corruption in government as a price to be paid in order to extract benefits from the system or to deal with police harassment. But the unbridled corruption of the López Portillo and the Salinas administrations drastically reduced such tolerance, and an upsurge in drug-related corruption in the 1990s—reaching into the highest levels of the government bureaucracy and the national security apparatus—angered many Mexicans. They feared that their government had been taken over by *narco-políticos*—public officials in league with corrupt police and drug lords. The slowness of the Vicente Fox administration to root out government and police corruption, despite its independence from the structure of corruption created under PRI rule, was a source of public anger by the end of Fox's term.

Despite much more competition in the electoral system since the 1980s, the average Mexican remains relatively uninterested in politics. At the beginning of the bitterly fought presidential election campaign of 2006, two-thirds of the interviewees in a national survey expressed little or no interest in politics, and 55 percent said they rarely or never discussed politics with other people. These percentages are essentially unchanged since the 2000 presidential campaign.[5]

In the last two national elections, however, Mexicans have shown themselves to be sensitive to short-term campaign stimuli, such as presidential candidates' debates, negative television ads, and news coverage. In fact, Mexicans appear more susceptible to persuasive campaign appeals than voters in the United States and other established democracies. Relatively more Mexicans change their party identification during the course of a campaign.[6] While such findings may indicate the absence of a core set of stable political beliefs, they reveal that Mexicans are paying close attention to the options provided by political competitors, at least during hard-fought national election campaigns.

MASS POLITICAL SOCIALIZATION

How do Mexicans form their attitudes toward the political system? In addition to the family, the schools and the Catholic Church are important sources of preadult political learning. All schools, including church-affiliated and secular private schools, must follow a government-approved curriculum and use the same set of free textbooks, written by the federal Ministry of Education. Although the private schools' compliance with the official curriculum is often nominal, control over the content of textbooks gives the government an instrument for socializing children to a uniform set of political values.

Under PRI rule, school-based political learning stressed the social and economic progress accomplished under postrevolutionary governments. The president was depicted as an omnipotent authority figure whose principal function is to maintain order in the country. Thus, despite the many egregious failures of presidential leadership that Mexicans have witnessed since the mid-1970s, many continue to express a preference for strong presidentialist government. However, mass public education has increased criticism of partisan politics and poor government performance. Higher levels of education are also associated with stronger support for the right to dissent and other democratic liberties.

The Catholic Church has been another key source of values affecting political behavior in Mexico. Church-run private schools have proliferated in recent decades. Along with secular private schools, they provide education for a large portion of children from middle- and upper-class families. Religious schools and priests have criticized anticlerical laws and policies, promoted individual initiative (as opposed to governmental action), and preached against abortion and gay marriage. They have also stressed the need for moral Christian behavior in public life.

As adults, Mexicans learn about politics from their personal encounters with government functionaries and the police. They also learn from participating in local community-based organizations and popular movements that seek collective benefits or redress of grievances from the government. There has been an impressive proliferation of popular movements in Mexico since 1968, when the student protest movement was violently repressed. The catalysts for this new wave of popular movements included gangsterism in government-affiliated labor unions, increasingly blatant PRI vote fraud in state and local elections during the 1980s, environmental disasters, and the implementation of neoliberal economic policies that adversely affected low- and middle-class segments of the society. While most of these popular movements are quite localized in scope and concerns, a few have grown to embrace thousands of Mexicans in many different states. The Civic Alliance—a coalition of hundreds of NGOs, independent labor unions, and popular movements—has mobilized tens of thousands of Mexican citizens and hundreds of foreign observers to scrutinize the conduct of every national election since 1994 and publish reports on election irregularities. Nevertheless,

nongovernmental organizations remain heavily concentrated in the Mexico City metropolitan area, where nearly 30 percent of the country's NGOs are registered. By contrast, the state of Chiapas hosts only 0.3 percent.

For seven decades, the PRI-government apparatus systematically used the mass media as an agent of political socialization. Although the government did not often directly censor the media, there were significant economic penalties for engaging in criticism or investigative reporting that seriously embarrassed the president. Since the PRI lost control of the presidency in 2000, the mass media have been much more openly critical of government performance. Many newspapers and news magazines retain their PRI partisan bias and energetically criticize the president and other PANista officials. The independent media have kept up their intense scrutiny of the executive branch and are also highly critical of what they see as incompetence and inefficiency in Congress.

The print media reach only a tiny fraction of the Mexican population (even the largest Mexico City newspapers have circulations under 100,000). As of 2003, newspaper circulation was just 93.5 per 1,000 Mexicans. Until recently, television was virtually monopolized by a huge private firm, Televisa, which had a notoriously close working relationship with the PRI-government apparatus and invariably defended the incumbent president's performance. One consequence of the Salinas administration's privatization program was the breakup of Televisa's virtual monopoly. A formerly government-owned television channel in Mexico City has grown quickly into a rival network, TV Azteca, and Televisa itself adjusted to the competition by giving much more coverage to opposition voices. In 2006, Congress approved a bill that would end government discretion in the awarding of specific parts of the television broadcasting spectrum. The Interior Ministry had in the past used its control of these concessions to guarantee positive media treatment of the government. The television spectrum would be auctioned off to the highest bidders. Opponents criticized this reform, claiming that it would exacerbate Televisa's monopoly because the corporation could often end up being the highest bidder. In 2007, the Supreme Court ruled that the new law unconstitutionally abdicated the State's authority over telecommunications. It became a question of weighing pluralism in the government against pluralism in the market.

POLITICAL PARTICIPATION

Traditionally, most political participation in Mexico has been of two broad types: (1) ritualistic, regime-supportive activities (for example, voting, attending campaign rallies) and (2) petitioning or contacting of public officials to influence the allocation of some public good or service. By law, voting is obligatory in Mexico, though there are no civil penalties for not voting. Evidence of having voted in the most recent election has sometimes been required to receive public services. People participate in campaign rallies mostly because attending might have a specific material payoff (a free meal, a raffle ticket, a T-shirt), or because failure to do so could have personal economic costs. In the past, as they went to the polls, Mexicans knew that they were not selecting those who would govern but merely ratifying the choice of candidates made earlier by the PRI-government hierarchy. Some voted because they regarded it as their civic duty, others because they wished to avoid difficulty in future dealings with government agencies. Some voted in response to pressures from local *caciques* and PRI sector representatives. And some, especially in rural areas, freely sold their votes in return for handouts from local officials.

As elections have become moments of genuine political confrontation in most parts of Mexico, the ritualistic quality of voting and participating in campaign activities has diminished. Since 1994, Mexico has experienced an explosion in political participation, evidenced not only by the virtually nonstop protests of citizens' movements of all types, but also by a sharp rise in turnout in federal elections. The turnout of registered voters rose from 49 percent in the 1988 presidential election, to 61 percent in the midterm 1991 elections, to 78 percent in the 1994 presidential election. In the highly competitive 2006 presidential election, over 41,800,000 Mexicans cast their votes, a turnout rate of 59 percent (see Figure 11.1). The total included 33,131 Mexicans abroad who were permitted to vote absentee in the presidential election for the first time.

Unfortunately, valid comparisons with electoral participation rates in the pre-1988 period are impossible, since the 1988 presidential election was the first for which reasonably accurate turnout figures were made public. In all previous national elections, the government inflated turnout statistics in an effort to convince Mexicans and the outside world that it had succeeded in relegitimating itself in impressive fashion.

As long as electoral politics remain as competitive as in the period since 1988 and potential voters continue to believe in the security of the electoral system, we can expect further, gradual movement toward a genuinely

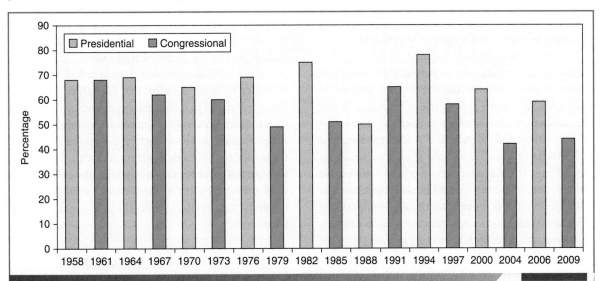

Turnout of Registered Voters in National Elections, 1958–2009*

FIGURE 11.1

Beginning in 1991, turnout rates reflect real increases in voter participation, not government padding.

*Beginning in 1970, the legal voting age was lowered from twenty-one to eighteen years.

Source: Data from Comisión Federal Electoral for 1958–1991; from Instituto Federal Electoral for 1994–2006.

participatory political culture in Mexico. In the 2010 national elections, voter turnout increased in all five states where the PAN and PRD ran coalition candidates to block PRI victories. It is reasonable to expect that left–right coalitions, by increasing competitiveness, will create stronger incentives to vote in future elections.

Rising educational attainment also will be crucial to boosting participation, as will greater involvement in nonpolitical, community-level organizations. Participation in such organizations builds **social capital**—the social networks, norms, and trust that enable people to act together more effectively to pursue shared objectives. Research has shown that Mexicans who are active in their communities and thereby connected to their neighbors are far more likely to participate politically.[7]

POLITICAL STRUCTURE AND INSTITUTIONS

Mexican politics has long defied easy classification. In the 1950s and 1960s, some U.S. political scientists depicted the regime as a one-party democracy that was evolving toward "true" (North Atlantic–style) democracy. They recognized certain imperfections, but in the view of these analysts, political development in Mexico was simply incomplete. After the government's massacre of student protesters in 1968 and 1971, most analysts described the system as authoritarian, but even this characterization was subject to qualification.

By the 1990s, Mexico seemed to belong to a rapidly expanding category of hybrid, part-free, part-authoritarian systems that did not conform to classical typologies. Such labels as "selective democracy," "hardline democracy," *democradura* (a Spanish contraction of "democracy" and "dictatorship"), and "modernizing authoritarian regime" have been applied to such systems. These are characterized by partly competitive (though not necessarily fair and honest) elections that install governments more committed to maintaining political stability and labor discipline than to expanding democratic freedoms, protecting human rights, or mediating class conflict.

Since the democratic breakthrough election of 2000, tolerance of undemocratic practices (for example, electoral fraud, selective repression of dissidents, and heavy-handed control of mass media) has declined. The functioning of all political institutions is scrutinized intensely, and they are held to much higher standards than ever before. The political design issue is no longer regime transition but how to improve democratic institutions already in place, especially to eliminate the structure of corruption that still supports abuses of authority and the electoral process at the local level in some parts of the country.

On paper, the Mexican government is structured much like the U.S. government: a presidential system, three autonomous branches of government (legislative, executive, and judicial) with checks and balances, and federalism with considerable autonomy at the state and municipal level (see Figure 11.2). Until the late 1990s, however, Mexico's system of government was in practice far removed from the U.S. model. Decision-making was highly centralized. The president, operating with relatively few restraints on his authority, completely dominated the legislative and judicial branches. Supreme Court justices were presidentially appointed and confirmed by a simple majority of the PRI-dominated Senate. Each incoming president replaced most justices, which made the judges agents of the executive branch. Until 1997, the ruling PRI continuously controlled both houses of the federal legislature. Opposition party members could criticize the government and its policies vociferously, but their objections to proposals initiated by the president and backed by his party in Congress rarely affected the final shape of legislation. Courts and legislatures at the state level normally mirrored the preferences of the state governors, many of whom themselves were handpicked by the incumbent president.

Since 1997, the government has lacked a majority in either or both chambers of Congress. President Vicente Fox had to lobby and negotiate with Congress on a routine basis to pass legislation, as does President Felipe Calderón. The era when Congress's sole functions were to serve as a debating arena for the opposition parties (and for factions within the ruling party until the whips were applied) and as a rubber stamp for decisions already taken by the president has clearly ended.

Federalism: A Double-Edged Sword

Despite the federalist structure of government that is enshrined in the 1917 Constitution and legal codes, with their emphasis on the *municipio libre* (the concept of the free municipality, able to control its own affairs), in practice, the Mexican political system has

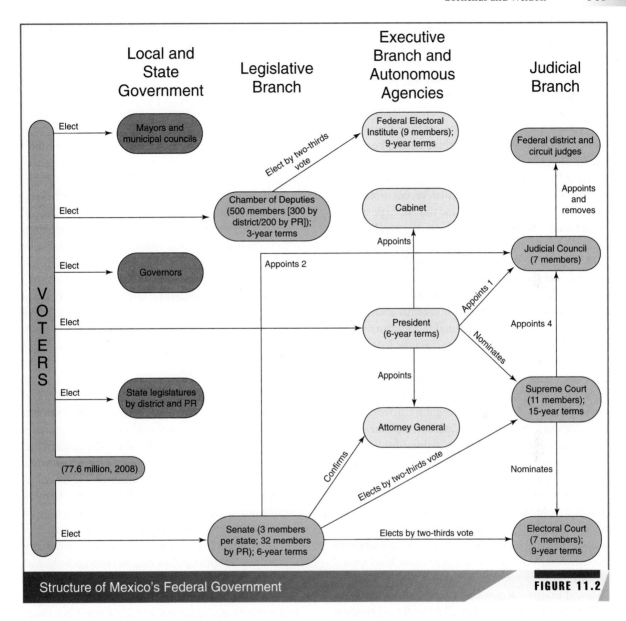

Structure of Mexico's Federal Government   **FIGURE 11.2**

usually functioned in a manner best characterized as **political centralism**.

From the 1920s through the Salinas presidency, the concentration of decision-making power at the federal level in most policy areas was continuous. Control over the preparation, conduct, and validation of elections—placed entirely at the municipal and state levels by the initial postrevolutionary electoral code, enacted in 1918—also passed to agencies that were part of the federal government apparatus or state-level entities controlled by federal authorities. A high degree of political centralism has been considered one of

the main factors underlying Mexico's long-term political stability, although research at the state and local levels has demonstrated that political control by the center has been far less complete than is commonly assumed.[8]

Mexico is divided into thirty-one states and the Federal District, each one divided into *municipios*—politico-administrative units roughly equivalent in size and governmental functions to county governments in the United States. Each of the country's 2,378 *municipios* is governed by an *ayuntamiento*, or council, headed by a *presidente municipal* (mayor). Municipal officials are elected every three years. Each successive layer of government in Mexico is significantly weaker, less autonomous, and more impoverished than the levels above it. In recent years, the federal government has raised well over 90 percent of total public revenues—one of the highest degrees of fiscal centralization in Latin America.[9] State governments now spend more than half of total revenues, but this is mainly because of federal revenue-sharing that provides the states with much of their budget.

All of Mexico's seven most recent presidents entered office pledging to renew the "struggle against centralism," but serious efforts to decentralize have been made only since 1984. Under de la Madrid and Salinas, a limited form of revenue-sharing was implemented, and the federal Constitution was amended to enhance the capacity of local governments to raise their own revenues. Partially successful efforts were also made to shift decision-making authority over public education and health care from the federal government to the states.[10] President Zedillo went so far as to sign an agreement with the country's state governors and mayors calling for constitutional amendments that would provide the legal framework for "a new Mexican federalism." Zedillo implemented a more equitable distribution of federal funds to the states and devolution of some functions that had been usurped by the federal government.

The state governors themselves represent a potential obstacle to the "new federalism." They retain control over all resources transferred from the federal government, and effective administrative decentralization down to the *municipio* level would require them to relinquish a major portion of their political power—something that they have successfully resisted. It is clear that, even under a president strongly committed to redistributing resources and sharing power with subnational units of government, movement toward U.S.-style federalism in Mexico will meet with opposition from many different quarters, including federal government agencies and the states themselves.

State-level elections have not democratized at the same pace as federal elections. Since the 1990s, governors of predominantly rural, PRI-dominated states like Tabasco, Oaxaca, Puebla, and Veracruz have attempted to keep tight control over local candidate selection and the state's electoral apparatus, often using state government resources to assure victory for the ruling party. One of these PRI governors, Manuel Bartlett of Puebla, secured passage of a law enabling him to divert the state's share of increased revenue-sharing funds approved by Congress from cities controlled by the opposition PAN to rural areas where the PRI was stronger. This mechanism was soon copied by other PRI governors across the country.

Rejuvenated federalism can thus be a double-edged sword, with the potential to consolidate authoritarian enclaves at the state and local levels. Even in the federal government's war against narco-traffickers, decentralization has had unintended consequences. President Calderón's strategy of breaking the cartels into smaller components supposedly manageable by local authorities has spawned greater competition among competing drug lords and, hence, more violence. In Mexico, less central control does not necessarily translate into more electoral democracy, better governance, and greater public security.

The Legislative Branch

Mexico's political system has been commonly described as presidentialist or presidentially centered. Nonetheless, these characterizations were based on observed practices in a dominant-party regime, in which the institutional rules of the party had overwhelmed the formal constitutional rules. A careful examination of the Mexican Constitution reveals a president who is among the more constitutionally constrained in Latin America and a Congress with strong, sometimes dominant powers over the other branches of government. The difference between the informal and formal institutions is the history of the PRI government.

The federal Congress has two houses: a 128-member upper chamber, the Senate, and a 500-member lower house, the Chamber of Deputies. Both chambers employ a mixed-member system in which some of the members are elected by plurality vote in single-member districts, while others are elected by a system of compensatory proportional representation on closed-party lists.[11] The current electoral rules for the Senate, dating to 1996, call for plurality elections in each of the thirty-two states whereby each party nominates a slate of two Senate candidates. The party that wins a plurality elects both candidates from the slate to the Senate. The party that places second sends the first candidate on the list to the upper chamber. Furthermore, thirty-two senators are elected by proportional representation on closed national lists, so that each party that wins at least 2 percent of the national vote elects its proportional share of the thirty-two list senators. The rules prevent any party from winning more than two-thirds of the seats in the Senate except under extraordinary circumstances (a party would have to place first in every state and win more than two-thirds of the national vote).

For the Chamber of Deputies, 300 members are elected by plurality in single-member districts, and an additional 200 deputies are elected by proportional representation in five regional closed lists. Each party that wins at least 2 percent of the national vote is entitled to its proportional share of the list deputies with a few restrictions. First, no party can ever have more than 300 total seats, which restricts the largest party to less than the two-thirds majority required for constitutional reforms. Second, no party's share of the total number of seats can exceed by more than 8 percent its share of the national vote. This means that in order to win a majority in the lower chamber, a party must win more than 42 percent of the vote and a sufficient margin of victory over the second-place party (usually around four percentage points) to win enough plurality districts.

The mixed-member system directly affects the party system. Usually, plurality systems lead to two-party systems, as the voters find that it is better to coordinate their votes toward one of the two leading parties rather than waste them on third-party candidates. PR systems tend to create multiparty systems, because votes for the larger minority parties are not wasted. In Mexico, the mixed-member system has yielded a three-party system, in which most regions now have two-party systems (respecting the tendencies of the plurality system), but nationally, the vote is split into three main blocs. The three parties with significant representation in the Mexican Congress in the Sixty-First Legislature (2009–2012) are the PRI (with 49 percent of the seats), the PAN (with 29 percent), and the PRD (with 14 percent). The low threshold allows small parties to attain representation in the Chamber of Deputies, as well; four small parties won seats in the Sixty-First Legislature (see Table 11.4).

Party Composition of the Congress				**TABLE 11.4**
	Seats Won by Plurality Vote	Seats Won by PR System	Total	Percentage
Chamber of Deputies				
Partido Revolucionario Institucional (PRI)	184	53	237	47.4
Partido Acción Nacional (PAN)	70	73	143	28.6
Partido de la Revolución Democrática (PRD)	39	32	71	14.2
Partido Verde Ecologista de México (PVEM)	4	17	21	4.2
Partido del Trabajo (PT)	3	10	13	2.6
Nueva Alianza	0	9	9	1.8
Convergencia	0	6	6	1.2
Total	300	200	500	100
Senate				
Partido Acción Nacional (PAN)	41	11	52	40.6
Partido Revolucionario Institucional (PRI)[2]	27	6	33	25.8
Partido de la Revolución Democrática (PRD)[1]	23	6	29	21.9
Partido Verde Ecologista de México (PVEM)[2]	2	4	6	4.7
Convergencia[1]	3	2	5	3.9
Partido del Trabajo (PT)[1]	0	2	2	1.6
Nueva Alianza	0	1	1	0.8
Total	96	32	128	100

[1] Alianza por el Bien de Todos.

[2] Alianza por México.

The mixed-member system complicates creating majorities in either chamber. Since the 8-percent rule on maximum overrepresentation was established in the lower house, no party has been able to achieve a majority. The Senate rules went into effect fully for the first time in the 2000 elections. Now, when the race is close between the first- and second-place parties, it is also unlikely that a majority party will emerge in the Senate. This means that the party of the president will rarely have a majority in Congress, thus creating a situation of divided government.

Like the U.S. Constitution, the 1917 Mexican Constitution lists the legislative branch first. The Congress is primarily responsible for enacting nearly all public policy, with only a few exceptions. The president has constitutional decree powers only over questions of land reform (expropriation decrees) and tariffs and quotas in international trade (in which he can unilaterally adjust tariffs and quotas if the circumstances call for modifications). All regular legislation must be approved by both chambers in the same form, and then submitted to the president for publication. The president must publish the bill within ten days or return the bill to the chamber of origin (see Box 11.3).

A presidential veto can take two forms: One is a regular veto, in which the president expresses his

---

How a Bill Becomes a Law in Mexico

BOX 11.3

- Bills can be introduced by federal deputies, senators, the president, or the state legislatures. All revenue bills, regardless of the sponsor, must be introduced in the Chamber of Deputies. Therefore, the president's annual economic package is sent to the Chamber of Deputies. However, senators can introduce revenue legislation directly in the Chamber of Deputies. All other legislation can begin in either the Chamber of Deputies or the Senate. The federal bureaucracy assists the president in preparing executive bills for introduction.

- All bills are sent to committees. There are twenty-nine committees in the Chamber of Deputies and thirty in the Senate. Committees amend most legislation before reporting it to the floor (77 percent in the Chamber of Deputies, and 67 percent in the Senate). The federal bureaucracy often sends commentary on pending legislation to the relevant committees. The legislators are not required to heed these opinions.

- All legislation reported by committee is voted on the floor. The chamber can amend legislation from committees, but only 32 percent of the legislation is amended on the floor in the Chamber of Deputies, and only 17 percent on the floor of the Senate. If a bill is approved by the first chamber, it is sent to the other chamber for approval.

- In the second chamber, bills are sent to committee. Routine legislation is usually reported to the floor without amendment. Important bills are usually amended in committee. If the second chamber

approves the bill on the floor without amendment, it is sent to the president; if the bill is amended, it is sent back to the first chamber for approval. Bills can be considered twice by each chamber before a final version is settled on.

- The president must sign or veto a bill within ten days, unless Congress has ended its session. In those cases, the president must dispatch the bills before the next session begins. The federal bureaucracy usually makes recommendations to the president on whether to sign or veto a bill. If the president vetoes a bill, it is sent to the first chamber for reconsideration. If the first chamber rejects the veto by a two-thirds vote, it is sent to the other chamber. If the second chamber also rejects the veto by a two-thirds vote, the president must publish the law. The president also has a corrective veto, in which he can return a bill to the first chamber, suggesting amendments. Each chamber may accept these amendments by a majority vote or reject the amendments by a two-thirds vote.

- The annual appropriations bill is considered by only the Chamber of Deputies. The president sends the appropriations bill to the chamber by September 8. The chamber must approve the bill, with or without amendments, by November 15, sending the bill back to the president. If the president vetoes the bill, the Chamber of Deputies can accept his suggestions by a majority vote or reject them by a two-thirds vote. The Senate never considers appropriations.

Note: Statistics pertain to the Sixtieth Legislature (2006–2009).

rejection of a bill, and the second is a corrective veto, in which the president requests that Congress amend the bill, usually because of technical errors in the text. In either case, Congress can insist on the original text of the bill by a two-thirds vote, after which the president must publish the legislation. In case of corrective vetoes, Congress often modifies the bill as requested and sends it back to the president for promulgation.

Each of the two chambers has exclusive powers and areas of specialization. The Chamber of Deputies specializes in fiscal legislation. All revenue bills must originate in the lower chamber. The Chamber of Deputies first approves the revenue and tax legislation, sending it to the upper chamber for Senate approval. However, only the Chamber of Deputies approves the appropriations legislation. This gives the Chamber of Deputies extraordinary influence over the federal public administration. Likewise, the lower chamber has exclusive powers over budgetary oversight and approves the public accounts.

The Senate has exclusive power to oversee foreign affairs. The upper chamber has the power to monitor foreign affairs, and it approves treaties submitted by the president by a majority vote. It approves presidential appointments of ambassadors and consuls, also by a majority vote. The Senate also has the power to remove state governors and depose state legislatures. The Constitution allows the Senate to topple state governments when it recognizes that the state can no longer provide for domestic security. This requires a vote of the upper chamber; afterward, the president proposes a list of three candidates from which the Senate elects the interim governor by a two-thirds vote. Prompted by PRI presidents, the Senate deposed many governors during the twentieth century, though usually for political reasons rather than for security motives. The Senate also regulates pacts between the federal and state governments concerning revenue-sharing and program administration.

Federal deputies and senators have shown extraordinary levels of party discipline in recent years (see Table 11.5). For example, during the last two years of the Fifty-Seventh Legislature (1997–2000), on average 99.6 percent of the PRIista deputies voted together on party bills. After 2003, PANista deputies voted together more than 98 percent of the time, nearly equaling the levels of PRI discipline when it held the presidency. High party discipline in Mexico has two main sources.[12] First, consecutive reelection for deputies and senators is

TABLE 11.5

Party Cohesion in Congress
Parties stick together in Congress on major party votes.

Legislature	PRI	PAN	PRD
Fifty-Seventh (1997–2000)	99.6	92.0	93.5
Fifty-Eighth (2000–2003)	89.3	93.6	92.5
Fifty-Ninth (2003–2006)	90.5	98.3	95.8
Sixtieth (2006–2009)	94.4	98.8	95.2
Sixty-First (2009–)	93.3	94.6	80.6

Note: Data for the Fifty-Seventh Legislature begins October 8, 1998; data for the Sixty-First Legislature ends April 29, 2010. Major party votes are roll calls in which at least one of the three parties dissented from the rest. Party cohesion is the percentage of the party voting with the majority of that party.

Source: For the Fifty-Seventh Legislature, Jeffrey A. Weldon, "Institutional and Political Factors in Party Discipline in the Chamber of Deputies, 1998–2002," presented at the First Latin American Political Science Congress, Salamanca, Spain, July 2002. Data for the last four legislatures calculated from the *Diario de los Debates* and the *Gaceta Parlamentaria* of the Chamber of Deputies.

prohibited. This nearly eliminates accountability of the representatives to their constituents. Voters can neither reward their legislators for good performance nor punish them for bad representation. Since federal legislators are not required to seek cues from their electorate, they look elsewhere for guidance, and the party leadership is more than willing to provide it.

Second, nomination procedures in each of the parties are relatively closed, with party leadership usually selecting candidates directly. This further focuses the legislators on party leadership, because without the support of the party elite, their political futures would be dismal. Each party generally votes as a bloc in Congress, which creates incentives for the leaders of each of the parties to negotiate bills among themselves rather than allow the rank-and-file members to work out compromises in committee. Together, these institutions create a highly centralized legislative branch.

The Executive Branch

Despite the constitutionally limited powers of the executive branch, no one would dispute that the president was the dominant political actor in Mexico for the greater part of the twentieth century. In addition to his rather modest constitutional powers, the

Mexican president possessed a broad range of unwritten but generally recognized "metaconstitutional" powers that traditionally ensured his dominance over all of the country's other political institutions.[13] Mexicans use the term ***presidencialismo*** to connote this extraordinary concentration of powers, formal and informal, in the hands of the president, with the implication that incumbents frequently abuse these powers in pursuit of personal and political ends.

On any issue of national political significance, the federal judiciary would take its cue from the incumbent president. Until very recently, the Supreme Court never found presidential decisions or legislation enacted at the behest of the president to be unconstitutional, and Congress never challenged presidential appointments to the federal judiciary. The president had the informal power to seat and unseat state governors, mayors, and members of Congress. From 1929 through 1994, the president also functioned as the "supreme head" of the official party, choosing its leaders, dictating his legislative proposals to the PRI delegation in Congress, shaping the party's internal governance, imposing his personal choices for the PRI's gubernatorial and congressional candidates, and—most important—controlling the selection of the party's next presidential nominee.

The absence of a rigid, fully elaborated political ideology made it possible for a Mexican president to have a pragmatic, flexible program and style of governance. The so-called ideology of the Mexican Revolution was never more than a loosely connected set of goals or symbols. The only "revolutionary" ideology that has been scrupulously observed is the constitutionally mandated no-reelection principle for the presidency: The president is limited to a single six-year term.[14]

During the PRI's seven decades of rule at the national level, three factors were required to create strong presidentialism.[15] First, the president's party had to have a majority in both chambers of Congress. Under **divided government**, the opposition majorities in Congress are unlikely to follow the dictates of the president. Second, there must be high levels of discipline in the majority party of Congress. Third, the president must be the leader of his party. In the 1930s, the first two factors were in place, but the leader of the party, Plutarco Elías Calles, received all of the benefits of the disciplined party, not the president. After Cárdenas reorganized the official party along lines of authority that led directly to himself, strong *presidencialismo* was finally achieved.

Executive–Legislative Relations

The dynamics of executive–legislative relations in Mexico used to be determined by the metaconstitutional powers of the president. The operation of the three key factors outlined earlier—unified government, high party discipline in the ruling party, and the recognition of the president as the de facto head of the party—explained a compliant Congress. Today, the first and third factors no longer hold. Executive–legislative relations follow constitutional rather than partisan norms, and Mexico either enjoys or suffers from the everyday republican conflicts of separation of powers.

Comparing levels of productivity during specific Congressional periods allows us to evaluate the executive's influence over the legislative branch under varying conditions of the metaconstitutional conditions listed earlier, as well as the relative strength of the president's party in the lower chamber (see Table 11.6). During the Fifty-Fourth Legislature (1988–1991), the PRI held a small majority of 52 percent of the lower chamber. Despite the marginal majority, 98.6 percent of the executive's public bills were approved. Of the 110 bills approved during the Fifty-Fourth Legislature, nearly two-thirds originated in the executive branch. In the Fifty-Seventh Legislature (1997–2000), divided government prevailed for the first time since 1928. The PRI held just under 48 percent of the seats in the lower chamber, while the PAN and the PRD each had about a quarter of the seats. Thus, the first of the conditions for metaconstitutional power—unified government—was eliminated. Under divided government, 90 percent of the president's bills were approved—a decline of nine percentage points from the previous legislature. Since 1928, a majority of the bills that the Chamber of Deputies approved had originated in the executive branch. In the Fifty-Seventh Legislature, this trend was abruptly reversed; only 31 percent of the bills approved in the term had been introduced by the executive, while nearly 60 percent had been sponsored by deputies.

By the time that the Fifty-Eighth Legislature had convened in 2000, metaconstitutional presidentialism had ended. The first condition—unified government—remained unfulfilled. President Fox's PAN held only 41 percent of the seats in the lower chamber. Nor was Fox treated as the head of his party. Nearly 90 percent of Fox's bills were approved during the 2000 to 2003 term.

TABLE 11.6

Presidential Party Strength and Executive Bills

The president now initiates much less legislation than members of Congress, and fewer of his bills are approved.

Legislature	% of Deputies from President's Party	% of Total New Bills Introduced	% of Total Bills Approved	% of President's Bills Approved
Fifty-Fourth (1988–1991)	52	22.8	65.1	98.6
Fifty-Fifth (1991–1994)	63	42.4	62.6	98.5
Fifty-Sixth (1994–1997)	60	33.8	74.2	98.9
Fifty-Seventh (1997–2000)	48	10.1	31.0	90.0
Fifty-Eighth (2000–2003)	41	6.8	23.7	89.9
Fifty-Ninth (2003–2006)	30	2.8	8.6	73.2
Sixtieth (2006–2009)	41	2.2	10.4	70.4
Sixty-First (2009–)*	29	2.1	11.3	61.9

*Data for the Sixty-First Legislature through April 29, 2010.

Source: Data compiled from *Diario de los Debates* and the *Gaceta Parlamentaria* of the Chamber of Deputies.

However, nearly every bill that Fox had sent to Congress had been extensively amended in at least one of the chambers. Never before had a higher percentage of executive bills been amended, either in committee or on the floor.

Mexico's first "opposition" president had difficult relations with a Congress in which the opposition parties—when united—had majority control. During the Fifty-Ninth Legislature (2003–2006), only 73.2 percent of the president's bills were approved, and a mere 8.6 percent of the bills approved by the Chamber of Deputies originated in the executive branch. Twice Fox attempted a tax reform, which would have increased the base of the value-added tax. Both times he was defeated.

In the fall 2004 term, the opposition coalition in the Chamber of Deputies amended Fox's federal appropriations bill, decreasing or eliminating a number of federal programs and increasing pork-barrel expenditures for PRI and PRD states. Fox vetoed the appropriations bill; this was the first budget veto cast by a president since 1933. The Chamber of Deputies disputed the veto by filing a suit in the Supreme Court, claiming that the president did not have the constitutional power to veto the budget (despite the fact that there had been forty-five vetoes of the budget between 1917 and 1933, none of which had been challenged on constitutional grounds by Congress). The Supreme

Court suspended the expenditures to which the president had objected, and later ruled that the budget veto was indeed constitutional. Such tests of will between the executive and legislative branches are increasingly common in Mexico's era of divided government, with the judicial branch assuming an increasingly important role as arbiter between the two branches.

Felipe Calderón enjoyed a legislative plurality in the Sixtieth Legislature (2006–2009), with the PAN holding 41 percent of the seats, and the PRI relegated to third place in the lower chamber. However, this was not enough to guarantee legislative success, as only 70.4 percent of his bills were approved in that term, representing only slightly more than a tenth of all of the bills approved. Nonetheless, the president has enjoyed legislative success despite divided government, accomplished by "logrolling" legislation with the PRI. For example, Calderón and the PAN won a major victory in tax reform through the creation of two new taxes.

Simultaneously, the PRI won an electoral reform to its liking. Party influence over the electoral authorities was increased, campaign financing was reduced, and officeholders can no longer promote themselves while in office. Negative campaign advertising (even if truthful) was banned. The law prohibits parties from buying television or radio time for their spots, instead using free media time allocated by the electoral authorities (this was opposed by the private television networks). However, no other person or organization can buy time to promote political ideas or candidates at any time. The president also won a series of major reforms in public security and police and judicial procedures.

Calderón also won a legislative victory yearned for by both Presidents Zedillo and Fox—a comprehensive energy reform. The president had asked for new interpretations of the laws prohibiting private investment in the oil industry, though he insisted that neither PEMEX nor any part of the process would be privatized. The committee report was a watered-down version of Calderón's bill, but the PAN and PRI passed the law, along with part of the PRD. After suffering numerous defeats in the 2009 midterm elections, the PAN presence in the Chamber of Deputies was reduced to only 29 percent, and Calderón's legislative success rate quickly fell; in the first year of the Sixty-First Legislature, only about 62 percent of the president's bills were approved.

RECRUITING THE POLITICAL ELITE

At least since the days of the Porfiriato, the Mexican political elite has been recruited predominantly from the middle class. The 1910 revolution did not open up the political elite to large numbers of people from peasant or urban laborer backgrounds. That opening occurred only in the 1930s, during the Cárdenas *sexenio* (six-year term), and then mainly at the local and state levels rather than the national elite level.

In the last three PRI-dominated administrations (1982–2000), the national political elite was drawn heavily from the ranks of *capitalinos*—people born or raised in Mexico City. Postgraduate education, especially at elite foreign universities and in disciplines like economics and public administration, became much more important as a ticket of entry into the national political elite. Over half of the cabinet members appointed by Presidents de la Madrid, Salinas, and Zedillo had studied economics or public administration, and over half of those who received training in these subjects at the graduate level did so in the United States. The economic policy debacles presided over by technocrat presidents and cabinet ministers in the 1990s discredited this breed of Mexican officials

in the eyes of the public as well as the party leaderships. Significantly, a national PRI assembly in 1996 removed most technocrats from the line of presidential succession by requiring the party's future presidential nominees to have previously held elective office.

Relatively few card-carrying technocrats found their way into the cabinet of Vicente Fox, who favored persons with nongovernmental experience, with a bachelor's or master's degree in business administration, educated in Mexico—like himself. Nearly half (45 percent) of Fox's top fifty-two appointees—many of them recruited through professional head-hunting firms—had no previous public-sector experience. The involvement of persons with private-sector experience in the Fox administration (46 percent) was far greater than in any of the PRI governments since 1929. Fox also broke with his PRI predecessors in recruiting more top officials from outside of Mexico City (60 percent of his top officials were from the provinces), and more who had received their undergraduate education in private rather than public universities (54 percent). Most strikingly, 75 percent of Fox's original top fifty-two appointees had no known political party affiliation. Fewer than one-fifth were recruited from the PAN.[16] Only four members of Fox's original cabinet had a history of militancy in the PAN, and the dearth of card-carrying PANistas was even more conspicuous at the subcabinet level. Some ministries were nearly devoid of PANistas.

In terms of professional background, Fox's successor, Felipe Calderón, is something of a throwback to the late technocratic PRI presidents. Calderón clearly had a *técnico's* skill set; he even had a master's degree from Harvard University. However, in contrast to the last five PRI presidents, Calderón also had extensive experience in party politics and elective office. His own economic cabinet was dominated by technocrats holding doctoral degrees from U.S. universities, including Chicago, Columbia, the Massachusetts Institute of Technology, and the University of Pennsylvania.

Since the 1970s, kinship ties have become more important as a common denominator of those who attain top positions of political power. Increasingly, such people are born into politically prominent families that have already produced state governors, cabinet ministers, federal legislators, and even presidents. Two of the three major presidential candidates in 2006

Mexicans Elect their Second Consecutive "Opposition" President

Felipe Calderón, presidential candidate of the PAN, celebrates his razor-thin election victory on July 5, 2006.

Wesley Bocxe/The Image Works

exemplify this pattern. Felipe Calderón's father was one of the founders of the PAN; Roberto Madrazo's father had been national chairman of the PRI. Only López Obrador was not born into a politically influential family.

These political families are increasingly interconnected: At least one-third of the government officials and politicians interviewed by one researcher for several books on the Mexican political elite were related to other officials, not counting those related through marriage and the traditional rite of *compadrazgo* (becoming a godparent to a friend's child).[17] Family connections can give an aspiring political leader a powerful advantage over rivals.

The growing importance of kinship ties and other indicators of increasing homogeneity in personal backgrounds causes some observers to worry that Mexico's political elite is becoming more closed and inbred. While its social base may indeed be narrowing, the modern Mexican political elite still shows considerable fluidity; the massive turnover of office-holders every six years is proof of that. This factor helps to explain why in Mexico—unlike other postrevolutionary countries, such as China and (until recently) the Soviet Union—the regime did not become a gerontocracy. In fact, the median age of cabinet members and presidential aspirants in Mexico has been dropping; in recent *sexenios*, most have been in their late thirties or early forties. Exemplifying this trend, Felipe Calderón was forty-four years old when elected to the presidency.

INTEREST REPRESENTATION AND POLITICAL CONTROL

In Mexico's presidentialist system, important public policies used to be initiated and shaped by the inner circle of presidential advisors before they were even presented for public discussion. Thus, most effective interest representation took place within the upper levels of the federal bureaucracy. The structures that aggregate and articulate interests in Western democracies (the ruling political party, labor unions, and so on) actually served other purposes in the Mexican system: limiting the scope of citizens' demands on the government, mobilizing electoral support for the regime, helping to legitimate it in the eyes of other countries, and distributing jobs and other material rewards to select individuals and groups. For example, the PRI typically had no independent influence on public policymaking; nor did the opposition parties, except where they controlled state or local governments.

From the late 1930s until the PRI's defeat in 2000, Mexico had a **corporatist** system of interest representation in which each citizen and societal segment was expected to relate to the state through a single structure "licensed" by the state to organize and represent that sector of society (peasants, urban unionized workers, businesspeople, teachers, and so on). The official party itself was divided into three **sectors:** (1) the Labor Sector, (2) the Peasant Sector, and (3) the Popular Sector, a catch-all category representing various segments of the middle class (government employees, other white-collar workers, small merchants, private landowners) and residents of low-income urban neighborhoods. Each sector in the PRI is dominated by one mass organization; other organizations are affiliated with each party sector, but their influence is dwarfed by that of the "peak" organization. Thus, the **Confederación de Trabajadores de México (CTM)** represents the Labor Sector, including most urban-dwelling labor union members. The **Confederación Nacional Campesina (CNC)** is the principal representative of the Peasant Sector, primarily *ejidatarios*—peasants who have received land through the agrarian reform program. The **Confederación Nacional de Organizaciones Populares (CNOP)** represents the Popular Sector, consisting of mostly urban-based service workers and small-business owners.

A number of powerful organized interest groups—entrepreneurs, the military, the Catholic Church—were not formally represented in the PRI. These groups dealt directly with the government elite, often at the presidential or cabinet level. They did not need the PRI to make their preferences known. They also had well-placed representatives within the executive branch who could be counted on to articulate their interests. In addition, the business community was organized into several government-chartered confederations. Since the Cárdenas administration, all but a small minority of the country's industrialists were required by law to join one of these employers' organizations, which channeled business interests into a few, well-controlled outlets. These confederations still exist, but the Supreme Court ruled in 1999 that compulsory membership was an unconstitutional restriction on the freedom of association.

Because the ruling party and the national legislature did not effectively aggregate interests in the Mexican system, individuals and groups seeking something from the government often circumvented their nominal representatives in the PRI sectoral organizations and the Congress, and sought satisfaction of their needs through personal contacts within the government bureaucracy. These **patron–client relationships** compartmentalized the society into discrete, noninteracting, vertical segments that served as pillars of the regime. Within the lower class, for example, unionized urban workers were separated from nonunion urban workers, *ejidatarios* from small private landholders and landless agricultural workers. The middle class was compartmentalized into government bureaucrats, educators, health-care professionals, lawyers, economists,

and so forth. Thus, competition among social classes was replaced by highly fragmented competition within classes.

The articulation of interests through patron–client networks assisted the PRI regime by fragmenting popular demands into small-scale, highly individualized, or localized requests that could be granted or denied case by case. Officials were rarely confronted with collective demands from broad social groupings. Rather than having to act on a request from a whole category of people (slum dwellers, *ejidatarios*, teachers), they had easier, less costly choices to make (as between competing petitions from several neighborhoods for a paved street or a piped water system). The clientelistic structure thus provided a mechanism for distributing public services and other benefits in a highly selective, discretionary (if not always arbitrary) manner. This system put the onus on potential beneficiaries to identify and cultivate the "right" patrons within the government bureaucracy. The prohibition on consecutive reelection prevented local elected officials from taking on the role of patron. As they could be neither punished nor rewarded for their performance, elected politicians abdicated this responsibility, and it was only natural that the bureaucracy would replace them in the role of patron.

Unquestionably, the PRI's vaunted political-control capabilities were weakened by the economic and political crises of recent *sexenios*. Nevertheless, the traditional instruments of control—patron–client relationships, *caciquismo* (local-level boss rule), the captive labor movement, and selective repression of dissidents by government security forces—are still effective in some PRI-controlled states.

In many of the states and localities where the PAN has come to power since the 1980s, officials have attempted to implement very different models of state–society relations aimed at increasing civic participation in public administration and placing greater reliance on public–private partnerships. For example, the Citizen Wednesday program, pioneered by the PANista mayor of León, Guanajuato, "encouraged citizens to make their particular needs and concerns known to the local government through weekly, one-on-one sessions with the heads of municipal departments for public lighting, paving, sewerage, water, public safety, and social welfare.... The program soon became the principal point of access between citizens and the government in León. It was quickly adopted by other PAN governments throughout Mexico."[18]

In other places, however, the limited success of PAN administrations in solving high-salience public-security and urban-development problems has undermined attempts to build new, enduring state–society relationships. For example, in 2004, disillusioned voters in the key Northern border city of Tijuana turned out the PAN after three terms, installing as mayor a traditional PRI politician with a reputation for corruption and authoritarianism. He quickly set about restoring the corporatist networks that his PANista predecessors had labored to dismantle.

POLITICAL PARTIES

The Partido Revolucionario Institucional

The PRI was founded in 1929 by President Plutarco Elías Calles to serve as a mechanism for reducing violent conflict among contenders for public office and for consolidating the power of the central government at the expense of the personalistic local and state-level political machines of the decade following the 1910 through 1920 revolution. Between 1920 and 1929, there had been four major rebellions against the national executive by these subnational political machines.

For more than half a century, the ruling party served with impressive efficiency, as a mechanism for resolving conflicts, for coopting newly emerging interest groups into the system, and for legitimating the regime through the electoral process. Potential defectors from the official party were deterred by the government's manipulation of electoral rules, which made it virtually impossible for any dissident faction to bolt from the party and win the election. Dissident movements did emerge occasionally, but before the neo-Cardenista coalition contested the 1988 election, no breakaway presidential candidacy had been able to garner more than 16 percent of the vote (by official count).

From the beginning, the official party was an appendage of the government itself, especially of the presidency. It was never a truly independent arena of political competition. A handful of nationally powerful party leaders, such as Fidel Velázquez, the patriarch of the PRI-affiliated labor movement until his death in 1997, occasionally constrained government actions, but the official party itself never determined the basic directions of government economic and social policies. Indeed, one of the key factors underlying the

erosion of party unity and discipline since the late 1980s and the PRI's overwhelming defeats in state-level elections beginning in 1995, leading to its loss of the presidency in 2000, was the party's inability to distance itself from the unpopular austerity policies made by the technocrats in the federal government.

The official party traditionally enjoyed virtually unlimited access to government funds to finance its campaigns. No one knew how much was actually being siphoned from government coffers to the PRI, because Mexico had no laws requiring the reporting of campaign income and expenditures. Reforms to the federal electoral code between 1993 and 1994 established minimal public reporting requirements for campaign income and expenditures, as well as Mexico's first-ever limits on individual and corporate contributions to electoral campaigns.

In the 1993 and 1994 electoral code reforms, ceilings on private contributions were set very high—the equivalent of $650,000 for an individual contribution. With its privileged access to financing from big business, the PRI continued to outspend its opponents by a huge margin, even without cash from government sources. It had even more money to spend on its campaigns, at all levels, than ever before, despite the contribution limits included in the electoral code reforms. In the same year, Roberto Madrazo, the PRI candidate for governor in the state of Tabasco (and 2006 presidential candidate), spent in excess of $50 million on his campaign—many times the limit for a gubernatorial race.

Yet another round of electoral reforms, passed by Congress in 1996, limited total private contributions to any party to 10 percent of the total amount of regular public financing to all parties, and no individual can contribute more than 0.05 percent of the total regular public financing. Also, the reforms greatly increased public funding for all parties. (In the 2006 presidential campaign, the three main candidates received and spent more than $200 million in public funds.) The law also added a new prohibition on "the use of public resources and programs to benefit any political party or electoral campaign."

Campaign finance abuses did not disappear, however. After the 2000 presidential election, the federal internal auditor discovered that the government-owned oil company, PEMEX, had made a $140 million loan to the oil-workers' union, one of the two most important PRI-affiliated labor unions. These funds were subsequently donated to the campaign of PRI candidate Francisco Labastida.

As the party in power, the PRI profited from a vast network of government patronage through which small-scale material benefits could be delivered to large segments of the population. The president himself controlled a large slush fund ("*la partida secreta*"), authorized each year by Congress as part of the federal government budget, that could aid PRI officials and finance the party's campaigns as needed. By the late 1990s, in the context of an increasingly competitive electoral system, such "incumbency advantages" were being intensely criticized by the opposition parties and the media. Responding to this pressure, Ernesto Zedillo virtually eliminated the presidential "secret budget."

Historically, the official party's most potent advantage over the competition was its ability to commit electoral fraud with relative impunity. A wide variety of techniques were used: stuffing the ballot boxes; disqualifying opposition party poll watchers; relocating polling places at the last minute to sites known only to PRI supporters; manipulating voter registration lists, padding them with nonexistent or nonresident PRIistas, and/or *rasurando* (shaving off) those who are expected to vote for opposition parties; issuing multiple voting credentials to PRI supporters; buying, "renting," or confiscating opposition voters' credentials, often in return for material benefits; organizing *carruseles* (flying brigades) of PRI supporters transported by truck or van to vote at several different polling places; and so forth.

Moreover, until 1996, the PRI held majority representation in all of the state and federal government entities that controlled vote counting and certification. The PRI could count on these bodies to manipulate the tallies to favor its candidates or, in cases where the opposition vote got out of control, nullify the unfavorable election outcomes. Adding votes to the PRI column, rather than taking them away from opposition parties, was the most common form of electoral fraud. In some predominantly rural districts, this practice led to election results in which the number of votes credited to the PRI candidate exceeded the total number of registered voters, or even the total number of adults estimated from the most recent population census. In a successful effort to build up domestic and international credibility for

the 1994 national elections, the Salinas government introduced a number of important safeguards against fraud (see Box 11.4).

The share of the vote claimed by the PRI had been declining for three decades, but until the mid-1990s, the erosion was gradual and did not threaten the party's grasp on the presidency and state governorships (see Figure 11.3). In the 1980s and 1990s, however, Mexican elections became much more competitive. The "Soviet-style" precincts that regularly delivered 98 to 100 percent of their votes to PRI candidates have disappeared.

In the four federal elections prior to 2006, the PRI did best among older voters, the less-educated, and low-income people. It has also held the loyalty of a plurality of union members. However, the corporatist vote in general is no longer a dependable source of support for the PRI, and the low mobilization of these voters was one of the major reasons for its defeat in the 2000 elections.

Another key factor accounting for the long-term decline in the PRI's effectiveness as a vote-getting machine is the massive shift of population from rural to urban areas that has occurred in Mexico. In 1950, 57 percent of the population lived in isolated rural communities of fewer than 2,500 inhabitants; by 2008, only 22.8 percent of Mexicans lived in such localities. The PRI is significantly weaker in cities with 100,000 or more inhabitants, where more than half of the Mexican population now lives. Mexico City has been a particular disaster area for the PRI in recent elections. The PRI lost the mayoral races in Mexico City by large margins in 1997, 2000, and 2006. Even in rural areas, however, the PRI's formerly safe vote continues to erode. While the PRI still gets a higher share of the vote in rural areas than any other party, the average vote for PRI candidates in rural precincts fell markedly from 1982 through 2006.[19]

The PRI has had to adjust from being an official party—a political machine based on incumbency advantages—to being a party out of power. PRI legislators for the first time have had to figure out how to vote without presidential leadership. The whole party has had to define its ideology as a political party, not as an instrument of power.

The PRI has recovered power since the 2006 debacle, when it found itself in third place in voter preference. It recovered the state of Yucatán from the PAN in 2007. In the 2009 midterms, the PRI and the Partido

BOX 11.4

Reforming Federal Elections in the 1990s

In 1994, Mexico's electoral law was amended to strengthen greatly and grant more autonomy to the IFE, which organizes and conducts federal elections. The PRI and its government representatives were denied a majority on the IFE's decision-making board. A new system of independent electoral tribunals was established to adjudicate election disputes, and a special prosecutor's office was established to investigate alleged violations of the electoral laws.

The new federal electoral law defined a broad range of electoral offenses not previously subject to prosecution as electoral crimes (though the special prosecutor was appointed by the president and reported to the federal attorney general, who was unlikely to bring charges against important PRI leaders or government officials). The role of independent, Mexican citizen observers in monitoring the casting and tallying of votes was formally recognized, and the presence of foreign electoral observers (euphemistically termed "international visitors") was legalized. Exit polls of voters and "quick counts" of the actual vote in sample precincts by the IFE as well as private organizations were authorized and publicly announced on election night. New, high-tech, photo-identification voter credentials were issued to the entire electorate.

Taken together, these innovations, which cost the Mexican taxpayers more than $1 billion, represented a major advance toward improving the security,

professionalism, and fairness of the Mexican electoral system. However, various types of irregularities—especially violations of ballot secrecy and efforts by local bosses to induce voters to support the PRI—were still widespread in the more isolated, rural areas. Subsequent state and local elections in various parts of the country have demonstrated that subnational PRI leaders continue to use direct threats and other forms of intimidation, particularly against peasant voters.

Another electoral reform, enacted in 1996, further increased the institutional autonomy of the IFE. The interior minister was removed as president of the IFE and replaced by a nonpartisan president and eight nonpartisan commissioners. These electoral commissioners are elected for a nine-year term by a two-thirds vote of the Chamber of Deputies. Since no party can control more than 60 percent of the seats in the lower chamber, the IFE commissioners are elected by consensus of all of the parties.

In the national elections from 1997 through 2009, there was very little evidence of systematic fraud. Since the IFE controls most of the process in a nonpartisan manner (for example, all poll workers are chosen at random from voter registration lists, as jurors are selected in the United States), the remaining sources of electoral fraud—still common in state elections—are vote-buying and the buying or renting of voter credentials. Both practices are illegal, but neither is easy for electoral authorities to police.

Verde Ecologista de México (PVEM) (the Green Party) together won an absolute majority of seats (258 of 500) as they campaigned against the ineffectiveness of the Calderón government in dealing with the worldwide recession that began in 2008. The PRI won back the states of Querétaro and San Luis Potosí, though it lost the Northwestern state of Sonora to the same party. It had also recovered many large cities from the PAN and PRD. In the 2010 gubernatorial elections, the PAN and PRD attempted to block the electoral recovery of the PRI. They formed left–right electoral alliances in five of the twelve states that were up for election, winning in three of them. However, the PRI recovered

Aguascalientes and Tlaxcala from the PAN, and Zacatecas from the PRD, all states without PAN–PRD alliances.

The Partido Acción Nacional

The PAN was established in 1939, largely in reaction to the leftward drift of public policy under President Lázaro Cárdenas, particularly his policies in support of socialist public education. Its founders included prominent Catholic intellectuals who espoused an early Christian democratic ideology, and the party has traditionally opposed government restrictions

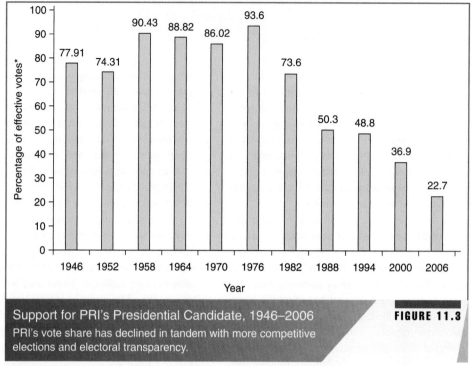

Support for PRI's Presidential Candidate, 1946–2006
PRI's vote share has declined in tandem with more competitive elections and electoral transparency.

FIGURE 11.3

*Percentage base includes annulled votes and those cast for independent candidates.

Note: The 1976 PRI candidate, José López Portillo, ran virtually unopposed because the PAN failed to nominate a candidate. The only other significant candidate was Valentín Campa, representing the Communist Party, which was not legally registered to participate in the 1976 election. More than 5 percent of the votes were annulled.

Source: Data from Comisión Federal Electoral, 1946–1988; and Instituto Federal Electoral, 1994–2006.

on church activities. The party attacked political centralism and advocated expanded states' rights long before it was fashionable to do so. The PAN's principal constituency has always been the urban middle class, but it has also attracted votes among socially conservative peasants and the urban working class.

Between 1964, when a primitive form of proportional representation increased opposition presence in the Chamber of Deputies, and the mid-1990s, when the PAN was governing many municipal and state governments, the focus of PANista representation was in the federal Congress, especially the lower chamber (the first PANista was elected to the Senate only in 1991). In these years, PAN deputies would typically begin their congressional terms fighting electoral fraud from the previous election in an attempt to increase the number of PANista deputies. Then they would settle in and begin to propose legislation. Until the Salinas years, these bills would almost always be ignored in the chamber at the time of introduction; but years later, most of the PAN's legislative proposals

were adopted by the federal executive and reintroduced and approved by Congress.

Among the PANista ideas later embraced by PRI governments were increased proportional representation in both chambers of Congress, autonomous electoral courts and electoral agencies, the permanent voting credential, increased municipal autonomy, increased autonomy and authority for the Supreme Court, increased self-governance for the Federal District (Mexico City), federal revenue-sharing with the states, liberalization of the social security systems, a national consumer-protection agency, and profit-sharing with employees.

The PAN's regional strongholds include the North, the Center-West, and some of the large municipalities of the states of México and Veracruz. Between 1989 and 2001, the PAN won gubernatorial elections in nine states (Baja California, Chihuahua, Guanajuato, Jalisco, Nuevo León, Querétaro, Aguascalientes, Morelos, and Yucatán). In 1995, the PAN retained control of the governorship of Baja California, thereby accomplishing something that no opposition party had previously done: the transfer of power from one elected opposition governor to another. The PAN picked up the governorship of San Luis Potosí in 2003, and took Tlaxcala in 2004 and Sonora in 2010. During these years, the PAN governed nearly all of the twenty largest cities in Mexico, with the conspicuous exception of Mexico City, and it also governed most of the capital cities of the country.

The ideological position of the PAN has been relatively constant over the last six decades. It could be classified as the center-right, with strong elements of Christian socialism (which covers a wide range of policies, from center-left on labor issues to right-of-center on abortion), combined with traditional liberal attitudes on trade, municipal decentralization, and general democratization. The party is affiliated with international Christian Democratic organizations. The PAN's relative position on the ideological spectrum has depended mostly on the positioning of the PRI, whose pendulum has shifted to positions clearly to the left of the PAN (as in the 1970s) or to the right of the PAN (as was the case from 1988 to 2000).

Roll-call votes in the Fifty-Seventh Legislature (1997–2000) placed the PAN at the center of the political spectrum, to the left of the PRI. Congressional debates suggest that the PAN held a similar position for most of the Salinas and Zedillo years. Despite the nationalist and populist background of their party, PRI deputies found themselves voting to the right of the PAN because they had to support the neoliberal economic policies and austerity measures of PRI presidents. However, since 2001, under a PANista president, PAN members generally vote to the right of the PRI. Now it is the PAN deputies who must support the austerity programs of their president, while PRI deputies are liberated to vote their conscience and constituencies rather than take cues from the president.

The PAN has worked long and hard to develop a strong network of grassroots militants, though it has always had several major organizational weaknesses. Since the mid-1970s, it has been divided into moderate-progressive and militant-conservative ("neo-PANista") factions, which have jockeyed for control of the party machinery and carried out purges of opposing faction members when they were in power.

Vicente Fox's ideology was closer to the moderate-progressives than to the neo-PANistas. This helped the PAN gain control of the presidency in 2000 by attracting an ideologically diverse group of voters, united mainly by their desire to remove the PRI from power.[20] During the Fox administration, the PAN continued its evolution toward a catch-all party, while still embracing with greater enthusiasm than its rivals the free-market, pro-foreign investment policies favored by the country's business community.[21] However, since 2006, many local PANista leaders and militants have complained that Calderón has interfered too much in internal party affairs (through the imposition of national party leadership and several gubernatorial candidates), mimicking in some ways old PRI traditions.

The Partido de la Revolución Democrática

Before 1988, the Mexican left had spawned political parties like the Partido Popular Socialista (PPS), which for decades served as a home for socialists and other left-of-center politicians willing to collaborate with the government and even to endorse the PRI's presidential candidates, in exchange for a seat in Congress. The more independent left—that is, those who did not cooperate openly with the ruling party—was traditionally represented by the Partido Comunista Mexicano (PCM). The Communists were allowed to compete legally in elections during the presidency of Lázaro Cárdenas, but their party was subsequently outlawed and did not regain legal representation until 1979, when its congressional candidates won 5 percent of the vote.

During most of the 1980s, even in the face of Mexico's gravest economic crisis since the 1910 Revolution, and despite a series of party mergers intended to reduce the fractionalization of the leftist vote, the parties on the left lost ground electorally. They were hampered by constant internal squabbling (motivated mostly by personalistic rivalries, and to a lesser extent by ideological cleavages), and an inability to do effective grassroots organizing.

The key to the left's rejuvenation in 1988 was a split within the PRI leadership—the most serious since the early 1950s. In August 1986, a number of nationally prominent PRI figures, all members of the party's center-left wing, formed a dissident movement within the PRI known as the Corriente Democrática (CD). The CD criticized the de la Madrid administration's economic restructuring program and sought a renewed commitment by the PRI to traditional principles of economic nationalism and social justice. Most urgently, CD adherents called for a top-to-bottom democratization of the PRI, beginning with the elimination of the *dedazo* (the unilateral selection by the outgoing president) as the mechanism for determining the party's presidential candidate. The CD's proposals were widely interpreted as a last-ditch attempt by the PRI's traditional politicos to recover leadership of the party by influencing the outcome of the 1987 and 1988 presidential succession. The CD's demands for reform were resoundingly rejected by the PRI hierarchy, and its leaders formally split from the party in October 1987.

Confronted with the defeat within the PRI, Cárdenas accepted the presidential nomination of the Partido Auténtico de la Revolución Mexicana (PARM), a conservative, nationalist party established by another group of dissident PRIistas in 1954. Later, four other parties—all on the left and including the remnants of the old Mexican Communist Party—joined the PARM to form a coalition, the Frente Democrático Nacional (FDN), to contest the 1988 presidential election, with Cárdenas as their candidate. Soon after the 1988 elections, however, the left's long-standing ideological and personalistic cleavages reasserted themselves, and by 1991, when midterm elections were held, most of Cárdenas's 1988 coalition partners had gone their separate ways, leaving the newly constituted PRD as the principal standard-bearer of the left. Even within the PRD, serious disagreements emerged over such issues as the degree of democracy in internal party governance and strategies for dealing with the government (dialogue and collaboration on certain issues versus permanent confrontation).

The left's problems in the early 1990s were not all self-inflicted. Under Salinas, the government showed no inclination to negotiate seriously with the Cardenista left. Salinas showed much greater willingness to recognize electoral victories of the PAN than those claimed by the PRD. And when the PRD's victories (all at the municipal level) were recognized, the city governments under its control were punished and starved for resources by PRI state governors. Conflicts between PRD militants and local PRI *caciques* were bitter, with hundreds of PRD activists murdered during the first five years of the party's existence.

President Zedillo opened a new chapter in PRD–government relations, recognizing Cuauhtémoc Cárdenas's overwhelming victory in the 1997 mayoral race in Mexico City. In 1998 through 1999, the PRD won gubernatorial elections in the states of Zacatecas, Tlaxcala, and Baja California Sur. In 2000, it picked up the state of Chiapas and again won the Mexico City mayoralty. In 2001, the PRD finally won Cárdenas's home state of Michoacán, after nominating his son, Lázaro, for governor. In all of these early victories, except for Mexico City and Michoacán, the PRD candidates were defectors from the PRI who had been passed over for the party's gubernatorial nomination. In 2005, the PRD continued its success by winning the southern state of Guerrero.

These outcomes illustrate a key advantage for the PRD in Mexico's current three-party competition: In places where the PRI organization is fractured by internal rivalries, where the local factions are unable to reach consensus on a candidate, the PRD is usually the main beneficiary. For PRIistas whose political aspirations are thwarted by their own party, the PRD—the party run by ex-PRIistas—is a natural new home.

Until 2000, the PRD continued to take policy positions to the left of the ruling party on some issues (for example, arguing against the use of any taxpayer money to bail out bankers who made bad loans during the Salinas *sexenio*). Its differences with most recent government policies were matters of degree, pacing, and how much was being done to ameliorate the social costs of these policies, rather than their basic direction.

In the Fifty-Eighth Legislature (2000–2003), the PRD took a more radical stance on policy issues and was more intransigent in its relations with the other parties. In part, this was due to the diminished presence of the party in the Congress—about 60 percent smaller than the PRD delegation in the 1997 through 2000 period. It introduced bills that, taken together, amounted to a sweeping restructuring of the Mexican political system, designed to weaken the federal executive. One bill would have introduced a parliamentary system with an elected president, akin to the presidential/premier system in France. In the Fifty-Ninth Legislature (2003–2006), the much larger PRD delegation increased its opposition to the federal government's economic policies. Once the party realized that it could win the presidency in 2006, it backed off pressing its bills to weaken the executive branch and to foment a parliamentary system.

In its early years, the PRD did a poor job of mobilizing previously uncommitted voters. It had retained many of the urban working-class voters who traditionally supported the parties of the independent left, but it was not very successful in establishing ties with the popular movements that had developed outside of the PRI-affiliated corporatist structures. However, its ties to the rural areas were underdeveloped, and the PRD had been dominated by Mexico City–based politicians and intellectuals for whom the provinces hardly existed. Central party leaders often shortchanged local organizers in their allocation of party funds. This trend was reversed in the 2006 election, when the PRD under

López Obrador proved much more effective at mobilizing rural voters.

Mexico's political left has yet to recover from the deep divisions within its leadership that emerged following López Obrador's narrow defeat in the 2006 presidential election. The tactic of forming coalitions with the PAN to block PRI victories, which the PRD pursued in 2010, may be its most effective electoral strategy in the short to medium term.

The Shifting Social Bases of Mexico's Parties

The social bases of political support for the parties shifted dramatically in the 2006 election (see Table 11.7).

TABLE 11.7

The Demography of Party Choice
Parties' supporters differ by where they live, gender, age, education, and income in 2006.

	PAN	PRI	PRD	Others
Type of Locality				
Urban	40	20	35	5
Rural	31	28	36	3
Region				
North	43	27	24	6
Center-West	46	20	27	4
Center	34	15	44	7
South	27	29	40	4
Gender				
Male	36	22	37	2
Female	38	23	32	4
Age				
18–29	38	21	34	6
30–49	38	21	35	4
50	34	26	37	2
Education				
None and primary	34	29	33	3
Secondary	37	21	35	5
University	42	14	38	5
Annual Income (dollars)				
Under $2,161	31	30	34	4
$2,162–$4,321	32	24	39	4
$4,322–$7,021	36	21	37	5
$7,022–$9,938	43	16	36	4
Above $9,939	50	14	30	5

Source: Nationwide exit poll conducted by *Reforma* newspaper (Mexico City), July 3, 2006.

Before 2006, the PRI's most dependable base was the rural voter. It also did relatively well with women and older voters. In 2006, the PRD's López Obrador did best among rural voters, and Madrazo of the PRI finished third among such voters, even behind Calderón (PAN). As in 2000, the PAN did best among urban voters, but the PRD finished ahead of the PRI for the urban vote in 2006.

There was a sizable gender gap in the 2000 election, with the PAN doing particularly well among male voters and the PRI relatively better among women. In 2006, the PRD took the male vote by a small margin, but Calderón did much better among women. In both cases, women tended to support the candidate who appeared to pose less of a threat to economic stability.

In 2000, the PAN did best among voters under age fifty, while the PRI was preferred by older voters. This was probably because this segment of the electorate remembered the social benefits and economic growth achieved in the better years of PRI rule. In 2006, the PAN again carried younger voters, but now voters over age fifty chose the PRD, possibly because, as mayor of Mexico City, López Obrador had introduced a pension plan for senior citizens.

In 2000, the PRI did better among voters with lower education, taking the vote among those with less than a secondary education. The PAN did best, by a large margin, among voters with higher levels of education. In 2006, education mattered less in determining the vote. Calderón attracted the most votes at all levels of education, and López Obrador placed second. López Obrador did relatively well among more highly educated voters because of the strong support that he received from public-university students.

In 2006, the PRD did best among the poor and the lower middle class. Both López Obrador and Madrazo promised reforms that would increase the spending power of voters with incomes below about US$10,000 per year (the PRD through subsidies, and the PRI through income tax cuts). The PAN did much better among higher-income voters, who were attracted by its probusiness platform and frightened by the populism of López Obrador.

In general, however, social class was not nearly as important to voters' choices in 2006 as was the region in which they lived. The PRD was weak in most of the Northern and Central states but had strong support in the Mexico City metropolitan area and the South,

while the PAN's support was concentrated in the North and center of the country. In 2006, region was as powerful a predictor of party preference as all other demographic variables combined (age, gender, income, education, skin color, urban versus rural residence). Thus, the dominant cleavage in Mexico's electorate today is not social class but region—especially the North/South split.[22]

GOVERNMENT PERFORMANCE

Promoting Economic Growth and Reducing Poverty

There is little debate about the importance of the state's contribution to the economic development of Mexico since 1940. Massive public investments in infrastructure (roads, dams, telecommunications, electrification) and generous, cheap credit provided to the private sector by Nacional Financiera and other government development banks made possible a higher rate of capital accumulation, stimulated higher levels of investment by domestic entrepreneurs and foreign corporations, and enabled Mexico to develop a diversified production capacity second only within Latin America to that of Brazil.

From 1940 until well into the 1970s, a strong elite consensus prevailed on the state's role in the economy. The state facilitated private capital accumulation and protected the capitalist system by limiting popular demands for consumption and redistribution of wealth, it established the rules for development, and it participated in the development process as the nation's largest single entrepreneur, employer, and source of investment capital. The state served as the "rector" (guiding force) of this mixed economy, setting broad priorities and channeling investment (both public and private) into strategic sectors. Acting through joint ventures between private firms and state-owned enterprises, the government provided resources for development projects so large that they would have been difficult or impossible to finance from internal (within-the-firm) sources or through borrowing from private banks.

The result, from the mid-1950s to the mid-1970s, was the much-touted "Mexican miracle" of sustained economic growth at annual rates of 6 to 7 percent, coupled with low inflation (5 percent per annum between 1955 and 1972). By 1980, the GNP had reached $2,130 per capita, placing Mexico toward the upper end of the World Bank's list of semi-industrialized or "middle-developed" countries. As sole proprietor of PEMEX, the state oil monopoly, the government was responsible for developing the crucial oil and natural gas sector of the economy. By the end of the oil boom (1978–1981), oil was generating more than $15 billion a year in export revenues and fueling economic growth of more than 8 percent per year—one of the world's highest growth rates.

It is the distributive consequences of this impressive performance in economic development and the manner in which it was financed by the PRI governments of the 1970s and 1980s that have been harshly criticized in retrospect. From Miguel Alemán (1946–1952) to the present, all but one or two of Mexico's presidents and their administrations reflected the private sector's contention that Mexico must first create wealth and then worry about redistributing it— the belief being that the state would quickly be overwhelmed by popular demands that it could not satisfy. By the early 1970s, however, there was convincing evidence that an excessively large portion of Mexico's population was being left behind in the drive to become a modern, industrialized nation.

This is not to say that some benefits of the development process did not trickle down to the poor. From 1950 to 1980, poverty in absolute terms declined. The middle class expanded to an estimated 29 percent of the population. From 1960 to 2008, illiteracy dropped from 35 to 8 percent of the adult population, infant mortality was reduced from 78 to 15 per 1,000 live births, and average life expectancy rose from fifty-five to seventy-six years. Clearly, the quality of life for many Mexicans—even in isolated rural areas—did improve during this period, although several other Latin American countries (Chile, Colombia, Costa Rica, Cuba, Ecuador, El Salvador, and Venezuela) achieved higher rates of improvement on indicators of social well-being than did Mexico during the same period.

Poverty and socioeconomic inequality have remained stubbornly high, however. During the period of Mexico's "economic miracle," ownership of land and capital (stocks, bonds, time deposits) became increasingly concentrated. Personal income inequality also increased, at a time when, given Mexico's middle level of development, the national income distribution should have been shifting toward greater equality, according to classical economic development theory.

Indeed, Mexico apparently had a higher overall concentration of income in the mid-1970s than in 1910, before the outbreak of the revolution. By 2007, the poorest 40 percent of Mexican families received only 13 percent of household income, while the richest 20 percent of families received 53 percent of income. In one recent period, 2003 to 2006, income inequality did diminish, but only by an annual average of 0.5 percent—far less than in most other Latin American countries.[23]

Moreover, by every indicator of economic opportunity and social well-being, there are vast disparities among Mexico's regions and between rural and urban areas. Unemployment and underemployment are concentrated overwhelmingly in the rural sector, which contains at least 70 percent of the population classified as living in extreme poverty. The rate of infant mortality in rural areas is nearly 50 percent higher than the national average. In 2006, 91 percent of urban-dwelling Mexicans lived in houses with a sewerage system connection, but only 48 percent of the rural population had improved sanitary facilities.

Interregional disparities in social well-being are equally extreme. In 2000, the percentage of persons with incomes lower than two minimum salaries (a bare subsistence level) ranged from 22 percent in Baja California to 76 percent in Chiapas. A composite index of social well-being in 2000 shows the Federal District (Mexico City) and the Northern border states as being the most privileged, and the Southern states (especially Chiapas, Oaxaca, and Guerrero) as the most marginalized. This pattern of extreme regional inequalities has remained essentially unchanged for several decades.

The policies and investment preferences of Mexico's postrevolutionary governments contributed much to the country's highly inegalitarian development. At minimum, the public policies pursued since 1940 failed to counteract the wealth-concentrating effects of private market forces. Evidence is strong that some government investments and policies actually reinforced these effects. For example, during most of the post-1940 period, government tax and credit policies worked primarily to the advantage of the country's wealthiest agribusiness and industrial entrepreneurs. Government expenditures for social security, public health, and education remained relatively low by international standards. By the late 1970s, Mexico was still allocating a smaller share of its central government budget to social services than some countries, such as Bolivia, Brazil, Chile, and Panama.

The slowness with which basic social services were extended to the bulk of the population in Mexico was a direct consequence of the government's policy of keeping inflation low by concentrating public expenditures on subsidies and infrastructure for private industry, rather than on social programs and subsidies to consumers. Even during the period between 1970 and 1982, when populist policies were allegedly in vogue and government revenues were expanding rapidly because of the oil export boom, public spending for programs like health and social security remained roughly constant, in real per capita terms.

The economic crisis that erupted in 1982, after an unprecedented run-up in Mexico's domestic and externally held debt, made it impossible to maintain even that level of government commitment to social well-being. By 1986, debt service was consuming over half of the total federal government budget, necessitating deep cuts in spending for health, education, consumer subsidies, and job-creating public investments. Social-welfare expenditures per capita fell to 1974 levels. Mexico's macroeconomic adjustment program was considerably more severe than those in other major Latin American countries that also experienced debt crises during the 1980s.

The severity of the adjustment is reflected particularly in minimum real wages, which fell by two-thirds between 1980 and 1989. Despite a modest resurgence of economic growth in the early 1990s, by the end of the Salinas *sexenio*, real wages for most Mexicans had still not recovered their levels of 1981. The peso devaluation crisis of 1995 and 1996 caused most Mexicans to lose whatever ground they had gained during the Salinas years. By 2004, nearly half of Mexico's population (47 percent) was living at or below the World Bank's official poverty level, and one-fifth were living in extreme poverty.

Under President Fox, macroeconomic stability was maintained through a combination of fiscal restraint and good fortune; government revenues were boosted by rising oil prices in global markets, and the U.S. market for Mexico's exports was strong after the U.S. economy recovered from the 2001 and 2002 recession. The absence of a major, end-of-*sexenio* economic crisis—for the first time since 1970—was a key factor in Felipe Calderón's victory in 2006. Calderón could plausibly claim that he was better-equipped

than his opponents to continue the economic policies that had averted such crises under Fox. Government spending on his watch has remained under control (except for spending on the antidrug war, which has mushroomed to $25 billion a year under Calderón), and inflation has been moderate (3.9 percent in 2010).

Under Mexico's four most recent presidents, the government has implemented a **neoliberal economic development model** stressing the need to give much freer rein to market forces. The primary objective of this "technocratic free-market revolution" has been to attract more private investment (especially foreign capital) and thereby push up Mexico's rate of economic growth. While drastically shrinking the public sector of the economy through a sweeping privatization program and opening up nearly all sectors of the economy to private investment (including those formerly reserved to the state), the technocrats were unwilling to completely surrender the government's traditional "rectorship" role in the economy.

This concern is reflected in the considerable spending by the last three administrations on social welfare initiatives, like Salinas's National Solidarity Program, Zedillo's PROGRESA program, and Fox's and Calderón's Oportunidades program—all efforts to construct a minimal safety net for the millions of low-income Mexicans who were the short-term "losers" from neoliberal economic policies and trade liberalization under NAFTA. But these carefully targeted social programs were not sufficient to offset the structural impoverishment caused by falling real wages, the elimination of millions of jobs, and the slashing of most consumer subsidies.

During the Fox administration, the government implemented a new health care program known as the **Seguro Popular** (Popular Health Insurance), designed to provide health services to people who were not covered by the Social Security Institute's health programs. Social Security in Mexico provides health coverage for salaried persons, but the unemployed, the self-employed, and many rural workers are excluded from the system. The Seguro Popular program requires beneficiaries to enroll in the program and pay relatively affordable premiums. The poorest Mexicans (the bottom 20 percent) do not have to pay premiums. The goal of the Seguro Popular is to achieve universal health-insurance coverage by 2013.

It is clear that the market-oriented development model of the past two decades has exacerbated—not alleviated—Mexico's poverty and inequality problems, even when the model was apparently working well in macroeconomic terms (that is, from 1989 through 1992).[24] Moreover, Mexico's experience with rapid economic growth during the "miracle" years of the 1950s and 1960s and the oil boom of the late 1970s and early 1980s suggests that without strong, sustained government action to correct for market failures and improve human capital endowments through education and job training, income concentration and associated social problems will continue unabated.

Establishing the Rule of Law

The one area of performance in which the Mexican government has been failing most conspicuously, especially since the mid-1990s, is the administration of justice. From the poorest urban workers to middle-class professionals to the richest business tycoons, Mexicans are appalled and incensed that the government seems totally incapable of dealing effectively with street crime—armed robberies, muggings, kidnappings, rapes, and homicides. Surveys in the late 1990s found that virtually every resident of Mexico City had either been a crime victim or had a close relative or friend who had suffered the same fate in recent years.

Nationally, homicide rates rose by nearly 20 percent in the 1990s, and by far more in many of the states (for example, 230 percent in Guerrero and 211 percent in Chihuahua). Statistics on street crime (robberies, assaults, muggings) showed an even steeper increase in the mid-1990s. In Mexico City, the total number of crimes reported to police doubled from 1993 to 1997. And official crime statistics have understated the magnitude of the problem because of widespread underreporting. Three-quarters of crimes go unreported due to citizens' low expectation that the perpetrators will be caught and punished, and to fears of reprisals by either criminals or the police.[25]

President Zedillo began tackling the rule of law problem by addressing the issue of the independence of the judiciary. In his first significant official act upon taking office in December 1994, he replaced all but two of the incumbent Supreme Court justices and reduced the size of the Supreme Court from twenty-four to eleven justices. He changed the terms of the justices from six-year periods, coinciding with the six-year presidential term, to fixed, fifteen-year terms. He also changed the requirement for confirmation of Supreme Court justices by the Senate, from a simple majority to two-thirds of the Senate. This means that the president's nominees must attract at least some votes from the opposition parties; they cannot be rubber-stamped by a PRI majority. Finally, Zedillo expanded the judicial review powers of the Supreme Court by explicitly granting the Court the ability to declare acts of Congress and other federal government actions unconstitutional.

The 1994 reforms made it possible for the opposition parties to bring various laws and government actions forward to the Supreme Court for constitutional review. However, several of these cases were dismissed on legal technicalities. In other cases, a six-to-five majority of the justices ruled against the federal government's position, but under the 1994 judicial reforms, it would have taken a *supermajority* of eight out of eleven justices to strike down a law or official action as unconstitutional, so the Court's decision had no practical impact in these cases.

These outcomes illustrate a major limitation of Zedillo's 1994 judicial reforms: The requirement that laws can be declared unconstitutional only with a supermajority ruling of Supreme Court justices is a very high threshold, one that can stymie the Court in dealing with the most sensitive political issues rulings.[26] In short, while Zedillo was willing to expand the Supreme Court's powers of judicial review and thereby reduce its subordination to the executive, he wanted to keep the Court on a fairly short leash.

Another major limitation of the 1994 reforms is that they apply only to the top level of the federal judiciary; state-level courts continue to function as before, and the federal Supreme Court must still rely on state-level officials to implement its rulings. Until Court decisions based on abstract principles of law cannot be undermined by political actors whose interests could be damaged by those rulings, the goal of a "government of laws, not men" will remain elusive in Mexico.

To the average citizen, what matters most is being liberated from the constant preoccupation with matters of personal security: how to avoid becoming a victim of violent crime. The causes of rising crime rates in Mexico are not difficult to identify. In the 1990s, Mexico became an increasingly important conduit for illegal drugs destined for the U.S. market. In states where drug trafficking is concentrated (Baja California, Chihuahua, Sinaloa, Durango, Tamaulipas,

Mexican Military Assumes Larger Role in War Against Drug Traffickers

Shortly after taking office in 2006, President Felipe Calderón launched an all-out effort to break the power of Mexico's drug cartels. Seen here are Mexican army soldiers patrolling Reynosa, a Northern border city wracked by drug-related violence.

Adriana Zehbrauskas/The New York Times/Redux Pictures

Michoacán, Guerrero), a high percentage of homicides and other violent crime is related to the operations of drug cartels and the federal government's war on narco-traffickers. As shown in Figure 11.4, such states account for a disproportionate share of drug-related killings, but what stands out is the pervasiveness of **narco-violence**; hardly any part of Mexico has been spared in recent years. Drug trafficking has also contributed mightily to the corruption of police, prosecutors, judges, and military personnel.

The Calderón government has invested heavily to bring the narco-traffickers under control, but progress has been halting. By 2010, as drug-related violence continued to rise, the government began to shift its strategy away from military operations and toward more spending on education and antipoverty programs to reduce opportunities for traffickers to buy local support, as well as efforts to reduce the demand for drugs within Mexico. A federal law was also enacted, decriminalizing the possession of small amounts of narcotics.

The police forces—federal, state, and local—themselves are a major source of Mexico's crime problem. Not only are they corruptible (because of low pay and low professionalization), they actually commit a sizable portion of crimes, especially in large cities. A remarkably large number of Mexican police officers are actually wanted for crimes, but the warrants for their arrest never get served because the offenders are protected by corrupt superior officers. Simply firing criminal elements in the police forces is not the solution, since they only return to the street as civilians, committing crimes with impunity. To help weed out corrupt officers and improve recruitment and training, in 2010 the Calderón administration proposed eliminating the nation's 2,200 municipal police departments and placing them under the command of state authorities, in coordination with the federal police.

Social and economic factors have also contributed powerfully to the recent epidemic of crime in Mexico. The rise in violent crime in the mid-1990s coincided with a sharp increase in the number of people living in

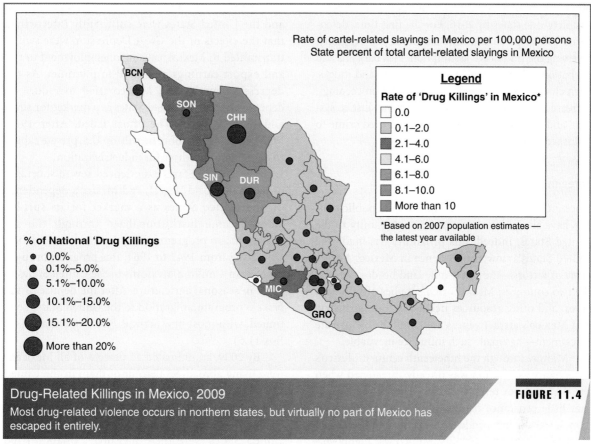

Rate of cartel-related slayings in Mexico per 100,000 persons
State percent of total cartel-related slayings in Mexico

Legend

Rate of 'Drug Killings' in Mexico*

☐ 0.0
☐ 0.1–2.0
■ 2.1–4.0
☐ 4.1–6.0
■ 6.1–8.0
■ 8.1–10.0
■ More than 10

*Based on 2007 population estimates — the latest year available

% of National 'Drug Killings

• 0.0%
• 0.1%–5.0%
● 5.1%–10.0%
● 10.1%–15.0%
● 15.1%–20.0%
● More than 20%

Drug-Related Killings in Mexico, 2009

Most drug-related violence occurs in northern states, but virtually no part of Mexico has escaped it entirely.

FIGURE 11.4

Source: State population figures for 2007 from Consejo Nacional de la Población (CONAPO). Statistics for 2009 on drug cartel–related slayings come from *Reforma* newspaper, Mexico City, compiled by the Trans-Border Institute, University of San Diego, San Diego, CA.

poverty and the number of unemployed and severely underemployed people—all consequences of the deep economic crisis that erupted in 1994. In a quantitative analysis of homicide rates in a national sample of 1,750 *municipios* in Mexico, a general index of poverty was, by far, the single most important predictor of homicide rates at the local level. Other indicators of economic distress—the unemployment rate and the degree of income inequality in a *municipio*—were also significant predictors. So were certain demographic variables, like the percentage of single mothers.[27]

Finally, the inefficiency or malfunctioning of the criminal-justice system is a major contributor to crime in Mexico. The actual probability of being caught, convicted, and serving substantial prison time is far too low to serve as a significant deterrent to crime. For example, out of every hundred crimes committed in Mexico in 2001, only twenty-five were reported to police, only 1.2 went to trial, and only 0.4 cases resulted in a jail sentence of more than two years.[28]

Potential remedies for Mexico's dysfunctional criminal-justice system include implementing tighter screening, testing, and monitoring of law-enforcement personnel; increasing the pay and improving the training for police; making criminal proceedings more transparent and efficient by introducing oral argument; giving public prosecutors greater autonomy to prevent undue interference from politicians; standardizing sentencing guidelines nationwide; making the corrections system more humane and effective in rehabilitation; and funding more ambitious crime-prevention programs aimed at young people. None of these possible remedies is a panacea, and most experts believe that real progress in reducing public insecurity will depend on addressing the root causes, including joblessness and extreme income inequality.

Nevertheless, significant reforms are being implemented. Oral trials before a trio of judges, open to the public, where forensic evidence is presented and crime victims and alleged perpetrators can confront each other, have been introduced in four states and will cover all thirty-one states by 2016. For the first time, defendants will be presumed innocent until proved guilty, reversing the traditional assumption. Plea bargains and probation will be available to prosecutors and judges. Such changes are expected to speed court proceedings, increase public confidence in the criminal justice system, and reduce opportunities for organized crime to influence outcomes.

International Environment

Since independence, Mexico's politics and public policies have always been influenced by proximity to the United States. Indeed, this proximity has made the United States a powerful presence in Mexico. A wide array of factors—the 2,000-mile land border between the two countries; Mexico's rich supplies of minerals, labor, and other resources needed by U.S. industry; and Mexico's attractiveness as a site for U.S. private investment—has made such influence inevitable.

Midway through the nineteenth century, Mexico's sovereignty as a nation was directly threatened when the U.S. push for territorial and economic expansion met little resistance in northern Mexico. Emerging from a war for independence from Spain and plagued by chronic political instability, Mexico was highly vulnerable to aggression from the north. By annexing Texas in 1845 and instigating the Mexican-American War of 1846 to 1848, the United States seized half of Mexico's national territory: disputed land in Texas; all of the land that is now California, Nevada, and Utah; most of New Mexico and Arizona; and part of Colorado and Wyoming. This massive seizure of territory, along with several later military interventions and meddling in the politics of "revolutionary" Mexico that extended throughout the 1920s, left scars that have not healed. Even today, the average Mexican suspects that the United States has designs on Mexico's remaining territory, its oil, and even its human resources.

The lost territory includes the U.S. regions that have been the principal recipients of Mexican immigrant workers in this century. This labor migration, too, was instigated mainly by the United States. Beginning in the 1880s, U.S. farmers, railroads, and mining companies, with U.S. government encouragement, obtained many of the workers needed to expand the economy and transport systems of the Southwest and Midwest by sending labor recruiters into northern and central Mexico.

By the end of the 1920s, the economies of Mexico and the United States were sufficiently intertwined that the effects of the Great Depression were swiftly transmitted to Mexico, causing unemployment to rise and export earnings and GNP to plummet. As the depression moderated, Mexico tried to reduce its dependence on the United States as a market for silver and other exports. The effort failed. After 1940, Mexico relied even more heavily on U.S. private capital to help finance its drive for industrialization.

The United States experienced severe shortages of labor in World War II, and Mexico's dependence on the United States as a market for its surplus labor became institutionalized through the so-called *bracero* program of importing contract labor. Operating from 1942 to 1964, this program brought more than 4 million Mexicans to the United States to work in seasonal agriculture. After the demise of the *bracero* program, migration to the United States continued, with most new arrivals entering illegally (see Box 11.5).

By 2009, an estimated 11 percent of all Mexicans were living abroad, 93 percent of them in the United States. This represents a seventeenfold increase in the Mexico-born population of the United States since 1970. Fifty-five percent of Mexican immigrants in the United States were there illegally.[29] Unauthorized migration has become the single most contentious issue in the U.S.–Mexico relationship, despite a preponderance of evidence that its net economic impact on the United States is positive.

The U.S. stake in Mexico's continued political stability and economic development has increased dramatically since World War II. In recent years, Mexico has been one of the three largest trading partners of the United States (with Canada and Japan). Employment for hundreds of thousands of people in both Mexico and the United States depends on this trade.

Despite the sharp fluctuations in its economy since the early 1980s, Mexico is one of the preferred sites for investments by U.S.-based multinational corporations, especially for investments in modern industries (such as petrochemicals, pharmaceuticals, food processing, machinery, transportation, and athletic footwear). In recent years, 55 percent of total foreign direct investment in Mexico has come from the United States. Subsidiaries of U.S. companies produce half of the manufactured goods exported by Mexico. Firms in Mexico's own private sector have actively sought

BOX 11.5

Dying to Get In
Mexicans Migrate Clandestinely to the United States

Each year, hundreds of thousands of Mexicans set out on a dangerous journey to the United States. They are drawn by jobs that do not exist in Mexico or do not pay enough to support their families, and by the desire to reunite with family members already living in the United States. Most migrants will pay $3,000 or more to a *coyote*—a professional people-smuggler—who will assist him or her in evading the U.S. Border Patrol. Most of this money is loaned by U.S.-based relatives—debts that take more than four months of work in the United States to repay.

Since 1994, the U.S. government has made it significantly costlier and riskier for Mexicans lacking legal entry papers to enter the country. Spending on border enforcement has quadrupled, and the Border Patrol has more than tripled in size. *Coyotes* have raised their prices in tandem with U.S. border fortification and because they lead their clients through increasingly remote and life-threatening areas; each year, more than eight hundred Mexicans perish in the deserts and mountains of the U.S. Southwest. More than 6,500 have died in border-crossing attempts since 1995.

But unauthorized migrants have not been deterred. They keep trying to get in until they succeed. Field research has found that more than nine out of ten who go to the border are able to enter eventually. Their tenacity is illustrated by the story of Briseida, a twenty-four-year-old undocumented migrant from the impoverished state of Oaxaca, who was caught by the Border Patrol six times in the month before she entered the United States successfully.

"The Border Patrol told me the first time, 'If we apprehend you a second time, we are going to put you in jail for two weeks. If we apprehend you a third time, it is going to be a month; the fourth time, three months. You could be in jail for up to a year.' I told them, 'Well, I just have to cross.' They asked me if I was sure. 'Maybe you should just go home,' they said. 'But I have to cross,' I told them. No matter what, the majority of us Mexicans are going to keep trying." (Interview by Mexican Migration Field Research and Training Program, University of California, San Diego, February 2008.)

foreign capital to finance new joint ventures and expand plant facilities.

Mexico's external economic dependence is often cited by both critics and defenders of the Mexican system as an all-encompassing explanation for the country's problems. In fact, economic ties between Mexico and the United States usually explain only part of the picture. And these linkages do not necessarily predetermine the choices of policy and development priorities that are set by Mexico's rulers. But Mexico's increasingly tight linkage to the U.S. economy limits the range of choices that can be made by Mexican officials, and economic fluctuations in the United States are a large source of uncertainty in Mexico's planning and policymaking. For example, the severe U.S. recession of 2007 through 2009 led to an even stronger economic contraction in Mexico, throwing millions of Mexicans out of work and sharply reducing the amount of money sent home by Mexicans working in the United States.

The international environment of Mexico's political system was transformed fundamentally by the signing of NAFTA in 1993. NAFTA made Mexico a much more attractive investment site for U.S. firms seeking low-cost labor and for Asian and European firms seeking privileged access to the U.S. market. The net macroeconomic impact of NAFTA has been positive for Mexico, as well as for the United States and Canada. However, NAFTA has not reduced the U.S.–Mexico income gap. GDP has risen in Mexico, but it has risen much more rapidly in the United States. Today, annual U.S. GDP per capita is more than six times that of Mexico.

If anything, NAFTA has increased unauthorized migration to the United States and made Mexico's economy more dependent on money remitted by its citizens working in the United States, who continue to send home more money each year than Mexico earns from any other source except oil exports. NAFTA created jobs in Mexico's manufactured-export sector, but

Migrant Deaths Escalate as U.S. Fortifies the Border

Coroner's staff remove the body of an undocumented Mexican woman who perished from dehydration while crossing California's Imperial Valley desert.

Peggy Peattie, San Diego Union-Tribune

competition from cheaper U.S. imports has put millions of small farmers out of work, and the nonagricultural jobs that have been created under NAFTA do not pay enough to lift most Mexican families out of poverty.

MEXICO'S POLITICAL FUTURE

In the months following Vicente Fox's victory in the 2000 presidential elections, there was a major debate among Mexican intellectuals and the political elite over whether the country had successfully completed its transition to democracy, with the alternation of power in the presidency, or whether further and deeper structural reforms would be necessary before Mexico should be classified as a democratic republic. In the aftermath of the 2006 election, particularly because of the disputed presidential result, precisely the same debates were rehashed.

It is certain that elections in Mexico at the federal level are now as democratic and transparent as nearly any other country in the Americas. Electoral law reforms have ended most forms of fraud that were typical in the past. The Federal Electoral Institute has a strong record as a guardian of democracy. Campaign-finance regulation is still deficient (disclosure rules for private contributions are very weak; the IFE can impose fines for violations only after the election), but

with generous public financing of all parties' campaigns, the playing field has been leveled. Considering that the PRI-government apparatus functioned as a political machine—in which maintaining power in the executive branch was absolutely necessary to maintain the incentive structure for the rest of the political elite—the end of PRI domination of the presidency arguably has concluded the authoritarian era of Mexican politics. At the same time, many argue that a mere alternation in power is insufficient to consolidate a democratic transition. They claim that structural reforms, especially a comprehensive state reform, are required before the transition to democracy can be completed.

The political strategies that follow from these two concepts of Mexico's political transition are very different. The notion that the transition was completed with the alternation in power in 2000 leads to political actors facing up to the problem of divided government, accepting that the electorate gave mixed signals on election day, and allowing each branch of government to make the best of the situation considering the constitutional powers that it holds. Therefore, the Congress should not consider executive bills to be untouchable (and considering the frequency with which they are amended in the chambers, this certainly seems to be the case). The president should use his constitutional decree powers and his veto as he sees fit, and not worry that their use be considered an affront to the legislative branch. The Supreme Court should arbitrate. Both the president and the parties in Congress should use publicity in the media to get their message out and pressure the other branch to give in. The opposing camp calls for national political accords and consensus on all basic matters of governance. They believe that the constitutional boundaries between the branches must be redefined, again by consensus. Proponents want to create a strong, flexible presidency, while those opposed want congressional dominance or even parliamentary government.

Whatever the outcome of this debate, there is little doubt that Mexico should now be classified as a democracy in terms of electoral transparency and even personal freedoms. Despite all of the sound and fury between the executive and legislative branches under divided government, there is little doubt that Mexico now has one of the best-functioning democratic political systems in Latin America—certainly closer to Chile and Costa Rica than to Brazil, Argentina, or Venezuela.

The results of the last three national elections suggest that the three-party system that took shape in the late 1980s, despite its imperfections, offers a solid basis for democratic consolidation. Mexican voters now seem quite comfortable with the idea of alternation in power, at all levels. Recent national elections have demonstrated that they are prepared to "throw the rascals out" for poor performance and corruption, regardless of party. Notwithstanding high levels of drug-related violence, Mexico is in little danger of becoming the "failed state" of which conservative U.S. critics have warned.

REVIEW QUESTIONS

- What explains the shift in Mexicans' party preferences between 2000 and 2006? Which parties benefit and which lose out in this change in public preferences?

- Have the 1996 electoral reforms been successful in stemming electoral fraud? What further reforms could improve electoral security and voter participation?

- What are the effects of the prohibition of immediate reelection of federal legislators? What are the effects of the absolute prohibition of reelection of the president?

- What are the benefits and costs of greater federalism in the Mexican political system? How can unintended consequences of decentralization be reduced?

- To what extent, and in what ways, do persistent poverty and socioeconomic inequality affect how democracy functions in Mexico today? What policies would be most effective in reducing such inequality?

- How does government performance in dealing with public security threats like drug trafficking affect political attitudes and behavior in Mexico? What is the trade-off between greater government control and public support for the government?

- What challenges do globalization and labor migration to the United States pose for Mexico's future development?

KEY TERMS

caciques

Confederación de Trabajadores de México (CTM)

Confederación Nacional Campesina (CNC)

Confederación Nacional de Organizaciones Populares (CNOP)

corporatist

divided government

municipios

narco-violence

neoliberal economic development model

North American Free Trade Agreement (NAFTA)

Partido Acción Nacional (PAN)

Partido de la Revolución Democrática (PRD)

Partido Revolucionario Institucional (PRI)

patron–client relationships

political centralism

presidencialismo

sectors (of the PRI)

Seguro Popular

sexenio (six-year term)

social capital

técnico

SUGGESTED READINGS

Bruhn, Kathleen. *Taking on Goliath: Mexico's Party of the Democratic Revolution*. University Park: Pennsylvania State University Press, 1997.

Camp, Roderic A. *Crossing Swords: Politics and Religion in Mexico*. New York: Oxford University Press, 1997.

———. *Mexico's Mandarins: Crafting a Power Elite for the Twenty-First Century*. Berkeley: University of California Press, 2002.

Centeno, Miguel Angel. *Democracy within Reason: Technocratic Revolution in Mexico*, 2nd ed. University Park: Pennsylvania State University Press, 1997.

Chambers, Edward J., and Peter H. Smith, eds. *NAFTA in the New Millennium*. La Jolla and Edmonton: Center for U.S.–Mexican Studies, University of California-San Diego and University of Alberta Press, 2002.

Chand, Vikram K. *Mexico's Political Awakening*. Notre Dame, IN: University of Notre Dame Press, 2001.

Cleary, Matthew R., and Susan C. Stokes, *Democracy and the Culture of Skepticism: Political Trust in Argentina and Mexico*. New York: Russell Sage Foundation, 2006.

Cornelius, Wayne A. et al., eds. *Subnational Politics and Democratization in Mexico*. La Jolla: Center for U.S.–Mexican Studies, University of California, San Diego, 1999.

Cornelius, Wayne A., David Fitzgerald, Pedro Lewin-Fischer, and Leah Muse-Orlinoff, eds. *Mexican Migration and the U.S. Economic Crisis: A Transnational Perspective*. Boulder, CO and La Jolla, CA: Lynne Rienner Publishers and University of California, San

Diego Center for Comparative Immigration Studies, 2009. Cornelius, Wayne A., and David A. Shirk, eds., *Reforming the Administration of Justice in Mexico*. Notre Dame, IN: University of Notre Dame Press, 2007.

Díaz-Cayeros, Alberto. Federalism, *Fiscal Authority, and Centralization in Latin America*. Cambridge: Cambridge University Press, 2006.

Domínguez, Jorge I., and Chappell Lawson, eds. *Mexico's Pivotal Democratic Election*. Stanford, CA and La Jolla, CA: Stanford University Press and Center for U.S.–Mexican Studies, University of California, San Diego, 2003.

Domínguez, Jorge I., and James A. McCann. *Democratizing Mexico: Public Opinion and Elections*. Baltimore, MD: Johns Hopkins University Press, 1995.

Domínguez, Jorge I., Chappell Lawson, and Alejandro Moreno, eds. *Consolidating Mexico's Democracy: The 2006 Presidential Campaign in Comparative Perspective*. Baltimore, MD: Johns Hopkins University Press, 2009.

Eisenstadt, Todd A. *Courting Democracy in Mexico: Party Strategies and Electoral Institutions*. Cambridge: Cambridge University Press, 2004.

Greene, Kenneth F. *Why Dominant Parties Lose: Mexico's Democratization in Comparative Perspective*. New York: Cambridge University Press, 2007.

Hamilton, Nora. *Mexico: Political, Social, and Economic Evolution*. New York: Oxford University Press, 2011.

Lawson, Chappell. *Building the Fourth Estate: Democratization and the Rise of a Free Press in Mexico*. Berkeley: University of California Press, 2002.

MacLeod, Dag. *Downsizing the State: Privatization and the Limits of Neoliberal Reform in Mexico*. University Park: Pennsylvania State University Press, 2004.

Magaloni, Beatriz. *Voting for Autocracy: Hegemonic Party Survival and Its Demise in Mexico*. Cambridge: Cambridge University Press, 2006.

Peschard-Sverdrup, Armand B., and Sara R. Rioff, eds. *Mexican Governance: From Single-Party Rule to Divided Government*. Washington, D.C.: Center for Strategic and International Studies, 2005.

Rubin, Jeffrey. *Decentering the Regime: Ethnicity, Radicalism, and Democracy in Juchitán, Mexico*. Durham, NC: Duke University Press, 1997.

Shirk, David A. *Mexico's New Politics: The PAN and Democratic Change*. Boulder, CO: Lynne Rienner Publishers, 2005.

Snyder, Richard. *Politics after Neoliberalism: Reregulation in Mexico*. Cambridge: Cambridge University Press, 2001.

Velasco, José Luis, *Insurgency, Authoritarianism, and Drug Trafficking in Mexico's Democratization*. New York: Routledge, 2005.

INTERNET RESOURCES

President's Office: **www.presidencia.gob.mx**.

Chamber of Deputies: **www.diputados.gob.mx**.

Senate: **www.senado.gob.mx**.

National Statistical Institute: **www.inegi.org.mx**.

National Population Council: **www.conapo.gob.mx**.

Federal Electoral Institute: **www.ife.org.mx**.

ENDNOTES

1. This percentage represents an undercount, since the census identifies as Indians only people over age fifty. Indigenous peoples of all ages constitute an estimated 15 percent of the total population.

2. The actual extent of irregularities in the 1988 presidential vote will never be determined. Within a few hours after the polls closed, with early returns showing Cárdenas ahead by a significant margin, top authorities ordered the computerized count to be suspended. When results for a majority of the country's polling places were announced six days later, Salinas had won. There is no corroborating evidence from exit surveys of voters, because the government denied permission for such surveys in 1988.

The PRI-controlled Congress later ordered the ballots stored in its basement to be burned, thereby eliminating any possibility of challenging the election outcome. Study of the partial, publicly released results and preelection polling data has led most analysts to conclude that Salinas probably did win but that his margin of victory over Cárdenas was much smaller than the nineteen-point spread indicated by the official results.

3. According to statistics of the IFE, Zedillo won 50.18 percent of the valid votes (i.e., excluding "spoiled" ballots and write-in votes cast for unregistered candidates). However, if the calculation is based on total votes cast (including those annulled by electoral authorities), his share of the vote declines to 48.77 percent.

4. See Roderic A. Camp, *Citizen Views of Democracy in Latin America* (Pittsburgh, PA: University of Pittsburgh Press, 2001).

5. James A. McCann and Chappell Lawson, "An Electorate Adrift?—Public Opinion and the Quality of Democracy in Mexico," *Latin American Research Review* 38, no. 3 (2003): 60–81; and Francisco Flores-Macías and Chappell Lawson, "Mexican Democracy and Its Discontents," *Review of Policy Research* 23, no. 2 (2006): 287–94.

6. McCann and Lawson, "An Electorate Adrift?"; and Jorge I. Domínguez and Chappell Lawson, eds., *Mexico's Pivotal Democratic Election* (Stanford, CA, and La Jolla, CA: Stanford University Press/Center for U.S.–Mexican Studies, University of California, San Diego, 2003).

7. Joseph L. Klesner, "Who Participates?—Determinants of Political Action in Mexico," *Latin American Politics and Society* 51, no. 2 (2009): 59–90. As used here, the term "social capital" derives from the work of Robert D. Putnam. See Putnam, "Tuning In, Tuning Out: The Strange Disappearance of Social Capital in America," *PS: Political Science and Politics* 28, no. 4 (1995): 664–83.

8. See Alan Knight, "Historical Continuities in Social Movements," in *Popular Movements and Political Change in Mexico*, ed. Joe Foweraker and Ann L. Craig (Boulder, CO: Lynne Rienner, 1990), 78–102; Jeffrey W. Rubin, *Decentering the Regime: Ethnicity, Radicalism, and Democracy in Juchitán, Mexico* (Durham, NC: Duke University Press, 1997); and Wayne A. Cornelius, Todd Eisenstadt, and Jane Hindley, eds., *Subnational Politics and Democratization in Mexico* (La Jolla: Center for U.S.–Mexican Studies, University of California, San Diego, 1999).

9. Alberto Díaz-Cayeros, *Federalism, Fiscal Authority, and Centralization in Latin America* (Cambridge: Cambridge University Press, 2006), 8, 143–47.

10. See Victoria E. Rodríguez, *Decentralization in Mexico: From Reforma Municipal to Solidaridad to Nuevo Federalismo* (Boulder, CO: Westview, 1997); and Peter M. Ward and Victoria E. Rodríguez, *Bringing the States Back In: New Federalism and State Government in Mexico* (Austin: Lyndon Baines Johnson School of Public Affairs, University of Texas, Austin, 1999).

11. For a recent discussion of mixed-member electoral systems in general, and comparisons between Mexico's electoral regime with similar systems, see Matthew Soberg Shugart and Martin P. Wattenberg, eds., *Mixed-Member Electoral Systems: The Best of Both Worlds?* (Oxford: Oxford University Press, 2001).

12. See Jeffrey A. Weldon, "Political Sources of *Presidencialismo* in Mexico," in *Presidentialism and Democracy in Latin America*, ed. Scott Mainwaring and Matthew Soberg Shugart (New York: Cambridge University Press, 1997), 225–58.

13. For a conventional interpretation of the powers of the Mexican president, see Luis Javier Garrido, "The Crisis of *Presidencialismo*," in *Mexico's Alternative Political Futures*, ed.

Wayne A. Cornelius, Judith Gentleman, and Peter H. Smith (La Jolla: Center for U.S.–Mexican Studies, University of California, San Diego, 1989), 417–34.

14. The purported rationale for this principle, applied to the president in the 1917 Constitution and extended to members of Congress in 1933, was to ensure freedom from self-perpetuating, dictatorial rule in the Porfirio Díaz style. However, the real reason for prohibiting the consecutive reelection of deputies and senators was probably to cut the ties between local political bosses and their federal legislators, at a time that the ruling party was seeking greater centralization of authority.

15. See Weldon, "The Political Sources of *Presidencialismo* in Mexico."

16. David A. Shirk, *Mexico's New Politics: The PAN and Democratic Change* (Boulder, CO: Lynne Rienner Publishers, 2005), 191–94.

17. Unpublished data from Roderic A. Camp. See also Roderic A. Camp, "Family Relationships in Mexican Politics," *Journal of Politics* 44 (August 1982): 848–62; and Peter H. Smith, *Labyrinths of Power: Political Recruitment in Twentieth-Century Mexico* (Princeton, NJ: Princeton University Press, 1979), 307–10.

18. Shirk, *Mexico's New Politics*, 181.

19. Joseph L. Klesner, "Electoral Competition and the New Party System in Mexico," *Latin American Politics and Society* 47, no. 2 (2005): 103–42; and Klesner, "Social and Regional Factors in the 2006 Presidential Election," unpublished paper, Dept. of Political Science, Kenyon College, August 2006.

20. Alejandro Moreno, *El Votante Mexicano* (México, DF: Fondo de Cultura Económica, 2003).

21. As Joseph Klesner has shown, both the PAN and the PRD now exhibit catch-all characteristics, driven by the dealignment of the electorate from the PRI and the desire of its rivals to broaden their constituencies by capturing these "delinked" voters. Klesner, "Electoral Competition and the New Party System."

22. Chappell Lawson, "Blue States and Yellow States: Preliminary Findings from the Mexico 2006 Panel Study," unpublished paper, Dept. of Political Science, Massachusetts Institute of Technology, July 27, 2006.

23. Nora Lustig, "Poverty, Inequality, and the New Left of Latin America," Woodrow Wilson International Center for Scholars, Latin American Program, *Democratic Governance and the New Left* series, no. 5, Washington, D.C., October 2009, p. 10.

24. A wealth of statistical data demonstrating these trends can be found in Enrique Dussel Peters, *Polarizing Development: The Impact of Liberalization Strategy* (Boulder, CO: Lynne Rienner, 2000).

25. Guillermo Zepeda Lecuona, "Criminal Investigation and the Subversion of the Principles of the Justice System in Mexico," in *Reforming the Administration of Justice in Mexico*, ed. Wayne A. Cornelius and David A. Shirk (Notre Dame, IN: University of Notre Dame Press, 1997).

26. Sara Schatz, "A Neo-Weberian Approach to Constitutional Courts in the Transition from Authoritarian Rule: The Mexican Case, 1994–1997," *International Journal of the Sociology of Law* 26 (1998): 217–44.

27. Andrés Villarreal, "Structural Determinants of Homicide in Mexico," paper presented at the annual meeting of the American Sociological Association, January 5, 1999.

28. Zepeda Lecuona, "Criminal Investigation."

29. Jeffrey S. Passel, "Mexican Immigrants in the United States," Fact Sheet, Pew Hispanic Center, Washington, D.C., April 2009.

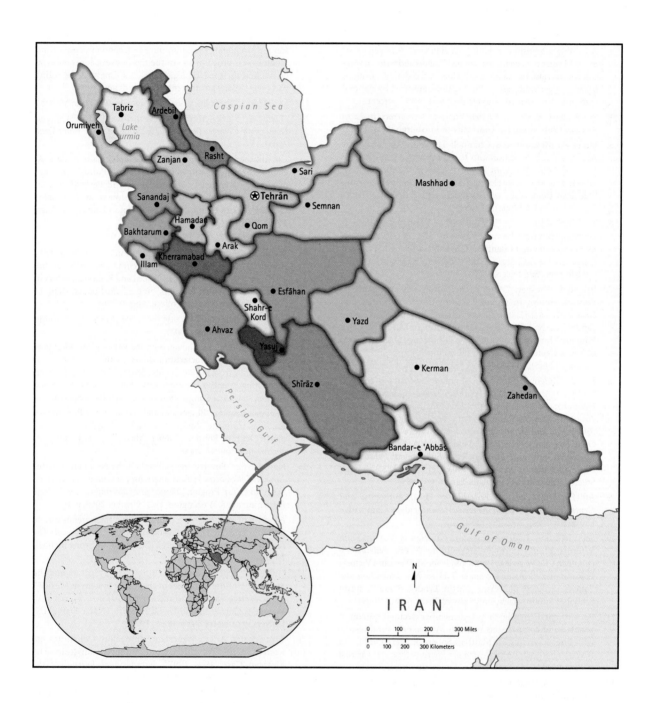

Caspian Sea

Tabriz
Ardebil
Orumiyeh
Lake
Urmia
Zanjan
Rasht
Sari
Mashhad
Sanandaj
☆Tehrān
Semnan
Hamadan
Qom
Bakhtarum
Arak
Kherramabad
Illam
Esfāhan
Shahr-e
Kord
Yazd
Ahvaz
Yasuj
Kerman
Shīrāz
Zahedan
Persian Gulf
Bandar-e 'Abbās
Gulf of Oman

N

I R A N

| 0 | 100 | 200 | 300 Miles |

| 0 | 100 | 200 | 300 Kilometers |

POLITICS IN IRAN

H. E. Chehabi and Arang Keshavarzian

Country Bio

IRAN

Population
72.4 million

Territory
636,296 square miles

Year of Independence
550 B.C.E.

Year of Current Constitution
1979, amended in 1989

Head of State
Ali Khamenei

Head of Government
Mahmoud Ahmadinejad

Languages
Persian, Azeri, Kurdish, and other regional languages

Religions
Twelver Shiite Muslim 90%, Sunni Muslim 10%, non-Muslims less than 1%

The Islamic Republic of Iran is the world's only **theocracy**, a form of government in which, ideally, all laws are grounded in religion and express the will of God, and a clergy exercises supreme power. While Islamic law has always been applied to varying degrees in Muslim states, it has almost always been complemented by some sort of nonreligious customary law. Moreover, various sultans, shahs, sheikhs, and, since the twentieth century, presidents or prime ministers have traditionally exercised political power in the Muslim world. Genuine theocracies have been very rare. Although the **ulema**, as religious scholars are called in the Muslim world, have sometimes been critical of rulers who strayed from the path of Islam, they almost never aspired to exercise power directly as they do in Iran today. Therefore, far from being a manifestation of Islamic conservatism, Iran's current theocratic regime constitutes a break with Muslim tradition.

The Islamic Republic of Iran was established in 1979, a few months after a popular revolution uniting poor with middle-class and religious with secular people overthrew **Mohammad-Reza Shah Pahlavi** (r. 1941–1979), the last ruler of the country's ancient monarchy. **Ruhollah Khomeini**, a charismatic clerical leader of Iran's majority Twelver Shiite community, who had authored a blueprint for theocratic government in the early 1970s, led the 1979 revolution. In this blueprint, Khomeini opposed democracy on religious grounds. Sovereignty, he argued, belongs to God alone. Divine law, known as the ***shari'a***, as interpreted and applied by the ulema, takes precedence over laws made by human legislators. In spite of Khomeini's preference for clerical dictatorship, the regime that was established and developed after the demise of the monarchy incorporated the ideals of a diverse revolutionary coalition including liberal nationalists, leftists of various proclivities, and lay Islamists, who imagined religious rule with only symbolic authority bestowed to clerics. Thus, the constitution enshrined some republican principles and rights, and consequently presidential, parliamentary, and local elections have offered citizens a choice of candidates advocating differing policies. The emergence of limited democratic practices and institutions under a regime founded on the negation of democracy is only one of many paradoxes found in Iran.

CURRENT POLICY CHALLENGES

The rulers of the Islamic Republic have faced a fundamental predicament ever since they replaced the monarchy. How could they reconcile the demands of Khomeini and his confidants to establish a political, social, and economic order that would be consistent with their understanding of Islam and simultaneously maintain the principles of republican government that would ensure representation of and accountability to citizens? As discussed in this chapter, it has not been easy to reconcile these principles. Not only may "God's sovereignty," popular sovereignty, and state interests conflict, but the successes and failures of the Islamic Republic's policies have also created new expectations and demands as well as new social and political actors.

During the first decade of the Islamic Republic, some redistribution of wealth took place as the government expropriated much of the property of the old prerevolutionary elite. The new leadership came mostly from humble or middle-class backgrounds and adopted populist policies that somewhat bettered the lot of the poorest. For instance, the new regime invested heavily in rural development, including in health, women's education, and roads. However, the postrevolutionary reality is far from ideal, and poverty, inequality, and underemployment continue to be major public grievances. Possessing the world's second-largest oil and gas reserves, the people expect Iran's government to improve the lives of ordinary Iranians and establish the basis for long-term and sustainable development. However, transforming natural wealth into economic productivity and diversification has proven difficult. In the ideological climate of the Islamic Republic, industrial entrepreneurs are seen as exploiters, and so private investment tends to go into speculation and rent-seeking rather than long-term investment aimed at enhancing exports and creating sustainable development. Consequently, job creation has been inadequate.

The need to increase economic output to provide employment for a rapidly growing labor force is perhaps the greatest challenge facing the government. Iran's population grows by about 600,000 every year.

Although the government has successfully brought down the birth rate, the effects of the lower population growth rate will not be felt for many years. Even under the best circumstances, it would be difficult to provide employment for the 800,000 men and women who enter the labor market every year, but Iran's anti-entrepreneurial outlook, as well as its unattractiveness to foreign investment, make the situation even worse. Regional conflicts and the continuing tension between Iran and the United States discourage both foreign and domestic investment. At the same time, a vastly expanded educational system means that many of the young unemployed hold academic degrees, which adds to their frustration and discontent. This discontent has produced massive migration. A 2006 IMF study of 90 countries ranked Iran as having the highest rate of brain drain with more than 150,000 Iranians with university degrees leaving per year.[1]

A new challenge concerns dissatisfaction with the status quo among some of Iran's ethnic minorities, especially those that are mostly Sunni, like the Kurds and Baluchis (see Figure 12.1).[2] Integrating these Iranian citizens into a national framework that is officially defined by its adherence to Twelver Shiism is increasingly difficult at a time when sectarian tensions are rising in the surrounding countries and fueled by complex geopolitical and regional rivalries.

Corruption makes matters even worse. The media increasingly report about corruption, and it is debated in Parliament and by politicians. As many Iranians struggle to find gainful employment and make ends meet, a new elite has made fortunes by exploiting personal connections to the officials who control access to hard currency, import licenses, and tax shelters. The relatives of former president **Ali-Akbar Hashemi Rafsanjani** are often cited as examples of the wealth nourished by privileged access and information.

For all these reasons, the promises of the Islamic revolutionaries concerning a more just and more moral society ring hollow with many Iranians, half of whom are too young to recall the corruption, political repression, and inequality under the Shah. As a result, the theocratic model of government has suffered a massive loss of legitimacy. While the people may still be religious, the ulema no longer command their deference and respect. In addition, practicing Muslims and thinkers are developing Islam in new directions by questioning the right of the ulema to rule and exposing different interpretations of texts and opinions among the clergy.

Shia ⌣   **Sunni** ⌣

▨ Azeri	▧ Turkmen
▨ Arab	▨ Baloch
▨ Kurd	

Map of Iran's Ethnic Minorities

FIGURE 12.1

www.lib.utexas.edu/maps/middle_east_and_asia/iran_ethnoreligious_distribution_2009.jpg

camps—those who wanted to enhance republican institutions and popular participation, and those who wanted to strengthen the pillars of Islamist rule and the office of the Leader.

In 2009, elite conflict and social d i s c o n t e n t merged into one after the results of the June presidential elections were a n n o u n c e d . O f f i c i a l l y , **M a h m o u d A h m a d i n e j a d** received 62 percent of the vote, with **Mir-Hossein Mousavi** trailing with less than 34 percent of the vote and Mohsen Rezaei and Mehdi Karroubi winning less than 2 percent each. Turnout was a staggering 85 percent and not challenged by any of the candidates or observers. As in 2005, Ahmadinejad had woven together support from core institutions of the Islamic republic, such as the office of the Leader (Ali Khamenei) and generals in the **Islamic Revolutionary Guard Corps (IRGC)**, as well as urban middle-class and lower-middle-class people who were mobilized by his populist message of redistribution, nationalism, and religious moralism. Yet Ahmadinejad's election victory was challenged by the reformist candidates and political leaders (including Hashemi Rafsanjani and Muhammad Khatami, both former presidents) and by Iranians drawn into what is known as the **Green Movement** (see Box 12.1).

While these social dynamics and tensions pose challenges to the regime, the political establishment also faces profound threats from within the ranks of the regime elite. Almost immediately after the establishment of the Islamic Republic, factions and fissures developed within the coalition of clerical and lay Islamists. During the 1980s, the war with Iraq, challenges from secular groups, and Khomeini's charisma and savvy politics helped unify the country's leadership. However, with the end of the war, Khomeini's death, and the massive challenges of normalizing revolutionary politics in the 1990s, disputes began to rage among the political elite. By the end of the regime's second decade, the political elite were divided into two broad

BOX 12.1

The Green Movement

During the 2009 presidential election campaign, former prime minister Mir-Hossein Mousavi's election team adopted the color green as their symbol. The selection was a savvy one. Green is associated with Islam and in particular *seyyed*s, or people who claim descent from the Prophet Muhammad. Thus, Mousavi, who is a *seyyed*, reminded religious Iranians of his pious background. In addition, in Iranian culture and literature, the color green symbolizes spring, rebirth, and joy. Thus, green reminded secular Iranians of Mousavi's reformist platform and his departure from Mahmoud Ahmadinejad. In the buildup to the election, Mousavi supporters publicly displayed their political allegiance by adopting and distributing green posters, bracelets, balloons, flags, and other campaign material. When the election results were announced on June 13 and large numbers of Iranians questioned irregularities in the election procedures and challenged the results, green became a unifying symbol for all those who challenged Ahmadinejad's reelection. In a series of rallies and other forms of civil disobedience, Iranians asked, "Where is my vote?" and called for a reelection, challenging the authority of the president and even the Leader; thus, Iran's "Green Movement" was born.

The Green Movement demands that unified these Iranians were associated with civil and political rights (e.g., right to assembly, greater government transparency, freedom of the press). Although initially focused on the election and its immediate aftermath, the aspirations of the participants in the movement have begun to diverge. Some "Greens," including Mousavi, Karroubi, and Khatami, call for strengthening the republican institutions and principles of the Islamic republic; others have broadened their goals and called for the eradication of the office of the Leader and the dismantling of the regime entirely. It is thus more precise to speak of different shades of green.

Source: Kaveh Ehsani, Arang Keshavarzian, and Norma Claire Moruzzi, "Tehran, June 2009," *Middle East Report Online*, June 28, 2009.

Who are Iran's so-called "Greens"? Given the harsh crackdown after the 2009 election, it is difficult to identify and analyze systematically the social backgrounds of supporters of the movement. Having said that, most active supporters seem to be urban, educated, under the age of forty, and drawn from those who voted for Mousavi or Karroubi. The movement is therefore sometimes referred to as a "middle-class movement." This is partially true, for members of the industrial working class (even union activists), the peasantry, and older Iranians have not joined these protests in large numbers. However, it is important to recall that urban, literate, and professional men and women comprise a significant portion of contemporary Iranian society (see demographic data pp. 556–7 and Table 12.2).

Thus, by responding to the Green Movement with massive violence and intimidation, the Ahmadinejad government and pillars of the regime have alienated a social constituency responsible for managing and running a functioning economy, society, and polity, while also angering key members of the Islamic Republic's political elite. Moreover, the brutal repression of the peaceful protests angered not only those citizens who were willing to accommodate themselves to the regime on account of its republican components, but also many pious Iranians who supported the Islamic Republic because they believed it represented a higher level of ethics and justice on the part of the rulers. The most immediate challenge faced by the Iranian government at the beginning of the new decade is therefore the heated debate within the political establishment and the regime's waning legitimacy in disparate segments of society.

HISTORICAL LEGACY

Iran, like China and Japan, is one of a handful of non-Western states that Europeans never formally colonized. Iran's borders were not drawn artificially by colonial powers but result from the historical balance of power between its shahs and their neighboring rulers. The Iranian state tradition is over twenty-five centuries old, but the current Iranian state was set up in the early sixteenth century by the Safavid dynasty. The dynasty's most lasting impact was the establishment of

Twelver Shiism as the official state religion and the conversion of most Iranians who had been **Sunnis** to Shiism. Historically, the shrine cities of Iraq had been the cradle of this branch of Islam, but with the establishment of a powerful Shiite state in Iran, Iran became the political center of the Shiite world.

Twelver Shiism

The split between Sunnis (who constitute about 90 percent of all Muslims) and the Shiites came about after the death of the founder of Islam, the Prophet Muhammad. Muhammad was not only the founder of a new religion but also a political leader. Therefore, after he died in 628 C.E., the nascent Muslim community had to find a leader to succeed him. A minority of believers, who later came to be known as *Shiites*, deemed the descendants of the Prophet to be his only rightful successors. Shiites call these hereditary successors to the Prophet *Imams*. Of particular importance is the Third Imam, Husayn, whose martyrdom in 680 C.E. symbolizes for Shiites the struggle of the just against the unjust. This event is still commemorated yearly in emotional processions that acquire a political dimension in times of political crisis.

While some Shiite sects believe in an unbroken line of Imams all the way to the present, the vast majority believe that the twelfth was the last of the Imams, hence their name. According to these Shiites, the twelfth Imam disappeared from view as a child in 874 C.E., but did not die. He is alive (rather like Elijah in the Jewish tradition) and will come forth and show himself to establish a just rule at the end of time. In other words, he is a messiah-like figure. From the moment the Twelfth Imam disappeared from public view, therefore, Twelver Shiite political thought faced a dilemma. The only figure who could exercise legitimate rule over the community of believers was not physically present, and no one knew when he would reveal himself. Most of the time, this dilemma did not matter in practice, because Shiites were a minority lacking political power, making their political theology inconsequential.

With the establishment of a Twelver Shiite state by the Safavid dynasty in the sixteenth century, the unavailability of the one truly legitimate ruler became an existential problem. In the absence of the Twelfth Imam, who had the right to rule in practice? Most ulema were willing to accord this right to the secular rulers, the shahs, so long as they ruled justly and in accordance with Islam. By the end of the seventeenth century, however, a minority of ulema argued that for the rule of a shah to be legitimate, he had to have the ulema's explicit endorsement. After the fall of the Safavids in 1722, Iran was in the grip of civil wars as various short-lived dynasties succeeded each other. The Qajar dynasty finally emerged victorious in 1796.

During the troubled eighteenth century, the ulema established themselves as an institution independent of the state. Since the state was in disarray much of the time, believers' tithes were increasingly paid to the ulema directly, assuring them of financial independence. Moreover, the center of Twelver Shiism, the city of Najaf, lay in Ottoman Iraq, outside the control of Iran's worldly authorities. Beginning in the nineteenth century, therefore, the ulema had greater social, political, and religious prominence in Iran than in the Sunni world. They had their own sources of income and were beyond the control of the state. Without this legacy, the establishment of a theocracy would not even have been conceivable in the 1970s.

In some ways, the role and function of the ulema resemble that of a clergy in Christian countries. However, while the Shiite ulema form a loose hierarchy, they are not organized in a pyramidal structure like the Roman Catholic Church. There is no equivalent of the pope, and no one leader can define dogma in a way that is binding for everyone else. Consequently, the ulema have often disagreed among themselves on political and even minor religious matters, a state of affairs that, as we will see, has not ended with the creation of an Islamic state.

A Multiethnic Nation

The population of Iran comprises a number of different ethnic groups defined by language. Persian speakers are the largest group and constitute roughly half the total population, the most important others being Azeri Turks, Kurds, Lurs, Baluchis, Arabs, and Turkmens (see again Figure 12.1). Historically, this ethnic variety did not pose a political problem. There are three main reasons for this. First, Iran's largest non-Persian population, the Azeri Turks, share the same religion with the Persians and have always been prominent among the country's elites. Second, the cultural prestige of the Persian language was such that non-Persian speakers acquiesced in its role as official language. Finally, the Iranian nation was defined territorially rather than ethnically, in the sense that "Iranian" meant coming from the land of Iran, which is the ancient name of the area between the Caspian Sea and the Persian Gulf.

Under the influence of ethnically defined European nationalism, the prerevolutionary elites of Iran defined Iran as a *Persian* country, ignoring its ethnic diversity. After the revolution, Twelver Shiism came to be the defining trait of the nation in the eyes of its leaders. This means that in recent Iranian history, two visions of what constitutes Iranian identity have contended with each other; one ignores the cultural specificity of non-Persian-speaking citizens, while the other marginalizes non-Twelver Shiites, of whom Sunnis are the largest community (approximately 10 percent). Additionally, these linguistic and religious divisions have been politicized by minorities lacking access to state resources and having fewer socioeconomic opportunities in the geographic margins of the country where the majority of Kurds, Baluch, Arabs, and Turkmen live.

Constitutionalism in Iran

Iran's geographic location between the Russian empire in the north and the British empire in the south allowed it to survive the heyday of European imperialism as an independent state. Both empires allowed it to remain a neutral buffer between their respective domains. Nevertheless, educated Iranians recognized the fragility of their country's sovereignty. As they became more familiar with Europe in the nineteenth century, they became more aware of their own backwardness. As long as Iran was less developed than Europe, it would forever remain vulnerable to imperialist encroachment. Consequently, "catching up with the West" became the major goal of Iran's intellectual and political elite. They believed that the rule of law was the secret of European superiority, whereas arbitrary rule prevailed in Iran. They concluded that constitutional government had to be introduced to strengthen the nation. Japan's victory over Russia in the war of 1905 confirmed Iranian constitutionalists in their view. For the first time, an Asian power had vanquished a European one, and Iranians argued that this reversal of fortunes occurred because Japan was the only constitutional power in Asia while Russia was the only autocracy among the major European powers.

In 1905, widespread dissatisfaction with the way the country was governed led to a popular movement that wrested a constitution from the Shah in December 1906. Shiite ulema played a major role in the constitutionalist movement. Until a few years earlier, the Iranian state had been characterized by an implicit contract between worldly and spiritual authorities. The Shah upheld the official religion and the ulema legitimated the Shah's rule. But by the early twentieth century, many politically active ulema shared the views of merchants and Western-educated intellectuals: that the powers of the monarchy needed to be curtailed. They believed that the citizenry had the right to elect a representative parliament, that the Shah could name a prime minister only in agreement with parliament, and that parliament could hold the government accountable. These very European ideas were criticized by conservative ulema for being alien to Islam, but constitutionalist ulema found ways to justify them in Islamic terms. Most famously, Ayatollah Muhammad-Husayn Na'ini argued that a despotic shah violated the rights of the Twelfth Imam and those of the people, whereas rule by the people violated only the rights of the Twelfth Imam. He concluded that while neither form of government was ideal, the latter was the lesser evil and thus preferable to the former.[3] This argument implied the novel idea that as long as the Twelfth Imam chose to remain in hiding, the believers themselves were his deputies. This elegant formulation reconciled Shiism's core beliefs with modern notions of constitutionalism and is a legacy that the revolutionaries of 1979 could not ignore as they set out to create an Islamic state.

The Pahlavi Monarchy

The Constitution of 1906 did not bring the hoped-for progress, however. In a 1907 secret agreement, Britain and Russia divided Iran into two spheres of influence. During World War I, belligerents repeatedly violated Iran's neutrality and fought each other on Iranian territory, causing much hardship to the population. By the end of the war, local warlords were challenging the authority of the central government in peripheral regions.

In 1921, a *coup d'état* put an end to the rule of the old establishment. The commander of the troops, Reza Khan, lost no time in extending government control over rebellious provinces and began an ambitious modernization program to develop and centralize state authority. By 1925, he ousted the ruling Qajar dynasty and had Parliament proclaim him the new ruler as Reza Shah Pahlavi. From his coronation in 1926 until his ouster by the British in the wake of the Allied occupation of Iran in 1941, he ruled as dictator, although he left the Constitution formally in place. Reza Khan initially enjoyed the support of most of the clergy. But in the 1930s, his relations with the ulema deteriorated after he implemented reforms that reduced their social functions and aimed at Westernizing the daily culture of Iranians, such as prohibiting women's veiling. With his departure into exile, politics opened up again. His twenty-one-year-old son and successor, Mohammad-Reza Shah Pahlavi, did not have the authority yet to continue his father's ways (see Figure 12.2).

Between 1941 and 1953, Iran's political system included three main camps. First, the pro-Western conservative establishment, including the Shah and the landlords, was supported tacitly by most of the ulema. Second was the pro-Soviet communist **Tudeh party**. Third was the neutralist National Front, which aimed at establishing the full rule of law within the country and consolidating its standing among nations. As the National Front saw it, the nation's sovereignty was compromised by British control over Iran's oil resources through the British-owned Anglo-Iranian Oil Company (AIOC). The Iranian government had no say in the company, not even the right to see its books. From 1945 to 1950, the total net profits of the AIOC were £250 million after deducting high British taxes, royalties, and exaggerated depreciation figures; at the same time, royalties paid to Iran for its oil amounted to merely £90 million.[4]

The leader of the National Front, **Mohammad Mossadegh**, advocated nationalizing the Iranian oil industry. This occurred in March 1951, and soon thereafter Mossadegh was elected prime minister by Parliament. Subsequent negotiations between the Iranian and British governments to resolve the oil dispute failed. Consequently, the British began plotting Mossadegh's overthrow, which was accomplished with the help of the U.S. Central Intelligence Agency (CIA) in August 1953.[5]

Iran's political system reverted to royal autocracy as the second ruler of the Pahlavi dynasty increasingly asserted himself and took full control over the emerging **rentier state** (see Chapter 7). With the help of a steady stream of oil revenue and U.S. support, in 1963, the Shah launched a reform program known as the "White Revolution," which included land reform and granting suffrage to women. In the 1950s, the Shah had enjoyed the support of the clerical hierarchy, but by the early 1960s, his dictatorial methods and Westernizing policies elicited the anger of religious traditionalists. These traditionalists rioted in June 1963 in support of a new oppositional member of the ulema, Ruhollah Khomeini. The government suppressed the riots with bloodshed, and Khomeini was arrested and exiled. He finally settled in the Shiite shrine city of Najaf in Iraq. He remained there until

Year	Head of State	President	Prime Minister
1941	Shah: Mohammad-Reza Pahlavi	—	—Various cabinets
1951	—	—	Mohammad Mossadegh (51–53)
—	—	—	—Various cabinets
1965	—	—	Amir-Abbas Hoveyda
1977	—	—	Jamshid Amuzegar
1979	Leader: Ruhollah Khomeini	—	Mehdi Bazargan
1980	—	Abolhasan Banisadr	—
1981	—	Ali Rajai, Ali Khamenei	Mir-Hosein Musavi
1989	Ali Khamenei	Ali-Akbar Hashemi Rafsanjani	Position abolished
1997	—	Mohammad Khatami	—
2005	—	Mahmud Ahmadinejad	—

Iranian Regimes

FIGURE 12.2

October 1978, when he was expelled by Saddam Hussein and sought refuge in Paris until his triumphant return to Iran on February 1, 1979.

Until 1963, opposition to royal autocracy was carried out in the name of the Constitution of 1906, which the two Pahlavi shahs were criticized for not respecting. Free elections were the opposition's main demand. After 1963, however, opponents of the Shah, increasingly driven underground or abroad, despaired of ever attaining constitutional rule by peaceful means and became radicalized. Gradually, the Constitution itself suffered a loss of legitimacy. Opponents of the Shah demanded the abolition of the monarchy and its replacement by a new regime. Given the Shah's suppression of civil society and of the secular opposition, mosques and religious circles became the only places where one could speak one's mind. Thus, religion became a more prominent political force, despite the secularist policies of the state. By the 1970s, Shiite activists, many of them university students or followers of Khomeini, were arguing about the shape of the ideal Islamic state.

While the Shah's regime was increasingly contested at home, it continued to receive support from the West in general and the United States in particular. Since the Shah's rule had been made possible through the direct intervention of the CIA, his opponents thought of him as an U.S. puppet whose policies were designed to benefit the United States rather than Iran. Opposition to the Shah thus logically entailed opposition to the United States and Israel, with which the Shah had contracted a strategic alliance directed against radical Arab states, such as Egypt, Iraq, and Syria. In recent years, evidence has appeared suggesting that at the height of his power in the early 1970s, the Shah, far from being manipulated by the United States, was actually successful in manipulating U.S. policymakers to achieve his ends.[6]

Although Iran's first revolution failed to produce a constitutional state based on the rule of law, during the seven decades of its life, Iran acquired the trappings of a modern nation-state. The government acquired a monopoly on the use of force; introduced unified legal codes; developed a functioning civil service, including a territorial administration that extended the writ of the state into distant provinces; and secured the country's international borders. State-building having been accomplished, the Islamic state created in the aftermath of the revolution of 1979 became an Islamic *republic*.

The Islamic Revolution

In 1977, Jimmy Carter became president of the United States and U.S. foreign policy began emphasizing respect for human rights by U.S. allies.[7] Unbeknownst to the public, the Shah had terminal cancer. To ensure a smooth transition to his heir at a time when U.S. support could no longer be taken for granted, he began liberalizing aspects of Iran's political system and removing longtime advisors and cronies. But various dissident and social groups with grievances took advantage of this liberalization to push for greater reforms. From late 1977 to early 1979, the calls for greater liberalization snowballed into a call for the abolition of the monarchy. This opposition coalition consisted of intellectuals, university and high school students and teachers, bazaar merchants, politically active clerics and seminarians, industrial workers, and, in the final stage, state employees and white-collar workers.[8] The popular movement against the regime's despotism, corruption, and alliances with the United States and Israel united such diverse ideological factions as liberal adherents of the 1906 Constitution, Marxist-Leninist leftists, and **Islamists**. The latter comprised democrats whose reading of Islam was decidedly liberal and noncoercive, leftists who stressed the egalitarian aspects of Islam, and direct followers of Khomeini who championed an Islamic state supervised by clerics. These activists organized massive meetings, demonstrations, and strikes, and they distributed anti-regime pamphlets in a largely peaceful manner.[9] In his reaction, the Shah vacillated between repressing the movement and making belated concessions. The result was that the activists became ever more radicalized during 1978, finally driving him and his family into exile in January 1979.[10]

In the course of the revolutionary uprising and immediately after the departure of the Shah's family, Khomeini's followers were the best-organized and most united force, and they rapidly sidelined the nonclerical currents in their coalition. The organizational power of Khomeini and his followers was enhanced by their access to independent sources of revenue, as traditionally observant Shiites pay their tithes directly to the ulema. In 1970, Khomeini had revived the strain in Twelver Shiite thought that called for clerical oversight of government and carried it to its logical conclusion. In a treatise titled "Islamic Government," he argued that God had revealed His laws to humankind, not

BOX 12.2

Velayat-e Faqih

Velayat-e faqih—the lynchpin of Iran's theocratic Constitution—is best translated as "guardianship of the jurisprudent." Ayatollah Ruhollah Khomeini described this while he was in exile in 1970 in Iraq. Khomeini argued that since God revealed the laws according to which Muslims should live and organize their community, Muslims should apply these laws in practice rather than just debating them theoretically. The most qualified people to supervise the application of these laws in the state, he wrote, are those who know them best (that is, the clerics who specialize in jurisprudence). He concluded that such a cleric must therefore be the head of state. In 1979, this principle was enshrined in the Constitution of the Islamic Republic of Iran, and Khomeini himself became the ruling jurisprudent, referred to henceforth as "Leader." For the first time in Iranian history, religious and worldly authorities were fused. *Velayat-e faqih* is not strongly grounded in scripture, and most Twelver Shiite clerics disagree with the principle. They see the task of the Shiite clergy as that of guiding the believers and advising rulers, as can be seen in post-Saddam Iraq.

so that they would be ignored until the moment the Twelfth Imam revealed himself, but in order to apply them here and now. Khomeini further observed that the people most suited to rule in accordance with divine law are those who know it best, namely the ulema themselves. This principle came to be known as **velayat-e faqih**, which is best translated as "guardianship of the jurisprudent"[11] (see Box 12.2).

Given Khomeini's charismatic leadership of the revolution, his followers enshrined this principle in the new 1979 Iranian Constitution. However, in deference to the preexisting constitutional tradition and to placate the many non-Islamists and moderate Islamists who had participated in the revolution, the Constitution maintained a parliament elected by universal suffrage. The shah was replaced with an elected president. The Islamic Republic was thus born with a mixed political system that is informed by both a version of Twelver Shiite political doctrine and by Western notions of popular sovereignty and division of powers.[12]

From 1979 to June 1981, secular moderates, leftists, moderate Islamists, and radical Islamists inspired directly by Khomeini competed for power. As time went on, the confrontation between adherents of *velayat-e faqih* and their opponents became ever more implacable and violent. In fact, far more people were killed in confrontations among the revolutionaries than had died as a result of the Shah's efforts to suppress the revolutionary mass movement. By the summer of 1981, Khomeini's supporters gained the upper hand and began instituting Islamic law in all spheres of public life. Their suppression of all who opposed them was facilitated by the war that was now raging with neighboring Iraq.

Iran–Iraq War

Soon after the revolution, Khomeini began calling for the overthrow of the Iraqi president, Saddam Hussein. This provoked Saddam Hussein to attack Iran in September 1980. The war that ensued lasted until 1988 and ended in a stalemate.

Officially termed the "imposed war" or the "sacred defense" in Iran, the war was a major watershed. Over 2 million Iranians were mobilized, with approximately a quarter of a million killed and more than double injured, many due to Iraq's use of chemical weapons. The war enabled the revolutionary regime to consolidate its hold on power by calling for national unity in the face of a foreign invasion. The war became a means to suppress dissent and public debate. The conflict created a "war generation" of young men who were shaped as much by their experiences at the front as by the revolution. Now many of these soldiers and officers are in their forties and fifties, and some are demanding a bigger say in national and local politics. These veterans have tended to call for more "social order" and a greater state role in providing for the lower classes who volunteered and perished in the war in disproportionately large numbers.

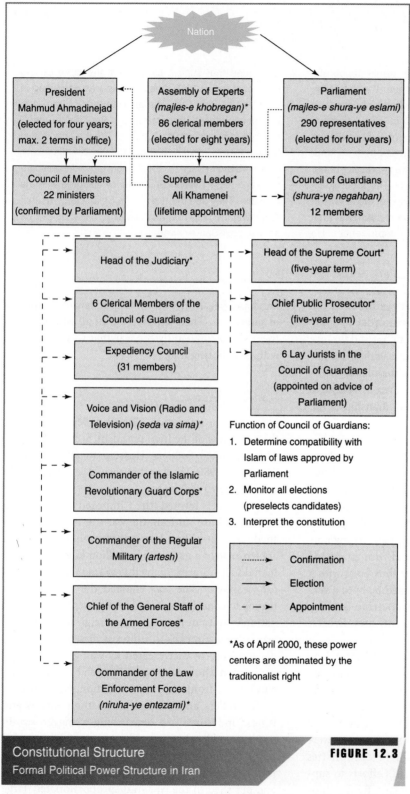

Function of Council of Guardians:

1. Determine compatibility with Islam of laws approved by Parliament
2. Monitor all elections (preselects candidates)
3. Interpret the constitution

- ·········> Confirmation
- ──────> Election
- ─ ─ ─> Appointment

*As of April 2000, these power centers are dominated by the traditionalist right

Constitutional Structure
Formal Political Power Structure in Iran

FIGURE 12.3

Source: Adapted from Wilfried Buchta, *Who Rules Iran? The Structure of Power in the Islamic Republic* (Washington, D.C.: Washington Institute for Near East Policy, 2000). © Wilfried Buchta, Rabat 2000.

INSTITUTIONS OF THE ISLAMIC REPUBLIC

Two types of institutions coexist in the political system of the Islamic Republic of Iran: appointed and elected offices. This dualism reflects the attempted synthesis between divine and popular sovereignty enshrined in the Constitution. The institutional structure of Iran is further complicated by the existence of what is known as **multiple power centers**, institutions created by the revolutionaries to supplement the activities of the traditional state institutions, with which they share overlapping responsibilities (see Figure 12.3).

Leader

The highest authority in the Islamic Republic is the **Leader**, who combines religious and temporal authority in accordance with the theocratic principle of *velayat-e faqih*. The position was tailor-made for Khomeini himself, who was both a high-level member of the ulema and a charismatic political leader. For his succession, the Constitution provided for a popularly elected **Assembly of Experts**, consisting of ulema who would choose the Leader from among the most learned ulema. By 1989, however, none of the ulema who had the requisite learning shared his notions of theocratic rule. Consequently, in April 1989, Khomeini appointed an assembly to revise the Constitution to relax the religious requirements of the office. Khomeini died on June 3, 1989. The Assembly of Experts chose **Ali Khamenei**, who had been president for eight years but was a low-level cleric, to be the new Leader. From the outset, much of the clerical hierarchy contested Khamenei's religious authority, reopening the split between state and "church" that the Islamic Republic had supposedly closed with its fusion of worldly and spiritual authorities. Additionally, unlike his predecessor, who avoided directly aligning with political factions or currents and instead maintained a position and status of mediator and arbiter, the current Leader has increasingly and publically sided with the hard-line conservative faction, which has dominated state institutions since the early 2000s. This was most dramatically and publically illustrated after the 2009 election, when Khamenei categorically supported Ahmadinejad and labeled the Green Movement as treasonous.

The Leader sets the overall policies of the state and appoints some of its key figures, such as the head of the Judiciary, half the members of the **Council of Guardians**, the members of the **Expediency Council,** the director of the state radio and television broadcasting monopoly, and the commanders of the IRGC. He also oversees the numerous parastatal economic foundations and organizations that were formed after the revolution out of the expropriated companies belonging to the previous economic elite. These organizations are ostensibly oriented toward charity and bear such names as the "Foundation of the Disinherited and War Injured" and the "Martyr's Foundation." In fact, they are major holding companies that benefit from state resources and subsidies without being accountable to or regulated by the elected government. Khamenei has used these "nonprofit" organizations as a means to distribute patronage[13] (see Box 12.3).

In theory, the Assembly of Experts, which is elected every ten years by universal suffrage, is more powerful than the Leader. It elects him and can dismiss him if he can no longer perform the responsibilities of his office or proves unworthy of it. However, candidacies to the Assembly of Experts are subject to the approval of the Council of Guardians, whose members are chosen by the Leader, who thus maintains his supremacy in practice.

BOX 12.3

The Martyr's Foundation

Among the most powerful **parastatal foundations** is the Martyr's Foundation (Bonyad-e Shahid) established in 1979. Its original mandate was to provide for the needs of families of those who were martyred or disabled in the Islamic Revolution and the Iran–Iraq war. The foundation supports 188,000 people by giving aid, priority admission for education, in-kind transfers, housing services, and other benefits. These services are funded by assets formerly belonging to supporters of the Shah, allocations from the state budget and the office of the Leader, and profits from the foundation's various firms. In the mid-1980s, reports stated that the Martyr's Foundation owned $3.3 billion in capital reserves, including sixty-eight industrial factories, seventy-five commercial firms, twenty-one construction companies, and many farms and pieces of urban property.

To administer this large and diverse economic conglomerate, the foundation employs 30,000 people and has a host of subdivisions, such as the International Relations Office and the Marriage Bureau for Widows of Wartime Martyrs. The foundation also publishes a magazine that spreads revolutionary ideology. In 1993, the foundation established the Shahid Investment Company to pool the savings of surviving relatives of the martyrs and invest them. By 2000, shareholders were complaining that the investment company never disclosed its accounts to the shareholders. Mehdi Karroubi was the president of the foundation from 1980 to 1992 and was the speaker of the Sixth Parliament (2000–2004). He ran for president in 2005 on a pro-welfare and distribution platform and came in third only narrowly behind Hashemi Rafsanjani and Ahmadinejad in the first round. He ran again for the presidency in 2009 and has become a vocal supporter of the Green Movement and staunch critic of Ahmadinejad.

Sources: Ali Saeidi, "The Accountability of Para-Governmental Organizations (*bonyads*): The Case of Iranian Foundation," *Iranian Studies* 37 (2004): 488; and Wilfried Buchta, *Who Rules Iran? The Structure of Power in the Islamic Republic* (Washington, D.C.: Washington Institute for Near East Policy, 2000), 75.

President

The president is elected by universal suffrage every four years. He must be a Twelver Shiite and male. However, a number of women have tried, always unsuccessfully, to become presidential candidates. Until 1989, the office was largely ceremonial and a prime minister chosen by Parliament headed the executive branch of the government. The 1989 constitutional revision abolished the office of prime minister, and the presidency became the chief executive. The president heads the executive branch except in matters reserved for the Leader, signs bills into law once they have been approved by the legislature, and appoints the members of the cabinet and provincial governors, subject to parliamentary approval. He can be impeached by Parliament, at which point the Leader can dismiss him. The president does not have to be a cleric, but between 1981 and 2005, three different members of the ulema held the office for two consecutive terms each, reflecting the hegemony of that group in the Islamic Republic. The June 2005 election of Mahmoud Ahmadinejad, a lay (that is, a non-ulema) Islamist supported by the IRGC and Basij, heralded the partial replacement of the clergy by the "war generation," men who risked their lives in the revolution and the war and feel that it is time that they reap the benefits of their sacrifices.

Parliament

Iran's unicameral parliament, the **Majles**, comprises about 290 members elected by universal suffrage for four-year terms. Members have to be Muslims, but the Constitution provides for five MPs to represent Christians (three), Jews (one), and Zoroastrians (one).

The Majles has lawmaking powers, but its legislative output must not contravene the Constitution or Islam, as determined by the Council of Guardians (as we discuss shortly). It has the right to investigate affairs of state, to approve or reject the president's cabinet appointments, and to call ministers to account and subject them to votes of no confidence. Interestingly, even the Seventh and Eight Parliaments (2004 to present) that have been dominated by conservatives have often used these powers to challenge Ahmadinejad's cabinet choices and ministers.

In his treatise on Islamic government, Khomeini assigned little importance to Parliament, arguing that Islam had already laid down laws for most matters. A legislative assembly's task was to draw up rules and regulations for minor issues not dealt with in Islamic jurisprudence. Since 1979, however, the Majles has shown remarkable dynamism and initiative. For one, the traditional corpus of Islamic law proved to be woefully inadequate for governing a modern state, requiring Parliament to fill some of the gaps. Furthermore, the legislative deputies have vigorously debated state business and held government officials accountable, the office of the Leader excepted.

In the first Parliament of the Islamic Republic, almost half of all deputies were clerics. Under the Shah, no free elections had taken place, so few people had enough name recognition to be elected to Parliament. Consequently, in many places, voters chose the local cleric. The percentage of clerics in the Majles has declined over time, as seen in Table 12.1.

TABLE 12.1

Who Is in the Parliament?
The number of women is increasing and the number of clerics is decreasing.

	Female MPs	Clerical MPs	Total MPs
First Majles (1980–1984)	4	131	263
Second Majles (1984–1988)	4	122	269
Third Majles (1988–1992)	4	77	267
Fourth Majles (1992–1996)	9	65	270
Fifth Majles (1996–2000)	10	53	274
Sixth Majles (2000–2004)	13	35	278
Seventh Majles (2004–2008)	12	42	281
Eighth Majles (2008–2012)	8	44	285

Although the ulema had generally opposed female suffrage in 1963, the founders of the Islamic Republic maintained women's active and passive suffrage in spite of their patriarchal disposition. Since 1980, every legislature has included female deputies, who often speak out on women's rights. Table 12.1 shows the evolution of the number of women in Parliament.

Nonetheless, two features of the political system seriously limit the Majles's legislative role. First, many policies, rules, and regulations are set by unelected specialized bodies. Second, all its bills are subject to the veto of the Council of Guardians. Under the Islamic Republic, the Majles is a forum where policies are discussed and proposals aired, and where some state officials are taken to account.[14]

Council of Guardians

In order to forestall any possibility of compromising the Islamic character of the state, the 1979 Constitution instituted a separate body for ensuring the conformity of legislation with Islam: the Council of Guardians. The body consists of six members of the ulema and six lay Muslim lawyers. The Leader appoints the ulema; the lawyers are nominated by the head of the Judiciary (who is himself appointed by the Leader) but approved by Parliament. The compatibility of laws with Islam is determined by the six ulema members only, their compatibility with the Constitution by the entire council. Through the years, the Council of Guardians has rejected numerous bills because it interpreted them as violating the Constitution and/or Islamic law.

The Council of Guardians also "supervises" the elections to the Assembly of Experts, the presidency, and Parliament. It has interpreted this provision of the Constitution to signify that it can vet candidacies. It uses this self-ascribed power to limit citizens' choice at elections by not allowing candidates of whose views it disapproves. When in 1991 the Majles passed a law stripping the council of these powers, the latter, unsurprisingly, declared the law to be contrary to the Constitution.

Expediency Council

Disagreement between Parliament and the Council of Guardians has been endemic in the Islamic Republic, resulting in legislative gridlock. As long as Khomeini was alive, he was the ultimate arbiter when a protracted stalemate arose, as all involved deferred to him. In 1988, Khomeini established a new collective body to arbitrate such cases, and it was aptly called the "Council for the Determination of What Is in the Interest of the Regime," an unwitting admission that conformity to the teachings of Islam now took a backseat to political expedience. Indeed, official Iranian documents render the name of this body in English as the "Expediency Council." Its existence was anchored in the constitutional revision of 1989.

The Leader directly appoints over thirty members of this body, who are chosen mainly from among top government officials, key cabinet members and military leaders, the ulema members of the Council of Guardians, and ulema chosen for their personal prestige. In addition to arbitrating conflicts between the Majles and the Council of Guardians, the Expediency Council has the constitutional mandate of advising the Leader in formulating overall state policy.

An Honestly Undemocratic Constitution

As our discussion shows, the authority of the elective offices of the Islamic Republic, essentially the presidency and Parliament, is systematically circumscribed by unelected bodies. To be sure, the Leader is chosen by an elected body, the Assembly of Experts, but there is no limit on his term, making him for all intents and purposes an unremovable leader with vast powers. By appointing the head of the Judiciary and the commanders of the police, army, and IRGC, he, rather than the president and Parliament, controls the coercive apparatus of the state.

The limited authority of the president and Parliament became startlingly blatant when reformists bent on liberalizing Iranian politics and society won a string of elections in the late 1990s. They gained control of the presidency in 1997 and 2001 with the election of **Mohammad Khatami**, and of Parliament in 2000. However, Leader Ali Khamenei openly sided with antireformist conservatives, whom he chose as the head of the Judiciary and as the members of the Council of Guardians. When the lawyers proposed by the Judiciary to fill vacant seats on the Council of Guardians failed to gain the endorsement of the reformist Parliament in 2001, the Leader simply refused to schedule the swearing-in ceremony of the reformist president, who had just been reelected with

77.9 percent of the popular vote. In the end, the lawyers took their seats without gaining majority support in Parliament, after which the Leader consented to swear in the president.

Although the reformists tried to bring about change by legal and constitutional means, they were ultimately stymied by the Leader, the Council of Guardians, and the Judiciary, using powers granted to them by the Constitution. This shows that the Constitution is, if not liberal and democratic, at least honest; its provisions need not be violated to prevent democratic governance.

The same can be said for citizens' rights. Although freedom of speech and association, as well as the safety of the person, are guaranteed, these are usually qualified by the clause "within the criteria of Islam," leaving the authorities considerable leeway to abridge them. The same is true for the equality of citizens. Christian, Jewish, and Zoroastrian Iranians are accorded some legal recognition and can practice their religion freely. However, Iran's largest non-Muslim minority, the adherents of the Baha'i faith, are considered heretics and systematically discriminated against; to this day, they may not attend university, for instance. Even Sunni Muslims, representing about 10 percent of the total population, are systematically discriminated against in the civil service and are not allowed to maintain a mosque of their own in Tehran. In the words of a prominent exiled Iranian human-rights lawyer, in the Islamic Republic, "the rights of the clerics do not equal those of nonclerics, the rights of Twelver Shiites do not equal those of non-Twelver Shiites, the rights of Shiites do not equal those of Sunnis, the rights of Muslims do not equal those of non-Muslims, the rights of 'recognized religious minorities' do not equal those of other 'minorities,' and the rights of men do not equal the rights of women."[15] The explicit denial of legal equality to citizens found throughout Iran's constitution and legal system stands in sharp contrast to the universalist language of many other Third World regimes.

Multiple Power Centers

When the revolutionaries took over the state in 1979, they inherited an administrative bureaucracy whose commitment to the new ideology they did not trust. Not content with purging state institutions of individuals they deemed counterrevolutionary, they built new ones whose competency overlapped with the old established ones. The idea was that the old institutions would more or less carry on with business as usual, while the new institutions would actively pursue the realization and defense of the new Islamic order (see again Figure 12.3). Examples include the Construction Jihad, which sent young people to rural areas to help develop them in parallel to the Ministry of Agriculture. The most important example is the IRGC. Their original function was to safeguard the revolution, but in time, they developed into a parallel army and even acquired an air force and a navy. These revolutionary institutions prevented the provisional government, which had taken over the Shah's administrative apparatus, from gaining control of the country.[16]

As Khomeini and his followers consolidated their rule in the mid-1980s, they attempted to merge state and revolutionary organizations. However, these attempts were mostly unsuccessful, and the revolutionary organizations are still active. In the late 1990s, as some state institutions came under the control of the reformists, conservatives created new parallel institutions under the aegis of the office of the Leader. Thus, when the Ministry of Information, as the secret police is called, came to be staffed mainly by reformists, the Judiciary, whose head is named by the Leader, proceeded to set up a parallel secret police (which even maintains a prison system for political prisoners). These multiple power centers complicate policymaking considerably.

ELECTIONS AND PARTIES

The Prerevolutionary Legacy

With the brief exception of the 1940s, between 1906 and 1979, competitive elections were rarely held in Iran. In 1963, the Shah gave women the active and passive suffrage. This action did not mean much in practice, because there were no free elections for the remainder of his reign, but it did establish standards that could not be undone. Although much of the ulema had vehemently opposed the extension of the suffrage to women in 1963, the mobilization of women in the course of the revolution was so important that it was not possible to deprive them of the right to vote again.

Under the monarchy, political parties were mostly weak and ephemeral. After World War II, two groupings succeeded in establishing a lasting societal presence: the Communist Tudeh party and the nationalist National Front of Mohammad Mossadegh. These two were revived in the course of the revolution of 1978. However, they were overshadowed by more radical leftist or Islamist groups that had emerged from the armed struggle against the Shah, such as the Marxist-Leninist Fada'iyan-e Khalq and the leftist Islamist Mojahedin-e Khalq. Initially, the Liberation Movement of Iran (LMI), a moderate Islamist offshoot of the National Front founded in 1961, fared somewhat better. Its leaders largely staffed the provisional government of Prime Minister Mehdi Bazargan that administered the country from February to November 1979, when they resigned in protest over radical students' seizure of U.S. diplomats as hostages. In 1981, the National Front, the Fada'iyan-e Khalq, and the Mojahedin-e Khalq were banned for advocating policies that contradicted the basic premise of the Islamic Republic. In 1983, the Tudeh party was disbanded and its leaders jailed for having spied for the Soviet Union. The LMI, for its part, has managed to maintain low-level activity within the country.

Postrevolutionary Parties

In early 1979, a group of Khomeini's loyal followers, including future President Rafsanjani and Leader Khamenei, founded a new party to work toward the realization of their version of an Islamic state: the Islamic Republican Party (IRP). Soon, however, separate factions crystallized within the IRP around different economic, social, and foreign policy agendas. Factionalism having rendered the party dysfunctional, Rafsanjani and Khamenei announced the dissolution of the IRP in a letter to Khomeini in June 1987. They said that the party had achieved its goal, the establishment of *velayat-e faqih*, and had thus ceased to have a *raison d'être*.

But the underlying reasons for the factionalism did not go away. Some regime figures advocated more state intervention in the economy on the grounds that Islam is the religion of social justice, and therefore an Islamic government must look after the interests of the poor. Others argued that Islam protects the sanctity of private property, and therefore more *laissez-faire* policies were in order as long as everybody adhered to the rules that Islamic jurisprudence established for economic activities. As the leaders of the Islamic Republic grappled with the problem of translating Islam into a political ideology that provides guidance for the solution to all problems, it became clear that divergent policy options could be derived from Islamic principles. In 1987, the Speaker of Parliament Rafsanjani admitted that there were "two powerful wings" within the Islamic Republic, adding that "basically they represent two unorganized parties. Indeed when they describe the positions they hold, they are two parties, not two wings."[17] The tensions came out into the open in 1988 when the Society of Militant Clergy, a pro-*velayat-e faqih* group, split in two as some less conservative members, including future president Mohammad Khatami, left to form the Association of Militant Clerics.

As long as Khomeini was alive, he acted as the ultimate arbiter among the factions. When government figures turned to him to break a factional deadlock over a policy, he would normally urge all to cooperate. But when pressed, Khomeini came out against the conservatives more often than not. After Khomeini's death in 1989, the fact that the leadership of the Islamic Republic included no high-ranking ulema combined with the rivalry of opinions among the ulema allowed many policy disagreements to remain unresolved. These disagreements were channeled into the political system and became the basis of electoral competition as different candidates espoused opposing views for which they sought people's votes. This factor has given Iranian elections a poignancy they lack in other nondemocratic states.

Ideological differences have become the basis of factional politics among three broad clusters in the political elite: conservatives, pragmatists, and reformers. The conservatives, who self-identify as "principlists," are clerics and lay politicians who favor stricter social rules (such as gender segregation in public places) and call for greater authority for the Leader at the expense of elected bodies, while simultaneously supporting freer, market-oriented economic policies.

Pragmatists, including Rafsanjani and many technocrats who staffed the ministries in the 1990s, are more accommodating on social issues and support economic liberalization and the privatization of state-owned and parastatal companies. Moreover, they toned down support for exporting the revolution and are somewhat more conciliatory regarding U.S.–Iranian relations. As their name suggests, depending on the issue, they align themselves with either the conservatives or reformists.

Finally, the reformers emerged in the 1990s. Many of the key members of this group were thought of as radicals, or the younger Islamist revolutionaries and clerics who were influenced by leftist and anti-imperialist politics. In the 1980s, they called for increased state control of the economy to ensure greater social justice and were active in supporting Islamist struggles in the Middle East. In the course of the 1990s, many of the radicals of the 1980s had a change of heart and moderated their views and came to be self-identified as "reformists." Their evolution had a number of reasons. For one, their exclusion from Parliament in 1992 brought home the importance of fair elections and political pluralism. Furthermore, the

A Poster from Mir Hossein Mousavi's 2009 election campaign

This poster depicts former reformist president Khatami bestowing a Green scarf on Mir Hossein Mousavi as a symbol of their shared descent from the Prophet Muhammad. The slogan at the top reads: "The Iranian nation's struggle today is a struggle between green-thinking and black-thinking," where "green" refers to the reformist agenda of the Mousavi campaign and "black" to the Ahmadinejad camp and its policies.

collapse of communism in the Soviet Union and Eastern Europe delegitimized the state-centric approach to social and political organization. At the same time, a group of Muslim intellectuals, some of them ulema themselves, challenged both the traditional jurisprudential approach to religion that led to the preeminence of the ulema and the survival of obsolete regulations and the ideologization of religion that led to the loss of spirituality and totalitarian government. As such, the reformists explicitly challenge the conservative faction in Iran. This more liberal approach to religion created a tentative connection between Islamic reformists and social groups that had hitherto not participated in politics, boosting participation rates at elections in the late 1990s and subsequently helping to forge the "Green Movement" in 2009.

As a result of the political liberalization linked to the election of Mohammad Khatami, a number of political parties appeared on the scene. With the possible exception of the Islamic Iran Participation Front, the leading component of the reformist coalition that backed Khatami's policies, most are vehicles for one man's political ambitions and lack any grassroots organization. Additionally, the politics, alliances, and membership of these factions tend to be quite fluid, making it difficult to predict definitively or explain the actions and positions of politicians and political organizations. Since strong parties are absent, journals, newspapers, and increasingly Web sites play a key role as vehicles for discussing, formulating, and disseminating ideological alternatives.

Presidential Elections

In January 1980, Iran held its first ever presidential election, resulting in the victory of a lay Islamist, Abolhasan Banisadr. But Banisadr was impeached by Parliament and deposed by Khomeini in June 1981. His more pliant successor and the prime minister were killed two months later by a bomb attack. The next four elections had predictable results, as close companions of Khomeini—Ali Khamenei in 1981 and 1985 and Ali-Akbar Hashemi Rafsanjani in 1989 and 1993—easily won against minor challengers. Consequently, the voting participation rate went steadily down, as can be seen in Figure 12.4.

The pattern seemed to repeat itself in 1997. Although Rafsanjani would have liked to run again, he could not because the Constitution provides for only one immediate reelection. The mere fact that the term limit was respected shows to what extent constitutional norms had finally come to govern Iranian politics. The speaker of Parliament, conservative cleric Ali-Akbar Nateq Nuri, was endorsed by most of the government and the politically active ulema, including the Leader. Most observers expected him to win. Instead, Mohammad Khatami, a moderate cleric who had resigned as Minister of Culture in 1992 after conservatives gained control over Parliament, ran a modern and effective campaign by reaching out to university students and active members of the nascent civil society, many of whom were the product of the regime's expansive educational and social policies (see below). He won a landslide victory. As an "outsider," Khatami appealed to all those who had been humiliated by the regime: educated people who felt that the state discriminated against them in favor of less educated but ideologically reliable Islamic activists, women who resented the legal restrictions and discriminations to which they were subjected, and young people who were tired of daily harassment by the guardians of public morality. To all these groups, Khatami promised greater cultural openness, personal freedoms, and a more transparent and accountable government. Although his reforms dwindled in 1999, he was easily reelected in 2001.

For the first time since 1981, there was no official government candidate in the 2005 presidential elections. Three allies of Khatami, four conservatives, and Rafsanjani ran for the highest elective office. No candidate having gained a majority, for the first time, there was a second-round runoff election, pitting Rafsanjani against the archconservative and populist mayor of Tehran, Mahmoud Ahmadinejad. At around 60 percent, voter participation in the two rounds was lower than in the previous two elections. Ahmadinejad won an upset victory amidst allegations that IRGC and Basij commanders had illegally urged troops to vote for him, and perhaps even engaged in stuffing ballot boxes to increase his vote share in the first round, in which he placed second. In any event, Ahmadinejad's message appealed to the poor whose concerns had not been addressed by the cultural liberalization of the Khatami years (see Box 12.4).

Parliamentary Elections

For the purpose of parliamentary elections, Iran is divided into multimember constituencies, the largest being Tehran with thirty MPs. Each voter can write

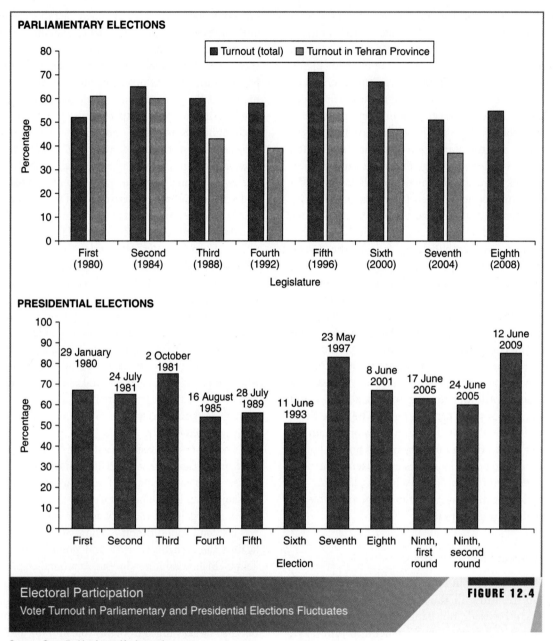

Electoral Participation

Voter Turnout in Parliamentary and Presidential Elections Fluctuates

FIGURE 12.4

Source: Compiled by Arang Keshavarzian.

down the names of as many candidates as there are seats in a constituency. The top vote-getters in each constituency are elected, provided they receive over 50 percent of the total vote. If a constituency has more seats than candidates who passed the 50-percent barrier, a second round determines the remaining MPs from among the runners-up. In the second round, the number of candidates is twice that of the seats that remain to be filled. In the absence of organized political parties, candidacies tend to be endorsed by a number of different political, religious, and cultural associations. This factor makes it difficult to deduce accurate figures about the relative popularity of different political groupings from the election results.

In the first legislative elections of 1980, a few National Front, LMI, and regionalist candidates were elected to Parliament. Since 1984, only candidates unequivocally committed to *velayat-e faqih* have been allowed to run. Radicals formed the majority in the Second (1984–1988) and Third Parliaments

BOX 12.4

Biography of Two Presidents and Two Generations

Iran's last two presidents—Mohammad Khatami (1997–2005) and Mahmoud Ahmadinejad (2005–present)—illustrate the changing face of Iran's political elite, from an older generation formed by the struggle against the Shah and the revolution to a younger one shaped largely by the events of the postrevolutionary era. Moreover, the socioeconomic differences between Khatami and Ahmadinejad are telling.

Khatami was born in 1943 into a family of notable clerics and landowners. He is a cleric educated in the seminaries of Qom and holds a B.A. in philosophy from a secular university. He has authored several works on philosophy, is fluent in Arabic, and knows some German and English. After the revolution, he became the Minister of Culture and Islamic Guidance (1982–1992), which regulates and censors all media and publications. There he was known to support freedom of speech and the press. Khatami carved out some space for his cultural activities thanks to his close relationships with Khomeini and his son, as well as with journalists and students who later supported his

presidency. Nonetheless, after growing pressure from hard-line conservatives, Khatami was forced to resign in 1992 and became the director of the National Library until he successfully ran for president.

Ahmadinejad was born in 1956 to a blacksmith and moved to Tehran at a young age. He is a product of the prerevolutionary secular education system and studied engineering. He participated in the Iran–Iraq war as a member of the IRGC. He later performed well during his three years as governor of the newly established Ardabil Province (1993–1996). In 1997, Ahmadinejad earned a Ph.D. from a technical university and continued to teach there. In 2003, he was part of the new conservative faction of younger politicians known as the "Alliance of Builders of Islamic Iran," which swept the Tehran city council elections, and he was elected as mayor.

What brings these disparate profiles and outlooks together is that both men were overwhelmingly elected president—against candidates favored by key elements of the establishment.

Sources: Wilfried Buchta, *Who Rules Iran? The Structure of Power in the Islamic Republic* (Washington, D.C.: Washington Institute for Near East Policy, 2000), 30; www.bbc.co.uk/persian/iran/story/2005/08/050801_pm-mv-khatami-profile.shtml; www.mardomyar.com/aspx2/aboutme.aspx.

(1988–1992), but after Khomeini's death, the conservative-dominated Council of Guardians gave itself the right to vet candidacies and proceeded to invalidate the candidacies of most radicals. Consequently, conservatives dominated the Fourth (1992–1996) and Fifth Parliaments (1996–2000), with pragmatist supporters of Rafsanjani forming the minority. In the wake of Mohammad Khatami's surprise victory in the presidential election of 1997, however, a record number of reformists became candidates. Since they were unknown to the Council of Guardians, they were allowed to run for office in 2000. They swept the elections, gaining around 70 percent of the vote.

For the 2004 parliamentary elections, however, the Council of Guardians disallowed about 2,000 reformist candidates, including about eighty sitting MPs. This was unprecedented, and many reformist personalities and associations called for an electoral boycott. Although participation diminished, 50 percent of the population still went to the polls. The

reason is that in many areas outside the main cities, voters do not judge candidates by their ideology but by what they can do (or have done) to further the interests of their constituents. Figure 12.4 shows that official turnout figures were again relatively high (55.3 percent) in 2008 despite the Guardian Council's vetting out a disproportionate number of reformist candidates.[18] Despite the conservative faction winning the vast majority of seats in the Eighth Parliament, new divisions have emerged among these self-proclaimed "principlists," with many of them becoming outspoken critics of Ahmadinejad's policies.

Local Elections

Although the Constitution of 1906 provided for elected local government councils, these bodies were never actually constituted. Similar provisions of the 1979 Constitution were first put into action in 1999, when Iranians for the first time went to the polls to elect city, town, and village councils.

Reformists won control over most councils, including Tehran. With the conservatives stymieing the reformist camp, apathy overtook voters. Voting came to be seen by many as a futile exercise, since ultimately, power rested with unelected bodies. In the second local elections in 2003, only 15 percent of the eligible voters in Tehran, mostly conservatives, bothered to vote, even though these were the freest elections in Iranian history. For the first time, the Council of Guardians had not vetted candidates, and even avowed secularists were allowed to run. Consequently, the nation's capital, home to about 15 percent of its total population, got a uniformly conservative city council, which elected as mayor the man who two years later used his position as a springboard for a successful bid for the presidency. Elsewhere in the country, however, campaigns were more centered on concrete problems and participation was thus higher, testifying to a relatively high level of civic engagement of the citizenry.[19] Participation sharply increased in the third local elections of December 2006, and supporters of President Ahmadinejad won only a few seats. As if to rebuke him for his incompetent management of the economy, his supporters won only three out of fifteen seats on Tehran's municipal council. They were led by his sister, Parvin Ahmadinejad. In 2010, the parliament voted to postpone municipal elections until 2013, rather than 2011.

POLITICAL CULTURE

To a large extent, Iran's political culture results from its place in the international system. Iran survived the age of imperialism as a nominally sovereign state, but this independence did not prevent outside powers, mainly Great Britain and Russia, from meddling in Iran's domestic affairs and controlling its economy.[20] Their country having been a long-standing member of the international society of nations, Iranians have tended to compare themselves more readily with the dominant countries of the West than with other Third World nations; nevertheless, transforming their country's formal independence into genuine sovereignty has always been a key concern of politically conscious Iranians.

One result of foreign meddling in Iranian affairs has been the Iranians' propensity to believe in conspiracies and to interpret politics in the light of conspiracy theories (that is, theories that purport to prove that politics is dominated by the ill-intentioned and conspiratorial machinations of small groups whose aims and values are profoundly opposed to those of the rest of society).[21] This was how the regime and some citizens reacted to the post-2009 presidential election events. In court cases, newspaper articles, Friday prayer sermons, and speeches by the Leader, the protests were dismissed; demonstrators were described as pawns of U.S., European, and Israeli secret services, and the Green Movement was described as a foreign-inspired group modeled after the revolutions that brought down regimes in Eastern Europe and Central Asia. Belief in conspiracies as a motor force in history is common in the rest of the Middle East as well.[22] But in the Iranian case, the plausibility of such theories is enhanced by the fact that Iran *has* indeed been the victim of conspiracies, most recently in 1953 when the U.S. and British governments conspired with Iranian conservatives to install the Shah. The main reason why the seizure of the U.S. hostages in 1979 was so popular at the time was that it symbolically ended the era of foreign interference in Iranian affairs by allowing Iranians to occupy what most believed was the epicenter of all conspiracies: the U.S. embassy.

System Level

Iran is not a country whose borders and statehood are a bequest of European colonialism, which helps explain why the modern polity enjoys considerable historic legitimacy among Iranians, in spite of their ethnic diversity: Iranians with different mother tongues have lived with each other for centuries. The Iranian nationalism propagated by the Pahlavi shahs included pride in the glories of ancient Persia and in a continuous "national" history of 2,500 years. This history was interpreted as conferring upon Iranians an intrinsic nobility that neighboring peoples and states cannot match.

This intense national pride survived the revolution but changed garb. While the glories of pre-Islamic Iran are now much less emphasized than before, the new authorities and their supporters considered Iran to be the vanguard of the Islamic world's struggle against Western domination. This position fuses commitment to Islam with Iranian nationalism. In recent years, however, Pahlavi-type ethnic Persian nationalism has been making a comeback among Iranians who are disenchanted with theocratic rule.

By the same token, ethnic nationalism has become stronger among Iran's non-Persian populations. This is particularly noticeable among the predominantly Sunni Kurds, who resent not only the poverty of the Kurdish areas but also discrimination on sectarian grounds. In the presidential election of 2005, for instance, a candidate who expressly addressed Sunni grievances carried the largely Sunni province of Sistan and Baluchestan. At the same time, an Azeri who emphasized his ethnicity carried the three largely Azeri-speaking provinces of northwestern Iran. In theory, there is no reason why this new ethnic assertiveness should not be compatible with a strong sense of Iranian civic nationalism, but that depends on how the central government will manage it. Repressive measures are likely to erode the identification with the Iranian state in the ethnic periphery.

One time-honored way governments shore up their legitimacy is by appealing to feelings of patriotism. In Iran, the government has recently hoped to unite Iranians around the issue of developing nuclear technology. The Iranian leaders' insistence that Iran has a "right" to develop nuclear energy has struck a sympathetic chord among ordinary Iranians, even among many of those who oppose Islamist rule. If Americans, Europeans, Chinese, Israelis, and even Indians and Pakistanis have nuclear weapons, many people ask, why should Iranians not have them too?

Process Level

One indisputable result of the Islamic revolution was the dramatic increase in the number of citizens who participated in politics. The millions of Iranians who poured into the streets to demand the departure of the Shah throughout 1978 refused to become mere subjects of a theocratic state after the revolution was over. The same cannot be said for those who opposed either the revolution or the Islamic state to which it ultimately gave rise. Many emigrated, and those who remained behind tended to consider the "Association of Militant Clerics" and the "Society of Militant Clergy" little more than Tweedledum and Tweedledee. It was these passive subjects of the Islamic Republic that Khatami had in mind when he repeatedly asserted that he wanted to be the president of *all* Iranians. They participated for the first time since the inception of the

new regime, carrying electoral participation rates to new heights. In the elections of 2004 and 2005, however, many of them boycotted the elections, feeling that their participation had not brought the country nearer to a more republican and less theocratic form of government. However, in 2009, the efforts of Mousavi's savvy campaign team combined with strong feelings toward Ahmadinejad's policies encouraged 85 percent of Iranians to go to the polls. After electoral irregularities and the extreme crackdown on protesters, it is unclear what course of action Iranian citizens will take in future elections.

Another key feature of Iran's political culture is extreme individualism and lack of trust. Most observers impute this to the country's long history of despotism, which never developed a state of law that made life predictable and governed by rules rather than personal connections. The conspiracy belief mentioned earlier added to this absence of trust. Political opponents tend to accuse each other of being in league with foreign powers, making compromise (necessary for deliberative politics) very difficult, for one cannot compromise or negotiate with a "traitor." In the Islamic Republic, the fact that the revolutionary credentials of the leaders of the various factions are equally strong has led to a certain mutual tolerance among those political leaders who remain faithful to *velayat-e faqih*. But even now, dissidents who question the system itself are invariably accused of doing the bidding of foreign (read: hostile) powers. The most consistent victims of this propensity to believe in conspiracies are religious minorities, especially Baha'is, who have been widely presented as agents of "Zionism." This charge is motivated by the fact that the world center of the Baha'i faith is located in Israel, which is a historic accident.

Distrust not only permeates the political elite, but is also evident among citizens. Recent results of the World Values Survey suggest that Iranians, like Turks, do not trust government (see Figure 12.5).[23] Since television channels are state-run and much of the press is owned by the state or heavily monitored by it, the low levels of trust in these institutions also illustrate a lack of trust in government. Meanwhile, the relatively high level of trust in the "mosque" should be interpreted with caution. As we will soon see, "the mosque" is far from a homogeneous entity and does not necessarily reflect a particular political agenda or culture.

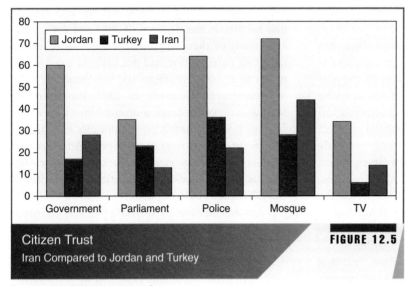

Citizen Trust
Iran Compared to Jordan and Turkey

FIGURE 12.5

Source: 2005–2006 *World Values Survey*.

This individualism and lack of trust are underlying causes for the absence of true political parties and the constant splits that the few parties that did come into existence have undergone. While all Iranians bemoan their inability to cooperate, it is this very inability that saved Iran from becoming a totalitarian state in the 1980s. If the ulema had the discipline and centralist organization of either the Roman Catholic Church or a Communist party, it is likely that their rule would be far more totalitarian and monolithic, and factionalism would never have been institutionalized.

A final consequence of the individualism and conspiracy belief prevalent in Iran's political culture is the periodic appearance of charismatic leaders. These leaders embody the yearning of the citizenry for overcoming the current order and the source of all problems—imperialists and autocrats. Mohammad Mossadegh, Ayatollah Khomeini, and even (to a much lesser extent) Mohammad Khatami and Mahmoud Ahmadinejad exemplify this tendency. Some have argued that Twelver Shiism, with its expectation of the Twelfth Imam, predisposes Iranians to put their hopes in a charismatic savior figure.

Policy Level

Given the fact that the Iranian state derives most of its income from oil, Iranians have tended to expect the state to provide welfare and material well-being for everybody and alleviate the gap between rich and poor. In other words, they want their share of the oil wealth. Part of the delegitimation of the Shah's regime occurred because people thought that not enough wealth trickled down to the poorer strata.

Corruption has been endemic in Iran, and fighting it has been an aspiration of Iranians of all political persuasions. Its persistence has been blamed on the regime, which has thereby lost some legitimacy, just like the Pahlavi regime in the 1960s and 1970s.

A noteworthy feature of Iran's contemporary political culture is the suspicion of private enterprise in the industrial sector. Beginning under Reza Shah (r. 1925–1941), the state took a leading role in the development of industry. Under Reza Shah's son, this statism was supplemented by an emerging class of capitalists who contributed considerably to Iran's industrialization in the 1960s and 1970s. But they were closely connected to the Shah and his relatives, they cooperated with foreign companies whose activities were suspicious for the mere reason that they were foreign, and some of them were members of religious minorities. Consequently, both the Islamists and leftists who carried the revolutionary movement opposed them and the mode of economic development they represented, calling them "exploiters." The legacy of this opposition is visible in Iran's Constitution, which puts heavy limits on foreign investment.

The populism propagated by the revolutionaries has intensified opposition to conspicuous consumption and privately owned large-scale economic activity. This has not affected rich bazaar merchants, who engage mostly in trade rather than production. Their activity is less immediately visible than that of an industrialist, as a merchant can deal in millions armed with nothing but a cell phone and sitting behind a desk in a small shop in the bazaar. In contrast, the factory and offices of an industrialist attract immediate attention.[24] This general distrust of industrialists means that citizens expect the state to be the main purveyor of development and increased living standards. Ahmadinejad mobilized this sentiment in his 2005 and 2009 campaigns, which highlighted his close affinity with "ordinary" Iranians and their needs and values.

While many Iranians thus expect the state to alleviate poverty and unemployment, others expect the state to provide an environment in which individual talent and creativity can flourish. Collectivism and individualism are both present in Iranian society, and the result is that Iran's political culture is highly conflictual. The citizenry is sharply divided over the very essence of the regime, with many, especially among

the more educated, considering Islamic theocracy, if not the Islamic Republic, to be an anachronistic form of government.

POLITICAL SOCIALIZATION

The political socialization of citizens is a process simultaneously driven from above by state institutions and from below by social practices. In Iran, state-controlled institutions—such as the education system, television, and the military—transmit many of the basic political values and norms in society and establish the framework for debating their meaning. Meanwhile, through their everyday practices as members of their family, neighborhood, or social group, Iranians negotiate, challenge, and even sometimes undermine these norms.

As in many postrevolutionary and postcolonial regimes, state-sanctioned political socialization in Iran has aimed at generating national unity and masking political, ethnic, and socioeconomic cleavages. The Pahlavi monarchy championed national unity in a mission to create a modern, industrial, and Western society. This vision presented the nation as secular, classless, and thoroughly Persian in identity. The schools, for instance, educated the entire Iranian population in the official language of Persian, a critical method to distance the significant numbers of Azeri (roughly 25 percent), Kurdish (8 to 10 percent), and Arabic (2 to 5 percent) speakers from their local and ethnic loyalties. The calls for greater economic equality, ethnic inclusion, and religious observance during the Islamic revolution dramatically questioned both the notion of national homogeneity and the perception that the Iranian nation accepted this image of itself. Under the Islamic Republic, the content of the official discourse and normative agenda has changed. However, the methods of socialization and the overwhelming elite desire to limit input from citizens and ignore the pluralistic nature of society remain quite similar to the prerevolutionary regime.

هموطن ، من آمده ام ، تو هم بیا ...

۲۲ خرداد : به احمدی نژاد رأی می دهیم

حامیان دکتر محمود مردمی نژاد

www.mardominejad.ir

A Poster from Mahmoud Ahmadinejad's 2009 Election Campaign

This campaign poster shows how Ahmadinejad presents himself as the protector of the oppressed and downtrodden, represented by the young disabled boy and the crowd of people holding up the candidate's image. The caption reads: "Fellow citizens, I have come [to the fore], you come too . . . [On] the 22nd of Khordad [election day of June 12, 2009]; we will vote for Ahmadinejad. Support Doctor Mahmoud Mardomi-Nejad." Mardomi-Nejad, meaning "Cut from the people's cloth," is a play on the president's name that reinforces his populism; the title "Doctor" reminds voters that he holds a Ph.D. in engineering.

Education System

The school system has been the principal agent of socialization for creating good Islamic citizens out of young Iranians. The school system was one of the first institutions to be Islamicized by the new regime. The government changed the school curricula to include a heavy dose of religious studies, yearly classes on the Islamic revolution, and more mandatory Arabic language courses. Meanwhile, rewritten textbooks present a state-sanctioned history of Iran, which highlights the role of the clergy in all "popular uprisings," erases or distorts any role played by nonreligious forces (such as liberal nationalists or leftist parties), and presents the Pahlavi monarchy (and all monarchs) as equally and continually oppressive and immoral.

Textbooks also depict the state's image of the family. Unlike the prerevolutionary textbooks that showed Iranian women as unveiled, families eating around a table, and children with non-Arabic and nonreligious names, the postrevolutionary textbooks depict all women as veiled (even inside the home), families sitting cross-legged around a simple spread on the floor, and children with Islamic names.[25] Schoolchildren also receive revolutionary doctrine by reciting chants and poems praising the greatness of Khomeini and the regime, while denouncing Israel and "the imperialists," most commonly the United States.

The authorities initially emphasized the role of primary and secondary schools for creating loyal and mobilized supporters. However, a group of Islamist activists and scholars also led a charge to "cleanse" the universities of "counterrevolutionary" elements by reviewing both the faculty and the curriculum. This "Cultural Revolution" was headed by what is now known as the Supreme Council for the Cultural Revolution. University campuses being the epicenter of anti-regime activism, the Cultural Revolution closed all universities for three years (1980–1983) and worked to develop links between the universities and the religious seminaries. When the universities were reopened, strict entrance requirements were established, including religious examinations, to give greater opportunities to those the regime expected would be more supportive of its ambitions. In addition, war veterans and relatives of those killed in the revolution and the Iran–Iraq war were allotted special quotas in all universities.

The regime also established institutions to create a new set of technocrats and teachers to staff the ministries and the universities. Domestically producing engineers, scientists, economists, and other professionals was essential for ensuring the Islamic Republic's independence and withstanding the U.S. attempt to isolate Iran. For instance, Imam Sadeq University (ironically on the campus of a former business school affiliated with Harvard Business School) was fashioned to produce technocrats. Another new aspect of the university system was the establishment of the "Islamic Open University," with 400 separate campuses all over the

country, including small towns. This university has offered higher education to Iranians living outside of the main population centers and provided opportunities for students who fail the highly competitive entrance examination for the elite national universities or whose families do not let them move to the larger cities.

The Islamic Republic transformed the content of higher education to promote and fund fields such as "Islamic Economics" and "Islamic Sciences" as ways to compete with what some viewed as the fundamentally distorted and anti-Islamic nature of Western academia. Over the years, the regime has also sponsored the establishment of pro-regime volunteer organizations (**Basij**) to monitor the political activities of students and faculty, and to mobilize students for pro-regime activities on the campuses.

The Islamic Republic's efforts to create obedient and loyal citizens out of the "children of the revolution" seem far from successful. Many of the investigative journalists exposing government abuses and incompetence or the staunchest supporters of reform and the burgeoning civil society (such as arts organizations and women's nongovernmental organizations) are products of the state school system and its post-Cultural Revolution higher-education establishments. In fact, the universities that the state tried so hard to control in the wake of the revolution are again full of students publishing political journals and declarations, organizing talks challenging the regime, and flaunting and mocking the social mores and the state's policies regarding gender relations. The large student demonstrations of 1999, 2003, and 2009 are indicative of the inability of the regime to manage this politicized space fully.

The Military and Veterans

Military conscription has been another fundamental mechanism for creating national unity, at least for young men. The shared experience of basic training and interacting with the military bureaucracy was augmented by the experience of the long war with Iraq. With approximately 4 to 5 million Iranians serving in the armed forces during the eight-year war, it directly affected a very large percentage of Iranian families.[26] Various public commemorations and war murals, as well as stories in cinema and fiction, act to foster emotional bonds between the war generation and those who preceded and followed it.

Politically, however, the war has been divisive, with part of the ruling establishment questioning the continuation of the war even after the Iraqi army was driven off Iranian soil in 1982.[27] Moreover, Iran's military includes the IRGC and the Basij, which have become distinct institutions with growing political influence. These latter institutions are under the direct supervision of the Leader and were integrated into a single hierarchy in early 2009. In the parliamentary election of 2004, over a hundred former members of the Revolutionary Guards won seats. In 2005, Ahmadinejad, himself a former member of the IRGC, ushered the way for several members to enter his cabinet. The IRGC's political relevance reflects their significant and growing role in construction projects, manufacturing (including the oil sector), communications, trade, and banking since the 1990s and increasingly so since Ahmadinejad's presidency. This goes a long way in explaining the IRGC leaderships' overt support for the incumbent in 2009.

Religion and Religious Institutions

While most Iranians consider themselves religious and consider religious matters and practices as important aspects of their lives, results from the 2000 to 2001 World Values Survey project suggest a more nuanced view.[28] Figure 12.6 shows that many Iranians believe religion is very important in life and participate in religious services, but at lower rates than in Jordan and Egypt. Moreover, while surveyed Iranians more often characterize themselves as "above all a Muslim" than as "above all a nationalist," about a third put nationalism first, far more than in either Egypt or Jordan.

Notwithstanding these aggregate findings, under the Islamic Republic, religion and religious practice have played a more divisive than unifying role. On the surface, religion permeates daily life. Official speeches and pronouncements are peppered with religious expressions and quotations, the calendar is full of religious holidays, and religious observance is often public and conspicuous. Shiite Islam plays a central role both in official discourse and as a means to regulate who can gain high office in the state. Friday congregational prayers and commemorations of religious anniversaries are state-regulated events that bring people from all walks of life together at neighborhood public spaces. As if to underline the emasculation of

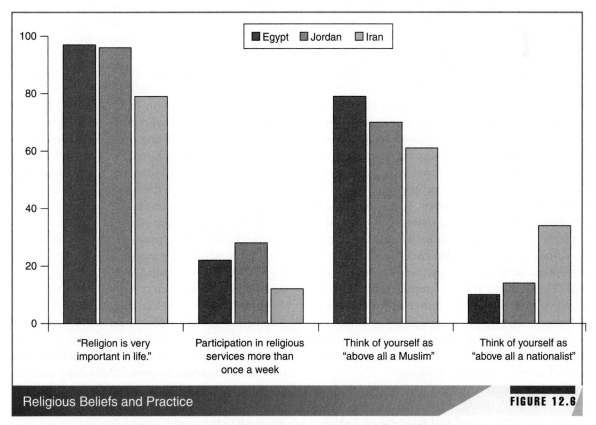

Religious Beliefs and Practice

FIGURE 12.6

Source: Mansoor Moaddel and Taghi Azadarmaki, "The Worldviews of Islamic Publics: The Case of Egypt, Iran, and Jordan," in *Human Values and Social Change: Findings from the Values Survey*, ed. Ronald Inglehart (Leiden, The Netherlands: Brill, 2003): 75.

Tehran University as the center of secular opposition to the Islamic regime, Tehran's official Friday congregational prayers are held on what used to be the campus's soccer field. On these occasions, leading members of the government give sermons in which they passionately weave together religious and moral issues and the pressing political problems of the day.

In staging these public and mass religious meetings, the state consciously attempts to mobilize citizens in support of the regime and also to transmit political messages. These events and state-owned radio and television are dominated by the well-versed and symbolic Shiite language of martyrdom and self-sacrifice, as exemplified by the Third Imam, in the name of justice and standing up to the great powers who usurp the rights of the innocent and faithful.

It is difficult, however, to monopolize the symbols, interpretations, and ephemeral beliefs that make up a religion. Over the years, the Islamic Republic has had difficulty controlling members of the political elite and clergy, let alone the hearts and minds of its citizens. Given the absence of a Shiite "pope," Iran's theocratic state has never fully imposed its politicized vision of Shiite Islam within Iran, let alone across the Shiite world. With the death of Khomeini and the appointment of the less religiously erudite and charismatic Khamenei, fundamental disagreements have emerged over the meaning of Islamic government and the role of religion in public life. For instance, the "reformist" political faction stresses the republican dimensions of the Constitution and the revolution. In contrast, the conservatives highlight the centrality of clerical authority and its right of oversight over the popular will. Meanwhile, lay religious intellectuals (such as Abdol-Karim Soroush) and clerics (such as Hasan Eshkevari) have called for a reformulation of the relationships among God, the individual, and political authority that explicitly challenges the basic assumptions of the current interpretation of *velayat-e faqih*. These debates not only percolate in the intellectual environments of the universities, seminaries, and magazines, but also shape more public discussions regarding the relationship between religion and politics, and resonate with the philosophical and political debates of ordinary Iranians.[29]

Finally, in more organizational terms, religious observance has always had a localized flavor. Numerous neighborhood and guild-based Koranic reading groups and religious associations cater to the spiritual needs of men and women of different regional, ethnic, and class backgrounds. These informal meetings act as grassroots and independent forums for religious practice, which by definition escape the watchful eye of those clerics who are affiliated with the regime. Sometimes escaping the attention of observers is the tension between the clerical state and the seminaries in the cities of Qom and Mashhad. With the vast majority of clergy historically shying away from politics and the seminary system historically maintaining financial independence, Khomeini's political innovation of clerical-led government has reconfigured "church"–state relations. For instance, job opportunities and income are available for clerics in the judicial system, in the ministries, and as Friday prayer leaders, the last being appointed by the office of the Leader. While the ulema, especially former students of Khomeini, have been prominent in the higher reaches of the regime, the actual running of the state has never been dominated by seminary graduates, and their presence has declined over the last quarter century. One indication is the decline in the number of clerics in the Parliament. In the very first Majles, almost half of the MPs were clerics, but by the late 1990s, clerics constituted less than 20 percent of MPs.

For the vast majority of clerics—who remain in the seminaries to teach, study, and interpret religious texts—the regime has in fact been intrusive. The authorities in Tehran have tried to monitor teaching in the seminaries by dictating curricula and identifying texts to be taught in Qom. In addition, the Leader has used his office and funds to support seminaries and teachers who are deemed to be "militant" and sympathetic to the regime's interpretations of Islam. But with the ascendancy of the IRGC after 2005 and especially after 2009, pro-regime clerics now find themselves increasingly marginalized, and their relationship with Ahmadinejad is an increasingly distant one. The most outspoken of his rival candidates in the 2009 elections, Mehdi Karroubi, is himself a cleric. Khomeini's grandson Hasan Khomeini's sympathy with the president's political opponents is so well-known that he was heckled by Ahmadinejad's followers on the anniversary of his grandfather's death in 2010.

The upshot is that mosque and state remain distinct entities despite the infusion of religion and seminarians into the constitution of the state.

Mass Media

The media play both a unifying and a divisive role in socializing Iranians. Radio and television are monopolized by the state and are one of the major means to transmit the official doctrine and to mobilize Iranians for elections and rallies across the country. Since the head of the Radio and Television Organization is directly appointed by the Leader, in recent years, it has reflected the interests of the conservative wing of the regime. The strong bias of state television was clearly demonstrated during the presidency of Mohammad Khatami (1997–2005) and the coverage of the 2009 presidential election and Green Movement, when news broadcasts either ignored or misrepresented many of the raging political debates.

In recent years, as satellite television has grown and the dishes have become less expensive, anti-regime Persian language programming from abroad and foreign news outlets (CNN and BBC) provide greater diversity for the viewing public. In response, the state has repeatedly tried to jam channels and outlaw private use of satellite dishes, although the law has not been applied consistently. The dishes can be seen on rooftops in major cities and even small towns.

The printed press has been the most diverse and fascinating form of media in postrevolutionary Iran. In the first decade of the revolution, newspapers and journals became increasingly uniform in their coverage. But as the regime began to feel more consolidated and elite competition became more open after the passing away of Khomeini, a growing number of independent newspapers and magazines appeared on the scene. These newspapers and magazines reflected specific schools of thought and critical views from intellectuals on the right and left, as well as the more republican and the more authoritarian wings of the regime. A flourishing nonstate press and burgeoning investigative journalism constituted the backbone of Khatami's surprising election victory in 1997 and underpinned the enormous popularity of the reformist movement in his first term. The critics of the government (many of whom were part of the revolutionary establishment) and the many young journalists writing critical articles presented a new political language of accountability, civil society, and participation to the educated, urban, and young population of Iran. In doing so, these newspapers both reflected and produced deep cleavages among the ruling establishment.

During the authoritarian backlash against the reformist movement since 2000, the conservative-controlled Judiciary has clamped down on the most vibrant aspects of this press. Currently, journalists have turned to the Internet to distribute their reports and publish their commentaries in online newspapers or in the mushrooming collection of blogs and even Facebook pages. Today, Persian is one of the most widely used languages on the Internet and in the "blogosphere." Politicians, political dissidents, journalists, poets, students, and others inside and outside of Iran use blogging as a means to do everything from expressing opinions to documenting events and human-rights violations. The Internet has been one of the battlegrounds between pro-Ahmadinejad and pro-Green Movement activists since the 2009 presidential election. Today, journalists and newspaper editors, some of whom have been imprisoned or physically attacked, have become the new political heroes of many of the youth.

The Family and Social Groups

Political socialization takes place in the private sphere as well as in the public sphere. This is particularly the case in more authoritarian contexts. In Iran, both under the monarchy and the Islamic Republic, the home has been a relatively free place to discuss politics by recounting the unofficial history of the country or debate current events with family members and friends. While patriarchy (and sometimes matriarchy) does prohibit unfettered debate in the family setting, the memory of key political episodes—such as the 1953 coup or the events leading up to the overthrow of the Shah in 1979—is transmitted in these settings. By retelling stories from earlier eras or speculating about the conspiracies behind them, older family members indoctrinate the family's younger generation in a political memory and culture that are at variance with the official story, as contained in school textbooks and official rhetoric.

As greater numbers of Iranians complete high school and attend universities, the family dynamic appears to have changed. Young men and women now have a certain authority, as they are the first generation in their families to graduate from high school and university. They interpret politics for their relatives by explaining differences between political factions and bringing campus politics into their homes. Over the last ten years, greater political freedoms, or at least a less fearful setting, allows for many of these types of discussions to take place while one waits for oven-fresh bread outside the local bakery, peruses headlines at the newspaper kiosk, or shares a collective taxi with total strangers. These ritualistic acts of resistance prevent the state from fully dominating politics, but at the same time, they do not challenge regime power.

In short, political socialization under the Islamic Republic has shifted from being solely the domain of the state to one that is contested by counterelite and popular voices. The early revolutionary message of unity and mobilization in the name of revolutionary Islam once taught in school textbooks and recounted in Friday sermons and newspaper pages has given way to greater pluralism and contestation, intriguingly by many of the same people who read those school texts and wrote those newspaper articles in the 1980s. The challenge today for the regime is either to accommodate and represent pluralistic discourse or to impose the single voice of unity. Their decision and capacity in this regard will determine whether Iran will move toward more democratic politics or authoritarianism.

RECRUITING THE POLITICAL ELITE

What kinds of people govern Iran? Under the Shah, the small class of educated and secular Iranians who could demonstrate personal loyalty to the monarch gained access to political offices. Many of the ministers came from landowning families and attended Western high schools and universities.[30] The Shah, however, carefully monitored his court to prevent the rise of potential competitors with strong personalities or independent bases of support. This policy produced a highly dependent inner circle whose members were unwilling to challenge the Shah and preferred to censor information and opinions in order not to offend His Imperial Majesty. This passive and dependent nature of the political elite prevented the Shah from acting in a timely and decisive manner as the revolts and political challenges of 1977 and 1978 snowballed into the revolution.[31]

Under the Islamic Republic, personalism also plays an important role, but in a broader sense. In the early years, political elites came from various backgrounds, but their most fundamental credentials were their revolutionary pedigrees. Those who could point to active participation in the Islamic revolution, and in particular the various groups associated with Khomeini and his students, leveraged this past experience into positions in ministries, the parastatal economic foundations, the IRGC, and various other institutions with access to state revenue. Thus, the new political elite that came to power immediately after the revolution was younger and less cosmopolitan; they were from more middle-class and lower-middle-class backgrounds, often hailing from the provinces rather than the capital.

In general, the state has expanded since the revolution. From 1976 to 1986, the number of employees in the public sector more than doubled, reaching more than 30 percent of all employed Iranians. In the 1980s, four-fifths of all new jobs created were in the public sector.[32] This expansion was due to a number of reasons, including the requisites of the war effort, the state-led economic development program, and the revolutionary agenda to restructure and Islamicize society from above.

Initially, the clergy who were recruited into the state were trained in the seminaries in Najaf and Qom, where Khomeini and his students taught during the 1960s and 1970s. The Fayziyeh Seminary in Qom was the principal seminary producing these new judges and ministers. Over time, the Haqqani Seminary in Qom has grown in importance, partially because many of its alumni include staunch conservatives who have dominated the Judiciary, the Council of Guardians, and the security apparatus. The head of the seminary, Ayatollah Mohammad-Taqi Mesbah Yazdi, is the leading hard-line cleric of the Islamic Republic, to the point where he advocates abolishing its republican components. The graduates of this seminary, known as the Haqqani circle, included important figures in the conservative backlash against Khatami's attempts to institutionalize political reform. Since then, it has cooperated with hard-line elements in the IRGC to ensure that hard-line candidates win in elections, including Ahmadinejad—who regards Mesbah Yazdi as his spiritual mentor—in 2005 and 2009.

Nonclerical parliamentarians and ministers tend to emerge from educational and military institutions. Many have attended the new Islamic universities. In the 1990s, think tanks and research centers were important in recruiting and producing political elites. Many of the reformists who dominated the Sixth

Parliament and supported President Khatami were based in the Center for Strategic Studies. These younger members of the elite often are too young to have significant revolutionary credentials, but their studies in these universities and institutes give them technical know-how, intellectual credentials, and the social networks to gain access to various government and state institutions.

More recently, many of the new elite have come from the ranks of the IRGC and the Basij. The current president, Ahmadinejad, the mayor of Tehran, Mohammad-Baqer Qalibaf, and many of the ministers were military figures from these corps or worked for the research institutes connected to the IRGC. It is worth noting that the regular army, navy, and air force have not had much influence in politics. This growing militarization of politics is a new phenomenon in modern Iranian history. Unlike neighboring Pakistan, Turkey, and Iraq, which have had numerous military coups and governments headed by generals, the Iranian political establishment was overwhelmingly civilian throughout the twentieth century.

Kinship ties are commonly used to gain political and economic power. Many of the sons and brothers, and on some rare occasions, daughters and sisters, of government officials use their family ties to gain access to the state. Often, their contacts are used as means for rent-seeking (receiving subsidized hard currency or special import licenses, or securing subsidized loans) and personal enrichment. In addition, marriage is used as a powerful way to cement political alliances and create bonds between prominent families.

INTEREST ARTICULATION AND AGGREGATION

The mix of electoral politics and authoritarian powers generates multiple and competing forms of interest articulation and aggregation under the Islamic Republic. The most institutionalized forms are regular presidential, parliamentary, and local elections. The least institutionalized, but probably the most prevalent and effective, is the use of personalistic ties and patron-client relations. As a consequence, representation under the Islamic Republic is highly fragmented, fluid, and contentious, although not fully pluralistic, competitive, and democratic.

Noninstitutional Forms of Interest Articulation and Aggregation

The principal means of interest aggregation in contemporary Iran is clientelism and the forging of relationships between political figures and citizens through patron-client networks. Given the state's access to external sources of revenue from the world oil market, Iranian political figures have exchanged political loyalty and support for access to such resources as subsidies, hard currency, subcontracts, and secure government jobs. This system of patronage can take a very direct form, where parliamentarians, ministers, or bureaucrats dole out these resources to kin, schoolmates, and people from the same city or province. Special access to powerful figures in the office of the Leader, state-owned banks, and economic foundations benefit these clients, while ensuring their dependence, if not loyalty, to the political system that plays more of a distributive, rather than an extractive, role. Since patron-client relations are based on the goods that the patron provides the client, if the patron loses power, so do his clients.

In a less targeted manner, the Islamic Republic distributes large subsidies as a social welfare net and to ensure the loyalty of large portions of the population. Food and medicine are subsidized at an annual rate of about $2 billion and particularly to benefit the urban poor. By contrast, the annual $10 billion energy subsidy for gasoline and electricity is quite regressive because it benefits the middle and upper classes that own automobiles, homes, and electrical equipment. This form of political aggregation undermines pretensions of institutional impartiality and meritocracy that are essential principles behind equal citizenship and participation.

Institutionalized Forms of Interest Articulation and Aggregation: Voting

Elections are regularized political events, but they do not provide complete pluralism nor necessarily entail a shift in power and policies, since the powers of the representative institutions are quite limited. Elections tend to function more as an act and measurement of regime legitimacy, and only secondarily as a means for citizens to express their interests by selecting among diverse sets of candidates with specified policy positions. Thus, except for the most recent elections, there has been more discussion about election turnout than candidates. The turnout in the ten presidential and eight parliamentary elections averaged about 60 percent (see again Figure 12.4).

The 1997, 2005, and 2009 presidential elections, however, indicated that under certain conditions, elections can be moments of interest articulation and offer information regarding the preferences of citizens. In 1997, it was quite clear that the regime candidate was Ali-Akbar Nateq Nuri, the sitting speaker of the Parliament and close confidant of the Leader. However, thanks in part to the burgeoning civil society and his low government profile, Mohammad Khatami, as "the outsider" and "nonregime" candidate, swept to victory with a surprising 70 percent of the vote. In somewhat similar fashion, although with a very different political agenda and significance, Mahmoud Ahmadinejad surprised many pundits by defeating Ali-Akbar Hashemi Rafsanjani, who has been one of the cornerstones of the Islamic Republic since its establishment. These surprising outcomes indicate that in spite of the limited nature of elections in the Islamic Republic, voters are able to express their views, and these preferences can matter even when they go against the wishes of the ruling establishment or the expectations of political experts. The most recent elections exposed the divisions with the political establishment, clerics, and society at large. Rather than processing these disputes through political forums and debates, the Leader and the neoconservatives turned the matter into a security issue and sought to silence the interests and views of a significant portion of society and even the regime's political establishment.

Given the weakness of party organizations, as mentioned earlier, political parties play no major role. The factions that contend for power and influence in Iran have not formed a clearly defined party system that would act as a mechanism for representing and aggregating the interests of constituents. Parties and political associations, such as the Society of Combatant Clergy or the Islamic Iran Participation Front, are groupings of members of the political elite that become active during elections. Yet until now, they have been unable to maintain party discipline with direct and formalized links to the citizenry. The inchoate structure of the popular protests following the 2009 elections testifies to the weakness of political parties.

Institutional Groups and Professional Organizations

While political parties are less developed, groups based in state organizations have a more corporate identity and a greater ability to shape policy, in much the same manner as controlled interest-group systems. The IRGC and the volunteer mobilization corps (Basij), consisting of 120,000 and 90,000 men, respectively,[33] are two of the most prominent arms of the state. They directly represent the state's interests in various policy-making areas, although they were established to mobilize support for the regime. These ostensibly military and security forces also play a role in the economy through their business subsidiaries, which are involved in large-scale construction projects as well as allegedly importing consumer goods. Since the 2003 local council elections, the IRCG and Basij have taken a more visible role in politics. A number of their high-ranking figures have run for local offices, Parliament, and the presidency. Finally, since they are in direct communication with the Leader, they have the ability to influence policy and coordinate actions beyond the oversight of the parliament.

Iran does have a host of associations representing the interests of labor, business, professional groups, and industrial sectors. However, the House of Labor or the Iranian Chamber of Commerce, Industries, and Mines, and other such organizations, operate more as a means for state officials to manage these corporate entities rather than as vehicles to represent specific interest and shape policymaking. Only in very recent elections have professional organizations endorsed different candidates, which may signal the emergence of an independent role for these corporate groups in political competition.

In the course of the struggle against the Shah and in the years following his overthrow, neighborhood councils and guild associations sprang up all over the country as grassroots initiatives to address ordinary citizens' needs during the revolution and the war years. Over time, they have become integrated into the patron-client system, and today, they are either mere appendages of state officials or means for the state to penetrate society.[34] Hence, there is no clear separation between interest groups and government officials. Moreover, since the revolution, the government has encouraged workers, merchants, and students to establish Islamic associations in universities, factories, and guilds as the principal means of aggregating the interests of these groups.

Nonetheless, in the 1990s and especially during the relatively less repressive administration of President Khatami, a large number of genuinely autonomous associations representing strata of society that had been largely sidelined by the revolutionary regime emerged. For instance, various women's organizations of both secular and reformist Islamist persuasion formed and started initiatives seeking to change discriminatory laws, provide services, and raise general consciousness regarding women's issues. Most notable is the 2003 Nobel Peace Prize winner, **Shirin Ebadi**. She was the first woman to become a judge under the Shah, but she lost her job when women were barred from that position following the revolution. Ebadi was active in a host of legal organizations championing and defending the rights of women, children, and political dissidents. Simultaneously, students and secular intellectuals took advantage of these opportunities to establish or reactivate associations and publications that were independently minded and represented alternative visions of politics. These organizations have been the backbone of the Green Movement as well as the target of repression by conservatives in the state apparatus.

Nonassociational Social Groups

Many social strata in Iran exist without independent associations aggregating and representing their interests. Among the historically and politically important social groups without corporate representation, it is worth mentioning the bazaari merchants. Among the more recent social groups, war veterans and the relatives of those killed in the war (referred to as "martyrs") stand out as well.

Bazaari merchants based in the historic covered bazaars of Iran, ranging from retailers and brokers to wholesalers and even international traders, have played a central role in various political episodes from the Constitutional Revolution (1905–1911) to the Oil Nationalization Movement (1951–1953) to the Islamic Revolution. Even though important differences exist among bazaaris in terms of socioeconomic status, political persuasion, and position in the international and national economies, they have a sense of solidarity because of the well-defined and vibrant physical space of the bazaar, which ensures socially embedded and crosscutting relations. Their political significance is enhanced both by their economic power and their close relationship with the ulema. Since the revolution, bazaari economic interests have been threatened by the state's domination of the economy, while the homogeneity of bazaari interests has been undermined by key pro-Khomeini bazaari families being coopted by the new regime.[35]

War veterans, the families of the martyrs, and those disabled in the Iran–Iraq war make up a large and politically important social group. They are ostensibly represented by various organizations and political groups, such as the Martyr's Foundation, the Foundation of the Disinherited, the Society of the Devotees of the Islamic Republic, and the Headquarters of the POWs. But these organizations have proved unable to address adequately the everyday demands of many of their constituents, and they have moved away from their original mandate of providing services to war veterans and their families. The state also supports this important constituency by setting up all kinds of affirmative action schemes (ranging from easier access to higher education to priority in flight reservations) and subsidizing consumer goods for veterans and relatives of both veterans and "martyrs" in order to enhance their socioeconomic standing. Yet these measures have not always worked adequately both to address the needs of this social group and to suppress challenges. Some prominent war veterans and former members of the IRGC have aligned themselves with the reformist faction, calling for greater political participation and freedoms. Others have accused the regime of turning its back on the wartime principles of self-sacrifice and justice. For much of the postwar era, there have been growing complaints by some war veterans that the memory of the war and respect for the sacrifices of the war generation have faded, while the veterans and relatives of the martyrs have not been sufficiently provided for. This position was given voice by some ultra-conservative newspapers, certain filmmakers engaged in producing war films, and outspoken figures of a group called Ansar-e Hezbollah (Partisans of the Party of God), who took it upon themselves to combat moral, political, and economic corruption.

Demonstrations and Public Protests

Given the closed nature of institutional interest representation and aggregation, many social groups and political tendencies have turned to civil disobedience to express their grievances. The relatively fresh memory of the demonstrations and strikes that constituted the revolution of 1978 and 1979 are a model for workers, students, activist women, and the urban poor to use public collective action to make their claims. Throughout the 1990s, industrial workers, for instance, protested against privatization policies, the selling of state-owned factories, and nonpayment of their wages. One high-profile tactic has workers blocking the main expressway connecting Tehran to the industrial satellite city of Karaj. On several occasions, these protesters blocked the selling of state-owned factories to private business interests they suspected of planning to lay off workers. Teachers, bus drivers, sugar-cane workers, and government pensioners in recent years have protested in front of Parliament to draw attention to their inadequate income. Women's groups also increasingly organize protests against the male bias enshrined in the Constitution. Ethnic political groups, especially Kurdish and Arab activists on the Iran–Iraq border, have vocally called for greater distribution of wealth and local authority in their provinces.

The most dramatic protests, however, have been based in the universities and spearheaded by students. During the summers of 1999, 2003, and 2009, student organizations staged sit-ins and demonstrations to protest against authoritarian measures by the regime. In the first case, they challenged the closure of a prominent reformist newspaper, and in the second case, the sentencing of an outspoken intellectual who had questioned clerical rule. These protests were originally based in Tehran University, but they spread to other cities and university campuses and persisted for several days. With little support or protection from reformist parties and other social groups (such as workers, bazaaris, and teachers), the volunteer forces (Basij) and police violently suppressed the demonstrators and prevented the movement from escalating. Yet in the aftermath of the 2009 elections, students and student organizations again were critical in coordinating actions and turning universities into sites of political dissent.

Although these and other events demonstrate that Iranian society is not completely passive in the face of government policies, the inability of these disparate groups to unite or coordinate their localized organizational capabilities is an indication of the overwhelming social atomization in contemporary Iran. Given the pervasive use of patron-client relations and lack of trust among Iranians, collective action and alliance-building is particularly difficult. Moreover, these noninstitutional forms of politics reflect the lack of efficacy of institutional politics and the belief in the part of many Iranians that their political voice cannot be heard unless it is in this form.

POLICY FORMULATION

In the Islamic Republic of Iran, state policy is set by a number of bodies, some of them explicitly mentioned in the Constitution, some not. Given the mixed nature of the political system, overlaps, duplications, and even contradictions abound, and it is not rare for different policymaking bodies to work at cross-purposes.

State Institutions Mentioned in the Constitution

As befits a theocracy in which, at least in theory, no state policy may contradict Islam, those who determine what does and does not contradict Islam have a preponderant voice in setting policy. In the Islamic Republic, this means first and foremost the Leader. The first Leader, Ruhollah Khomeini, on numerous occasions used his authority to determine state policy by issuing religious edicts (*fatwas*). On a few occasions, these edicts broke with established religious tradition, which is not astonishing given the charismatic nature of his leadership.[36] One of the earliest examples was his ruling on caviar. According to Shiite (and Jewish) dietary laws, a fish can be eaten only if it has scales. The sturgeon, however, has no scales, and traditionally, its meat and by extension its roe (caviar) were not deemed permissible. But caviar is one of Iran's main exports, and so the matter was revisited. A specially appointed state commission concluded that the sturgeon does indeed have scales, but that they are of a peculiar shape. Taking note of this finding, in 1983, Khomeini issued a *fatwa* declaring that caviar could be eaten. In 1988, he broke with other time-honored legal traditions by authorizing the playing of chess, provided no bets were made on the outcome, betting and gambling being forbidden in Islam. He also liberalized the early republic's stifling cultural life by relaxing the rules pertaining to music and television programming.[37]

Khomeini's interventions in the state's policy-making were often made necessary by continued deadlock between Parliament and the Council of Guardians, as mentioned earlier. To avoid paralysis, in 1988, Khomeini amended his doctrine of *velayat-e faqih*, guardianship of the jurisprudent, by issuing an edict that gave the state, as embodied by its Leader, authority to override religious law when that is expedient. This "absolute dominion of the jurisprudent" (*velayat-e motlaqeh-ye faqih*), he stated, was the "most important of divine commandments and has priority over all derivative divine commandments . . . even over prayer, fasting, and the pilgrimage to Mecca."[38] This reinterpretation of the theocratic principle was enshrined in the 1989 revised Constitution.

Needless to say, most traditional Muslims and most members of the ulema were horrified by this subordination of religion to reason of state. The whole purpose of an Islamic state was the exact opposite. Moreover, no person other than Khomeini could conceivably get away with disregarding religion when it was expedient for the state to do so. As a result, shortly before his death, Khomeini invested the newly established Expediency Council with the authority to advise the Leader on invoking the absolute authority. As president (1981–1989), Khamenei had been a member of the conservative faction, but as Leader he initially tried to give the impression of remaining above the fray. However, with the onset of the Khatami presidency in 1997, he abandoned all pretense of neutrality and became the de facto leader of the conservatives who did their best to stymie the reformist zeal of the elected officials.

The Expediency Council is the institution that decides the most vital policies of the nation. For instance, in Iran's international negotiations about its nuclear program, the top Iranian negotiator, Hasan Rowhani, did not come from the foreign ministry or the Atomic Energy Organization of Iran, but is an engineer-turned-cleric who was the secretary of the National Security Council and as such a member of the Expediency Council. Politically identified with Hashemi Rafsanjani, he resigned from his position as chief negotiator after the election of Mahmoud Ahmadinejad to the presidency in June 2005. With Ahmadinejad's election, the old establishment became apprehensive about the new president's ultraconservative and populist policies, policies that threaten not only the domestic status quo but also Iran's security.[39] And so, in 2005, the chairman of the Expediency Council since 1997, none other than Ali-Akbar

Hashemi Rafsanjani, extracted a letter from the Leader that granted the Expediency Council broad supervisory powers over all three branches of government. Despite the presidency's and Parliament's being dominated by conservatives since 2005, the combination of institutional checks and balances and various intrafactional disputes have limited the ability of Ahmadinejad and his supporters to make sweeping changes, although he has used his executive powers to direct state funds to key supporters.

In the course of the 1988 revision of the Constitution, a body formed some years earlier was added to the official institutional structure: the National Security Council, whose members include the heads of the three branches of government, top military commanders, the Foreign Minister, the Minister of Information (that is, intelligence), and a few other figures named by the Leader. It is the nation's highest policymaking body in matters of foreign and security policy, which, in the case of the Islamic Republic, includes the struggle against what is officially called "Western cultural aggression."

The Council of Guardians does not have a direct role in policymaking, but its six lay members are present in Parliament when it is in session and have at times attempted to work with sympathetic MPs to introduce legislation. As for Parliament itself, it has been largely emasculated as a policymaking body by the unelected bodies mentioned earlier. Legislative proposals come before it either from the cabinet or from a minimum of twenty-five MPs, and while successive Parliaments have tried to create frameworks for conducting economic policies and changing the penal and civil codes, much of their activity has been stymied by the Council of Guardians.

The executive branch of government and Parliament have had an impact on policies of setting the state budget, providing and regulating social and welfare services, and handling territorial administration, which includes redrawing provincial borders. Beginning in the mid-1980s, for instance, the MPs of the northwestern city of Ardabil campaigned for the creation of a new province around their city. Young men from Ardabil having died in disproportionate numbers in the Iran–Iraq war, the people of the city used the moral leverage that their sacrifices gave them to renew their demands with greater fervor after the war ended in 1988. All sorts of civic associations mobilized for the demand, which was expressed inside

Parliament by the MPs. In the end, the administration of President Hashemi Rafsanjani introduced a bill in Parliament providing for the new province. The bill was hotly debated, and it finally passed in a secret vote in early 1993.[40]

The extensive powers of the Leader and the existence of such unelected decision-making bodies as the Council of Guardians, the Expediency Council, and the National Security Council severely limit the policymaking role of the elected officials: the president, the individual cabinet members named by him and approved by Parliament, and Parliament itself. Popular sovereignty is thus severely undermined.

State Institutions Not Mentioned in the Constitution

The role of elected officials is further limited by councils that are not mentioned expressly in the Constitution and that were established for the express purpose of formulating state policy in a particular field. The most prominent of these is the Supreme Council for the Cultural Revolution, which was set up by order of Khomeini in 1986 to perpetuate the policies unleashed during the Cultural Revolution of the early 1980s that purged universities of leftists and secularists. Its tasks include determining not only state policies in the realms of culture, education, and research, but also "the spread and reinforcement of the influence of Islamic culture in all areas of society." Its supremacy over Parliament is seen from the fact that the Council of Guardians has at times vetoed legislation on the grounds that it contradicted policies determined by the Supreme Council for the Cultural Revolution, the latter having the approval of the Leader.

Power Centers and the Difficulty of Policy Coordination

Given the existence of multiple power centers, policies are often not coordinated, as some state institutions make and implement their own policies independently of the relevant ministries. This includes the Judiciary, which does not limit itself to implementing the law but in fact takes it into its own hands, and the Revolutionary Guards, who wage their own struggle against dissent and pursue a foreign policy independent of that of the foreign ministry and even the National Security Council.

The impact of these inconsistencies became particularly apparent under President Khatami, when the dispute between reformists and conservatives added an ideological dimension to the diffuse, ill-defined, and overlapping competencies of many state bodies. A few examples will illustrate this.

Under Khatami, the Ministry of Culture, which controls censorship and issues licenses for newspapers and journals, adopted more liberal policies, inaugurating a period of press freedom and diversity. But the Judiciary, headed by a conservative ally of the Leader, used its powers to close down newspapers and indict and jail reformist journalists and editors who had incurred the displeasure of conservatives. For every newspaper that was closed down, the Ministry of Culture would issue a new license and the newspaper would appear under a new name.[41] But by 2000, the most critical voices had been silenced by the Judiciary and its allies in the armed forces.

Another example comes from the security apparatus. In late 1998, six months after the commander of the Revolutionary Guards had threatened violence against opponents of the regime, a number of opposition politicians, journalists, and writers were killed in what became known as the "chain murders." Khatami insisted on an investigation and persuaded Khamenei to give his consent. Soon, it became clear that members of the Ministry of Information had carried out the murders. This led to a purge in the ministry, which operates under the authority of the president and of Parliament.[42] While the Ministry of Information subsequently became more tolerant of dissent and respectful of the law, the Revolutionary Guards and the Judiciary set up their own parallel intelligence organizations, replete with prosecutors and prisons, to pursue the conservatives' agenda of suppressing dissent.[43]

A final example is from foreign policy. Beginning at the end of the 1980s, a number of Foreign Ministry officials began calling for a policy that would privilege Iran's national interest in light of *realpolitik* rather than the pursuit of worldwide revolution. Tirelessly arguing their case and demonstrating the cost for Iran of remaining on the margins of world diplomacy, they managed to inflect foreign policy with a number of countries, except the United States and Israel. But while government officials engaged in diplomacy denied that Iran meddled in the internal affairs of other countries, various state or parastatal institutions pursued separate activist foreign-policy agendas.

Thus, when in 1998 the Ministry of Foreign Affairs reached an agreement with Britain to the effect that Iran would do nothing to carry out the death penalty imposed by Khomeini in 1988 on British author Salman Rushdie, the parastatal Second of Khordad Foundation immediately increased the $2 million bounty it had put on the author's head in 1989. These inconsistencies have seriously damaged Iran's credibility on the international scene, as Iranian negotiators seem unable to deliver on their commitments.

The result of the multiplicity of policymaking bodies is frequent incoherence and sometimes paralysis. On a positive note, this incoherence has prevented the system from becoming totalitarian, as the overlapping spheres of activity of various state institutions have made centralized control of public life well nigh impossible.

Economic Policymaking

One of the most contentious topics in the postrevolutionary era is economic policymaking. From the very outset, the founders of the Islamic Republic and the new elite in the ministries and parastatal organizations had fundamentally differing views on the best approach to foster economic development. Those who favored a more state-centered approach to development initially dominated policymaking through the Parliament, ministries, and such institutions as the Construction Jihad. In the 1980s, the state played a critical role in rationing hard currency, setting prices for consumer goods, and using the public banking system to distribute loans to key sectors of the economy. The logic of state control found support at the time in large part due to the requirements of war, the political necessity of redistributing the assets of the numerous industrialists who had been forced into exile, and the fact that international investment had come to a standstill.

A liberal approach to development that placed greater emphasis on the private sector and market mechanisms began to dominate policymaking circles in the late 1980s. This was encouraged by the conclusion of the Iran–Iraq war and the global rise of neoliberal development agendas in the wake of the Soviet Union's demise. The major impetus to redirect economic policies, however, was the poor performance of the economy (see Figure 12.7 and discussion later in this chapter). Thus, both the Rafsanjani and Khatami administrations tried to restructure Iran's economy by selling state-owned assets, lifting trade restrictions, and encouraging private and foreign investment. These policy initiatives had mixed results. Iran liberalized its trade regime, with ministries and procurement boards now playing a less pronounced role. Furthermore, private banks and industries take advantage of incentives to export goods. Nonetheless, the deregulation of the economy also led to hardship and has therefore faced opposition. On the one hand, many state employees and those who rely on state subsidies have been hurt by economic insecurity and inflation. On the other hand, the government's attempt to reform the economy has challenged the economic powers and vested interests of the large economic foundations that control large portions of Iran's commercial, industrial, and agricultural sectors, and that are largely unaccountable to the Parliament, the central bank, and development policymaking bodies. Khatami's and the reformists' attempt to introduce greater transparency and competition into the economy was limited by the economic foundations' and parastatal organizations' autonomous and privileged access to resources and markets. Thus, any attempt to reform the economy, boost productivity, or direct investment toward exports must address the inequality and inconsistencies of the parallel economy controlled by these organizations.

Under Ahmadinejad, economic policymaking has combined populist rhetoric of redistribution and various forms of highly publicized handouts with the simultaneous privatizing of state firms and functions.[44] While the language of social justice and attacking "the corrupt" aimed at shoring up a social base of support, privatization of manufacturing and allocating construction contracts aimed at rewarding Ahmadinejad's key political allies. For instance, under Ahmadinejad, key contracts in the oil and gas sector and telecommunications were given to companies affiliated with the IRGC. While for decades there has been domestic debate and international pressure from lending agencies such as the IMF and World Bank for Iran to reduce and remove its generous energy and consumer subsidies, ironically, it was Ahmadinejad in 2010 who took the first concrete steps in removing subsidies that act as a social welfare net. Thus, these IMF-lauded policies threaten to exacerbate inequalities and create a new class of oligarchs, as was the case in Russia. Moreover, the transformation of the subsidy system may become a highly contentious issue for the many Iranians from middle and working class

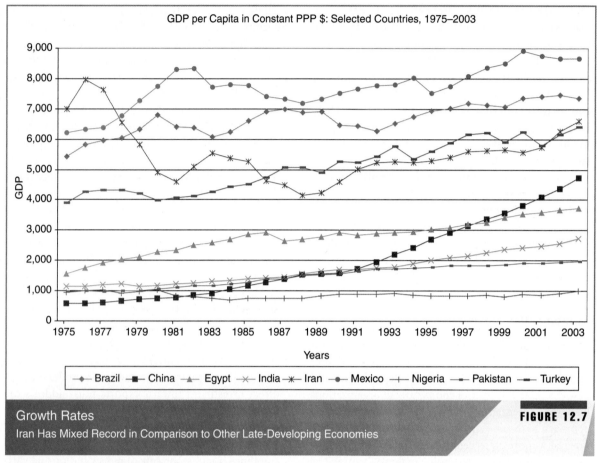

GDP per Capita in Constant PPP $: Selected Countries, 1975–2003

Legend: Brazil — China — Egypt — India — Iran — Mexico — Nigeria — Pakistan — Turkey

Growth Rates

Iran Has Mixed Record in Comparison to Other Late-Developing Economies

FIGURE 12.7

Source: Based on data from Massoud Karshenas and Hassan Hakimian, "Oil, Economic Diversification, and the Democratic Process in Iran," *Iranian Studies* 38, no. 1 (March 2005): 67–90.

backgrounds who survive economically thanks to the robust welfare system provided by the regime.

POLICY OUTCOMES

Spreading Progress and Prosperity

The chief complaint of the revolutionaries had been that the Shah's policies failed to benefit the majority of Iranians. While succeeding administrations in the Islamic Republic have been on the whole indifferent to the interests of the educated upper-middle class, they have tried to adopt policies that will improve the lot of the poor.

The state educational system is astonishingly good, given the limitations imposed by the political system. Iranian students regularly win medals at international science olympiads, and literacy rates have continued rising, reaching 89 percent for men and 80 percent for women by 2006, while the gap between sexes has narrowed from 1976 levels, when 59 percent

of men were literate compared to only 35 percent of women.[45]

After pronatalist policies in the 1980s, the government realized that birth rates had to be brought down, and it inaugurated a multifaceted policy of facilitating birth control. All forms of contraception are widely distributed and subsidized both in cities and in villages, everywhere clinics offer free sterilization to men and women, and the state actively encourages couples to have "only two children, be they boys or girls." All over Iran, couples do indeed have fewer children than their parents' generation. But for the foreseeable future, Iran's population will keep rising, as the very numerous Iranians born in the 1980s are beginning to have children of their own. The current growth rate of the Iranian population is approximately 1 percent, one of the lowest in the Middle East.

Health care is another area of considerable progress. Small clinics staffed by paramedics serve many villages, and there is no shortage of physicians. While the quality of medical care may not always be very high, it has astutely emphasized prevention and its availability to the general population is respectable even when compared with rich Western countries. These rural social and economic development programs are successful partly because they are spearheaded by the local communities rather than by experts from distant urban areas who typically are unaware of the local needs or social and cultural conditions.[46]

Much effort has gone into improvements in the countryside. Paved roads now connect all towns and many villages, and many villages have clean water and electricity. In spite of the state's efforts to create a welfare state financed by oil income, most Iranians struggle to make ends meet. To some extent, this is because the middle class has grown tremendously. People whose parents were illiterate and poor peasants now aspire to a middle-class lifestyle; they expect to eat meat every day, send their children to good schools, and have decent housing. Table 12.2 compares some basic human development indicators for Iran for 2007 with those of a few comparable countries.[47]

The provision of basic services to the general population has been quite successful. Obviously, more than three decades of steady oil income have made a difference. In many ways, the indicators for Iran are closer to those of Turkey than to those of Egypt or Pakistan. However, many Iranians are unwilling to credit the government for this, and impute it to the natural development of a country with a large oil income. It is often argued that with better planning, more competent management, and an acceptance of Saddam Hussein's offer to end the Iran–Iraq war in 1982, the situation might be much better still. Moreover, as Figure 12.7 reveals, over the last three decades, Iran's overall macroeconomic performance has fallen behind the newly developing countries in Latin America or East Asia. The per capita growth rates have not kept pace with the emerging economic powers of China and India.[48] In fact, Iran's growth indicators have been quite volatile, with a rather extended period of depression in the 1980s due to war, sanctions, high birth rates, and deficient industrial policies. Even with the gradual improvement in per capita GDP since the early 1990s, which was largely due to the rise in oil prices, unemployment remains the number-one worry for young people, and the growth rate of the economy is not nearly enough to absorb the growing population. In fact, youth unemployment increased from 14.8 percent in 1996 to 27.5 percent in 2001.[49]

Islamicization of Society

Another motivation of much policymaking is the desire to roll back secularism and spread Islamic moral values among the population. Since the early 1980s, alcohol consumption is banned except for the

		TABLE 12.2
Iran Compared: Iranian Social Conditions Compared to Other Developing Nations		

Country	Population 2007	Annual Population Growth 2005–2010 (%)	Life Expectancy 2007 (years)	Percentage of Population Not Using an Improved Water Source (%)	Literacy/ Men Aged 15 and Above (%)	Literacy/ Women Aged 15 and Above (%)	GDP/ PPP* $
Iran	72.4 million	1.3	71.2	6	87.3	77.2	10,955
Turkey	73.0 million	1.2	71.7	3	96.2	81.3	12,955
Egypt	80.1 million	1.9	69.9	2	74.6	57.8	5,349
Pakistan	173.2 million	2.3	66.2	10	67.7	39.6	2,496
India	1.16 billion	1.4	63.4	11	76.9	54.5	2,753
China	1.32 billion	0.7	72.9	12	96.5	90.0	5,383
Mexico	107.5 million	1.4	76	5	94.5	91.4	14,104
Nigeria	147.7 million	2.4	47.7	53	80.1	64.1	1,969

*PPP: purchasing power parity

Source: UNDP *Human Development Report*, 2009.

non-Muslim minorities, veiling is enforced in public spaces, the state is in theory committed to minimizing contact between unrelated men and women, the religious content of education is vastly expanded, and gruesome physical punishments chastise adulterers, homosexuals, and other offenders of religious morality.[50] Divine law, as interpreted by the state, also allows capital punishment. In 2008, the number of death penalties carried out in Iran (at least 346) was second only to China (at least 1,718), and more than in the United States (at least 111) and Saudi Arabia (at least 102), which were the next two highest practitioners of the death penalty.[51]

Outwardly, the Islamicization of society has been a success. Women cover their hair in public, people are in general more familiar with religious doctrine than before the revolution, the country has more mosques, Friday congregational prayers are routine in towns and cities, and all flights of Iran Air (the national airline) begin with a prayer. Even the best hotels serve no alcohol, even to foreign guests. Underneath the surface, however, the situation is more complicated. Prostitution is rife, driven by poverty. Over 2 million Iranians are drug addicts. Bootlegging flourishes, often with the connivance of the forces of order, who get a cut. As education has become longer and the marriage age has gone up, young people are much more likely to have premarital sex than their parents' generation, at least in Tehran. Corruption operates at almost all levels, from the petty official who will do his job only if he is paid a bribe to the relatives of the top leaders who have enriched themselves by controlling economic life.

All of this should not be construed to mean that Iranians have become irreligious. But religious practice has become more private, as the influence of clerics over religious life has declined. One study, comparing data gathered in 1975 and in 2001, demonstrates that while levels of personal religiosity (such as frequency of prayer) have remained relatively constant, participation in organized religion (such as attendance of congregational Friday prayers) has declined, reflecting a growing ambivalence toward state-sponsored public religious practices.[52]

Iranian Islam has always contained an anticlerical strain, as believers have always criticized clerics for their greed and hypocrisy. The ulema's assumption of power in the Islamic Republic has given a new fillip to this tendency. Taxi drivers are known not to stop for clerics,

many of whom have taken to wearing civilian clothes in public. Foreign observers are often astonished by how few turbaned clerics one sees in the streets of Tehran.

The rise of anticlericalism has led some of the more thoughtful members of the Shiite clergy to revisit the relations between "church" and state and to call for a separation of the two. They do so not because they advocate secularism, but out of concern for the collective reputation of the ulema. In the Muslim world, advocates of the separation of "church" and state had always been secularists. In Iran, for the first time, *religious* arguments are being made for that separation on the grounds that coercively imposed religion harms spirituality.[53] One may even wonder whether some of the pious people who voted for Mahmoud Ahmadinejad in the 2005 and 2009 presidential election did so in order to rebuke the ulema, many of whom—such as the 2005 losing candidate, Hashemi Rafsanjani—have joined the country's ruling class and are seen to have been corrupted by power. Moreover, during his tenure in office, Ahmadinejad has often confronted staunch criticism from the traditional clerical establishment for his sometimes unorthodox and messianic understanding of Shiism. This relationship reached an all-time low in the aftermath of the 2009 elections, when only one of the top clerics congratulated him on his "victory."

Gender Relations

One of the key reproaches that Islamists addressed to the Shah's regime before the revolution was that its promotion of Western lifestyles turned women into sex objects and was generally conducive to moral corruption and sexual depravity—hence the effort to reorder gender relations and place them on an authentic Islamic footing.

Looked at from a Western perspective, the legal status of women improved under the Pahlavi monarchy, whereas the majority of society remained more conservative than the laws governing it. After the revolution, much of the legislation that reduced the gender gap was repealed. According to the Islamic penal code introduced in 1981, the value of a woman's life is half that of a man's, in the sense that the law of the talion ("an eye for an eye") instituted by that code explicitly states that the blood-money of a woman is half of that of a man.[54] In practice, this means that if a man kills another man, the relatives of the victim can either ask for the execution of the murderer or accept a legally fixed amount of blood-money. But if a man kills a woman, her relatives can ask for the murderer's execution only if they pay half a man's blood-money. By the same token, in courts of law, the testimony of one man is worth that of two women. In some cases (such as adultery or murder), a woman's testimony does not count at all. A man can easily divorce his wife, whereas in principle a woman can initiate divorce proceedings only under exceptional circumstances; polygamy is recognized under the law. To travel abroad, a wife needs the formal permission of her husband, but the latter can leave the country as he pleases. The foreign wife of an Iranian man can easily acquire Iranian citizenship, whereas an Iranian woman cannot obtain Iranian citizenship for her foreign husband and her children from that husband.[55]

In addition to these legal restrictions on women's rights, the Islamic Republic has instituted all sorts of ad hoc discriminations. In the early years of the Islamic Republic, many fields of study, such as agronomy and mining engineering, were closed to female students at the universities on the assumption that they were too rough for women. Women's sports were severely restricted because the attire worn by female athletes is incompatible with veiling. This differential treatment of men and women is in stark violation of the International Convention on Civil and Political Rights, an international treaty that prohibits discrimination on religious and gender grounds. Iran acceded to the Convention in 1975 and remains a party after its regime changed. But from the point of view of theocracy, divine law obviously supersedes obligations incurred under international law.

Despite *and* because of these legal restrictions, Iranian women have continuously increased their participation in public life and their presence in the public sphere since strict Islamic law began to be enforced in the early 1980s.[56] At the same time, they have challenged the logic of patriarchy. There are a number of reasons for this seemingly paradoxical development. The widespread participation of women in the mass anti-Shah demonstrations of 1978 made it unlikely that their interest in public affairs would end once the revolution was over. During the Iran–Iraq war, millions of men were serving at the front, and this forced many women to do jobs hitherto performed by men. Many women became their families' main breadwinners. Furthermore, the aspiration to a middle-class existence awakened by the revolution, coupled with the slow growth of the economy, has meant that women increasingly supplement their husbands' income by joining the labor force. Given the strictly enforced rules on veiling and gender interaction in the public sphere, more traditional women feel more at ease entering the public sphere. In addition, more traditional men are less reluctant to let their wives, daughters, or sisters work outside the house. Restrictions that are offensive and limiting to nontraditional women have thus had a liberating effect on religiously observant women—and these constitute, after all, a majority of the female population.

The relative strength of the antitraditional attitude toward women's roles in society is reflected in the comparative results of the World Values Survey. For instance, while only 4 percent of Egyptians and 12 percent of Jordanians disagree with the statement that "marriage has become an outdated institution," 17 percent of surveyed Iranians agree.[57] A plurality of surveyed Iranians disagree with the statement that "women need to have children in order to feel satisfied," whereas only 12 percent of Egyptians and 9 percent of Jordanians disagree with it.[58] Finally, 40 percent of Iranians agreed with the statement that "a working mother can develop intimate relationships with her children just like a nonworking mother," a rate that is double that of surveyed Egyptians and Jordanians.[59] Thus, despite the regime's initial attempts to inculcate a traditional image and role for women in the family and society, Iranian men and women seem to hold a less narrow view of women.

The visitor to today's Iran encounters women everywhere; they staff government agencies, work in offices, sell goods in shops, and own and run businesses. Most dramatically, women now constitute over 60 percent of the student body at the universities, restrictions on what they can study having been gradually lifted throughout the 1990s to the point where none remain. In Persian literature, the traditional emphasis on poetry has given way to a boom in the writing of novels—and most novelists are women. In sports, a daughter of then-president Hashemi Rafsanjani took over women's sports in the early 1990s. Using her father's clout, she instituted a system whereby women compete under international rules and in normal athletic gear but at locations to which no men are admitted. This change led, incidentally, to many more women becoming coaches, referees, paramedics, and state sports officials.[60] Even veiling is now enforced less strictly, and the partial covering of the head that hard-liners call "mal-veiling" has spread. None other than Khomeini's granddaughter complained in an interview with a U.S. journalist about the state's intrusiveness in this regard.[61]

The widening gap between women's growing participation in public life and the legal system governing their society, and the many-voiced debates about this discrepancy, have had repercussions for Islam itself in Iran. Given the impossibility of criticizing any state of affairs from a secular perspective, feminists couch their arguments in Islamic terms. This has led to the emergence of "Islamic feminism," which is espoused both by truly observant Muslim women and by secular women who have no other way of articulating their demands. Given the continued religiosity of Iranians in general, Islamic feminism has been arguably more effective in raising the gender consciousness of the average woman than secular feminism would have been. These Islamic feminists are discreetly supported by a few sympathetic clerics who have helped them to contest discriminatory policies or laws by proposing ways to circumvent them or even suggesting alternative readings of the relevant scriptural passages and legal principles. Small gains have thus been made. Take the issue of divorce: According to Islamic law, marriage is a contract whose clauses have to be agreed on freely by both husband and wife. A woman has always had the right to ask that her marriage contract include a clause giving her the right to initiate divorce proceedings, but this clause had to be added on to the standard contract issued by the state. Very few bridegrooms consented to it. Since the early 1980s, however, the standard contract includes the clause, meaning that for the woman not to have the right to divorce, bride and bridegroom have to ask for its removal—to which, nowadays, few educated women consent. Since Ahmadinejad's ascendancy, there has been greater cooperation between secular and religious women's activists. This new solidarity may be a model for other opposition groups that have been divided by secular/religious disputes.

The greater success of women in higher education and the fact that the vast majority of Iranian drug addicts are men, coupled with the continued existence of domestic violence against women, have led Shirin Ebadi, the woman who more than any other personifies women's struggles and occasional successes, to quip that Iran has not a "women's question" but a "men's question."

Foreign Policy

Like the French, Russian, Chinese, and Cuban revolutionaries before them, Iran's Islamic revolutionaries saw themselves as the vanguard of a vast revolutionary wave that would also encompass other countries. According to the preamble of the Constitution of 1979, the role of the army and the IRGC is not limited to "securing the borders" of the country but includes "struggling to spread the rule of divine law in the world." Managing the inherent tension between an ideological commitment to help overthrow or weaken other governments on the one hand, and dealing with these governments on a daily basis on the other, poses a tremendous challenge.

Beginning in the early 1990s, "national interest" rather than "export of the revolution" dominated the foreign policy agenda. The best example is the discreet support Iran gave to Christian Armenia in its conflict with Muslim (and predominantly Shiite) Azerbaijan in the war that followed the breakup of the Soviet Union. But, as elsewhere in the world, there is little consensus as to what constitutes a nation's national interest. Many Iranians argue that the national interest demands the solidification of its ties with the rest of the Islamic world.

Ultimately, the foreign policy of the Islamic Republic is driven by a "Third Worldist" desire to escape the hegemony of the Western world. In the parlance of Iran's leaders, Western hegemony is referred to as "world arrogance." In its struggle against "world arrogance," Iran has sought alliances, and these can be conceptualized in terms of three concentric circles. The outermost circle consists of Third World nations, the middle circle is made up of Muslim countries and movements, and the innermost one is constituted by the Shiites in West and South Asia (Lebanon, Iraq, Bahrain, Afghanistan, and Pakistan).

Iran's regional foreign policy enjoys an economic dimension related to the movement of people and goods. Iran now trades a greater share of goods and services with countries in the Middle East and the rest of Asia than it previously did. Some of this is driven by the economic growth of East Asian economies, and it reflects the desire of Iranian leaders to participate in the world economy without being dependent on Western economies, as was the case under the Pahlavi monarchy. Additionally, Iran has forged formal and informal commercial relations with Dubai's entrepôt economy and the war economies of Iraq and Afghanistan. Alongside this trade, weapons, drugs, and humans are trafficked to, from, and through Iran. Conflicts in neighboring countries also resulted in Iran's becoming home to one of the largest refugee populations in the world. Finally, ordinary Iranian citizens have turned to new destinations for tourism and pilgrimage. Given tight visa restrictions for travel to Western Europe and North America, Dubai, Syria, Turkey, China, Malaysia, and Indonesia are now places where vacationers and pilgrims increasingly head, only to encounter Iranian businessmen and politicians on their voyages. Contemporary Iran's economy and society, hence, are far more integrated and engaged with regional dynamics than was the case during the Pahlavi era.

Many Third World countries greeted the revolution of 1979 with sympathy. However, the subsequent triumph of hard-line Islamists put a damper on pro-Iranian sympathies in non-Muslim nations. In recent years, President Ahmadinejad's defiance of the United States, which is perceived as an arrogant "bully" by many people in the Third World, has made Iran popular in a number of countries, especially in Latin American states with strong populist movements. Consequently, political cooperation and trade links with such countries such as Venezuela, Ecuador, Bolivia, and even Brazil have grown substantially.

Sunni Islamists, for their part, were divided over support for revolutionary Iran. As the *Shiite* nature of the *Islamic* Republic became ever more apparent, and as Khomeini refused to accept Saddam Hussein's offer to end the Iran–Iraq war, thus causing continued intra-Muslim bloodshed, most Sunni Islamists turned away from Iran. This estrangement was encouraged by Saudi Arabia, because its Wahhabi version of Sunni Islam is hostile to Shiism. With U.S. connivance, Saudi money helped create a Sunni *cordon sanitaire* around Iran to contain the spread of revolutionary Shiism in

such countries as Afghanistan and Pakistan; the Taliban operation in these two countries was an unanticipated consequence of that policy. Today, Iran maintains very few client movements among Sunnis, most notably the Palestinian Islamic Jihad.

This leaves Twelver Shiites as the only group among which Iranian efforts to spread the revolution have been somewhat successful. The founding of Lebanon's Hezbollah in the early 1980s was facilitated by Iran, and Iran continues to support the party and its social-welfare activities financially. Iran also sponsored formation in Iran of the Supreme Council for the Islamic Revolution of Iraq (SCIRI). The party, ironically, played a major role in Iraq after the ouster of the Saddam Hussein regime in the wake of the U.S. intervention of 2003, which resulted in Twelver Shiites becoming the politically dominant community in Iraq.

While increasing Iran's influence in the Middle East, Saddam Hussein's ouster also affected Iran's domestic politics. The consolidation of a semi-independent Kurdish state in northern Iraq has emboldened the Kurds of Iran, some of whom now regard it as an alternative to Iran that they would like to emulate or join. Likewise, the Arabs in Iran's Khuzistan province, until now loyal to the Iranian state because they are mostly Shiites, may become less certain of their national affiliation now that their kith and kin rule in Iraq. All of Iran's ethnic minorities straddle the country's borders with neighboring states (see again Figure 12.1). Until recently, this did not matter much, since they constituted minorities on the other side as well. But the events in Iraq and the breakup of the Soviet Union, which resulted in the emergence of an independent Azerbaijan that exerts a certain attraction on Azeris in Iran, has changed the situation. Iran's relations with its neighbors are now inextricably intertwined with its domestic ethnic politics.

In its relations with the West and the Soviet Bloc, the early Islamic Republic had as its motto "Neither East nor West." Iran was a U.S. ally under the Shah, but after the revolution, it joined the nonaligned movement. In practice, however, Iran's foreign policy in the first decade of the Islamic Republic, like that of many other Third World "nonaligned" countries, was far more anti-Western than anti-Soviet. In the case of the Islamic Republic, this stance reflected the revolutionaries' mistrust of a West that had supported the hated Shah, and the geographic proximity of the Soviet Union, whose occupation of neighboring Afghanistan in December 1979 was a constant reminder of the need for caution. Today the Islamic Republic maintains cordial relations with Russia, but Iran has not had diplomatic relations with the United States since the United States severed them in response to the seizure of U.S. diplomats as hostages in 1979. Iranians have paid a heavy price for their government's hostility to the West. In the last stages of the war against Iraq, most Western powers discreetly assisted the Iraqi side. The United States maintains an economic embargo on Iran. For instance, Iranian airlines have difficulty purchasing a sufficient number of modern passenger aircraft and adequate spare parts for the old ones, forcing them to keep flying old Russian planes or Boeing jets purchased before the revolution. As a result, "Iran's civil aviation sector suffers from one of the world's highest rates of accidents and incidents."[62]

After Khomeini's death, Presidents Hashemi Rafsanjani and Khatami tried to lessen Iran's diplomatic isolation. Relations with Arab countries, most of which had supported Iraq in the war, improved, and Iran made an effort to mend its ties with Europe and Japan. In the 1990s, the EU embarked on a policy of "critical dialogue" with Iran, which offered Iran concessions in exchange for improvement in the field of human rights. During the Khatami years, the policies of the government did indeed become less repressive, but given the overall control of unelected bodies, none of these liberalizing measures could be institutionalized.

In the aftermath of September 11, 2001, Iran found itself surrounded by U.S.-installed governments in Afghanistan and Iraq, and by U.S. troops and military bases in the countries to the north and south. This partially explains the anti-Western belligerence of the Ahmadinejad administration and its attempts to forge alliances with such countries as Russia and China.

The main issue confronting current Iranian diplomacy in its relations with the West is Iran's nuclear program. Since the days of the Shah, successive Iranian governments have declared that they are not interested in developing nuclear weapons. The official line of the government of the Islamic Republic is that all weapons of mass destruction are contrary to

Islamic ethics. Iran is a signatory of the Nuclear Nonproliferation Treaty, whose Article IV grants its signatories the "inalienable right" to "research, develop, produce, and utilize" nuclear technology for peaceful purposes. On that basis, the Iranian government embarked on a vast program to develop a self-sufficient nuclear industry by mastering the fuel cycle in which uranium is enriched to produce the fuel needed to power reactors. Western countries worry that this knowledge will allow Iran to produce highly enriched uranium or plutonium that could be used for nuclear weapons. What lends this worry a certain plausibility is Iran's development of long-distance missiles to which nuclear warheads could be fitted, and the fact that some nuclear facilities and experiments were kept secret. To allay Western fears, the Khatami administration agreed to negotiate with France, Germany, and the United Kingdom, while temporarily suspending the enrichment program and allowing international inspectors greater access to Iran's nuclear facilities. When these negotiations failed, Iran resumed the enrichment program in 2004. Given President Ahmadinejad's virulent verbal attacks on the West and on Israel, not to mention his questioning of the veracity of the holocaust, the Iranian government's claim that its nuclear program is of an entirely peaceful nature has met with widespread skepticism in the West. While inspectors of the **International Atomic Energy Agency** have regularly visited Iranian installations, the government's cooperation has not been deemed satisfactory either by the agency or by Western governments. The U.S. military commitments in Iraq and Afghanistan having made a preemptive attack on these installations impractical, the United States has pursued a policy of ever-tightening sanctions against Iran, both unilaterally and within the UN Security Council. Most recently, on June 9, 2010, the Security Council imposed a wide-reaching set of economic sanctions on Iran, which the Ahmadinejad administration immediately dismissed as irrelevant.

While the sanctions imposed on Iran have hurt Iranian businesses and made life more difficult for ordinary Iranians, the relative high price of oil has enabled the government to withstand the pressure. Foreign trade has been largely redirected to Asian countries, especially China, which in 2008 surpassed Germany as Iran's largest trade partner.

Western sanctions against Iran have thus had the paradoxical result of globalizing Iran's foreign policy ambitions by inducing it to find alternative trading partners.

CONCLUSION

Iranian politics in the twentieth century were tumultuous. The century started with a constitutionalist movement seeking to make a monarchy more accountable, and ended with a reformist movement striving to make a theocracy more republican. Between these two bookends, nationalist, religious, secular, and Marxist ideologies competed for followers, while social relations were restructured by processes associated with modernization. The Pahlavi monarchy promised to usher Iran into the modern industrial age, and because of both its successes and failures in doing so, the Shah was overthrown by a revolution that established a republic, but one that, unlike other revolutionary regimes, incorporated the clergy.

To manage the many objectives of the revolutionaries, the Islamic Republic has created a bewildering set of institutions and organizations, many of which compete with one another and occasionally work at cross-purposes. The regime has been in continuous conflict with the United States and some regional powers, such as Israel. It has provided social welfare to many of its citizens, which has resulted in outcomes that were unintended by the establishment, whose authority has been challenged by the increasingly educated, urban, and individualist society. By the admission of many of its own leaders, "the economy is sick" and "social pathologies" tarnish all layers of society. Unlike most other states in the region, which have almost completely muzzled dissent, contestation is pervasive and sometimes public even among state officials. The Islamic republic is an authoritarian regime that circumscribes participation and contestation, but because it was born out of a mass revolution has sustained a norm of public participation and engagement.

How has a regime that faces so many challenges and contradictions survived for over three decades, and what are the prospects for significant change? The irony is that the same institutions that have created contestation and allowed a degree of pluralism in Iran have also contributed to the regime's survival and

ability to withstand opposition.[63] The fragmented nature of the state enables differences to emerge and persist, but it is this very fragmentation that prevents the aggregation of interests and demands of a dynamic society. Thus, even though many of the founders of the Islamic Republic have defected from the regime or called for quite fundamental changes, they have not had the leverage to restructure the regime, which continues to enjoy a robust coercive apparatus, is financially solvent due to oil revenue, and enjoys the ideological sympathies of some citizens. Elite politics in Iran today is factional politics, not party politics encompassing debates over specific policies and specified platforms and visions of the future.

Meanwhile, a myriad of patron-client networks, in conjunction with a coercive apparatus and an individualist political culture, creates a fragmented state with divisions at all levels of society. Corporate and associational interests are ill-defined and undermined by personalism, and even ideologically similar groups often battle one another over access to assets. State-society relations as they are constituted now hinder coordination and trust between citizens and rulers as well as ultimately preventing the emergence of public deliberation and consensus-building.

The problems faced by the Islamic Republic have reopened the debate on the proper relation between religion and politics in Iran. Going farther than revisiting Islamic law, some reformist Muslims are questioning whether religious law is as central to Islam as, say, ethics or personal experience of transcendence. These reformers impute the current preoccupation with Islamic law in Muslim governance to the prominence of the ulema in Muslim society, pointing out that the ulema are, after all, merely legal scholars.

As we said at the beginning of this chapter, Iran was the first state in which Islamists were able to exercise political power. The problems they have faced, the forces they have unleashed, and the responses they have elicited from society could have profound implications for political Islam in the rest of the world. In practice, however, Iran's experience remains of limited relevance to Islamists elsewhere. The experience of both the rulers and the ruled in the Islamic Republic is shaped more by Iran's historical trajectory, socioeconomic conditions, cultural configurations, and geopolitical context than a static religious doctrine and uniform model of political Islam.

REVIEW QUESTIONS

- How do the republican components of Iran's institutional structure interact with the Islamic ones? Has their relative importance changed over time?

- How does Iran's prerevolutionary legacy of constitutionalism affect its current politics?

- *Theocracy* literally means "government by God." Since God does not rule directly, how is the idea of divine government implemented in practice in Iran?

- What is meant by elite politics being factional politics? What are these factions, what issues divide the elite, and how are their rivalries managed?

- Which social groups participated in the revolution of 1978 and 1979, and why? What factors led to the overthrow of the Pahlavi monarchy and support for Ayatollah Khomeini?

- The founders of the Islamic republic sought to create an Islamic society composed of Islamist citizens. How did they seek to do this, and how successful were they?

KEY TERMS

Ahmadinejad, Mahmoud
Assembly of Experts
Basij
Council of Guardians
Ebadi, Shirin
Expediency Council
Green Movement
Hashemi Rafsanjani, Ali-Akbar

International Atomic Energy Agency
Islamic Revolutionary Guard Corps (IRGC)
Islamists
Khamenei, Ali
Khatami, Mohammad
Khomeini, Ruhollah
Leader

Majles
Mossadegh, Mohammad
Mousavi, Mir-Hossein
multiple power centers
Pahlavi, Mohammad-Reza Shah
parastatal foundations
rentier state
shari'a

Sunnis
theocracy
Tudeh party
Twelver Shiism
ulema
velayat-e faqih

SUGGESTED READINGS

Abrahamian, Ervand. *A History of Modern Iran.* Cambridge: Cambridge University Press, 2008.

Adelkhah, Fariba. *Being Modern in Iran.* New York: Columbia University Press, 2000.

Amir Arjomand, Saïd. *After Khomeini: Iran under His Successors.* New York: Oxford University Press, 2009.

Asadi, Houshang. *Letters to My Torturer: Love, Revolution, and Imprisonment in Iran.* Oxford: Oneworld, 2010.

Atabaki, Touraj. *Azerbaijan: Ethnicity and Autonomy in Twentieth-Century Iran.* London: British Academic Press, 1993.

Azimi, Fakhreddin. *Iran: The Crisis of Democracy, 1941–1953.* New York: St. Martin's, 1989.

Bayat, Assef. *Making Islam Democratic: Social Movements and the Post-Islamist Turn.* Stanford: Stanford University Press, 2007.

Chehabi, H. E. "Religion and Politics in Iran: How Theocratic Is the Islamic Republic?" *Daedalus* 120 (Summer 1991): 69–91.

Gasiorowski, Mark. *U.S. Foreign Policy and the Shah: Building a Client State in Iran.* Ithaca, NY: Cornell University Press, 1991.

Gheissari, Ali, ed. *Contemporary Iran: Economy, Society, Politics.* New York: Oxford University Press, 2009.

Keshavarzian, Arang. *Bazaar and State in Iran: The Politics of the Tehran Marketplace.* Cambridge: Cambridge University Press, 2007.

Kurzman, Charles. *The Unthinkable Revolution in Iran.* Cambridge, MA: Harvard University Press, 2004.

Martin, Vanessa. *Islam and Modernism: The Persian Revolution of 1906.* London: I. B. Tauris, 1988.

Moin, Baqer. *Khomeini: Life of the Ayatollah.* London: I. B. Tauris, 1999.

Moslem, Mehdi. *Factional Politics in Post-Revolutionary Iran.* Syracuse, NY: Syracuse University Press, 2002.

Mottahedeh, Roy. *The Mantle of the Prophet: Religion and Politics in Iran.* Oxford: Oneworld, 2000.

Paidar, Parvin. *Women and the Political Process in Twentieth-Century Iran.* Cambridge: Cambridge University Press, 1995.

Sanasarian, Eliz. *Religious Minorities in Iran.* Cambridge: Cambridge University Press, 2000.

Tajbakhsh, Kian. "Political Decentralization and the Creation of Local Government in Iran: Consolidation or Transformation of the Theocratic State?" *Social Research* 67 (2000): 377–404.

Vahdat, Farzin. *God and Juggernaut: Iran's Intellectual Encounter with Modernity.* Syracuse, NY: Syracuse University Press, 2002.

INTERNET RESOURCES

Iran Daily (English-language daily newspaper): **www.iran-daily.com**.

Ministry of Foreign Affairs, Islamic Republic of Iran: **www.mfa.gov.ir**.

Payvand (news and information portal): **www.payvand.com**.

Encyclopaedia Iranica: **www.iranica.com/**.

Iranian Studies Group at Massachusetts Institute of Technology: **www.isg-mit.org**.

The Middle East Research and Information Project: **www.merip.org**.

ENDNOTES

1. Frances Harrison, "Huge Cost of Iranian Brain Drain," BBC News, 8 January 2007, http://news.bbc.co.uk/2/hi/middle_east/6240287.stm. From the Washington Institute (accessed at http://washingtoninstitute.org/templateC05.php?CID=1556).

2. Sonia Ghaffari, "Baluchestan's Rising Militancy," *Middle East Report* 250 (Spring 2009): 40–43.

3. Abdul-Hadi Hairi, *Shiism and Constitutionalism in Iran* (Leiden, The Netherlands: Brill, 1977).

4. Nikki R. Keddie, *Modern Iran: Roots and Results of Revolution* (New Haven, CT: Yale University Press, 2003), 123.

5. Mark Gasiorowski, "The 1953 *Coup d'État* in Iran," *International Journal of Middle East Studies* 19, no. 3 (1987): 261–86.

6. See James A. Bill, *The Eagle and the Lion: The Tragedy of American-Iranian Relations* (New Haven, CT: Yale University Press, 1988), 319–78.

7. Richard W. Cottam, *Iran and the United States: A Cold War Case Study* (Pittsburgh, PA: University of Pittsburgh Press, 1988), 156–69.

8. Ahmad Ashraf and Ali Banuazizi, "The State, Classes, and Modes of Mobilization in the Iranian Revolution," *State, Culture, and Society* 1 (1985): 3–39.

9. Misagh Parsa, *Social Origins of the Iranian Revolution* (New Brunswick, NJ: Rutgers University Press, 1989).

10. Ironically, even the Shah himself believed in the omnipotence of the United States and Britain; after his ouster, he blamed these countries for having engineered his demise.

11. Ruhollah Khomeini, "Islamic Government," in *Islam and Revolution: Writings and Declarations of Imam Khomeini*, trans. and annotated Hamid Algar (Berkeley, CA: Mizan, 1981).

12. See H. E. Chehabi, "The Political Regime of the Islamic Republic of Iran in Comparative Perspective," *Government and Opposition* 36 (2001): 48–70.

13. See Suzanne Maloney, "Agents or Obstacles? Parastatal Foundations and Challenges for Iranian Development," in *The Economy of Iran: Dilemmas of an Islamic State*, ed. Parvin Alizadeh (London: I. B. Tauris, 2000), 145–76.

14. Bahman Baktiari, *Parliamentary Politics in Revolutionary Iran: The Institutionalization of Factional Politics* (Gainesville: Florida University Press, 1996).

15. Abdol-Karim Lahiji, "Moruri bar vaz'-e hoquqi-ye Iranian-e gheyr-e mosalman," *Iran Nameh* 19 (1379–80/2001): 19. On the legal discrimination of women, see section on gender relations in this chapter.

16. Mehran Kamrava and Houchang Hassan-Yari, "Suspended Equilibrium in Iran's Political System," *Muslim World* 94 (October 2004): 495–524.

17. Asghar Schirazi, *The Constitution of Iran: Politics and the State in the Islamic Republic* (London: I. B. Tauris, 1998), 134.

18. See Farideh Farhi, "Iran's 2008 Majlis Elections: The Game of Elite Competition," *Middle East Brief: Crown Center for Middle East Studies, Brandeis University*, no. 29 (May 2008), www.brandeis.edu/crown/publications/meb/MEB29.pdf.

19. Kian Tajbakhsh, "Political Decentralization and the Creation of Local Government in Iran: Consolidation or Transformation of the Theocratic State?" *Social Research* 67 (2000): 377–404.

20. Before World War I, Westerners considered Iran and other non-Western but nominally sovereign countries, such as China and Thailand, to be "semi-civilized" nations, which had some but not all of the attributes of a full-fledged member of the international community. See Gerrit Gong, *The Standard of "Civilization" in International Society* (Cambridge: Cambridge University Press, 1984).

21. Houchang E. Chehabi, "The Paranoid Style in Iranian Historiography," in Touraj Atabaki, ed., *Iran in the 20th Century: Historiography and Political Culture* (London: I. B. Tauris, 2009), 155–176, 294–303.

22. See L. Carl Brown, *International Politics and the Middle East* (Princeton, NJ: Princeton University Press, 1984), 233–52.

23. Mansoor Moaddel and Taghi Azadarmaki, "The Worldviews of Islamic Publics: The Case of Egypt, Iran, and Jordan," in *Human Values and Social Change: Findings From the Values Survey*, ed. Ronald Inglehart (Leiden, The Netherlands: Brill, 2003), 81.

24. This line of reasoning is based on Azadeh Kian-Thiébaut, "Entrepreneurs privés: entre développement statocentique et démocratisation politique," *Les Cahiers de l'Orient* 60 (2000): 65–92.

25. Peter Chelkowski and Hamid Dabashi, *Staging a Revolution: The Art of Persuasion in the Islamic Republic of Iran* (New York: New York University Press, 1999), 130–31.

26. Kaveh Ehsani, "Islam, Modernity, and National Identity," *Middle East Insight* 11(1995), 51.

27. Farideh Farhi, "The Antinomies of Iran's War Generation," in *Iran, Iraq, and the Legacies of War*, ed. Lawrence C. Potter and Gary G. Sick (New York: Palgrave Macmillan, 2004), 101–20.

28. Moaddel and Azadarmaki, "The Worldviews of Islamic Publics."

29. Ahmad Sadri, "The Varieties of Religious Reform: Public Intelligentsia in Iran," in *Iran: Between Tradition and Modernity*, ed. Ramin Jahanbegloo (Lanham, MD: Lexington Books, 2004), 117–28.

30. Marvin Zonis, *The Political Elite of Iran* (Princeton, NJ: Princeton University Press, 1971).

31. Khosrow Fatemi, "Leadership by Distrust: The Shah's *Modus Operandi*," *Middle East Journal* 36 (1982): 48–61.

32. Mehran Kamrava, *The Modern Middle East: A Political History Since the First World War* (Berkeley: University of California Press, 2005), 261.

33. Figures are from Wilfried Buchta, *Who Rules Iran? The Structure of Power in the Islamic Republic* (Washington, D.C.: The Washington Institute for Near East Policy, 2000), 68.

34. Assef Bayat, *Street Politics: Poor People's Movements in Iran* (New York: Columbia University Press, 1997).

35. Arang Keshavarzian, "Regime Loyalty and *Bazari* Representation under the Islamic Republic of Iran: Dilemmas of the Society of Islamic Coalition," *International Journal of Middle East Studies* 41, no. 2 (May 2009): 224–246.

36. In his discussion of charismatic authority, Max Weber points out that charismatic leaders oppose tradition, and he summarizes this attitude in the famous statement ascribed to Jesus: "It has been written . . ., but *I* say unto you." *Economy and Society* (Berkeley: University of California Press, 1976), 1115.

37. Schirazi, *The Constitution of Iran*, 67–68.

38. Quoted in Saïd Amir Arjomand, *The Turban for the Crown: The Islamic Revolution in Iran* (New York: Oxford University Press, 1988), 182.

39. In fact, Ahmadinejad belongs to a current of thought that considers the return of the Twelfth Imam imminent. This messianic expectation sets him apart from most other leaders of the Islamic Republic and may yet be the source of friction.

40. For details, see H. E. Chehabi, "Ardabil Becomes a Province: Center-Periphery Relations in the Islamic Republic of Iran," *International Journal of Middle East Studies* 29, no. 2 (May 1997): 235–53.

41. For an inside account, see Elaine Sciolino, *Persian Mirrors: The Elusive Face of Iran* (New York: Free Press, 2000), 248–60.

42. For details see Buchta, *Who Rules Iran?*, 156–70.

43. How this multiplicity of power centers affects individuals is seen in the story of Dariush Zahedi, an Iranian-American political scientist who had met with dissidents while visiting Iran one recent summer for his research. He was arrested by the Ministry of Information and held prisoner for two months before being told that, as far as the Ministry was concerned, he was innocent—except that upon leaving the prison, he was immediately rearrested by the intelligence agency of the Revolutionary Guards, who held him for another two months in solitary confinement and subjected him to similar interrogations as his preceding jailers, only in a less respectful tone. He was finally released and returned to the United States through the intervention of a number of Iranian diplomats after academics in the United States publicized his plight.

44. Kaveh Ehsani, "Survival through Dispossession: Privatization of Public Goods in the Islamic Republic," *Middle East Report* 250 (Spring 2009): 26–33.

45. Zahra Mila Elmi, "Educational Attainment in Iran," in *The Iranian Revolution at 30* (Washington, D.C.: Middle East Institute, 2009) 62–69.

46. Ervand Abrahamian, "Why the Islamic Republic Has Survived," *Middle East Report* 250 (Spring 2009): 10–16; Homa Hoodfar, "Activism under the Radar: Volunteer Women Health Workers in Iran," *Middle East Report* 250 (Spring 2009): 56–60; and Eric Hooglund, "Thirty Years of Islamic Revolution in Rural Iran," *Middle East Report* 250 (Spring 2009): 34–39.

47. The data are from the UNDP Human Development Index, 2009.

48. Massoud Karshenas and Hassan Hakimian, "Oil, Economic Diversification, and the Democratic Process in Iran," *Iranian Studies* 38, no. 1 (March 2005): 67–90.

49. "Youth Employment in Islamic Republic of Iran" (report prepared by the Department of International Affairs of the National Youth Organization, October 2004).

50. Mehrangis Kar, "*Shari'a* Law in Iran," in *Radical Islam's Rules: The Worldwide Spread of Extreme Shari'a Law*, ed. Paul Marshall (Lanham, MD: Rowman & Littlefield, 2005), 41–64.

51. The numbers are from Amnesty International.

52. Abdolmohammad Kazemipur and Ali Rezaei, "Religious Life under Theocracy: The Case of Iran," *Journal for the Scientific Study of Religion* 42, no. 3 (2003): 347–61.

53. See Mahmoud Sadri, "Sacral Defense of Secularism: Dissident Political Theology in Iran," in *Intellectual Trends in Twentieth-Century Iran*, ed. Negin Nabavi (Gainesville: University Press of Florida, 2003), 180–92.

54. Mahmud Abbasi, *Qanun-e Mojazat-e Eslami* (Islamic Penal Code) (Tehran: Hoquqi, 2002), 108.

55. Following the victory of the Mujahidin in Afghanistan, as the Iranian government became keen on repatriating Afghan refugees to Afghanistan, tens of thousands of Iranian women who had married Afghan refugee men in Iran were told by the authorities that they faced the choice of either seeking a divorce from their husbands or following them to their country.

56. Mehrangiz Kar, "Women's Political Rights after the Islamic Revolution," in *Religion and Politics in Modern Iran: A Reader*, ed. Lloyd Ridgeon (London: I. B. Tauris, 2005), 253–78.

57. Moaddel and Azadarmaki, "The Worldviews of Islamic Publics," 77.

58. Moaddel and Azadarmaki, "The Worldviews of Islamic Publics," 78. Forty-five percent of Iranians agree with this statement, while 88 and 89 percent of Egyptians and Jordanians agree, respectively.

59. Moaddel and Azadarmaki, "The Worldviews of Islamic Publics," 79.

60. For details, see *The International Encyclopedia of Women and Sport* (New York: Macmillan, 2001), s.v. "Iran," 586–87. For an eyewitness account by a Western journalist, see Geraldine Brooks, *Nine Parts of Desire: The Hidden World of Islamic*

Women (New York: Anchor Books, 1995), 201–11, "Muslim Women's Games."

61. Asked whether she would ever "want to throw off the head scarf in public," she answered: "Do you want to issue me my death sentence?" *International Herald Tribune*, April 3, 2003, 2.

62. Najmedin Meshkati, "Iran's Nuclear Brinkmanship, the U.S. Unilateralism, and a Mounting International Crisis: Can Civil Aviation Industry Provide a Breakthrough?" *Iran News*, July 26, 2004, 14.

63. Arang Keshavarzian, "Contestation Without Democracy: Elite Fragmentation in Iran," in *Authoritarianism in the Middle East: Regimes and Resistance*, ed. Marsha Pripstein Posusney and Michelle Penner Angrist (Boulder, CO: Lynne Rienner, 2005), 63–88.

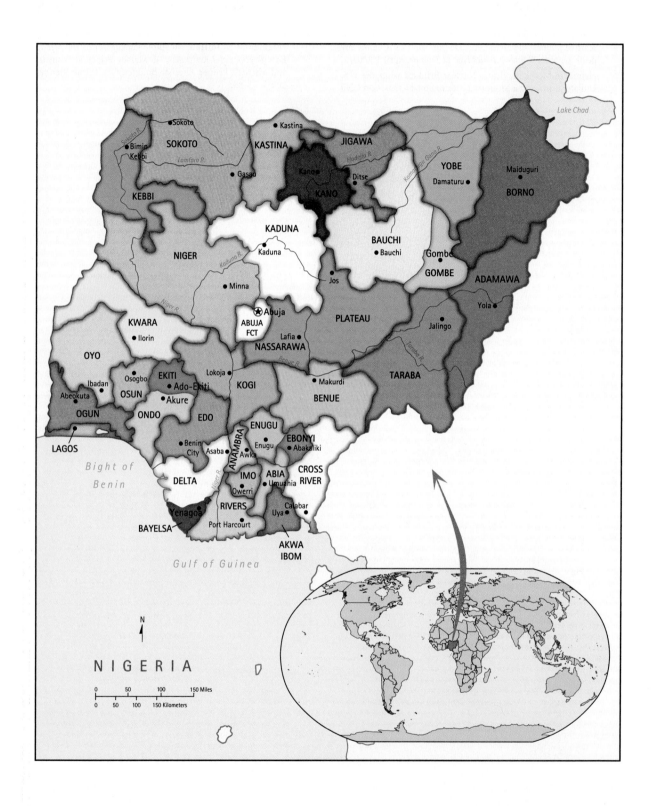

NIGERIA

Lake Chad

Sokoto R.

Sokoto

SOKOTO

Bimin
Kebbi

Gasau

KEBBI

Kastina

KASTINA

JIGAWA

Kano

KANO

Ditse

Hadeja R.

Komadugu Gana R.

YOBE

Damaturu

Maiduguri

BORNO

Lomfaro R.

KADUNA

Kaduna

NIGER

Kaduna R.

Minna

Jos

BAUCHI

Bauchi

Gombe

GOMBE

ADAMAWA

Yola

Niger R.

Abuja

ABUJA
FCT

KWARA

Ilorin

Lafia

NASSARAWA

PLATEAU

Jalingo

Jamba R.

TARABA

OYO

Ibadan

Osogbo

EKITI

Ado-Ekiti

Akure

OSUN

Abeokuta

OGUN

ONDO

EDO

KOGI

Lokoja

Benue R.

Makurdi

BENUE

LAGOS

*Bight of
Benin*

Benin
City

Asaba

ANAMBRA

Awka

ENUGU

Enugu

EBONYI

Abakaliki

CROSS
RIVER

DELTA

Niger R.

IMO

Owerri

ABIA

Umuahia

Uya

Calabar

Yenagoa

BAYELSA

RIVERS

Port Harcourt

AKWA
IBOM

Gulf of Guinea

N

N I G E R I A

| 0 | 50 | 100 | 150 Miles |
| 0 | 50 | 100 | 150 Kilometers |

POLITICS IN NIGERIA

A. Carl LeVan, Oladimeji Aborisade, and Robert J. Mundt

Country Bio

NIGERIA

Population
151 million

Territory
356,668 square miles

Year of Independence
1960

Year of Current Constitution
1999 Constitution, based on the 1979
Constitution (including revisions drafted in 1995)

Head of State
President Goodluck Jonathan

Head of Government
President Goodluck Jonathan

Languages
English (official), Hausa, Yoruba, Igbo, and 250
other ethnic groups

Religions
Muslim 50%, Christian 40%, indigenous beliefs 10%

In the African context, Nigeria is a megastate. Even on a world scale, Nigeria is a major country. Larger than France or Britain, it claims over one-fifth of the people in Africa and has the world's largest black population. Its petroleum and its substantial standing military force guarantee its prominence in international relations, and with 104 universities, Nigeria contains a large proportion of Africa's centers of learning and research.

For these reasons alone, one should know about Nigeria. But learning about Nigeria is also an efficient approach to learning about Africa, because Nigeria embodies much of the variety of African political experience within its borders. Its traditions include the large-scale emirates of the North and the small kingdoms and village-level republics of the South. Although both were administered by Britain, the North and South of Nigeria experienced different versions of colonial rule. Its culture is divided by ethnicity and by religion, especially between Christians and Muslims. Its history since independence includes coups, countercoups, and civil war; recently, along with many other Africans, Nigerians have been groping toward a renewal of democracy. The problems and prospects of many African ministates are found in Nigeria, but at a more daunting scale and level of complexity. To know Nigeria is not necessarily to know Africa, but to one who is well-acquainted with the Nigerian experience, there will be little that is surprising in politics elsewhere on the continent.

Nigeria's prominent place in the world is more potential than real, however, because in recent years, Nigeria has been a *sick* giant. Its economy is in shambles and the provision of public services has broken down. This chapter examines the causes of this illness and assesses the democratic government's remedies to it.

CURRENT POLICY CHALLENGES

Nigeria is now enjoying the longest period of civilian rule in its history, but it faces failures of governance and ongoing challenges to constitutional authority that keep democracy in a precarious state. The country's ethnic, regional, and religious divisions have intensified in recent years. Leading political elites and some violent groups argue for breaking up the country into a weak federation or even completely independent states if political power and economic resources are not distributed more justly. The declining quality of elections, persistent inequalities, and failures of government performance all contribute to popular skepticism about democracy.

The transition to democracy in 1999 began hopefully with the election of **Olusegun Obasanjo** as president and then a new democratic legislature a few weeks later. In 2003, President Obasanjo was reelected in a landslide, and his party also captured most other important political offices. A new president, **Umar Musa Yar'Adua**, was elected in 2007, but only after a failed attempt by Obasanjo's supporters to change the constitution to extend his stay in office another term. The constitution faced a fresh test when President Yar'Adua disappeared from public view after falling seriously ill in November 2009. After months of inaction, the National Assembly voted to appoint the vice president as acting president—even though it lacked explicit constitutional authority to do so. When Yar'Adua passed away in April 2010, Nigeria seemed to survive another transition when Vice President **Goodluck Jonathan** was officially sworn in as president.

Beyond these political tests, Nigerians remain frustrated with the failure of democracy to harness their country's wealth to provide basic human needs, education, potable water, reliable transportation, and communications. Power generation has actually declined since 1999, creating an expensive and difficult climate for private investment into the expanding economy. Income levels per capita are barely a tenth of income in the United States or Western Europe; in 2009, the UN ranked Nigeria 158th among the 182 nations in its Human Development Index. This is a slight improvement over recent years, moving the country into the bottom of the "medium human development" group. The failure to prosecute rampant corruption impairs economic development, and the country's ranking in the Corruption Perceptions Index, developed by Transparency International, declined in 2009. Nigeria now ranks 130th out of 180 countries due to inaction on dozens of major cases.

The current regime has thus far avoided the fate of previous attempts at democracy. But with poor government performance, persistent sectarian tensions along ethnic, regional, and religious lines, and struggling democratic institutions, the allure of authoritarianism has not entirely faded. In the discussion that follows, the reader should consider the historic and structural roots of the country's challenges as well as the evolving social values that inform political behavior. Whether the country consolidates democracy or reverts back to familiar and destructive political patterns depends upon some combination of principled leadership, civic activism, and sound institutions that inspire the confidence of citizens and investors.

Political Violence Reaches Abuja

Until recently, political and religious violence generally took place outside the capitol. This changed in 2010, when MEND blew up the cars pictured here during a celebration on the anniversary of Nigeria's independence.

AP Images

THE EFFECTS OF HISTORY

More than forty years ago, anthropologist Clifford Geertz titled an essay on the developing nations "Old Societies and New States."[1] This title is an apt characterization of Nigeria, for although the concept of Nigeria dates only to 1914, and the independent state only to 1960, the cultures that compose it have ancient roots.

In one sense, then, there are many Nigerias. That is, there are distinct political cultures with precolonial origins, and there are the varied colonial experiences of North, East, and West. We will consider these causes of variety separately.

The Enduring Effects of Precolonial Events

Our images of precolonial Africa have been plagued by misunderstandings, sometimes in the form of simple ignorance but often the result of prejudice. Many in the industrial world still view traditional Africa as "primitive," composed of a series of "tribes."[2] As we shall see from the case of Nigeria, even early civilizations organized at the village level developed complex systems of political limitations on their rulers. All these peoples interacted in trade, cultural diffusion, and war for many centuries before the creation of today's nation-states, and their belief systems were as complex and nuanced as any in the world. To reiterate, there was no single Nigeria a century ago. The **Hausa** people began forming city-states in northern Nigeria between 1000 and 1200 C.E., and came under the influence of Islam no later than the fifteenth century. By the next century, mosques and Koranic schools were flourishing, and Hausa princes were international rivals of Morocco and the Ottoman Empire. The fortunes of these systems waxed and waned through the centuries, but they were decisively changed when non-Hausa court officials rose against them early in the nineteenth century. These officials were **Fulani,** a people with their origins in western Sudan who had entered into the Hausa lands as herders and, more important, as teachers, traders, and eventually court advisors. A Fulani scholar and preacher, Usman dan Fodio, inspired a religious and political revolt against the Hausa kings. A Fulani-dominated caliphate was established in Sokoto, now northern Nigeria. This Fulani Empire controlled most of the North until the

British defeated it in 1903. Sokoto retains its role as the Muslim religious capital of Nigeria to this day. The Hausa and Fulani cultures have become so intertwined, with extensive intermarriage and with Hausa the primary language of both, that the dominant culture of the North is usually referred to as **Hausa-Fulani.** The descendants of the rulers of the Hausa-Fulani kingdoms, identified by the Islamic title *emir*, continue to hold court in the major cities of northern Nigeria.

In the forest region of the Southwest, the **Yoruba** and Bini peoples began forming kingdoms between the twelfth and fifteenth centuries at Oyo, Ife, and Benin. In the seventeenth and eighteenth centuries, the kingdom of Oyo subdued its rivals and extended its control over the entire southwestern part of Nigeria. These political systems developed intricate methods of limiting the powers of their rulers. For example, the ruler of Oyo, the Alafin, was chosen by a council of chiefs. Historians believe that if the council felt the Alafin had exceeded his powers, they could compel him to commit suicide. To ensure that the council did not abuse this authority, one of their members had to die with the Alafin.[3] Other peoples inhabiting the land that now constitutes Nigeria organized themselves without kingdoms or states. For example, the **Igbo** communities in the Southeast governed at the village or extended family level. "The political system is conciliar and competitive," explains one anthropological study. "Leadership is democratic in character, and the village government gives much latitude to the youth. It is *ability* rather than *age* that qualifies for leadership."[4] The Yoruba and the Igbo examples illustrate how accountability and limited government come in a variety of forms.

Because Nigeria was defined through the colonial experience, we must ask how and why the eventual British domination occurred. The immediate cause for British interest in West Africa was trade, and the first such international trade of any importance was in slaves. Coastal groups began exchanging captives for goods with European trading ships as early as the sixteenth century. Wars among the various kingdoms ensured a plentiful supply of captives, particularly in southwestern Nigeria. For the next 300 years, this trade was sustained: Benin, Lagos, Bonny, and Calabar thrived as slave trade centers, exporting upward of 20,000 persons per year to the Americas.

In 1807, the British Parliament outlawed the slave trade. In a remarkable turnabout, the British navy replaced British slave ships and began patrolling the West African coast to cut off the trade, which was not completely eliminated until about 1850. The established slave-trading patterns were gradually converted to other goods. British consuls established themselves on the coast and began to intervene in local politics, favoring those candidates for ruling positions who would give them commercial advantages over other European traders. The British succeeded in obtaining treaties of British protection and trade along the coast. These were treaties between unequals, increasingly favorable to the British as they established first commercial and then political control.

The Colonial Interlude (1900–1960)

In order to avoid war resulting from the competition for colonies, the great European powers met as the Conference of Berlin in 1884 and 1885 and divided Africa into spheres of influence. In effect, the European powers decided to seize control of the continent rather than merely trading with its rulers and merchants. In a wave of negotiations, imperialist wars, and conquests, their efforts were successful, and by the beginning of World War I in 1914, maps of Africa showed clearly drawn lines with areas color-coded according to the European power claiming control. Thus, in 1886, the Royal Niger Company was granted a royal charter to control Nigerian trade. That charter was replaced in 1900 by the creation of the Colony of Lagos and the Protectorates of Northern and Southern Nigeria. Like most Africans, Nigerians remain sensitive to this history of external interference. Indeed, the name "Nigeria" itself was coined by an Englishwoman who later married Sir Frederick Lugard, the architect of colonial Nigeria.

There was an unfortunate interaction between the colonial penetration and West Africa's natural environment: Cultures tend to be affected by climate and ecology, as people adapt differently to life in the rainforest, grasslands, or desert. In West Africa, the prevailing climate and ecological zones run east and west (see Figure 13.1). However, the colonial thrust was from the coast of the Gulf of Guinea inland, and colonial boundaries were established on the coast and then extended northward, intersecting the climate zones. This virtually guaranteed that the colonies thus established would be composed of peoples coming from vastly different cultures.

Nigeria first became an entity in 1914, when the Northern and Southern Protectorates and Lagos were brought under a single colonial administration. This unifying action was largely symbolic, however, as its two parts continued to be governed separately. The Northern and Southern Provinces replaced the Protectorates, each under a lieutenant governor. Northern Nigeria remained apart as such political structures as a legislative council evolved in the South. Northerners did not sit on the Nigerian Legislative Council until 1947. Indeed, the

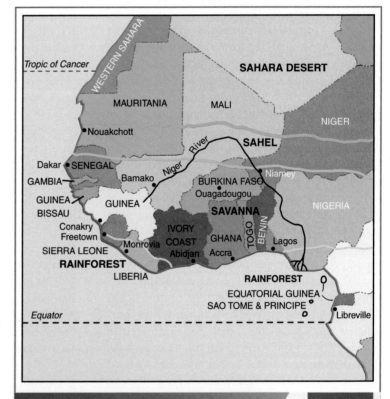

Political Boundaries in Tropical West Africa   **FIGURE 13.1**

The unification of Northern and Southern Protectorates into what is today Nigeria brought together peoples from vastly different climates, cultures, and histories.

North proved to be the perfect setting for the "indirect rule" elaborated by the governor, Lord Lugard: The British administration would not intervene directly into everyday life in its colonies but would support the rule of traditional leaders, such as the Fulani emirs. This, Lugard argued, was the most efficient means of controlling the colonies. As part of the understanding, the British also prohibited Christian missionaries from proselytizing in the North, a largely Muslim region. In southern Nigeria, Western-educated elites challenged the authority of the traditional rulers where they existed (as among the Yoruba); this complicated the strategy of indirect rule. In southeastern Nigeria, among the Igbo and other peoples, there really were no traditional kings or chiefs. Attempts to create village chiefs where the concept was unknown produced results that were sometimes comical and often tragic. As a result of these different traditions, the applicability of indirect rule served to distinguish further the political experiences of the regions.

The British colonial administration also faced the problem of incompatible objectives. In order to make the colony self-sustaining, Britain needed an export economy. However, the conversion of peasant societies from subsistence to a market orientation eroded the foundations of traditional rule. Except in the North, chiefs and kings had no traditional right to collect taxes, yet this became a central duty in the colonial system. Also, the development of a modern system of transportation and communication, necessary to stimulate commerce, encouraged the movement of people from the countryside to cities and from one part of the country to another, all under the protection of the colonial authorities. Urbanized populations and immigrants from other cultures could scarcely be expected to show deference to traditional rulers, nor did they see any good reason for paying taxes.

Along with commerce and administration, the British brought missionaries and education. Missionaries of many denominations—Anglicans, Presbyterians, Catholics, Baptists, Adventists, and others—brought the Gospels to Nigeria, although only to the South; the Northern emirates had an understanding with the British that Christian proselytizing would not be permitted in their domains. Christianity spread especially rapidly in the Southeast and somewhat less so in the Southwest; with it went formal schooling. As Nigerian children learned the English language and customs, they acquired the tools with which to challenge colonial rule on the rulers'

own terms. However, the Western-educated elite that emerged came largely from the South. Thus, the culture is divided North and South along religious lines, but the difference has to do with much more than religion.

Modern constitutional development began within a few years of the creation of Nigeria as a single colony, with elective office first provided in 1922. An early nationalist leader, Herbert Macaulay, established a political party soon thereafter. As a Nigerian-centered political life grew up among the formally educated, other organizations arose, and the British colonial administration was pressed with demands for participation.

From then on, constitutions promulgated by various governors (and named after them) were always somewhat behind the expectations of Nigerian political activists. What Southern politicians judged conservative, however, was usually seen as radical by the conservative elites in the North. These differences of opinion among Nigerians resulted in 1954 in the creation of a federal system of three regions: Northern, Eastern, and Western. A single ethnic group dominated each region: the Hausa-Fulani in the North, the Igbo in the East, and the Yoruba in the West. Under pressure from their leaders, the Eastern and Western Regions received self-government in 1957; the North became self-governing in 1959, a few months before national independence.

Nigerian Independence

As Nigeria approached independence, there was a general consensus that the nation should come to independence as a single country. Independent Nigeria was born on October 1, 1960. Nigeria's independent governments at the federal and state levels experienced a very short "honeymoon." Within two years, conflict had torn apart the ruling coalition in the Western Region. The next year, suspicions about the national census (as we will see later) destroyed what little trust there was among the regions. Finally, in 1965, law and order broke down in the Western Region over election-related fraud and violence, and the military ended the First Republic in a January 1966 coup.

ENVIRONMENTAL POTENTIAL AND LIMITATIONS

Nigeria has made great economic progress in recent years, pointing to a new wellspring of optimism. Controlling for PPP, per capita GDP was $1,940 in

2008, up from $1,130 in 2000. Its GDP in 2008 was $212.1 billion, recording an impressive 5.3 percent growth rate. (We will discuss Nigeria's GDP later in this chapter; see Table 13.4 and accompanying text.) This constitutes a vast improvement over an earlier era, when per capita GNP actually declined by 1.7 percent annually between 1980 and 1991. At the aggregate level, these figures appear to suggest that Nigeria may be climbing out of the UN classification for "low-income countries."

Yet these statistics translate into very limited concrete improvements in the daily lives of average citizens, and whether we can attribute progress to political reform and better policy decisions remains an open question. Policy options remain limited, in part due to the colonial legacy of uneven development within the country, and the Nigerian economy is highly dependent on a single commodity—oil. The country thus weathered the recession of 2008 to 2009 reasonably well, partly out of sheer luck that world oil prices remained so high. The economic diversification necessary to stabilize these gains requires overcoming a difficult physical environment and complex socioeconomic challenges.

Conditions Affecting Agricultural Production and the Sale of Primary Commodities

Colonial policies not only retarded Nigeria's political development but also had profound, if mixed, effects on its economy. Since early in the colonial period, Southern Nigerians have been producing cocoa, palm oil, timber, and rubber. The timber, sold mostly as tropical hardwoods for use in furniture and construction, came from the now-dwindling rainforests in the South. In the North, the principal market products were cattle, hides and skins, cotton, and peanuts.

The growth of trade in these commodities was not entirely spontaneous. The British interest in Nigeria was primarily commercial, with its origins in the United Africa Company (UAC). When the UAC was granted a charter as the Royal Niger Company in 1886, it was given police and judicial power, and it was authorized to collect taxes and to oversee commerce. Not surprisingly, its policies aimed at developing the Nigerian economy to be compatible with British needs. Also, public sentiment in Britain never solidly favored creating a colonial empire, and powerful voices in Parliament favored keeping the costs of the empire to a minimum. Colonial administrations were

under heavy pressure to be self-sufficient—to develop local sources of revenue to cover their costs of administration. As a result, colonial administrators pressured peasant farmers away from subsistence agriculture and into commercial farming, particularly of export crops. Furthermore, cost-efficient marketing meant emphasis on just a few of the most needed products; in Nigeria (and elsewhere in West Africa), these turned out to be palm oil, cocoa, peanuts, and cotton. Thus, British raw material priorities and the need to provide a self-sufficient colonial administration distorted African economies toward dependence on the sale of a small number of primarily agricultural commodities.

The combination of population growth and the commercialization of agriculture strained relationships between agricultural techniques and the ecology that had been in place for centuries. Colonial officials sometimes assumed that productivity could be greatly increased in tropical regions with the introduction of "modern" methods, without recognizing the different ecological conditions of production in a tropical setting. Lush tropical rainforest could not simply be replaced by plantations. Rainfall, temperature, and soil conditions meant that farming techniques effective in England or North America would be unsuccessful or even disastrous in Nigeria. Only gradually, and much later, were the efforts of agronomists applied to maximizing agricultural production in the tropics, especially to food production for local consumption.

Nigeria broke with some colonial economic development policies, especially the need to diversify production, because it offered a large, ecologically diverse environment. But the need for foreign exchange meant that agriculture continued to emphasize exportable commodities, even as investment capital was largely directed toward industrialization. Economists in both the industrial and Third World countries associated industry with prosperity, and agriculture was seen as the "cash cow" from which to extract savings for investment in other areas. Also, Nigerian government officials, trained in the need to balance budgets, balanced appropriations bills with overly optimistic estimations of "expected revenue." When these fell short, the difference was made up from cash reserves accumulated by the Central Produce Marketing Board, a government agency that purchased all the goods from farmers. However, "since those reserves were derived from the price differential between what was paid to the farmer and what the

Board earned in export earnings . . . for close to a decade, Nigeria existed only through the exploitation of her farmers."[5]

In addition to keeping agricultural prices low to provide such reserves, Nigerian governments also tried to satisfy urban demands for cheap food by holding down the price paid to farmers in the domestic market. This action contributed to the unattractiveness of agricultural work and enhanced the lure of the cities.

Disease

Physical illness is a part of the human condition, and the higher disease rates of poorer nations are largely explained by the lack of resources to acquire medicines, medical facilities, and personnel. But environment contributes as well; some of the most common human diseases, including malaria, can survive only in tropical climates. In tropical Africa, virtually every long-term resident carries the malaria virus, and large proportions of the population are affected by it. It is usually not fatal, but it is extremely debilitating, and it has a documented effect on labor productivity. Various river-borne diseases also account for long-term illness and fatalities, contributing especially to the high mortality rate among children. As with agricultural problems, research can attack these diseases, yet a vastly disproportionate share of the world's resources applied to health problems is focused on ailments more common to the industrialized world. In recent times, AIDS has topped the list of the most dreadful diseases in Africa. The Joint UN Program on HIV/AIDS reported in 2008 that 3.1 percent of all Nigerians between the ages of fifteen and forty-nine were infected. Incredibly, this constitutes an improvement over recent years, which is attributable to a massive influx of external assistance, as well as a serious commitment from President Obasanjo's administration. In many African countries, the AIDS epidemic slows down national productivity and especially agricultural productivity because it requires so much labor effort.

Population Growth

Nothing is more striking to a visitor to Nigeria than the youth of the population; everywhere there are multitudes of children. About 45 percent of the Nigerian population is less than fifteen years of age.[6]

Children are considered a valuable resource in labor-intensive agricultural societies, and in a country with high infant mortality rates and no social security system, parents would be imprudent not to have enough children so that some would grow up to provide for them in their old age. This behavior becomes dysfunctional at the societal level, of course, as increasing populations struggle to survive on a limited physical environment. Figure 13.2 illustrates the projected population growth through 2020. Between 1975 and 2000, the population of Nigeria grew an average of 2.9 percent annually. Even with a high economic growth rate of 6.6 percent since 2000, rapid population growth brings the figure down to only 4 percent in per capita terms. In this environment of rapid population growth and urbanization, children become economic liabilities. Thus, the "dependency ratio" (the proportion of the nonworking population to the working population) has steadily risen since the early 1960s, placing a great strain on the country's underdeveloped facilities for social welfare and education.[7]

Counting the population in Nigeria has always been controversial because of its implications for the distribution of resources and political districting. There has not been a widely accepted census since 1963. Protests and some violence followed the most recent government census in March 2006. The National Population Commission released results a

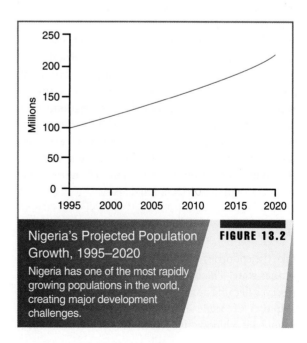

Nigeria's Projected Population Growth, 1995–2020

FIGURE 13.2

Nigeria has one of the most rapidly growing populations in the world, creating major development challenges.

year later, and they were forwarded to the president in November 2008. They remain so controversial that they still have not been formally approved.

Urbanization

Nigeria shares a pattern of urbanization common in Africa: Although the country is still primarily rural, it is urbanizing rapidly. Between 1970 and 1995, the share of Nigeria's urban population increased from 20 to 39 percent. By 2000, 42 percent of the population lived in urban areas, a figure that now stands at 48 percent. Due to internal migration, the need for urban infrastructure adds to the long list of demands on government. For example, the government ministry in charge of **Abuja**, the federal capital, announced in 2002 that the population of the city had exceeded 4 million, whereas city planners had estimated that the population would be only about 1.5 million at this stage of development.[8] In an effort to discourage additional migration, the federal minister in charge of Abuja implemented oftentimes harsh policies, including the destruction of informal housing. Nigeria's largest city is **Lagos**, within the state by the same name. Lagos State recently reversed years of decline after increasing tax enforcement, attracting new foreign investment, and investing in infrastructure. Since it is one of the few states run by a governor belonging to the country's opposition party, many people are watching to see if good governance will have a spillover effect into other states.[9]

The population shift means that a smaller proportion of the labor force is available for agricultural work. That is a normal pattern of modernization, of course, but unless the productivity of agricultural workers increases, it means a drop in food production per capita. Urbanization also has political consequences, since dense living arrangements are conducive to organizing; this was in fact one reason for the military's decision to create Abuja as a new capital in an area with low population density.

Petroleum

Like the countries discussed in Chapter 7, Nigeria is a rentier state. The magnitude of Nigeria's petroleum reserves became apparent in the 1950s, with the first shipload of crude exported in 1958. Nigeria was engulfed in a bloody civil war from 1967 to 1970, which brought a halt to oil exports. At war's end, however, Nigerian petroleum production began to boom, and it grew at a dramatic rate through the 1970s. Although such a valuable mineral resource is an asset to any country, its effects on Nigeria were not all beneficial. The country's economy became distorted by the great disparity of value between petroleum and the traditional agricultural products; soon, young workers were abandoning their farms and villages, and flocking to the cities and the oil fields. Figure 13.3 shows that the source of Nigeria's hard currency shifted dramatically from agricultural products to petroleum in the early 1970s.

Oil revenues hit a peak in 1979. World demand for oil decreased each year from 1979 to 1983. At the same time, oil production in countries that were not part of OPEC, especially Mexico, Norway, and the United Kingdom, grew substantially. Nigeria's planners were slow to realize the implications of rising supply and stagnant demand. The glory days of seemingly limitless oil revenues ended abruptly in April 1982,

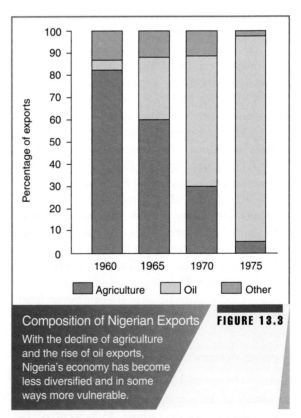

FIGURE 13.3

Composition of Nigerian Exports

With the decline of agriculture and the rise of oil exports, Nigeria's economy has become less diversified and in some ways more vulnerable.

Source: Peter O. Olayivola, *Petroleum and Structural Change in a Developing Country* (New York: Praeger, 1987).

when production of crude oil in Nigeria dropped from 2.1 million to 0.9 million barrels per day; oil export revenues fell correspondingly, from $1.35 billion to $0.7 billion per month. In the preceding decade, Nigeria had become dependent on oil revenues for imports and large-scale development projects. As was commonly the case in the Third World, Nigeria fell behind in its debt payments, which forced the government to impose unpleasant austerity measures. A further fall in oil prices in 1986 pushed the country into a severe recession.

Over time, Nigeria's economic fortune became even more closely tied to oil revenues. Today, petroleum accounts for over 90 percent of export earnings. After world oil prices increased due to the Iraq War that began in 2003, Nigeria again began earning huge revenues. It applied this windfall toward its foreign debt, which has helped insulate the country from the effects of the global recession since 2008.

The Geographic Distribution of Natural Resources: Political Effects

Nigeria's oil fields are found in the Niger Delta basin, an area of 43,500 square miles, or 8 percent of the country. As a natural resource that is both geographically concentrated and far more valuable than any other, Nigerian petroleum presents a classic problem for distributive justice. Its potential value was an important motivation behind the Eastern Region's declaration of independence as **Biafra** in 1967, and oil certainly helps explain why the rest of the country was so obstinately determined to keep the region within Nigeria. But had Biafra maintained its independence, the question of oil-field ownership would not have gone away, for the people who traditionally inhabited that area were minorities in Igbo-dominated Biafra. And even though the federal government won the civil war, local peoples continue to protest the spread of oil wealth over the whole country while their land pays the price of environmental degradation from the oil operations. The underdevelopment in the oil-producing region generates widespread resentment, and the current regime has struggled to accommodate the region's grievances through democratic channels.

As a result, bitter and violent combat has broken out among various youth organizations in the Delta. Protests organized by groups such as the Movement for the Actualization of the Sovereign State of Biafra

(MASSOB) are testing Nigeria's commitment to democratic freedoms by resurrecting memories of the civil war. If these groups feel impeded from expressing themselves, though, they may become more militant. This seems to be the case with the **Movement for the Emancipation of the Niger Delta (MEND)**, which has taken dozens of foreigners hostage in protest over conditions in the oil-producing areas. Militant groups and numerous criminal gangs seeking profit engage in oil theft known as "bunkering," which has cost the government at least $100 billion between 2003 and 2008. As many as 300,000 barrels a day are lost to "blood oil" being used either to finance the rebellion or to line the pockets of complicit government officials.[10]

The International Environment

Nigeria, like most African countries, has been profoundly affected by its birth at the height of the Cold War, and by the sudden end of the bipolar war with the dissolution of the Soviet Union. During the Cold War, new nations were pressured to choose sides. The West and East granted foreign aid to developing nations as a reward for loyalty. Nigeria at independence was considered to be conservative and "pro-Western."

Many Nigerian intellectuals equated the West's capitalism with colonialism, however, which they contended continued after independence through **neocolonial** economic ties. Political discourse through the first thirty years of Nigerian independence was often based on the ideological poles of capitalism and socialism, and relationships with the major powers involved staking a position between the two camps. In the civil war that resulted from the Eastern Region's declaration of independence as Biafra in 1967, the Soviet Union sided with the Nigerian federal government, while the U.S. government attempted to maintain a neutral position, even though the Biafran cause was widely supported by Americans. Economics finally dictated Nigeria's international position: The West was best-equipped to prospect for Nigeria's oil fields, and only the West had the technology to extract and market this natural resource. Thus, a close relationship developed between the Nigerian federal government and some of the world's major oil companies.

The end of the Cold War brought a new era to the relations between Nigeria (and other poorer nations) and the industrial world. The West's fear of the spread of communism had caused it to pay some attention to

Public Education to Encourage Farming

As the oil boom drained the rural workforce, signs urged Nigerians to return to agriculture.

Bruno Barbey/Magnum Photos, Inc.

even the smallest and least-endowed countries. In the colonial period, Britain had provided virtually all foreign aid to Nigeria. In the Cold War environment at independence, Nigeria adopted a deliberate policy of diversification that diluted British influence and brought aid from the United States, Canada, the European Common Market (now the EU), Japan, and Sweden. By the 1990s, however, those Third World countries without significant resources or with serious developmental problems were simply less interesting to the developed world; it is commonly perceived that Africa particularly has been "marginalized." The first decade of the twenty-first century suggests that the situation may be turning around, especially among democratic countries where good governance is stimulating economic growth.

Nigeria shared in a common Third World experience following the oil crisis of 1973 as it accumulated massive international debts. A sudden boom in oil prices resulted in huge new deposits in the world's banks, which made credit plentiful. The military governments of the decade failed to invest sustainably in infrastructure, and an overvalued currency led to inflation as elites bought imports that were now inexpensive. Borrowing to spend seemed to make sense to all sides until commodity prices collapsed. Third World debt mushroomed in the 1980s, and several governments defaulted. Nigeria's indebtedness grew

from $8.9 billion in 1980 to $34.5 billion in 1991; by 1995, it represented 274.5 percent of the annual value of the country's exports and 140.5 percent of GNP. After the transition to democracy in 1999, President Obasanjo made debt reduction a high priority for his administration, and in 2000, Nigeria rescheduled $20 billion of its debt. In 2006, thanks in large part to earnings from the high price of oil, Nigeria became the first African country to pay off its Paris Club debt, reducing its total debt by $30 billion. It still owes money to the World Bank and some private lenders.

A final aspect of Nigeria's international environment is its regional context—West Africa. As an accident of colonial rule, Nigeria is entirely surrounded by former French colonies: Benin (formerly Dahomey), Niger, and Cameroon. France and the French-speaking West African countries have been suspicious of Nigeria's intentions and have developed close economic ties among themselves. Nigeria is increasingly a regional leader, though, due to its strength, size, and influence in Africa's regional organizations.

POLITICAL CULTURE AND SUBCULTURES

The political culture of Nigeria is extremely heterogeneous and complex. Analysis of it must take into account a Western value system overlaid on those of its various precolonial traditions; it must assess the impact of a variety of religious beliefs and of the continuing effects of Christian and Muslim proselytizing efforts. Since the colonial experience have come new divisions based on social class and on the different experiences of urban and rural dwellers. The whole range of modern political ideologies is found among the belief systems of the politically active population. Here we will give greatest attention to the political implications of ethnic identity, religious beliefs, social and economic status, contact with urban life, and civil society.

Ethnic Identity

Because of the geographic separation of ethnic groups, Nigerians can be easily identified based on language and cultural traits. These groups vary tremendously in size, and only three of them—the Hausa, Igbo, and Yoruba—are particularly numerous and influential in the country's politics. The influence of these three major groups is a cause of great concern to the remaining minority groups. Because there has been a high degree of geographical separation of ethnic groups in Nigeria (a result of the country's policies during and since the colonial period), Nigerians can easily identify the origins of their fellow citizens by observing their dialect (or accent in English), their manner of dress (if it is traditional), and in some cases "tribal marks," patterned facial scars that formerly were created as part of rites of passage to indicate ethnic identity. There are also differences in wealth and political awareness.

In the absence of a widely accepted census, the size of Nigerian ethnic groups can only be approximated. Approximately one-half of the country's population is in the North and about one-fourth each in the Southeast and Southwest. The Hausa represent about two-thirds of the North's total population, the Igbo about two-thirds in the East, and the Yoruba about two-thirds in the West. Thus, other groups represent about one-third in each region and one-third overall. Here we will briefly consider the three largest groups.

Hausa-Fulani The Hausa-Fulani people live mostly in the northern half of the country. As noted earlier, this hyphenated identity came from the imposition of Fulani rule over the Hausa population in the nineteenth century. The two cultures became intricately intertwined, although they have never become completely homogenized. Thus, the term "Hausa" is often used as a short form of "Hausa-Fulani." "Hausaland" actually straddles the border between Nigeria and Niger to the north, a former French colony, and the people in these two countries maintain many cultural and commercial ties. A greater proportion of Hausas engage in subsistence agriculture and live in rural villages than is true of Southern Nigerians. There are sizable Hausa communities in cities all over Nigeria, where they carry on trade and commercial activities while maintaining kin and client relationships with their home region. The vast majority of Hausas are Muslim. The Hausa heartland is itself still organized as a series of emirates: Each of the major cities in Northern Nigeria is the seat of an emir, one of the kings through whom the British applied their indirect rule. There is no official role for the emirs in modern Nigeria, and their unofficial role is hotly disputed, even in the North. Yet they retain great influence in their localities and, through Hausa prominence in national politics, in the rest of the country as well.

Igbo The Igbo (also spelled *Ibo*) occupy the southeastern part of the country, from the banks of the Niger River east. Most of the region is developed for market agriculture, with Igbo farmers growing palm products, rice, and yams. The Igbo people lived in politically independent, socially endogamous villages, usually no larger than 8,000 people, and did not have a sense of common Igbo identity until the colonial period.

The Igbo are known for the fervor with which they adopted Western culture. Although the encounter with British colonialism was a wrenching shock forcefully described in Chinua Achebe's novel *Things Fall Apart*, the Igbo responded enthusiastically to Western education and the missionaries who brought it. They used new skills and knowledge to seek advancement in modern commerce and civil service. Igbo people also emigrated widely throughout the country and seem less concerned than other groups with maintaining separate communities where they are "strangers." (In Nigeria, the term "stranger" refers specifically to a person living outside his or her "home" community.) They are employed on the basis of their education and modern skills in all parts of the country, including the North.

Igbo officers led the first military coup in 1966, and thousands of Igbos living in Northern cities were attacked and killed in reaction to that coup. The Igbos retreated to their home region. The next year, they followed the call of one of their own, Lieutenant Colonel Ojukwu, in the secession from Nigeria of Igbo-dominated Biafra. The three-year civil war that ended in the defeat of Biafra in 1970 caused great hardship, but within a few years, Igbos were again active in commerce (they were by then generally barred from government work in other localities) across the land. Nevertheless, the Biafran experience and the civil war left long-term mistrust between the Igbos and other Nigerians.

Yoruba The Yoruba live mostly in the southwestern part of Nigeria, including the sprawling metropolitan area of Lagos, the former federal capital. Traditionally subsistence farmers, rural Yoruba people began growing cocoa and palm products for export in the colonial period. Although they share a common language, traditional religion, and myths of origin, the precolonial Yoruba were divided into a number of independent and warring kingdoms that give them separate identities today. The Yoruba have a long tradition of commerce, and both men and women are prominent in trade networks and markets throughout West Africa.

The Yoruba kingdoms were marked by complicated institutions that balanced power between an *oba* (king) and lineage chiefs. In their effort to impose indirect rule, the British upset these structures by supporting the obas against all challengers. In the process, the obas frequently became autocratic and lost much of their legitimacy with their own people; their influence in contemporary politics varies greatly but is generally much less than that of the Northern emirs.

Because the Yoruba had, on the one hand, a highly stratified society complete with kings, but were, on the other hand, quite receptive to missionaries and their schools, they are often seen as being in an intermediate position between the stratified and change-resistant Hausa and the egalitarian and innovative Igbo. In their sometimes strident assertion of their identity and interests, they also have provoked their share of mistrust among other Nigerians, as their candidates have generally been shut out of national leadership positions.

Given the ethnic-based strife so common in the world today, it should not come as a surprise that group identities are deeply rooted and emotionally charged in Nigeria as well. Ethnic rivalries often have their roots in precolonial warfare and are frequently refreshed by economic rivalries. While nationalism may serve as a cement where the feeling is shared by a country's entire population, the same feeling at a subnational level can destroy a political system.

Because the major ethnic groups are regionally based, political issues affecting such groups are often defined geographically, and Nigeria has preserved a sense of permanent attachment between a people and its "traditional" homeland to the degree that it is more difficult to become a "citizen" of another state in Nigeria than it would be for a Nigerian to acquire citizenship in many foreign countries. Discrimination against "non-indigenes," referring to people who may have migrated into a given state decades ago, has been regularly linked to tensions and sometimes serious violence even during the current democratic regime.[11]

Multiple ethnic identities even at the local level have had a fragmenting effect on political structure. Particularly since 1976, there have been numerous disputes over the site of local government headquarters, with the "loser" often petitioning to the state and federal governments for a division of the local government area. The conflict between the Ife and Modakeke in Oranmiyan local government (see Box 13.1) is but one of many examples that could be cited. Local ethnic conflict affects policy outputs as well, where local governments build health centers or markets that are not used by some ethnic groups, thus throwing off planners' projections.

Religion

Each of the groups identified in the previous section had traditional religious institutions and beliefs in place long before the arrival of Christianity and Islam. In some cases, these earlier beliefs have maintained their vigor, especially among many Yoruba. However, the missionaries brought their religion with formal education in the Southern regions; most major Christian churches are well-established in the South, and indigenous Christian sects have split off from them in a myriad of denominations. Not surprisingly, the Christian denominations themselves tend to be geographically and ethnically concentrated, with a higher proportion of Roman Catholics among the Igbo, a Baptist concentration among the Yoruba of Ogbomoso, the Evangelical Church of West Africa predominant in Igbomina and Kwara State, and so on. A significant proportion of Yoruba—perhaps half—are Muslim. Under the agreement between the

BOX 13.1

The Conflict between Modakeke and Ile-Ife

Early in the nineteenth century, Yorubas from Old Oyo were driven south by a Fulani invasion, and some settled in and around Ile-Ife. They were at first well-received by Ile-Ife's traditional ruler, the Ooni, but soon got into a violent quarrel with the local population. The Oyo refugees were then reduced to servitude, and some were sold into slavery. Later, however, in an internal dispute, they sided with the ruler, who rewarded them with a settlement of their own, Modakeke. Strife continued between the two groups, and in an 1882 battle, the Modakeke burned down the sacred city of Ife. Throughout the colonial period, the Ooni often used their conflict to play one group against the other. As independence neared, Modakeke sought a local government independent of Ife. Also, the Ife leaders supported the Action Group (party), while Modakeke supported the National Council of Nigeria and the Cameroons (NCNC).

After independence, Ife and Modakeke were in the same local government (Oranmiyan), but they fought constantly until Oranmiyan was split in 1989. There was peace until August 1997, when the government moved one local government from an Ife to a Modakeke location and then to supposedly neutral ground. Violent conflict broke out among young men of each side. Whole villages were burned, and hundreds of lives were lost. In January 1999, the Osun state administrator invited the two communities to an open meeting, at which both groups agreed to a ceasefire. The Ooni stated that he had in fact requested General Abacha to create a new state and that Abacha had declined but had given him the new local government as a consolation prize. The traditional leader's request and the government's response inadvertently rekindled historic animosities, with tragic results. In April 2002, the federal government mandated Osun State to create an Area Office for Modakeke as part of a peace process. The Area Office was created without delay, and it is yielding some positive results within the Modakeke community.

colonial administration and the Northern emirates, Christian proselytizing was barred from the North; except for the "strangers" living there, almost the entire population is at least nominally Muslim, and the Hausa bring their religion with them when they move South. This movement is offset by the establishment of churches in Northern cities by immigrants, mostly from the South.

Missionaries built and staffed the great majority of schools during the colonial period. Thus, the North–South education gap, with its effect on political awareness, attitudes toward civil rights, and the like, itself derives from the prohibition of missionaries in the North. There is, then, an overlay of religion on ethnicity that intensifies the North–South cultural split, and the case can be made that the most sensitive issues now involve religion rather than ethnicity. These overlapping cleavages are more dangerous because they accentuate regional differences. Because some fundamentalists among Christians as well as Muslims have found it unacceptable to live in a pluralist society, those seeking a basis for political stability in Nigeria must be sensitive to finding a balance between the two

major faith groups, which each constitute about half of the population. Religious harmony has been elusive, though, when additional factors accent these cleavages. In the 1980s, the Maitatsine Islamic movement, composed largely of young men marginalized by the socioeconomic changes, rioted against the Christian presence in Northern Nigeria (as well as against police repression), with loss of life estimated in the thousands. Not long after, Southerners vociferously protested when President **Ibrahim Babangida** proposed in 1986 that Nigeria join the Organization of the Islamic Conference (OIC), a group of more than fifty predominantly Muslim countries. Shortly after the 1999 transition, Nigeria experienced a new wave of ethnic and religious tension. Riots between Christian Igbos and local Muslims in the Northern city of Kaduna left hundreds dead in brutal violence. The sensitivity over Islam in Nigeria was highlighted again in 2002, when the Miss World beauty pageant took place in Abuja. A newspaper suggested that the contestants were so beautiful that the religion's founding prophet would have chosen one of them. Over two hundred people died when tensions between Christians and Muslims flared up.[12] Overall, it was reported in 2010 by the Human Rights Watch that at least 13,000 people had been killed since 1999.

The return of democracy has possibly contributed to the heightened religious and regional identities. Surveys in 2008 reported that nearly three-fourths of Nigerians say they belong to religious associations, and half of Nigerians describe themselves as active members. Sometimes this has contributed to fundamentalism, as with the Maitatsine Movement or with the Izala movement—an acronym for the Society for the Removal of Heresy and Reinstatement of Tradition. Christians have also mobilized against, for example, the implementation of Islamic criminal law in the North. Organizations such as the Christian Association of Nigeria have opposed these changes as violations of Nigeria's constitution. A core challenge for democratic consolidation is thus balancing these regional identities with a sense of Nigerian nationhood, and also resolving ongoing questions about the state's relationship to religion.

The Evolution of Nigerian Nationalism

All of our preoccupation with Nigerian subcultures should not obscure the fact that the British colonial administration was responding to Nigerian nationalist forces when it granted independence in 1960. There were three major sources of nationalist sentiment. The first was a small number of freed slaves from North America and others of African descent from the Caribbean who settled on the West African coast and developed a culture unrelated to any of those indigenous to the country. Second, nationalist fervor

grew out of the experience of Nigerians who fought for the British in World War II and felt frustration at the lack of recognition of their service. A third category of nationalists consisted of those Nigerians who studied in England and especially in the United States, including one of the most prominent among them, **Nnamdi Azikiwe** (see Box 13.2). Although they came from a variety of ethnic backgrounds, in their quest for independence, these activists developed a sense of Nigerian nationalism and succeeded in forming cross-ethnic alliances.

Civil war also stimulated Nigerian nationalism. The two military coups before the Biafran war were clearly ethnic in their origins. However, the Biafran conflict brought together a military force that was cross-ethnic (excluding, of course, Igbos, who were at the heart of the Biafran succession). Although the officer corps is increasingly dominated by Muslims, it has continued to recruit nationally.

A study of Nigerian political culture must focus on orientations toward national (federal) political institutions. Nigerians oriented toward public political activities can be identified by (1) exposure to formal education and (2) involvement in the modern economy. As concerns interest in public policy, many Nigerians, particularly in rural areas and in the North, may be less engaged in issues of general political concern. Yet they still have to deal with local government officials on issues affecting themselves and their families. In Nigeria, as elsewhere in Africa and the Third World, such concerns are likely to be handled through personal-interest contacting. In most cases, such contacting is part of a *clientelist* arrangement: Citizens go to an individual who is politically influential for help

---

BOX 13.2

The Story of Nnamdi Azikiwe

Although an Igbo, Nnamdi Azikiwe was born in Zungeru in northern Nigeria in 1904. He received his basic education in Nigeria and then went to the United States, where he studied at Lincoln University in Pennsylvania, Stores College in West Virginia, and the University of Pennsylvania. He also worked in the United States as a coal miner, laborer, and dishwasher. Upon his return home, he joined the Nigerian Youth Movement. His interest in self-rule led to his presence at the founding

of the National Council of Nigeria and the Cameroons (NCNC) and to his founding of a pro-self-rule newspaper, the *West African Pilot*. He then moved to the Gold Coast (now Ghana), where he published an article, "Has the African a God," that resulted in a sedition charge. He won his case on appeal and went on to serve as the premier of the Eastern Region, and from 1963 to 1966 as president of Nigeria. He died in 1996 at the age of ninety-two.

and expect to "pay" for help through a long-term arrangement that may include payment in kind (as in bribes), or by turning out to vote when asked to do so, even while remaining uninterested in politics. Political activity is widespread and virtually all-embracing; interest in public affairs is strongly conditioned by education and employment.

Democratic Norms and Values

In order to assess Nigeria's chances for achieving political democracy, we must first consider the distribution of norms that might support democratic institutions. The legitimacy of opposition, manifested as tolerance for criticism, opposition, and competition for control, is an obvious prerequisite for stable democracy.[13] The history of political activism in Nigeria since 1960 suggests problems, even under democratic civilian regimes. As single parties gained control in each region, opponents were treated very roughly, with armed thugs hired to disrupt their meetings and attack their leaders. Harassment of political opposition by the government still occurs, and incumbents often use their position to gain unfair advantages.

Nevertheless, strong support has emerged for democratic norms since the military's exit in 1999. Since then, support for democracy has remained high, with 72 percent of Nigerians reporting in 2008 that "democracy is preferable to any other form of government." However, during the same period, the number of Nigerians who actually described the country as democratic (42 percent) has precipitously declined. This points to a wide gap between demand for and supply of democracy, and implies a good deal of disillusionment about government performance over the last decade.[14]

The Political Role of Women

In Nigeria's ethnic diversity, the position of women varies considerably. In Igbo, Yoruba, and other Southern Nigerian traditions, women had considerable control over their own affairs in what anthropologists label "dual-sex" systems. That is, there were parallel systems of political and social organization for men and women. Scholars of colonial history contend that women lost most of their autonomy under colonialism, because British custom at the time gave women less control of their own affairs than did the African societies they controlled.

In the North, Islamic custom greatly restricts women's roles in society. Although Hausa women have considerably more freedom than their counterparts in the Middle East, including significant roles in local production and trade, they generally were not allowed an active political role at the time of independence. Northern women voted for the first time in 1979.

The contemporary involvement of women in political leadership is similar to that of many countries; in most parts of the country, Nigerian women vote in equal numbers with men but are generally underrepresented in politics. Women have made only very modest gains under democracy. The 2007 elections brought twenty-six women to the 360-seat House of Representatives, up from only fifteen in 1999. Ten Senate seats (out of 109) are held by women, up from only three. Yet men still hold about 90 percent of the elected and appointed positions. Women are even more poorly represented in state governments, and there are sharp regional disparities. For example, not a single woman was elected to the state houses of assembly in any of the six states in northwest Nigeria.[15]

Political Corruption

A traveler on Nigerian roads meets frequent police checkpoints and barricades. Ostensibly in place to check for arms and smuggled goods, their actual function is to extort payments from travelers by uncovering various minor violations. Many Nigerians do not take offense at this behavior, noting that police officers' pay is low and often comes late.

Pervasive corruption has been a problem ever since the late colonial era; it was the central theme of Chinua Achebe's novel *No Longer at Ease*, in which an idealistic young administrator is gradually pressured by personal problems and the prevalence of corruption into accepting bribes. Achebe is only one of many Nigerians to condemn corruption; each political regime comes to power promising to eliminate the practice and punish offenders, only to fall into the same pattern. The huge sums of money that passed through officials' hands as a result of the oil boom greatly aggravated the problem; unprecedented forms of flagrant corruption appeared when oil revenues began to fill the federal treasury of General Yakubu Gowon in the early 1970s. His military governors spent large sums on openly lavish lifestyles, thus tarnishing the image of the military, which had supposedly come to power in reaction to the corruption of the First Republic. The coup against Gowon in 1975 was a direct result, as was the assassination of his successor, General Murtala, in 1976.[16] Achebe asserts that corruption has grown more "bold and ravenous" under each new regime.[17] It is widely believed that the leader **Sani Abacha** and his family in the 1990s channeled enormous sums of money from petroleum revenue accounts into their private coffers at home and abroad. As part of its campaign to promote transparency in government and fight corruption, the Obasanjo administration successfully recovered $2 billion from the Sani Abacha family. Since the return of democracy, the National Assembly has removed several leaders, including a Speaker of the House who directed public funds to remodel her houses.

In 2002, the National Assembly passed the **Economic and Financial Crimes Commission (EFCC)** Establishment Act. Its purpose is to "prevent, investigate, prosecute, and penalize economic and financial crimes." Crimes within its jurisdiction include money laundering, Internet fraud, bank fraud, bribery, and misuse of public funds. The EFCC was often accused of selective prosecution of the president's political enemies. For example, it launched an investigation of Vice President Atiku Abubakar in 2006, when he was running for president. The Commission's critics suspected that the charges were brought because Abubakar had opposed President Obasanjo's efforts to amend the Constitution so as to make him eligible for a third term in office.[18] In light of the charges, the **People's Democratic Party (PDP)** suspended him from the party just before the December 2006 presidential primaries to prevent him from contesting. During President Yar'Adua's tenure, EFCC prosecutions virtually ground to a halt, and the United States suspended some of its technical assistance out of concern for its integrity. The new president, Goodluck Jonathan, has considered plans to bring back the previous EFCC commissioner, who claims credit for recovering over $5 billion and successfully prosecuting eighty-two people when he served during Obasanjo's administration.

POLITICAL SOCIALIZATION

Nigerians develop their political beliefs and attitudes through the influence of socialization "agents," such as the family, religious organizations, primary and secondary groups, formal education, the media, and government-sponsored activities.[19] A caveat is necessary, however, when comparing the political socialization process in Nigeria with the established liberal democracies. Political socialization in the developed world occurs through fairly stable institutions. We treat the fluidity of party alignments in France or events such as the Vietnam War in the United States as exceptional, whereas in Nigeria, people have grown up under political arrangements that shift constantly, even to their very core. Add to this the upheaval of urbanization and the sudden and dramatic impact of petroleum on the culture and the economy, and the need for a different perspective on socialization is apparent. Nevertheless, there is a universal quality to the importance of the agents of socialization we have identified, even as the nature of those institutions and the objects of political attitudes and values they shape may differ greatly from those in Europe or North America.

The Family

The family, whether nuclear or extended, remains the core unit of political activity in Nigeria. In many Nigerian traditions, families are identified with a particular trade or role in society. Thus, among the Yoruba, a family of warriors is called *Jagunjagun*, farmers are *Agbe*, and traders are *Onisowo*. To traditionally minded Nigerians, such identification remains important to the determination of one's appropriate role in modern politics.

Many Nigerians have grown up in polygamous families.[20] There is no law preventing a man from taking more than one wife, although Muslims are theoretically limited to a maximum of four and Christians of mainstream denominations to one. All indigenous traditions in Nigeria accept polygamy, and little stigma is attached to the practice. Some Christian denominations in Nigeria enforce monogamy only on those men who hold office in the church.

The large family units that result from polygamous households and the broader definition of family give kinship special political importance. A politician may be able to count on the support of literally hundreds of actual kin, and even larger numbers if one considers clan affiliations based on a sense of kinship even where exact genealogical ties cannot be demonstrated. Kinship provides the most powerful sense of identity and loyalty to many in Nigeria and elsewhere in Africa, and it is the model (and often the real-world basis) for clientelist relationships.

Schools

In most contemporary nations, schools play a central role in developing a sense of community. This is clearly an important mission in Nigerian schools, and balancing various loyalties is a delicate task for Nigerian educators. Also, formal education is one of the principal benefits Nigerians expect from government. The school certificate is highly regarded throughout the developing world as a means to economic and social advancement, and this is especially true in Nigeria.

As Nigeria approached independence in the 1950s, the two Southern regions invested massively in expansion of their educational systems, especially at the primary level. There is a broad consensus that primary education should be free and universal. Beyond that basic agreement, however, Nigeria has struggled with how to shape the curriculum and how to make it available.

There was only one university in 1948 and five in 1962. The oil boom of the 1970s stimulated a massive wave of secondary and postsecondary school expansion, even though amid this prosperity there was a lack of properly trained instructors at all levels. Today there

are 104 universities, including 41 new private universities created since the 1999 transition; the higher-education system also includes 75 polytechnics and colleges of technology and of education.

Enrollment rates in Nigerian universities doubled every four to five years in the 1960s, 1970s, and 1980s. They slowed somewhat in the 1990s but increased after the 1999 transition to democracy. Between 2000 and 2006, the primary enrollment rate went from 61 to 64 percent, and the secondary school enrollment rate increased from 24 to 32 percent. However, equal access has remained illusory for years, and the problem becomes more acute as one moves from the primary to the secondary and then postsecondary level. The bias is on the one hand socioeconomic—children of the elite occupy a disproportionate share of the enrollments—and on the other hand reflects gender. Enrollment of girls has hit an unfortunate plateau, as democracy has never pushed girls' enrollment above 45 percent, showing little difference in 2007 compared with the previous decade.

Another important disparity exists between the North and South.[21] There have been indirect political effects of the education gap across regions. As the number of secondary graduates increased in the South, many of them sought jobs in the North and were embittered at Northern rejection. At the same time, Northerners grew alarmed at the prospect of being inundated by educated Southerners. Differences

Graduation at the University of Ibadan

At the time of independence, the University of Ibadan boasted modern structures and a 100,000-book library. After years of decay, the government is trying restore the University to its previous elite status.

George Esiri/Reuters/Landov

in educational achievement thus contributed to the resentments that exploded in violence in 1966. Today, Northern political dominance in the face of higher-educational achievement in the South continues to aggravate interregional political conflict. In 2009, hundreds of people died in violence after a group calling itself *Boko Haram* (meaning "education is a sin") said they wanted to cleanse northern Nigeria, which is "polluted by Western education, and uphold *shari'a* (Muslim religious law) all over the country."[22]

Language is an aspect of community-building that is often taken for granted, but language usage in school can have a major impact on political attitudes. As noted previously, English is the official language of Nigeria and remains the vehicle of instruction in Nigeria from primary school through the university. Furthermore, English is the language of government and, for the most part, of the mass media. Because English is a second language in most Nigerian homes, school plays an especially critical role in enabling access to the political system.

As a nation-building effort, the three major indigenous languages—Hausa, Igbo, and Yoruba—are also taught through secondary school and are topics in the Senior School Certificate Examinations. Proficiency in English is required for admission to a university, where the local languages are used only in programs where they might specifically be required. The connection between English usage and government activities gives added weight to the usual relationship between education and political efficacy.

Whatever the effect of intentional socialization in the schools, studies of political culture invariably affirm the effect of education on political participation. This is especially true in less-developed countries, where the cultural gap between those with and without formal education is especially great.

The Mass Media

The presence of a lively and politically independent press goes back at least to Azikiwe's *West African Pilot*. By the time of independence, a considerable number of competing newspapers existed in Nigeria. The political effect of the press is naturally limited in a country where one-third of the adults are illiterate. A 2008 survey found that only 25 percent of Nigerians get their news from newspapers at least a few times a week. But that same survey reported that 57 percent of

Nigerians are somewhat or very interested in public affairs.

Most Nigerians get their news from radio, and 58 percent of Nigerians list television as a source of news at least once a week. For decades, radio and television were state-controlled media and were therefore faithful purveyors of the government's perspective on political events. After 1999, citizens enjoyed a variety of new choices through exposure to independent stations, satellite news, and dozens of new privately owned newspapers. While few Nigerians can afford computers, Internet cafés are common and inexpensive in cities, thus increasing access to other independent news sources.

The authoritarian regimes imposed a substantial number of restrictions on the media. According to the Center for Free Speech, a Nigerian watchdog organization, the military issued twenty-one decrees between 1966 and 1995 limiting press freedoms or even proscribing particular publications outright. There was a high level of tension between military governments and the press, and the life of a journalist was not easy. Many journalists were arrested, and in 1986, a prominent critic of the government was killed by a letter bomb.

The 1999 Constitution reversed many media restrictions instituted under the previous military rulers. Although it guarantees broad freedom for the media, journalists can still face criminal punishment for defamation of public officials, and a 1999 decree requires them to be accredited by a government-run media council. The Committee to Protect Journalists reported in 2009 that ruling party officials harassed journalists with impunity, and President Yar'Adua threatened to revoke a television station's license for reasons of "national security." Journalists—and increasingly bloggers—remain subject to physical harassment, and some have had to flee the country.[23]

The State

Nigerian political attitudes are far more likely to be affected by everyday contact with the state than by the state's direct, intentional efforts to shape attitudes. In Nigeria's federal system, direct contact comes largely through local officials. Rural residents without English-language proficiency find that, even at the local level, officials are much more educated than they and generally expect and get deference. Government is remote and must be approached through some form of informal mediation. For those with formal education, contact with local government is relatively simple; furthermore, because Nigerian policy is to hire civil servants from their home areas, there is neither a social nor a cultural difference between the educated citizen and the public servant. Nigerians expect to pay for expeditious service, and while they are aware of norms of honesty and ethics that are higher than the behavior they perceive, they are not scandalized by the difference. Perceptions of policymakers are not usually the result of direct contact.

Nigerians generally express great cynicism about the motivations of policymakers at all levels, civilian or military, but for the most part, this results from media accounts of venality and corruption. Whether through direct contact or media portrayal, they most often get what they expect from governmental officials.

One would expect that the unhappy experience with military rulers would leave Nigerians cynical and disillusioned. There certainly have been such effects,

but there is a remarkably abiding faith in the importance of politics, especially among the educated. There is an impact here of the oil economy. Profits from the sale of petroleum have flowed through the central government, so that the stake in access to those in government, especially at the top, is high. For many intellectuals, however, the knowledge that important resources will be distributed through the government is offset by the uncertainty of the outcome of any attempt to become involved. They tend, thus, to leave the political field to a collection of seasoned politicians, those who have assembled a voter base every time a regime has offered the prospect of new elections.

POLITICAL RECRUITMENT

All the chief executives of Nigeria since independence are identified in Table 13.1. Several features of Nigeria's political leadership stand out. First, Northerners have dominated the leadership of the country under both civilian and military rule, in the

Nigerian Chief Executives, 1960–2010

TABLE 13.1

Until the transition to democracy in 1999, coups and uncertainty characterized the political system.

Dates	Name	Title	Ethnicity	Cause of Departure
1960–Jan. 1966	Tafawa Balewa	Prime Minister	Hausa-Fulani (North)	Coup (killed)
1963–Jan. 1966	Nnamdi Azikiwe	President [appointed]	Igbo (East)	Coup (removed)
Jan.–July 1966	Agusi Ironsi	Military Head of State	Igbo (East)	Coup (killed)
July 1966–1975	Yakubu Gowon	Military Head of State	Tiv ("Middle Belt")	Coup (removed)
1975–1976	Murtala Muhammed	Military Head of State	Hausa-Fulani (North)	Coup (killed)
1976–1979	Olusegun Obasanjo	Military Head of State	Yoruba (Southwest)	Handed power to civilian government
1979–1983	Shehu Shagari	President	Hausa-Fulani (North)	Coup (removed)
1983–1985	Muhammed Buhari	Military Head of State	Hausa-Fulani (North)	Coup (removed)
1985–1993	Ibrahim Babangida	Military Head of State	Gwari (North)	Forced out of office
Aug.–Nov. 1993	Ernest Shonekan	Interim Head of State [appointed]	Yoruba (Southwest)	Forced out of office
Nov. 1993–June 1998	Sani Abacha	Head, Provisional Ruling Council	Kanuri (North)	Died in office
May 1998–May 1999	Abdulsalami Abubakar	Head, Provisional Ruling Council	Gwari (North)	Handed power to civilian government
May 1999–May 2007	Olusegun Obasanjo	President	Yoruba (Southwest)	Civilian-to-civilian transfer
May 2007–April 2010	Umar Musa Yar'Adua	President	Hausa-Fulani (North)	Died in office
May 2010–present	Goodluck Jonathan	President	Ijaw (south south)	—

first case because the population of the North is about the same as in the East and West combined, and in the case of the military regimes, because of increasing dominance of the officer corps by Northerners.

In the early years of independence, a military career lacked prestige, especially among educated Southerners. In an effort to speed the replacement of remaining British officers, the Balewa government actively recruited university graduates into the officer ranks. One result was the introduction of large numbers of educated Igbos into officer ranks; another was the politicization of the army.

When the military controlled the country between 1983 and 1999, an officer's commission came to be seen as the most regular path to political power. The first coup leaders in 1966 professed great regret at the necessity to intervene and promised that their stay would be temporary. They were removed and killed in the second 1966 coup before their sincerity could be tested. The longevity of General Gowon's regime was made necessary by the need to prosecute the civil war and then to lay a constitutional framework for civilian rule. When Gowon seemed inclined to settle in for the long term, he was removed, and General Obasanjo set and abided by his 1979 deadline. Thus, through the first period of military rule, although there was serious profit-taking on the part of many military leaders, none of them expected to have long-term political careers.

The second round of military power (1983 to 1999) produced a gradual change in the perspectives of at least some military officers. Many observers have wondered about the military leadership's annulment of the 1993 presidential election results and the abolition of state and local elective offices already filled. Most feel that if the presumed winner, Moshood Abiola, had been allowed to assume power, he would have been unable to deal effectively with the country's problems, would quickly have lost an already dubious legitimacy, and would thus have prepared the way for a return of the military with acceptance by the population. As it was, the Abacha regime faced massive resistance and was able to rule only on the basis of force, at least in much of the South. Many observers assume that Abacha's actions, while certainly supported by elements in the North that could not stomach a Yoruba president, also reflected the strong desire of a new generation of military officers to enjoy the fruits of power that come from oil revenues and from the potential

profits that flow from the corruption of public office. The country witnessed open jockeying for positions as state governors or "chairmen" of local governments, which were allocated according to military rank. National-level offices were usually filled by generals, brigadiers, or colonels; state governors were mostly colonels; and local chairmen were lieutenant colonels and majors, often retired from active service. Politics in Nigeria is still largely a game of money; therefore, the retired military, the business group, and some retired civil servants dominate the elective positions, while a few academics have political appointments, like minister, commissioner, or in the foreign service.

Today there are more routes to professional advancement than simply joining the military, and education has arguably become more important. Nigerian universities produce large numbers of trained public administrators, and they follow long-term careers in federal, state, or local administration that usually are not affected by changes at the top. By the time of the 1979 transition, 89 percent of the bureaucrats at the assistant-secretary or permanent-secretary level held university degrees.[24] An appropriate educational level had come to be expected in the civil service. This is not to say that the civil service offered a stable career; an estimated 11,000 administrators were removed when Murtala Muhammed came to power in 1975 and took vigorous action against corruption. But to the degree that the administrative system continues to function through the many regime changes, it does so because of the permanence of the civil service.

Recruitment into political positions at the local and state levels generally excludes "strangers," even though they may be long-time residents of a community and, of course, Nigerian citizens. There are some exceptions: Where "strangers" are sufficiently numerous, they can run and win. In most places, however, regulations have expressly limited candidacy to indigenous candidates. In addition to simple democratic fairness, the advantage of creating a multiethnic council is that it stimulates identity and participation in the community on the part of populations that are otherwise excluded. An important characteristic of recruitment into political or administrative office, however, is the effort to "reflect the **federal character** of Nigeria" faithfully. In practice, this has become Nigeria's own version of affirmative action, which fills government positions with regard to identity. This reduces fears of political exclusion by attempting to ensure that government is an ethnic microcosm of the locality or state it controls.

In the past, appointments of military personnel to government posts also reflected the country's federal character: Northern officers were appointed in the Northern states, Yorubas and others from the Southwest to states in that region, and so on. Even today, ethnic politics still very much dominate the politics of Nigeria. However, the federal government has increasingly made use of the zoning structure, which breaks Nigeria into six divisions for the purpose of appointments and the distribution of infrastructures. After all, it is easier to distribute appointments on the basis of six units rather than thirty-six states. In recent years, this appointment process has increasingly been challenged for a variety of reasons. Qualified people have to be "rotated out" in order to fill the position with someone from another zone. The Majority Whip of the House explained in 2010 that this approach helped stabilize the country after the transition and build confidence among previously marginalized communities, but it also deprives the National Assembly and many government agencies of experienced officeholders.[25]

POLITICAL STRUCTURE

Before we can assess—or perhaps appreciate— Nigeria's political structure, it is critical to understand the instability that preceded the current "dispensation," as Nigerians frequently refer to regimes. After a tumultuous postindependence history with five successful coups, three civilian constitutions, and Babangida's annulment of the 1993 elections, the country seemed to heave a sigh of relief when Obasanjo was sworn in as president in 1999. It is thus important to evaluate the mixed democratic progress since then, bearing in mind the 2003 elections and the country's first peaceful transfer of civilian authority in 2007. After decades of constitutional fragility and failures of previous constitutional arrangements discussed in this section, the shortcomings of the Obasanjo, Yar'Adua, and Jonathan administrations may start to sound like small setbacks outweighed by the relative stability experienced by the political system under their stewardship.

The first political institution in which Nigerians participated as Nigerians was the legislative council mandated by the Clifford Constitution of 1922, which provided for elected representatives from Lagos. Elections were introduced in this way and stimulated political activity. Through successive constitutional changes in the 1940s and 1950s, elective office was extended to local and regional governments, and the first provisions for a federal structure were introduced. Because of the numerous military interludes after independence, constitution drafting and large-scale reform efforts almost seem like a regular part of politics. The current constitution closely resembles the one promulgated in 1979. But the transition that made the current constitution possible and the various political bargains it enshrines are perhaps best understood by starting with a discussion of the failed transition in 1993.

The Development of the Constitution of 1999

As Babangida postponed the return to civilian rule in 1993, his standing with the population, and even within the military, moved ever lower. When he delayed announcing the outcome of the June 12, 1993, presidential election, apprehensions grew, for it was popularly believed that Moshood Abiola had won. Two days after the election, initial results released by the National Election Commission (NEC) showed that Abiola had won in eleven of fourteen states. Later, a private human-rights coalition, the Campaign for Democracy (CD), published election results indicating that Abiola had won in nineteen of the thirty states. A few days later, the military government declared the election invalid. At the same time, Babangida promised new elections and once again promised a return to civilian rule. He appointed a transition committee chaired by a Yoruba, Ernest Shonekan, and Babangida vacated the capital without fanfare—in a technical sense meeting his deadline for the restoration of civilian rule. However, Shonekan had virtually no support and was pushed aside by General Sani Abacha three months later in November 1993. General Abacha maintained the myth of a return to civilian government and created the Constitutional Conference to draft yet another governing document. The Constitutional Conference was inaugurated on June 27, 1994, but two weeks earlier, on the anniversary of the annulled election, Moshood Abiola had declared himself president. Abiola was arrested on June 23, 1994, and charged with three counts of treason. Abacha seemed to manipulate the system to remain president, but his strategy was aborted by his death of a reported heart attack in May 1998. Meanwhile, Abiola had maintained his claim from prison, but he also died of a reported heart attack two months after Abacha, just as he was negotiating his release with Abacha's successor, Abdulsalami Abubakar. The succession of deaths, first of Shehu Yar'Adua in prison (November 1997), then Abacha (May 1998), and then Abiola (July 1998), was seen by many Nigerians as an entirely improbable set of events. Even though the departed represented an extreme range of political positions, conspiracy theories have since then been widely floated.

From 1983 to 1999, politics in Nigeria took the form of a succession of military regimes that constantly planned a return to democracy. Administrative and judicial proceedings continued as though a constitutional structure were in place. The 1995 Constitution was widely discussed and even cited as the basis for election procedures in 1997 and 1998—yet the document was only officially promulgated by General Abubakar in May 1999 as he handed power over to a civilian regime. The overall structure of the current Constitution is outlined in Figure 13.4.

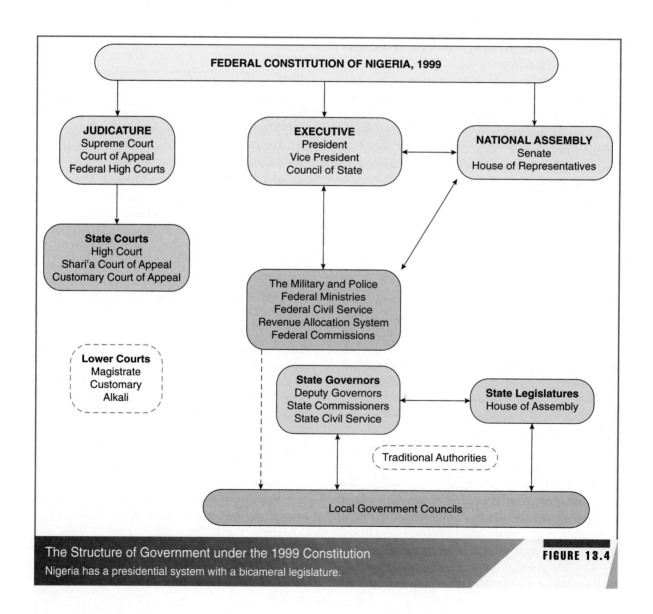

The Structure of Government under the 1999 Constitution
Nigeria has a presidential system with a bicameral legislature.

FIGURE 13.4

Federalism

In a country as vast and complex as Nigeria, many political decisions are not made at the national level. A federal system was established as Nigeria moved to independence in 1954. In a uniquely Nigerian scenario, two of the regions, the Eastern and the Western, gained self-governing status in 1957; the North followed in 1959. Thus, a very decentralized federal system was already in effect at independence. The Constitution of 1960 was explicitly federal, dividing responsibilities between the federal government and the three regions. Federalism has been a constant in the three constitutions (1963, 1979, and 1989) since that time, and in the constitution developed but never promulgated under Abacha in 1995. For the return to civilian rule in 1999, Abubakar drew upon these federal traditions and a strong commitment to presidentialism.

In the face of formal federalism, however, stands a fiscal condition that calls the federal concept into question: All levels of government derive the largest portion of their revenues from the national oil monopoly, distributed through the national government. Beyond this fiscal fact of life, there has been the control of Nigeria by military governments for twenty-nine of its fifty years of independence. It is difficult to define federalism under a military chain of command. Nonetheless, any permanent civilian constitution will undoubtedly be genuinely federal. As political activists in the South have become convinced that Northerners are bent on dominating any central government in Nigeria, they have argued for greater state or regional autonomy. Moreover, with the emergence of militant groups, such as MEND, the federal government has had to confront an increasingly visible and viable secessionist movement in the South.

State-level politics has often been dominated by local ethnic rivalries, as states are called upon to settle local government boundary disputes and to decide on the competence of various traditional institutions. Pressures analogous to those at the local level have led to an expansion of the number of states. The three colonial regions, which became the states of federal Nigeria, quickly became four. With the outbreak of civil war in 1967, the country was divided into twelve states, a number that was increased to nineteen in 1976, to thirty in 1991, and to thirty-six in 1996 (plus the Federal Capital Territory; see Figure 13.5). The number of local government areas within the states has progressively increased, too, with different ethnic or subethnic groups vying for representation.

All these tensions finally converge at the national level, the source of most government resources. Recent federal governments have attempted to calm the ethnic struggle with a Nigerian version of affirmative action based on the country's federal character. Various regions—and thus ethnic groups—are guaranteed a proportionate share of federal positions. This is an application of the consociational model, a common solution where countries are deeply divided by religion or ethnicity.[26] If appointments were made on competence alone, the educational advantage of the southernmost populations would result in their having a disproportionate share of civil-service jobs. Federal character is thus widely accepted as a means of integrating the government and building confidence among disparate groups. In recent years, this approach has been used in the appointment process even at most local levels; federal character is no longer merely for appointments at the federal level.

Both the 1979 and 1989 Constitutions establish a three-level federalism. In such other large federations as the United States, Canada, and Australia, the constitution focuses on the federal–state relationship, with local government principally in the domain of the state or province. The fact that Nigerian constitutions have specified a uniform structure and common functions for local government is rather unusual. While there are no doubt advantages to this uniformity of structure and function, it does not allow for local governments to reflect the diversity of local cultures present in the country, nor is experimentation possible of the sort that has produced the manager and commission systems at the local level in the United States. Since colonial times, however, local government has really been little more than local administration of federal policy, a situation unlikely to change until local governments acquire independent sources of revenue. Clearly, in an oil-centralized system, the demand for local governments cannot be explained by the control of decision-making. Rather, ever more local government is attractive because of the formula-driven allocation of funds that supports local activities. In 1981, the Second Republic's National Assembly decided to allocate 10 percent of federal revenues and 10 percent of state revenues to the localities. However, not only were state governments unwilling to abide by this

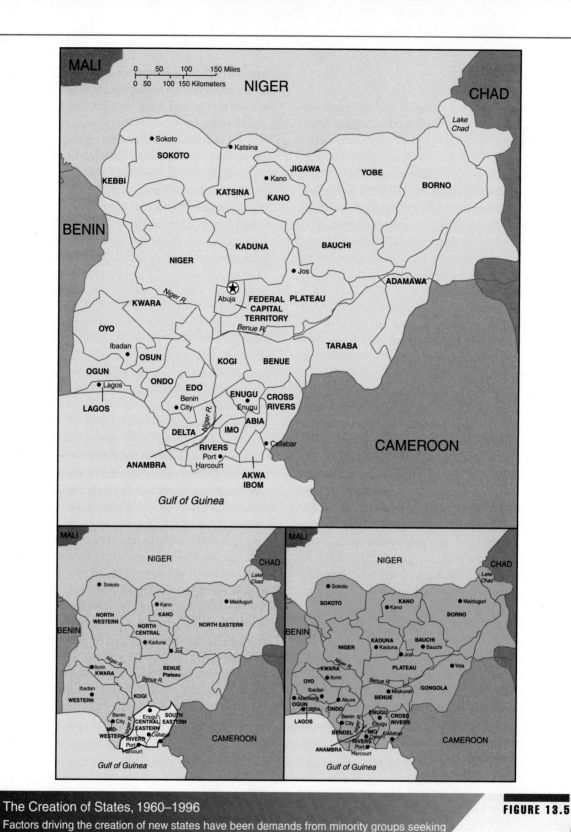

The Creation of States, 1960–1996

Factors driving the creation of new states have been demands from minority groups seeking distinct representation and the revenue allocation system of federal grants.

FIGURE 13.5

Note: Lower left: Dark border (lower left map) shows original three regions, increased to four by the creation of the Midwestern Region, and to twelve in 1967. Lower right: Nineteen states, 1976–1991. Above: Thirty states, 1991–1996. (Current thirty-six states are shown at the beginning of the chapter.)

mandate, they also frequently tapped for their own purposes the federal allocation that was transmitted to them for distribution at the local level. To remedy this situation, the 1989 Constitution provided direct payment of the federal allocation to local governments; in 1990, that allocation was increased to 15 percent, and a few years later, to 20 percent of federal revenues, where it stands today.

The process of subdividing administrative and political units has fueled a growth of the public sector. Employment in the public service is an indicator of the growth of government. At independence, there were 71,693 employees of federal and regional government; by 1974, there were about 630,000, not counting the 250,000 in military service. A study of local governments in 1978 and 1979 found another 386,600 positions at that level, not counting general laborers or district or village heads. The drop in oil revenues in the mid-1980s brought an end to government growth. However, the Buhari administration imposed a 15-percent across-the-board personnel reduction that started a long period of stability in government employment.[27] Since 1999, competition among states for the distribution of federal revenues is acute in two arenas: first in disagreements between the president and the National Assembly over the amount of money that should be returned to the oil-producing areas, or what Nigerians refer to as the "derivation formula." Second, the controversy has played out between the states and the federal government in a series of major Supreme Court decisions in 2002 concerning states' entitlement to offshore oil revenues and the federal government's right to exempt certain expenses from funds distributed under the derivation formula.

Some observers suggest that a genuine federalism would help to cure Nigeria's political problems, which almost always involve the tremendously large stakes in the oil-rich nation's federal government. Perhaps a national government with limited resources would result in a federation that is not viewed as a high-stakes zero-sum game.

Parliamentary versus Presidential Government

Without exception, British colonies came to independence with a parliamentary system based on the mother country's Westminster model. Initially, Nigeria followed the Commonwealth pattern, with a ceremonial governor-general named by the British monarch.

In 1963, the formal structure was redesignated a republic, with Nnamdi Azikiwe as president with mostly ceremonial powers; the parliamentary system was maintained, with a prime minister as head of government. Because Nigeria's first experience with civilian rule ended disastrously in 1966, it is not surprising that the previous system was called into question as a new constitution was being framed in the 1970s. The drafters decided that the Westminster parliamentary model promoted majority rule with few checks and balances, which alienated much of Nigeria's population. Their solution was to model the Constitution of the Second Republic unabashedly after the U.S. presidential model: An independently elected president was balanced against a two-house National Assembly at the federal level, with governors and legislatures following the same model at the state level. The disorder in the Second Republic might have brought presidentialism into disrepute as well, but the principal aspects of the presidential system have been maintained in the more recent constitutions.

The 1999 Constitution provides for an independently elected president and a dual-chamber National Assembly at the federal level. Governors and single-house legislatures follow the same basic model at the state level. The Speaker of the House presides over the House of Representatives, while the president of the Senate, who is in the line of presidential succession after the vice president of the republic, presides over the upper chamber. Each of Nigeria's thirty-six states has three senators (plus one for the Federal Capital Territory of Abuja), while population determines the number of constituencies in each state for a total of 360 representatives. Senators and representatives serve four-year terms and are elected at the same time, rather than in staggered elections. The number of standing committees has increased in recent years, fragmenting the jurisdiction over issues and often making it impossible for members to carry out their responsibilities. For example, in 2010, there were eighty-six standing committees in the House of Representatives! Members demand chairmanships because of the additional resources, benefits, and power they offer. Committees are still getting accustomed to their role in the legislative process, and many bills are not amended or debated until they reach the floor for debate. As permitted by the Constitution, the Executive Branch introduces the federal budget and other major pieces of legislation, and how much the

National Assembly can or should modify these bills has been a hotly contested issue since the transition to democracy. Differences of opinion between the two branches of government have been dramatic, even though the president's party has consistently enjoyed a majority in both legislative chambers since 1999.

Nigeria's problems with achieving stable constitutional rule have made it an important case study in arguments over the relative advantages of presidentialism compared to parliamentarism in conditions of cultural pluralism. On the face of it, the fault may seem to lie with defects in the various constitutional frameworks, but the problem may actually be the intractable nature of Nigerian pluralism. A constitutional document cannot succeed at papering over a lack of trust among the country's subcultures. The lack of trust has led to suggestions of a "zoning" arrangement, which would require that the presidency and other top posts rotate automatically among the various geographical "zones" in the country, such that every major group could have a turn. The Constitutional Conference of 1995 gave a general endorsement to zoning at all levels of government—that is, for governorships of states and chairmanships of local governments as well as at the federal level. The National Assembly proposed similar constitutional reforms in 2001.

The Judiciary

Nigeria came to independence with a well-established legal system that included a court system and a thriving legal profession in the British tradition. The federal and state courts are integrated into a single system of trial and appeal courts. Thus, the 1999 Constitution provides a Supreme Court, a Court of Appeal, and state and federal High Courts with original and appellate jurisdictions. Traditional authorities maintain their greatest influence in their judicial powers, for states are explicitly allowed to constitute customary and *shari'a* (Muslim Koranic law) courts, both original and appellate. A dozen Northern states maintain *shari'a* courts, a point of contention between Muslim authorities and those who see such official recognition as divisive.

Successive military regimes undermined the judiciary as the country's dictators ruled by decree, often whimsically. Abacha seemed to deliver the final blow to judicial independence because his government had little inclination to respect the legal system. It reacted to court orders by changing the rules and establishing special military tribunals, even for common crimes such as robbery.

INTEREST ARTICULATION

There are at least two aspects of political influence in Nigeria. First is the effect of organized interest groups, such as unions and trade associations and religious bodies. The second involves the more informal channels of participation through individual relationships often described by the term "clientelism."

The activities of formal associations and institutions often offer the most vigorous expression of societal independence from a government. Characteristically, voluntary associations were either brought under control or abolished in the authoritarian regimes that took hold in Africa soon after independence. This was not, however, the case in Nigeria, where even during military regimes, organizations such as the Nigerian Women's Union have maintained an independent existence, even as their political influence was reduced.

Ethnic and Religious Associations

Many of the first formal associations in Nigeria had an ethnic base. The Igbo Federal Union (later the Igbo State Union) was "inaugurated by politically conscious representatives of the Igbo intelligentsia."[28] The Egbe Omo Oduduwa was organized among young, urban, Yoruba professionals. Minority groups especially found comfort in formal associations such as the Ibibio State Union, the Edo National Union, the Urhobo Renascent Convention, and others. These associations often formed the organizational base for parties and contributed to the latter associations' ethnic orientations. In the North, where individual clientelist ties are relatively stronger, associations even of the ethnic type have played less of a role. An ethnic association of contemporary significance is the Movement for the Survival of the Ogoni People (MOSOP), founded by **Ken Saro-Wiwa**. MOSOP claims to speak for the 500,000 Ogoni people whose land is now occupied by Shell Oil drilling rigs. In the 1990s, the Ogoni complained that they have borne the brunt of the inconvenience of Nigeria's oil industry and have received little in return. Tensions reached a peak when four Ogoni chiefs were murdered by young militants. Saro-Wiwa and fourteen other Ogonis were arrested and charged with murder for inciting the youths. In a blatant frame-up and an example of how Abacha's government undermined the courts, he and eight co-defendants were summarily convicted and hanged in 1995. This shocked world leaders and highlighted the deplorable state of human rights in Nigeria. The South African leader, Nelson Mandela, himself recently released from prison, said at the time, "General Sani Abacha is sitting on a volcano, and I am going to make sure that it blows up under him."[29] In November, the Ogonis were hanged, despite pleas of clemency from around the world. Saro-Wiwa's legacy remained sensitive, and it was not until 2002 that the federal government allowed the families to exhume bodies of Ken Saro-Wiwa and the others for a proper burial.

As in many other countries, religious institutions and associations play an important part in Nigerian politics. These groups are especially durable and resilient because when political activity is repressed, they remain organized around denominational objectives, and where an ethnic association might have to play a less obvious role, neither Christian nor Muslim religious groups and leaders find it necessary to camouflage their identities. As in other countries, religious-based interest groups take several forms: the formal institutions (churches, Koranic schools); leadership roles such as bishops, pastors, and *mallams* (Muslim teachers and learned men); and voluntary denominational associations. The effectiveness of religious institutions in articulating concerns to government has been reduced by intergroup conflicts, most frequently between Christians and Muslims, which put the government in the role of mediator.

Not surprisingly, associational life is most active in the South; however, the North is home to an Islamic "mystic brotherhood," the Tijaniyya, which is particularly influential among lower-class Hausa Muslims and is looked on with suspicion by the representatives of orthodox Islam (another brotherhood, the Khadiriyya, is identified with the traditional elite of the North). The existence of such groups blurs the distinction between "modern" associations and "traditional" institutions. A new breed of ethnic organizations has emerged under democracy, with groups such as the Arewa People's Congress, which declares its mission as "defending Northern interests," and the Odua People's Congress militating for its version of Yoruba interests in the Southwest.

Associational Groups

In the more urban and industrialized areas of the country, one encounters a range of associational interest groups common to the politics of any modern nation. Trade unions have played a role in Nigerian politics since the colonial period, sometimes collectively through the Nigerian Labor Congress (NLC) and its affiliated unions. However, labor action is organized more frequently by sector. Groups representing the petroleum workers can have an immediate impact on the national economy and consequently have the potential for great political influence, as was demonstrated in 1994 strike actions by the **National Union of Petroleum and Gas Workers (NUPENG)** and the Petroleum and Natural Gas Senior Staff Association (PENGASSAN). Groups such as the Nigerian Union of Local Government Employees (NULGE) are especially influential because of their immediate impact on government.

Professional organizations—such as the Nigerian Bar Association, the Nigerian Medical Association, and especially the Nigerian Union of Journalists—are politicized as issues concern them directly. Military governments periodically force the dissolution of such groups by arresting their leaders. The universities are another modern sector that has a tradition of political activism. Faculty as well as students were some of the earliest critics of military rule, and military governments have tried to marginalize their role in the country. Strikes by staff and students are common; it is not unusual for a student's undergraduate education to take six or seven years.

During the long periods of military rule, politicians at all levels who were turned out by the military have constituted an interest group united around their desire to be allowed back into the circles of power. They were a force pushing for the return to civilian rule, even as many of them were content to be "co-opted" into administrative service under the military.

Civil society groups such as such as the National Democratic Coalition (NADECO) and the CD were at the forefront of the struggle for democracy. After Abacha died in 1998, a new coalition, the Transition Monitoring Group (TMG) emerged as an advocate for electoral form and a watchdog against electoral fraud. In 2007, it trained over 20,000 election monitors who fanned out across polling stations, and their final report condemned widespread electoral fraud.

Nonassociational Groups

A clear Nigerian example of the nonassociational interest group, but shadowy in its definition, is the famous "**Kaduna Mafia**." Hardly any informal conversation on Nigerian politics fails to mention this network of powerful Northern leaders, who are said to maintain strong influence over the military and Nigerian politics. Richard Joseph offers this description:

> In a general sense [Kaduna Mafia] refers to members of the Northern intelligentsia who assumed positions of political and social influence during the decade of military rule after the civil war. These individuals are, on the whole, better educated than their predecessors in the emirate North who held similar positions in the first decade after independence. [They also] were less dependent on the patronage of the traditional rulers to advance in their careers.[30]

This group was highly influential in the Babangida years, but Sani Abacha distanced himself from it. General Yar'Adua, a political reformer and a leading figure in the Kaduna Mafia who served in military administrations in the 1970s, died in prison in 1997. When his brother, Umar Musa Yar'Adua, was elected president in 2007, some saw this as a return of their influence.

Given that most of Nigeria's labor force is involved in agriculture, one expects to find strong associational activity among farmers. However, the ethnic divisions in the country have prevented the formation of any national-level farm organizations. Those groups that do exist are usually engaged in local cooperative activities and are not active beyond the regional level. More commonly, the interest articulation activities of farmers are relatively spontaneous and unorganized, or take the form of clientelism (as we will discuss later).

Finally, one institution is far more than an interest group: the military itself. We will address its political role later. The Nigerian military is not a cohesive interest, as was demonstrated in the transition from Abacha to Abubakar. The enlisted personnel and lower-ranking officers have not seen any direct benefit from military rule, and many supported efforts to return to civilian rule. Also, the country's ethnic divisions are reflected in the military as well, although they compete there with a well-ingrained military professionalism. The military rank-and-file were originally drawn mostly from Northern non-Hausa minorities. Later recruitment drew from all over the country, but the minorities, especially from the "Middle Belt," remain disproportionately numerous. The early preponderance of Igbo officers ended with the second coup and the Biafran civil war, which resulted in the Northern dominance in the officer corps that is present today. However, there is wide ethnic diversity among the officers, and ethnicity is only one factor in the complex disputes within the military. There is a constant possibility that new factions will emerge to challenge the current leadership, to forestall or delay the return to civilian control.

Patron–Client Networks

An alternative structure for interest representation is found in the **patron–client network**. Powerful Nigerian political figures are able to mobilize support through personal "connections" with subordinates, who may themselves serve in a corresponding role of "patron" for a yet-lower set of "clients." **Clientelism** was an integral aspect of political life in the larger-scale precolonial systems of the Hausa, the Yoruba, and others. Those who are not represented by formal associations may be able to take advantage of their connections to achieve political ends, particularly at the local level and where traditional rulers and their political systems maintain some influence. Furthermore, the pattern of personal contacts is ingrained in the culture and thus remains important as an approach to powerful modern figures independent of any local traditional context.

Resting on these patron–client networks in Nigeria is a patronage system in which a ruler or an official gives a public office to an individual client in return for his loyalty in delivering political support at some lower level. The prevalence of such a system in Nigeria is not dependent on particular regimes, civilian or military.[31] Their durability makes the "restructuring" of Nigerian administration difficult when regimes are under pressure to develop an "austerity" budget.

POLITICAL PARTICIPATION

Given the lack of either good census data or reliable voter registration figures, it is difficult to be precise about voter turnout figures, but estimates are in the range of 40 to 60 percent in some earlier elections, an impressive level for a majority poor and illiterate populace. Some of the explanation is found in the prevalence of patron–client systems, the "machine politics" that ties ordinary voters into the electoral process through personalistic ties with political activists.

Interest in elections, even in the mobilization of patron–client networks, declined during the long transition to civilian rule, but it rose again with the return to civilian rule. In the presidential election of February 1999, turnout was estimated at 52 percent. Voter turnout for the 2003 election was an estimated 69 percent. Reflecting the underlying problems with the 2007 election, official estimates of turnout are unavailable, but unofficial estimates are around 57 percent.

Violence also is employed frequently, from the use of "thugs" by political parties in both republics to the confrontations with police in Lagos and the Southwest during the last days of the Babangida regime and in the challenges to Abacha's seizure of power. Violence by the state, although less common than in many authoritarian regimes, has played a major role in Nigeria politics: Upward of fifty people were executed for participating in the failed coups of 1986 and 1990; death sentences against those accused in 1995 were not carried out, only because members of the Provisional Ruling Council (PRC) could not agree among themselves on whether to do so. The greatest example of political violence was, of course, the Biafran civil war from 1967 to 1970. Nigeria experienced over 2 million deaths in wars from 1960 to 1992, the vast majority of them during the civil war. Though on a lesser scale, the government remains complicit in human-rights violations following the 1999 transition. Violence often takes the form of reprisal attacks—often on a large scale—by security forces after one of their own is killed. Extrajudicial killings by police are not unusual, either.[32]

Nigeria has been a highly politicized country ever since independence. If democracy offers better representation, rule of law, and improved government performance, it will, it can be hoped, reduce the sense of alienation and frustration that inspires much of this violence.

PARTIES AND ELECTIONS

Nigeria's early political parties were influenced by the divisive effects of colonialism, which strengthened regional attachments, as well as nationalist opposition to British rule. The National Council of Nigeria and the Cameroons (NCNC) emerged as a diverse nationalist movement in 1944 under the leadership of Nnamdi Azikiwe.[33] This organization advocated increased representation in the Nigerian colonial government. Political reforms creating indirect elections to regional assemblies strengthened ethnic attachments in the 1950s, and the NCNC broke up along ethnic lines. The Action Group (AG), an opposition party with its stronghold in the West, emerged under the leadership of a young Yoruba lawyer, Obafemi Awolowo. From the beginning, there were forces within both the NCNC and the AG arguing for movement in a multicultural, issue-based, cross-regional direction. However, the AG was split on how quickly to proceed to independence via a cross-regional strategy or along more conservative, ethnic-based, evolutionary lines. Azikiwe was particularly committed to action at the national level, but the NCNC played to its strength in the East when it became clear that he needed a regional power base. Thus, the NCNC came to be identified with that region and the Igbo people, while the AG was identified with the opposition in the West (see Table 13.2).

Unlike the NCNC and AG, the major Northern political parties never really tried to obtain political support outside their own region. Britain's successful application of indirect rule in the North had resulted in an alliance between the colonial administration and the traditional emirs that impeded the formation of

TABLE 13.2			
Ethnic Distribution of Party Leaders, 1958			
Even before independence, Nigeria's political parties acquired a strongly regional character.			
Party*	**Igbo**	**Yoruba**	**Hausa-Fulani**
NCNC	49.3	26.7	2.8
AG	4.5	68.2	3.0
NPC	—	6.8	51.3

*NCNC: National Council of Nigeria and the Cameroons; AG: Action Group; NPC: Northern People's Congress.
Source: Richard Sklar and C. S. Whitaker, Jr., "Nigeria," in *Political Parties and National Integration in Tropical Africa*, ed. James S. Coleman and Carl Rosberg (Berkeley: University of California Press, 1964).

modern political movements. Although reformist political organizations were formed—notably the Northern Elements' Progressive Union (NEPU)—they operated only at the margins and tension points of the emirates. A more conservative movement, the Northern Peoples' Congress (NPC), was taken over by the Sardauna (a traditional title) of Sokoto and a Hausa commoner, Abubakar Tafawa Balewa. The NPC, the traditional emirates, and the preindependence administrative structure were intertwined such that young administrators could run successfully for public office, but only if they had the support of their administrative superiors and of the local traditional elite. This political structure grew up among a population that was not as educated (less than 15 percent were literate) as in the South and that was much more loyal to their traditional authorities. The elite origins of the party's officers and candidates were deemphasized through both communal (ethnic) and religious (Islamic) appeals to the electorate. Not surprisingly, the NPC did not give high priority in its program to achieving national independence.

When General Ironsi assumed power following the breakdown of political order in the Western Region and the first coup, one of his first moves was to abolish all parties and a large number of political associations. It was a move imitated by later dictators, who sought either to eliminate political competition to consolidate power or to limit it as part of a managed transition to democracy. The country operated without political parties during General Yakubu Gowon's tenure from 1966 to 1975. When Murtala Muhammed then took over, he set in motion a process to return to civilian rule, including drafting a new constitution and establishing strict rules for political parties, which he thought should be "genuine and truly national political parties."[34] The constitution drafters in response specified that to be elected president, a candidate would have to poll at least 25 percent of the votes cast in each of at least two-thirds of the states. Parties were required to register with an electoral commission, and their governing boards had to reflect the country's "federal character"—specifically, coming from at least two-thirds of the states.

The elections of 1979 and 1983 are difficult to analyze because five parties competed for president, Senate and House seats, and state assemblies with varying degrees of success. Looking at the Senate, House, and state assemblies overall, most states were controlled by a single party. For example, Awolowo's party dominated five of the nineteen states, all in the Yoruba West and the Midwest (a "minority" area). Azikiwe's party carried three states, two of which were in the Igbo-dominated East. The ethnic factor was complicated by the success of the NPN in building cross-regional alliances. The NPN controlled eight states; five of these were in the North, but three were in the Southeast.

Following the military coup in 1983, Nigeria went nearly ten years before it held national elections again. After Babangida voided the national elections of 1993 and Abacha came to power, party activities were banned in Nigeria. Abacha artificially created five parties to contest local and state elections, which were allowed to exist only as long as they refrained from any criticism of the government. Reflecting their weak sense of political independence, all five endorsed Abacha as their presidential candidate.

In 1998, the Abubakar regime allowed new parties to be formed. In order to participate in the elections of 1998 and 1999, parties were required to demonstrate a nationwide organization. On the basis of the cases they submitted, nine parties were qualified to compete in the local elections of December 1998. The three parties that received the highest number of votes in the 774 local governments were then allowed to compete in the state and national elections of 1999. The PDP won in 389 local governments, the All People's Party (APP) in 182, and the Alliance for Democracy (AD) in 100, with other parties winning in the remaining 103. As the presidential elections of February 1999 approached, the APP and AD negotiated to present a single candidate—in other words, the normal effect of a winner-take-all situation pushed toward the creation of a two-party system. There were ultimately just two candidates: Olusegun Obasanjo, representing the PDP, and Olu Falae, leading the APP. Obasanjo won with 62.8 percent compared with Falae's 37.2 percent. The **Independent National Election Commission (INEC)**, created by the Abubakar regime for this election, declared Obasanjo the winner.

In 2003, Obasanjo ran for reelection. The APP, which had in the meantime renamed itself the All Nigeria People's Party (ANPP), selected Muhammed Buhari, another former military ruler, as its presidential candidate. The PDP increased its majority in both houses of Congress and won twenty-eight out of thirty-six governorships. Obasanjo was reelected by a landslide, winning almost twice as many votes as Buhari. He and the PDP particularly improved their position in the Southwest, where they captured five governorships from the AD.

The 2007 election season began with a campaign by President Obasanjo's supporters to change the constitution in order to allow him a third term in office. Because his vice president, Atiku Abubakar, wanted to run, this led to an acrimonious battle within the PDP that carried regional dimensions too, since Abubakar is from the North. Abubakar failed to win the nomination in highly suspect primaries, and the dispute has left a lasting scar on the party.

After the third-term bid failed, Umar Musa Yar'Adua won the nomination and went on to be elected president in 2007 (see Table 13.3). At every level, the PDP remained dominant. It secured large majorities in the House and Senate again, and it won most of the governorships. International and domestic observers widely condemned the elections as fraudulent, and the courts threw out at least eleven gubernatorial and nine senatorial elections. In fact, the 2007 election of President Yar'Adua was not upheld by the Supreme Court until December 2008.

Nigeria loomed on the edge of constitutional crisis starting in November 2009, when Yar'Adua disappeared from public as his heart-related ailments increased. The cabinet (loyal to the chief executive in a presidential system) declined to assess his condition, as called for by the constitution. Under pressure from global leaders and new civil society organizations such as the Save Nigeria Group, the National Assembly swore in Vice President Goodluck Jonathan as "acting president." When Yar'Adua died in April 2010, Jonathan was formally sworn in as president, ending an awkward—and potentially explosive—impasse. Jonathan's administration

has an ambitious reform agenda; he began by refusing to reappoint the top INEC official who oversaw the troubled elections of 2003 and 2007.

Ethnic Solidarity and Party Loyalty

Arguably, ethnicity still drives much of the political organizing in the country, and political leaders undermine truly national parties through ethnic appeals. The PDP today is so large that it seems to transcend such differences, but in other ways, it merely operates as a coalition of ethnic and regional elites. Figure 13.6 shows the formation of Nigerian political parties, notably their reemergence with the same regional ethnic bases they had in the 1960s, even before the military regimes. Ethnicity and regionalism complicate the role of political parties as instruments of interest aggregation and articulation. Until the election of Obasanjo in 1999, Hausas captured the top office in national elections. The annulment of the 1993 elections denied the South an apparent victory, which compounded the frustration for a region that had lost the presidency in 1979 and 1983. The annulled elections also created a "political debt" of sorts to the Yorubas, which heavily factored into the political party formations during the 1999 transition.

In 1979, the Hausa-dominated NPN won the ultimate prize, the presidency, essentially on the basis of a combination of Northern voters and minority voters in the Southern regions. The most significant difference for parties between the First and Second Republics turned out to be the carving-up of the original three regions into nineteen states. Ethnic groups other than the "big three" were dominant in a number of these states and had thus broken free of regional ethnic dominance. Party strategists henceforth combined a strong

Results of 2007 National Elections

TABLE 13.3

In 2007, the PDP won the presidency and both chambers of the National Assembly by huge majorities.

	PDP (%)	ANPP (%)	AC (%)	Others (%)
Presidential vote	69.8	18.7	7.5	4.0
House of Representatives	73.0	17.5	8.3	1.1
Senate	79.8	12.8	5.5	1.8

Note: PDP: People's Democratic Party; ANPP: All Nigeria People's Party; AC: Action Congress.
Source: The Independent National Electoral Commission, results, www.inecnigeria.org.

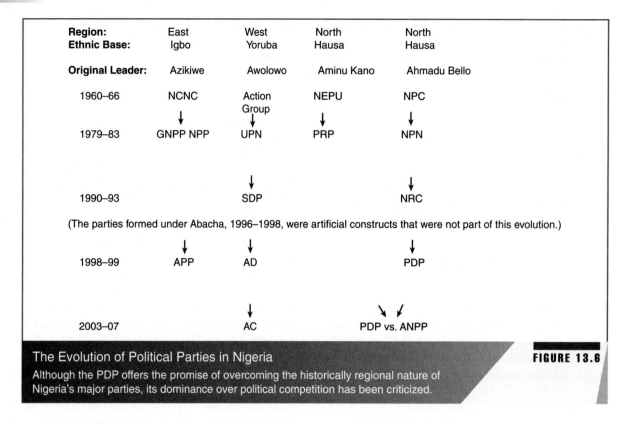

Region:	East	West	North	North
Ethnic Base:	Igbo	Yoruba	Hausa	Hausa
Original Leader:	Azikiwe	Awolowo	Aminu Kano	Ahmadu Bello
1960–66	NCNC	Action Group	NEPU	NPC
	↓	↓	↓	↓
1979–83	GNPP NPP	UPN	PRP	NPN
		↓		↓
1990–93		SDP		NRC

(The parties formed under Abacha, 1996–1998, were artificial constructs that were not part of this evolution.)

	↓	↓		↓
1998–99	APP	AD		PDP
		↓		↘ ↙
2003–07		AC		PDP vs. ANPP

The Evolution of Political Parties in Nigeria   **FIGURE 13.6**

Although the PDP offers the promise of overcoming the historically regional nature of Nigeria's major parties, its dominance over political competition has been criticized.

base in one of the main ethnic group areas with a successful appeal for support among minorities and potentially among dissident groups in the home bases of the other two major groups.

The same five parties remained in existence through the four years of the Second Republic and contested again in 1983 for the presidency, seats in the Senate and House, and state-level positions. However, the smallest parties, the PRP and the GNPP, had been weakened by their lack of access to resources. And, as is normal in a presidential system where the ultimate prize, the presidency, is a winner-take-all election, there were pressures on the two major opposition parties to combine against the incumbent. Such cooperation proved impossible, however, when neither Azikiwe nor Awolowo would defer to the other as presidential candidate. In a campaign marked with violence and vote-rigging, the NPN won a solid victory, recording gains against the opposing parties in their home areas. The NPN victory was short-lived, though. Three months into its second term, it met an early demise at the hands of Nigeria's fourth military coup. This time, the military's abolition of political parties had some political support because the parties were seen as so corrupt.

The two-year reign of Muhammed Buhari (1983–1985) presented no timetable for a return to electoral politics. However, Buhari's successor, Ibrahim Babangida, began outlining conditions for a return to civilian rule in 1986 that revealed his view of the country's problems. Between 1987 and 1989, a series of decrees created the NEC to replace the defunct Federal Election Commission (FEDECO) in managing the electoral process. The NEC provided for nonpartisan local council elections in 1987; set a timetable for the creation of political parties and the sequential election of legislators and executives at the local, state, and national levels; and promulgated a constitution to come into effect in 1992.

The military favored a two-party system, and it eventually overruled NEC and created two by fiat. Babangida then asked the NEC to examine the various documents of the dissolved parties and synthesize them into two discrete philosophies, one for a party "a little to the left," the other to fit a party "a little to the right" on the political spectrum. Even the parties' names were assigned by the government: The party on the left would be the Social Democratic Party, that on the right the National Republican Council (NRC).

Nigerians reacted to these developments with a mixture of cynicism and hope. It was difficult for intellectuals to accept a "democracy" based on parties and elections mandated by an authoritarian government, yet it promised to bring the country back to civilian rule. This transition process suffered a setback late in 1992, when the regime nullified the results of the parties' efforts to produce presidential candidates. The process had indeed been so poorly handled as to justify a postponement of the process. Yet Nigerians were ever more skeptical as to whether the military really intended to leave, or was just playing an elaborate game to buy time.

Babangida scheduled a new election for June 1993, ordered the parties to produce new candidates, and set August 27, 1993, as the date for turning over power to the civilian government. Under more careful control, the parties reconvened their national conventions and nominated new candidates. The NRC selected a relatively unknown figure, Bashir Tofa (a Kanuri from the Northeast), while the Social Democrats nominated a rich businessman from the Southwest, Moshood Abiola. The election finally took place on **June 12, 1993.** Nigerian and international observers reported that it was a generally fair election, and the NRC did not announce any plans to contest the outcome. Perhaps equally as important as its relative fairness, the election seemed to promote national unity. Abiola, from the South, appeared to have won a majority of the votes in nine Northern states, including his opponent's home state of Kano. The results seemed to suggest that under a two-party system, factionalism in each region and state could be exploited to prevent a strictly regional outcome.

The 1993 results were never officially announced, however, and two weeks later, Babangida annulled the election. "June 12" became a term forever etched into Nigerian memory, particularly for political activists in the Southwest who claimed the Yoruba had been denied the presidency. Party politics, even the contrived variety invented by the Babangida regime, had once again proved to be an exercise unacceptable to the military leadership and their allies. The Abacha regime announced guidelines for the creation of new parties in June 1996, and political entrepreneurs immediately began forming alliances, even though NADECO and other opposition groups denounced the exercise as a sham. The five parties certified for local elections in March 1997 all nominated Abacha for the presidency.

On July 20, 1998, Abubakar announced the dissolution of the five parties, the nullification of the local and state elections, and a new start toward democracy with freely formed parties and a promise to hand over power to an elected president on May 29, 1999. A new organ, the INEC, was created to supervise the electoral process. Of the nine parties originally certified in October 1998, the three that survived the local elections represented some degree of continuity with earlier party formations—each with a base among one of the three major ethnic groups. However, because of the requirement to have a national base and for other strategic considerations, the candidates of each party were not necessarily of the ethnic group presumably dominant in it. Most importantly, even though the PDP is said to have its base in the North, its leaders threw their support for the presidential nomination to General Obasanjo, who had only recently been released from Abacha's prison. As both a Southerner (both he and his principal opponent, Olu Falae, were Yoruba) and a former military ruler, Obasanjo was seen by many both inside and outside the country as the individual most likely to provide effective leadership in the postmilitary state. However, some of those active in the various human-rights and democracy movements were dubious that a former authoritarian leader was an appropriate president for a democratic state, and his Northern backing raised doubts among many Southerners. And the question still remained: Would the military be ready to return to the barracks? The answer came with the inauguration of Obasanjo as president on May 29, 1999.

For Nigeria's third attempt at democracy to succeed, it will have to tackle significant problems, including corruption driven by substantial new oil revenues, a bureaucracy in need of retraining, ongoing ethnic and religious conflicts, and serious economic inequalities. Even though the president's party has held a majority in the National Assembly, there have been significant tensions between the executive and legislative branches. Since 1999, corruption investigations have resulted in two changes of leadership in the Senate and two in the House. The elections of April 19, 2003, in Nigeria were the first civilian-conducted elections in twenty years. This development represents a big step toward establishing an enduring democracy in Nigeria. President Olusegun Obasanjo won with 62 percent of the votes to Muhammed Buhari's 32 percent; other candidates had 6 percent, including

Odumegu Ojukwu, the former seccessionist leader of Biafra (1967–1970). Olusegun Obasanjo's PDP captured most of the governorships, along with super-majorities in the House and Senate. Election observers reported significant irregularities, concluding that they "severely limited and even denied in some parts of the country the ability of Nigerians to express their franchise" during both the legislative and presidential elections. The National Democratic Institute's observation report continued: "The cumulative effect of these problems seriously compromised the integrity of the elections where they occurred." Despite these flaws, Obasanjo was widely accepted as the winner, and the international community interpreted the elections as a step toward democracy.

Umar Musa Yar'Adua, the governor of Katsina State, emerged as the winner of the 2007 presidential contest. The election marked the first civilian-to-civilian transfer of power in the country's history, although power remained firmly entrenched in the ruling PDP. Yar'Adua received nearly 70 percent of the votes, while the party that took second place received less than 13 percent. International observers and domestic monitors criticized election preparations and the conduct of voting even more harshly than in 2003. The major national civil-society coalition, the Transition Monitoring Group, called for the results to be canceled outright. The EU's Observation Mission said that the "State and Federal elections have fallen far short of basic international and regional standards for democratic elections." A report issued immediately after the elections noted "significant evidence of fraud" and concluded that the elections "cannot be considered to have been credible." The defeated vice president, Atiku Abubakar, and other candidates challenged the 2007 election results, which the courts did not formally resolve for over a year. Election tribunals sifted through hundreds of other results, overturning

Goodluck Jonathan Launches His Campaign

Goodluck Jonathan's political intentions were unclear during his term as "Acting President" and even after he was sworn in as president. He formally declared his candidacy in September 2010 at this rally.

Afolabi Sotunde/Reuters/Landov

several key governorships, further confirming the fundamental problems with the voting process. The election also marked the return of power to the North, since Yar'Adua came from a traditional Hausa-Fulani background. When Yar'Adua passed away in 2010, many Northerners were uncomfortable with the presidency reverting to the vice president, who was from the South. This tension was captured—and often critiqued—in many spirited newspaper editorials and cartoons, reflecting the central importance of political balancing between the Northern and Southern regions.

POLICY FORMATION AND IMPLEMENTATION

In comparing Nigeria's various civilian and military regimes, the ultimate question must always be their *performance*. This is certainly the "bottom line" for Nigerians, whose support of these various regimes is based on the quality of life they experience under them. This section thus focuses on the *decisions* governments have made, particularly in raising revenues, dispersing funds, and implementing programs. It will also discuss some background issues, such as planning and conducting the federal census, the results of which underlie all policy. Finally, it presents the constraints imposed on Nigerian decision-making by the outside world, particularly in the World Bank–supported **Structural Adjustment Program (SAP)**. Dealing with "SAP," as the economic restructuring program is commonly called, leads us back to the discussion of environment with which we began. Policy relating to Nigeria's international economic situation has responded to initiatives from other African countries, world powers, international organizations, and multinational firms. Here we consider the critical constraints that the world economy puts on the choices available to a Third World country, even one as large and resource-rich as Nigeria.

Extractive Performance

Nigeria inherited a fiscal system in 1960 that depended mainly on taxes on international trade. Indirect taxes provided 64 percent of total revenues, direct taxes only 16.5 percent, and other revenues 19 percent. The colonial system had developed a revenue system that operated through agricultural marketing boards. Ostensibly created to provide price stability to farmers, marketing boards accumulated surplus funds in good years that tempted government officials with development projects in mind. Peasant farmers also paid direct taxes, of which they were much more aware. Widespread tax riots broke out in the Western Region in 1968 and 1969, a period during which tax collection was halted, eventually to be replaced by a lower, much simpler flat tax.

In the First Republic and under the Gowon administration, the state governments collected the personal income, sales, and poll taxes. Tax collections generally declined as new states were created, without fiscal institutions in place and with smaller tax bases than the old regions. At the same time, rising oil revenues strengthened the fiscal position of the federal government (and those states with oil fields).

Oil production began in earnest in 1958. At independence, the federal government was collecting modest royalties from private Western oil companies. In 1971, within a few years of the Biafran civil war, Nigeria joined the **Organization of Petroleum Exporting Countries (OPEC)** and also formed the **Nigerian National Oil Corporation (NNOC)** to participate directly in oil production. NNOC acquired a one-third interest in the AGIP Company and Elf, both French-controlled firms. At the time, this was seen as retribution for French support of the Biafran separatist effort, but within a few years, the government had acquired a majority interest in all oil-production activities. The NNOC was merged with the Ministry of Petroleum Resources to form the Nigerian National Petroleum Corporation. Over this same period (the mid-1970s), petroleum prices had risen dramatically, from $3.30 per barrel in 1972 to $21.60 in 1979. Thus, the sale of crude oil directly by the Nigerian federal government to multinational oil companies came to provide the greater part of federal government revenues and, through the federal system, of state and local revenues as well.

In a pattern typical of Third World oil-exporting countries, Nigeria today depends almost entirely on the revenues from this single industry. Since there is no indication that the world's appetite for oil will diminish in the near future, it is a reliable revenue source that substitutes for the various forms of taxes on private income. Nigerians are fortunate that they have not been directly burdened with the cost of supporting government programs; they are perhaps unfortunate that governments, especially authoritarian military regimes, can tap this vast wealth without risking the wrath of taxpayers. The exceptions to this general rule are enterprises and property owners in Lagos State, which has a large share of the country's modern enterprises and generates over half its revenues, and the Ogonis and other peoples who inhabit the oil-producing region, who do not feel they benefit from the natural resources of their home area.

Given their control of vast petroleum reserves, Nigerian regimes have not actively sought large amounts of direct foreign aid. They have, however, used the country's oil reserves as the collateral for massive borrowing from foreign and international banks in the 1970s and 1980s. The funds supported massive capital expenditures and gave Nigeria an enormous external debt, which rose from 10 percent of GNP to 140.5 percent between 1980 and 1995. Oil wealth did not bring the country financial independence; to the contrary, the debt gave international lenders a predominant voice in Nigeria's allocation of public funding. With the debt payoffs in 2005 and 2006, Nigeria will now be substantially insulated from such outside influences.

Distributive Performance

As a producer of high-grade petroleum, Nigeria has an unusually great potential to move out of the ranks of the less developed into the middle-income nations. In the 1970s, impressive projects, such as road development and irrigation projects, as well as the launching of Abuja as the nation's capital, were signs that potential might become reality.

Unfortunately, political corruption grew apace and probably began consuming a higher proportion of national wealth than in the pre-oil period. When oil revenues suddenly began their decline in 1980, "corruption and mismanagement prevented any kind of disciplined adjustment," and "the economy was plunged into depression and mounting international indebtedness. . . . Sucked dry of revenue by the corruption, mismanagement, and recession, state governments became unable to pay teachers and civil servants or to purchase drugs for hospitals, and many

services (including schools) were shut down by strikes."[35]

In spite of the country's raw material advantage, Nigerians have not seen their lives improve in recent years. The UN Development Program publishes the Human Development Index based on three factors: life expectancy at birth, adult literacy, and per capita GDP (see Table 13.4). Nigeria has a rank of 158 out of 182 countries on the HDI and a rank of 141 on per capita GDP alone. It is not surprising to find the less-developed countries low on these listings. However, per capita GDP is a good measure of distributive potential. Thus, the comparison of per capita GDP and the HDI ratings can be an indicator of how well a country has done for its people compared with other countries with similar capacity. Because Nigeria's per capita GDP ranking is much higher than its HDI ranking, this suggests that the Nigerian advantage in oil revenue has had little noticeable impact on the overall quality of life.

Budgetary priorities are important in analyzing distributive performance. In the case of a country ruled by the military for most of the last decade, one might expect that military expenditures would loom especially large. In Nigeria, the military budget increased from $234 million to nearly $1.5 billion between 2000 and 2009. However, there are believed to be significant additional military expenditures that are not publicly reported. Extremely modest in size at independence, Nigeria's armed forces grew to 250,000 at the height of the Biafran civil war. Then the Gowon regime began a program of gradual attrition that reduced the force to about 100,000 in the mid-1980s. Further shrinkage since then has resulted in a total force of 85,000. This still leaves Nigeria a major military force, meaning that firm civilian control of the military remains central to the stabilizing of the country's nascent democracy. In a continental context, Nigeria's army remains one of the more professional. As we will discuss later, Nigerian leaders have used this military strength to maintain a high profile in West Africa.

Nigerians have a great enthusiasm for education, and parties and regimes have promised universal access to it. Some progress can be noted. In 1964, Nigeria ranked twenty-ninth among African nations in enrollments, with 5 percent of the school-aged population in primary school; it was nineteenth in secondary enrollments, with 5 percent of the appropriate age group in

Nigeria's Ranking on Per Capita GDP and Human Development Index (HDI)

TABLE 13.4

Even with its tremendous oil wealth, Nigeria still ranks among the lesser developed countries.

Country	Life Expectancy at Birth, 2007	Adult Literacy Rate (%) 2007	Real GDP per Capita 2007*	Human HDI 2007
United States	79.1	99.0	45,592	0.956
Japan	82.7	99.0	33,632	0.960
Britain	79.3	99.0	35,130	0.947
Mexico	76.0	92.8	14,104	0.854
Botswana	53.4	82.9	13,604	0.694
Indonesia	70.5	92.0	3,712	0.734
China	72.9	93.3	5,383	0.772
Nigeria	47.8	72.0	1,969	0.511
Benin	61.0	40.5	1,312	0.492

*Note: These figures are in U.S. dollars converted at purchasing power parity (PPP) rates.
Source: United Nations Development Program, *Human Development Report 2009*.

school. Ten years later, 24 percent of the school-age population was in school, and Nigeria was fifteenth in Africa on this measure. Primary enrollments stood at about 64 percent in 2006; youth literacy was 87 percent in 2008, up from 65 percent in 1985.

The Nigerian government's performance in the area of health has been mediocre overall. Nigeria's infant mortality rate has dropped from 185 in 1960 to 139 in 1970, 114 in 1980, and 96 in 2008. However, nearly one-fifth of all children die before reaching the age of five, a figure that improved only slightly between 2000 and 2007. These statistics reflect an unfortunate and perhaps surprising trend, mirrored in old age: In 2007, life expectancy was only forty-eight years, showing surprisingly little improvement over earlier data. The government has recently poured more resources into the health sector. In fact, Nigeria ranked fifteenth globally for spending on health in 2006 in per capita terms adjusted for PPP, and this may translate into progress in the health sector.

With petroleum firmly established as the major source of foreign exchange in Nigeria, and with that industry under government control, the distribution of wealth is heavily influenced by policy decisions. Private consumption surged as oil revenues multiplied in the 1970s, about 8 percent per year. This average figure conceals tremendous increases in wealth at the top; the lower 40 percent of the population benefited very little. Government expenditure grew at an even greater rate than private consumption, both in absolute terms and as a proportion of GDP.[36] This aspect of expenditure, of course, includes sums lost in corrupt payments to individuals. Nigeria should have reaped another windfall during the Gulf War, as petroleum prices temporarily shot up, but increased revenues never showed up in national accounts. In 1994, economist Pius Okigbo examined the books of the Central Bank of Nigeria; he reported (as he left the country) that $12.6 billion was not accounted for. The skimming of oil profits had indeed reached astronomical proportions.

Income distribution is also affected by inflation, which followed from the rapid increase in the money supply during the 1970s oil boom and continued apace later on, as governments followed a time-honored approach to balancing budgets when revenues decline: They printed money. The result was continuous inflation, a problem that became especially serious in the 1990s, as shown in Figure 13.7. The case study (see Box 13.3) shows the effect of this inflation on individual income. Consumer inflation peaked at 75 percent in 1995. Since the return of democracy, it has

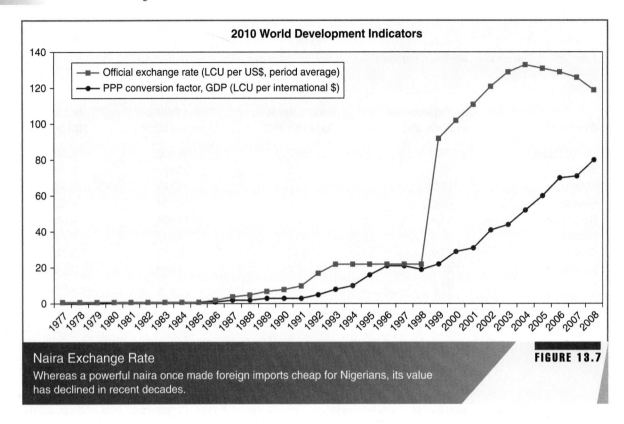

Naira Exchange Rate

Whereas a powerful naira once made foreign imports cheap for Nigerians, its value has declined in recent decades.

FIGURE 13.7

fluctuated but has hovered in the low teens since 2007. This is still a great financial burden for most people in a poor country.

Governments have attempted to deal with inflation by enforcing an official exchange rate for the **naira**, Nigeria's national currency. The result was a huge divergence in official and market exchange rates, causing chaos in the financial system. That chaos dried up investments and stimulated corruption, since anyone with access to foreign exchange at the official rate

The Effects of Inflation: A Case Study

BOX 13.3

A young graduate with a new doctoral degree won a position as an instructor at a Nigerian university in 1977. His salary and benefits totaled 6,000 naira per year. At that time, one naira equaled $1.50, so his salary was the equivalent of $9,000—modest by industrial-world standards but very comfortable in Nigeria. Twenty years later, this same man achieved the rank of full professor, at a salary of 51,000 naira per year, with fringe benefits raising his total annual compensation to 90,000 naira. However, at the parallel market exchange rate of 80 naira to the dollar, his salary was the equivalent of $1,125 per year, a figure not taking into account

the effect of inflation on the purchasing power of the dollar since 1977. In 1998, a national review of faculty salaries increased the professor's salary to the equivalent of $5,000 per year. This discussion implies that salaries are regularly paid. However, in early 1999, the Abubakar government was in such financial straits that it failed to provide salary payments at all. In 2000, President Obasanjo improved the workers' pay generally and moved university teachers' pay to 130,000 naira per month, the equivalent of $1,000 per month. He did this to discourage brain-drain in Nigeria and to promote high-level productivity in all sectors.

can then sell the foreign currency "on the street" for a large profit. Since 1999, the government has reduced its role in stabilizing the currency, allowing the value of the naira to be largely determined by forces of supply and demand.

As a policy issue, distribution in a large country such as Nigeria is also seen as a geographic question, not just one of policy priorities. Nigerians have a fondness for referring to the national budget as the "national cake," and they see state and local governments as the major recipients of "slices." The federal government now spends between two-thirds and three-fourths of public monies and also has great control over how the money distributed to state and local governments will be spent. On the contentious question of how to distribute resources as the number of states and local governments expanded, governments settled on relatively straightforward formulas, a combination of equality (across-the-board distributions to all states) and population. States other than Lagos now depend on the federal Revenue Allocation System (RAS) for 70 to 90 percent of their recurrent revenues. In order to fund local governments, the RAS was extended to cover them directly in 1981. Beginning in 1982, federal revenues were shared according to set percentages among the three levels of government. Given the set formulas in the RAS, it is not surprising that regions and localities strive for statehood and local autonomy and that population counts loom large as a political issue.

Dealing with Debt and Structural Adjustment

Nigeria's recent debt repayments are historic—both for the country and for Africa. It solves a problem that began with fiscal indiscipline during the 1970s oil boom, when the government paid insufficient attention to the lack of productivity of public spending. Much of the money was applied to an increase in welfare expenditures, to developing an unprofitable steel industry, and to building the new capital at Abuja. Late in the 1970s, commodity prices fell, while oil prices remained high. African governments borrowed at an even faster pace, and the continent's total indebtedness increased. As African governments became unable to make debt payments, international financial institutions, principally the IMF and the World Bank, were called in to monitor a restructuring and rescheduling of the debt. Nigeria's total indebtedness continued to increase in the 1980s. By 1991, it represented 257 percent of the annual value of the country's exports and 109 percent of GNP. The annual cost of servicing the debt consumed 25 percent of the value of exports (up from 4 percent in 1980); the weight of this burden almost ensured that the debt would continue to grow. Throughout the past decade, the question of how to deal with the external debt has been a principal focus of political discussion in Nigeria.

The debt problem that began under military rule became much more acute during the Second Republic (1979–1983). The Buhari regime approached the IMF for relief in the form of new loans and more favorable repayment terms, but it rejected the severe conditions the IMF attached to its help. The naira would have to be devalued, trade restrictions would have to be dropped, and subsidies for domestic gasoline consumption ended. These and similar measures have been the issues involved in Nigeria's SAP. It was clear to the military leadership that such measures would be extremely unpopular with the Nigerian public and would lead to outbursts of political violence. When Ibrahim Babangida seized power in 1985, he opened a "national debate" on the issue. He claimed to fashion a Nigerian version of structural adjustment (while at the same time negotiating with the IMF). As the program's austerity measures began to be felt, the SAP became extremely unpopular. In his parallel program of moving back toward civilian rule, Babangida forbade candidates to criticize the program, but at the same time, he eased off on the necessary austerity measures. The net result was that, although Nigerians were suffering from the country's poor position in international finance, the SAP did not reduce the debt or reform the financial system.

Rather than allow the naira to float as urged by the IMF, the Abacha regime fixed an official exchange rate. In 1995, the exchange rate was partially opened to market forces, but this neither stabilized the economy nor satisfied the international sector. The total external debt reached almost $8 billion, and the Nigerian National Petroleum Corporation owed over $1 billion to its foreign partners. In responding to gasoline shortages, however, the government lowered the subsidy on petroleum products. However, the sharp price rise seemed one more hardship to endure for the poor, who were already suffering from rapid inflation. The discomfort increased when extreme fuel shortages reappeared in 1997, bringing long lines at official stations and in turn prompting a black-market rate of nearly seven times the normal price per liter.

There could hardly be a more dramatic demonstration of policy failure: a country rich in petroleum incapable of providing its citizens with fuel. By late 1998, disruptions in the oil-producing areas were having a serious impact on Nigerian oil production, a situation that complicated the inauguration of a stable civilian government. After President Obasanjo was inaugurated in May 1999, he tried to bring calm to the situation by voiding all contracts awarded in the six months prior to his administration. Since then, each attempt by the government to raise the price at the pump has been met with widespread protests and long lines at filling stations. Efforts to reduce government spending by eliminating the petroleum subsidy for domestic consumption remain highly controversial, because those efforts impact not only the cost of public transportation but also food and other daily essentials. For this reason, an academic study in 2010 concluded: "Virtually every fuel price hike that was announced by the government has been massively unpopular and has in almost all cases been resisted by most Nigerians."[37]

Regulative Performance

At independence in 1960, the Nigeria Police Force was essentially regionalized. Because the police were frequently mobilized for political purposes during the rough-and-tumble politics of the 1960s, the military regime decided to consolidate the police function at the national level. It is this national police force that now enforces traffic laws and other government legislation. However, it is often still the case that "law and order" is maintained in individual communities—especially in rural areas—through traditional institutions and norms. Traditional leaders not only prevent deviant behavior but also take responsibility for the welfare of the "strangers" who, in accord with accepted procedures, have taken up residence in their communities.

Although Nigeria was under military rule from 1983 to 1999, the average citizen has not felt oppressed by an authoritarian state. That citizen is aware of the police presence at checkpoints along the country's highways, but fear of authority does not restrict citizen's

actions to a significant degree. As in most Third World countries, there simply are not the resources available to the Nigerian government to keep close tabs on its large population.

Nigeria's judicial system remains vigorous, and until the advent of Abacha's period in office, it had been surprisingly diligent at following a rule of law through the various informally constituted regimes. Still, military regimes intruded on that rule of law. The regime imposed the State Security (Detention of Persons) Decree in 1984, which allows detention without trial of those "suspected of posing a threat to national security." State officials seemed to intervene with increasing frequency into the judicial system where political questions are involved. Though Nigeria's democratic regime appears committed to ending such arbitrary exercises of authority, detention without trial remains a serious problem due to inefficiencies, inadequate resources, and few public defenders. Amnesty International reported in 2008 that nearly two-thirds of Nigeria's inmates were being held without trial—often in the most miserable prison conditions.

The Census Issue One policy issue, the census, has overshadowed all the others since independence, because the outcome often determines how political goods will be distributed. A minor policy issue in some countries, in Nigeria, the population counts have been fraught with conflict. In a country where federal subsidies make up the lion's share of budgetary allocations at all levels, the distribution of population directly affects the distribution of resources.

> After a false start in 1962, a national census was conducted in 1963. It reported a total population of 55.6 million, making Nigeria the tenth-largest country in the world. However, it found a majority of that population (30 million) to be in the North, a finding that was then, and since then, questioned by Southern Nigerians, who maintain that a flyover or drive through the North and South will easily demonstrate that population densities are higher in the latter (although it is also true that the area of the North is much larger). Nevertheless, the 1963 census, or straight-line projections from it, remained the official source of population statistics for almost twenty years. Even in 1973, when General Gowon's regime placed the integrity of the military on the line by having unarmed soldiers accompany enumerators, people rejected the results. In particular,

the figures inspired profound anxiety among Southerners, who alleged overcounting in the North. Fears of regional domination are never too distant within Nigeria.[38]

After almost two additional decades of continued reliance on the 1963 figures, the Babangida government commissioned a new census to be conducted by a National Population Commission. Following methodical pretesting and sampling, a census in November 1991 put the country's total population at 88.5 million, a substantial downward revision from estimates that had exceeded 100 million. According to this census, the highest population concentrations were in the states of Bauchi, Kaduna, Kano, Katsina, and Sokoto in the North, and Lagos, Oyo, and Rivers in the South. The census caused new consternation in the South, where feelings ran high that the figures had again been "cooked" to favor the North. As mentioned earlier, the recent 2006 census effort fared only slightly better.

Conclusions on Performance

While our judgments on performance should be nuanced, given the complexity of Nigeria's political environment and the problems it faces, an overall conclusion emerges unfailingly. In comparison with other countries with equivalent natural resources, skilled human resources, and size, Nigeria has not done well.

That outcome caused Chinua Achebe to write *The Problem with Nigeria*, in which he concluded that the "problem" was leadership. Until Nigerians can settle on a constitutional arrangement that provides responsive leadership from the national to the local levels, the country will continue to fall far short of its potential. Although the Second Republic failed, it was a significant improvement over the first in reining in the politicization of ethnicity. There was reason to be optimistic that the Constitution developed in the later years of the Babangida regime would introduce another increment of correction. Although Abubakar was able to move the country to civilian rule, his decision to base the transition on the poorly articulated Constitution drafted under Abacha in 1995 did not inspire confidence in most Nigerians that the new regime would be based on the rule of law. Democracy cannot be "delivered" by a military regime; indeed, further progress in democratization

will depend on the formation and maintenance of a coalition with the strength to force the country in that direction.

A fatal flaw in political culture may have developed in Nigeria since independence, and it is part of the "curse of oil": Public policy is often seen in Nigeria as the "national cake," and the unfortunate analogy suggests that "they"—the government—bake a cake that is distributed in slices sized to match the political influence of various constituencies. At least at the mass level, constituencies are defined in ethnic terms, and politics becomes a competition among ethnic groups for larger slices of cake. The analogy could of course be used to describe the politics of many countries, but not to the extreme degree to which it applies in Nigeria. There, communities look to the government to provide for them. A successful Nigerian constitution not only must provide responsive leaders, it also must shift responsibility so that extractive and distributive performance come from the same budget, and so that there is some relationship between the amounts one pays into and receives from the public sector. Public goals based on community effort were the norm in most Nigerian traditions; that norm must be rediscovered.

NIGERIA IN AFRICA AND IN THE WORLD

Nigeria has the population and resource base to be a regional power, and it has stimulated hopes and fears among its neighbors concerning that potential. Under the First Republic (1960–1966), Nigeria generally focused inward and played a rather minor role in the continent's turbulent politics. But then came the civil war over Biafra in 1966; Nigeria's army grew from 10,000 to 250,000, the country's oil potential became known, and, as we have seen earlier, world powers took an interest in the war's outcome.

Some West African governments offered clear support to Biafra, a support Nigerians suspected grew from a desire to see their country divided up and thus reduced in influence. This was thought especially to be the case with Cote d'Ivoire (the Ivory Coast) under President Houphouet-Boigny, who favored Biafra with French support. When the war ended, relations among these countries were, as might be expected, strained.

Subsequently, Nigeria under General Gowon took a leading role in establishing, in 1975, the **Economic Community of West African States (ECOWAS)**, hoping to bring Nigeria closer to other West African countries while at the same time countering French influence in the region. The Ivoirian government had taken the lead in forming the Economic Community of West Africa, an exclusively French-speaking organization, and was wary of the predominant position that Nigeria might play in a wider regional organization. But Nigeria was successful in first approaching Togo, Benin, and Niger, the French-speaking countries with which it already had close ties, offering attractive economic inducements that included special petroleum prices. With this group in hand, Nigerian diplomats cast their net wider, and the representatives of sixteen West African governments signed the Treaty of Lagos. The ECOWAS treaty specified a two-year phase during which intracommunity tariffs would be frozen, followed by an eight-year period that would end with the removal of duties on trade among members. Finally, a common external tariff wall would be created.

Thus, West Africa under Nigerian leadership is partaking in the worldwide movement toward free-trade zones. As elsewhere, however, progress has been difficult. Ten years after its creation, ECOWAS reported that it had not made "tangible progress in practical terms," and by 1989, the member governments were $80 million in arrears in their contributions to the organization. The proportion of intracommunity trade in the member countries' total international trade has not changed since 1980. At the same time, ECOWAS has had better success as a regional political organization, especially in mediating disputes among member states, and in 1990, a Nigerian proposal was approved that created a standing mediation committee.[39]

Because of its prominence on the continent, Nigeria's international financial problems have been especially embarrassing. Forced along with other African nations to accept stringent structural adjustment planning from the World Bank and IMF, Nigeria has reacted with frustration and anger. It has led the region's governments in their critique of international lenders' policies, hosting the meeting that led to the Lagos Plan of Action as a response to international debt-structuring proposals. When the Obasanjo administration renegotiated and paid off most of the country's debts, this move was seen as liberating the country from foreign pressures, allowing Nigeria to assume its rightful place as a giant on the continent. Sub-Saharan Africa's great powers—Nigeria, Kenya, and South Africa—increasingly believe that Africa deserves permanent representation on the UN Security Council.

Of all the world powers, France plays the most prominent role in West Africa. Although the French interest focuses on its own former colonies, in recent years, the French have come to believe that Nigeria's size and potential wealth should not be overlooked, and France actively promotes closer economic ties with Nigeria, a move that upsets Nigeria's French-speaking neighbors. The Western powers, especially Britain and the United States, were openly critical of Nigeria's military rulers and supported the country's return to civilian rule, especially during the Babangida regime and once again with Abdulsalami Abubakar. The United States and Britain condemned Babangida's 1993 election annulment, and they suspended aid as a result. However, this relationship was not important enough to Nigeria's rulers to modify their behavior. Presumably, an embargo on purchases of Nigerian oil would have had that effect, but the industrial nations' governments did not have the will to take such a drastic step. Most observers saw the Abacha regime's treatment of dissenters as a calculation of how far it could silence opposition without provoking more severe international sanctions. In contrast, many Nigerians were critical of what they saw as the West's premature zeal over actions that until then were only *promised* by Abubakar in 1998. Western support returned with enthusiasm upon Obasanjo's inauguration.

Nigeria has played a prominent role in the region through commitment of its substantial military capacity, notably in supplying the leadership and the majority of troops for the Economic Community of West African States Monitoring Group (ECOMOG), the ECOWAS-sponsored peacekeeping force in Liberia. That operation was viewed as a success, with armed conflict halted and elections held. Nigerian troops have also been stationed in Sierra Leone to protect that country's borders from incursions of Liberian rebels, and have confronted a Sierra Leonean military junta that overthrew an elected civilian government, an action more than a bit ironic given the origins of the Abacha regime. Nigeria has participated in wider-ranging UN operations in Lebanon, Rwanda, the former Yugoslavia, and Somalia.

Nigeria moved beyond peacekeeping during the Obasanjo and Yar'Adua administrations, demonstrating regional leadership on a variety of other foreign-policy issues. The Chief of Defense Staff affirmed the military's respect for civilian authority in 2010 and then went on to note that the military needs to be "more proactive and responsive to nonmilitary stimuli and developments."[40] This is reflected on issues such as drug and human trafficking, which led the government to establish new agencies to confront these growing transnational criminal networks. Nigeria recognizes that some of these security problems originate within its borders, too, for example as international ties of some militant groups have been exposed. The United States is very concerned both about the incubation of Islamic extremism in the North and threats to the flow of oil in the Niger Delta. Nigeria often prefers to treat such challenges as domestic problems first, although ECOWAS is becoming increasingly important to its foreign policy and as a lens for formulating a regional understanding of terrorism and other security threats.[41]

PROSPECTS FOR DEVELOPMENT

Nigeria's political and economic setbacks do not equal the tragedies of Rwanda, Sudan, or Somalia, but the frustrations are nonetheless deep and enduring. Billions of desperately needed naira have been wasted, a few people have grown rich at the expense of the poor, and accountability in government has proved highly elusive. Poet Tanure Ojaide captured this frustration in "No Longer Our Own Country," written in 1986:

> We have lost it,
> the country we were born into.
> We can now sing dirges
> of that commonwealth of yesterday—
> we live in a country
> that is no longer our own.[42]

In much of the world, the attraction of democracy has been its association with prosperity. Like other people, Nigerians are more interested in the outcome of the political process than in the process itself. Calls for better leadership and the welcome initially extended to some military regimes suggest that Nigerians' highest priorities are economic security and

the rule of law. If these could be provided by generals, the country would probably accept an authoritarian system. However, at least since Plato we have known that benevolent authoritarianism is an elusive concept. Western democracies have developed on the premise that democracy is a necessary, if not sufficient, condition for accountable leadership. And Nigerians have had enough opportunities to compare the results of military rule with their expectations that a majority of them are ready for another try at elective civilian rule. Perhaps another constitutional correction will be enough to usher in the long-term political stability for which they have hoped.

This discussion highlighted so many different problems (alongside a few hopeful solutions) that the reader might feel overwhelmed by the sheer complexity of the Nigerian case. There are a handful of enduring questions, though, that characterize Nigeria's past, present, and future challenges. First is the relationship between the state and the economy. "Stable democracy is associated with an autonomous, indigenous bourgeoisie, and inversely associated with extensive state control over the economy," writes Larry Diamond. "In Nigeria, and throughout much of Africa, the swollen state has turned politics into a zero-sum game in which everything of value is at stake in an election, and hence candidates, communities, and parties feel compelled to win at any cost."[43]

Oil wealth exacerbates the problem because so much money accrues to the central government, giving federal politicians vast resources for patronage. Part of the answer appears to be the emergence of a vigorous private sector capable of counterbalancing political power emanating from the capital. Nigerians have a reputation for entrepreneurship around the world, and the recent economic development of Lagos gives us some idea of what such a political counterweight might look like—especially since it is one of the few states controlled by a governor from the opposition party. Another part of the answer lies in creating an environment conducive to such investment, where rule of law protects the political rights of citizens and entrepreneurs do not have to spend huge portions of capital on generating power or surviving poor roads.

A second and related problem stems from the exploitative and destructive nature of oil itself. The vast environmental destruction throughout the Niger Delta gave rise to the Ogoni movement and, later, more militant groups such as MEND. Unlike the

Biafran secession movement, their rallying cry has often been "resource control," rather than demands for political independence. Even though Goodluck Jonathan is the first president to come from the Niger Delta region, he must reassure the area that his policy promises are more credible than the years of betrayal and neglect these communities have suffered. A broad amnesty plan brought nearly 20,000 militants out of the swamps and into a rehabilitation and reintegration process in 2009 and 2010, but such progress may fall by the wayside absent sustained political commitment and massive public investment in the region. As a technical committee convened by the federal government in 2008 concluded, the region does not necessarily need new ideas or government agencies; it merely needs the government to implement the critical recommendations of seventeen previous committees on the Niger Delta.

Finally, representation remains a central debate within the political structure and across society. Born of an awkward amalgamation of two distinct colonies

a century ago, Nigeria's two regions may not always exist in harmony, but they do create a political equilibrium that has helped the country survive. After eight years of a Southern president, there was a broad national consensus in 2007 that there must be a "power shift" to the North. Tensions over succession after Yar'Adua fell ill in late 2009, however, highlighted how quickly such traditions become complicated by unforeseen circumstances, as many Northern elites protested a vice president from the South (Jonathan) taking the helm of government. Whether Nigerians will continue to insist on power shift, federal character, and other efforts to balance ethno-regional identities remains a pressing question. Beyond those fundamental distinctions between North and South, the country's system of zones, states, and local governments adds progressively complex layers of representation, often at the core of civil tensions. Nigerians have a wealth of ideas, abundant resources, and a rich history on which to draw in formulating solutions for Africa's twenty-first-century giant.

REVIEW QUESTIONS

- What factors—cultural, historical, or otherwise—explain Nigeria's ongoing underdevelopment despite its tremendous oil wealth?

- After so many failed democratic transitions, why did the one in 1999 succeed?

- How have Nigeria's constitutional structures and political traditions attempted to deal with the country's tremendous ethnic and religious diversity?

- What were some of the lasting influences of colonialism on politics after independence?

- What are some examples of the informal nature of politics in Nigeria, where political recruitment and interest aggregation often take place?

- Why has civil conflict remained such a problem, even though support for democracy appears to be strong?

KEY TERMS

Abacha, Sani
Abuja
Azikiwe, Nnamdi
Babangida, Ibrahim
Biafra
clientelism
Economic and Financial Crimes Commission (EFCC)
Economic Community of West African States (ECOWAS)

federal character
Fulani
Hausa
Hausa-Fulani
Igbo (Ibo)
Independent National Election Commission (INEC)
Jonathan, Goodluck
June 12, 1993
Kaduna Mafia

Lagos
Movement for the Emancipation of the Niger Delta (MEND)
naira
National Union of Petroleum and Gas Workers (NUPENG)
neocolonial
Nigerian National Oil Corporation (NNOC)

Obasanjo, Olusegun
Organization of Petroleum Exporting Countries (OPEC)
patron–client network
People's Democratic Party (PDP)
Saro-Wiwa, Ken
Structural Adjustment Program (SAP)
Yar'Adua, Umar Musa
Yoruba

SUGGESTED READINGS

Achebe, Chinua. *A Man of the People*. New York: Doubleday-Anchor, 1967.

———. *The Trouble with Nigeria*. Enugu: Fourth Dimension Press, 1983.

Adichie, Chimamanda Ngozi. *Half of a Yellow Sun*. New York: Random House, 2006.

Balogun, M. J. *The Route to Power in Nigeria*. New York: Palgrave Macmillan, 2009.

Beckett, Paul, and Crawford Young, eds. *Dilemmas of Democracy in Nigeria*. Rochester, NY: University of Rochester University Press, 1997.

Coleman, James S. *Nigeria: Background to Nationalism*. Berkeley: University of California Press, 1958.

Diamond, Larry. *Class, Ethnicity, and Democracy in Nigeria: The Failure of the First Republic*. Syracuse, NY: Syracuse University Press, 1988.

Diamond, Larry, Anthony Kirk-Greene, and O. Oyediran, eds. *Transition without End: Nigerian Politics and Civil Society under Babangida*. Boulder, CO: Lynne Rienner, 1997.

Falola, Toyin, and Matthew Heaton. *A History of Nigeria*. Cambridge and New York: Cambridge University Press, 2008.

Graf, William D. *The Nigerian State: Political Economy, State Class and Political System in the Post-Colonial Era*. Portsmouth, NH: Heinemann Educational Books, 1988.

Ikein, Augustine, D. S. P. Alamieyeseigha, and Steve Azaiki, eds. *Oil, Democracy, and the Promise of Federalism in Nigeria*. Boulder, CO: University Press of America, 2008.

Joseph, Richard A. *Democracy and Prebendal Politics in Nigeria: The Rise and Fall of the Second Republic*. Cambridge: Cambridge University Press, 1987.

Koehn, Peter H. *Public Policy and Administration in Africa: Lessons from Nigeria*. Boulder, CO: Westview, 1990.

Lewis, Peter M., Pearl T. Robinson, and Barnett R. Rubin. *Stabilizing Nigeria: Sanctions, Incentives, and Support for Civil Society*. Washington, D.C.: Brookings Institution Press, 1998.

Nafziger, E. Wayne. *The Economics of Political Instability: The Nigeria-Biafran War*. Boulder, CO: Westview, 1983.

Ohiorhenuan, John F. E. *Capital and the State in Nigeria*. New York: Greenwood Press, 1989.

Oyediran, O., ed. *Nigerian Government and Politics under Military Rule 1968–79*. London: Macmillan, 1979.

Paden, John. *Muslim Civic Cultures and Conflict Resolution*. Washington, D.C.: Brookings Institution Press, 2005.

Smith, Daniel Jordan. *A Culture of Corruption: Everyday Deception and Popular Discontent in Nigeria*. Princeton, NJ: Princeton University Press, 2007.

Soyinka, Wole. *You Must Set Forth at Dawn*. New York: Random House, 2006.

Suberu, Rotimi T. *Federalism and Ethnic Conflict in Nigeria*. Washington, D.C.: U.S. Institute of Peace, 2001.

INTERNET RESOURCES

www.AllAfrica.com

Federal government of Nigeria: www.nigeria.gov.ng.

Current information on Nigeria, including news from the major daily papers in Lagos, can be obtained through the Nigeria page of *Africa South of the Sahara: Selected Internet Resources*: www-sul.stanford.edu/depts/ssrg/africa/guide.html.

http://234next.com

www.pambazuka.org/en/

www.thisdayonline.com/

www.africanexaminer.com/

ENDNOTES

1. Clifford Geertz, *Old Societies and New States: The Quest for Modernity in Asia and Africa* (New York: Free Press of Glencoe, 1963).

2. The term "tribe" has been applied indiscriminately to small groups of villages or whole empires, and often in conjunction with the adjective "primitive." Thus, "tribe" has lost any specific meaning and imparts prejudicial notions.

3. Michael Crowder, *The Story of Nigeria* (London: Faber and Faber, 1978).

4. Victor Chikezie Uchendu, *The Igbo of Southeast Nigeria* (Fort Worth, TX: Harcourt Brace Jovanovich College Publishers, 1965), 103.

5. Billy Dudley, *An Introduction to Nigerian Government and Politics* (Bloomington: University of Indiana Press, 1982), 230.

6. World Bank, "World Development Indicators," in *World Development Report, 2006* (Washington, D.C.: World Bank, 2006).

7. Patrick Smith, "Economy," in *Africa South of the Sahara 1994* (London: Europa, 1994), 660.

8. "Abuja Faces Population Explosion Crisis," *This Day*, September 12, 2002.

9. Kaye Whiteman, "At Last, Something Is Happening in Lagos," *New African* 479 (2008): 50–52; "Nigeria; Strategy for Reversing Development Crisis," *This Day*, August 12, 2009.

10. Judith Burdin Asuni, "Blood Oil in the Niger Delta," U.S. Institute of Peace Special Report 229 (August 2009).

11. A. Carl LeVan and Patrick Ukata, "Nigeria," in *Countries at the Crossroads* (New York: Freedom House, 2010).

12. Associated Press, "Hundreds Flee Nigerian City Swept by Riots," November 25, 2002.

13. Robert A. Dahl, *After the Revolution* (New Haven, CT: Yale University Press, 1971); see also the discussion in Dudley, *An Introduction to Nigerian Government*, 80–83.

14. Afrobarometer Briefing Paper No. 67, "Neither Consolidating Nor Fully Democratic: The Evolution of African Political Regimes, 1999–2008" (May 2009).

15. Mustapha Muhammad, "In the Shadows of Men: Women's Political Marginalisation," *InterPress Service*, March 12, 2010; Ghaji Badawi, "Libraries and Women's Participation in Nigerian Politics," *IFLA Journal* 33 (2007): 168–75.

16. See the discussion in Dudley, *An Introduction to Nigerian Government*, 80–83.

17. Chinua Achebe, *The Trouble with Nigeria* (Enugu, Nigeria: Fourth Dimension Press, 1983), 42.

18. BBC News, "Nigerian Leaders 'Stole' $380 Billion," October 20, 2006; BBC News, "Nigeria Governors in Graft Probe," September 28, 2006; and BBC News, "Obasanjo Accuses Deputy of Fraud," September 7, 2006.

19. The discussion that follows draws on Crawford Young's treatment of socialization in his chapter on "Politics in Africa" in earlier editions of this book.

20. In anthropological usage, *polygamy* is a general term for marriage to more than one spouse. *Polygyny* is preferred to describe the marriage of one man to more than one woman (and *polyandry* for the reverse). However, *polygamy* is the term in general use in Nigeria and elsewhere in English-speaking Africa.

21. *A Handbook of Information on Basic Education 2003* (Abuja: Federal Ministry of Education and UNESCO, 2003).

22. David Smith, "Nigerian 'Taliban' Offensive Leaves 150 Dead," *The Guardian* (UK), July 27, 2009; Segun Awofadeji, "150 Killed in Bauchi Religious Crisis," *This Day*, July 27, 2009.

23. Committee to Protect Journalists, "Attacks on the Press 2009: Nigeria."

24. Peter H. Koehn, *Public Policy and Administration in Africa: Lessons from Nigeria* (Boulder, CO: Westview, 1990), 16.

25. Interview with Honourable Emeka Ihedioha, March 17, 2010, Abuja.

26. As noted in Chapter 5, the concept of consociational arrangement comes from Arend Lijphart, *Democracy in Plural Societies* (New Haven, CT: Yale University Press, 1977).

27. Koehn, *Public Policy and Administration in Africa*, 17–18, cites various sources for these totals.

28. Richard Sklar and C. S. Whitaker, Jr., "Nigeria," in *Political Parties and National Integration in Tropical Africa*, ed. James S. Coleman and Carl G. Rosberg, Jr. (Berkeley: University of California Press, 1964), 636.

29. Wole Soyinka, *You Must Set Forth at Dawn* (New York: Random House, 2006), 421.

30. Richard A. Joseph, *Democracy and Prebendal Politics in Nigeria* (Cambridge: Cambridge University Press, 1987), 133–34.

31. Joseph, *Democracy and Prebendal Policy in Nigeria*. Joseph calls the Nigerian version of patronage prebendalism "patterns of political behavior which rest on the justifying principle that such offices should be competed for and then utilized for the personal benefit of officeholders as well as for their reference or support group. The official public purpose of the office often becomes a secondary concern, however much that purpose may have been originally cited in its creation or during the periodic competition to fill it" (8).

32. A. Carl LeVan and Patrick Ukata, "Nigeria," in *Countries at the Crossroads* (New York: Freedom House, 2010).

33. "Cameroons" here refers to the English-speaking portion of the contemporary country of Cameroon (French Cameroun) on Nigeria's eastern border. The former German colony of that name was divided into League of Nations Trust Territories after World War I under British and French control. The NCNC was meant to include members from the British trust territory as well as from Nigeria, but in a preindependence plebiscite, the English-speaking Cameroonians opted for incorporation into Cameroon. The NCNC then was renamed the National Convention of Nigerian Citizens.

34. Address of Brigadier Murtala Muhammed, reprinted as the preface to the *Report of the Constitution Drafting Committee* (Lagos: Ministry of Information, 1976), quoted in Dudley, *Introduction to Nigerian Government*, 127.

35. Diamond, "Nigeria," 53.

36. I. William Zartman with Sayre Schatz, "Introduction," in *The Political Economy of Nigeria*, ed. I. William Zartman (New York: Praeger, 1983), 13. The military figures cited here come from Ruth Sivard, "World Military and Social Expenditures 1996" (Leesburg, VA: WMSE Publications, 1996), and Ruth Sivard, "The Military Balance 2001–2002" (London: Oxford University Press, 2001).

37. Obiora Chinedu Okafor, "Between Elite Interests and Pro-Poor Resistance: The Nigerian Courts and Labour-Led Anti-Fuel Hike Struggles (1999–2007)," *Journal of African Law* 54 (2010), 95–118.

38. Claude E. Welch, *No Farewell to Arms?* (Boulder, CO: Westview, 1987), 10.

39. The preceding treatment of the formation of ECOWAS is drawn from Carol Lancaster, "The Lagos Three: Economic Regionalism in Sub-Saharan Africa," in *Africa in World Politics*, ed. John W. Harbeson and Donald Rothchild (Boulder, CO: Westview Press, 1991), 249–67.

40. Air Chief Marshal Paul Dike, Preface to *Winning Hearts and Minds: A Community Relations Approach for the Nigerian Military*, ed. Ebere Onwudiwe and Eghosa Osaghae (Ibadan, Nigeria: John Archers, 2010).

41. Cyril Obi, "Nigeria's Foreign Policy and Transnational Security Challenges in West Africa," *Journal of Contemporary African Studies* 46 (April 2008), 183–96.

42. Tanure Ojaide, *The Blood of Peace and Other Poems* (London: Heinemann, 1991), 9.

43. Diamond, "Nigeria," 69.

POLITICS IN THE UNITED STATES

Thad Kousser and Austin Ranney

Country Bio

UNITED STATES

Population
310 million

Territory
3,475,031 square miles

Year of Independence
1776

Year of Current Constitution
September 17, 1787, effective March 4, 1789

Head of State
President Barack Obama

Head of Government
President Barack Obama

Languages
English, Spanish (spoken by a sizeable minority)

Religions
Protestant 50%, Roman Catholic 25%, Muslim 1%, Mormon 1%, Jewish 1%, none or not stated 20%

> And what should they know of England
> Who only England know?
>
> RUDYARD KIPLING[1]

Why a chapter on the United States in a book on comparative politics? One reason is that most of its readers are Americans,[2] and politics in the United States affects our lives far more than politics in any other country. Moreover, however feeble we may feel that our personal power is to influence the actions of our government, it is certainly greater than our personal power to influence the actions of other nations' governments.

The question Rudyard Kipling asked about the English in the quotation above can be asked with equal relevance about Americans. There are, of course, many excellent textbooks on the American political system written by American authors and intended for American students. But most of them make few references to, let alone systematic comparisons with, other political systems. Thus, viewing American politics with a special focus on how it resembles, and differs from, politics in other nations will help us better meet

our version of Kipling's challenge. It may even give us some insight into how the distinctive ways of American politics are likely to affect our country's ability to meet the enormous challenges it will face in the years ahead.

CURRENT POLICY CHALLENGES

Still fighting our nation's longest war, grappling with the persistent unemployment that followed our deepest recession since the Great Depression, and battling an oil spill that looks to be the worst environmental disaster in national history, the United States faces a daunting series of policy challenges. All of these challenges—wars in Afghanistan and Iraq, a worldwide financial crisis and a looming national debt with trillions of dollars owed to the central banks of other nations, and an oil spill from a British-owned rig—are global in nature. Responding to them requires domestic decisions made with an eye toward America's place in the world that recognizes both the opportunities and the limits of standing as the world's leading economic and military power.

As in any democracy, our political system serves as the battleground of ideas for confronting these challenges. American democracy not only allows but encourages internal conflict, bringing the competition between diametrically opposed approaches to policy challenges into the open during electoral campaigns and legislative debates. This sort of democracy can often appear loud, bitter, and messy. Indeed, politics in the United States today has featured the most expensive campaigns in history, while the level of partisan polarization—the magnitude of the ideological gulf between Republican and Democratic elected officials—has grown unabated for a generation. A quick glance at cable television news shows evidence of the decline in civility.

These trends pose political challenges, but not insuperable ones. By making the fight between divergent approaches toward the nation's policy challenges transparent to voters, today's rancorous American democracy presents the electorate with clear choices. Through a series of nail-biting, momentous elections over the past decade, voters placed control of government fully in the hands of Republicans in 2000, then shifted power completely back to Democrats by 2008, and finally split control between a Democratic chief executive and a Republican House of Representatives in 2010. The two parties, led by Presidents George W. Bush and Barack Obama, moved policy dramatically in the directions that they and their supporters desired. Rather than bringing a stalemate, these combative politics delivered sweeping changes in both international and domestic policy over the past decade.

Though he was elected by the narrowest of margins in 2000, George W. Bush quickly moved beyond the controversies of butterfly ballots and hanging chads in Florida to make his imprint on the nation's policy direction. He may have lacked a strong electoral mandate, but the Republican Party controlled majorities in both the House and the Senate, and—once the Supreme Court issued its *Bush v. Gore* decision confirming his election—Democrats in Congress did not challenge the legal legitimacy of his victory. President Bush pushed for and won a major tax cut in his first year in office. The policy challenges facing the United States radically shifted from domestic to international with the events of September 11, 2001, the most lethal terrorist attacks committed against the United States on American soil. Planned and executed by members of Al Qaeda, an international terrorist organization led by Osama bin Laden, the attacks were met by a U.S.-led "war on terror" that has been fought not only against Al Qaeda but also against any organization or nation-state that has sheltered terrorists, financed them, or supported them in any way.

The new war is unlike any other in American history. The enemy is not another nation-state, such as Nazi Germany or Imperial Japan as in World War II. There are not organized armies to be defeated in battle by U.S. armed forces, there are no enemy governments to acknowledge or appeal to, and there is no true way to determine when the war is over. The tactics used to fight this war—surveillance both on the ground in dozens of other countries and in the air through interception of wireless communications, some originating in America—are new and often controversial. Through legal cases and debates in Congress, the nation has had an open, ongoing discussion on the proper balance between tightening security and loosening liberties. Signs of progress have come when attempted terrorist attacks have been thwarted. Under both the Bush and Obama administrations, failed attempts to down aircraft headed to Miami (in 2001) and to Detroit (December 25, 2009) have left officials both heartened that security measures helped prevent another tragedy and shaken by the close calls. Nearly a decade has passed since the 9/11 attacks, but the threat of another terrorist attack remains a pressing policy challenge.

The 9/11 attacks also spurred American involvement in two conventional wars, one in Afghanistan and one in Iraq. Because Al Qaeda planned its attack on New York City from remote bases in Afghanistan, under the tacit protection of the ruling Taliban regime, the U.S.-led invasion of this isolated nation was swift and uncontroversial in domestic and international political circles. Many other nations lent troops and support to the war, which appeared to be immediately successful. It began less than a month after September 11, 2001, and by December of that year, the Taliban had been toppled from power and Al Qaeda driven into hiding. Hamid Karzai became Afghanistan's first elected president in 2004, but by the time he was reelected in a contest marred by fraud in 2009, his administration was tainted by allegations of corruption and struggled to control outlying areas such as the Kandahar province. Al Qaeda resurgence there has posed a challenge to American forces and the

Afghan military that they are training. Early in his presidency, Barack Obama both increased U.S. troop levels by 30,000 and promised a drawdown beginning in 2011, but heightened violence in early 2010 led Obama to squash any hopes that American involvement in the troubled region would end soon. Though U.S. casualties in Afghanistan have been relatively low, at 1,139 troops killed in action, this conflict overtook Vietnam as America's longest-running war on June 7, 2010.

The second war that followed in the wake of 9/11 was much more controversial, both in America and across the globe. While only a single member of Congress had voted against the invasion of Afghanistan in 2001, the resolution to authorize an attack on Iraq—which was not directly involved in the terrorist attacks—was opposed by 133 U.S. representatives and 23 senators. President Bush's decision in March 2003 to invade Iraq despite the U.S. failure to win endorsement from the UN Security Council also met with international opposition from traditional allies such as France and Germany. The war was quick, with Saddam Hussein's regime in Baghdad falling within weeks. Yet winning the peace proved much more difficult than winning the war, as it became clear that the United States committed too few troops and was too optimistic in its hopes to be welcomed as a liberator.

Ongoing conflict with insurgents claimed the lives of more than 4,400 American troops, though the intensity of this war subsided after reaching its highest levels in 2007. Barack Obama, a critic of the war since its inception, campaigned openly against the Bush administration's policies during the presidential contest, and began a troop drawdown shortly after he was inaugurated, planning a full withdrawal from Iraq by the end of 2011.

An immediate challenge to the daily lives of most Americans has been the impact of the worldwide recession of 2008 and 2009. Stocks crashed sharply in September 2008 as home foreclosures and a credit crunch sent America, and then much of the world, into a spiraling recession (see Box 14.1). The economy of nearly every developed nation abruptly contracted, consumer spending plummeted, and unemployment reached sustained levels not seen in America since the Great Depression of the 1930s. The decisive actions that both the Bush and Obama administrations took to combat the financial crisis illustrate both the responsiveness to policy challenges that the American system can allow and the partisan perils that quick action can entail. During the initial days of the credit crisis in September 2008, President Bush's treasury secretary and officials at the Federal Reserve Bank acted quickly to direct billions of dollars toward banks

---

BOX 14.1

The Worldwide Recession of 2008 and 2009

This global crisis was precipitated when the American housing bubble—the sharp, spectacular rise in home prices that prompted many buyers to take loans that they could only hope to repay if the market continued its rise—suddenly burst. Many homeowners stopped paying their mortgages, banks foreclosed on them, and the effects reverberated across the world's financial system. Lenders had repackaged their risky home loans as complex financial instruments traded from investor to investor to investor across the globe, with the ultimate holders of these investments losing sight of their risk. Foreclosures in places like Phoenix, Arizona, and the suburbs of Las Vegas, Nevada, soon led to losses on Wall Street, in Europe, and in Japan. Stung by the losses and uncertain about the future, major

financial institutions stopped making the short-term loans upon which companies rely to expand operations, to invest in new technology, and even to pay their employees. The world economy abruptly contracted as governments scrambled to keep banks in their countries from failing and to pass stimulus packages that substitute government spending for the consumer spending that was fast disappearing.

In the short term, these quick governmental interventions appeared to stop a recession from becoming a depression. However, by committing governments to spend more at the same time that their tax revenues were slipping, this approach to fiscal policy set the stage for a potential debt crisis in nations such as Greece, Portugal, and Spain in 2010.

and other financial companies on the brink of collapse, worried that their failure would reverberate throughout the nation's economy. This immediate executive-branch action was followed by a dramatic back-and-forth in Congress, where a $700 billion Wall Street bailout bill supported by President Bush was initially defeated, leading to the largest one-day drop in stock-market history. Congress reversed itself and passed the bill four days later. The bailout became a key issue in the 2008 elections, propelling Barack Obama to a comfortable victory as voters placed blame for the crisis on the Republican administration. Yet once President Obama took office, tackling the economic downturn became his political responsibility. With the support of Democratic majorities in both the House and Senate, in February of 2009, Obama passed a $787 billion economic stimulus plan—a mixture of tax cuts and spending increases—without a single Republican vote in the House. Since then, American voters have generally held President Obama responsible for the state of the economy, with his approval ratings falling as the nation's economic recovery has remained sluggish.

With lagging popularity but loyal majorities in Congress, President Obama pressed to pass two more pieces of legislation that, combined with the stimulus bill, amount to perhaps the sharpest policy shifts since Franklin Delano Roosevelt's "New Deal." Succeeding where Presidents Truman, Nixon, and Clinton had failed before him, Obama championed a **health-care reform** package that set the country on a path toward universal medical coverage through publicly subsidized private insurance. After nearly a year of debate on this controversial overhaul, Congress passed the bill by a razor-thin margin in March 2010. Another enormous bill passed by miniscule majorities was the financial reform bill that enacted a strong set of consumer protections and banking regulations in July 2010.

In reaction both to these sharp leftward policy swings and to the slow pace of economic recovery, voters put the House of Representatives back into Republican hands in the 2010 midterm election. While the president's party nearly always loses seats in midterm elections, the 63 seats that then-Speaker Nancy Pelosi's Democrats lost signified a major electoral swing and ensured that President Obama would be forced to compromise with incoming Speaker John Boehner's Republican majority in Congress until at least the 2012 elections.

The events of the twenty-first century's turbulent first decade have demonstrated both America's vulnerability and power on the world stage as well as the responsiveness of its political system. The nation moved sharply over the course of the decade: from economic boom to bust, from unified Republican control of government to unified Democratic control, from a series of tax cuts to major enlargements of government services, from unchallenged superpower to an embattled yet still potent world player. The American political system has not always delivered such sharp partisan swings or reacted so nimbly to policy challenges, but its basic features, described in this chapter, have remained unchanged.

HISTORY

Founding of the Nation

Ever since its founding as the world's first modern democracy, America has been dramatically expanding its place in the world. Americans have been renegotiating exactly who will be included within our democracy. The nation has grown more and more prominent in the global community throughout its history, transforming itself from a loose confederation of thirteen states surrounded by the colonial holdings of European powers into a continental power, then a hemispheric player, and, finally, taking its current position as a world superpower. The path of American democracy has been less straightforward and linear than the route of America's global influence. Under the Founders, America was a democracy constituted of white males who owned property. The electorate expanded slowly, with the nation at times reversing its course to take away voting rights from those who once possessed them. Today, men and women of any race or ethnicity can vote, though differences in turnout rates across these categories persist. There are many parts to tell in the story of American history, so this brief retelling focuses upon changes in our nation's place in the world as well as upon how inclusive its democracy has been.

The revolution by a disparate set of colonies against the English throne was a long shot from the start that remained a risky proposition through the nation's early history. Putting their lives and their considerable fortunes at risk, the signers of the

Declaration of Independence began a guerilla war against the British, the world's leading imperial power at the time. George Washington and his fellow colonists took advantage of the military training that they had received by fighting for the British in the French and Indian War, as well as the more steadfast commitment of their troops, to win a shocking victory. The first government that they crafted, organized under the Articles of Confederation, was largely a failure, too weak to provide a common defense against threatening foreign powers or to bring the new states together in the pursuit of unified goals. The truly exceptional step that marked America's historical path as unique and magnificent came next, when the weak confederation was replaced not by a strong dictator but by a muscular democracy. The other major revolutions in world history—in France and in Russia—eventually led to tyranny, but America's revolution of 1776 led to the crafting of the Constitution in 1787. This successful system produced the stablest democracy that the world has seen, and has influenced the design of governmental systems the world over. Its essential characteristics—separation of powers, presidentialism, judicial independence, and, in its first ten amendments, a Bill of Rights that limits the government's powers—have appeared in whole or in part in constitutions from the Philippines to Latin America to modern Russia.

Still, at the edge of a continent controlled by rival European powers, the Americans remained in peril. The War of 1812, in which the British burned the new capital city of Washington, served as a reminder of the young nation's vulnerability. Yet with a strong constitution keeping the agriculture-based, slave-reliant colonies of the South in a strained but workable alliance with the industrial, antislavery colonies of the North, America prospered and used some of its wealth to purchase land from France (in the 1803 Louisiana Purchase) and Russia (acquiring Alaska in 1867). Assembling a military that became the preeminent power in the Western Hemisphere, America also expanded its borders to the Pacific Ocean after the Mexican-American War ended in 1848.

Also growing during the nineteenth century was the size of the electorate eligible to vote in America. After the revolution, states imposed various requirements that white men had to own property or hold wealth to vote, every state barred women from taking part in most elections, and only a few Northern states granted the franchise to African-Americans. By 1792, France had surpassed the United States in the scope of its democracy when the new republic there granted universal male suffrage (though this expansion of rights ended as the republic became Napoleon's Empire). American states gradually caught up in the early 1800s, reducing property-holding requirements so that white men of every class could vote. The Democratic-Republican Party, led by the charisma of war hero Andrew Jackson and the organizational genius of professional politician Martin Van Buren, helped to turn this legal right into electoral reality when its grassroots party groups ushered in an era of high turnout among white men. While the energetic advocates of women's voting rights won partial victories when twenty states allowed women to vote in referendums to prohibit alcohol sales, and when Wyoming became the first state to allow female suffrage in 1869, the final victory for this movement did not come until the ratification of the Nineteenth Amendment, giving all American women the right to vote in 1920. Even more discouraging was the fight for African-American voting rights, which were won and then lost in the South after the Civil War.

Civil War

The Civil War (1861–1865) is the United States' great historical watershed. Before 1861, it was a much-disputed question as to whether the United States was merely a convenient alliance made among independent sovereign states—states that had every right to secede whenever they wished—or an indissoluble sovereign nation whose people chose to divide power between the national government and the state governments. In the terminology introduced in Chapter 6 of this book, the United States was a "confederation" during this period. After 1865, in both law and fact, it was established that the United States was, as every American schoolchild is drilled to know, "one nation, indivisible," and not a federation of sovereign states.

Before 1861, many Americans, especially those in the eleven Southern states that seceded to form the Confederacy, felt that they were first and foremost citizens of their states and thus derived their American citizenship from the membership of their states in the union. (The most famous example was Robert E. Lee; he strongly opposed both slavery and secession, and yet when Virginia seceded, he refused command of the

Union Army and cast his lot with Virginia because he felt he owed his primary loyalty to his state, not his nation.) The Fourteenth Amendment to the Constitution, ratified in 1868, removed all doubt by declaring, "All persons born or naturalized in the United States and subject to the jurisdiction thereof, are citizens of the United States and of the State wherein they reside." In short, all Americans are now primarily citizens of the United States, and derivatively become citizens of the state in which they reside. (Interested readers can see the broader discussion of federalism in Chapter 6.)

By cementing the union of American states, the Civil War also solidified American power abroad. The vast military might assembled to fight this internal war left the nation able to challenge even European powers, as it did successfully in the Spanish-American War of 1898. More difficult was the fight to transform America into a nation that uniformly accepted civil rights. Passed in the Civil War's wake, the Fifteenth Amendment guaranteed voting rights to American citizens regardless of "race, color, or previous condition of servitude." Still, it took the might of the North's military occupation of the South to keep polls open to former slaves. When the troops left the South in 1876, massive political violence made African-American voting dangerous, and a series of state laws began to make it nearly impossible. By 1900, these laws— including poll taxes that imposed fees on all voters, literacy tests that could be administered in a discriminatory fashion, and blunter instruments like the "white primary"—reversed the voting rights gains won in the Civil War and left black voter turnout below 10 percent in the South.

Twentieth Century

After experiencing staggering, if uneven, industrial growth in the late 1800s, America was ready to take its place as an economic and military leader on the world stage by the turn of the century. Theodore Roosevelt's mediation of the Russo-Japanese War (1905) and America's belated entry (1917) into World War I (1914–1918) signaled the nation's willingness to engage in world affairs beyond its own hemisphere. Ever since America emerged from World War II (1939–1945) as a clear military victor and the strongest remaining economy, it has been a leading player on the world stage. Of course, superpower status has come

with immense dangers and costs. From 1948 to 1989, world politics was dominated by the "Cold War" between the two great superpowers and their allies: the United States, leading an alliance of Western capitalist/democratic nations, and the Soviet Union, leading an alliance of Eastern communist/authoritarian nations. The Cold War came to an end in the early 1990s when the Soviet Union was formally dissolved (see Chapter 12) and Eastern European nations established their independence.

The defining internal struggle in American politics during the century was again the fight for African-American political rights. During World War II, many blacks fought valiantly abroad, while others migrated from the South to cities across the country to work in factories. These geographic and economic migrations brought social change and a well-organized push for civil rights in the South and across the country. Galvanized by the Supreme Court's 1954 *Brown v. Board of Education of Topeka* decision, the push to integrate schools and other public institutions moved from Kansas to Little Rock to the University of Alabama. When some Southern leaders reacted with explicitly racist rhetoric and police officers met the Rev. Martin Luther King's peaceful protests with violence, popular opinion across the nation turned toward the side of African-American rights. Congress passed important Civil Rights Acts in 1957 and 1964, but it was the Voting Rights Act of 1965 that finally enfranchised black Americans in practice by giving the federal courts and the U.S. Department of Justice the power to enforce voting rights. The political and social transformation that followed in the South and in other areas of the country have served as an example to civil-rights advocates around the world, demonstrating the potential for translating legal changes into vast societal shifts.

America Today

With an expanded electorate, America now has a much more diverse set of elected leaders. In 2007, 74 of the 435 U.S. Representatives in Congress were women, 42 were African-American, 23 were Hispanic, and 4 were Asian-American or Pacific Islander. Comparing this representation of women to other democracies, America ranks ahead of Russia, Iran, Ireland, Japan, and South Korea, but behind the United Kingdom, Mexico, and France, and far behind Germany, the

Netherlands, and Argentina. The election of President Barack Obama is an obvious watershed event in the representation of racial and ethnic minorities, but it should be viewed as the culmination of a series of advances rather than a singular event. George W. Bush's administration featured two African-American Secretaries of State in Colin Powell and Condoleezza Rice. Although the nation has never elected a female president, Hillary Clinton was an early favorite for the Democratic nomination in 2008, and Sarah Palin played a very prominent role as the vice-presidential nominee on the Republican ticket that year.

Of course, political rights and equality also do not guarantee economic equality. Women earn less than men, on average, in America, and the problem of the economic and social status of African-Americans remains high on the agenda. While African-Americans today are in many respects better off than they were a generation ago, they still lag behind whites in many areas, including family incomes, crime and imprisonment rates, formal education, housing quality, family stability, vulnerability to such diseases as AIDS and prostate cancer, and life expectancy. The nation's attention was focused on many of these inequalities after Hurricane Katrina flooded and destroyed many areas of New Orleans, a heavily African-American city, in August 2005. The lack of planning for this frequently predicted emergency and the agonizingly slow response to it by all levels of government led many, both black and white, to question whether the race and poverty of New Orleans residents put them especially at risk.

Immigration into America has increased its social diversity at the same time that it has moved the politics of diversity beyond black-and-white divides. In the new millennium, our nation of immigrants will once again debate immigration policy and the nature of U.S. citizenship. The acceleration in recent decades in the ethnic and linguistic diversity of nearly every state, along with a rise in the number of illegal immigrants, has led to demands for a more inclusive citizenship policy as well as calls for increased border security. Immigrant-rights activists demonstrated their organizational muscle when millions of people in cities from Chicago to Dallas to Los Angeles participated in marches held on May 1, 2006, to protest Congressional legislation that would have classified illegal immigrants and anyone who aided them as felons. That bill eventually died, but because neither legal nor illegal immigrants may vote in state and federal elections today, their political power is often limited. Voters concerned with illegal immigration have also been passionately engaged on this issue, and won a victory in April 2010 when Arizona passed a law mandating a crackdown on illegal immigrants in that border state. Conflicts over immigration policy, affirmative action, and the use of languages other than English will surely continue well into the twenty-first century.

SOCIAL CONDITIONS

Geography

The United States has jurisdiction over a territory totaling 3,475,031 square miles. This makes it geographically the fourth-largest nation in the world, smaller only than Russia (6,592,800 square miles), Canada (3,849,674 square miles), and the People's Republic of China (3,696,100 square miles).[3] The United States is bounded by the Atlantic Ocean on the east, the Pacific Ocean on the west, Canada on the north, and Mexico on the south. This secure location—great oceans on two sides, militarily weak nations on the other two sides—made feasible the foreign policy of isolation from alliances and wars with foreign countries that the United States pursued until the end of the nineteenth century. In these days of intercontinental ballistic missiles, orbiting spy satellites, and international terrorism, however, no nation, including the United States, can count on its geographical location to keep it isolated from world politics.

Population

The U.S. Bureau of the Census estimated that the total population in the United States surpassed 310 million in 2010. This makes it the third most populous nation in the world, behind China with 1.3 billion and India with 1.2 billion.[4] The U.S. rate of population increase has been impressive. The first census in 1790 reported a total population of 3.9 million, so the 2010 figure represents a staggering increase of 7,949 percent in 220 years. Over 50 million people have moved from other parts of the world to the United States—a phenomenon characterized by British analyst H. G. Nicholas as "the greatest movement of population in Western history."[5] Accordingly, one of the most important facts to recognize about the United States is that, more than any other nation in history, it is a nation of immigrants. The census classifies only 1.2 percent of the population as being of Native American, Alaskan native, or Hawaiian ancestry;[6] the rest are immigrants or descendants of immigrants from all over the world.

Most immigrants came in one or the other of three historic waves: first, 1840 to 1860, mainly from Western Europe, Britain, and Ireland; second, 1870 to 1920, mainly from Asia, Eastern Europe, Italy, and Scandinavia; and third, 1965 until the present, mainly from Latin America and Asia. In the 1920s, Congress imposed a ceiling on the number of immigrants allowed, and the immigration rate dropped sharply. It rebounded after the Immigration and Nationality Act was amended in 1965 to eliminate caps on the number of people who could migrate from each country. Today, about 700,000 to 1 million *legal* immigrants continue to arrive in America every year. In addition, an estimated 11 million *illegal* immigrants—those who are foreign-born and enter the country without inspection or violate the terms of a visa—reside in the United States.[7] Figure 14.1 divides up America's foreign-born population (including both legal and illegal immigrants) according to places of birth.

Thus, from its beginnings, the United States has received far more immigrants than any other nation in history, and it has the most ethnically and culturally diverse population that the world has ever seen (only India comes close). Later, we will consider some of the consequences for American politics.

Economy

Even after the "dot.com" bust of 2000 to 2003 and the global financial crisis of 2008 and 2009, America remains the world's largest economy. In 2007, its gross national income (GNI), or the total value of all the goods and services it produced plus income from foreign sources, was calculated at $13.9 trillion, compared with Japan's $4.8 trillion and Germany's $3.2 trillion.[8] The American dollar continues to be the world's basic monetary unit; the value of most nations' currencies is customarily measured by how many euros, pounds, rubles, yen, and other units it takes to exchange for part or all of a dollar.

Some economists believe that American economic dominance has ended. The United States, which for many years was the world's greatest creditor nation, has become the world's greatest debtor nation, in part because Americans continue to buy billions of dollars more of foreign goods than foreigners buy of American goods, and in part because of the long-standing enormous deficits in the federal government's budget. From 1980 through 1997, the federal government spent a total of $3.1 trillion more than it took in, then ran modest surpluses from 1998 to 2001, but has returned to record-setting deficits since then. By 2009, the accumulated gross national debt was more than $12.9 trillion.[9]

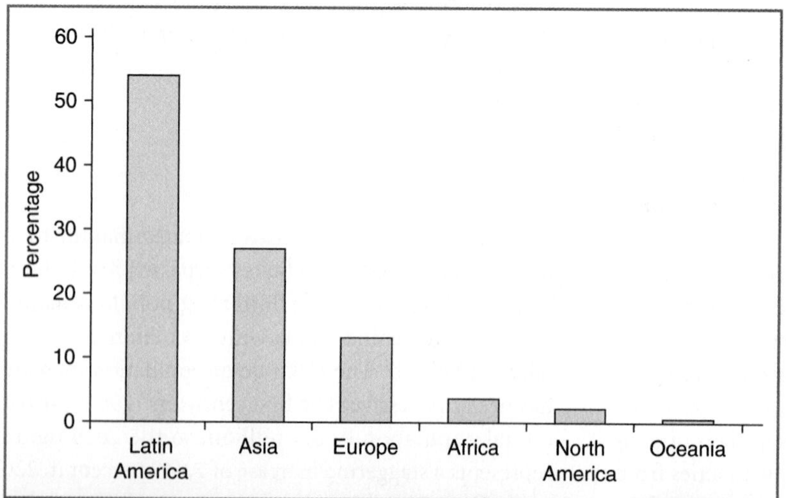

America has long been regarded as the citadel of capitalist economic ideas and institutions, and the main antagonist of people and nations who believe in socialism. Yet American economic institutions and practices have never come close to meeting the standards for completely free enterprise laid down by such *laissez-faire* economists as Adam Smith in the eighteenth century and Milton Friedman in the twentieth. These economists advocated the barest

Birthplaces of Foreign-Born Population, 2005

FIGURE 14.1

Source: *Statistical Abstract of the United States: 2010* (Washington, D.C.: Bureau of the Census, 2010), Table 44.

minimum of government interference in economic affairs, including no government regulation of the operations, profits, and wages paid by successful businesses, and no government subsidies or "bailouts" for unsuccessful businesses.

Yet even before Congress authorized a $700 billion bailout of financial institutions and other large corporations in the fall of 2008, American governments have subsidized American businesses in many ways. They conduct research that businesses can use to develop new products and pay to market American products in other countries. State, local, and federal governments work together to provide public goods, such as education and a transportation infrastructure. Congress imposes tariffs and import quotas on certain foreign manufactured goods so as to prevent them from undercutting American manufacturers. Federal laws guarantee that all workers will be paid a certain minimum wage regardless of what they would get in a truly free market, and this wage has been raised repeatedly in recent decades. Quasi-public enterprises like Fannie Mae and Freddie Mac, put under full federal conservatorship in 2008, make it easier for homebuyers to obtain loans. Federal tax law subsidizes the pensions and health plans that businesses offer to their employees, creating a hybrid public/private safety net that works something like a European welfare state, though only for those who get jobs with good benefits.[10] As the effects of the health-care reform bill passed in 2010 begin to phase in, America will look even more like a European nation by mandating and subsidizing universal coverage. Most of these policies have come from political pressure by business associations, labor unions, and other pressure groups. Thus, it seems fair to say that, while most Americans say they believe in free enterprise, they prefer to practice safe enterprise. The recent economic disaster and the massive bailout of private enterprise that it spurred serve as reminders that free-market ideologies can yield quickly in a time of crisis and that the public treasury assumes the risks of private corporations deemed "too big to fail."

THE CONSTITUTIONAL SYSTEM

As in most modern nations (Great Britain and Israel are two notable exceptions), the basic structure of the American system of government is set forth in a written constitution—the Constitution of the United States, a document drawn up in 1787, ratified in 1788, and inaugurated in 1789. It is the world's oldest written constitution still in force.

Of course, the Constitution of today differs from that of 1789 in a number of important ways. It has been formally amended twenty-seven times, the most recent being the 1992 amendment that provided that no law changing the compensation for members of Congress shall take effect until an election of members of the House has been held.[11] The first ten amendments, known collectively as the **Bill of Rights**, list the rights of individuals that the national government is forbidden to abridge (see Box 14.2).

One of the most important amendments is the Fourteenth Amendment, ratified just after the Civil War. It makes national citizenship legally superior to state citizenship, and prohibits the states from violating the "privileges and immunities" of U.S. citizens—which, by judicial interpretation, has come to mean nearly all the rights guaranteed against the national government by the first ten amendments. Other major amendments have outlawed slavery (the Thirteenth), guaranteed the right to vote to former slaves (the Fifteenth) and women (the Nineteenth), limited presidents to two elective terms (the Twenty-Second), and spelled out the conditions under which an incapacitated president can be replaced (the Twenty-Fifth). Even with these amendments, most of the basic elements of the 1789 Constitution have remained in force, whereas the written constitutions in many other countries and in most of the American states have been replaced altogether several times. Thus, if durability is a mark of constitutional strength, the Constitution of the United States is one of the strongest in history.

Yet the words in the Constitution do not tell all there is to be told about the basic structure of the American constitutional system. A number of customs, usages, and judicial decisions have significantly altered our way of governing without changing a word in the Constitution. Examples are the addition of judicial review, the development of political parties, and the conversion of the presidential selection process from a closed process by small cliques of insiders to popular elections open to all citizens.

Taken together, the provisions of the written Constitution of the United States and their associated customs and usages add up to a constitutional system

The U.S. Bill of Rights

BOX 14.2

1. Freedom of religion, speech, press.
2. Right to bear arms.
3. Freedom from quartering soldiers without owner's consent.
4. No unreasonable searches and seizures.
5. Trial of civilians only after indictment by a grand jury; no double jeopardy; prohibition against compelled self-incrimination; no deprivation of life, liberty, or property without due process of law; no taking of private property for public use without just compensation.
6. In criminal prosecutions, right to speedy and public trial by an impartial jury; defendant must be informed of the nature and cause of accusations;

defendant has power to compel testimony by witnesses in his or her favor; right to assistance of counsel.
7. Guarantee of trial by jury where the amount in controversy is over twenty dollars.
8. No excessive bail, no excessive fines, no cruel and unusual punishments.
9. Enumeration of certain rights in the Constitution shall not be construed to deny or diminish others retained by the people.
10. Powers not delegated to the national government nor prohibited to the states are reserved to the states or to the people.

---

that has three distinctive features: federalism, separation of powers, and judicial review.

Federalism

Federalism is a system in which governmental power is divided between a national government and several subnational governments, each of which is legally supreme in its assigned sphere. This system has some ancient precursors, notably the Achaean League of Greek city-states in the third century B.C.E. and the Swiss Confederation founded in the sixteenth century C.E. But the men who wrote the American Constitution established the first modern form of federalism. They did so because they had to. The 1787 convention in Philadelphia was called because its members felt that the new nation needed a much stronger national government than the Articles of Confederation provided, but the representatives from the small states refused to join any national government that did not preserve most of their established powers. The framers broke the resulting stalemate by dividing power between the national and the state governments, and gave each state equal representation in the national Senate. Only thus could the large and small states agree on a new constitution.

Even so, some of the framers regarded federalism as more than a political expedient. James Madison, for example, believed that the greatest threat to human

rights in a popular government is the tyranny of popular majorities that results when one faction seizes control of the entire power of government and uses it to advance its own special interests at the expense of all other interests. He saw a division of power between the national and state governments, combined with separation of powers, as the best way to prevent such a disaster.

Federalism has been widely praised as one of the greatest American contributions to the art of government. A number of nations have adopted it as a way of enabling different regions with sharply different cultures and interests to join together as one nation. The clearest examples of such nations today are Australia, Canada, Germany, Nigeria, Russia, and Switzerland, but significant elements of federalism are also found in systems as disparate as those of Brazil, India, and Mexico.

The American federal system divides government power in the following principal ways:

- Powers specifically assigned to the federal[12] government, such as the power to declare war, make treaties with foreign nations, coin money, and regulate commerce between the states.
- Powers reserved to the states by the Tenth Amendment. The main powers in this category are those over education, marriage and divorce, intrastate commerce, and regulation of motor vehicles. However, the federal government often

grants money to the states to help them build and operate schools, construct and repair highways, make welfare payments to the poor and the sick, and so on. The states do not have to accept the money, but if they do, they also have to accept federal standards governing how the money is to be spent and federal monitoring to make sure it is spent that way.

- Powers that can be exercised by both the federal government and the states, such as imposing taxes and defining and punishing crimes.

- Powers forbidden to the federal government, mainly those in the first eight amendments, such as abridging freedom of speech, press, and religion, and various guarantees of fair trials for persons accused of crimes.

- Powers forbidden to the state governments. Some of these are in the body of the Constitution, but the main ones are the Fourteenth Amendment's requirements that no state shall "abridge the privileges or immunities of citizens of the United States; nor shall any State deprive any person of life, liberty, or property without due process of law; nor Deny to any person within its jurisdiction the equal protection of the laws." A series of U.S. Supreme Court decisions have interpreted these phrases to mean that almost all the specific liberties guaranteed against the federal government in the first eight amendments are also guaranteed against the state governments by the Fourteenth Amendment.

When all is said and done, however, perhaps the most important single point to note about the nature of American federalism is made in Article VI of the Constitution:

> This Constitution, and the laws of the United States which shall be made in Pursuance thereof; and all Treaties made, or which shall be made, under the Authority of the United States, shall be the supreme Law of the Land; and the Judges in every State shall be bound thereby, any Thing in the Constitution or Laws of any State to the Contrary notwithstanding.

In short, while the federal government cannot constitutionally interfere with the powers assigned exclusively to the states, whenever a state constitution or law is inconsistent with a law or treaty the federal government has adopted in accordance with its proper powers, the conflicting state constitution and law must yield. Moreover, it is the Supreme Court of the United States, an organ of the federal government and not of the state governments, that decides which acts of the federal government and the state governments are within their respective powers. Thus, to the extent that the American federal system is a competition between the national government and the states, the chief umpire is a member of one of the two competing teams.

Separation of Powers

Since most analysts of the American system maintain that separation of powers is the most important single difference between the U.S. system (which is called a **presidential democracy**) and most other democratic systems (which are called *parliamentary democracies*), let us be clear on the institution's main features.

Separation of powers means the constitutional division of government power among separate legislative, executive, and judicial branches (see Figure 14.2). The Constitution of the United States specifically vests the legislative power in Congress (Article I), the executive power in the president (Article II), and the judicial power in the federal courts, headed by the Supreme Court (Article III). The constitutions of many other nations, including most of Latin America's democracies, are presidential systems modeled after America's system of separated powers.

The three branches are separated in several ways, the most important of which is the requirement in Article I, Section 6: "No Person holding any Office under the United States, shall be a Member of either House during his Continuance in Office." This provision means that each branch is operated by persons entirely distinct from those operating the other two branches. Thus, for example, when Representative Norman Mineta was appointed secretary of transportation in 2001, he had to resign his seat in the House before he could take up his new post. This, of course, is the direct opposite of the fusion-of-powers rule in many parliamentary democracies, such as Great Britain, which require the head of the executive branch to be a member of Parliament.

The persons heading each branch of the U.S. government are selected by different procedures for different terms. Members of the House of Representatives

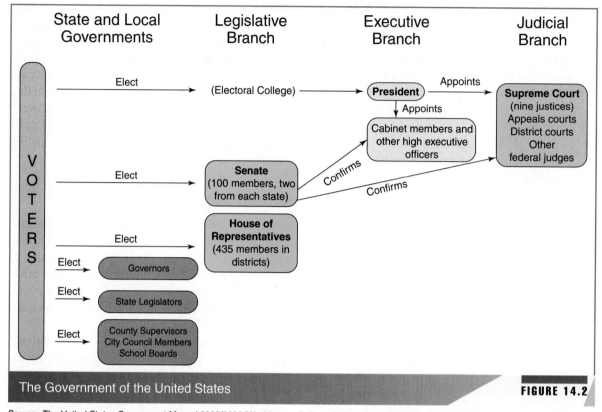

The Government of the United States

FIGURE 14.2

Source: *The United States Government Manual 2005/2006* (Washington, D.C.: U.S. Government Printing Office, 2005), 21.

are elected directly by the voters for two-year terms, with no limit on the number of terms they can serve. Members of the Senate are elected directly by the voters for six-year terms without term limits, and their terms are staggered so that one-third of the Senate comes up for election or reelection every two years.[13]

The president is elected indirectly by the **electoral college** (which is selected by direct popular election) for a four-year term, and is limited to two full elected terms. All federal judges, including the members of the Supreme Court, are appointed by the president with the approval of a majority of the Senate, and they hold office until death, resignation, or removal by Congress.

The other main devices ensuring the separation of powers are the **checks and balances** by which each branch can keep the other two branches from invading its constitutional powers. For example, the Senate can disapprove top-level presidential appointments and refuse to ratify treaties. The two chambers of Congress acting together can impeach, convict, and remove the president or federal judges from office. They can (and

often do) deny the president the legislation, appropriations, and taxes he requests. The president, in turn, can veto any act of Congress, and the Constitution requires a two-thirds vote of both chambers to override the veto. The president also makes the initial appointments of all federal judges. Presidents have normally nominated judges who are likely to agree with their political philosophies and policy preferences, but once appointed and confirmed, judges rule without political supervision.

Some scholars believe that the American system is more accurately described as a system of "separated branches exercising shared powers," since getting government action usually requires some kind of joint action by the Congress and the president, with the acquiescence of the Supreme Court. Separation of powers is what most political scientists have called this feature of the system since the time of the *Federalist Papers*. Whatever it is called, this constitutional feature, more than any other, makes the American system different from most other democratic systems.[14]

Judicial Review

Judicial review can be defined as the power of a court to render a legislative or executive act null and void on the ground of unconstitutionality. All American courts, including the lower federal courts and all levels of the state courts, exercise this power on occasion. But the final word on all issues involving an interpretation of the national Constitution (which, as we have seen, is "the supreme law of the land") belongs to the U.S. Supreme Court. The Supreme Court can declare any act of the president or Congress null and void on the ground that it violates the Constitution. Such a decision can be overturned only by a constitutional amendment or by the Court, usually with new members, changing its mind.

Although every democracy has to determine who has the final word on what its constitution allows and prohibits, the United States is one of the few democracies in which that power is given to the top appellate court of the regular court system. Some countries, such as Italy, give the final word to special tribunals rather than to bodies in their regular court systems, while in others (such as Mexico and Switzerland), the power includes only the "federal umpire" power, and not the power to override decisions of the national executive and legislature. Thus, judicial review is a prominent but not exclusive feature of the American constitutional system.

Because of the important authorities granted to the Supreme Court by the American Constitution, the Court plays an active role in shaping policies that affect the everyday lives of Americans. Abortion rights are an issue of utmost importance both to right-to-life and to pro-choice activists, and ever since the Court's 1973 *Roe v. Wade* decision created federal protections for basic abortion rights, the drive to overturn or uphold this decision has motivated much political participation. The landmark decision applied a constitutional right to privacy to abortion rights, while those advocating a right to life have won some restrictions on late-term abortion practices in Congress and in the Court. This has not been the only major debate decided by the Supreme Court in recent years. In the 2010 session alone, the Court issued landmark opinions granting corporations the right to spend unlimited amounts of money on elections, broadening Second Amendment protections by casting the constitutionality of state and local gun-control laws into doubt, and narrowing the rights of criminal defendants. With the Court's impact looming so large, and with presidents able to reshape the Court when they nominate new members to replace departing justices, the direction of the judicial branch becomes an important part of presidential elections in America.

POLITICAL CULTURE AND SOCIALIZATION

The American constitutional system, though important to how Americans make political decisions, is not the whole story. To a considerable degree, the American political system functions as it does because it is operated by Americans rather than by Britons, Italians, Mexicans, or Iraqis, and it does what it does because Americans have a distinctive **political culture** that underlies, animates, and shapes all of the formal institutions we have reviewed.

Chapter 3 of this book discusses political culture and socialization in a comparative perspective, and America's unique political culture deserves close attention here.

Melting Pot or Patchwork Quilt?

Most Americans are immigrants or descendants of immigrants who came from many different cultures in Africa, Asia, Western and Eastern Europe, and Latin America. In this sense, globalization has always played a role in shaping America. Throughout most of its history, the United States has had to deal with how best to fit the immigrants and their different cultures into American economic, social, and political life.

Throughout our history, two visions of how immigrants should become incorporated into society have clashed in intellectual discourse, policy debates, and actual practice. One vision is of a "**melting pot**" that blends all the different cultures of immigrants into one uniquely American culture, which was to be expressed and passed on in one language, the American version of English. Some room was left for such special ethnic folkways as Polish weddings, Irish wakes, and Mexican food, but the paramount task given to the educational system was to turn everyone into English-speaking Americans imbued with the main values and attitudes of the nation's political culture.

Democratic Diversity in America

The voting coalition that put Barack Obama, a candidate with a multiracial heritage, into office and which supported his party's congressional candidates in 2010 was made up of voters from many racial and ethnic groups. The demographic diversity of America constantly shapes its politics.

Jim Watson/AFP/Getty Images

A contrasting vision sees America as a true cultural **"patchwork quilt"** (the phrase is Jesse Jackson's)—an array of the languages, history, customs, and values of each of the nation's major ethnic groups, each receiving the same attention, respect, and importance as every other, with none dominant. This view rejects the melting-pot idea that the ancient and distinct cultures of immigrant groups should be homogenized into one prevailing national culture—a culture that, they say, is not truly a blend of all cultures but rather the culture of Western Europe, especially Great Britain. While the patchwork quilt metaphor was recently coined and is today associated with some leaders among the African-American, Latino, and Asian communities, members of various immigrant groups have sought to cling to their cultural identities and native languages for over a century. Italian, Irish, and especially German immigrants often resisted melting into America's customs and language, and reshaped the mainstream culture and even the English language.

Among the policies advocated by adherents to the patchwork-quilt vision are bilingual education (educating minority-group children in their native languages rather than forcing them to learn English as their primary language), printing ballots and other official documents in languages other than English, and broadening school curricula so as to give full and fair attention to the contributions of African, Asian, and Latin cultures as well as of British and Western European cultures.

Some opposition has set in against this movement. One manifestation is the laws adopted by several states and the May 2006 vote by the U.S. Senate declaring English to be the official language. Political scientist Sam Huntington's book, *Who Are We? The Challenges to America's National Identity*, offered a controversial defense of the Anglo-Protestant culture against a threatened erosion by today's wave of immigration from Latin America. The clash between the competing melting-pot and patchwork-quilt visions of immigrant assimilation will likely continue throughout the twenty-first century.

Main Elements of the Traditional American Political Culture

The first dimension of political culture that political scientists usually consider is the level of trust in government that a nation's residents exhibit. In 1958, when the National Election Study first asked Americans whether they trusted their government to do what is right, 73 percent replied that they trusted government just about always or most of the time. In the decades since then, trust in government has eroded, with a sharp increase occurring during the Vietnam War and after the Watergate scandal followed by fluctuations that followed the path of the nation's economy since then. For the last thirty years, Americans have trusted their government in boom times yet looked more skeptically at Washington during bust years. After the global financial crisis of 2008 and 2009, unemployment levels rose to historic highs while trust in government plummeted to historic lows. By the year 2010, only 22 percent of Americans trusted their government to do the right thing all or most of the time.

Yet the Americans who do not always trust their government remain deeply proud of their nation and willing to sacrifice for it. Comparing Americans with Western Europeans on these dimensions is instructive. Studies have shown that more Americans say they are very proud of their country (80 percent) and are willing to fight for it (71 percent) than the citizens of Great Britain, Spain, Italy, France, and Germany say about their countries (where the proportions range from 55 and 62 percent in Great Britain to 21 and 35 percent in Germany).[15] Thus, while Americans may trust their governments to do what is right less than some Western Europeans do, they are nevertheless more patriotic than many Western Europeans. How can we explain this paradox?

The answer may lie in the fact that throughout history, most Americans have strongly held two ideas that may be logically (but not emotionally) inconsistent. One is the idea that ordinary Americans are good, solid, reliable folks with plenty of common sense, and that America is a wonderful country. Conversely, they feel that the *government*, which is not the same thing as the country, is, as former president Ronald Reagan put it, "the problem, not the solution," and they feel that the professional politicians who fill its offices, lead its parties, and conduct its business are self-seeking lightweights more interested in winning votes and getting reelected than in making courageous and forward-looking policies to solve the nation's problems. Thus, many Americans love their country but distrust the politicians who run its governments.

Another dimension of political culture is the degree to which ordinary people believe that their preferences significantly influence public officials. One of the findings of the first major comparative study of political cultures was that Americans score higher on this dimension than people in Great Britain, Germany, Italy, and Mexico, and that in all five countries, better-educated people score higher than less-educated people.[16] Subsequent studies have confirmed that Americans generally feel more "politically efficacious" in this sense than do the citizens of most other nations.

Another exceptional feature of our nation is the depth of the conviction among most Americans—black and white, women and men, young and old—that they have certain basic rights and that the best way to make sure they get their rights is often not to wait for executives, legislatures, and bureaucrats to do the right thing, but to file lawsuits to force public officials—and other private individuals—to honor their rights. The **litigiousness** of Americans—that is, their tendency to file lawsuits against government officials and other private citizens for violating their rights—gives the courts a central role in America. American legal scholar Robert Kagan argues that litigation in the United States accomplishes (at a much higher cost) the same things that European nations accomplish through regulation.[17] America has pursued this different path most likely because of the notion, espoused by populists like President Andrew Jackson, that the common man has enough wisdom to supervise everything, even his government.

Political Socialization

Political socialization is the process by which children are introduced to the values and attitudes of their society, shaping their notions of what the political world is like and which people, policies, and institutions are good and bad. That process in America is much the same as in every other modern, populous, industrialized democracy. The main agencies shaping Americans' political socialization are their families (especially their parents), schoolteachers, friends, schoolmates, work associates, and the mass communications media. While parents have historically had the most powerful impact on socialization, the influence of the mass communications media in the past few decades, and especially of social networking Web sites in the past few years, has begun to reshape the process of political socialization.

The term **mass communications media** includes all the devices used to transmit information, thought, or feeling to a mass audience that does not see the communicator face-to-face. They fall into two categories: the print media (newspapers, magazines, books, and pamphlets) and the electronic media (the Internet, broadcast television, cable and satellite television, and radio).

The United States, like most other industrialized democracies, has a mixture of publicly owned and privately owned television and radio stations and networks. The privately owned media are much more important than the publicly owned in America; there are three times as many private as public broadcasting stations, and the public stations usually have only about 10 percent of the viewers. Additionally, nearly all high-circulation newspapers, magazines, and Web sites are privately owned and supported by advertising revenues and subscribers.

The political content produced by print media outlets is almost entirely unregulated by government because of the First Amendment's protection of freedom of the press (see again Box 14.2). About the only restrictions on what is printed are libel and slander laws, but in the landmark case of *New York Times v. Sullivan* (1964), the U.S. Supreme Court held that public officials and public figures cannot collect damages for remarks made about them in the print media unless those comments are (1) knowingly false or made with a "reckless disregard" for their truth and (2) made with proved "malice" as a deliberate attempt to damage the victim's public reputation and standing—a charge that is very difficult to prove.[18]

By contrast, radio and television stations are much more closely regulated than the print media. They can broadcast only if they are granted a license by the Federal Communications Commission (FCC). That license requires that the political content of programs meet certain standards. For example, the stations must make available to all candidates for a particular political office an equal opportunity to make their appeals; they do not have to *give* any of them free time, but if they do give time to one candidate, they must give it to all. If they sell time to one candidate, they must sell it to all at the same rates and offer comparably desirable times. They cannot charge political advertisers higher rates than they charge commercial advertisers.

The U.S. Supreme Court has consistently upheld the government's power to impose such restrictions on the electronic media while denying government any comparable power over the print media. The reasons have to do with what is generally called the **scarcity doctrine**: The Court has found that there is no limit, other than economic, on the number of newspapers, books, magazines, or pamphlets that can be printed and circulated. But there is a physical limit on the number of television or radio stations that can operate in a given portion of the broadcast spectrum.

Accordingly, said the Court, broadcasting is a public resource, much like the national parks or navigable rivers; this gives the government the right not only to allocate frequencies, but also to set standards to ensure that their use will promote "the public convenience, interest, or necessity."[19]

Much less regulated are the Web sites, Facebook pages, and Twitter feeds that today play an ever more prominent role in transmitting political fact and opinion and breaking scandals, real or manufactured. Independent Internet sites, which are not subject to licensing requirements, do not have to stay in the good graces of a large range of advertising clients, and have little reputation to lose if they publish news reports that become discredited. Web logs, or "blogs," authored by activists from every part of the ideological spectrum, play an increasingly important (and often criticized) role in campaigns, with their ability to spread fact, rumor, and baseless accusation across cyberspace with unchecked speed. Because of the Internet's rising importance in politics, regulation of its political content is an evolving area of policy and jurisprudence.

POLITICAL PARTICIPATION AND RECRUITMENT

Participation by Voting

Since voting in elections is the main way in which ordinary citizens in all democracies actually participate in their nations' governing processes, most political scientists believe that **voting turnout**—the percentage of all the people eligible to vote who actually do so—is one of the most important indicators of any democratic system's health. Studies of voting turnout in the world's democracies, like that in Table 14.1, usually find that the turnout is lower in the United States than in most other democracies.

Many commentators in America have also pointed to figures suggesting that U.S. voter turnout has declined dramatically over the past few decades as signs of a deep sickness in U.S. politics. They have claimed, variously, that it is a symptom of too much negative campaigning, too few good candidates, the rising role of money in campaigns, the diminishing role of parties in grassroots politics, and many other ills. However, recent research shows that these are false diagnoses of what turns out to be a healthy patient;

Levels of Turnout, 2000s	TABLE 14.1
Nation	**Turnout (%)**
Italy[†]	86
Belgium[†]	85
Sweden	76
New Zealand	75
Germany	70
Japan	65
United Kingdom	58
United States	53*
France	52
Switzerland	37

[†]Compulsory voting law

*Presidential election turnout in the United States, parliamentary elections in other countries

Source: Russell J. Dalton, *Citizen Politics in Western Democracies*, 5th ed. (Washington, D.C.: C.Q. Press, 2008), 37.

turnout has remained fairly stable in America over the past thirty years.

The conventional wisdom that turnout had dropped was wrong because it relied on a misleading approximation of turnout, which calculated the percentage of those old enough to vote who actually did so. The problem with this measure is that many people who are old enough to vote in the United States are not eligible to cast a ballot, some because they are not citizens and some because they are convicted felons living in states that bar them from voting. As the percentage of Americans who are noncitizens (including both legal and illegal immigrants) or felons has grown in recent decades, a smaller portion of the voting-aged population has been eligible to vote. Scholars who counted up these groups and correctly calculated the percentage of eligible voters who participate found that turnout in presidential elections has remained steady at 55 to 60 percent since 1972 (after the Twenty-Sixth Amendment gave eighteen-year-olds the right to vote, and turnout in fact dropped).[20]

Further scrutinizing what goes into these turnout figures makes America look better compared to the rest of the world, and points out a key obstacle to voter participation. When voting turnout is counted in exactly the same way in the United States as it is in other democracies—as a percentage of registered voters—the American record looks much better. In America, as in most of the world's other democracies, citizens' names must appear on voting registers before they can legally vote. But the United States differs from other nations in one important respect: In most other countries, getting on the register requires no effort by the voter. Public authorities take the initiative to get all eligible citizens enrolled, a job often made easier in countries that have a national list of residents. As a result, almost every citizen of voting age is registered to vote.

In the United States, by contrast, there is no list of residents, and each state regulates **voting registration**. In most states, would-be voters must make an effort to get on the register; no public official will do it for them. Moreover, in most democratic countries, when voters move from one part of the country to another, they are automatically struck off the register in the place they leave and are added to the register in the place to which they move, all with no effort on their part. In contrast, when people move from one U.S. state to another, they are not automatically added to the register in their new state.[21] One study that compared turnout of registered voters in the United States, which averages 86.8 percent, with turnout of registered voters in twenty-four other democracies found that the United States ranks eleventh-highest on this measure.[22]

This ranking is still lower than many might expect from the world's self-described citadel of democracy. Another explanation for America's low voting turnout arises from the fact that American voters are called on to cast far more votes than the citizens of any other country (only Switzerland comes close). In the parliamentary democracies, the only national elections are those for the national parliament, in which voters normally vote for one candidate or for one party. They also vote periodically for a candidate or a party in the elections for the city or rural district in which they live. In the federal systems, they also vote for a member of their state or provincial parliament. Hence, in most democracies other than the United States and Switzerland, the typical voter makes a total of only four or five voting decisions over a period of four or five years.[23]

In the United States, the combination of separation of powers, federalism, the direct primary, and, at the state and local levels, the initiative and referendum means that citizens may be faced with several *hundred* electoral decisions in a period of four years. At the national level, voters are called on to vote in the presidential primaries of their parties, and in the general election to decide (mostly) between the Democratic and Republican candidates. They are also expected to vote in primary elections and general elections every two years for members of the House of Representatives and twice in every six years for members of the Senate. At the state and local levels, not only are the leading executive officials (governors and mayors) and members of the legislatures nominated in primary elections and elected in general elections, but in most states and localities, a considerable number of other offices that are appointed positions in most other democracies—for example, state secretaries of state, attorneys general, treasurers, superintendents of education, judges, school superintendents, and members of local school boards, sanitary commissions, park commissions, and so on—are selected by much the same primary-plus-general-election procedures.

Direct democracy processes, such as the **direct initiative** (a proposal for a new law that goes before voters if enough of them sign a petition), and the **popular referendum** (a vote on whether to keep an existing law), give many Americans even more choices to make at the ballot box. Although the U.S. federal government has never held a direct democracy election, twenty-four states and many local governments make the initiative process available, meaning that about 70 percent of Americans live in a city or state with the initiative.[24] This sometimes adds as many as thirty complex policy choices to a ballot.

Thus, American citizens are called on to vote far more often and on more questions than those of any other country except Switzerland (where voters in many cantons also have direct democracy). Surely the opportunity to vote in free, fair, and competitive elections is a *sine qua non* of democratic government, and therefore a good thing. Yet a familiar saying is that there can be too much of a good thing, and many Americans leaving their polling places after casting their ninetieth (or more) vote of the year are likely to conclude that the sheer number of voting decisions in America is a case in point.[25]

Participation by Other Means

Voting, of course, is only one of several ways citizens can participate in politics. They can also serve in office; work in political parties; donate money to candidates, parties, and causes; attend rallies; take part in street demonstrations; send letters, telegrams, faxes, and e-mail messages to their elected representatives; write letters and op-ed pieces to newspapers; call radio and television talk shows; try to persuade families and friends; file lawsuits against public officials; and so on. These other forms of participation have not been studied as extensively as voting, but Russell Dalton has collected some interesting comparative data on conventional and unconventional forms of participation in the United States and some Western European countries (see Table 14.2).

Nonvoting Forms of Political Participation in Four Democracies (in percentages) TABLE 14.2				
Activity	**United States**	**Great Britain**	**France**	**Germany**
Campaign Activity				
Attempted to convince others how to vote	44	44	28	29
Participated in campaign	30	25	7	7
Contacted by party/candidate	47	26	13	7
Communal Activity				
Worked with others in community in the past five years	35	23	20	26
Protest Activity				
Signed a petition in past year	35	34	21	35
Boycotted a product in past year	24	23	29	34
Attended protest in past five years	6	12	24	12

Source: All figures are from Russell J. Dalton, *Citizen Politics in Western Democracies*, 5th ed. (Washington, D.C.: C.Q. Press, 2008). Campaign activity figures are taken from pp. 44–46, communal activity from p. 49 and p. 68, and protest activity from p. 68.

The responses in Table 19.2 show that citizens of France are more likely than citizens of the United States, Great Britain, or Germany to participate in demonstrations and political strikes, whereas Americans are more likely to persuade other people how to vote, attend a campaign meeting and/or rally, work with citizen groups, sign a petition, and/or join in a boycott.

Several other studies have found that the form of participation most frequently claimed by Americans is voting in elections (53 percent), followed by stating their political opinions to others (32 percent), contributing money to campaigns (12 percent), displaying political bumper-stickers and signs (9 percent), and attending political meetings or rallies (8 percent). Only 4 percent report belonging to a political club or working for a political party.[26]

In short, Americans participate in politics in ways other than voting in elections as much, or more, than the citizens of the other Western democracies for whom we have reliable information. These data certainly do not support the conclusion that Americans are in any way more alienated or lazier than the citizens of other democracies.

RECRUITMENT OF LEADERS

Recruitment is the process whereby, out of the millions of a nation's citizens, emerge the few hundreds or thousands who hold elective and appointive public office, play leading roles in parties and pressure groups, decide how the mass communications media will portray politics, and, within the limits permitted by the general public, make public policy.

Many scholars have studied leadership recruitment in many countries and have found certain general tendencies that are also evident in American politics. For instance, American leaders, like leaders in other countries, are drawn disproportionately from the middle and upper ranges of wealth and status. The reason lies not in the existence of any conspiracy to oppress the lower classes but rather in the kinds of knowledge and skills a person must have to win the support needed for selection as a leader. These skills are more likely to be acquired and developed by well-educated rather than poorly educated people. For example, people's chances to climb in a political party or a pressure group, to be selected for public office, or to be appointed to higher administrative offices are considerably enhanced if

they have the ability to speak well in public, and, for elected officials increasingly, to look and sound good on television.

The federal and state governments choose most of their administrative employees by procedures and standards other than the unabashed political patronage that prevailed until the late nineteenth century. In today's system, initial selection is made according to the applicants' abilities to score well on standardized examinations or possession of other abilities and experience desired by their employers, and salary increases and promotions depend on job performance rather than on party connections. Since the merit system was established in 1883, an increasing number of federal positions have been placed under it or under the "general schedule" category, and today, only about 1 percent are available for purely political appointments.

Accordingly, in most respects, elite recruitment in the United States differs very little from its counterparts in other advanced industrialized democracies. But in one aspect of that process—the nomination of candidates for elective office—the United States is unlike any other nation in the world.

The Unique Direct Primary

We can divide the process of electing public officials into three parts: (1) *candidate selection*, the process by which political parties decide which people to name as their standard-bearers and campaign for; (2) *nomination*, the process by which public authorities decide which people's names will be printed on the official ballots; and (3) *election*, the process by which the voters register their choices among the nominees.

Many political scientists believe that candidate selection is the most important of the three processes. After all, the recruitment of public officials is essentially one of narrowing the choices from many to one. For example, in 2010, about 176 million Americans satisfied all the constitutional requirements for being elected president. Theoretically, all 176 million names could have been printed on the ballot, and each voter could have had an absolutely free choice among them. But, of course, no voter can possibly make a meaningful choice among 176 million alternatives, and so a practical democratic election requires that the choices be narrowed down to a manageable number. The same is true for elections to office in all democratic countries.

In the United States, as in every other democracy, the narrowing process is accomplished mainly by the political parties. Each party chooses its candidates and gives their names to the election authorities, and those names appear on the ballot.[27] Accordingly, in 2008, the Democrats chose Barack Obama to be their presidential candidate over Hillary Rodham Clinton, John Edwards, Bill Richardson, Dennis Kucinich, Joe Biden, Mike Gravel, Christopher Dodd, Tom Vilsack, and Evan Bayh. Contesting the Republican nomination were John McCain, Mike Huckabee, Mitt Romney, Ron Paul, Fred Thompson, Duncan Hunter, Rudy Giuliani, Sam Brownback, Jim Gilmore, and Tom Tancredo. By narrowing the field from twenty candidates to two, these nominations made it relatively easy for the voters to make the final choice between Obama and McCain.

Given the crucial role of candidate selection in democratic elections, it is important to recognize that the United States is the only nation in the world that makes most of its nominations by direct primaries. In nearly all the parliamentary democracies, the parties' candidates for parliament are chosen by the parties' leaders or by small groups of card-carrying, dues-paying party members. A few countries, such as Germany and Finland, require the parties to choose their candidates by secret votes of local party members in procedures that resemble, but strictly speaking are not, direct primaries. Consequently, in every nation except the United States, the candidates are selected by only a few hundred, or at most a few thousand, party insiders.[28]

In the United States, nominations for almost all major elective public offices are made by **direct primaries**, in which candidates are selected directly by the voters in government-conducted elections rather than indirectly by party leaders in caucuses and conventions. Direct primaries make candidate selection in the United States by far the most open and participatory in the world. Moreover—and this is the key difference between America's direct primaries and the primary-like procedures in other countries mentioned earlier—public laws, not party rules, determine who is qualified to vote in a particular party's primary. In 2002, twenty-seven states held **closed primaries**, in which only persons preregistered as members of a particular party could vote in that party's primary. Eleven states held **crossover primaries**, which are the same as closed primaries except that voters do not have to make a public choice of the party primary in which

they will vote until election day. Nine states held **open primaries**, in which there is no party registration of any kind, and voters can vote in whichever party primary they choose (they can, however, vote in only one party's primary in any particular election) with no public disclosure of their choice.[29] In its 2000 *California Democratic Party v. Jones* decision, the U.S. Supreme Court prohibited California's **blanket primary** (which allowed voters to switch back and forth between the parties in voting for nominees for particular offices) on the grounds that it violated a party's First Amendment right to free association. This decision, which also caused Alaska and Washington to alter their primary systems, makes clear the extent to which nomination procedures are formal, regulated by the government, and structured by the Constitution.

Direct primaries make candidate selection in the United States by far the most open and participatory in the world. As noted earlier, in all other countries, only a few thousand dues-paying party members at most participate in choosing candidates; in the United States, they are chosen by any registered voter who wants to participate, and millions do in every election cycle. To give just one example, although American presidential candidates are formally selected by national nominating conventions, a great majority of the delegates to both conventions are chosen by direct primaries. In 2008, a grand total of 58,140,064 votes were cast in the Democratic and Republican presidential primaries.[30]

The American system for choosing its presidents may be wiser or more foolish than the ways other democracies select their top political leaders, but it is far more participatory.

INTEREST ARTICULATION: PACS AND PRESSURE GROUPS

As we have seen throughout this book, every society has a number of different and conflicting political interests, and the more advanced the economy and the more heterogeneous the society, the more individuals and groups there are with interests that to some degree conflict with other interests. The inevitable clash of these interests generates the political process, which consists of two main parts: (1) interest articulation, by which the persons and groups make known their desires for government action or inaction; and

Wall Street Lobbyists

A group of lobbyists and government officials watch a Senate hearing on the "Wall Street Transparency and Accountability Act," the financial-reform bill that drew the attention of hundreds of lobbyists throughout the spring of 2010.

AP Photo/Harry Hamburg

(2) interest aggregation, by which various demands are mobilized and combined to press for favorable government policies.

In most democracies, interests are articulated mainly by pressure groups and political parties, and the governing parties also aggregate interests in formulating and implementing their programs. In the United States, however, the political parties are much weaker and less cohesive than those in most other democratic systems. Consequently, pressure groups play a major role in both interest articulation and aggregation in the United States.

Many foreign observers of America's peculiar politics have been especially struck by the great variety and power of our organized political groups.[31] Today, they are even more numerous and important than in the past. They take two main forms, each of which specializes in a particular technique for influencing government: (1) political action committees and campaign contributions, and (2) pressure groups and lobbying.

PACs and Campaign Contributions

Strictly speaking, a **political action committee (PAC)** is any organization that is not formally affiliated with a particular party or candidate and spends money to influence the outcome of elections. PACs differ from political parties in two main respects. First, unlike parties, they do not nominate candidates and put them on ballots with PAC labels; rather, they support or oppose candidates nominated by the parties. Second, PACs are interested mainly in the policies that public officials make, not in the party labels those officials bear. Hence, a PAC will often support candidates of both major parties who are sympathetic to the PAC's particular policy preferences.

Such organizations have operated in American politics at least since the Civil War, and some of them have had considerable success. For example, the Anti-Saloon League, which was founded in 1893 to support both Democratic and Republican candidates for Congress, pledged to support a constitutional amendment outlawing the manufacture and sale of alcoholic beverages. Most historians believe that it deserves much of the credit (or blame) for the adoption of the Eighteenth Amendment (prohibition) in 1919. One of the most powerful organizations in the second half of the twentieth century was the Committee on Political Education (COPE) of the American Federation of Labor and Congress of Industrial Organizations (AFL-CIO), which has supplied millions of dollars and thousands of election workers for candidates (mostly but not entirely Democrats) sympathetic to organized labor.

The most important PACs can be classified in one of three main categories: (1) *narrow material interest PACs*, which are concerned mainly with backing candidates who will support legislation that favors a particular business or type of business; (2) *single, nonmaterial interest PACs*, which promote candidates who favor their positions on a particular nonmaterial issue such as abortion or gun control; and (3) *ideological PACs*, which support candidates committed to strong liberal or conservative ideologies and issues.

The greatest increase in the number and activity of PACs in American history has come since 1974 as an unanticipated (and, by many, unwanted) consequence of that year's amendments to the Federal Election Campaign Act. The amendments set low limits on the amount of money individuals could contribute to a candidate or a party, but considerably higher limits on what organizations could contribute. They also stipulated that although labor unions and business corporations could not directly contribute money to election campaigns, they could sponsor PACs, and their PACs could make campaign contributions as long as the funds came from voluntary contributions by sympathetic individuals rather than by direct levies on union and corporate funds.

In ruling on the constitutionality of these rules, the Supreme Court upheld the limits on direct contributions, but said that limiting the amounts of money that an individual or an organization can spend on behalf of a candidate (that is, by broadcasting or publishing ads *not* controlled by candidates or parties) was a violation of the First Amendment's guarantee of free speech.[32]

These changes in the substance and interpretation of the campaign finance laws led most politically active interests to conclude that forming a PAC was the best way to influence election outcomes, and that is just what they have done. In 1974, only 608 PACs operated in national elections; by 2009, the number had exploded to 4,611 (see Box 14.3).

At present, each PAC must register with the Federal Election Commission and periodically report its receipts (who contributed and how much) and its expenditures (to what candidates it gave contributions and how much, and how much it spent on its own independent campaigning). A PAC can contribute $5,000 to a particular candidate in a primary election and another $5,000 in the general election. Yet there is no limit on the total amount it can contribute to all candidates and party committees. There is also no limit on the amount it can spend on behalf of a particular candidate or party as long as its beneficiaries have no say in how the money is spent. The enactment in 2002 of the McCain-Feingold bill prohibited all "soft money" contributions—formerly unlimited contributions that were made to federal, state, and local political parties. However, a perceived loophole in this law has allowed "527 Committees" (a name that comes from their categorization in the tax code) to play the

---

Top Ten PACs in Overall Spending, 2007–2008

BOX 14.3

Rank	PAC Name	Overall Spending ($)
1	ACTBLUE	53,547,065
2	Service Employees International Union Committee on Political Education	45,956,641
3	Moveon.org PAC	38,123,090
4	Emily's List	25,061,526
5	Fred Thompson Political Action Committee	24,316,838
6	American Federation of State, County & Municipal Employees-PEOPLE	19,319,462
7	National Rifle Association Political Victory Fund	15,588,823
8	UAW-V-CAP (United Auto Workers Voluntary Community Action Program)	13,116,234
9	DRIVE (Democrat Republican Independent Voter Education) PAC for International Brotherhood of Teamsters	13,077,646
10	National Association of Realtors PAC	11,893,975

Source: Harold W. Stanley and Richard G. Niemi, *Vital Statistics on American Politics, 2010* (Washington, D.C.: Congressional Quarterly, 2010), Table 2-13.

role that parties formerly played by collecting the same sorts of unlimited contributions and spending them independently to influence campaigns.

Although many PACs take some part in presidential election campaigns, the federal government finances most of the costs of those campaigns. Thus, most PACs make most of their contributions to House and Senate campaigns. It is estimated that they now contribute about 34 percent of all the funds for those campaigns.[33]

The most important PACs can be classified in one of three main categories:

1. *Narrow material interest PACs.* These are PACs concerned mainly with backing candidates who will support legislation that favors a particular business or type of business (for example, Chrysler, Coca Cola, General Electric, General Motors, Texaco), and many other corporations have their own PACs, as do many labor unions, including the Air Line Pilots Association, the American Federation of State, County, and Municipal Employees, and the American Federation of Teachers. In addition, a number of PACs represent the interests of whole industries, such as the Dallas Energy Political Action Committee (oil), the Edison Electric Institute (electric power), and the National Association of Broadcasters (radio and television).

2. *Single, nonmaterial interest PACs.* These PACs promote candidates who favor their positions on a particular nonmaterial issue. For example, the National Abortion Rights Action League (pro–choice) and the National Right to Life Committee (anti-abortion) are concerned with the abortion issue, and the National Rifle Association (anti–gun control) and Handgun Control, Inc. (pro–gun control) focus on the gun control issue.

3. *Ideological PACs.* Finally, a number of PACs support candidates committed to strong liberal or conservative ideologies and issues. Liberal PACs include MoveOn, the National Committee for an Effective Congress, and the Hollywood Women's Political Committee. Conservative PACs include the Republican Issues Campaign and the Conservative Victory Committee.

Pressure Groups and Lobbying

Another tactic that PACs use to advance their interests is **lobbying** through their Washington representatives. This stratagem concentrates on inducing public officials already in office to support government action (including administrative and judicial rulings as well as legislative acts) the groups favor and to block those the groups oppose.

In the "bad old days," pressure groups often used straight bribes in the form of cash payments or guarantees of well-paid jobs after retirement. Sadly, bribes are still occasionally offered and accepted, but the laws against them are strict and the mass media's investigative reporters love to expose bribe-taking. In a recent example, the San Diego *Union-Tribune*'s 2005 investigation of Congressman Randall "Duke" Cunningham for accepting over $2 million in bribes in exchange for influencing defense contracts led to an eight-year prison term for Cunningham, as well as a Pulitzer Prize for the newspaper. Congress reacted to the Cunningham scandal and the investigations that forced the resignation of House Majority Leader Tom DeLay and sent former lobbyist Jack Abramoff to jail by considering new ethics legislation. These scandals played a major role in the Democratic surge in the 2006 congressional elections (see Box 14.4). Ethics investigations of prominent Democratic Representatives Charlie Rangel and Maxine Waters, though less serious than Cunningham's, also hurt their party on the eve of the 2010 congressional contests. Calls for reform are likely to fade, though, as the scandals pass. Such was the case with the "Teapot Dome" influence-peddling scandal of the 1920s, which caused huge outrage at the time but is now a quaint historical footnote. Bribery is quite rare in everyday American politics, since most interest groups and public officials have decided that giving or taking bribes is either too immoral, too risky, or both.

The main tactic of lobbyists is now *persuasion*—convincing members of Congress (and their staffs, who play key roles in making most members' decisions) that the legislation the lobbyist seeks is in the best interests of the nation and of the member's particular district or state. After all, almost all members of Congress feel that their job is to do the best they can for the interests of their particular constituents. Since it is those constituents rather than the rest of the nation who determine whether the members will be reelected, their likely reactions must be the members' first concern.

Accordingly, lobbyists for all interests use the most persuasive evidence and arguments they can to convince a particular member that the actions their groups want will be in everyone's best interest—the voters in the particular district or state, the member's, and the nation's. Lobbyists who work for interest groups that

For the second time in a short four-year period, voters shifted control of the House of Representatives during the 2010 midterm elections. Democrats led by Nancy Pelosi had capitalized on voter dissatisfaction with President George W. Bush's handling of the Iraq War and with the Republican Congressional leaders' handling of a multitude of scandals to pick up thirty-one seats and claim control of the House in the 2006 elections. Four years later, the political pendulum swung sharply back. With voters in the political middle unhappy with President Barack Obama's handling of the economy and with the leftward turn that Congress had taken in policy areas such as health care and deficit spending, Republicans led by John Boehner captured sixty-three seats to gain a comfortable 242-192 majority in the House.

Democrats also lost six seats in the Senate, but after the election still clung to a 53-47 edge in the upper house. One factor that may have prevented the Republicans from gaining total victory in both houses was the role played by the "Tea Party," a loosely-organized faction of Republican voters and activists who were focused primarily on fiscal conservatism (but who gave voice to many other strands of political conservatism in areas such as social issues, immigration, and race relations). Tea Party activists worked within the Republican Party to nominate House and Senate candidates with staunchly conservative views and often little electoral experience. In some cases, these candidates energized the Republican base and drove home the party's anti-incumbent message. In several key Senate races, however, nominating conservatives appeared to cost Republicans the opportunity to gain seats. Christine O'Donnell, lampooned on the *Daily Show* for her views on sex education and for dabbling in witchcraft, lost badly in Delaware, and her fellow Tea Party favorite Sharron Angle lost a winnable race in Nevada. Although the 2010 elections brought a clear landslide victory for the Republican Party, political observers debated whether the Tea Party movement helped or hindered the cause.

also have PACs may sometimes hint that the PAC will be contributing to the campaigns of legislators who see the light on their issues. Surprisingly, however, most lobbyists and PACs work quite independently of one another, and a great volume of studies by political scientists have failed to provide any clear evidence that campaign contributions influence the votes cast by legislators. Contributions may ensure access to politicians, scholars have found, but they do not buy votes.

Although American interest groups most frequently employ electioneering and lobbying, they sometimes use tactics that are more widely used in other countries, such as mass political propaganda, demonstrations, strikes and boycotts, nonviolent civil disobedience, and sometimes even violence. There is one tactic, however, in which the United States leads the world: the use of **litigation** for political purposes. In their book, *Politics by Other Means: The Declining Importance of Elections in America*, political scientists Benjamin Ginsberg and Martin Shefter note that from 1955 to 1985, the number of civil cases brought in federal district courts increased from 50,000 a year to over 250,000 a year. One of several reasons for that enormous increase, they say, is the fact that a growing number of interest groups that have done poorly in both elections and lobbying have filed suits in the courts to reverse their losses in other arenas:

> Civil rights groups, through federal court suits, launched successful assaults on Southern school systems, state and local governments, and legislative districting schemes. . . . Environmental groups used the courts to block the construction of highways, dams, and other public projects that not only threatened to damage the environment but also provided money and other resources to their political rivals. Women's groups were able to overturn state laws restricting abortion as well as statutes discriminating against women in the labor market.

Conservative groups have countered by trying to ensure that **conservatives** rather than liberals or feminists are appointed to the Supreme Court and other federal judgeships. Liberal groups have also organized campaigns to influence appointments and confirmation battles in order to populate the judicial branch with those who are sympathetic to their goals. Ever since Democrats in the Senate failed to confirm President Ronald Reagan's nomination of Robert Bork to the U.S. Supreme Court in 1987, nearly every appointment to the nation's highest court has been fought with intense lobbying, with public pressure, and even with avalanches of television ads. The fact that interest groups are involved in judicial battles far more in America than in any other democracy should not surprise us, because the popularity of pursuing one's individual rights through litigation is one way in which the political culture of America differs significantly from the political cultures of most other countries.

The most important special trait of interest articulation and aggregation in the United States, however, is the very different party environment in which they take place. In most of the democracies discussed in this book, most interests operate closely within political parties. (Indeed, in several instances, particular interest groups are formally associated with particular parties, such as the trade unions with the British Labour Party.) Their main tactic is to persuade the parties with which they are associated to give their demands prominent places in the parties' programs and actions in government.

In contrast, American political parties are so much weaker and so much less important in the policymaking process that the interest groups operate largely outside the parties and are little concerned about whether they are helping or hurting the parties. In 1980, for example, the National Organization for Women (NOW) fought for a rule in the Democratic Party to prevent the party from helping to elect any Democratic candidate who opposed the Equal Rights Amendment. In 1984, NOW said that it would refuse to support the party's national ticket unless a woman was nominated for the vice presidency (and, indeed, Geraldine Ferraro was nominated). In the 2008 election, Emily's List, a PAC supporting women candidates, spent a total of $25 million to help women's campaigns, the second-largest amount spent by any PAC.[34]

The same observation applies to the Republican Party. For some time before 1994, many business PACs contributed much more campaign money to incumbent Democrats than to their Republican challengers, even though the Republican political philosophy is much closer to that of business. The national leaders of the Republican Party complained bitterly about what they regarded as treason to the party and to conservatism, but Doug Thompson, the leader of the National Association of Realtors, rejected the Republicans' complaints and has spelled out his PAC's political priorities:

We are a special interest group. Our interest is real estate and housing issues; it is not Contra aid, it is not abortion, it is not the minimum wage. . . . Our members are demanding a lot more accountability. Gone are our free-spending days when we poured money into a black hole called "challenger candidates." Our marching orders on PAC contributions are very clear: Stop wasting money on losers.[35]

In short, interest articulation and aggregation are in many respects different in the United States because its political parties are in most respects very different from those in any other democracy.

THE SPECIAL CHARACTERISTICS OF AMERICAN POLITICAL PARTIES

A Two-Party System

The American party system is usually a nearly pure two-party system—that is, one in which two major parties are highly competitive with one another and, taken together, win almost all the votes and offices in elections.[36] The most notable exception since the 1930s came in 1992, as Figure 14.3 shows, when independent H. Ross Perot won 19 percent of the popular votes for president (Democrat Bill Clinton won 43 percent and Republican incumbent George H. W. Bush won 38 percent). After the election, Perot founded the Reform Party and ran as its presidential candidate in 1996, but, as the figure shows, his vote share fell to 8.6 percent. He did not run in 2000, but his party's presidential candidate, Pat Buchanan, received less than 1 percent of the votes.[37]

In 2008, in addition to Republican John McCain and Democrat Barack Obama (see Box 14.5), there were presidential candidates from seventeen other parties on the ballot in at least one state. However, all these other parties polled a combined 1.4 percent of the popular vote. In addition, nearly all the members of the House and Senate for the past several decades have been affiliated with one of the two major parties. Although the 2010 elections were marked by the emergence of the "Tea Party," this group was in fact not a party but a faction of energetic voters and organizers who worked almost exclusively within the Republican Party to nominate and support fiscally conservative Republican candidates. The United States is one of the most distinctive two-party systems in the world.

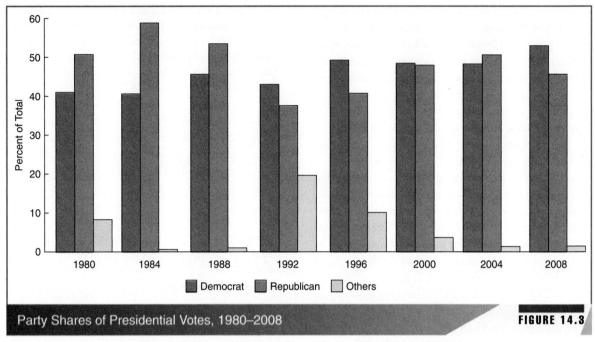

Party Shares of Presidential Votes, 1980–2008   **FIGURE 14.3**

Source: *Statistical Abstract of the United States: 2010* (Washington, D.C.: Bureau of the Census, 2010), Table 385.

The "Americanization" of Electioneering

Electioneering—what parties and candidates do in campaigns to maximize their votes in elections—has changed considerably in most democratic nations since the 1950s, and the United States is generally credited with (or blamed for) leading the way. Before the 1950s, electioneering in democracies was conducted mainly by party leaders and workers. The party workers made direct contacts with their candidates' known and potential supporters, and used the mass media mainly to publish newspaper advertisements and to print pamphlets and flyers for the party workers to distribute.

Since the 1950s, American parties and candidates have replaced the old techniques. They now depend mainly on paid television advertisements and broadcasters' interviews and talk shows to showcase their candidates and policies to the voters. They employ experts to conduct frequent polls of the voters to test how well their strategies are working. They store and analyze information about the demographics, past electoral behavior, and vast amounts of consumer behavior of individuals in computerized "microtargeting" databases. They also have transferred control of electioneering from party politicians to paid professional campaign consultants trained in advertising agencies rather than party organizations.

They have made televised debates among the candidates the most important events in campaigns.

Party leaders and candidates in other democracies have watched U.S. electioneering. Many have deplored it, and some have vowed never to "Americanize" (their term) their own campaigns. Nevertheless, campaigners in most democracies have adapted some or all of the high-tech American methods for their own uses. For example, the United States held its first nationally televised debates between presidential candidates in 1960. Similar debates among leading parties and candidates are now regularly held also in Brazil, Chile, Denmark, France, Germany, Mexico, Norway, Sweden, and Venezuela. Most parties in most democracies now hire professional campaign consultants, some of them American or trained in America, to plan their campaigns. They use private polls to assess the effectiveness of their campaigns, and they use the mass media, especially television, as their main device for soliciting the voters' support. They have followed America's lead by increasingly using negative advertising to sharpen the contrasts between candidates or to ruin an opponent's reputation. In short, while the "Americanization" of electioneering may or may not be a healthy development, it has happened to some degree in all democracies and to a considerable degree in many.[38]

BOX 14.5

The Presidential Election of 2008

Candidate	Popular Votes	Electoral Votes
Barack Obama, Democrat	69,456,897 (52.9%)	365
John McCain, Republican	59,934,814 (45.7%)	163
Others	1,865,617 (1.4%)	0

The 2008 election garnered even more worldwide attention than American presidential contests usually do, because in Barack Obama it featured a multiracial candidate with African ancestry whose positions on foreign affairs and environmental policy fit much more closely with European viewpoints than President Bush's. In fact, when he toured Europe after securing the Democratic nomination, Obama was greeted like a rock star, with more than 200,000 adoring fans swarming his July 24, 2008, speech in Berlin. Yet Americans were less quick to embrace Obama, who faced a well-respected challenger in Vietnam War hero and "maverick" senator John McCain. While Obama's eventual triumph came by a margin much larger than the razor-thin victories that Bush had won in 2000 and 2004, the contest remained close throughout the summer and early fall and was sealed only when voters blamed September's massive stock-market collapse on the incumbent Republican administration.

Both Obama and McCain began their party's nomination contests as underdogs. A law professor who had only recently begun his political career, Obama rose from the Illinois state senate to the U.S. Senate in 2004 and to national prominence with an impressive speech at that year's Democratic national convention. Still, he began trailing New York senator Hillary Rodham Clinton, whose credentials in foreign affairs were exceeded only by the extent of her personal political connections. By focusing on an often ambiguous message of political change, a clear and consistent opposition to the war in Iraq, and a brilliantly organized grassroots campaign, Obama rocketed ahead of Clinton in the Iowa caucuses and retained his lead through a bruising primary season.

McCain, the "maverick" Republican who mixed conservative policy stances on most issues with support for environmental regulations, criticism of the Bush administration's policies on torture, and leadership on campaign finance reform, initially trailed Republican contenders such as Rudy Giuliani and actor-turned-senator Fred Thompson. In part because he seemed to stand a better chance against the Democratic candidate in November, McCain drew enough support from Republican primary voters to capture his party's nomination. When he accepted it at the Republican National Convention, his appearance was overshadowed by the phenomenon of Sarah Palin's electrifying convention speech. McCain's vice-presidential pick won immediate fans—pulling the McCain-Palin ticket nearly even with the Obama-Biden team in polls—but her support withered over the course of the fall as her inexperience and policy positions came under scrutiny.

The major event of the campaign, however, was the sharp and staggering financial crisis and each candidate's reaction to it. McCain, already on the defensive because he had called the fundamentals of the economy "sound" and because his party's president was taking the blame for its collapse, called for a temporary halt to the campaign, then reversed that plea. Obama hammered at his message of "change" from the "Republican recession," and finally pulled away in the polls in October. He won a historic victory in November, the first ever by a candidate with African-American heritage in a country that has been so often divided along racial lines, but did so with the very traditional strategy of running against the incumbent party during a time of economic turmoil.

Differences between the Major Parties

Throughout the 1950s and 1960s, foreign observers (and many Americans) saw few differences between the Democratic and Republican parties. Today, however, the split between the two major parties is sharp and meaningful, and there is a vast gap between the views of Democratic and Republican voters on issues like health-care reform, abortion rights, and foreign policy. In Congress, the Democratic caucus has moved further and further to the left since 1970, just as Republicans have become increasingly conservative.[39] Thus, the level of mass and elite **partisan polarization**

Presidential Debate in 2008

During the first debate of the 2008 general election campaign, Democratic presidential candidate Barack Obama (R) speaks to Republican presidential candidate John McCain (L) at the University of Mississippi campus at Oxford, Mississippi.

Larry W. Smith/epa/Corbis

in America is now quite high, as it is in most European nations.

This does not mean that there is no one left in the middle of the American political spectrum; indeed, most Americans see themselves as moderates who lean only slightly in the liberal or conservative direction. Instead, the increase in partisan polarization reflects the fact that Americans today have sorted themselves into the party that most accurately reflects their ideology.[40] No longer are there many conservative Democrats in the South or liberal Republicans in New England or the Midwest. This sorting has taken place among elected officials, party activists, and ordinary voters alike. Because of it, the parties now differ significantly in both the social composition of the voters who identify with them and the policy positions taken by their elected leaders.

As is shown in Figure 14.4, by 2008, Americans were more likely to identify themselves as Democrats (51 percent) than as Republicans (38 percent) or independents (11 percent). (It should be noted also that most of these independents lean toward one party and vote for its nominees quite loyally.)[41] Democrats have greater support among women than men, among blacks than whites, and among people with lower incomes and educations than upper-status people. Other research shows that the link between income

and party affiliation has grown in recent decades: "The relatively poor are increasingly Democratic and the rich Republican."[42] There are, of course, many, many rich Democrats, but the overall trend is that Americans with higher incomes are more likely to be Republicans. Thus, as income inequality has increased in America, the gap between the two parties has widened. Finally, the parties now differ more than ever in how religious their members are, with Republican presidential candidates doing better among regular churchgoers than Democrats.[43]

These rising differences in each party's social base help to explain why Democratic and Republican members of Congress increasingly take different policy positions. Table 14.3 explores these divisions by looking at roll-call votes on some significant issues before the House and Senate from 1993 to 2003. It shows that there are significantly more liberals than conservatives among the Democrats in both houses of Congress and significantly more conservatives than liberals among the Republicans—although on most issues, some Democrats vote for conservative positions and some Republicans vote for liberal positions.

Generally, Democrats tend to believe that government should take a major and active role in dealing with the nation's problems, while most

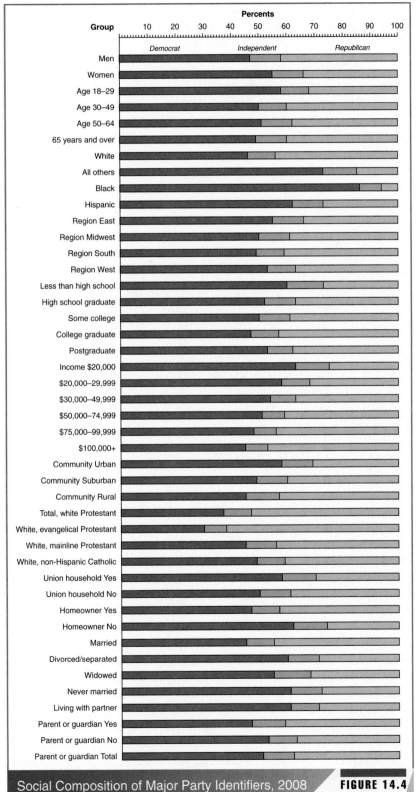

Percents

Social Composition of Major Party Identifiers, 2008   **FIGURE 14.4**

Republicans tend to agree with Ronald Reagan that "big government *is* the problem." Thus, compared with Republicans, most Democrats favor higher levels of government spending on aid for the poor and homeless, education, medical care, public housing, and the like. On these economic issues, the two parties are quite consistent and predictable in translating their ideologies into policy positions. On the so-called social issues, the parties take positions that sometimes appear contrary to their ideological principles. Democrats tend to favor less government intervention in people's moral, religious, and intellectual lives, though they often support governmental action to reduce tobacco use or to require motorcycle riders and young bicyclists to wear helmets. Many Republicans favor policies that allow greater government involvement in such social matters as outlawing abortions and encouraging prayer in the public schools, while they oppose taxpayer support of art or films that they may consider obscene.

Democrats tend to be more egalitarian than Republicans. That is, Republicans tend to support measures for equal opportunity (giving every citizen an equal chance to engage in fair competition for material riches and the other good things in life), while Democrats tend to support measures for "equal conditions" (giving all citizens a guaranteed minimum of the good things in life—such as health insurance—even if they cannot earn them by their own efforts).

Selected Votes in Congress, 1993–2003						**TABLE 14.3**

	Republicans			Democrats		
	Liberal	Conservative	Cohesion Index*	Liberal	Conservative	Cohesion Index*
House						
Lift ban, leave gays-in-military issue to Clinton	101	157	22	163	11	88
Welfare reform	30	165	70	226	4	96
Impeach Clinton for perjury	5	223	98	200	5	98
Bush-proposed tax cut, 2001	0	219	100	197	10	91
Iraq War	6	215	95	126	81	22
Partial-birth abortion ban	4	218	96	137	63	37
Bush-proposed tax cut, 2003	1	224	99	198	7	93
Senate						
"Brady bill" for handgun control	8	47	70	28	16	28
Welfare reform	1	51	96	23	23	0
Bush-proposed tax cut, 2001	0	50	100	38	12	52
McCain-Feingold campaign finance reform	12	38	52	47	3	88
Iraq War	1	48	96	21	29	16
Partial-birth abortion ban	3	47	88	30	17	28
Bush-proposed tax cut, 2003	3	48	88	46	2	92

*The cohesion index is a measure of the extent to which members of a particular party in a legislature vote alike on a matter of public policy. The percentages of the members voting each way are calculated, and the smaller percentage is subtracted from the larger. If they all vote alike, the index is 100. If they split evenly, the index is 0. If they split 75 to 25, the index is 50.

Source: *Congressional Quarterly Reports, 1993–2003.*

Although there are some issues on which legislators from both parties agree—in fact, many bills in Congress are passed by unanimous votes—a number of contentious issues reveal a split between the parties in America that is deep and growing.

Decentralized Organization

Most political parties in most democracies are organized as **hierarchies**, with a national leader and national organization at the top holding the power to supervise the activities of local and regional party organizations. In sharp contrast, the American Democratic and Republican parties are organized, in Samuel Eldersveld's apt phrase, as "**stratarchies**."[44] That is, their organizations at the national, state, and local levels have little power, legal or extralegal, over the organizations at the other levels. Moreover, within

each level, most parties have an executive organization and a legislative organization, and neither has any power over the other.

At the national level, for example, the Democrats and Republicans each have a **presidential party** and a **congressional party**. For the party that holds the presidency, the presidential party consists of the president, the national committee, the national chairman, and the national nominating conventions. The party that does not hold the presidency has no single person as its universally acknowledged leader.

Each party in each house of Congress has a caucus consisting of all the party's members in the particular chamber (and thus equivalent to what in most democracies is called the *parliamentary party*). A floor leader is selected by the caucus to serve as the main coordinator of the party's legislative strategy and tactics. A policy committee, chosen by the caucus, advises the floor leader and the caucus on matters of substantive policy and legislative tactics. The whips are chosen by the caucus to serve as channels of communication between the leaders and the ordinary members. The campaign committees are chosen by the caucus to raise money and distribute it among the campaigns of selected candidates for the particular chamber.

We should emphasize, however, that the presidential party has little formal connection with the congressional party, and that any effort by the president (to say nothing of the national committee or the national chairman) to intervene in the congressional party's selection of its leaders or the determination of its policies or strategy is resented and rejected as "outside interference." In many other nations, this would be viewed as the normal course of party politics.

At the state level, both parties usually have a gubernatorial party and a legislative party. The gubernatorial party consists of the governor (the other party has no single, acknowledged leader), the state central committee, the state chair, and the state conventions. The legislative parties, like the congressional parties, usually have caucuses, elected floor leaders, policy committees, and whips. But each state's gubernatorial and legislative parties have no power over one another, and the national parties have no power over any part of the state parties. The national and state parties are simply different strata, not higher and lower levels in a chain of command headed by the national agencies.

At the various local levels, there are congressional district committees, county committees, city committees, ward and precinct committees, and others too numerous to list here. In most states, the local party committees and conventions are, both in law and in fact, independent of the state and the national party agencies. Hence, they constitute a third stratum, which is just as independent from the state agencies as the state agencies are from the national agencies.

Far more than almost any major party in any other modern democratic nation, then, American party organizations are agglomerations of hundreds of different leaders and committees distributed among various organizational strata, each of which has little or no power to command or obligation to obey any other agency in its own stratum, let alone any agency in any other stratum. Former Georgia governor and senator Zell Miller's speaking career exemplifies this. A moderate Democrat from a state with many such voters, he delivered the keynote address to the Democratic National Convention in 1992. After growing disenchanted with national Democrats and supportive of President Bush, Miller gave the keynote at the Republican National Convention in 2004, but remains a Democrat. Even more tellingly, Connecticut senator Joe Lieberman went from being Al Gore's vice-presidential running mate in 2000 to losing the Democratic primary for Senate in 2006 to running (and winning) that year as a third-party candidate on the "Connecticut for Lieberman" party label. In America, candidates can use parties when they are helpful in campaigns and abandon parties when they are an electoral hindrance, the opposite of the candidate–party relationship in most nations.

Low Cohesion

The parliamentary parties in most modern democratic nations have high **party cohesion**, a term that denotes the degree to which the members of a legislative party vote together on issues of public policy. Abstentions and even votes against the party leaders' wishes are not unknown in those parties, and in some countries, their frequency has increased, though very slowly, in recent years. But these are, at most, minor deviations from the norm that all the members of parliamentary parties in other countries vote solidly together in most parliamentary votes.

By sharp contrast, the only matters in either chamber of Congress on which all Democrats regularly vote one way and all Republicans vote the other way relate to "organizing" the chamber—that is, selecting the speaker of the house, the president pro tem of the Senate, and the chairs of the leading standing committees. On all other issues they rarely vote unanimously, though most usually vote together.

On the issues shown in Table 14.3, party cohesion was generally higher among House Democrats than among Senate Democrats, and even higher among House and Senate Republicans. On some issues, one party or the other approached the cohesion levels of most major parties in other democracies. For example, the House Democrats' opposition to President Clinton's impeachment was very high, while House Republicans had perfect cohesion for President George W. Bush's tax-cut proposal in 2001. On the other hand, House Democrats split more evenly on gays in the military and Bush's tax cut.

Consequently, the congressional parties have some party cohesion. It is especially high on such issues as higher spending for social-welfare measures and greater regulation of business—with the Democrats usually voting predominantly (but not unanimously) in favor and the Republicans usually voting predominantly (but not unanimously) against. On the other hand, on issues that cut sharply across party lines—especially moral issues such as abortion, capital punishment, and the regulation of pornography—both parties regularly split relatively evenly. Thus, in comparison with the major parliamentary parties in most other democratic nations, the American congressional Democrats and Republicans have low cohesion on most issues.

This situation has important consequences for the role of American parties in the policymaking process, which we will consider later. It also has several causes, the most important of which is the fact that, compared with most other democratic parties, the leaders of the Democrats and the Republicans have very weak disciplinary powers.

Weak Discipline

The leaders of most major parties in the world's democracies have a number of tools to ensure that the legislators bearing their parties' labels support the parties' policies in the national legislatures. For one, they can make sure that no unusually visible or persistent rebel against the party's positions is given a ministerial position or preferment of any kind. If that fails to bring the fractious member into line, they can expel him or her from the parliamentary party altogether. Many parties in many countries give their leaders the ultimate weapon: the power to deny the rebel reselection as an official party candidate at the next election.

In sharp contrast, in the United States, any person who wins a party's primary for the House or Senate in any congressional district or state automatically becomes the party's legal candidate for that office, and no national party agency has the power to veto the nomination. On one notable occasion, called by historians "the purge of 1938," Franklin D. Roosevelt, an unusually popular and powerful national party leader, tried to intervene in the primary elections of several states to prevent the renomination of Democratic senators who had opposed his New Deal policies. He failed in twelve of thirteen attempts, and most people have since concluded that any effort by a national

party leader to interfere in candidate selection at the state and local levels is bound to fail.

To be sure, presidents and their parties' leaders in Congress can, and often do, plead with their fellow partisans to support the president's policies for the sake of party loyalty, or to increase the party's chances at the next election, or to keep the party from looking foolish. If persuasion does not work, leaders can (but rarely do) promise to provide future campaign funding to a reluctant member or grant a hearing to a stalled bill authored by that member. Unless they have some strong reason to do otherwise, most members of Congress go along. However, unlike the leaders of most parties in most other countries, neither the president nor his party's congressional leaders have any effective disciplinary power to compel their members in Congress to vote in ways contrary to their consciences—or to what they perceive to be the interests and wishes of their constituents.

A Special Consequence: Divided Party Control of Government

In a pure parliamentary democracy, one party cannot control the legislature while another party controls the executive. If the parliament refuses a cabinet request, the cabinet either resigns and a new cabinet acceptable to the parliament takes over, or the parliament is dissolved, new elections are held, and a new cabinet is formed that has the support of the new parliamentary majority. There can never be more than a short interim period in which the parliamentary majority and cabinet disagree on any major question of public policy.

In the United States, in contrast, separation of powers and the separate terms and constituencies for the president, the members of the House, and the members of the Senate make it possible for one party to win control of the presidency and the other party to win control of one or both houses of Congress. How often does it actually happen? From the election of 1832 (when most historians say the modern electoral and party systems began) through the election of 2008 there have been a total of eighty-nine presidential and midterm elections. Each of these elections could have resulted in either divided party control or unified party control. In fact, fifty-six (63 percent) produced unified control, and thirty-three (37 percent) produced divided control.

Even more noteworthy is the fact that since the death of Franklin D. Roosevelt in 1945, **divided party** control has occurred so frequently that many observers feel it has become normal, not exceptional. In the period from 1946 through 2008, there have been thirty-two elections. Only thirteen (40 percent) have produced unified control (ten with a Democratic president and congress, and three with a Republican president and congress), and nineteen (60 percent) have produced divided control (see Figure 14.5).

The election of 2000 initially produced unified Republican control, with President George W. Bush joining the Republican-controlled Congress. But it did not last long; in 2001, Senator James Jeffords of Vermont announced that he was leaving the Republican Party to become an Independent, and that he would vote with the Democrats. That gave the Democrats only a 50-to-49 margin, but with Jeffords's support, they regained control of the Senate and once again became part of a divided government. In 2002, the voters restored control of both houses to the Republicans, but then delivered both the Senate and the House of Representatives to Democrats in 2006 and the presidency to Democrats in 2008. In the 2010 midterm elections, voters once again switched control of the House to the Republican Party, and left Democrats clinging to a narrow majority in the Senate (see Figure 14.5).

The most obvious cause for this situation (which is both unknown and impossible in parliamentary democracies) is the fact that the chief executive and the members of both houses of Congress are, as we have seen, elected separately by overlapping constituencies and with different terms. The constitutional structure thus makes it possible for American voters to do something that voters in most parliamentary democracies cannot do, namely, "split their tickets"—that is, vote for a member of one party for president and for a member of the other party for Congress.

Ticket-splitting explains the increasing frequency of divided party control. Figure 14.6 shows the changing percentages of respondents in the National Election Studies of all presidential elections from 1952 through 2008 who reported voting for the presidential candidate of one party and a candidate of another party for the House of Representatives. This figure shows that split-ticket voting rose steadily from 1952 until 1980. It has fallen since then, as partisan polarization in the electorate has increased, but in 2008, it was still higher than it was in 1952.

However, divided government apparently does not significantly weaken (or strengthen) the federal

Year	Congress	President
1946	Republicans	
1948	Democrats	Harry S Truman, Democrat
1950	Democrats	
1952	Republicans	Dwight D. Eisenhower, Republican
1954	Democrats	
1956	Democrats	
1958	Democrats	
1960	Democrats	John F. Kennedy, Democrat
1962	Democrats	
1963	Democrats	Lyndon B. Johnson, Democrat
1964	Democrats	
1966	Democrats	
1968	Democrats	Richard M. Nixon, Republican
1970	Democrats	
1972	Democrats	
1973	Democrats	Gerald R. Ford, Republican
1974	Democrats	
1976	Democrats	James E. Carter, Democrat
1978	Democrats	
1980	S–R, H–D	Ronald W. Reagan, Republican
1982	S–R, H–D	
1984	S–R, H–D	
1986	Democrats	
1988	Democrats	George H. W. Bush, Republican
1990	Democrats	
1992	Democrats	William J. Clinton, Democrat
1994	Republicans	
1996	Republicans	
1998	Republicans	
2000	S–D, H–R	George W. Bush, Republican
2002	Republicans	
2004	Republicans	
2006	Democrats	
2008	Democrats	Barack Obama, Democrat
2010	S–D, H–R	

FIGURE 14.5
United/Split Party Control of the Presidency and Congress, 1946–2010

government's ability to make public policies. David Mayhew's careful study of the most important pieces of legislation passed from 1946 to 1990 shows that the rate of production was about the same in periods of divided party control as in periods of unified control.[45]

THE POLICYMAKING PROCESS IN AMERICA

When we consider the policymaking process in the United States, we must first understand that the constitutional framework within which the process operates was carefully designed to keep government from doing bad things, not to make it easier for it to do

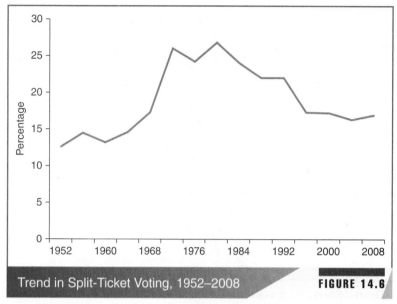

Trend in Split-Ticket Voting, 1952–2008   **FIGURE 14.6**

Source: American National Election Studies, Inter-University Consortium for Political and Social Research, University of Michigan, compiled by Gary Jacobson. Data points are the percentage reporting a different vote for the presidential and House of Representatives elections; third-party candidates are excluded from the calculations.

good things. To be sure, in writing the Constitution, the men of Philadelphia hoped to achieve a more effective national government than that provided by the Articles of Confederation. But making and implementing effective, coherent, and forceful national policies was not their prime goal.

They believed that government should never be regarded as some kind of benevolent mother, doing whatever is necessary to keep all her children well-fed and feeling good. We should never forget, they warned, that government is a powerful and dangerous institution created by fallible human beings. Its prime objective—indeed, its only legitimate reason for existing and being obeyed—is to secure every person's right to life, liberty, and property. Anything that government does beyond that, they believed, is not only less important but not even acceptable if it in any way abridges those basic rights.

The best way to make a government strong enough to secure the rights of its citizens without becoming so powerful that it overrides them, they believed, is to disperse its power among many different agencies—among the federal and state governments by federalism, and within the federal government by separation of powers. The power should be divided, they held, so that no single faction would likely ever get control of the whole power of government and promote its interests at the expense of all the others.[46]

Accordingly, they did not think that policy deadlocks, in which the government cannot act because one of its parts blocks action by other parts, are some kind of terrible failure that should be avoided wherever possible and unblocked as soon as possible. Rather, they regarded such deadlocks as highly preferable to any government action that rides roughshod over the interests and objections of any significant part of the community. Consequently, whenever a deadlock blocks today's government from making effective policies to deal with budget deficits, mounting national debt, crime, health care, campaign finance, the war on terror, or any other public problem, the least we can say is that the policymaking process is operating as the framers intended.

The governmental apparatus they assembled to slow down policy movement to a deliberative pace is depicted in Figure 14.7. This rough schematic of how a bill becomes a law illustrates the parallel paths that legislation must take through the two houses of Congress that represent very different constituencies. To become law, versions of a bill must first pass both the House (where each of the 435 representatives vote on behalf of districts containing roughly 650,000 residents) and the Senate (where pairs of senators represent states that range in population from 520,000 in Wyoming to 38 million in California). In each body, legislation is assigned to a committee, making it vulnerable to the will of the committee's chair and its members, and then must pass on the floor. This is an especially difficult hurdle in the Senate, where sixty votes out of one hundred are needed to end a potential filibuster on any bill other than the annual budget resolution and the policy changes necessary to reconcile law with the new budget. (This "reconciliation" process opens the door to passing major legislation with a fiscal effect, such as President Obama's health-care reform bill, with only fifty-one rather than sixty votes, but such a step is rarely taken.) Even after both houses act in tandem, they must agree on a final bill that sorts out any differences between the Senate and House versions, and pass it. Then the bill moves on to the president's desk, where the leader of the executive branch can always veto the measure and ask

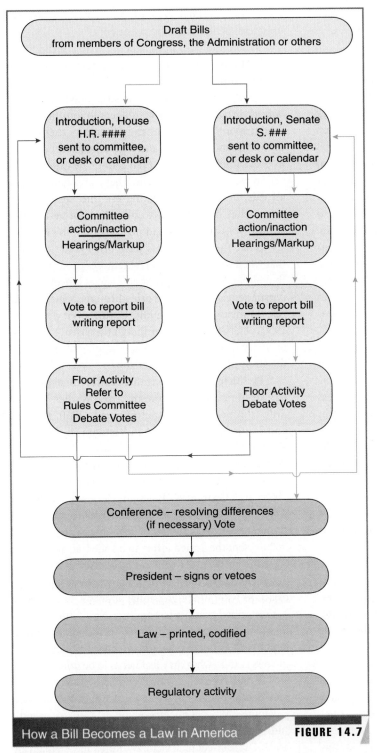

Draft Bills
from members of Congress, the Administration or others

Introduction, House
H.R. ####
sent to committee,
or desk or calendar

Introduction, Senate
S. ###
sent to committee,
or desk or calendar

Committee
action/inaction
Hearings/Markup

Committee
action/inaction
Hearings/Markup

Vote to report bill
writing report

Vote to report bill
writing report

Floor Activity
Refer to
Rules Committee
Debate Votes

Floor Activity
Debate Votes

Conference – resolving differences
(if necessary) Vote

President – signs or vetoes

Law – printed, codified

Regulatory activity

How a Bill Becomes a Law in America   **FIGURE 14.7**

Source: Lexus Nexis: http://www.google.com/imgres?imgurl=http://wiki.lexisnexis.com/
publib/images/8/85/Bill2law.gif&imgrefurl=http://wiki.lexisnexis.com/publib/index.php%3
Ftitle%3DCongressional&usg=__Fj1u5xcgCXzK3-MJrBoBNGz-bGY=&h=558&w=
432&sz=103&hl=en&start=1&um=1&itbs=1&tbnid=4KLeBog6Ho-pEM:&tbnh=
133&tbnw=103&prev=/images%3Fq%3DCRS%2Bhow%2Ba%2Bbill%2Bbecomes
%2Ba%2Blaw%26um%3D1%26hl%3Den%26client%3Dsafari%26rls%3Den%26tbs
%3DIsch:1

for legislative changes. Compared to the parliamentary systems that fuse their legislative and executive branches and often privilege one house above the other, the American system of policymaking puts in place many roadblocks where a bill can be stopped.

Traditional Ways of Avoiding Deadlocks

From the opening of the First Congress in 1789 to the twenty-first century, Americans have found that, however dangerous to human rights it may be, the government of the United States has to make and implement at least *some* policies. It has to regulate interstate and foreign commerce, increase or decrease the supply of money, conduct relations with foreign nations, levy taxes, make appropriations, and so on. Americans have developed ways of getting policies made despite the constitutional system's many roadblocks and general tendency toward inertia. One set of ways has been traditionally used in ordinary times, and the other set has been called on in times of great crisis.

In ordinary times, public policies in America have been made mainly by putting together ad hoc, issue-specific coalitions of interests by bargaining and cutting deals among their representatives. The main coalition-builders have included public officials of all kinds, including presidents and their chief political aides in the Cabinet and the Executive Office of the President; members of Congress and their professional staffs; political heads and permanent civil servants in the executive departments and the independent agencies; and federal judges and their clerks. At least as active and often as powerful as these inside players are the outside players, especially the lobbyists representing the major organized interest groups that feel they have major stakes in the policy outcomes. The usual result is that, while each contest over each policy produces winners and losers, it never produces total victory or total defeat for any highly involved interest. Each contestant gets something of what it wants but never all, and each manages to stave off total disaster.

Many commentators, past and present, have been highly critical of this process. They claim that it usually takes far too long to get anything done, and that what is done is usually messy, full of inconsistencies, self-defeating, and in constant need of repair. They are also struck by how difficult it is to get closure on any major policy. Typically, when a coalition loses in the presidency, it tries in the Congress; when it loses in the Congress, it tries in the bureaucracy; when it fails to persuade incumbent elected and appointed officials, it tries to replace them; and when it loses everywhere else, it turns to the courts to upset or water down policies made by the other agencies.

In recent years, for example, environmentalists have increasingly focused their efforts on lobbying the federal agencies that implement natural-resources legislation rather than only the members of Congress who pass it. As another example, when civil-rights advocates in the 1950s failed to get Congress to abolish racial segregation in the schools, they turned to the U.S. Supreme Court and won their victory in the landmark decision of *Brown v. Board of Education* (1954). Those who today advocate same-sex marriage rights have found success in several court cases while they have generally lost in legislative fights and in initiative battles.

Without doubt, the ordinary-times process falls far short of the neat, orderly, and swift policymaking process that parliamentary democracies usually enjoy because of their fusion of powers and the consequent impossibility of prolonged deadlock between the executive and the legislature. Yet the American process has undeniably produced a large number of major national policies, many of them quite successful: for example, the establishment of Alexander Hamilton's economic development program in the 1790s, the western expansion of the country in the nineteenth century, the absorption of millions of immigrants, the Progressive reforms of the early 1900s, the New Deal, the constant (though to some too slow) advance in the status of African-Americans since the end of slavery, the Great Society welfare and health-care programs of the 1960s, the drastic overhaul of the tax system in 1986, and so on. Even at its best, however, the ordinary-times process has always taken a great deal of time to produce results, and there have been occasions in American history when the danger that it would not work rapidly enough to meet the needs made the nation turn to a less rigid but more controversial type of policymaking process: unilateral action taken by presidents.

When the Southern states started seceding in 1861, Abraham Lincoln took a number of steps that were far outside the ordinary policymaking process. By executive proclamations, he suspended the writ of *habeas corpus*; called for volunteers to join the Union Army; spent government money to buy them food, uniforms, and weapons; and made the fateful decision to provision Fort Sumter even though he expected the action would start a civil war. Then, after having done all this, he summoned Congress into session, told them what he had done, and asked for retroactive authority—which they had no choice but to give him.

Since then, presidents have often taken the view that when the national interest requires prompt action, they either should do it on their own, as Lincoln did, or persuade Congress to rush through their radical reform measures, as Franklin D. Roosevelt did in the 1930s when it seemed clear that in the absence of extraordinary measures, the economy would collapse under the stress of the Great Depression.

Presidents usually exert these extraordinary powers in foreign rather than domestic crises, as when Truman ordered American troops into Korea in 1950; Kennedy and Johnson followed suit in Vietnam in the 1960s; George H. W. Bush ordered troops to Panama, the Persian Gulf, and Somalia in the 1980s and early 1990s; Clinton sent troops to Haiti in 1994 and to Bosnia in 1995; and George W. Bush in 2001 and 2002 sent American soldiers and airmen to Afghanistan to overthrow the terrorist-sheltering Taliban government, and in 2003 sent the armed forces to invade Iraq and depose Saddam Hussein. The War Powers Act of 1974 was designed to limit the president's power to take this kind of action without congressional approval, but in fact it has restrained presidents very little. No one doubts that in any future crisis, especially in foreign affairs, presidents will again bypass the ordinary policymaking process and do what they feel needs to be done.

Recent experience, however, makes it clear that the **presidential dictatorship** escape valve does not stay open indefinitely. When a military action drags on for months and years with huge expense, many casualties, and little hope of a clean-cut final victory—Korea and Vietnam are so far the leading examples, and Iraq and Afghanistan may take their places on the list—the president eventually loses popular and then congressional support, and the nation returns to the ordinary process. In any case, a leader who is held to account for his actions in free elections every four years is no dictator.

He can also be checked by the courts and by the press, which happened to President George W. Bush with increasing frequency. The *New York Times* revealed in December 2005 that the National Security Agency, at the president's request, was conducting surveillance on domestic and international telephone calls without obtaining court warrants as proscribed by the Foreign Intelligence Surveillance Act (FISA). The Bush administration argued that the presidency's inherent powers justify bypassing this congressional act during a time of war, but the president faced tough questioning on this issue from reporters and from some members of Congress. In June 2006, the U.S. Supreme Court ruled that detainees held at Guantanamo Bay could not be put on trial before secretive military commissions, in part because the commissions were created without congressional authority. This landmark case points out the limits of executive power, even in wartime.

POLICY PERFORMANCE

Tax Policies

When considering policy performance in the United States, it is important to remember that we are dealing with the outputs of many governments, not just the one in Washington, D.C.[47] In 2007, there were over 89,000 governmental units in America, including the federal government, 50 states, 3,033 counties, 19,492 municipalities, 16,519 towns and townships, 13,051 local school districts, and 37,381 special districts—each of which had some constitutional or statutory power to make policies.[48]

Of these 89,527 authorities, the federal government extracts the greatest share of revenues; it collects 57 percent of revenues from all sources. Its share is, of course, smaller than the shares taken by the national governments of unitary nations—such as Great Britain, Japan, and Sweden—but it is larger than those taken by the national governments in any of the federal systems except Austria.[49]

Table 14.4 displays the main types of taxes as percentages of total revenue in the United States and six other industrialized nations in 2000. This table shows that the United States relies more on personal income taxes than any other nation. Social Security taxes paid by employees in America are higher than average. The United States relies less on sales and other taxes on consumption than any other country. Part of the reason is that, unlike most European governments, the U.S. national government has never levied a sales tax or a value-added tax, although most American states levy sales taxes as well as income taxes. Accordingly, the tax structure in the American federal system as a whole is more progressive (in the sense of placing the heaviest burden on people with the greatest ability to pay) than that in most but not all other nations.

Americans frequently complain about the heavy tax burden they bear, and Republican presidents Ronald Reagan, George H. W. Bush, and George W. Bush all made cutting taxes the cornerstones of their economic programs. Just how great is the tax burden of Americans compared with that borne by the residents of other industrialized democracies?

The answer depends on what measure is used. Expressed as a percentage of GDP, American taxes take

Tax Sources as Percentages of Total Revenue, 2007						TABLE 14.4
	Personal Income	**Corporate Income**	**Employees' Social Security**	**Employers' Social Security**	**Sales and Consumption**	**Specific Goods**
Great Britain	29.8	9.4	7.7	10.4	18.2	9.7
Canada	37.6	11.4	5.6	8.1	13.6	8.4
France	17.3	6.6	9.2	25.2	17.0	7.1
Germany	25.5	5.9	16.1	17.4	19.4	8.8
Italy	25.9	8.7	5.3	20.8	14.4	8.5
Japan (2000)	20.2	13.2	13.9	18.2	8.7	7.7
United States	37.7	11.4	10.3	12.0	7.6	5.9

Source: *Statistical Abstract of the United States: 2010* (Washington, D.C.: Bureau of the Census, 2010), Table 1325.

a total of 25.6 percent, the lowest figure among the major industrialized nations (Sweden, at 50.6 percent, is the highest). Moreover, its take from GDP has increased at a slower rate than in any other industrialized democracy since 1980 (again, Sweden leads with the highest rate of increase).[50] In summary, compared with the tax systems of most other industrialized countries, the American system is one of the more progressive in its structure but takes a smaller proportion of the GDP than any of the others.

Distributive Performance

Figure 14.8 gives an overview of how the federal government spent its $3 trillion budget in 2008. This figure shows that the federal government spent 61 percent of its budget on domestic welfare and education functions, 21 percent on defense-related functions, 8 percent for interest on the national debt, and 10 percent in other areas. State and local governments in America also spend more than $2 trillion on their own, with the bulk of this spending going toward education, health care, and welfare.

Among the world's other democratic governments, only Israel spends as high a proportion of its budget on defense as the United States. (Some developing countries, such as North Korea, Oman, and Saudi Arabia, spend even higher proportions.) Some Americans argue that defense spending is far too high, especially now that the Cold War has ended. Others counter that the events of September 11, 2001, demonstrate that the world is still a dangerous place, and America needs to spend whatever it takes to win the **war on terror**. Whatever the merits of these positions, the trend up to 2001 was toward lower proportions of federal spending on defense, but defense spending then climbed from 2002 through 2008.

Other international comparisons show that U.S. per capita expenditures on health care are by far the highest in the world, followed at some distance by Switzerland and Germany.[51] And in proportion of the GDP spent on education, the United States (with 7.3 percent) ranks second behind South Korea (8.2 percent) and ahead of Denmark (7.1 percent), Iceland (6.7 percent), and Sweden (6.5 percent).[52]

Regulatory Performance

Like all modern industrialized democracies, the United States is a welfare state in the sense that many of its policies proceed from the conviction that government has an obligation to guarantee certain minimum levels

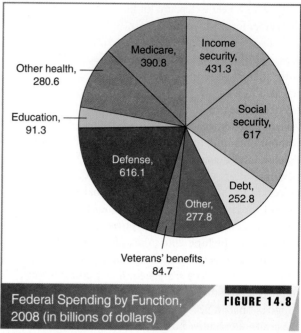

Federal Spending by Function, 2008 (in billions of dollars)

FIGURE 14.8

Source: *Statistical Abstract of the United States: 2010* (Washington, D.C.: Bureau of the Census, 2010), Table 461.

of life's basics to all its citizens, especially to those who cannot provide them for themselves. However, nations differ markedly both in the particular items of basic needs that government should provide and the levels at which they should be provided. In this section, we briefly review the major policies adopted by American governments in three main problem areas.

Social Insurance The United States was among the last of the modern industrialized nations to embrace the goals of the welfare state, and today, the proportion of the nation's GDP spent on public-welfare programs is lower than that in most industrialized nations. Even so, the federal, state, and local governments together have a wide range of policies intended to put a floor beneath the income and living conditions of the poor. For that purpose, they use two main instruments: social insurance and welfare, as well as public assistance.

1. *Social insurance and welfare.* This category includes programs to protect citizens against the risk of loss of income due to old age, retirement, sickness, industrial accidents, and unemployment. The basic federal legislation is the Social Security Act of 1935, which established a fund from mandatory contributions by employees and employers from which all wage-earners are entitled to receive cash payments at retirement or on

reaching a certain age. Since the benefits are available to all who contribute, most Americans regard its benefits as entitlements, not handouts. No stigma attaches to receiving Social Security checks, and most Americans of all income levels approve of the program.

2. ***Public assistance.*** This category includes both direct cash and in-kind payments to poor people, such as cash aid to families with dependent children, food stamps, free milk for young children, and day care for children of working mothers with low incomes. Unlike Social Security, these programs are noncontributory and thus constitute obvious income transfers from upper-income to lower-income people. As a result, some social stigma does attach to receiving public-assistance benefits, and these welfare programs are much more controversial than the social-insurance programs.

For years, there were many complaints that the welfare system, especially Aid for Families with Dependent Children (AFDC), was removing recipients' incentives to work and making them into lifelong dependents on government handouts. Then, in 1996, the Republican Congress passed, and President Clinton signed, a bill for **welfare reform**. The new law ended the federal guarantee of direct AFDC payments to all eligible families. Instead, the federal government gave $16.4 billion in block grants to the states to develop and fund their own new welfare programs, *provided* that the states impose work requirements for welfare recipients, develop job-training programs for them, and put time limits on welfare benefits (thereby replacing welfare with "workfare," according to the new law's advocates).[53]

Education In the United States, as in other industrialized nations, education is provided mainly by schools financed and operated by the government, although there are more privately owned and operated schools, especially universities, in America than in most other countries (they are also important in Japan and Great Britain).

What sets the American school system apart from systems in other countries is its high degree of decentralization. Most schools, from kindergartens through universities, are financed and regulated by state and local governments, although the federal government provides considerable subsidies for many special programs, each of which carries restrictions on how the money is to be spent. For example, in awarding federally funded scholarships and other forms of financial aid for students, schools may not discriminate against applicants because of their race or gender.

The local financing and regulation of schools has many consequences, not the least of which is the fact that schools in poor states and poor districts generally spend considerably less money per pupil than schools in richer states and districts.

Whatever the consequences of these differences, the United States still has a higher proportion of its population with secondary or university degrees than any other nation. It also has the second-highest proportion (after Japan) of seventeen-year-olds in secondary schools, the highest proportion of twenty-one-year-olds in colleges and universities, and the highest proportion of college graduates going on to graduate and professional schools.[54]

A number of industrialized nations operate on the theory that higher education should be reserved for only the most talented and accomplished students. They therefore require that only those students who do well in demanding, nationally administered tests after finishing one level may advance to a school at the next higher level. The United States, in contrast, operates on the theory that as many people as possible should be given a chance at a college education. Consequently, it is much easier for American eighteen-year-olds to enter some kind of post-secondary education—a four-year college or university, or a two-year community college—than for their peers in any other country, and many more do so. In 2006, 30 percent of Americans between the ages of twenty-five and sixty-four had university educations—a higher proportion than in any other industrialized democracy.

What about the *quality* of American education? Many scholars, school administrators, and politicians in America have long and inconclusively debated that question, and the literature on the subject is far too vast and complicated to survey in detail here. We will note only that U.S. students score just above the mean for industrialized countries on a combined reading scale and just below the mean on math and science scales.[55]

Environmental Protection Of the policy areas considered here, environmental protection is the most recent to take center stage, not only in the United States but in most other industrialized nations as well. From the beginning of the Industrial Revolution in the late eighteenth century until well after World War II, one of the highest goals of every nation was economic growth—constantly increasing the nation's production of goods and services, both for home consumption and for sale abroad.

For many purposes, that goal remains highly desirable today, since economic growth allows governments to reach a diverse set of policy goals, including boosting their military strength and diplomatic clout; providing more food, shelter, and medical care for the poor; and increasing the coverage and improving the quality of health care and education. In recent years, however, policymakers in many nations, including the United States, have come to realize that economic growth, especially unrestrained and rapid growth, has great costs. Nowhere is this cost greater than in the area of toxic emissions and solid wastes that have been the by-products of large-scale industrialization.

As a result, policymakers in the United States and elsewhere have become increasingly aware that they must grapple with environmental problems. Some nations, especially Japan and Great Britain, have approached these problems less by relying on government regulations than on encouraging corporations and labor unions to work together to develop their own plans for dealing with pollution. Early in the era of environmental policy, the United States took a quite different approach. It enacted a series of stringent laws, beginning with the Clean Air Act of 1970. These laws require manufacturers to reduce sharply their emissions that pollute the air and water by installing expensive devices (such as smoke-scrubbers and water-purifiers) to recycle solid wastes, and to clean up, mostly at their own (and/or their insurance companies') expense, the toxic waste dumps they had created. The federal government established a special agency, the Environmental Protection Agency (EPA), to make sure that these laws are strictly enforced.

More recently, U.S. policymakers have moved away from stringent regulations and toward incentives, voluntary industry goals, and tradable permits that seek to reduce pollution in the most cost-effective way possible. Perhaps the clearest indication that the United States has moved away from the forefront of environmental regulation is the federal government's refusal to ratify the Kyoto Protocol, an international agreement designed to stave off global warming by reducing emissions of "greenhouse gases," such as carbon dioxide. Opponents have argued that abiding by the protocol's targets would slow down economic growth in the United States, and that it places too much of a burden on industrialized nations while putting much looser limits on developing countries. During his campaign, Barack Obama argued against this position, promising swift action to limit greenhouse gas emissions and more energetic American leadership in the fight against global warming.

AMERICAN EXCEPTIONALISM: MYTH OR REALITY?

The Idea in History

During much of its history, many of the United States' leaders and citizens—and some foreign commentators and many of the millions of immigrants who left their native countries to become Americans—have regarded the United States as not just another polity in a world of many polities, but as significantly different from other political systems. Some have viewed it as a great social experiment from which all political systems can and should learn lessons relevant to founding and reforming their own systems.

In his first Inaugural Address, George Washington said, "The preservation of the sacred fire of liberty, and the destiny of the republican model of government, are justly considered as deeply, perhaps as finally staked, on the experiment entrusted to the hands of the American people."[56]

In December 1862, when the very existence of the American system was at stake in the Civil War, Abraham Lincoln said to the Congress, "We of this Congress and this administration, will be remembered in spite of ourselves. . . . The fiery trial through which we pass, will light us down, in honor or dishonor, to the latest generation. . . . We shall nobly save, or meanly lose, the last, best hope of earth."[57]

How True Is It?

It seems altogether fitting and proper that we should end this chapter by asking not whether the idea of **American exceptionalism** is noble or vainglorious, but rather how true it is. That is, in what respect and to what degree does the American system resemble and differ from the world's other political systems? Our conclusions are summarized in Table 14.5.

How the American System Closely Resembles Other Systems It is a government that has jurisdiction over a certain territory and peoples. It makes laws governing their behavior and enforces them with means up to and including capital punishment.

American society is composed of many different groups with different interests, and its political process is essentially a contest among them to advance their interests. Few if any policies benefit all groups and interests equally, and most political decisions have, relatively speaking, some winners and some losers.

The United States Compared with Other Nations: A Summary			**TABLE 14.5**

Characteristic	How the U.S. Is Like Other Nations	How the U.S. Resembles a Few Nations but Differs from Many	How the U.S. Is Unique, or Nearly So
Society	Consists of many different groups with different interests	Large population of immigrants and descendants of immigrants High religious diversity	
Political System	Has a government, which makes and enforces laws	Is a democracy	
Structure of Government		Based on principles of constitutionalism Federal system	Extensiveness of system of checks and balances
Executive Branch	Has a chief executive	Presidential system rather than parliamentary system Chief of state and head of government roles performed by same person President is directly elected through an electoral college	
Legislative Branch	Has a national legislature	Both houses of the legislature are directly elected	Legislative committees play a critical role
Judicial Branch	Courts settle civil and criminal disputes	All national judges appointed; some state and local judges elected Most courts have power of judicial review	Many political issues settled by courts rather than by parties or legislatures
Parties and Elections	Has regular elections	Has a two-party system Elections use single-member districts and plurality decisions Elections held on fixed dates; no power of dissolution Parties closely regulated by law Executive and legislative branches can be and often are controlled by different parties	Candidates selected by direct primaries Voter registration is decentralized and responsibility of voter Voters have many elections and many choices at each Party leaders have no power to admit or expel party members Parties are decentralized and largely undisciplined and uncohesive

In addition, this book's basic theoretical scheme for comparing governments is as applicable to the United States as to any other nation.

How the American System Resembles a Few Nations but Differs from Most As Table 14.5 notes, the United States is a democracy along with other democracies. It is based on the principle of constitutionalism. Its society is diverse in the ethnic and religious makeup of its residents.

The United States is a presidential democracy rather than a parliamentary democracy, based on the separation of powers rather than on their fusion. The head of government is elected rather than hereditary. Furthermore, the roles of chief of state and head of government are performed by the same official.

The United States is also unusual because it is a federal system rather than a unitary system. State governments and the local governments that they create exert a strong, independent influence over the lives of Americans, bringing meaningful representation to voters on a much smaller and more accessible scale.

The legislative system displays differences from other systems. The presiding officers of its legislative chambers are partisan rather than neutral. Its legislative

The New Immigrants

Mexicans crossing the Rio Grande to enter the United States.

J.P. Laffont/Sygma

committees play a critical role in the legislative process. And American legislators are largely free of party discipline and control their own votes.

The U.S. legal system is based on the English common law rather than on the continental European civil law. This means that our legal precedents are derived from the prior decisions of judges rather than from an extensive codification of principles constructed by legislative or executive branch officials. Also, its highest court has the power to declare acts of other government officials and agencies unconstitutional and thereby render them null and void.

U.S. elections use the single-member, plurality system rather than proportional representation. Because of this, they are almost always contested by only two major parties. Not only can different parties control different branches of government at the same time, but they often do. American elections are held on fixed dates, and there is no power of dissolution. The practice is well-established by law and custom that members of the national legislature must live in the states and districts they represent. Particularly in some states and localities, though not at the national level, there is extensive use of popular initiatives and referendums.

How the United States Is Unique, or Nearly So Finally, Table 14.5 highlights many of the unique aspects of the American political system. For instance, committees within Congress are more powerful and autonomous than committees in nearly every other national legislature.

American political parties choose most of their nominees for office by direct primaries conducted and regulated by public law, not by party rules. Many of its executive officers, particularly at the state and local levels, are directly elected and nominated by direct primaries; consequently, the U.S. voter faces more frequent elections and more decisions to make at each election than voters in any other democratic nation except Switzerland. In addition, America's systems for

The New Republican House Leadership in 2010

Just four years after Democrats won control of the US House of Representatives and elected Speaker Nancy Pelosi after the 2006 elections, Republicans regained control of the House with a landslide victory in November 2010. Controlling a majority of House seats set them up to elect Ohio congressman John Boehner, shown here celebrating his party's victory on election night, as the next speaker.

Tom Williams/Roll Call Photos/Newscom

registering voters are largely decentralized and put most of the burden on the voters.

Political parties are closely regulated by law. But political parties do not control who can become and remain their members, and the parties are, compared with those in other democratic systems, uncohesive, undisciplined, and decentralized.

Because candidates run as individuals rather than as local representatives of national party teams, and because no publicly financed free media time is given to parties or candidates, the raising and spending of large amounts of money are more important in American elections than in most other democracies.

The court system is also unusual. A higher proportion of political issues are settled in the courts than in any other democracy. Consequently, lawyers play a more important role in the American political system than in any other.

CONCLUSION

It seems fitting to end this chapter comparing the American political system to the world's other systems with a quotation from one of its greatest foreign observers, the English scholar and statesman, Lord Bryce:

> All governments are faulty; and an equally minute analysis of the constitutions of England, or France, or Germany would disclose mischiefs as serious . . . as those we have noted in the American system. To any one familiar with the practical working of free governments it is a standing wonder that they work at all. . . . What keeps a free government going is the good sense and patriotism of the people . . . and the United States, more than any other country, are governed by public opinion, that is to say, by the general sentiment of the mass of the nation, which all the organs of the national government and of the State governments look to and obey.[58]

REVIEW QUESTIONS

- Why is voter turnout lower in the United States than it is in most democracies?

- How has immigration policy changed over the past century? What effect has this had on American political culture?

- What impact has the direct primary had on the power of political parties in the United States? Why?

- How has America's traditional approach to environmental issues differed from the strategies pursued in Europe? In what ways has our approach changed recently?

- On which areas of government does the United States spend more than the rest of the world does?

KEY TERMS

American exceptionalism
Bill of Rights
blanket primary
checks and balances
closed primaries
congressional party
conservatives
crossover primaries
direct initiative
direct primaries
divided party control

electoral college
federalism
health-care reform
hierarchies
judicial review
litigation
litigiousness
lobbying
mass communications media
melting pot

open primaries
partisan polarization
party cohesion
patchwork quilt
political action committee (PAC)
political culture
popular referendum
presidential democracy
presidential dictatorship
presidential party

scarcity doctrine
separation of powers
stratarchies
ticket-splitting
voting registration
voting turnout
war on terror
welfare reform

SUGGESTED READINGS

Abraham, Henry J. *The Judiciary: The Supreme Court in the Governmental Process*, 10th ed. New York: New York University Press, 1996.

Ansolabehere, Stephen, Roy Behr, and Shanto Iyengar. *The Media Game: American Politics in the Television Age*. New York: Macmillan, 1993.

Bryce, James. *The American Commonwealth*, 2nd ed. London: Macmillan, 1889.

Davidson, Roger H., and Walter J. Oleszek. *Congress and Its Members*, 7th ed. Washington, D.C.: Congressional Quarterly Press, 2000.

Fiorina, Morris P. *Culture War? The Myth of a Polarized America*. New York: Pearson-Longman, 2005.

Ginsberg, Benjamin, and Martin Shefter. *Politics by Other Means: The Declining Importance of Elections in America*, rev. ed. New York: Basic Books, 1999.

Hamilton, Alexander, James Madison, and John Jay. *The Federalist Papers*, ed. Clinton Rossiter. New York: New American Library, 1961.

Jacobson, Gary C. *A Divider, Not a Uniter: George W. Bush and the American People*. New York: Pearson-Longman, 2007.

Kenski, Kate, Bruce W. Hardy, and Kathleen Hall Jamieson. *The Obama Victory: How Media, Money, and Messages Shaped the 2008 Election*. New York: Oxford University Press, 2010.

King, Anthony S. *Running Scared: Why American Politicians Campaign Too Much and Govern Too Little*. New York: Martin Kessler Books, 1997.

Mayhew, David R. *Divided We Govern: Party Control, Lawmaking, and Investigations, 1946–1988*. New Haven, CT: Yale University Press, 1991.

McCarty, Nolan, Keith T. Poole, and Howard Rosenthal. *Polarized America: The Dance of Ideology and Unequal Riches*. Cambridge: Massachusetts Institute of Technology Press, 2006.

Neustadt, Richard E. *Presidential Power and the Modern Presidents: The Politics of Leadership from Roosevelt to Reagan*. New York: Free Press, 1990.

Nicholas, Herbert G. *The Nature of American Politics*, 2nd ed. New York: Oxford University Press, 1986.

Peltason, Jack W. *Corwin & Peltason's Understanding the Constitution*, 14th ed. Fort Worth, TX: Harcourt Brace 1997.

Polsby, Nelson W. *Congress and the Presidency*, 4th ed. Englewood Cliffs, NJ: Prentice Hall, 1986.

Rourke, Francis E. *Bureaucracy, Politics, and Public Policy*. Boston: Little, Brown, 1984.

Schlozman, Kay Lehman, and John T. Tierney, *Organized Interests and American Democracy*. New York: Harper & Row, 1986.

Tocqueville, Alexis de. *Democracy in America*, 2 vols. Henry Reeve text, rev. Francis Bowen, ed. Phillips Bradley. New York: Alfred A. Knopf, 1945.

Wildavsky, Aaron. *The New Politics of the Budgetary Process*, 2nd ed. New York: HarperCollins, 1992.

INTERNET RESOURCES

White House: **www.whitehouse.gov.**

U.S. Senate: **www.senate.gov.**

U.S. House of Representatives: **www.house.gov.**

U.S. Courts: **www.uscourts.gov.**

Library of Congress: **lcweb.loc.gov.**

National Political Index: **politicalindex.com.**

ENDNOTES

1. "The English Flag," in *Barrack-Room Ballads and Other Verses* (London: Methuen, 1892), stanza 1.

2. Strictly speaking, "America" means all the nations located in North and South America, including Canada and the countries in Central America, the Caribbean, and South America. Yet for better or worse, most people around the world use "American" to label anything connected with just one of those nations, the United States of America. With apologies to the citizens of other Western Hemisphere nations, we will use this common, though technically incorrect, label in this chapter.

3. *The World Almanac and Book of Facts 2002* (New York: World Almanac Books, 2002), 782, 804.

4. *Statistical Abstract of the United States: 2010* (Washington, D.C.: U.S. Census Bureau, 2010), Table 1296.

5. H. G. Nicholas, *The Nature of American Politics*, 2nd ed. (New York: Oxford University Press, 1986), 4.

6. *Statistical Abstract of the United States: 2010*, Table 11.

7. See *Statistical Abstract of the United States: 2010*, Table 4, for figures on legal immigration, and Table 47, for estimates and definition of illegal (or unauthorized) immigration.

8. *Statistical Abstract of the United States: 2010*, Table 1312.

9. *Statistical Abstract of the United States: 2010*, Table 458.

10. See Jacob Hacker, *The Divided Welfare State: The Battle Over Public and Private Benefits in the United States* (New York: Cambridge University Press, 2002).

11. The Twenty-First Amendment repeals the Eighteenth (prohibition) Amendment, so there are, in effect, only twenty-five amendments. The resistance to amending the Constitution even with quite popular provisions was demonstrated in June 2006, when an amendment that would have given Congress the power to ban flag-burning fell one vote short of gaining the required two-thirds majority in the U.S. Senate. See Johanna Neuman and Faye Fiore, "Flag Measure Fails by 1 Vote," *Los Angeles Times*, June 28, 2006.

12. A word about this usage: Strictly speaking, the government in Washington, D.C., is the "national" government, and the whole divided-powers system of national and state government is the "federal" government. However, most Americans use the terms "national" and "federal" interchangeably to mean the government in Washington, D.C. We will do the same, but the reader should be aware of the ambiguity of this usage.

13. Fifteen states have term limits for members of their legislatures. A number have also tried to impose similar limits on their members of Congress, but the U.S. Supreme Court ruled in 1995 (*U.S. Term Limits, Inc. v. Thornton*) that the states have no constitutional power to limit the terms of national legislators.

14. In recent years, an old dispute has been revived by a number of political analysts who argue that presidential democracy is inherently inferior to parliamentary democracy and that the United States should convert to a system of parliamentary democracy similar to Great Britain's. Other analysts reply that, judging by the results—effective policies, loyal citizens, and stability—the American system has done at least as well as the parliamentary systems. See Chapter 6 for a discussion of the issues and arguments in the dispute's current version.

15. James Q. Wilson and John J. DiIulio, *American Government*, 6th ed. (Lexington, MA: D. C. Heath, 1995), 81, Table 4.3.

16. Gabriel A. Almond and Sidney Verba, *The Civic Culture: Political Attitudes and Democracy in Five Nations* (Princeton, NJ: Princeton University Press, 1962), 186.

17. Robert A. Kagan, *Adversarial Legalism: The American Way of Law* (Cambridge, MA: Harvard University Press, 2003).

18. *New York Times v. Sullivan*, 376 U.S. 254 (1964).

19. The two key cases are *National Broadcasting Co. v. United States*, 319 U.S. 190 (1943), and *Red Lion Broadcasting Co. v. Federal Communications Commission*, 395 U.S. 367 (1969).

20. See Michael P. McDonald and Samuel Popkin, "The Myth of the Vanishing Voter," *American Political Science Review* 95, no. 4 (December 2001), 963–74.

21. In 1993, Congress passed the "Motor Voter" act, which was intended to make registration much easier and thereby increase voting turnout. The legislation requires the states to allow citizens to register when applying for a driver's license, to permit registrations by mail, and to provide registration forms at public assistance agencies, such as those distributing unemployment compensation and welfare checks. While most political scientists applaud the new law, its effectiveness

is not yet clear. Turnout of eligible voters, which stood at 61 percent in the 1992 presidential election, *dropped* to 53 percent in 1996. It rose to 56 percent in 2000, and then to 61 percent in 2004.

22. David Glass, Peverill Squire, and Raymond E. Wolfinger, "Voter Turnout: An International Comparison," *Public Opinion* (December 1983/January 1984), 49–55.

23. Russell J. Dalton, *Citizen Politics*, 2nd ed. (Chatham, NJ: Chatham House, 1996), 45–47.

24. See John G. Matsusaka, *For the Many or the Few: The Initiative, Public Policy, and American Democracy* (Chicago: University of Chicago Press, 2004).

25. One distinguished foreign observer of American politics argues persuasively that American public officials, such as members of the House of Representatives, face elections far more frequently than do their counterparts in other democracies. Consequently, he says, they have to spend large parts of their time in office raising money, touring their districts, appearing on television, and otherwise preparing for the next election. These necessities leave them less time than is needed for the careful study of public issues and the formulation of good public policy. See Anthony S. King, *Running Scared: Why America's Politicians Campaign Too Much and Govern Too Little* (New York: Martin Kessler Books, 1997).

26. Robert S. Erikson, Norman R. Luttbeg, and Kent L. Tedin, *American Public Opinion*, 4th ed. (New York: Macmillan, 1991), 5, Table 1.2.

27. In the United States, as in many democratic countries, voters can write names other than the parties' nominees on their ballots, but few voters do so, and write-in candidates almost never get more than a handful of votes. An exception came in the 2004 mayor's race in San Diego, when write-in candidate Donna Frye came within a few hundred votes (and a disputed vote tabulation procedure) of getting elected mayor of the nation's seventh-largest city.

28. See Reuven Y. Hazan, "Candidate Selection," in *Comparing Democracies 2*, Chapter 5.

29. William J. Keefe and Marc J. Hetherington, *Parties, Politics, and Public Policy in America*, 9th ed. (Washington, D.C.: CQ Press, 2003), 61–63.

30. Federal Election Commission, *Election Results for the U.S. President, the U.S. Senate and the U.S. House of Representatives* (Washington, D.C.: Federal Election Commission, 2008).

31. See, for example, Alexis de Tocqueville, *Democracy in America*, vol. 1, Henry Reeve text, rev. Francis Bowen, ed. Phillips Bradley (New York: Alfred A. Knopf, 1945), 191–93; and Michel Crozier, *The Trouble With America*, trans. Peter Heinegg (Berkeley: University of California Press, 1984), 81.

32. *Buckley v. Valeo*, 424 U.S. 1 (1976).

33. Harold W. Stanley and Richard G. Niemi, *Vital Statistics on American Politics 2009–2010* (Washington, D.C.: Congressional Quarterly, 2010), Table 2–10.

34. Stanley and Niemi, *Vital Statistics on American Politics 2009–2010*, Table 2–13.

35. *New York Times*, November 21, 1988.

36. Arend Lijphart puts the United States at the top of his list of democratic nations with the smallest number of effective legislative parties, closely followed by New Zealand, the United Kingdom, and Austria: *Democracies: Patterns of Majoritarian and Consensus Governments in Twenty-One Countries* (New Haven, CT: Yale University Press, 1984), Table 7.3, 122. Austin Ranney's ranking of "two-partyness," based on the somewhat different measure of "party fractionalization," which includes both the number of effective parties and the closeness of electoral competition between them, ranks the U.S. parties second behind New Zealand (although in 1995, New Zealand adopted proportional representation, and since then it has had a multiparty system): *Governing: An Introduction to Political Science*, 8th ed. (Englewood Cliffs, NJ: Prentice Hall, 2001), Table 8.6, 181.

37. Richard Scammon, Alice McGillivray, and Rhodes Cook, *America Votes,* 24 (Washington, D.C.: Congressional Quarterly Press, 2001), 8.

38. For a recent survey of changes in electioneering in the United States and other democratic nations, see David Butler and Austin Ranney, eds., *Electioneering: A Comparative Study of Continuity and Change* (New York: Oxford University Press, 1992).

39. Gary C. Jacobson, *A Divider, Not a Uniter: George W. Bush and the American People* (New York: Pearson-Longman, 2007), Chapters 1 and 2.

40. Morris P. Fiorina, *Culture War? The Myth of a Polarized America* (New York: Pearson-Longman, 2005), 18, 5.

41. Bruce E. Keith et al., *The Myth of the Independent Voter* (Berkeley: University of California Press, 1992).

42. Nolan McCarty, Keith T. Poole, and Howard Rosenthal, *Polarized America: The Dance of Ideology and Unequal Riches* (Cambridge: Massachusetts Institute of Technology Press, 2006), 12. But note that the very rich often vote for and contribute to Democrats, making the 90210 postal code in Beverly Hills a top fundraising area for the Democratic Party.

43. Fiorina, *Culture War?*, 70.

44. Samuel J. Eldersveld, *Political Parties in American Society* (New York: Basic Books, 1982), 133–36.

45. David Mayhew, *Divided We Govern* (New Haven, CT: Yale University Press, 1991).

46. The fullest exposition of this philosophy is, of course, *The Federalist Papers*, especially the tenth paper, by James Madison. See Clinton Rossiter, ed., *The Federalist Papers* (New York: New American Library, 1961).

47. Hundreds of books have been written comparing American public policies with their counterparts in other nations. We have drawn heavily on two: Arnold J. Heidenheimer, Hugh Heclo, and Carolyn Teich Adams, *Comparative Public Policy*, 3rd ed. (New York: St. Martin's Press, 1990); and Harold Wilensky and Lowell Turner, *Democratic Corporatism and Policy Linkages* (Berkeley: Institute of International Studies, University of California, 1987).

48. *Statistical Abstract of the United States: 2010*, Tables 416, 418, 457.

49. Heidenheimer, Heclo, and Adams, *Comparative Public Policy*, 198, Table 6.5.

50. OECD, *Revenue Statistics 1965–2004* (Washington, D.C.: OECD, 2005), Table 3, 68.

51. *Statistical Abstract of the United States: 2006*, Table 1323, 871.

52. OECD, *OECD in Figures, OECD Observer 2005/Supplement 1* (Washington, D.C.: OECD, 2005), 66–67.

53. For the law's details, see *Congressional Quarterly Almanac, 1996* (Washington, D.C.: Congressional Quarterly Press, 1997), 6–13 to 6–24.

54. Heidenheimer, Heclo, and Adams, *Comparative Public Policy*, 30, Table 2.1.

55. *Statistical Abstract of the United States: 2010*, Table 1333.

56. *The Addresses and Messages of Presidents of the United States*, vol. 1, compiled by Edwin Williams (New York: Edward Walker, 1846), 32.

57. Address to Congress, December 1, 1862, in Roy P. Basler, ed., *The Collected Works of Abraham Lincoln*, vol. 5, (New Brunswick, NJ: Rutgers University Press, 1953), 537.

58. James Bryce, *The American Commonwealth*, vol. 1, 2nd ed. (London: Macmillan, 1889), 300–301.

Abacha, Sani 95, 107, 393, 396, 400–403,
406–410, 413, 419, 421
Abiola, Morashood 400–402, 413
Abramoff, Jack 451
Abubakar, Abdulsalami 402–403, 410, 413,
418, 421–422
Abubakar, Atiku 396, 411, 414
Achebe, Chinua 395–396, 421
Acton, Lord 8
Afghanistan 6, 12, 42, 54, 144, 155, 159,
222, 373–374, 430–431, 464
Taliban 6, 54, 430, 464
Aging population 34, 133, 155, 290
Agrarian parties 83
Ahmadinejad, Mahmoud 335–336,
343–344, 349, 351–354, 357–358,
361–362, 365, 367, 370, 373–374
AIDS 22, 387
Al Qaeda 430
Alemán, Miguel 321
Algeria 54, 199, 206
Alternative vote 184, 192
American exceptionalism 429, 468–471
Amnesty International 67, 180, 420
Anarchism 6, 127
Angola 145
Antigua 154
Argentina 95, 112, 161, 329
Aristotle 29–30
Armenia 197, 372
Attlee, Clement 165
Aubry, Martine 222
Australia 12, 151, 154, 158, 403
Austria 70, 91
Austro-Hungarian Empire 11
Authoritarian rule 23–24, 56, 67, 102, 108,
112, 115, 120, 124, 135, 245, 282, 375
Awolowo, Obafemi 409–410, 412
Azerbaijan 372–373
Azikiwe, Nnamdi 394, 398, 405,
409–410, 412
Babangida, Ibrahim 393, 401, 409–410,
412–413, 421–422
Bagehot, Walter 167
Bandaranaike, Sirimavo 112
Bangladesh 112, 140, 146, 159
Banisadr, Abolhasan 349
Bartlett, Manuel 304

Basques 14
Bayrou, François 220
Belarus 203, 220
Belgium 10
Benin 390, 422
Bennett, Andrew 31
Besancenot, Olivier 222
Biafra 389, 392, 394, 409, 414, 416, 421,
424
Bicameral legislature 109
Bin Laden, Osama 430
Black Block 65
Blair, Tony 89, 154, 158, 161–163,
166–167, 172, 180, 184, 187, 189–190
Boehner, John 432
Bolivia 298, 322, 373
Bolsa Familia see entry under Brazil
Bolshevik Revolution see entry under
Russia
Bono 20
Bosnia-Herzegovina 14, 50, 144, 146, 464
Botswana 18
Brazil 5, 18, 20–21, 47, 64, 70, 86, 93, 95,
103, 105–109, 111, 121, 131, 135,
137, 139–143, 145, 298, 320, 322,
329, 373
Bolsa Familia 131
Brezhnev, Leonid 202
British Empire 154, 158
Brown, Gordon 152, 161–162, 164, 166,
181–182
Brown v. Board of Education 434
Brundtland, Gro Harlem 112
Buchanan, Pat 453
Buhari, Muhammed 405, 410–413, 419
Bureaucracy 66, 72, 81, 110, 118–121 see
also entries under individual
countries
Burma see Myanmar
Bush, George 453, 464–465
Bush, George W. 154, 162, 237, 430–431,
460–461, 464–465
Cabinet 103–104, 110, 115–117 see also
entries under individual countries
Cable, Vince 168
Calderón, Felipe 295–298, 302, 304,
309–311, 317, 320, 322, 324
California Democratic Party v. Jones 448

Callaghan, James 160, 164, 166
Cambodia 6
Cameron, David 152, 161, 164, 167, 173,
183–184, 192
Cameroon 390
Canada 11, 15, 45, 48, 69, 84, 107, 151,
158, 28, 390, 403, 435
Cárdenas, Cuauhtémoc 294, 318
Cárdenas, Lázaro 94, 292–294, 297, 308,
310, 315, 317
Carter, Jimmy 340
Case study 31
Centralization 12, 181, 233, 202, 213, 304
Channels of political access 71–75
Chechnya 146, 198, 210–211, 222, 227, 237
Checks and balances 91, 440
Chief executive 111–118
Chile 95, 112, 298, 322, 329
China 6, 9, 11–12, 14, 18, 20–22, 31, 36,
38, 46–47, 51, 57, 68, 71, 76, 92, 95,
104, 106–107, 111, 113, 115,
120–121, 129, 131, 135, 137–139,
141, 143, 145–146, 240, 199,
244–283, 290, 336, 370, 374, 435
Central Military Commission 254,
256, 258
Communist Party 36, 92, 113, 115, 243,
246, 250–251, 253–261, 264–270,
275–276, 283
Central Committee 254–255, 257
Cultural Revolution 248, 255, 258–259,
261, 265, 267, 269
Democracy Movement 268–269
government-organized
non-governmental organization
(GONGO) 270
Great Leap Forward 248, 265, 280
Leading small groups (LSG)
272–273, 275
minorities 250, 280
National People's Congress (NPC) 36,
110, 251, 253–254, 259–260, 266,
270, 273–274, 278
Nationalist Party 246, 282
one child policy 280–281
party-state 250–254
Politburo 36, 254–258, 271–272, 274
political culture 262–264

political participation 264–269
"socialist market economy" 243, 245, 267, 277
State Council 36, 251, 253–254, 271, 273–274, 278
state-owned enterprises (SOEs) 277
Supreme People's Court 254
Tiananmen massacre 243, 269, 282
village committee 266–267
Chirac, Jacques 197, 211, 215, 217–219, 221–222, 225–227, 229
Churchill, Winston 136, 152, 154, 160, 164–165, 174, 176
Citizenship 9, 48
Civil society 68–69
Civil war 7, 15, 144–145, 394, 403, 433–434
Clegg, Nick 152, 165, 167, 183, 192
Clientelism see patron-client network
Clinton, Bill 3, 108, 161–162, 453, 460, 464, 467
Clinton, Hillary 455
Coalitions 89–90, 116–117
Cold War 2, 14, 102, 146, 199, 237, 389–390, 434
Collective action problem 66
Collor de Mello, Fernando 109
Colonialism 13–15, 93, 281, 291, 336, 352, 384, 386, 391, 409
Colosio, Luis Donaldo 294
Common Agricultural Policy (CAP) see entry *under* European Union (EU)
Commonwealth of Nations 154, 158, 405
Communist Party (China) see entry under China
Communist Party (France) see entry under France
Communist Party (Russia) *see entry under* Russia
Community building 3, 13, 20, 44, 50, 135–136
Comparative method 29–33
Confederal system 106, 433
Congress Party see entry under India
Congruence theory 50–51
Constitution 100–102, 106–108, 112–113, 200 see also entries under individual countries
Corporatism see entry under interest group systems
Corruption 121, 127, 221, 213, 236, 244, 275–276, 299, 334, 354, 370, 395, 416, 418
Costa Rica 112, 329
Cote d'Ivoire 421
Creel, Santiago 295
Crosland, Anthony 178
Cuba 46, 92, 95
Cultural Revolution see entry under China
Cunningham, Randall "Duke" 451
Czechoslovakia 11, 14
Daley, Richard 79
Dalton, Russell J. 446

Decision rules 100–101
DeLay, Tom 451
Denmark 82, 119, 200, 209, 236
Democracy 23–24, 32, 46–47, 58, 84, 93, 97, 102, 120, 125, 129
representative 23
Democratization 4, 23–25, 32, 57, 75, 95, 100, 140, 151, 229
Third Wave of 24, 105, 262
De Gaulle, Charles 82, 199, 202, 216–217, 219, 224, 226, 229, 232
De la Madrid, Miguel 294, 304, 310
De Soto, Fernando 134
De Tocqueville, Alexis 29, 31, 63, 151
Democratic Party (US) see entry under United States
Deng, Xiaoping 247, 256, 259, 268–269, 271
Diamond, Larry 423
Díaz, Porfirio 291–292
Díaz Ordaz, Gustavo 293
Divided government 104–105, 308, 328, 460–461
Douglas-Home, Alec 164, 166
Downs, Anthony 86
Duverger, Maurice 85
Duverger's Law 85, 88–89
East Germany see entry under Germany
Ebadi, Shirin 363, 372
Economic Community of West African States (ECOWAS) 422–423
Ecuador 109, 373
Eden, Sir Anthony 160, 164–165
Effective number of parties 86, 88–89
Egypt 54, 340, 357, 369, 371
Elections 23, 45, 56, 61, 63, 83–84, 89, 94, 102, 108, 111, 117 see also entries under individual countries
primary 85, 224, 226, 447–448
Electoral authoritarianism 93, 95
Electoral systems 84–89, 116
majority runoff 85–86, 224, 226
mixed 305–306
proportional representation (PR) 85–86, 88, 105, 117, 183–184, 206, 304, 316
single-member district plurality (SMDP) 84–86, 88–89, 182–184, 192
Elías Calles, Plutarco 308, 313
Elizabeth II 164
Emily's List 453
England 156, 158, 182, 186 see also Great Britain
European Convention of Human Rights 163, 171
European Court of Justice 171
European Union (EU) 9–10, 24, 100, 102, 104, 198, 239, 374, 390, 414 see also entries under individual European countries
Common Agricultural Policy (CAP) 200, 214, 239
Exclusive governing party 92

Externality 5, 134
Federal system 106, 109, 204, 304, 403, 438–439
Federalist Papers 440
Ferraro, Geraldine 453
Fiji 96
Fillon, François 229
Finland 70
Flatto-Sharon, Shmuel 82
Fox, Vicente 295–296, 299, 302, 308–310, 322, 328
Fragmented authoritarianism 273
France 9–10, 12, 14–15, 20, 31, 48, 54, 64, 69, 72–73, 82, 85, 89–91, 104–107, 109, 113–114, 117, 119, 121, 128–129, 130–132, 135, 138, 140, 142, 145–146, 151–152, 197–240, 374, 390, 422, 433, 447
and European Union (EU) 239–240
anti-clericalism see secularism
bureaucracy 208, 210, 215
Cabinet (Council of Ministers) 227–228
Cohabitation (divided government) 197, 222, 229
Communist Party 86, 201, 211, 213, 221–224, 231, 238
Confédération Française Démocratique du Travail (CFDT) 213
Confédération Générale du Travail (CGT) 213
Constitution 200–201, 224, 227–233
Constitutional Council 225, 231–233, 238
Council of State 233
Cumul des mandats 235
decentralization 234–235
elections 223–224, 226–227
Fédération de l'Education Nationale (FEN) 213
Fédération nationale des syndicates d'exploitants agricoles (FNSEA) 214
Fifth Republic 197, 199, 201, 203, 208–209, 221–222, 224, 227, 229–230, 239
Force Ouvrière (FO) 213
Fourth Republic 91, 199 209, 211, 214, 221, 227, 232
French Council of the Muslim Religion (CFCM) 205
French Revolution 198, 202–204
grandes écoles 208, 210
grands corps 210
immigration 198, 205, 207, 220, 237, 239
Mouvement Démocrate (MoDem) 220
Mouvement des Entreprises de France (MEDEF) 214
National Assembly 197, 209–211, 217, 223, 229–232
National Front 83, 86, 213, 218, 220, 224, 228–229
party system 216–223
political culture 202–206

France (*continued*)
   Rally for the Republic (RPR) 86,
      217–219
   referendums 221, 224–225, 227
   secularism 201, 203, 205, 221
   Senate 109, 231–232
   Socialist Party 86, 205, 209, 211,
      214–215, 220–222, 224, 231, 238
   Third Republic 199, 204, 214, 221, 227
   Union for a Popular Movement (UMP)
      216–219, 226, 231
   Union for French Democracy (UDF)
      218–220
Franco-Prussian War 199
Fréchette, Louise 25
Free riders 66
Freedom House 135
Freedom of speech 5, 127, 141
Friedman, Milton 436
Fundamentalism 17
G8 (Group of 8) 65
Gandhi, Indira 112
Gandhi, Mahatma 82
Geertz, Clifford 383
Gender 25, 54, 83, 139
George, Alexander 31
Georgia 197, 214, 237
Germany 10, 12, 14–15, 20, 24, 45, 49, 51,
      70, 72–73, 83, 86, 89–90, 100,
      105–107, 109–114, 116–117,
      120–121, 129–132, 137–138,
      145–146, 174, 209, 236, 374, 447
   East Germany (German Democratic
      Republic; GDR) 52, 202
   Greens (die Grünen) 83
   Nazi (National Socialist German
      Workers' Party) 24, 195, 199
   unification 202
   Weimar Republic 91
Gini Index 233
Ginsburg, Benjamin 452
Giscard d'Estaing, Valéry 217, 219, 232
Glasnost 202, 220
Globalization 2, 9–10, 34, 50, 58, 75, 134,
      144–145, 153–155, 239
Gorbachev, Mikhail 46, 115, 202–203, 213,
      222, 226, 234, 237
Gore, Al 32, 431, 459
Government functions 3–6, 35
   problems of 6–8
Gowon, Yakubu 395–396, 400, 410, 415,
      420, 422
Grameen Bank 140
Great Britain 8, 12, 15, 21, 36 ,44, 48, 51, 53,
      58, 64–65, 69, 71–72, 82, 84 86, 89–90,
      101–102, 105–108, 110–112, 114, 117,
      119–121, 130, 135, 137–139, 142,
      145–146, 151–192, 200, 209, 236, 238,
      240, 282, 339, 352, 374, 383–385, 388,
      390, 409, 422, 447
   and European Union (EU) 153, 155,
      158, 160–161, 171, 185, 190
   British National Party (BNP)
      159–160, 183

   bureaucracy 162, 167–169, 172,
      177–178, 189
   Cabinet 36, 167–168, 178
   coalition government 152–153,
      155–156, 165, 167, 169, 172, 186,
      190–191
   Confederation of British Industries 179
   Conservative Party 36, 56, 89, 117, 119,
      152–153, 155, 157–158, 160, 171,
      173, 176, 180, 182–184, 186–187
   Constitution 163
   devolution 156, 161–162, 187, 192 see
      also Northern Ireland, Scotland,
      Wales
   Green Party 183
   House of Commons 36, 89, 101, 110,
      152, 154, 162, 164, 167, 169–170,
      175, 178
   181, 183
   House of Lords 8, 162, 167, 170–171,
      178
   immigration 158–159, 184
   Labour Party 36, 56, 80, 89, 152–153,
      155, 157–162, 171, 175–176,
      179–180, 182, 184, 187–189, 191,
      221
   Liberal Democrats 36, 86, 117, 152–153,
      155–157, 160, 165, 168, 171, 173,
      182–184, 186–187
   National Health Service 152, 160, 188,
      190
   Northern Ireland Assembly *see entry
      under* Northern Ireland
   Parliament 36, 156, 160, 162–164,
      168–169, 171, 384
   party system 181–185
   Plaid Cymru (Party of Wales) 157, 182
   political culture 173–174
   political participation 176–177
   quasi-autonomous non government
      organizations (quangos) 188
   Scottish Nationalist Party (SNP) 157,
      173, 182, 187, 192
   Scottish Parliament 156, 184, 187
   Supreme Court 171
   Trades Union Congress (TUC) 179
   UK Independence Party (UKIP) 183
   Welsh Assembly 157, 184, 187
Great Depression 51, 131, 136, 326, 464
Greece 130–131
Green Movement *see entry under* Iran
Green parties 83–84 see also entries under
      individual countries
Greenpeace 62, 67, 74
Griffith, J.A.G. 163
Gross domestic product (GDP) 18, 20,
      129–131, 133, 327
Gurr, Ted Robert 73
Haiti 464
Hamas 74
Hamilton, Alexander 102
Haugaard, Jacob 82
Heath, Edward 160, 166
Henry, Patrick 127

Hidalgo y Costilla, Miguel 291
Hitler, Adolf 2, 145 *see also* Third Reich
Hobbes, Thomas 3–4, 108, 128, 134, 142,
      147
Hong Kong 57, 159, 261, 263, 281–282
Hu, Jintao 245, 255–256, 258
Human Development Index (HDI) 18,
      382, 416
Human rights 6, 24–25, 58, 161
Human Rights Watch 394
Hung parliament 152
Huntington, Samuel P. 52, 129, 442
Hussein, Saddam 6, 340–341, 369, 373,
      431, 464
Hutus (Rwanda) 14
Immigration 83 see also entries under
      individual countries
Impeachment 108–109
Inclusive governing party 92–94
Income inequality 5, 20–21, 140–141, 143,
      235, 321
India 10–12, 14, 17–18, 20–22 ,24 ,64, 70,
      74, 76, 80, 84, 88–89, 102, 105–107,
      112–113, 115, 121, 130–132,
      135–143, 145–146, 151, 154,
      158–159, 283
   Congress Party 56, 82
   Supreme Court 107
Indonesia 74
Inputs of political system 34
Interdependence 34, 69, 75
Interest aggregation 37–38, 79–97, 110,
      224
Interest articulation 37–38, 61–76, 110 see
      also interest groups under individual
      countries
Interest groups 8, 26, 35, 55, 61, 65–69, 81,
      118 *see also entries under individual
      countries*
   anomic 64
   associational 67–68, 73, 75, 80
   institutional 66–67, 73, 81
   non-associational 66, 71
Interest group systems
   controlled 70–71
   corporatist 70, 80, 181, 214–215, 311
   pluralist 69, 221
International Atomic Energy Agency 374
International Convention on Civil and
      Political Rights 371
International Monetary Fund (IMF) 160,
      231, 334, 367, 419, 422
Internet 56–57, 68–69, 71, 76, 139, 145,
      176, 209, 261, 359, 444
Iran 16, 35, 38, 45, 56, 105–106, 111–112,
      115, 129, 131–132, 135, 137, 139,
      141, 143, 145, 282, 333–375
   Assembly of Experts 342–343, 345
   Basij 356–357, 361–362, 364
   Constitution 333, 338–342, 344–346,
      351, 354, 358, 364–366, 372
   Council of Guardians 35, 343–346,
      351–352, 360, 365–366
   elections 349–352

Expediency Council 343, 345, 365–366
Green Movement 335–336, 343, 349, 352, 359, 363
Islamic Republican Party (IRP) 347
Islamic Revolution 145, 340–341, 343, 346–347, 353, 360, 363–364, 375
Islamic Revolutionary Guard Corps (IRGC) 335, 345–346, 349, 351, 357–358, 360–363, 366–367, 372
Leader 343, 345–346, 352, 359, 362, 365–366
Majles *see* parliament
minorities 334, 337–338, 346, 353, 354, 364, 373
National Security Council 365–366
parliament 338, 344–345, 349–351, 358, 365–366
political culture 352–355
Qajar dynasty 337, 339
Tudeh Party 339, 347
Twelver Shiism 334, 337–338, 341, 344, 373
ulema 333, 337–338, 342, 354, 358, 370, 375
Iraq 6, 154, 162, 172, 190, ?198?, 335, 337, 340–341, 357, 361, 373–374, 389, 431
Ireland 16, 151, 156–157
Irish Republican Army (IRA) 157–158, 171 see also Northern Ireland
Iron law of oligarchy 84
Israel 12, 14, 16–17, 34, 74, 82, 85, 112, 340, 353, 356, 374–375
Italy 10, 66, 89, 91, 117–118, 174, 238, 263
Jackson, Andrew 433
Jackson, Jesse 442
Japan 13–15, 20, 24, 34, 45, 58, 69, 71, 73, 80, 86, 105–107, 109–110, 113–114, 130–133, 135, 137–139, 146, 240, 244, 246, 336, 338, 374, 390
malapportionment 255
Jefferson, Thomas 101
Jeffords, James 461
Jiang, Zemin 256, 259
Jolie, Angelina 20
Jonathan, Goodluck 382, 396, 411, 424
Jordan 357, 371
Joseph, Richard 408
Jospin, Lionel 221–222
Judicial review 38, 107, 232–233, 441
Juppé, Alain 219
Kadyrov, Ramzan 211
Kagan, Robert 443
Karroubi, Mehdi 335–336, 343, 358
Karzai, Hamid 430
Kashmir 46
Kenya 93, 422
Khamenei, Ali 31, 345, 347, 359, 358
Khatami, Mohammad 345, 347, 349, 351, 353, 359–363, 366–367, 374
Khodorkovsky, Mikhail 221–222
Khomeini, Ruhollah 333–334, 339–342, 345–347, 349, 351, 354, 356, 358, 360, 364–365, 367, 372
Khrushchev, Nikita 115, 202

King, Reverend Martin Luther 434
Kipling, Rudyard 429
Kohl, Helmut 108
Korea, North 10, 24, 92, 282
Korea, South 18, 21, 34, 74, 108, 244
Kosovo 14, 83, 144, 146
Kurds 14, 353, 364, 373
Kyrgyzstan 233
Labor unions 53, 55, 64, 67, 70–71, 74, 76, 80, 83, 110, 176, 179–180, 207, 211–213, 215, 221, 223–224, 312, 407
Large-N study 31–32 see also comparative method
Lebanon 50, 91, 373, 423
Labastida, Francisco 314
Labour Party see entry under Great Britain
Legislative committees 109–110, 118, 170, 229, 231, 207, 405
Legitimacy 45–46, 48–49, 57, 93–95, 101, 115, 136, 354
Lenin, Vladimir 201, 250
Le Pen, Jean-Marie 218, 220
Leviathan 3, 108
Li, Keqiang 244
Liberal Democratic Party of Russia (LDPR) see entry under Russia
Liberal Democrats see entry under Great Britain
Liberation theology 16
Libertarianism 6–7, 127
Lieberman, Joe 459
Lijphart, Arend 107
Lincoln, Abraham 464, 468
Litigation 452
Lobbying 72, 451–453
Locke, John 3–4, 102, 134
López Obrador, Andrés Manuel 296–298, 311, 319–320
Louisiana Purchase 433
Lugard, Sir Frederick 384–385
Lula, Luiz Inácio da Silva 131
Luxembourg 10, 12, 200
Luzhkov, Yuei 228
Maastricht Treaty 104, 221, 225, 238
Macaulay, Herbert 385
Macmillan, Harold 160, 164–165
Madero, Francisco I. 292
Madison, James 7, 102, 438
Madrazo, Roberto 295–297, 311, 313, 320
Major, John 104, 160, 164, 166
Mandela, Nelson 400
Mandelson, Peter 162
Manufactured majority 89
Mao Zedong 92, 243, 246–249, 256, 271, 282
Markets 5, 58, 129, 135, 322 see also privatization
Mayhew, David 461
McCain, John 448, 453
McGuiness, Martin 158
—Media 8, 20, 23, 48, 56, 68, 71–72, 102, 120, 176, 197, 217, 359
Median voter 86

Medvedev, Dmitrii 115, 197–199, 212–214, 217, 228, 233, 235–237
Meir, Golda 112
Merkel, Angela 111–112
Mesbah Yazdi, Mohammad-Taqi 360
Mexico 20, 47, 51, 64, 70, 74, 86, 94, 105–106, 109, 111, 114, 121, 131, 139–143, 263, 289–329, 388
caciques 292, 301
Chamber of Deputies 295–296, 304–309, 315–316
Chiapas rebellion 294
Civic Alliance 300
Confederación de Organizaciones Populares (CNOP) 312
Confederación de Trabajadores de México (CTM) 312
Confederación Nacional Campesina (CNC) 312
Congress 300, 302, 304, 306–309, 313–314, 328–329
Constitution 291, 297, 302, 304, 306–307
indigenous population 291
local governments 302–304
migrants 326–327
Partido Acción Nacional (PAN) 94, 295–296, 302, 304–305, 308–312, 315–317, 319–320
Partido Communista Mexicano (PCM) 317–318
Partido de la Revolución Democrática (PRD) 296, 298, 302, 305, 308, 310, 318–320
Partido Revolucionario Institucional (PRI) 93–94, 106, 114, 289–290, 293–298, 300–302, 304–305, 307–321
Partido Verde Ecologista de México (PVEM) 315
party system 313–320
political culture 297–299
political participation 301–302
presidencialismo 308
Senate 295, 304–307, 323
Supreme Court 300, 302, 308–309, 312, 323, 329
Michels, Robert 84
Miliband, Ed 162
Military coup 94, 96, 385, 391, 400
Military government 93–95, 115, 400, 407, 423
Miller, Zell 459
Minorities at Risk Project 140
Mitterrand, François 201, 221–222, 224, 227, 229, 239
Mixed electoral system see entry under electoral systems
Mobutu Sese Seko 7
Modernization 48, 57, 64, 75
Moldova 45
Monarchy 113–114, 173
Monopoly 5, 7
Montesquieu 102

Morelos y Pavón, José María 291
Mossadegh, Mohammad 339, 347, 354
Mousavi, Mir-Hossein 335–336, 353
Mugabe, Robert 7, 154
Multiparty system 86, 89–91, 116, 182, 226
Myanmar 10, 112
Na'ini, Muhammad Husayn 338
Napoléon Bonaparte 198, 207, 238
Napoléon III 199, 223
Nateq Nuri, Ali-Akbar 349, 362
Nation building 4, 9 see also community building
Nation state 9
National Front see entry under France
National identity 9, 14, 45
Nationalization 214, 237
Nazis see entry under Germany
Nehru, Jawaharlal 82
Netherlands 10, 70, 85, 89, 91, 117, 225
New York Times v. Sullivan 444
New Zealand 69
Nicholas II 201
Nicholas, H.G. 435
Niger 96, 390–391, 422
Nigeria 13–14, 17–18, 20, 24, 47, 70, 95, 102, 105–107, 111, 115, 121, 129, 132, 136–139, 142–144, 381–424
    All Nigerian People's Party (ANPP) 410
    bureaucracy 400
    Constitution 382, 394, 398, 401–403, 405–406, 421
    Economic and Financial Crimes Commission (EFCC) 396
    elections 410–415
    Hausa-Fulani 383, 385, 391, 393, 395, 398, 407–408, 411
    House of Representatives 395
    Igbo 383–385, 391–392, 395, 398, 400, 406
    Independent National Election Commission (INFC) 410
    Kaduna Mafia 408
    local government 392–393, 403, 405, 419
    Movement for the Emancipation of the Niger Delta (MEND) 389
    Movement for the Survival of the Ogoni People (MOSOP) 406
    National Assembly 382, 396, 401, 403, 405–406, 413
    National Union of Petroleum and Gas Workers (NUPENG) 407
    Nigerian Labor Congress (NLC) 407
    Nigerian Union of Local Government Employees (NULGE) 407
    party system 409–414
    People's Democratic Party (PDP) 396, 410–411, 413–414
    political culture 390–395
    political participation 408–409
    Structural Adjustment Program 415, 419
    Supreme Court 405–406, 411

Transition Monitoring Group (TMG) 407
    Yoruba 383, 385, 391–392, 395, 398, 407–408, 411, 413
Nixon, Richard 108
Nomenklatura 120, 218–219, 256–258
North American Free Trade Agreement (NAFTA) 290, 322, 327–328
North Atlantic Treaty Organization (NATO) 14, 34, 145, 237
Northern Ireland 13, 44, 46, 50, 74, 105, 151, 156–158, 161–162, 173, 182–183, 187–188, 191
    Northern Ireland Assembly 158, 184
    party system 158
    Sinn Fein 158
Norway 70, 111–112, 119, 129, 133, 155, 209, 388
Nuclear Non-proliferation Treaty 374
Obama, Barack 430.432, 435, 448
Obasanjo, Olusegun 95, 382, 387, 390, 396, 400–401, 410–411, 413–414, 418, 420, 422
Okigbo, Pius 417
Oligarchy 24
Ombudsman 120, 170
Organization for Economic Cooperation and Development (OECD) 130
Outputs of political system 34, 38, 49, 64, 124, 127
Oxfam 177, 180
Pahlavi, Mohammad-Reza Shah 333, 339–340, 344, 346, 352–354, 360
Pakistan 11, 14, 16, 112, 144, 146, 154, 158–159, 361, 369, 373
Palin, Sarah 455
Panama 322, 464
Paraguay 109
Paris Commune 199
Parliamentary system 103–105, 108–109, 112, 114–117, 318, 405
Participatory values 48, 50–51, 64, 75
Partido Acción Nacional (PAN) see entry under Mexico
Partido de la Revolución Democrática (PRD) see entry under Mexico
Partido Revolucionario Institucional (PRI) see entry under Mexico
Party discipline 104, 362
Party family 83
Party of power see entry under Russia
Party platform 85
Party system 81–83 see also entries under individual countries
    authoritarian 81
    competitive 81, 89, 95–96
    conflictual 90–91
    consensual 90–91
    consociational 90–91
    personalistic 82
Patron-client network 79–81, 312, 361, 364, 394, 406, 408–409
Patten, Christopher 282

Peak association 70 see also corporatist interest group system
Pelosi, Nancy 432
People's Democratic Party (PDP) see entry under Nigeria
Perestroika 202
Perot, H. Ross 453
Peru 74, 134
Pétain, Marshal Philippe 199
Pew Global Values Survey 58
Philippines 24, 74, 80, 108, 112
    People Power Revolution 24, 74
Poland 16, 45, 71
Policymaking 37, 52, 100–121
Political action committees (PACs) see entry under United States
Political communication 38–39, 118, 135
Political culture 4, 34, 44–58, 79, 96, 173
    see also entries under individual countries
    subculture 49, 53
Political goods 124–127
Political parties 8, 23, 26, 35–36, 56, 66, 72, 79, 81–93, 96, 102, 109, 111 see also entries under individual countries
Political recruitment 38–39, 54, 110, 114
Political socialization 38–39, 44, 52–57, 68, 110
    agents of 53–57
Political system 1, 8–10, 16–17, 23, 33–42, 50, 124
    functions of 38–39, 41
Pompidou, Georges 217, 219, 224, 232
Ponting, Clive 172
Populist parties 83
Portugal 10, 15
Presidential system 102–103, 105–106, 108–110, 112, 114–117, 302, 412
Privatization 160, 188–189, 200, 209–210, 217, 237–238, 231–232, 277, 322
Property rights 4–5, 134
Proportional representation see entry under electoral systems
    closed-list 85, 304
    open-list 85
Protests 62, 64, 72–73, 215, 267–268, 364
Przworski, Adam 32
Public goods 4–5, 140
Public policy 127–147
Putin, Vladimir 82, 115, 197–199, 208, 210–215, 217, 219–220, 227–229, 233, 235–237
Qualified majority 101
Quebec 16
Queen Victoria 152
Raffarin, Jean-Pierre 210
Rafsanjani, Ali-Akbar Hashemi 334, 343, 347, 349, 351, 362, 365–366, 370, 374
Rally for the Republic (RPR) see entry under France
Rangel, Charlie 451
Reagan, Ronald 3, 58, 161, 443, 453, 457, 465

Redistribution 6, 128–133, 141, 236, 367
Regulation 38, 124, 127, 133–135
Relative deprivation 73
Rentier state 129, 339, 388
Rent-seeking 7, 84, 92, 121, 134
Republican Party (US) see entry under
    United States
Resource distribution 38, 127, 131–133,
    321, 417
Resource extraction 34, 127–130
Reza Shah 338–339, 354
Robinson, Peter 158
Roosevelt, Franklin D. 136, 154, 432,
    461–462, 464
Roosevelt, Theodore 434
Rousseau, Jean-Jacques 3, 6
Rowhani, Hasan 365
Royal, Ségolène 211, 222
Rushdie, Salman 367
Russia 11–12, 18, 21, 31, 38–41, 45, 47–48,
    70, 85, 90–91, 105–106, 108,
    113–115, 121, 129–131, 135, 137,
    140–143, 145–146, 197–238, 250,
    338, 352, 367, 374, 433, 435
    Bolshevik Revolution 146, 201
    bureaucracy 40–41
    Communist Party 40, 208, 226–229
    Constitution 203–204
    Constitutional Court 208, 210, 236
    Duma 205–208, 225–226, 228
    elections 225–229
    Fatherland party 228
    Federal Security Service (FSB) 204, 235
    Federation Council 109, 206–209
    Federation of Independent Trade
        Unions of Russia (FITUR) 221,
        223–224
    Liberal Democratic Party of Russia
        (LDPR) 226–227
    oligarchs 213, 220–221
    Parliament 40–41
    party of power 224–225, 227–228
    party system 224–228
    political culture 213–217
    political participation 217–218
    Public Chamber 206
    Regional governments 40, 196,
        210–212
    Russian Union of Industrialists and
        Entrepreneurs (RUIE) 221
    Security Council 205
    shock therapy 231
    State Council 206, 233
    Supreme Court 208–209
    United Russia Party 207–208, 224–226,
        228–229
    Yabloko 226–227
Rwanda 6, 13–14, 423
Salinas, Carlos 295–296, 297, 299, 304,
    310, 318, 322
Sarkozy, Nicolas 197–198, 211, 219–220,
    222, 226, 229, 239
Saro-Wiwa, Ken 406–407

Saudi Arabia 34, 113, 370, 372
Schmidt, Helmut 108
Schumpter, Joseph A. 84
Scientific process 29
Scotland 50, 151, 156, 158, 161–162, 171,
    182–183, 187, 192
Semi-presidential system 104
Sen, Amartya 22, 47
Separation of powers 102, 104, 118,
    438–440
Serbia 14
Shari'a law 333, 398, 406
Shefter, Martin 452
Shonekan, Ernest 401
Sierra Leone 144, 422
Single European Act 190
Skocpol, Theda 31
Small-N study 31–32 see also comparative
    method
Smith, Adam 436
Social contract 2–3, 134
Socialist Party (France) see entry under
    France
Somalia 95, 144, 423, 464
South Africa 24, 44, 64, 75, 91, 422
Sovereignty 9–10, 126
Soviet Union 6, 10–11, 14, 24, 39, 42, 46,
    57, 84, 92, 102, 115, 120, 124, 127,
    145–146, 201–202, 210, 214–216,
    231, 234, 246–247, 276, 347, 349,
    374, 389, 434
    Communist Party 39–40, 46, 84,
        201–202, 218, 220, 226, 235
Spain 10, 15, 291
Sri Lanka 112, 144
Stalin, Joseph 6, 24, 146, 201, 231
State of nature 2–3
Statistical method 31–32
Strategic voting 86
Structural-functional approach 38
Sudan 6, 95
Suu Kyi, Aung San 112
Swaziland 18
Sweden 14, 70, 82, 107, 111, 119–120, 130,
    133, 209, 334, 390
Switzerland 11
Syria 340
Taiwan 10, 18, 21, 246–247, 263, 282
Taliban see entry under Afghanistan
Tamils 14
Tanzania 93
Taxation 128, 130, 134, 187, 190, 235–236,
    415, 465–466
    direct 128, 130
    indirect 128–129, 236
Terrorism 17, 34, 74, 159, 211, 237
Terrorist attacks
    Bali 17, 74
    London 4, 17, 74, 159, 192
    Madrid 4, 17, 74
    September 11 4, 17, 74, 198, 211, 237,
        374, 430
Thailand 46, 96

Thatcher, Margaret 58, 89, 112, 160–161,
    163, 166, 169, 173, 176, 181, 185,
    187–189, 191
Theocracy 16, 45, 333, 355
Third Reich 2
Third Way 161
Thompson, Doug 453
Tiananmen massacre see entry under
    China
Togo 422
Totalitarianism 24, 92, 244
Trade unions see labor unions
Transparency International 382
Treaty of Versailles 9
Treaty of Westphalia 9
Truman, Harry S. 464
Turkey 45, 353, 361, 369
Tutsis (Rwanda) 14
Two-party system 85–86, 91, 116, 182
Ukraine 46, 74, 197, 203, 214, 220
Ulema see entry under Iran
Unicameral legislature 109
Union for a Popular Movement (UMP)
    see entry under France
Union for French Democracy (UDF) see
    entry under France
Unitary system 106, 109, 156
United Kingdom see Great Britain
United Nations (UN) 10–11, 14, 20, 22,
    25, 126, 145, 423
    Commission on the Status of Women
        25
    Millennium Development Goals 126,
        137–139
    Security Council 374, 422, 431
    United Nations Development Program
        (UNDP) 18
United Russia Party see entry under Russia
United States 4, 8–12, 14–15, 17, 20–21,
    31, 34, 42, 45, 48, 54–56, 58, 63–64,
    66–67, 69, 72, 75–76, 80, 82, 84–86,
    89–90, 10, 102–103, 105–108, 110,
    114, 119, 121, 124, 130–133, 135,
    137–143, 145, 151–152, 154, 158,
    183, 198–199, 236, 240, 237, 276,
    282, 290, 310, 322, 326–328, 334,
    339–340, 352, 356, 370, 373–374,
    389–390, 403, 422
    Articles of Confederation 106, 433, 438
    Bill of Rights 433, 437–438
    bureaucracy 447, 465
    Civil Rights movement 434, 452,
        463–464
    Civil War 433–434
    Congress 101, 110, 169, 439–441, 464, 467
    Constitution 107, 109, 163, 306, 433,
        437–440
    Declaration of Independence 126
    Democratic Party 86, 432, 435, 451,
        453, 455–459, 461
    electoral college 440
    Environmental Protection Agency
        467–468

Federal Communications Commission 444

health care reform 432, 437, 462–463

House of Representatives 439–440, 456–457, 462–464

immigration 435–436, 446

lobbying 451–453

minorities 434–435, 442

National Security Agency 464

partisan polarization 455–456

party system 453, 455–459

political action committees (PACs) 449–451

political culture 441–443

political participation 444–447

Reform Party 453

Republican Party 86, 430, 448, 452–453, 455–457, 459–461, 465

Senate 108, 116, 439–440, 442, 456–457, 463–464

Supreme Court 107, 233, 439–441, 444, 448, 450, 464–467

Tea Party 453

War on terror 466

Uppsala Conflict Data Project 144

Urbanization 18, 22–23, 48, 134, 142, 221, 388

Uruguay 95

Van Buren, Martin 433

Vatican 10–12, 83, 204

Velázquez, Fidel 313

Venezuela 109, 329, 373

Veto power 38, 118

Vietnam 45, 55, 92, 283

Vietnam War 42, 431, 464

Villa, Pancho 292

Vote of no confidence 104, 108, 231, 344

Voting 61, 63–64, 83

Wales 151, 156, 158, 161–162, 182–183, 187

Walesa, Lech 71

War of 1812 433

Washington, George 433

Waters, Maxine 451

Weber, Max 14, 119

Wei, Jinsheng 268

Weimar Republic *see entry under* Germany

Welfare state 131–133, 136, 141, 160, 162, 235–236

Wen, Jiabao 245, 253, 255, 258

Wilson, Harold 160, 166

Working class 53, 67–68, 83, 111, 175, 205, 207, 220–222, 293, 336, 367

World Bank 20, 321–322, 367, 415, 419, 422

World Trade Organization (WTO) 65, 214, 239, 221, 282

World Values Survey 47, 173, 353, 357, 371

World War I 9, 101–102, 146, 158, 199, 338, 434

World War II 9–10, 45, 51, 81, 101–102, 136, 146, 199, 202, 204, 200–201, 326, 394, 434

Wu, Bangguo 258

Xi, Jinping 245

Yabloko *see entry under* Russia

Yar'Adua, Umar Musa 382, 396, 398, 408, 411, 414–415, 424

Yeltsin, Boris 115, 198, 202–206, 210, 212–213, 220, 226–227, 237

Yugoslavia 11, 13–14, 50, 146, 423

Yunus, Muhammad 140

Zaire 7

Zambia 154

Zapata, Emiliano 292, 297

Zedillo, Ernesto 294, 304, 310, 314, 318, 322–323

Zhao, Ziyang 256, 258, 268–269

Zhirinovsky, Vladimir 226

Zimbabwe 7, 95, 154